UNDER THE GENERAL EDITORSHIP OF
WILLARD B. SPALDING
CHAIRMAN, DIVISION OF EDUCATION
PORTLAND STATE COLLEGE

MENTAL HYGIENE IN TEACHING

Second Edition

Fritz Redl   WAYNE STATE UNIVERSITY

William W. Wattenberg   WAYNE STATE UNIVERSITY

Harcourt, Brace & World, Inc.
New York, Chicago, San Francisco, Atlanta

Library of Congress Catalog Card Number: 59–7739

Printed in the United States of America

CONTENTS

EDITOR'S FOREWORD

Generalizations are dangerous, and nowhere more dangerous than in the field of education. But I am willing to hazard the generalization that today's teachers have both a richer grasp of the necessary conditions underlying mental health and a firmer sense of what classroom teachers can (and cannot) do to foster healthy, integrated personalities in their students than was true even a decade ago. If this is indeed the case, credit must be given in no small part to the movement reflected in such outstanding textbooks as *Mental Hygiene in Teaching*. That the teacher can and must assume some share of responsibility for the emotional as well as the intellectual development of his students is today a truism. That he cannot and should not try to assume all the responsibilities of parents, counselors, and clinicians is perhaps more obvious today than was true in the first flush of enthusiasm with which teachers hailed their discovery of the implications of modern psychology.

Both aspects of this awareness were fully reflected in the first edition of the present book. One of its greatest merits was that it gave teachers a realistic, down-to-earth, and yet psychologically sound introduction to the forces—psychological, biological, social—which affect the development of the human personality, and that it offered concrete and practical suggestions for dealing with these forces constructively in the classroom. Another strength was that it was careful to point out the limitations of this process: classroom teachers can perform one of their most useful functions not by treating, but by identifying (often for the first time) and referring to competent specialists those children whose behavior indicates the possibility of serious emotional disturbance. Yet good mental hygiene is *preventive* mental hygiene, and the authors took it as their primary function to show the positive steps that could be taken day by day in the classroom to strengthen the emotional development of the normal child.

In this new edition the authors have not been content simply to update the references. They have taken the opportunity to reshape most of the chapters; they have added three entirely new and highly stimulating chapters; and they have greatly increased the range of citations from the professional literature. The result is markedly to strengthen an already well-received text.

WILLARD B. SPALDING

PREFACE TO THE FIRST EDITION

Teaching is one of the most complicated of all occupations. Teachers, from students in training to the veterans of the profession, must learn to cope with a multitude of problems. Curriculum revisions, innovations in method, and shifts in philosophy are part of a continuous process of change, because schools must be adjusted to utilize new knowledge and to meet the needs of society.

Mental hygiene is one of the fields of study which increasingly demand attention from all people who are responsible for guiding the growth of children. Within recent years scores of excellent books on the general subject of mental hygiene have been published.

The present volume, however, has a specific objective. Its main purpose is to bring to teachers some basic principles of mental hygiene as these relate to the work of guiding young people in school. By translating these understandings into practice, teachers will strengthen children psychologically, and thus increase their chances of becoming happy and effective adults. As a result, teachers will find greater satisfaction in their work.

As the introduction indicates, the authors have drawn upon many common school situations to which mental hygiene principles apply. The situations are based largely on the experiences of the authors and on incidents related to them by either experienced teachers or student teachers in training. However, the authors have substituted fictitious names for those of real persons and have otherwise altered all identifying data, so that any resemblance to any person living or dead is purely coincidental.

The book is divided into five major sections. After the two introductory chapters in Part A there follow, in Part B, chapters on behavior mechanisms, developmental psychology, and the influence of important factors in individual development. Part B concludes with a discussion of the concepts of maturity, adjustment, and normality.[1]

Part C deals with ordinary classroom problems. The authors first consider relationships between mental hygiene and learning.[2] Next they take up the group factors which make every classroom a complex interplay of psychological forces. Understanding this interplay may help teachers to develop a desirable atmosphere and spirit in their classrooms. The succeeding chapter considers the way in which the teacher as a person influences and is influenced by the group forces. The next one describes methods of applying theory to classroom situations. This is followed by a study of influence techniques: the tools which teachers use in on-the-spot efforts to guide behavior. The final chapter deals with various dilemmas which trouble some teachers as they think of modifying their accustomed ways in the light of mental hygiene principles.

Aside from the normal classroom problems, teachers have other difficulties with which they must deal. Some of these difficulties are discussed in the chapters of Part D. First, there is the question of giving special help to those children whose problems are too great to be handled effectively within the limits of ordinary classrooms. Another topic, discussed in Chapter XV,[3] is the relationship between teachers and parents. Since teachers must live with themselves, as well as with children, no book on mental health in education could be complete without a discussion of mental hygiene as it applies to teachers themselves. In the concluding chapter, the authors analyze the limitations of mental hygiene in education.

The sequence of chapters is one which the authors have found convenient in the light of their own predilections. Undoubtedly, other instructors will want to modify it. The interests of different classes usually vary sufficiently to warrant such alteration. Therefore, topics are presented in relatively self-contained form so that their order can be rearranged without any marked difficulty. The one exception is that Chapter III, on behavior mechanisms, and Chapter IV, on developmental tasks, are interdependent and should precede the remaining chapters in Parts B, C, and D, which lean more or less heavily upon the concepts developed in them.[4]

---

[1] In the second edition a new chapter has been added in Part B; see p. xiii below.
[2] For a description of the new chapter inserted at this point, see p. xiii.
[3] Now Chapter 17.
[4] The new Chapter 3, Motivation, Conflict, and Control (see p. xiii), should be included in this category.

This book can be used in a number of different ways. Some instructors will employ it as a text in the traditional sense of the term. They will use the chapters as basic reading. They will assume that by study the students will derive the theoretical concepts to be developed more fully by lectures and by class discussions.

In a number of places, instructors may wish to build the program of readings and discussions around individual studies of youngsters or group situations, made and reported by class members. Where such an approach is used, this book can serve as one resource to stimulate thoughtful analysis.

There are a number of institutions where, for one reason or another, a separate course of mental hygiene in teaching is not offered, or is offered only to graduate students. In such places the instructors of educational psychology or methods may wish to go more deeply into mental hygiene than the regular texts permit. They may find it wise to have their students read this book for general viewpoint and approach rather than for detailed analysis.

Mental Hygiene in Teaching, too, we believe, offers an opportunity for independent study to teachers who are no longer taking formal courses but who are continually improving their professional understanding, either as individuals or in study groups.

Terminology is a special problem, because so much of mental hygiene knowledge is derived from psychology and psychiatry. Furthermore, disciples of different schools of thought in both disciplines tend to express themselves in a more or less esoteric vocabulary. It often happens that students who have been required to learn the specialized terminology of one school find it difficult to understand related ideas, because these ideas are cloaked in the pet phrases of a different school. Although scientific terminology may serve a useful function of communication for those who have become skilled in its use, the authors feel that for the purposes of this book it is better to strive to express ideas in generally used words. For the benefit of those readers who would like to have a better grasp on scientific terminology that they may encounter in other readings, we have provided in Appendix II the meanings of frequently used psychiatric terms.

Despite these good intentions concerning vocabulary, readers may nevertheless find some words or phrases which we have employed in unusual meanings or in combinations that appear strange. Where this has happened there is nothing sacrosanct about the terminology; certainly the reader would be wise to recast the ideas into phrases he prefers.

The details of sequence and terminology are dwarfed in importance by the spirit with which the subject is approached. The instructor who teaches mental hygiene has a special responsibility in setting in his own classes an example through which students may receive greater light on just what is meant by education for mental health. The students themselves share in this responsibility; they can show their own developing grasp of the subject not so much by the power of their intellectualizations as by the skill with which they help each other work out the problems involved. They can make clear their growing mastery not so much by the brilliance of their insights as by the thoughtfulness with which they bring these insights to bear on real problems.

The authors are indebted to so many people for help with this volume that the full list would be too long to print. There were our own teachers, and the many pioneers who worked out theory and practice. From our colleagues we received inspiration, ideas, and helpful criticism in developing methods of presentation. Teachers with whom we have held countless discussions, both in classes and in their schools, gave us the illustrations used throughout the book. They contributed many valuable suggestions on how to apply theory in the strenuous day-to-day job of teaching. Most important of all, through the powerful nonverbal language of behavior, children have taught us many lessons which we hope some day to interpret more fully. To all of these people we owe a debt. Our hope is that in this book we may partially repay that debt by helping through you, its readers, to make life more rewarding for at least a few teachers and children.

Detroit, Michigan   FRITZ REDL
January, 1951   WILLIAM W. WATTENBERG

PREFACE TO THE SECOND EDITION

Almost a decade has passed since the material for *Mental Hygiene in Teaching* was compiled. In the intervening years, much important work has been carried on by clinicians, research teams, and teachers. New understandings have been developed; new ways of applying old ideas have been tested. To incorporate these into the original edition is our primary reason for undertaking a revision.

Three new chapters have been added; one which appeared in the first edition has been deleted. Chapter 3, which deals with unconscious motivation, conflict, and the extent to which children have conscious control over their behavior, has been added at the suggestion of instructors who have used the textbook with their classes and have found a need for fuller discussion of those issues. Chapter 9, which deals with unusual learners—the problems presented to teachers by the "slow," the gifted, and the many children who seem unable to work at their capacity—is a response to the many teachers who have sought help in dealing with such pupils. Chapter 16 is written in recognition of a major development, the appearance of widespread efforts to help young people develop insight, to the end that they will find better ways of dealing with life's issues. Evidence has accumulated as to successes achieved along these lines through both group discussion and informal talks.

The chapter which has disappeared was one on personality distortions, which dealt largely with home situations out of which major behavior problems often arise. What appeared useful has been added to the present Chapter 6, "Influences That Shape Lives." The decision to make this change reflects the growing recognition that it has been too easy to attribute all of children's problems to their parents, and that research has developed strengthening evidence of the part played by heredity, biological forces, and social conditions.

Previous users of this book will recognize two shifts in emphasis and approach. To aid students and teachers confronted by certain aspects of current criticism of education, we have attempted to document more fully the scientific bases for much that is said. We have also attempted to focus increased attention on the ways in which information pointing to the causes of children's difficulties can be used in devising constructive programs for coping with those difficulties. In addition, as an aid to students and instructors we have briefly annotated the lists of additional readings and audio-visual aids at the ends of the chapters.

By and large, most people who deal with children try to do their best. All of them need and should receive useful support in making that best a little better. It is to that proposition that this revision is dedicated.

Washington, D.C.   FRITZ REDL
Detroit, Michigan   WILLIAM W. WATTENBERG
January, 1959

PART A

INTRODUCTION

chapter **1**

FOOD FOR THOUGHT

A real school with live youngsters is a fascinating place. Day after day there is a never-ending series of surprises. Often the learning activities flow smoothly; sometimes there are disturbances.

Each of the twelve situations described in this chapter involves principles of mental health. In later chapters those principles will be developed and discussed. At this point our purpose is simply to illustrate the range of problems found in schools.

Charles: A "Troublemaker"

Anyone who often visits schools will sooner or later run across some boy or girl who has been temporarily banished from a classroom because a teacher felt his behavior was upsetting the class. Perhaps he will be sitting in the principal's office. Then again, he may be standing alone in a cloakroom or supply closet, or in some other place of exile. He may be crying, he may be pretending indifference, or he may be indignant. For example:

We found Charles Gordon kicking at the baseboard in the hall outside Room 107. When he heard us, he turned around to glower sullenly, as though daring us to do or say something. In his mind (he later told us), a vengeful scene had been taking shape as he rehearsed it over and over again. In his imagination, he was being welcomed back to Ridgetown after having captured a gang of enemy spies. As a conquering hero, he had been asked if there was anything Ridgetown could do for him. He had ordered Miss Chase (his present teacher) brought before him. She had promptly fallen to her knees, clasped his legs, and begged him to forgive her. With a kick he spurned her, and then relented upon her tearful promise to reform and to write, "I am an old sour-puss," fifty times on a blackboard which had miraculously appeared in the middle of Soldiers' Square.

Why had he been put out in the hall? Charles's explanation was quite incomplete. According to him, Miss Chase had been picking on him. She had always had it in for him. He had done nothing serious, nothing that other pupils had not also done. He was a victim of arbitrary malevolence.

What was Miss Chase's side of the story? Ten-year-old Charles had surpassed his usual impudence that day by such willful defiance of her authority that she had had to do something to discipline him. She never *had* liked the boy; he was a disrespectful little smart aleck. That particular day she had known there would be trouble when the boys had come piling into the room after recess. Coming through the door, Charles had shoved the boy ahead of him so hard that the other youngster almost fell. Miss Chase had made Charles go back and come in again "like a gentleman." He obeyed, but had affected so mincing a stride that several pupils snickered. In taking his seat, he deliberately knocked a book to the floor. While the class was working on arithmetic, she caught him reading a comic magazine. Then, instead of doing his own work, he copied from the girl in front of him. Miss Chase asked him to go to the board and do one of the examples for the class. On the way to the board, he jostled the arm of one of the other boys and knocked over a small globe. When she told him to go back and walk up right, he muttered something that sounded like "stinker."

Angrily she demanded, "What did you say?"

Charles: "Nothing."

Miss Chase: "Don't lie to me, I heard you." She wanted to hit him, but after striding toward him, held herself back.

He glared at her and shouted, "It's a free country, isn't it?"

That did it. She took him by the shoulders, shook him hard, and announced in a quivering voice, "You've been asking for this. Now, get out of this room and stay in the hall until you're ready to apologize."

Any teacher involved in an incident of this sort—and practically every teacher has been through something similar, not once but dozens of times—has questions to ask. Why did the child act the way he did? Will the punishment prevent a future repetition? Why did that particular child make the teacher so angry? What effect did the incident have on the rest of the class? What could have been done in advance to avoid this clash? Later, as we study various psychological mechanisms, we may pick up some clues.

Agnes: A "Clinging Vine"

Although beginning teachers are most worried about keeping order and control, they face many other types of problem. To name but one: whenever children are asked what they expect of teachers, a large number answer, "They should be fair." When a class feels a teacher has pets or is favoring one or two children, the others may think less of him. Yet in some cases the teacher may feel he has to give one child special attention. For instance:

High-pitched screams echoed through the halls; the noises were coming from the kindergarten room. Surprisingly, Mrs. Benson, the kindergarten teacher, was walking slowly down the hall; she motioned to us to do nothing. Intrigued, we looked through the window in the upper part of the closed door. The children were sitting and looking with strained curiosity at a little girl who was having a terrific temper tantrum. She had thrown herself to the floor, and was alternating violent screeches of rage with vicious kicks at the door.

Mrs. Benson made comic gestures of holding her fingers to her ears, but her usually kindly face was a study in anxiety and despair.

"It's Agnes," she said. "I don't know what to do. I just had to do something, so I did this. Maybe it will work. I hope so. I hope it's the right thing, but I had to do something.

"It started the very first day. As soon as her mother left her, she began to cry. She kept it up for an hour and then asked to go home. She said her mother had told her that if she cried, I'd phone home.

"I knew that if I did that, she would never get used to school, and every day would be the same story. So, I told her I couldn't send for her mother but that she could stay close to me. I took her hand and kept her with me all morning. That made her feel better, and she stopped crying.

"Ever since, she has clung to me. When I went to the front of the room, she would come with me. When I went to the back, she'd tag along. Even when I'd go to the supply room or the office, she would stay with me. It was very annoying, but I figured that she had an extra need for security. It kept up for three weeks.

"Yesterday, some of the other children complained. They wanted to know why they couldn't come with me, too. I could see that things just couldn't go on that way forever. So, today I told her to sit at one end of the little tables and play while I was taking care of some of the other children.

"She obeyed but looked hurt. Then, just to test her out, I left the room. When she saw me leave, she came after me. I deliberately shut the door in her face. You heard the rest."

By this time, Agnes' screams had stopped. Mrs. Benson sighed. "I guess I can go back now."

We watched her go into the room. She picked Agnes up, shook a finger at her, and pointed to a table where another little girl was making paper baskets. Agnes meekly took a chair, and then picked up a scissors and began cutting paper. On the surface, at least, she looked quite calm and content.

Like Mrs. Benson, many a teacher has felt forced to take action, even though she was not sure what to do. Why had Agnes acted as she had? Was the complaining of the other children as serious as Mrs. Benson had thought? Was the lesson "good for" Agnes? Could Mrs. Benson have handled the affair without having to take such drastic action? What effect will the incident have on Mrs. Benson? What effect will it have on the way the other children treat Agnes?

Jerry: A "Spelling Problem"

For children, the main business of school is learning. The material is reading, drawing, writing, music, and other subjects. Although most of it may appear to involve sheer intellectual activity, often there are emotional implications. For many different reasons, children may be stirred up by particular subjects. Some children show an intense drive to master certain material. In other children, emotions hamper learning. For example:

Jerry's spelling was a problem for Miss Chilton, his third-grade teacher. Although he successfully learned many difficult words, on others, including rather simple ones, he would produce weird distortions. When corrected, he seemed very irritated. Worse yet, after he had practiced the right spelling and seemed to have mastered it, he would go back to the original error a week or two later. His spoken language was extraordinarily poor. He used an unusual amount of slang and violated almost every rule of grammar.

What made all this so much of a problem was that Miss Chilton knew that he came from a fine home and was quite bright. His mother was a college graduate who had taught speech in the local high school before her marriage to his father, a highly respected engineer. To add to Miss Chilton's puzzlement, the first-grade teacher reported that Jerry had had no such trouble in her class; in fact, he had spoken unusually well and had quickly learned to write new words.

One day, Miss Chilton was called to the office for a conference with Jerry's mother and father. The mother was quite distraught. She explained that Jerry had heard only the most correct English in the home; they had not even used baby talk. She traced all Jerry's troubles to comic books. When he first showed interest, they had read the books to him but had carefully corrected the language usage. However, as soon as he could read for himself, he had discovered the deception. At first, he used the incorrect expressions to tease his parents. Now, he seemed genuinely unable to avoid bad English. Miss Chilton and the principal suggested that possibly Jerry was only going through a passing phase. They readily agreed that something ought to be done about the comics, but that it would be unwise to forbid Jerry to read comic books all his friends had.

During the conference Jerry's father had said very little. He did emphasize the care both he and his wife took to speak very correct English. When they left the office, he lingered for a moment after his wife. The seriously solicitous look on his face gave way to a mischievous grin. He winked understandingly at the principal and said, "You know, I think all this yak-yaking is sorta silly, but I can go along with a gag."

In a case like this, a teacher may wonder whether the child knew what he was doing. Was he deliberately teasing adults, or had he actually become unable to learn? Did subjects involving English usage arouse in him a resentment at the strict standards his parents had tried to enforce? Had he sensed his father's amusement and developed a feeling that learning correct language rules was a silly business which a true he-man should disdain? Was he going through a stage that would end of itself? What could his teacher do?

Rhoda Is Upset

For many young people, especially those in their teens, school is a place for social life, which is much more important to them than teachers, books, and academic learning. This part of life may be full of perplexities for young people. Now and again, some incident in a classroom will reveal the resultant strains. For instance:

Mr. Lawrence had often wondered what he could do for Rhoda. In a "slow" general mathematics class, she did so poorly he felt she was "lost." Moreover, she was quite unpopular.

Although one would expect young people who are all having trouble in school to be sympathetic to each other, in this particular group anyone who made an error was likely to be subjected to raucous laughter. Most of the youngsters could weather such incidents, but Rhoda was sensitive. Not only that, but her voice had a harsh, jarring sound so out of keeping with her appearance that it almost invited ridicule.

One day, when she was working a problem at the blackboard, she became hopelessly confused about the meaning of proportions. While Mr. Lawrence, working hard to sound patient and sympathetic, was trying to help her out of the difficulty with leading questions, a boy's voice in a stage whisper commented, "It's no use. She'll never learn the score."

Apparently this sally had a double meaning familiar to many of the class. In any event, it evoked a loud chorus of mocking snickers. Mr. Lawrence turned on the class, angry disapproval showing clearly in his face. The laughter subsided; but several boys and girls placed their hands over their mouths as though trying strenuously not to show obvious glee.

Rhoda flushed, and tears came to her eyes. The quiet was broken by another boy's whisper, "And she's a crybaby, too."

At this Rhoda lost all control of herself. In a brassy, screeching voice she shouted, "You're not funny," and then in furious tones berated the class. Toward the close of her tirade, she became incoherent, gasping out wild epithets. Both the class and Mr. Lawrence were shocked by the spectacle she presented.

Recognizing that she was too upset to understand any calm reasoning, Mr. Lawrence knew only that he had to get Rhoda out of the room. Then, after giving the class a good talking-to, he could have a helpful chat with her.

Quickly, he apologized to her for the class, and then turned to Theresa Nolan, a girl who he knew had a reputation for being helpful. "Take her to the girls' room and stay with her until she is calm," were his instructions.

After the two girls had left, the class held a discussion. Mr. Lawrence was popular enough with the group for his disapproval of teasing to make most of them contrite. There was a general agreement that in the future all of them would try to help Rhoda, just as they wanted to be helped when they had trouble. Thinking about their reactions later, however, Mr. Lawrence could not quite evaluate an undercurrent of giggling among the students that he had suppressed during the discussion. He was not sure whether it represented a secret reservation against the agreement or was merely a perverse symptom of guilt.

In thinking about an outburst like this, we naturally have quite a few questions: Why did Rhoda's resentment give rise to a temper outburst? What other forms might it have taken? Mr. Lawrence will not always be around to protect her; how can she learn how to face her own problems? Why did the boys have to be so nasty? Would they have acted the same way if they had been confident of their ability to learn? How permanent a change in the group could Mr. Lawrence make?

Karl: An Unhappy "Prodigy"

Karl's teachers would have told you that here was a boy who would get places. All through school, he had been studious, respectful, and a credit to his class. His straight-A record was all the more surprising because there had been several in the class who had much higher I.Q.'s. But the teachers also would have said that for years Karl's classmates had sneered at him. They were not mean to him, or cruel. Rather, when his name was mentioned, they shrugged their shoulders or made grimaces of distaste. They had much preferred the company of less diligent boys and girls.

When he came back to visit Rosewood, Miss Carney, the principal, remembered him right away. She thought of the pale youth of sixteen who had appeared so lonely in the group waiting for graduation six years before. He had worked so hard that she felt he ought to be happy. She knew that he almost never played or wasted time. Every afternoon he had gone right home and studied for four or five hours. Two summers, he had given up his vacation to come to summer school.

His parents had been proud of him, no question of that. Miss Carney thought they had a right to be. In America only fifteen years, they had an intense interest in succeeding. Karl's father or mother had come to school often to find out how he was doing. You could almost feel their driving worry that someone might do better than their son.

Now, six years later, there he was in the outer office. There could be no question: there was the same pale, tense, unhappy face. When he saw Miss Carney, he arose awkwardly and, as though not sure of himself, jerkily extended his hand. Miss Carney was unpleasantly surprised at his clammy handshake.

"It is good to see you again," she told him.

Karl seemed ill at ease. He said nothing for a while, then blurted, "Is it O.K. for me to use your name as a reference for a job?"

"Of course it is."

"Thanks."

Miss Carney was puzzled. "I thought you were going to become a doctor."

He looked very unhappy. "I was, but the doctors say I have to rest. I studied too hard and cracked up."

Then he told her the whole story. He had won a scholarship and, in the premedical courses, had done well enough to get into a good medical school. In college, his marks had given him a little trouble; despite all his trying, he had begun to get B's and even a C.

In medical school again, he did above-average work, but somehow he could not get back up to the A average he felt people expected of him. The competition was too tough. He had increased his study hours, but without success. Then, this year at examination time, he had tried getting along on four hours of sleep. He got through, but his marks were still all B's and C's. At least, that is what they had told him in the infirmary. After the last examination, he said, "I guess I just came apart at the seams. Anyway, they say I must relax and have some fun or I'll have a real breakdown."

He seemed thoroughly bewildered.

Miss Carney said, "After a year you'll be back on your feet, and then everything will be fine."

He acted morose, sat for a while without saying anything, and then rose to go. "Thanks for letting me use your name."

"Glad to do it, Karl." Then Miss Carney asked, "What will you do for a good time?"

He answered wearily, "I don't know. I've never had one, you know."

In schools and colleges, boys or girls like Karl are called "grinds," "bones," "creeps," or other names of distaste or pity. Many young people look down on them. Are they right? What makes one youngster study intensively while others have a good time? Do all diligent students have exceptional drive? Did the attitude of his classmates keep Karl from having a good time? What part did his parents play? Could the teachers have done anything to make his life happier?

Eighth-Grade Bedlam

The social attitudes of young people differ with age. Hitting and fighting in the classroom occur quite often in kindergarten and nursery schools. Social pressures such as those that bedeviled Rhoda are far from unusual in high schools. Each age level has its own problems. For example:

Miss Devers was beginning to regret that she had ever volunteered to teach the class in Social Living to eighth-graders in the Rowtown Junior High School. This was her first year, and she had been eager to help the principal in his campaign to "loosen things up." On his part, he had seen very quickly that her youthful jauntiness made her an ideal person to put life into the course, which previously had been made dull by the prissy correctness of Miss Gorham.

The first month, things had gone marvelously. The students responded wonderfully in discussions. Lately, however, she had been miserable and was ready to call herself a failure. The trouble had started when the class began discussing dating and dancing parties. The girls were almost all interested, but the boys began misbehaving. They acted like immature little brats, making silly, childish, leering wisecracks. One or two did tell her that they did not like what the others were doing, but in class they refused to expose themselves to the derision of the "kids." The girls retaliated by making snippy remarks. (Miss Devers felt they were justified.) When she tried to talk to the boys, she found they turned against her. At a class Halloween dance they raced around the floor like little Indians and so terrorized each other that the girls had to dance together, and even that was disrupted by volleys of catcalls and crude shouts. No matter what she did, the boys kept getting worse. On the rare days when they seemed to be calm, some girl was almost certain to stir things up again by an ill-timed derogatory comment.

Many teachers who have gone through such experiences have decided to stick to safer activities. Yet, the very same type of incident may disrupt a class in history or algebra. A teacher seeking a way to curb such disorders would want to know not only how such forces can be handled but what effect they have. Would early participation in such sex warfare influence later attitudes toward marriage? Can group pressures force an individual to hold to immature behavior patterns? In the incident discussed, could Miss Devers have helped matters by siding with the boys instead of the girls? If she had been stern and squelched the first boy who got out of line, what would have happened? Was it a mistake to let the class discuss dating at all? Just how can you help junior high school students to work out their problems of social adjustment?

Dick Quits School

For many children, school is an unpleasant experience. We are not talking now about the moth-eaten legend that all children hate school. We are talking about those boys and girls who feel bored, browbeaten, or betrayed, for endless days. Some vent their hostility in the dramatic gesture of truancy; others remain physically present but escape in other ways. Many "serve their time" and then quit as soon as they pass the legal age of compulsory attendance. Their reasons for leaving are many and frequently complicated. Some are doing poor work, and their teachers are relieved at their going. Others quit because they are lonesome in school, or they say their families need the money, or give other reasons that are polite masks for truths they either do not know or would rather not air. For instance:

According to the school records, Richard Kane had an I.Q. of 115, stood about in the middle of his class, had passed all his subjects with mediocre grades, had never been in trouble, and had engaged in a minimum of extracurricular activities.

Mr. Herrick, boys' counselor at the West Gilbert High School, leafed through the very uninformative cumulative record. He had sent for Dick because of a note from the home-room teacher saying that the boy planned to leave school in April, the day after his seventeenth birthday. The school policy was to interview all such students. Mr. Herrick did not remember Dick. He watched the boy very carefully when he came in. Dick was of medium height, clean, a little stocky, and somewhat timid. He opened the conversation. "You sent for me, sir?"

Mr. Herrick motioned for him to take the chair alongside his desk.

"Yes. Your home-room teacher said you are planning to leave us, and I thought you would want to talk with me before making a decision which could influence the rest of your life."

Dick smiled. "Thank you, sir. I've thought it all out."

"Your mind is made up," echoed Mr. Herrick.

"You bet. I've got a job."

"You have a job?"

Dick's tone was confident as he explained: "Last summer I worked over at the Eagle Gadget plant, and they told me they'd be glad to have me work there any time. I went to see them last week, and they promised me a job right away. They said they needed workers right away. And, the pay is good."

Although he had been trained not to use any form of coercion in such interviews, the counselor could not help putting a sly dig into his next reply: "The pay is good for beginners?"

Dick saw the point, "Oh, it's not a blind alley. Plenty of men get promoted from the assembly line. Experience counts there. The manager over there never went to high school, and I'll bet he earns more than you do, sir."

Mr. Herrick tacitly admitted defeat on that point, and said, "You feel you have a good chance for promotion. Do you think this is really a fine opportunity?"

"You bet. I get on with people O.K., and that's what counts. I can get along with everybody, I guess, except maybe my father."

"You and your father have fights?"

"Not exactly fights, sir. He just treats me like a kid. I'm grown up now, and can take care of myself."

"You feel that if you earn money, your father will treat you differently?"

"That's it. I can make enough to live on if I want to. Then I won't have to take orders from anyone, my old man or teachers or anybody. I'm sick and tired of being bossed around. Sure, I do what I'm told, 'cause what's the use of getting in a row, but I'm not a kid any more. You folks here mean well, but you are awful bossy, and you really don't know the score."

Mr. Herrick began to understand. Here was a boy who, for the moment at least, prized independence more than anything. There were more facts to discover. Was this attitude a temporary phase of adolescence, or was it a deep-seated antipathy to all authority? Would Dick go through life concealing his hate for bosses beneath a surface of pleasing obedience while he planned to escape from them? Would he become a vocational rolling stone? Why had no teacher been able to find out how he felt? Had his teachers really been needlessly bossy? Why had no subject caught his interest? Mr. Herrick sighed. What could he do next? He suspected he would be unable to influence Dick. Forty per cent of the boys and girls at West Gilbert left school without finishing, as soon as they were seventeen. He wondered what changes in the school could improve the situation. Yet, he realized that there were aspects of the problem the school could not touch.

Mr. Brown's School:
The Machinery Squeaks

As a complicated social institution, a school must have rules. Rules may protect groups from interference with learning, they may make record keeping easier for administrators, they may make life simpler for children who like to know what is expected of them. But rules can also cause trouble if they negate basic needs of teachers or learners, if they create mechanical difficulties for the teaching process, or if they cause hostility within the school. For example:

Mr. Brown was a principal who prided himself on his ability to work out a system to take care of any situation. His school was noted for the machine-like precision of its operation.

Visitors to Mr. Brown's school could not help but admire the pains-taking care given to even minor details. The principal was particularly proud of a new system for dismissing classes, explaining that his school held two thousand children and that the sidewalks outside were so narrow that children might be forced into the very busy and dangerous bordering highways "if classes left helter-skelter and the children were allowed to loiter."

The scheme he had worked out required each class to leave in a designated order. The older children went through the exits first. Because they walked faster, this arrangement avoided any crowding of the streets caused by older children overtaking and trying to pass slower-moving little children.

On a typical day, a warning bell sounded promptly at 2:56. Quickly doors opened, and teachers lined their classes up outside the rooms. Each line faced toward the exit designated for the class.

As Mr. Brown surveyed the scene, his satisfaction gave way to swift, displeased action when he saw no line outside Room 113. In the room a girl was reading a report. The teacher, Miss Keith, began to explain: "Janet has worked very hard, and I didn't want to deprive her of the opportunity to show how well she could do. This is her first really good piece of work——"

"You're holding up the whole school," Mr. Brown said, interrupting her. "She can finish that tomorrow."

The teacher stopped the report and told the class to put on their wraps.

In the hall, a hubbub became audible. Children, impatient at delay, shifted in line and started to talk to each other. The teachers, with forced smiles and well-practiced airs of confidence, patrolled their charges to quiet them down. Miss Keith, now obviously flustered, shouted impatiently to her group to hurry.

When he was satisfied that all was ready, Mr. Brown nodded at his clerk, who was watching from the office doorway. She pressed a button; the bells sounded two sharp rings. From the second floor, the lines of older pupils swiftly descended the stairs and moved through the halls to their exits. For a few brief minutes, all was smooth movement, as the building quickly emptied. The principal glowed with pride at the orderly bustle.

Outside, however, a circle of interested first graders had gathered around a weeping little girl. They took up a jeering chant, "Kindergarten baby, wash your face in gravy!"

As the girl's mother came up, one of her classmates explained, "Marilyn wet herself."

"Why didn't you tell the teacher?" the mother asked roughly. Her gestures bespoke impatience.

Marilyn sobbed. "I did, but it was after recess. She said I could wait till I got home."

The mother, still annoyed with the girl, objected. "You could have gone while the big children were coming out."

Marilyn explained, "You're not allowed to cross the lines."

In working out his plans, Mr. Brown was doing his level best to safeguard pupils from physical dangers. He liked to keep as many factors as possible under control because he worried lest some untoward incident endanger a child while the school was responsible. He wanted to be absolutely sure that every boy and girl was accounted for and safely out of the building at dismissal time. In setting up arrangements for recesses, he was anxious to guard against even the remote possibility of some older boy or an intruder molesting one of the little girls.

Despite all this, we can see that he upset Miss Keith, spoiled an experience valuable for Janet, and unwittingly subjected Marilyn to a vividly unpleasant series of events. In cases like these, does the mental hygienist condemn rules and regulations? Could the rules be made more flexible? Exactly how damaging were the incidents to the people involved? What would be the ultimate emotional effect upon the other teachers and pupils? What is the relation between the way this school runs and Mr. Brown's own personality? Would it be different if there were another principal?

Jean: A "Mental Casualty"

Much happens in every class and in every school that principals and teachers do not notice. In this book, we will be concerned not only with incidents that disturb classes, but also with events which often go unnoticed but can be highly significant. For example:

The Elton School was highly regarded, largely because of a little group of four old teachers, admired by pupils and parents alike for their affection toward youngsters and their effectiveness in developing skills and imparting knowledge. The four had been at the school fifteen years, and seemed to know all the families. In fact, the children of their first pupils were beginning to attend the school.

In the teachers' lunchroom, they always sat at the same table. There, and during their bridge parties, they shared gossip.

"Do you remember Jean Warpatch?" Miss Alberty asked her cronies one day. As she obviously had something to tell, they waited.

"I met her mother yesterday," she added.

Miss Cormon rose to the bait. "Did she tell you anything about Jean?"

Miss Alberty dropped her bombshell. "Yes, she went out of her mind and had to be put away."

All looked shocked. Then they began comparing their memories of the girl.

"I never had any trouble with her."

"Come to think of it, she was always a little queer. Nothing you could put your finger on. She would just sit with a faraway look on her face."

"I always had a little trouble making her pay attention, but she was such a good girl you could forgive that."

"She did get into one fight in my room. She had been sitting and daydreaming when one of the boys pulled her hair, not hard, just teasing. She flared up as though she wanted to kill him. I didn't do anything about it because she had always been so good; and, after all, he started it."

"They tell me her aunt was a bit queer."

"When Jean came to kindergarten, she used to hang on to her mother. Not that she was glad to see her, but she just hung on as if she was afraid to let go."

What is unusual about the above scene is, first, that the teachers remembered Jean and, second, that they learned what had happened to her. Statistics indicate that, on the average, 2 children in every class of 32 will spend part of their lives in a mental institution. This startling fact is one of the reasons for the present-day emphasis on mental health. The figure in itself is shocking enough; but, even more important, there is good reason to believe that if mental illness can only be recognized and treated in its early stages, many of these tragedies can be prevented.

In the things her teachers remembered about Jean, there were several plain clues to emotional disturbances. What were they? What other signs of mental instability could teachers learn to recognize? What agencies will give help? How do you go about talking to parents in such cases? Upon the answers to these questions the future happiness of thousands of children depends.

Too Conscientious?

Mrs. Blount, principal of the Patton School, worried a good deal about Louise Nagler, the third-grade teacher. If ever there was a thorny administrative problem where "no matter what you do, it's wrong," the question of what to do about that teacher (or to her or for her) was one.

Miss Nagler was a strict, hard-working woman of thirty-two, who looked ten years older. She was sick and unhappy. Mrs. Blount and the other teachers agreed that "Louise is working herself to death." They tried to tell her that she should spare herself. But she would have none of their pity, and insisted that her first duty was to the children in her class.

During the eleven years she had been teaching, Miss Nagler had accumulated a large collection of teaching aids. She had made flash cards for difficult words and for arithmetic facts. She had hectographed work sheets. She had made cardboard games in which her classes found exciting fun. Despite the fact that her health was not too sturdy, she still found time to add to her collection and to invent new games. Every night she took home papers to correct.

But it was also true that Miss Nagler had been showing almost uncontrolled impatience with children who did not do well. She tried to spur laggards by holding them up to ridicule. She slapped children who repeated errors in spelling or arithmetic drills. None of this happened when Mrs. Blount or a visitor was in the room; then Miss Nagler was the picture of gentleness.

Very few parents or children ever complained; when they did, Mrs.

Blount could refer to Miss Nagler's reputation as an effective teacher and thus back her up. Indeed, throughout the community the teacher was highly regarded as a stern taskmaster who got work out of the children. There was little doubt that one large group of parents highly approved of her methods. Among the other teachers, there likewise was an admiring consensus: "Whatever you may think of her methods, when you get children from her, they know their spelling and arithmetic."

Mrs. Blount was not so sure. It was true that Miss Nagler's more capable pupils often took a spurt in accomplishments which involved memorization, but those in the lower half of the group often appeared to go backward in her class. Mrs. Blount had several times put forth the view that Miss Nagler should concentrate on rebuilding such a child's self-confidence.

As a principal, she did not see what she could do. She had attempted several times to suggest that Miss Nagler should seek medical care; but she had not been able to find a way to bring up the possible need for psychiatric care. After all, one can hardly portray devotion to duty as a bad symptom. Certainly, it would be impossible to find any charges on which to force her out of teaching.

A situation of this type raises a cluster of issues. What provisions should be made for teachers who have emotional problems? If those problems result in behavior harmful to children, what should be done? Is stern pressure always a bad way to obtain achievement? Should teachers be concerned with the effect on "weak" pupils? Should administrators back up teachers in actions of which they do not entirely approve? How should members of a school staff act when one teacher does things the others feel are damaging to some children?

The Morris Boy, Snakes, and a Teacher

Many teachers are already doing a great deal to help children with problems. Some have learned what to do in psychology and mental hygiene classes; others have a "natural feel" for people and use an uncommon amount of common sense in dealing with them. For example:

The boiler room of the Kinnawalk Consolidated School was a favorite hangout for the teachers. By unofficial tradition it was the one place in the building where they could smoke. The main attraction, however, was Chuck Johnson, the janitor. When he was around, somehow everyone relaxed; there was a great deal of joking, and troubles managed to dissolve.

"Your room looks like a drunkard's nightmare," he told Miss Fogner as she came in during the ten o'clock recess.

"You mean the snakes?" She grinned.

Miss Upstead made a face. "Snakes, ugh!"

Chuck added, "If you get any pink elephants, let me know, or this school'll be getting a new janitor."

"It was your idea," Miss Fogner said.

"How come?"

"Remember what you said about the Morris boy?"

"You mean the farm kid with the lame leg?"

"The same. He has been getting in trouble. You know, low I.Q., no good at games, clothes all patched, his folks have no money, and his mother ran away. There was nothing he could do right."

Chuck nodded. "Uh-huh. I remember. He was starting to swipe stuff, and using the money he got from selling it to buy candy for the town boys."

"And you said he was not bad, just trying to show off."

"Check. You teach him to do something the others can't, and he'll straighten out."

Miss Fogner looked triumphant. "Snakes!"

"You taught him about snakes?"

"I didn't have to. He knew. He spends his spare time finding them and watching them."

"So?"

"So, my room is having a contest to see who can bring in the most different kinds of snakes. Today was the judging. You should have heard him tell about his entries."

"He won?"

"Right. Haven't been missing anything around here lately, have you?"

The bell rang, and Miss Fogner had to go back to class.

Chuck watched her go. He nodded approvingly, and then made a mental note to check her room carefully that night. Some of the town children in the other classes might get upset if they found snakes in their rooms the next morning.

The basic principle involved in this incident has nothing to do with snakes or with contests. It has a great deal to do with finding the roots of a child's problem and then helping him to get in school the affection or admiration or security he needs. To provide such emotional tonics is one of the basic strategies of mental hygiene in education.

The Kilroy Faculty Has a Meeting

Although the focus of education will always be upon students, the key person in any classroom is the teacher. In some instances, as with Miss Nagler, or Miss Fogner, the way they act toward children is largely a product of their personal values. But we must also recognize that conditions in a school may lead to emotional tensions and dissatisfactions among teachers, and that their classes may feel the indirect effects. We can never afford to overlook the fact that teachers are people, who have their own ways of meeting new problems involving other people. For example:

During the final period messages had been brought to all teachers at the Kilroy Junior High School ordering them to a staff meeting right after school. Mr. Sharpe, the principal, told the meeting that during the lunch hour there had been a rock-throwing incident on the playground, and one boy had received a gash so bad that he had been sent to the hospital. In order to forestall criticism and to do all they could to prevent any future incidents, the staff would have to keep one teacher on duty in the playground during the lunch hour. He announced that a list of the faculty with the dates they were to be on duty had been posted on the office bulletin board.

Miss Mendota rose to ask if the culprits were known, and, if so, what was being done to them. She advised that they be expelled from school and their parents forced to pay all damages.

With tears in her voice, Miss Macy objected. "The poor children are suffering enough as it is. I'm sure it must have been an accident. These young people need our sympathy."

Mr. Queen grumbled that the teachers were already overworked. He thought the whole thing was the fault of the administration and the school board. He said he had been hired as a teacher, not a policeman.

During this speech, Mrs. Meade had been shaking her head. She said that she was sure Mr. Sharpe's plan was the best, and volunteered to take charge of the playground the very next day.

That night, Miss Mendota revised a test she had been planning to give. She added a few very hard questions. Feeling thoroughly righteous, she told herself that the young hooligans needed discipline and that she was the person to give it to them.

Miss Macy felt quite doleful. She attended a sad moving picture and had a good cry. She resolved to show her pity by making her classes more pleasant the next day and decided to have the children take up a collection and buy flowers for the injured boy.

Indigestion spoiled Mr. Queen's dinner. He was boiling mad both at Mr. Sharpe for having ordered the staff around and at the staff for having taken the indignities without protest. Mentally he composed a little speech to give to his classes to show them what he thought of the new playground-guard arrangement.

As for Mrs. Meade, she telephoned Mr. Sharpe to ask him if there was anything she could do to help the situation at school. She also thought that the incident might be turned to advantage by preaching to her classes a little sermon on the importance of giving implicit obedience to all school rules and regulations.

We cannot but wonder how the students would be affected by these teachers. Equally important, why did each act as he did? How could each be helped to secure greater happiness in the school situation?

In this chapter we have described twelve incidents typical of those which arise in almost every school system. By the use of concrete examples, we have tried to show the kinds of problems that can take on new meaning in the light of ideas developed in the field of mental hygiene. In later chapters, we shall treat some of the psychological forces that come into play, and relate these to events with which teachers have to cope in a classroom setting.

ADDITIONAL READINGS

Division of Child Development and Teacher Personnel, American Council on Education. *Helping Teachers Understand Children.* Washington: American Council on Education, 1945. Tells how a group of teachers learned about the children in their classes. Contains many anecdotes describing individual behavior and class situations.

Fuess, Charles, and Emory Bradford. *Unseen Harvests.* New York: Macmillan, 1947. Drawn largely from novels and other well-known literature, passages exemplifying the effects of schools and teachers are compiled in a thought-provoking sequence.

Langdon, Grace, and Irving W. Stout. *These Well-Adjusted Children.* New York: Day, 1951, Part 3. Sketches of nine well-adjusted children and their families show the variety among individuals.

McDaniel, Henry B. *Guidance in the Modern School.* New York: Dryden Press, 1956, Chap. 5. Describes the guidance needs of young people and presents eight case studies.

Morse, William C., and G. Max Wingo. *Psychology and Teaching.* Chicago:

Scott-Foresman, 1955, Chap. 2. What goes on in schools is pictured as a preliminary to the discussion of educational psychology.

National Society for the Study of Education. *Fifty-Fourth Yearbook, Part II: Mental Health in Modern Education.* Chicago: U. of Chicago Press, 1955, Chap. 1. Harry N. Rivlin discusses the role of mental health in education.

Teachers! Are These Your Children? Brooklyn: Board of Education of the City of New York, 1946. Describes various kinds of child behavior that are often of concern to teachers.

AUDIO-VISUAL AIDS

Self-Conscious Guy, a 10-minute sound film by Coronet, which depicts the problems of a high school boy hampered by the feeling he is conspicuous.

When Should Grown-Ups Help? a 14-minute sound film by the Department of Child Study, Vassar College, in which situations at the nursery-school level are depicted and the audience asked to decide what should be done, and why.

chapter **2**

WHAT IT IS ALL ABOUT

The purpose of a course or a book on mental hygiene for teachers is to enable them to make life better, both now and in the future, for themselves and for the children in their classes. The principles of mental hygiene, as you will see, apply to all people. An understanding of this branch of knowledge, therefore, should increase the likelihood that we can help all children develop into happier, more confident, and more stable adults. Teachers should be able to aid the growth of character and personality more effectively. Equally important, school life can become an ever more pleasant and significant part of young people's lives. Finally, teachers themselves can learn to obtain greater satisfaction from the hours spent earning a livelihood in the classroom.

In the very recent past, the major objective for many mental hygienists was to instruct teachers in the signs of mental disease. This was done in the hope that victims of such disorders could be brought to treatment early and therefore cured more surely. As our knowledge of psychological forces has increased, we have realized that this cannot be the sole, or even the most important, objective of mental hygiene for teachers. It will always be a significant purpose, but more and more emphasis is placed on those principles and techniques which can be applied day in and day out to most of the young people in the schools.

Specifically, what may teachers hope to do better after studying mental hygiene? They can expect that more of the events in a classroom will make sense to them. The reasons why individual children do hitherto puzzling things should become clearer. Teachers thereby should have better intellectual tools with which to analyze what happens in their classes and to work out a plan for meeting situations which otherwise might be mishandled.

23

All this implies several other possibilities. First of all, it means that teachers should be more capable of spotting those children who are mentally sick and who need expert help. More than that, it implies that teachers will be sensitive to the forces which cause personality distortion and will guide their classes in ways that will minimize further damage to already vulnerable children. Beyond that, knowing about the course of mental and emotional development, they will have greater skill in providing constructive experiences for children. As their grasp of these ways of analyzing new situations improves, they should be able to meet future incidents with greater flexibility.

The Nature of Mental Hygiene

Being a relatively new field, mental hygiene has been the victim of many misunderstandings. We shall mention and comment upon a few of these.

One common belief is that if you study mental hygiene—assumed to be an occult science—you will somehow become "different." In many people's minds the mental sciences may still be associated with hypnotism, penetrating eyes behind thick-lensed glasses, diabolically clever whispers in foreign accents, and spine-chilling music. Such images may be echoes of scenes from Hollywood thrillers. Actually, the subject is not mystical; there is a large body of rigorously scientific experiments behind mental hygiene theory. Moreover, as it has developed over the years, this knowledge has had to meet the test of practice in clinics, homes, and classrooms. Mental hygiene is a science, not a magic.

Some people are apprehensive because they think that studying mental hygiene will turn them into introverts who will spend too much of their time examining their own inner lives. To some degree, an increase in self-awareness is inevitable. For instance, when medical students study diseases, even the healthiest think they detect in themselves the signs of many disorders, but they soon get over this. The same thing happens to many students of mental hygiene. For example, when we discuss mental mechanisms and various peculiarities, you are almost certain to discover that your own actions include most of the mechanisms and resemble many of the peculiarities. For the average stable person, however, such speculations about themselves usually prove to be both entertaining and useful. Understanding a type of behavior does not produce it, but does help you to use your intelligence in dealing with it. A few people who apparently just have to worry about themselves become anxious about their mental balance after studying mental hygiene. But even if such people avoided the subject, they would still worry about themselves, though in other ways.

A number of students are always a little disappointed because they expected that a course in mental hygiene would enable them to solve practically all their problems and to cure themselves, their friends, relatives, and pupils of all maladjustments. This expectation is as unrealistic as the hope that a course in anatomy will qualify one to remove an appendix. The most one can expect to gain is a greater understanding of people and some general principles to help determine what to do in many classroom situations. Such an awareness is the first step in helping people.

WHAT MENTAL HYGIENE IS.   Most of you who read this book have taken courses in health or physical hygiene in high school or college. In such courses you learned how to keep your body healthy; you learned about its needs for food, rest, and air. You discussed such dangers to physical health as germs, bad posture, and narcotics. Most important, you were taught some simple but very general rules for strengthening your resistance to disease. You were never given the impression that you had learned exactly how to diagnose and treat any physical disorder. You learned the components of a good diet, but you were not given recipes for cooking meals.

Mental hygiene is in many ways similar in purpose to physical hygiene, but its main concern is with mental phenomena. The term "mental" is taken to include all psychological aspects of the individual, whether these involve his intellectual activity, emotional reactions, personality traits, or character development. Mental hygiene helps us to understand people's psychological needs and how to meet them. It aids in dealing with situations in which mental health may be endangered, but it makes no pretense at giving exact rules for treating mental disturbances.

Most of our rules for health, both physical and mental, have resulted from study of diseases. For example, we discovered vitamins through doctors' successful attempts to get at the causes of scurvy, pellagra, rickets, and other ailments. In the same way, as psychiatrists treated mentally disturbed patients, they learned of such needs as security, affection, and acceptance.

There are striking differences between the study of physical hygiene and mental hygiene. The causes of physical diseases are usually objective and visible in the sense that we can take X-ray photographs, make chemical tests, or take bacteriological cultures, which numerous observers will interpret in the same way. We can sometimes take out of the affected person a sample of the organism or chemical which has caused trouble, and introduce it into an experimental animal. For example, we can prove that certain bacteria cause tuberculosis because we can take them from the victim, grow them in a test tube, and show that they will cause the disease in another organism. That is to say, it is possible to repeat experiments without hurting any more people.

The subject matter of mental hygiene is the entire mind and the entire personality. It deals with such things as emotions, character structure, attachments, and feelings. These are not directly visible. Moreover, they have no existence independent of human beings. We cannot take a sample of a negative self-concept out of one person and introduce it into someone else. Because the conditions underlying psychological disturbances involve the whole life history of a person, it is much harder to duplicate the particular situation for experimental purposes. Psychologists do make some use of animal experiments, as, for example, in attempts to create experimentally induced neuroses in rats and goats. But these, while of interest, are limited in their application to human beings. Although many clear-cut experiments have been carried out with human beings, the methods are harder to develop, and more time is needed to show conclusive results because human beings are more complex and develop more slowly than laboratory animals.

The apparent lag of mental hygiene can be linked to the fact that physical hygiene has a much longer history of research behind it. Medical experimentation now benefits from centuries of scientific study during which many wonderful instruments for observation were developed. On the other hand, serious scientific study of mental disease had barely started ninety years ago. Even today, many more millions of dollars go into research on a single physical disease, such as cancer, than into the study of all mental and emotional ailments.

Today, public opinion readily accepts most medical findings concerning physical phenomena. This is true only because our schools and other agencies of education have made most people familiar with the basic concepts. We find it hard to believe now, but such ideas as the germ theory of disease and the value of vaccination were terrifically disturbing to many people at first. Today, these theories are so much a part of our cultural heritage that they are no longer questioned. With the possible exception of campaigns against venereal diseases, few people nowadays are upset by efforts to eradicate bodily illnesses. Only a most unusual individual would feel an emotional urge to defend cancers or influenza viruses, or have a sense of outrage at the pasteurization of milk or the inspection of meats.

To too large an extent, the opposite is true for mental hygiene measures. There has been comparatively little education in the field. Large numbers of otherwise highly literate people still have only a sketchy understanding of the nature of psychological science. In addition, the findings may weaken the self-esteem of certain people and shake their faith in long-established patterns of behavior. For example, a mother may get satisfaction from keeping her children strongly dependent on her. The suggestion that this might be harmful and that she ought to change her ways is highly unpleasant. She may meet the danger by refusing to believe the mental hygienist or by shrugging him off as a crackpot. Similarly, a man whose own personality has been distorted may take pride in the very qualities which make him unhappy or socially undesirable. The bigot not only may admire his own bigotry but may want to spread it; the confirmed criminal may boast of how tough he is, and look with contempt on law-abiding citizens; the man so indecisive that he avoids making choices may think of himself as prudent and want to pass the same quality along to his children. To such people and others like them, the conclusions of the mental health sciences are menacing. Consequently they dare not accept the new ideas.

Despite these differences between physical hygiene and mental hygiene, both are basically alike in striving to apply scientific knowledge, much of it derived from the study of disease, to the prevention of ill health and the protection of human beings. As protective and constructive sciences, they depend upon certain qualities of thinking which we shall now discuss.

Clear Thinking About Mental Health

The fields of both physical and mental hygiene suffer from a common curse: Because people worry about their own well-being, quacks have found great profit in publishing half-baked or completely incorrect newspaper columns, magazine articles, and books dealing with mental or physical health. Such irresponsible material can frequently be spotted by two characteristics: its authors affect a very positive tone, and they give sweeping rules without reference to scientific findings. A reader has a right to be suspicious of any mental hygiene book that is not based on concrete facts. Serious efforts to use mental hygiene theory require hard, disciplined thinking. We shall now consider some problems which arise as we attempt to put mental hygiene theory into practice.

DISCIPLINED THINKING VERSUS MAGICAL BELIEF.   Certain ancient peoples thought that headaches were caused by spirits inside the brain and therefore cut holes in the skull to let the spirits out. Others thought insanity was caused by demons and had medicine men dance in fearful costume to frighten them away. We call this type of thinking magical because it is based on the belief that some type of behavior is powerful even though it has no proved relation to the situation that is supposed to be modified. One can hear an occasional college student ascribing a poor score on an examination to the fact that she forgot to wear her "lucky sweater." Like other magic, such beliefs enable people to avoid facing their own poor grasp of the subject. In modern life, the magical assumption may be cloaked in scientific words. Thus, some people act on a belief that all headaches are caused by "acid indigestion" and accordingly dose themselves with alkaline powders.

The scientist proceeds in a different fashion. When confronted with a condition that needs changing, he looks for the real causes. When he thinks he has a clue, he checks his results. Then, he looks for a treatment to get at the causes. This, also, he tests with care. The same symptom may have different causes in different people. In one famous case, for example, it was found that a man's headaches came from wearing collars that were too tight! In yet other cases, headaches have been traced to brain tumors, to high blood pressure resulting from noise, to reading under bad lighting conditions, to improper eyeglasses, and to many other causes. In each case, the method of treatment was different.

The same thing is true in mental and emotional difficulties. There, too, we have traditional magic. For example, when a child "talks back," teachers often decide without further investigation that he is "spoiled," that is, has not been "disciplined" sufficiently at home. The traditional cure is to "teach him respect for his elders" by punishing him. In high schools, when classes become restless and boys and girls pay more attention to each other than to the teacher, school officials may promptly blame everything on sex. One traditional cure is to "burn up the energy" by giving students strenuous exercise. In some circles it is believed that "nervousness" on the part of unmarried adults is caused by "sexual frustration," and can be cured only by indulgence.

Clear thinking on these and similar problems would take an altogether different course. A careful investigation would be made in each instance to discover what the "talking back" or the restlessness or the "nervousness" really meant and what its cause was. For example, the "talking back" might mean only that the boy was trying to be friends. Perhaps the adults he knew made a habit of bantering insults when they got together for a good time. If this were the case, punishment would embitter him; a friendly explanation of other techniques of having pleasant conversation with people might help him. Another possibility is that the "talking back" might be a symptom of a deep rebellion against adults, caused by his being punished frequently at home for no reason. If this were so, additional punishment at school would only add to his difficulties; to be helpful, adults must let him see that there are many grownups who do like children and are fair to them. In still another case, however, the boy's behavior might be an attempt to exploit a presumed special privilege by "getting away with murder" to amuse the other children. A wisely chosen form of reproof or other punishment would help him to establish clear limits for his future behavior. There are many other possible meanings, each calling for its own special handling.

The same principle of seeking out the cause-and-effect relationship holds true for the other examples we have given. A high school class could be restless because the subject was dull, the teacher irritated them, they were hungry, there was quarreling between cliques, they were keyed up in anticipation of a big game, the seats were poorly designed, or a combination of a dozen other possibilities. Success in coping with the restlessness would depend in each case on finding a suitable method. "Nervousness" in adults, of course, can cover a multitude of conditions.

An illustration of the need for thorough examination of the causes of any problem is found in a study of children with reading disabilities whose records are in the files of the Queens College Educational Clinic and the Brooklyn College Educational Clinic, both in New York.[1] Twenty-five children reading at 20 per cent below capacity were compared with 25 normal readers matched as to age, I.Q., grade, sex, type of school, and dominant side of body. The study found a number of patterns responsible. For instance, some poor readers, because of overindulgence at home which had deprived them of opportunities to find out how much they could do for themselves, had poor expectations of their performance; others kept a rigid control over emotional expression. Contrary to

---

[1] Myron H. Gordon, *A Clinical Study of Personality Patterns in Children with Reading Disability,* Ph.D. dissertation, New York University, 1952, University Microfilms Publication No. 4518.

expectations, the poor readers were less tense and anxious than the children sent to the clinics for other reasons. Clearly, children with reading problems are not one group, all sharing the same condition, which will yield to one program of treatment.

The fact that we have stressed the importance of scientific attitudes does not imply that good mental hygiene could or should be practiced by a cold-blooded thinking machine. On the contrary, the establishment of an emotionally happy relationship between the teacher and his group generally increases his sensitivity to the various forces that make them tick and also makes his efforts to help them more effective. "Emotion" becomes dangerous to the thinking process only when its intensity blocks vision, understanding, or both.

Nor does being clearheaded exclude using intuition. In fact, in many cases an intuitive awareness of what is going on may supply valuable hunches that then can be subjected to more deliberate exploration. Thus an experienced and sensitive teacher may have an intuitive hunch that the particular noisiness of his room has a peculiarly aggressive undertone, that it differs from the kind of noise resulting from fatigue or boredom. On the basis of this hunch, he is likely to react more intelligently. In the long run it is wise, however, even for a teacher with great confidence in his intuitive skills to check on himself from time to time. Let him predict what a child will do or how a situation will develop, and keep track of his accuracy.

RESPECT FOR REALITIES VERSUS WISHFUL BLINDNESS. Denying unpleasant implications of facts is natural to all of us. Even on issues as well understood and generally accepted as some facts of medical care, we may cover up symptoms by prolonged wishful thinking. Thus, the discomfort of going to the dentist may tempt us to ignore the twinges which warn of a growing cavity and the necessity of taking the only step that can keep it from growing worse, though we know that all the wishful thinking and cold compresses in the world will not stop tooth decay.

Facts must be faced as they really are, not as we would find them convenient. In the physical field we do not let ourselves get away with violating this rule to any marked degree. For example, we would not think much of a doctor who did not detect and treat anemia simply because that condition gave his patient an interestingly esthetic appearance. Or again, suppose parents who were planning a long-anticipated dinner party noticed their little girl was acting irritable, seemed very warm, and had a red rash. We can understand that they might be irate at the prospect of having to call off their dinner party, and would be likely to say she had "played a dirty trick" on them. But we would be very critical if they punished her or even if they thought that giving her an aspirin to bring down the fever would cure her.

The temptation to substitute wishful blindness for realism is even greater with psychological facts. When faced with unpleasant behavior, we feel better if we can somehow take action that gets rid of our feelings. Thus, it may be very tempting to blame children for conduct over which they really have no control. When we can believe they are deliberately being bad, we can be righteously indignant and "give them what they deserve," even though we know it will not change their behavior patterns. Glaring examples of this are supplied in the punishment of hundreds of hard-of-hearing children for disobedience of instructions they did not hear. Records in many clinics show that the disability of such youngsters may go undiscovered for years, partly because no one bothers to hold off giving punishment until the reason for the alleged misconduct can be discovered. Indeed, even after evidence of poor hearing is established, an occasional teacher may continue to punish on the grounds that the child "is taking advantage of his defect."

Another reason for wishful blindness is that we dislike inactivity in the face of a difficulty. Doing something, anything, right now, just for the sake of being active, makes us feel better. For example, when a class contains quite a few children who are tardy, an instructor whose plans are spoiled is quite likely to open the day by bawling out the class. At the moment he may completely forget that the children present are not the audience to which his little sermon should be directed.

In so important a matter as recognizing that a child is unusual to the point of needing treatment, teachers have a special advantage. Not only are they likely to be less emotionally involved than parents, but they see children in new types of situations and in comparison with other young people. More than a half century ago, an early "medico-pedagogical clinic" noted that many mental anomalies which had easily been ignored in the family seemed to be brought out by the school environment.[2] Classroom activities call forth reactions which can reveal that the child is unusual. A teacher who can afford to be objective recognizes the signs of serious disturbance and can take appropriate action.

---

[2] Jean Philippe and G. Paul-Boncour, *Les Anomalies Mentales chez les Écoliers,* Paris, Félix Alcan, 1907.

THE CONCEPT OF MULTIPLICITY OF CAUSES. Underlying some wishful blindness is a tendency to seek simple explanations for any situation. Yet one of the most valuable intellectual tools we have in the field of mental hygiene is the realization that behavior is rarely the result of a single, simple cause, operating all by itself. Usually several factors, interacting with each other, furnish the real explanation. Healy and Bronner,[3] as a result of decades of nationally admired work with delinquents and other disturbed children, report that in the hundreds of cases they have studied, the number of significant factors required to explain personality distortions averaged more than 3 per case.

To illustrate this concept, let us look at John Pentoll, who is coughing badly. Why is he coughing? First of all, he had a bad cold. The doctor ordered him to bed and instructed his mother to put a vaporizer in the room where he slept. His mother did not follow instructions. Where did he get the cold? "He caught it from a girl in his class." However, the other children did not get colds—why did he fall victim? His teacher suspects he was run-down. Why? His mother says he has always been sickly. The doctor knows he has badly infected tonsils. Besides all this, he is not getting enough sleep because he shares a room with an older brother, who disturbs him at night by making noise and turning on the light while getting ready for bed.

Now, we can see a few of the possible reasons why John is coughing: (1) he may be constitutionally weak; (2) he has infected tonsils; (3) he does not get enough sleep; (4) he was exposed to a cold virus; and (5) he has a mother who did not follow the doctor's orders. It might be interesting to discover why his mother ignored the doctor's advice. We might find an equally complicated interaction of factors. In this complex situation, what is the doctor doing? He has decided that John's tonsils should come out, but first, to build him up, John is getting a tonic and cough medicine so that he can sleep better. The parents have been sternly instructed to change their living arrangements and to use a vaporizer.

For another example, take Don Edgeman, who has a record of repeated truancies and auto thefts. Here are a few significant items in his life story:

He grew up in a neighborhood where quite a few boys were delinquent. His mother was aware of the danger, and, even when he was

---

[3] William Healy and Augusta Bronner, in National Society for the Study of Education, *Forty-Seventh Yearbook, Part I: Juvenile Delinquency and the Schools*, Chicago, U. of Chicago Press, 1948, p. 31.

twelve, she made him be home by nine o'clock. His father died when he was six; his stepfather wanted Don to like him and therefore never disciplined the boy until he was ten. At that time Don had accidentally injured another boy quite seriously in a playground incident. Although the police exonerated Don, his sister often taunted him about the incident. His mother had forbidden him to go swimming in a neighborhood pool because the boys were rough and she was afraid he might drown. He went to a distant beach with a group of boys who engaged in petty thefts. On several occasions, afraid to come home late, he slept at friends' homes. His stepfather then beat him severely, and his mother took him to the police. The police tried to make arrangements for Don to join a Boy Scout troop which had access to a swimming pool, but there was a delay in completing the arrangements, by which time he found his gang more exciting. He is now a thoroughly embittered boy, who feels the only real friends he has are his companions in delinquency.

In a case like this we can see how each factor added its influence to the others to produce the final result. We can also see that Don's progress toward delinquency could have been stopped at a number of points along the line. If he had lived in a different neighborhood, or if his mother had been more understanding, or if his stepfather had been more positive, or if his sister had shown a different attitude, or if the neighborhood pool had been better supervised, or if the Boy Scout leaders had acted more quickly, the chain of circumstances might have been broken, especially if the results of the previous mishandling had been properly treated at any point. If all the people dealing with the boy had handled him wisely all along the line, the chain would never have existed.

Multiple causation can also exist as the explanation for desirable or praiseworthy outcomes. For instance, in an autobiographical sketch Marjorie Borrows, editor for many years of *Child Life Magazine,* traced her intense interest in children's literature to a rather unusual combination of circumstances in her childhood:

> As I was not too husky, my doctor-father kept me out of school and until I reached college my home education was decidedly sketchy. But my world was filled with books and these I read omnivorously.[4]

In real-life situations, many people prefer to overlook the principle of multiplicity of causes, because the price of accepting the idea is to lose

---

[4] Louise M. Jacobs and Mabel Thorn Lulu, "Chicagoland Authors and Illustrators of Children's Literature," *Chicago Schools Journal,* Vol. 3 (1951), Suppl., p. 3.

the fun of being able to throw blame on someone else or to claim a sure-fire, easy solution. Thus, at a recent conference on youth problems, while moving picture theater owners smugly held that "there are no delinquent children, only delinquent parents," parents in the group wanted to concentrate on a campaign against "bad moving pictures." Each felt quite pleased with arguments that placed the blame on the other. Their emotional satisfaction would have disappeared if they had faced the fact that delinquency is a product of many causes, to which each group made some contribution.

Even when we know all this, we still have to contend with our desire to find a simple solution to our problems. The fewer factors we notice, the easier the answer seems to be. We like advice that can be put to use at once. If we face all the facts involved in a complicated situation, easy solutions no longer satisfy us. Then we have to live with our doubts. Instead of getting simple advice, we are told to investigate further, get more facts. That is irritating and, therefore, another reason we are tempted to ignore the principle involved.

SURFACE SMUGNESS VERSUS SUBSURFACE CURIOSITY.   When told that his well water was contaminated with typhoid, many a farmer in former days held up a sample of clear liquid and shook his head in heartfelt disagreement. Because he could not see the bacteria, he preferred to believe they were not there. Yet, sad history tells us that many lives have been taken by deadly bacteria, viruses, or chemicals that no one could see, or taste, or smell. Surface appearances can be deceptive. Thanks to scientists whose curiosity led them to probe beneath such surfaces, we are now able to guard ourselves against many hidden perils.

In dealing with human behavior, it also pays well to look beneath the surface and to see what else may be observed. Here is an example:

In a seventh-grade class, Albert Warner had been the "best" pupil. His teacher had rewarded him with lavish praise. Then, his work fell off. During a science lesson on light which the teacher had always disliked because it was too hard for most children, she asked him the difference between convex and concave mirrors. Surprisingly, he said he did not know. When she accused him of not reading the assignment, he shrugged his shoulders. She made a mental note to talk to his parents and find out why he had become lazy. What she had not noticed was the proud sideways look he gave Tom Richards, the class ringleader in mischief, and the return nod of approval. Later in the day she stopped Albert in the corridor to ask if things were all right at home.

"Sure," was his answer.

"Why didn't you read the lesson on light?" she asked.

He grinned. "I did. I knew the answer all right, but the fellows don't like you if you act too smart."

In the field of mental and emotional phenomena, it is well to examine simple and apparently satisfactory explanations of conduct in order to make sure they do not mask forces with which we would certainly want to deal. The reader will recall Jean Warpatch, described in the previous chapter, beneath whose apparent quietness lurked the beginnings of mental disease. When she exploded with violence against a boy who teased her, the incident was overlooked on the ground that because she had always been a "good" girl, she must have had justification for the outburst.

Many an adult is filled with rage when a group of children bring tears to the eyes of a classmate with a physical defect by shouting in chorus such epithets as "fatso," "runt," "four-eyes," and "gimpy." Time and again we rest content with the observation, "Children are cruel little beasts." A little subsurface curiosity would ruffle the grown-up complacency with which such verdicts are accepted. Various experiments, which will be cited later, have shown that incidents of this type occur most frequently among children exposed to dominating, arbitrary, or inconsistent adult leadership. The solution in such cases is not to wipe out the cruelty by means of punishment, but to destroy its unseen roots by relaxing the pressures on the group.

SURFACE DETAILS CAN BE CLUES.   Once people accept the idea that observable conduct is usually only a symptom of something deeper, they may carry it too far. It may be made an excuse for a do-nothing attitude, on the grounds either that one is sure to make mistakes if he acts before all the causes are known or that there is not enough time or knowledge to ferret out the causes. Although our purpose in mental hygiene is to get beyond the symptoms and reach the real causes, the symptoms and the surface details may provide all the clues needed to start helping a person.

Consider the case, described earlier in this chapter, of the girl with a red rash. The fact that she was acting differently from normal and that she had red spots was enough to tell her parents that she was sick and that, even though they did not know the exact reason for her illness, they should put her to bed and send for the doctor. While the doctor knew the red spots were only a symptom, his experience had taught him that differences in appearance were valuable hints—some types pointed to measles; others, to allergies; and still others, to insect bites. Once he had seen the spots, he had a fairly good idea what to do next.

Here is an example of wise use of this principle by teachers: In a school in a poor neighborhood, a boy took several dollars from a girl who had been collecting milk money. It was the third time he had been caught stealing. The first thought of the teachers naturally was that the boy was a very deprived child or one without adequate moral concepts. They were struck, however, by the fact that although he had normal intelligence, he made no attempt to hide his thefts. When discovered, he acted quite differently from other youngsters caught stealing, who usually had a tougher defense against discovery and against confessing. Because of this lack of toughness, the teachers had a hunch that this particular youngster was in great need of being the center of adult concern. They promptly made plans among themselves to see that each of them would show him more friendly interest in connection with ordinary classroom activities. They also took steps to learn more about his home. What they found out seemed to corroborate their hunch. At home, every morning his parents gave him two dollars, but also told him not to come home until ten at night.

The significant point in this illustration is that the teachers were able to start on the right track for helping this youngster before a more complete causal picture had been obtained. They had paid attention to their observations of little details in the way this boy's stealing and the incidents around it differed from that of other children. Thus, it was the study of the very surface itself which gave them the clue to its possible meaning and also enabled them to tackle the problem without too much delay.

The differences among children and the differences in the way they do things which are apparently similar are important indicators. The expressions on faces, differences in habitual postures, and the manner of talking, all provide clues. Many an adult has learned to chuckle at the famous remark, "It wasn't what she said, it was the way that she said it." There is even greater wisdom in watching how children act. It is not so much what they do, but the way in which they do it that can speak volumes to anyone who pays close attention. A very dramatic illustration is supplied by the film *Balloons,* produced by the Department of Child Study at Vassar College. In the film two boys are seen hitting balloons. One strikes them with tense gestures; after the blows, his fists remain partially clenched. The second boy hits with smooth, confident motions, after which his hands and arms fall relaxed. The differences in behavior are interpreted to mean that the first boy is bottling up strong destructive impulses, which he also feels are very naughty; the second boy has no such conflict.

IMMEDIATE RESULTS VERSUS LONG-RANGE EFFECTS.   Each step in dealing with a difficulty need not produce a surface improvement. Most people would agree that there are times when it is wise to accept a momentary sacrifice in order to achieve a desirable result in the future. Thus, if a man is walking badly because of a broken bone in his foot, they would accept the fact that an operation which temporarily would prevent him from walking at all could ultimately be helpful. Conversely, measures which meet with immediate success may provide only temporary solutions to a problem. A watch in bad repair may often be made to run by shaking it. Few would pretend, however, that shaking watches is a reliable technique for making permanent repairs.

Too often, we react only in terms of immediate results when human behavior is at stake. When children are restive and disorderly, their conduct may be improved in the classroom by laying down stringent rules which are enforced with firmness. That such an apparently good solution often leaves the youngsters fundamentally unchanged is shown when the group reverts to wild disorder if the teacher has to leave the room unattended for a while. Yet, faith in the method is upheld by the argument, "It gets results," and the teacher quiets the subsequent outbursts with more and larger doses of the same palliative.

On the other hand, efforts to teach children to develop internal respect for orderly procedures by permitting them varying degrees of self-management are often prematurely abandoned. This method works well in the long run. However, during the early stages bedlam may sometimes reign. At this point, the verdict is often rendered that the method does not work, before it has really been given a chance to take effect.

Especially where a child's problems grow out of long-established home conditions, the process of treatment takes a seemingly zigzag course. Frequently the youngster temporarily becomes more demanding or more openly hostile before making the desired adjustment.

Some Common Resistances

One of the most interesting findings in the field of mental hygiene is the discovery that when people get an inkling that they may learn something which will require a reorganization of their behavior patterns, they try to ward off the impending new knowledge. This tendency is called resistance. In the next two chapters and elsewhere in this book, we shall discuss some of the specific devices in detail. However, there are some resistance techniques so common to the mental hygiene field that we shall take them up here. Speakers and teachers who deal with aspects of mental health soon become familiar with one or more of the following dodges:

ASKING MEANINGLESS EITHER-OR QUESTIONS.   A favorite trick is to squeeze a complex situation into a seemingly simple either-or alternative. A typical perennial: "Is reward better than punishment?" We can see the naïveté of such a question by transposing it to the physical realm: "Is it better to operate or to give medicine?" There are two troubles with these queries: (1) Both reward and punishment are end points in a scale which includes many possibilities. (2) Until we know what the situation is, we cannot know what method to use. Such questions, of course, may be asked in a sincere effort to secure understanding, and may merely show lack of skill in wording a query on the spur of the moment. However, in some cases the questioner is urged on by a wish to keep the speaker busy talking on a topic which causes no uneasiness. He may fear that the trend of discussion might otherwise prove upsetting. The either-or question is especially suitable because it is essentially meaningless and can precipitate a lengthy explanation. However, other questions that are basically irrelevant may be used to make the discussion take a tangent.

DEMANDING "PRACTICAL"ADVICE IN VAGUELY DESCRIBED SITUATIONS.   Another method of resistance is to "prove" that your talk is of no practical value by demanding that you give definite answers to more or less vaguely described situations. Trap questions of this sort are, "What is the best punishment?" and "What should I do about a child who steals?" The first is like asking, without specifying the purpose of a surgical operation, "What is the best way to operate?" There is no answer. To questions of the second type, a good answer can be given only after the child and the situation are both known in considerable detail. As a conscientious speaker, you would refuse to provide a prescription on the basis of incomplete and secondhand information. Everything you may say later may then be ignored on the grounds that it is not practical.

HIDING BEHIND LABELS.   It may look like compliance when members of a group encountering mental health concepts take a new-found delight in looking for the proper label to pin on a particular form of conduct, but this may also be a form of resistance. Having named the behavior, they may then be inclined to rest on their laurels. The labeling is merely a substitute which helps them to establish intellectual prestige. The feeling of accomplishment they gain enables them to forget that the cause-and-effect relationships at bottom remain unsolved or uninvestigated, and to pass on to other matters. There is a tremendous gap between knowing what to call a particular type of behavior and having really helped the child who displays it.

DISPROOF BY ASSOCIATION.   A very neat dodge is set in operation by finding out where the mental hygienist stands on a local issue concerning which feelings are strong. The first move is for someone to ask, usually a little out of context, a key question such as, "What do you think of scholastic eligibility rules for varsity athletes?" or "Are you in favor of special classes for the gifted?" If the speaker gives a categorical reply, he is taken to have lined up with anyone and everyone who holds the same view on that issue, and statements on other matters may be treated as mere propaganda for that purpose. The basic technique is to label the mental hygienist and then use the label as a just reason for opposing what he says.

FEAR THAT MENTAL HYGIENE MAKES PEOPLE "SOFT."   Quite a few people fear that too much understanding of children will make them weak, incapable of maintaining discipline. It is true that when we understand children, it is hard to maintain previously blind harshness. However, the knowledge may help us act more wisely, and need not lead to indecision. Understanding the nature of a disease does not paralyze a surgeon; it does enable him to take drastic action when necessary. Juvenile court judges have found that the more they know about a child in trouble, the more skillfully they can make plans for helping him and for protecting society. Popular belief to the contrary, you will find that mental hygiene teachings can play an appreciable part in maintaining classroom control, and that skillfully applied punishment, when it is needed, is very much a part of helping some children.

In addition to the resistances discussed, there will be others which are more varied and subtle. Material may be misread or misunderstood. Students may welcome being distracted from the subject by feelings concerning fellow students. In one case, even concern with parking problems took priority over mental health material and was used to ward off discussion.

Mental hygiene is a field of applied science devoted to helping increase the amount of mental and emotional good health in the world. In this area, educators will be concerned primarily with those forces which affect children and with the part that teachers and schools can play in providing a healthy framework for child development. Like any branch of knowledge, mental hygiene requires honest and disciplined thinking. To gain most from its study, we must be wary of the many emotional reactions that can distort our view.

ADDITIONAL READINGS

Bernard, Harold W. *Mental Hygiene for Classroom Teachers.* New York: McGraw-Hill, 1952, Chap. 1. Emphasis is given to the need for a mental hygiene viewpoint among educators.

Buhler, Charlotte, Faith Smitter, and Sybil Richardson. *Childhood Problems and the Teacher.* New York: Holt, 1952, Chap. 1. A discussion of what teachers should obtain from a study of the psychology of childhood.

Lindgren, Henry Clay. *Mental Health in Education.* New York: Holt, 1954, Chap. 1. A description of attitudes basic to mental health.

Moloney, James Clark. *The Battle for Mental Health.* New York: Philosophical Library, 1952, Chaps. 1 and 2. A psychiatrist's answer to the question, "What is mental health?"

Patty, William L., and Louise Snyder Johnson. *Personality and Adjustment.* New York: McGraw-Hill, 1953. A presentation of the need for, and various approaches to, mental health.

Preston, George H. *Substance of Mental Health.* New York: Rinehart, 1943. A well-written book for popular consumption, describing mental health principles.

Ryan, W. Carson. *Mental Health Through Education.* New York: Commonwealth Fund, 1938. A pioneering text in the application of mental health principles to school situations.

Witty, Paul, and C. E. Skinner. *Mental Hygiene in Modern Education.* New York: Farrar & Rinehart, 1939. A thoughtful summary of basic ideas and their application.

AUDIO-VISUAL AIDS

Balloons, a 20-minute sound film produced by the Department of Child Study at Vassar College, in which the behavior of two boys in response to an invitation to break balloons is seen to be indicative of deep personality trends.

Search for Happiness, a 16-minute "March of Time" sound feature, which describes in semicomic fashion some of the poorly thought out panaceas to which people have turned for solutions to their problems.

PART B

SOME FUNDAMENTALS

chapter **3**

MOTIVATION, CONFLICT, AND CONTROL

The purpose of this chapter is to examine the control systems of young people and to outline the nature of the psychological conflicts which give rise to otherwise puzzling behavior. It has been observed that teachers who have learned to think in terms of the hidden needs responsible for many of the actions of children will tend to deal with children more effectively and make classroom living more fruitful for pupils and more satisfying to themselves.

An illustration of these positive effects was found in a study by Fleming[1] in an elementary school at Dobbs Ferry, New York, where a group of teachers volunteered for an in-service program. Films and group discussion were used to familiarize the teachers with the needs underlying certain pupil behavior. An indication of the effects of the program was obtained by seeing what happened to children in the first five grades of the school who were suffering from illnesses such as stomach upsets, stuttering, headaches, allergies, and "nervousness," which physicians had identified as having some psychological roots. There were 26 such children in the classes of the teachers who volunteered for the program; 12 in the classes of teachers who did not. Although such psychosomatic diseases could hardly be cured by school activities alone, it is reasonable to expect that the afflicted children would respond somewhat to changed classroom conditions. That is exactly what happened: In the classes of the teachers who sought understanding, the absence rate of these young people dropped from an average of 12

---

[1] Robert S. Fleming, *An Exploratory Study of an In-Service Education Program on Children with Symptoms of Psychosomatic Illness,* Ed.D. dissertation, New York University, 1949, University Microfilms Publication No. 1487.

days during the previous year to 8 days; in the other classes it went up from 6 to 10. On a new physical examination, physicians noted improvement in 64 per cent of the children who had teachers in the special group and in 40 per cent for the other classes.

Motivation

To understand the behavior of any organism, human beings included, it is essential to know what drives set it in motion, what needs it is seeking to satisfy. Motivation is thus a key concept in the study of behavior. Psychologists differ, often heatedly, as to the nature of motivation and the list of drives and needs. Some prefer to think in terms of forces which push from within; others, of goals which have a strong attraction. Some explain human behavior in terms of long lists of highly specific instincts. In recent years, the tendency has been to accept the idea that there are a few general drives which become attached to specific goals through learning. The present authors will not attempt to describe all the existent theories, but rather will point out some aspects of motivation which may aid in the making of judgments about the behavior of young people.

TYPES OF MOTIVATION. To survive, an organism must eat, drink, breathe, rest, and keep warm. If the species is to persist, it must reproduce itself. Some part of every person's conduct is thus motivated by physiological drives—the necessity of satisfying physical needs. This much is simple and clear-cut. What is of moment is that, except for breathing, the nature of the goals which can satisfy the need has to be learned. To cite the simplest case: What foods are considered attractive varies widely throughout the world. Tomatoes, a favorite now, were once considered poisonous and repulsive. In addition, learning soon adds new needs to old ones. For instance, money, which might be considered only a means to the end of purchasing necessities, can become an end in itself.

There are other needs whose origin may not be so clear but whose existence is obvious. Many are products of the importance of group life. Here, for example, we find that it helps to understand a person's actions if we think of them as motivated by his need to have other people think well of him.

AWARENESS OF MOTIVATION. Whether or not a person recognizes his own goals may make quite a difference. When he knows what he needs, he can seek it directly and efficiently. Thus, most of us know when we are hungry. Knowing it, we decide what to do about it.

There are, however, many instances in which people act as though they are under the influence of forces of which they are unaware. The clearest evidence on this point has been accumulated in psychiatric treatment, although most people recognize evidence of it in everyday life. For example, all of us have forgotten things, wondered why, and perhaps found out later that the forgetting served some purpose. We have observed other people acting as though they wanted to be talked about, but have encountered genuinely angry denials when we suggested that was what they sought. Such *unconscious motivation* is encountered time and again in the clinic or the consulting room. Teachers will witness its operation dozens of times every day. In the later sections of this chapter, we will find this concept fundamental to an understanding of two major facts: (1) Children have to cope with conflicts the full nature of which they cannot understand. (2) Children have incomplete control over a great deal of their behavior.

Conflict

At times we observe both adults and children giving evidence that they are uneasy, tense, or anxious. This is often a sign that they are experiencing the effect of inner conflict. One simple way of picturing the origin of much conflict is to consider the personality structure of every person as having several somewhat inharmonious aspects: a system of uncivilized impulses, a conscience, an ego, and an ego ideal. We shall now look briefly at each of these.

THE IMPULSE SYSTEM.   The system of impulses (called the *id* by psychoanalysts) involves love and hate, self-preservation and self-protection—the energy-giving drives of human life. These make themselves felt to a person in the form of desires, wishes, cravings, and needs. The fulfillment of drives which are basic at any stage in life is an essential condition for the happiness of an individual, and also for his mental health. A source of valuable incentive, they are a major element in the personality, given appropriate expression. Of necessity, every one of us has some impulses that have to be kept in check at times. This means that we are bound to have some inner conflict whenever our impulses have to be curbed or we meet with obstacles to their legitimate realization.

THE CONSCIENCE. One type of control over the impulses is represented by the conscience, that inner sense of right and wrong which Freudians call the *superego*. By the time he reaches school, every child has acquired an emotionally potent value system. There are some things he cannot even contemplate doing without feeling uneasy. Other actions make him glow with self-approval.

One important quality of the conscience is that it can operate regardless of our wishes. In fact, that is what it is expected to do. A conscience would be of little use if it did not send out warnings at the very time when the person most wanted to avoid its dictates.

In a sense, the conscience represents an internalized version of social and moral values as they are represented to us, first by our parents and then by other people important in our lives. When any of the impulses pushes a person toward conduct or even thoughts which would violate those values, the conscience goes into action by producing feelings of uneasiness and discomfort. It warns against impending violations; if the warning is not heeded, the temporary triumph of the impulses is marred by feelings of guilt. Indeed, there are some children whose consciences seem to be very weak on the preventive side but quite potent afterward. These include the delinquents who have a post-action conscience; they engage in all sorts of mischief but feel sorry later.

Individuals differ in the strength of their consciences, the territory covered, and the mode of operation. Some consciences appear to be stern and panicky; they forbid almost any enjoyment. Others are weak and spotty; they let their possessors get away with a wide range of misbehavior without remorse. Whatever the situation—and for most people it is between these extremes—every child and every adult is bound to find himself in situations where his impulses push him in one direction while his conscience orders him to take another. He will find himself wanting to engage in behavior which his conscience makes him feel wicked and unworthy for just thinking about.

The necessary role the conscience plays, and the feelings of conflict and discomfort with which individuals must cope as a result, are aptly expressed in Mark Twain's complaint that if he had a yellow cur as mean as his conscience he would drown it. Weak or strong, potent or powerless, its action is bound to produce inner conflict.

THE EGO. A third aspect of the personality, usually called the *ego,* is much more complicated. It performs a complex and necessary series of functions, such as enabling a person to predict the consequences of his actions, giving him an understanding of the real world, controlling his impulses when necessary, helping him satisfy his impulses in ways acceptable to his conscience, and finding ways of avoiding impasses of inner conflict. This is only a partial list of jobs the executive department of the personality must carry out; here we shall deal with only a small sample of its functions.

One important aspect is the so-called reality-testing function. Any normal human being must be able to predict reasonably well the actual consequences of his behavior. If you hit people, they get angry and hit you back. If you know the answer to a question and give it in the way required by classroom routines, most teachers will tender you approval. If you spend your money on candy, it is gone, and you cannot use it to buy a ball. All of us have impulses to do things that involve no moral issues but do have unfortunate consequences. At such points, the executive department, reminding us of reality, comes in conflict with the impulse structure.

At some points, the task of the ego is to deal with demands of the conscience, some of which may be unrealistic and unreasonable. The demands may involve no important moralities but would create difficulties if met. A not too uncommon situation is that of the girl whose conscience bade her tell the exact truth, no matter what. Gradually, she began to realize that this not only made her unpopular but led to her hurting people. In such a situation, the ego may try to get the conscience to reduce the rigidity of its demands. The girl may recognize some untruths as being "tactful," and take pride in them.

Another important ego function is that of self-appraisal in relationship to tasks. A competent individual must have a fairly good idea of what he or she is able to do. Almost every teacher has been irritated by children who are weak in this quality, who volunteer to answer questions but turn out not to know the answer. Other young people are quite expert in forecasting their performance on a task.

This self-knowledge is an aspect of the *self-concept,* the person's inner picture of himself as he thinks he is. A great deal of research has recently been done on this aspect of the personality by psychologists who believe that much behavior is motivated by a need to enhance the self-concept and to protect it from threat of various kinds. A brief discussion of its development will be found in Chapter 5.

The present description of ego functions has been held, deliberately, to a very incomplete sample of the many areas in which the personality's executive department has jobs to do. The purpose at this point is simply to acquaint the reader with the concept so that he can recognize the probability of conflict among the major aspects of a child's inner world.

EGO IDEAL.   Some of the internalized values to which the ego is also expected to be sensitive involve not moral values as described under the concept of conscience, but aspects of a desired image of oneself. These characteristics are technically called the *ego ideal*. In contrast to the self-concept, which is a person's inner picture of himself as he thinks he is, the ego ideal is his concept of himself as he feels he ought to be. An example would be a teacher's picture of himself as being calm in the face of provocation. Violation of this ego ideal would not so much make us feel guilty as leave us disconcerted, embarrassed, or ashamed.

PSYCHIC CONFLICT.   Since a complete personality will have an impulse structure, a conscience, an ego, and an ego ideal, each individual will have to cope with feelings generated by the conflicts in his own goals, inclinations, and behavior which result. Here are a few typical examples:

In many school districts these days, parents and teachers feel that fighting is a bad method of settling disputes. Children have been raised to feel that fighting is wrong. The consciences of many have come to accept the prohibition against hurting other children. This is likely to be the case for both sexes, but even more true for girls. Yet, every child, girl as well as boy, will encounter some situations in which his or her wishes are thwarted by another person. The impulsive reaction to being thwarted is to get angry and attack. Yet, conscience says this is bad. Here is a conflict. How will it be resolved? In the next chapter we will look at some of the solutions which are available. The possibilities in this particular case are numerous. A girl might take physical action and then feel remorseful. She might bottle up her anger and get a headache. She might find and use a "ladylike" way of hurting her foe, as by spreading a bit of nasty gossip. She might go off by herself and viciously crumple a sheet of paper.

There are neighborhoods in which fighting is expected of children. Here, the boys especially are expected by parents to settle differences by physical combat. Consider the very different type of conflict which would be felt by a boy who has been angered by someone he knows is a better fighter. Here the wish to hit and hurt is checked by the realization that his blow will start a fight painful to him. In this case, there are many ways such an inner conflict might end. The boy could launch an attack with the desperate onslaught so typical of street fighting, where the object is to disable the antagonist with the first blow. If this succeeded, he might find himself trembling from his own unrealized fear. If it didn't work, he might take a beating but comfort himself on having put up a good battle. He might not tackle his immediate foe but find an excuse to pick a fight with someone he could master. He might make his attack in school, where, he knows, teachers would soon stop the fight, leaving him in a position to receive credit in his group both for having defended his rights and for showing a socially approved disdain for school rules.

Not all conflicts involve aggression or even directly involve specific impulses. In some cases, differing demands of conscience are at issue. For example, if a teacher asks one child whether he knows who committed some offense, the group code against tattling comes into effect. If the youngster has been brought up to tell the truth, his conscience will bid him to give the teacher the facts. But in most classes above the fourth or fifth grade, he will also know that his popularity with his classmates will drop if he tells. Here the conflict is between conscience and ego ideal. There are many ways this can be handled: He can tell the truth, and then do something to win his way back into his friends' respect. He can say he doesn't know and then convince himself that this is really so. He can appear to protect his classmate, but so unskillfully that the teacher is given a hint as to the identity of the culprit. He can obey the taboo on tattling and then satisfy his conscience by privately criticizing the offender.

Another type of conflict results from the fact that most people want to think well of themselves. In some cases, the self-concept is thrown into question by reality: for example, a young person who would like to feel competent has repeatedly failed on spelling tests. How can he protect his self-esteem? He can decide the tests were unfair. He can decide that spelling does not count. He can face the facts and feel bad. He can daydream of working so hard he amazes everyone.

Examples of inner conflict could be multiplied. By this point, however, the reader will have recognized that this phenomenon is universal among human beings of all ages. With this in mind, we can now move along to descriptions of behavior resulting from conflict and to the problems which arise from the need to control such behavior.

Variations in Control

There is a great deal of variation in the extent to which young folks—and adults, too—are able to exercise conscious control over specific items of behavior. There are areas of living where no one can deliberately change his behavior; other areas where practically everyone can assume full responsibility for his actions. There are individuals who are helpless victims of forces acting upon them; others who are substantially masters of their fate. All, to some degree, are impelled by unconscious motivation.

SOME BEHAVIOR IS NOT SUBJECT TO CONTROL. The clearest illustrations of the fact that human beings engage in some behavior without conscious will power being able to start or stop it are supplied by the physical operations of the body. Such phenomena as digestion, perspiration, and heart action go on when we sleep as well as when we are awake. It would be news indeed if an individual could shut off and resume any of these processes merely by deciding to do so.

Allied to these mechanical and automatic body functions are such bits of behavior as blushing, stage fright, and jumping when startled. Some individuals try to control such actions; occasionally a teacher or parent spurs their efforts. Although a training program over a period of time may change the responses of the body, this cannot be done by simple persuasion. A blushing girl of ten does not want to blush; at times she would give much for power to control this phenomenon.

Other examples appear in children with physical afflictions. A boy or girl with chorea will fidget. The child with a thyroid deficiency will be slow-moving, may tire easily, and will seem lazy. Young people with overactive thyroids may be irritable. In none of the above-mentioned instances will nagging or punishment alter the pattern of behavior. The child may want to try to do as teacher or parent wishes. But all the trying in the world will not increase the output of the thyroids nor cure chorea. Attempting to impose control on such behavior is like ordering an early-maturing girl to remain a child, and then penalizing her for allowing hair to appear in her armpits.

SOME BEHAVIOR CAN BE CONTROLLED. In the daily living of every reasonably normal child, there are many things that he does because he decided to do them and which, if he wanted, he could do differently or not at all. He can at least go through the motions of most class activities. He can hold his conduct within the limits usual for young people in the school and grade which he attends. If he has an inclination toward mischief, he can usually be deliberate about selecting the opportunity which suits his purpose, choosing the words or actions that fit his design, and making appeals to evade or reduce the anger of adults.

EFFECTS OF UNCONSCIOUS MOTIVATION AND CONFLICT. The fact that all humans engage in behavior which is motivated by unconscious forces means that much of what we do is at the moment beyond our own understanding. For instance, a child will often find himself consciously "wanting" to concentrate on his studies, but "something" keeps luring him into daydreams. What that something is he does not know. We recognize the existence of imperfect conscious control most clearly in respect to feelings. At times, for no apparent reason, children will be happy or sad, trusting or sullen, anxious or confident. A particular child may dislike or be afraid of a teacher who is a very nice person. Young people will form friendships that are hard to understand, or hold unfounded grudges.

In the realm of visible behavior, there are a host of "nervous habits," beginning with thumb sucking and including nail biting, head scratching, and doodling. The extent of unconscious habits and tendencies was indicated by a study of "nervous traits" among first-grade children in the schools of Butler County, Ohio, conducted jointly by Ohio State University, the Ohio Agricultural Experiment Station, and the Division of Mental Hygiene of the Ohio State Department of Public Welfare, in co-operation with the Butler County Mental Hygiene Association.[2]

In a group of 543 first-graders, interviewing revealed the following: Forty-six per cent bit their nails, 30 per cent were unduly tired, 26 per cent had bad dreams, 17 per cent had insomnia, 12 per cent had frequent illnesses, and 9 per cent cried often. In some cases, physical conditions over which a child would have no control were at the root of the behavior. Among children who had gross physical defects, 34 per cent showed 4 or more nervous traits. However, among youngsters with no noticeable defect, 22 per cent had the same concentration of characteristics.

---

[2] R. H. Woodward and A. R. Mangus, *Nervous Traits Among First Grade Children in Butler County Schools,* Hamilton (Ohio), Butler County Mental Hygiene Association, 1949.

A closer look at this list of actions—and it is only a sample of the types of behavior often found to have an element of unconscious motivation—will enable the reader to recognize the phenomenon that all children engage in some behavior of whose real causes they are unaware and in which they engage despite their apparent intentions to the contrary.

Nail biting belongs to the family of *oral habits,* like thumb sucking, pencil chewing, gum chewing, and pipe smoking. A review of forty-six studies on the subject[3] led to the following conclusion:

> Nail-biting is one of the most common habits observed in children and young adults. It begins between the ages of 3 and 12 years. The incidence rises sharply from 4 to 6 years of age, remains level between 7 and 10 years, and rises again to a peak during puberty.
>
> Nail-biting is "normal" between the ages of 4 to 18 years as indicated by high prevalence during these years. Simple, occasional nail-biting merits little attention other than the fact it is evidence of some degree of internal tension.

Anyone who has bitten his nails will know how many times he has decided to stop the habit and then, despite himself, found that his resolve was forgotten. "Something" made him backslide repeatedly. We should note here, incidentally, that the tension out of which nail biting arises can be relatively mild; this action is "normal" in the sense that many basically stable people have been or now are nail biters.

Feelings of fatigue that are not caused by physical effort or lack of sleep are common. This, also, is often a result of tension, in many cases within the limits of ordinary experience. Although a few people have trained themselves to relax, most adults and almost all children often become tense or feel tired, not because they want to, but because "something" makes them.

Bad dreams occur while the individual is asleep and therefore obviously cannot consciously control what is going on in his mind. Insomnia and other sleep disturbances, such as bed wetting, are especially annoying because their victims try to avoid them.

An analysis of most common "nervous habits" reveals that, although the individual may, and probably does, decide to end the difficulty, "something" makes it continue. That "something" which is so resistant to "will power" and rational insight is what has previously been described as unconscious motivation, the aspect of everyone's per-

---

[3] Maury Massler and Anthony J. Malone, "Nail-biting—A Review," *Journal of Pediatrics,* Vol. 36 (1950), pp. 523-31.

sonality which "makes" him engage in some behavior for reasons of which he is unaware and over which he may have no direct control. The intensity of this unconscious motivation makes a difference. Where it is light, the individual may exert conscious control if it is worth his while. If the intensity is heavy, this possibility may be slight.

OTHER MANIFESTATIONS OF UNCONSCIOUS MOTIVATION. The operations of a child's or an adult's "unconscious" is by no means limited to nervous habits. It shows itself in many forms. At points which may be crucial in the learning process, for example, it may exert great influence over the ability to pay attention, to develop interests, and to put forth effort, as well as being at the base of many behavior problems.

Almost every person has had the experience of having his attention distracted from either study or work by worry over some event or by persistent daydreams. Many a reader has discovered that although his eyes have been following the lines of print, his mind has wandered off into a train of thought in no way related to what is written.

Interest in particular subjects, which may give rise to attention or get in its way, is a peculiarly personal experience. Many factors go into the development of an interest or into boredom. Every teacher has known children who have had intense interest in one or more subjects, not all of which are necessarily in the curriculum. Equally, some young people who may have considerable ability have found it impossible to muster enthusiasm for art, music, arithmetic, languages, science, or other particular activities. In some cases, unconscious motivations are an important ingredient in the pattern of causes.

On occasion, one even finds children who seem to want to do poorly. In the following quotation, Thomas De Quincey, referring to his relationship to his older brother, makes explicit a pattern of motivation which operates much less consciously in many pupils who have "stopped trying":

> But it happened, on the contrary, that I had a perfect craze for being despised. I doted on it; and considered contempt a sort of luxury that I was in continual fear of losing. . . . To me, at that era of life, it formed the main guarantee of an unmolested repose. . . . The slightest approach to any favorable construction of my intellectual pretensions alarmed me beyond measure; because it pledged me in a manner with the hearer to support this first attempt by a second, by a third, by a fourth——O heavens! There is no saying how far the horrid man might go in his unreasonable demands upon me. . . . Professing the

most absolute bankruptcy from the very beginning, giving the man no sort of hope that I could pay even one farthing in the pound, I never could be made miserable by unknown responsibilities. . . .

Sometimes, indeed, the mere necessities of dispute carried me, before I was aware of my own imprudence, so far up the staircase of Babel, that my brother was shaken for a moment in the infinity of his contempt: and, before long, when my superiority in some bookish accomplishments displayed itself, by results that could not reasonably be dissembled, mere foolish human nature forced me into some trifle of exultation at these retributory triumphs. But more often I was disposed to grieve over them. They tended to shake that solid foundation of utter despicableness upon which I relied so much for my freedom from anxiety; and, therefore, upon the whole it was satisfactory to my mind that my brother's opinion of me, after any little transient oscillation, gravitated determinably back towards that contempt which had been the result of his original inquest.[4]

SUPERIMPOSED CONTROL IS POSSIBLE.   For every type of behavior cited above as an example of unconscious motivation over which individuals have incomplete control, the reader may know of instances in which an individual's actions were changed by drastic measures. For instance, if an attractive enough promise is made, many young people can stop biting their nails, at least until they get the reward. If threatened with failure and serious consequences, a boy uninterested in foreign languages can be forced to work intently, at least until the final examination. If a teacher, parent, or class group insists, a child given to stage fright may give a public recitation.

There are times, of course, when it is essential to provide a child with superimposed control. Not only may the necessities of group living, for instance, demand that a teacher keep a child from running around the room or from starting a fight, but control may be required for the immediate protection of an individual. There are instances in which physical safety is at issue. In a sense, the safety-patrol boy represents a program of superimposed control: young children might not be able to check their impulses to dart into the street without looking both ways. Also, in a sense, the presence of an umpire at a game illustrates the possibility that, in order to hold to a level of behavior needed to achieve social acceptance, some individuals need controls from without.

Useful and necessary though they may be, superimposed controls

---

[4] Thomas De Quincey, *Selected Writings,* New York, Modern Library, 1949, pp. 79-81.

may sometimes look more effective than they really are. "Successful" applications may well prove to have three elements in common: (1) The control over behavior is not that of the individual but of an outsider. (2) It may be short-lived. And (3) there can be unfortunate side effects. For example, the coerced nail biter, if he doesn't backslide, will probably develop a new nervous habit. Once the final exam is over, some boys forced to study foreign languages may have a stronger antipathy to them, or may even have a deepened feeling of antagonism to school. Among children who are compelled to stand before a group and speak, some may later in life join the ranks of people who sit silent at meetings, even though they have good ideas. One reason this may happen is that the pressure does not solve unconscious problems but merely suppresses their manifestation.

MENTAL ILLNESS.   Some adults and some children act almost all the time as though important parts of their behavior were beyond control. Depending on the degree of the difficulty, these people may be considered "emotionally disturbed" or "mentally ill." For example, some suffer from depression—periods of low energy during which they experience an intense extreme of the feelings most folks would call the blues, and without good reason. They feel sad, helpless, and disheartened. Some reach the point where they do not want to live.

To an outsider who wants to help, an obvious attack on the problem is to "cheer them up." For instance, one might tell a child with such a tendency how well he has been doing, what the future can hold for him. Or, one could try to make him laugh or smile by telling jokes, or by having his classmates engage in exciting nonsense. A third attack would attempt to "snap him out of it" by punishment or threat. The classic speech here goes, "See here, young man. You have nothing to mope about. You just buckle down to work, or you'll flunk this course."

Now, if the young person's depressive feelings are part of an emotional illness, none of these measures will have more than a temporary effect. Most observers will recognize this, and come to the conclusion that there is something seriously wrong. Once the label "mental illness" is applied, people nowadays generally understand that the victim cannot help himself, that rational persuasion has little hope of success, and that punishment would be cruel as well as useless.

In this chapter, two concepts fundamental to the mental health sciences have been introduced and illustrated. The first is that all people, children and adults, are at times under the influence of forces of which they are unaware and over which they have little or no conscious control. This is the fact of unconscious motivation.

The second key consideration is that each individual's personality structure is such that he will experience inner conflict. The urgings of his impulses and his conscience are bound to clash. The executive aspect of his psychic life, here called the ego, may have to check his conscience as well as his impulses. In the interest of maintaining a favorable inner picture of himself, he has to deal with disquieting realities as well as inner dissatisfactions.

These two factors lead to an important generalization about behavior: Much of what an individual does takes place beyond the limits of his control. This means that there are limits to what will power can accomplish. Although we must not now go to the extreme of saying or implying that all conduct is determined, that a person can exercise no control, we must be clear that some physical phenomena, some behavior expressive of unconscious motivation, and acts based on mental illness, do take place without the person involved being aware of what he is doing. In some instances, he does want to behave differently but finds himself incapable of doing so.

ADDITIONAL READINGS

Hadfield, J. A. *Psychology and Mental Health.* London: Allen & Unwin, 1950, Chap. 2. An interesting treatment of the sources of behavior.

Hilgard, Ernest R. *Introduction to Psychology.* 2nd ed. New York: Harcourt, Brace, 1957, Chap. 8. The phenomena of conflict and frustration are described from a psychological viewpoint quite different from that of this book.

Horney, Karen. *The Neurotic Personality of Our Time.* New York: Norton, 1937, Chaps. 3 and 4. Deals with the question of how anxiety is aroused and what it does.

Martin, William E., and Celia Burns Stendler. *Child Behavior and Development.* New York: Harcourt, Brace, 1959, Chap. 7. The processes whereby children are socialized are described from a psychoanalytic approach.

Maslow, A. H. *Motivation and Personality.* New York: Harper, 1954, Chap. 7. The nature of basic human needs is discussed.

Menninger, Karl A. *The Human Mind.* New York: Knopf, 1937, Chap. 4. A discussion of human motives by one of the greats among American psychiatrists.

Shaffer, Laurance Frederic, and Edward Joseph Shoben, Jr. *The Psychology of Adjustment.* 2nd ed. Boston: Houghton Mifflin, 1956, Chaps. 2, 4, and 10. A systematic presentation of psychological evidence relating to motivation, conflict, and anxiety.

AUDIO-VISUAL AIDS

Overdependency, a 32-minute sound film, produced by the National Film Board of Canada, in which the development of sick feelings in the case of one person is accurately portrayed and explained.

chapter **4**

BEHAVIOR MECHANISMS

In dealing with inner conflicts—and their variety is infinite—human beings use a great many devices. Frequently they work out a somewhat stereotyped way of coping with the outside world and the world within themselves. These we shall call behavior mechanisms. They are rather similar in a way to the reflexes, such as eye blinking and head ducking, by which we automatically deal with sudden physical threats. These mechanisms, of many ingenious types, help people to work out their problems, each in his own way. They are unconscious, in the sense that a person may be unaware of their operation.

While some of these devices, used to excess or inadequately, may be an expression of mental illness, they also provide stability. They supply a psychological protection which, for most people, makes living more pleasant. Much depends on how adaptable the individual remains in using them and in dealing with both his internal feelings and the outside world of reality. It is essential to realize that normal people employ practically all the mechanisms described below in some measure. Neither do normal people seem to specialize in using any one mechanism. This was brought out in a study by Goldstein,[1] which set out to prove the opposite. Using a test, called the Blacky Test, composed of a series of dog pictures designed to evoke reactions linked to powerful psychological forces, he found that only a minority of a group of 104 normal college students showed any consistent preference for particular defense mechanisms. With these facts in mind, let us glance now at some very common behavior mechanisms.

---

[1] Stanley Goldstein, *A Projective Study of Psychoanalytic Mechanisms of Defense,* Ph.D. dissertation, University of Michigan, 1952, University Microfilms Publication No. 3501.

For purposes of study, we shall group the mechanisms into three major classifications: (1) those by which we *ignore* or *overlook* important facts; (2) those by which we *escape* or *evade* potentially unpleasant situations; and (3) those by which we alter the form of the conflict by techniques of *substitution* or *shift*. All have in common several important characteristics: (1) All can be normal behavior. (2) Any one, if used to the point where it dominates a person's life or removes him from effective relationships to the world about him, may be a sign of mental illness. (3) Any is likely to be seen in the behavior of an entire group as well as in the actions of single individuals.

Some deliberate oversimplification appears in the above classification. In actual behavior, the several elements are often combined in complex interplay. To illustrate this fact, the description of simple mechanisms will be followed by two sections, one on the development of physical symptoms and one on "nervous habits," which bring out some of the possible interrelationships.

Mechanisms of Denial

A very simple way to deal with a conflict is to ignore, deny, explain away, or mask the facts on which it rests. By making believe there is no conflict, we can spare ourselves the turmoil it would create. There are several ways this is done.

SIMPLE DENIAL.   The easiest course to follow is to remain unaware of those facts which could create one side of a conflict. An example that is particularly annoying to grownups occurs when children do not hear instructions which would mean the end of group play or other enticing sport. (Denial is a quite different thing from deliberate pretense, in which the individual knows something but decides to make believe that he doesn't.) Although the parent or teacher may have spoken loudly and plainly, the children will say they heard nothing. In fact, what was said was not allowed to penetrate their consciousness. If it had, they would have had either to abandon their pleasure or be torn by guilt at their disobedience.

Another commonplace illustration of the same thing is observed in adults who may prefer not to think about the fact that high school students can fall strongly in love with each other. How do they dodge the fact? It is easy to dismiss everything with a joke about "puppy love," and then go on serenely oblivious to what may be happening.

Many such denials are quite normal. In fact, anyone who realized and frankly acknowledged every possible danger facing him would lead a frightening life. The possibilities in our civilization for accidents and crises are so numerous that if we could not ignore some of them, our lives would be a perpetual nightmare of frantic precaution.

Occasionally, too, the denial helps a person delay facing up to a problem until he is capable of developing the insight to deal with it. The youngster who ignores sex talk and a group's dating practices for a while may be following a course of wisdom. Today he may not be ready to cope with the problems; in a year or two his growth may have increased his emotional capabilities.

Denial is not used just by individuals; it can also be shared by an entire group. For example, when a child of a different race or nationality joins a class, the pupils may act as though nothing had happened, even though the event is being discussed heatedly by the adult community.

This mechanism has been the subject of more scientific experiment than any other as a result of the debate aroused by a pioneering study by McGinnies[2] in which he had a group of southern women college students, in the presence of a male experimenter, read a list of words presented to them at great speed. Included in the list were some terms which many people are embarrassed to employ. These were not recognized in many cases: students made nonsensical errors. But during the period in which they had not yet recognized the words, physical apparatus used in the experiment detected clear evidence of a rise in emotionality, which would indicate that the nonrecognition policy involved psychological energy of which they were not aware.

As might be supposed, many psychologists doubted that there could be any reaction to stimuli of which a person was unaware. These results go to the very heart of the concept of unconscious motivation, discussed in Chapter 3. To check directly on this aspect, Lazarus and McCleary[3] tried an experiment in which they repeatedly gave individ-

---

[2] Elliott McGinnies, "Emotionality and Perceptual Defense," *Psychological Review*, Vol. 56 (1949), pp. 244-51.

The basic point made by critics of this experiment was that the findings could be accounted for on the basis of differences in the frequencies with which the words were used. In later experiments McGinnies attempted to control this factor and to show that the phenomenon appeared in different form among mental patients. The present authors feel he has adequately replied to his critics.

[3] Richard S. Lazarus and Robert A. McCleary, "Autonomic Discrimination without Awareness: A Study of Subception," *Psychological Review*, Vol. 58 (1951), pp. 113-22.

uals an electric shock while reading certain nonsense syllables but not when others were read. Then, later, while the experimental subjects were hooked up to an apparatus, somewhat like a simple lie detector, which records the presence of perspiration on the skin, the same nonsense syllables were shown too rapidly for conscious recognition. The persons showed evidence of fear much more often at the presentation of syllables where shock had been given.

Denial can come into play with spoken words and even with feelings. An example appeared in an experiment by Rosenbaum[4] in which he described various people to a group of normal individuals and to a group of persons suffering from schizophrenia, a mental disease in which the individual tends to withdraw from people. The descriptions included reference to personal warmth and tenderness. That element of the descriptions apparently was sensed by the schizophrenics as a threat against which they had to protect themselves. At any rate, they tended to act as though they were oblivious of that portion of the descriptions.

While many examples of denial are found in normal people, there are times when it can be carried too far, or when it is so inflexible or so compulsive that it is a sign of emotional disturbance. Determining such occasions in children is a matter of judgment, based on familiarity with them.

REPRESSION.   Where a conflict is due to forces active within ourselves, we often forbid ourselves to recognize their existence. Such repression differs from simple denial, by which we overlook facts. In a manner of speaking, the forces still exist and are still active, but at the unconscious level. Typically, in repression mental energy is used to enforce nonrecognition of some aspect of ourselves. Consequently, we become alarmed or angry when some person or event threatens to call our attention to the quality we are working so hard not to see. The conceited boy or girl may be totally unable to admit, even privately, his or her conceit or envy. A teacher who tries to prove to such a youngster that he is displaying these traits will often be met by a strong emotional display, such as crying or rage.

Repression is usually a response to an inner conflict. It may be used to bury feelings which are loaded with anxiety or guilt. For ex-

---

4 Gerald Donald Rosenbaum, *Forming Impressions of Persons from Verbal Report: A Study of Schizophrenic and Normal Groups,* Ph.D. dissertation, Columbia University, 1952, University Microfilms Publication No. 3915.

ample, nothing is more normal than occasional feelings of rivalry or nostility between brothers and sisters. Under ordinary circumstances, youngsters will be aware of these emotions, express some of them openly, but gain control of their more harmful wishes, just as they gain command over anger-producing inclinations in other areas. In some cases, however, where parents put such a heavy demand on "loving" a brother or sister, the child cannot even allow himself to perceive such hostile feelings as he may have. He will have to repress them all. That means he will not be aware of having them, even when they color his actual behavior or appear disguised in his dreams.

Here, as with denial, some very careful experiments have been performed in recent years. Zeller,[5] for example, had students learn semi-nonsense syllables under several conditions, including artificially created failure. Later, not only did they tend to "forget" the words associated with the failure, but this spread to related tasks. Although in general people tend to remember their successes and forget their failures, Taylor[6] showed in an experimental study that this depends upon how they feel toward an instructor and a class. The more a student liked his teacher, the more he remembered his successes and forgot his failures in problem solving in class. But students who disliked the class remembered their failures better than their successes.

An even more cogent illustration of how repression enables individuals to protect their self-esteem appeared in an experiment by Flavell[7] in which thirty-eight college students were asked to tell what words came to their minds when they heard certain nonsense syllables. A psychology professor "interpreted" these associations to the students: For half the nonsense syllables, he declared, the word association indicated "abnormal" psychological conditions. Among the students given this "treatment," the "abnormal" syllables were forgotten on a subsequent test more often than the "normal" syllables. Even when the trick was explained, the effect persisted.

There is nothing wrong with repression in itself; some repressions perform a mentally helpful function. Other repressions, however, are

[5] Anchard Frederic Zeller, "An Experimental Analogue of Repression: III. The Effect of Induced Failure and Success on Memory Measured by Recall," *Journal of Experimental Psychology,* Vol. 42 (1951), pp. 32-38.

[6] James William Taylor, *An Experimental Study of Repression with Special Reference to Success-Failure and Completion-Incompletion,* unpublished Ph.D. dissertation, Washington University, 1952.

[7] John Hurley Flavell, *Selective Forgetting as a Function of the Induction and Subsequent Removal of Ego-Threat,* unpublished M.A. thesis, Clark University, 1952.

a source of disturbance. This is especially true where repression takes place before a problem is solved and where the repression does not settle the conflict.

Disturbing repressions are the most frequent source of neurotic behavior. To treat resultant problems, the repression must be lifted under conditions where the individual can work successfully on the real problem. The goal in such treatment is the achievement of control; if this does not take place, destroying the repression may do more harm than good. For this reason, and because people may react strongly to attempts to remove the repression, attempts at curing neurotic behavior should be undertaken only by experts.

In working with children, the repressed feelings are frequently brought out into the open by special play with toys or art work. Normal children will quite often take care of their own problems. As they do so, a teacher may witness them giving vent to their feelings in dramatic play, art, and discussions. This can be very healthy. Without prying, teachers can help such youngsters by giving them freedom instead of stifling emotion-laden expression.

Many books on psychology do not make a distinction between denial and repression, but deal with both phenomena under the heading of repression. In others, special emphasis is given to something called *suppression*. In suppression, the individual, although recognizing a conflict, deliberately holds back from expressing his feelings. Thus, a boy who is angry at a teacher may bottle up his rage because he feels it would be wrong to act on his hostility to a source of authority, even though he is aware of his anger. In repression, he would be ignorant of the feeling of hostility itself. In denial, he would not realize what the teacher had done, and would not be angry.

RATIONALIZATION. A somewhat different tactic is to avoid the conflict by explaining it away. Finding an alibi for otherwise untenable behavior is a favorite human pursuit. Whenever we ask anyone why he did something questionable, we expect to get some sort of "good" excuse. We use rationalizations, not only to win approval from other people, but, more important, to elude the dictates of our own consciences.

When an individual finds himself in a situation where undue restraint of basic drives is demanded, rationalization offers one way out. For example, if the school tries to keep children too quiet and to inhibit muscular activity, children become more expert in finding excuses for moving around. Usually these "excuses" lack logic, and teachers may feel the children are fibbing. In most cases, the children themselves firmly believe the stories they are telling.

Another reason for rationalization is to protect ourselves from the guilt and shame of recognizing primitive impulses for what they are. Much cruelty to children is camouflaged with the argument that this is a harsh world and therefore it is good for children to meet failure. This argument may be maintained even in the face of evidence that failure was destructive in a particular case.

PROJECTION.   Colloquially the term "projection" is used for any attempt to avoid blame or to ascribe responsibility to outside forces, while ignoring one's own contribution to an event. Some children who get into a great many fights may, despite all evidence to the contrary, apparently really believe that the other fellow always starts things.

In its essential psychological sense, projection is a device whereby we believe we see in other people a quality which would trouble us greatly if we had to admit it was our own. There are several ways in which this is done.

In the kindergarten and lower grades, some of the most persistent tattlers are children who on the surface may be very well behaved but who are having a hard time following classroom rules. Such children are employing the mechanism of projection by pointing to something happening outside as a way of denying their own desire to break rules. It is essential to realize, though, that the person who does the projecting feels quite sincere; no conscious hypocrisy is involved.

The range of projections seen in the average classroom is very great. Children who are doing poorly often are very critical of the teacher or other pupils. Also, they frequently act as if they were expecting a teacher or another child to display toward them the hatred, love, suspicion, or contempt which they themselves feel.

At times, projection works in reverse. A young person whose desires for affection have often met disappointment may convince himself that an individual he unconsciously loves is going to persecute him. When teachers go out of their way to be nice to a child who has had a bad home life, sometimes they are spurned. The boy or girl shows suspicion instead of the anticipated gratitude. Tempted strongly to enjoy the affection and become "soft" but afraid of being betrayed, the young person saves himself conflict by picturing his would-be friends as clever tricksters who mean no good.

Similarly, sex interests which run counter to strong taboos can be dealt with by projection. Thus, girls may act on the assumption that all boys are "nasty," out of the necessity to deny their own desires. More than one teacher has been falsely accused either of making advances to or of being down on some adolescent when the actual problem lay in the child himself.

Carried to extremes or used too frequently, projections are a sign of mental ill health. The most extreme form appears as delusions of persecution. Here we find such individuals as the girl whose life is dominated by elaborate plans to keep a gang, to whom she is hardly known, from killing her.

All of us use some projections. Projections may lead a child, for instance, to be very wary in dealing with other youngsters. However, if most of his contacts with people are based on realistic estimates of how they act or feel, we have little cause for worry. When projection is used only in a few areas to avoid painful self-insight, it is a far different matter than when a person blames outside forces for practically everything he does.

In any case, before acting on the assumption that an individual is using projection, it is wise to find out the facts. For instance, many children will claim that "everyone has it in for me." Once in a while, some youngster really is the victim of many unfair attacks. In such cases his claim may be exaggerated, but it does have a grain of truth.

DEFENSE THROUGH THE OPPOSITE. When our deeper feelings might frighten us, we often cover them up for ourselves by acting in the opposite way. Thus, a tiny girl who would like to get dirty but fears to lose her parents' favor may conceal her impulse by being excessively clean. Similarly, a brother may deny his real hostility for a sister by acting ever so loving. The exceptionally good behavior of a class after a wild episode in a neighboring room is a temporary use of the same device for resisting temptation.

Teachers' reactions to children are often products of this phenomenon. At marking times, guilt over the possible effects of poor grades which they felt they had to give may be buried by a blithe unconcern or a forbiddingly irritable, crusty manner. The rather abrupt cruelty of Mrs. Benson, the kindergarten teacher mentioned on page 6, is an example of the same thing. Of course, the opposite may also be true: a teacher who feels apt to give way to temper outbursts may put on for himself a very convincing show of being sweetly nonpunitive.

In normal doses, this mechanism is a good way of coping with fears. The often-offensive callousness of the medical student performing his first human dissection may be necessary if he is ever to become a coolly efficient surgeon. The horseplay of children handling biology exhibits is a method of overcoming their fright. The giggling of children during a serious discussion of moral or social issues, as in Mr. Lawrence's class after the incident involving Rhoda's outburst, on page 9, may merely be a cover-up for embarrassment at their own serious concern, and does not necessarily mean they are taking the matter lightly.

When defense through the opposite becomes incorporated in relatively permanent character traits, psychiatrists call it *reaction formation.* This phrase originally meant that when a person's impulses threatened to violate a strong taboo, he strengthened his controls by making his behavior conform excessively to the standards. Thus, a youngster who really is assailed by strong urges to do things he or she regards as wicked may react by making an especially striking display of virtuousness. Teachers will sometimes refer to a boy or girl as "too neat" or "too nice." In this way they voice their recognition that reaction formation may have taken place. They have an inkling, with which psychiatrists would agree, that such all-too-intensive neatness or niceness does not come naturally to children. They sense it is primarily a device to keep in check very strong impulses to do the opposite.

Mechanisms of Escape

A different strategy for handling conflicts is to run away from the activity or the area in which the contending forces would operate. There are several means by which we make such escapes.

WITHDRAWAL.   An obvious tactic is to withdraw from the situation itself. Thus, school children who have failed in a subject often lose interest, cease trying, and escape involving themselves in the efforts and tensions of striving for accomplishment. Outside school, the same thing is very commonly noted in the way boys and girls develop hobbies, only to drop them as soon as the possibility of falling short of high standards is felt.

Frequently, young people find that the ordinary social behavior of other youngsters might lead them to violate the strict dictates of their consciences. Rather than face the resultant conflicts, they concentrate on solitary pursuits, shun companionship. They do not dare be with their age-mates.

Daydreaming is one of the most common types of escape. By living for brief periods in a safe make-believe world, we can withdraw from harsh realities. In fact, so commonplace are excursions into fantasy that much literature, both good and bad, serves this function. So do the comics, radio, and television. The frequency of this use of what could truthfully be called "externally controlled fantasy" was brought out in interviews of 332 mothers in Cambridge, Massachusetts.[8] They reported their 622 children spent an average of one and one-half hours a day in passive fantasy in front of television sets.

In some individuals, preoccupation with a fantasy world reaches the point where there is only flitting contact with real people and real things. Then, mental health is in danger. In a study of 60 normal, 60 neurotic, and 60 schizophrenic children, Halpern[9] found that among the schizophrenic children there was more indication of anxiety and of flight reactions.

Nevertheless, much withdrawal is perfectly normal. When adults expect too much of a child, his escape from their demands is healthy self-protection. When the alternative to escape is knocking one's brains out against a brick wall, the withdrawal is to be preferred. Indeed, inability to withdraw from overwhelming situations, as shown by the man or woman who just has to be successful in everything, can be a sign of poor emotional balance.

Withdrawal can also be a group phenomenon. The reader will recall the boys described in Chapter 1 who held together in refusing to engage in social dancing. If any of the boys had given in while others held out, the integrity of the group would have been destroyed. The ones who danced would have felt isolated. The others would have felt left out of things. Firm friendships might have suffered strain. Sensing this peril, they withdrew in united fashion. Similarly, when any group of young people displays apathy or shows loss of interest in a program, a specific analysis needs to be made; some aspect of the program may threaten to create a conflict.

INTELLECTUALIZATION.   School people, who are trained in the use of words and the value of theory, are apt to be taken in when a

---

[8] Eleanor E. Maccoby, "Television: Its Impact on School Children," *Public Opinion Quarterly,* Vol. 15 (1951), pp. 421-44.

[9] Florence Cohn Halpern, *An Investigation into the Nature and Intensity of Anxiety Experienced by Three Clinical Groups of Two Different Age Levels and of the Defenses They Develop Against Their Anxiety,* Ph.D. dissertation, New York University, 1951, University Microfilms Publication No. 2763.

youngster employs the technique of escape by indulging in excessive theorizing. As a substitute for dealing with a problem or a conflict, the person engages in building theories about it. The significant aspect is that the theory in those cases actually is used to *avoid* action.

In view of the frequent use of discussion techniques in schools, teachers should be aware of this propensity to theorize. Children will engage in intellectualization in the lower grades, and it is a favorite technique of adolescents. Usually powerless to put their ideas into action, they nevertheless delight in seemingly endless talk about religion, money, war, freedom, friendship, and love.

An interesting use of this mechanism appears in a very full case study of an intellectually brilliant boy, Paul, presented by Blos.[10] Paul could and did discourse at length about girls and women. Actually, he seemed to be very uneasy with people. At a party his clumsy approach to a girl would be a question as to the comparative merits of Latin and Greek.

In school situations, intellectualization may perform a useful function in helping people get ready to deal with their real problems. It is of value to individuals during periods when they have to wait or when they are powerless to act. The development of theory, itself, is a necessary and very important activity of great value. However, when it is used consistently as a substitute for action, that is another matter. The danger is that young people may become satisfied with talking a good game while remaining blind to the fact that in their own home and life problems they follow a passive, do-nothing pattern.

COMPULSIVE FUN SEEKING.   Dramatists love to portray the young man or woman disappointed in love who throws himself into a round of wild pleasure. It is true that fun can keep a person from having to think about his troubles. Young people often learn this trick. Unhappy children display the strongest and most persistent greed for such pleasures as moving pictures, sports spectacles, amusement parks, and parties.

As a means of release from problems, fun has definite values. Quite significant is the person's inner freedom to choose what to do, to decide upon an alternate activity. But where he seemingly cannot help himself, where the pleasure-seeking pattern is a compulsive habit, deeper troubles are indicated.

In addition, one should realize that pleasure seeking may serve

---

[10] Peter Blos, *The Adolescent Personality*, New York, Appleton-Century-Crofts, 1941, pp. 113-219.

specific secondary purposes. For example, by getting a bad reputation and bringing disgrace upon their parents, young folks may be taking revenge for real or fancied wrongs. Added spice may be given to wild fun in a classroom during a teacher's absence by the thought that it might get her in bad with the principal. In fact, the pleasure seeking may be merely a mask for other purposes. Under the guise of "fun," some people tease and otherwise torture individuals they would not dare attack openly. Also, a revolt against authority may be conducted as an exhibition of "high spirits." To serve this purpose, activities which have been forbidden may be vested with an aura of being fun.

However, we should never forget that fun is enjoyable for itself, and a child's wish for fun does not always have a deeper significance. Unless there is good reason for thinking otherwise, it is safer to assume that a person seeks pleasure for its own sake.

ESCAPE INTO WORK AND PERFECTIONISM. In order to achieve the same goal of preventing thought about deep personal problems, some people use the opposite trick—they immerse themselves in work. They may set themselves standards of perfection for the unconscious purpose of justifying time-monopolizing and painstaking effort. It is as though they are afraid of finishing tasks and exposing themselves to the hazard of being so unoccupied that dreaded conflicts will come to attention.

Intuitively, many teachers invoke this device after a disturbing classroom incident. They feel correctly that if they can only get the class busy and have everyone working hard, emotional upsets will be calmed. That accomplished, they can deal more effectively with the individual or the situation responsible for the trouble.

In a mild and temporary form, this mechanism may help us over rough spots in life's road. A child from a home torn by bickering may throw himself with zest into the learning activities of school-work because the activity drives out of his mind the terrifying thoughts of what may happen to him. Later, when he is older and emotionally more developed, he may be able to face his problems.

There is a danger, however, that young people whose escape into work has seriously unhealthy roots will be confirmed in this technique by the praise of teachers. Such children turn in phenomenal quantities of work. They drag out tasks by spending a great deal of time in extra embellishments of neatness and do work over because of minor imperfections. It is hard not to be impressed and to hold such youngsters up for praise as models the others should emulate. Yet what these children really need is help with the problems which are driving them to such apparently praiseworthy lengths.

REGRESSION.   Under the impact of conflict or fear, people may return to a previous phase of development. They are, so to speak, trying to live again in "the good old days" when they did not have to wrestle with a particular problem. Parents often see this behavior in a child when a younger brother or sister is born. At that time there may be a reversion to crawling on the floor, babyish eating patterns, and other outgrown habits.

High school teachers are forever being surprised by the amazing way, for instance, that girls who one minute are a picture of adult sophistication can suddenly switch over to childishly pouting crybabies as a result of a sharp reprimand. Many adolescents temporarily run away from the problems of growing up. For instance, a few may enjoy sitting and shivering in safe terror at an eerie television horror story. At the time, they revel in a childish fear of the dark because it feels so much more comfortable than the more-difficult-to-deal-with agonies of acting their age in a world of critical grownups.

As with other behavior mechanisms, some regressions help maintain a healthy mental balance. Young people may feel more relaxed and more able to face their problems after a party where everyone has done "silly" things, such as riding on the toys of the host's younger brother and making mock by talking to each other as would excited kindergartners. The baby talk of lovers gives some a feeling of safety in an otherwise frightening new relationship.

Ability to regress when professionally necessary is an asset to teachers and other leaders of youth groups. Some can actually enter into the fun of youthful jokes and really enjoy parties and similar times of juvenile gaiety. The genuine joy they have is readily sensed by youngsters and may be a big factor in establishing a fine group relationship. The essential requirement in such professional regression is that the leader be quite flexible, retain adult responsibility, and easily resume a full adult role when that is required for the welfare of the class. He does not feel compelled to be childish. (Special problems which may arise for young teachers will be discussed later, in Chapter 11.)

Regression can be a very serious matter when it is persistent or becomes a habitual response to all problems. At its extreme, regression is typical of severe forms of mental illness. When a young person uses this technique often, it can be a sign of deep and very unhealthy troubles. Judging its seriousness requires skillful weighing of the person's maturity. Some of these considerations will be discussed at length in Chapter 7.

Mechanisms of Shift and Substitution

There is yet another strategy people use in dealing with conflict. Instead of denying its existence or running away from it, they deal with it indirectly. They shift some aspect of the conflict to another area where they can meet it successfully. They make one activity or desire substitute for others.

DISPLACEMENT.   One way of doing this is to express in one area feelings which we are unable or afraid to show in another area. In an experiment with rats, Miller[11] trained the animals to attack each other in response to an electric shock. When they could not use this method because there was no rat present, they would attack a rubber doll, which had always been in the cage but previously had been ignored.

Much adolescent sauciness in school can also be explained in this manner. Boys and girls may be irked by restrictions at home but dare not talk back to their parents. Instead, they turn their feelings against teachers and other persons in authority.

Even in the early grades, children from very strict homes may use against teachers the strong hostilities they feel toward, but dare not show, their parents. When a teacher talks to such parents, they often hint that the teacher must be inadequate, since the child doesn't give a bit of trouble at home. When the child is very bad in school, the teacher may falsely suspect the parents of lying, and may even say so. However, the truth may be that a displacement has taken place. Sometimes, this process can work in the opposite way. Now and then, parents will come to school because their children are misbehaving at home and express surprise that in school they are little angels. If the school or the teacher is very strict, the displacement may have taken a reverse route.

In some young people, violent prejudices may contain an element

---

11 Neal E. Miller, "Theory and Experiment Relating Psychoanalytic Displacement to Stimulus-Response Generalization," *Journal of Abnormal and Social Psychology*, Vol. 43 (1948), pp. 155-78.

of displacement. For instance, in Mussen's study[12] of 106 white boys attending an interracial camp, some of the more prejudiced boys gave evidence of harboring strong hostility to their parents, even to the point of sometimes unconsciously wishing their death. These feelings, however, were not openly directed against the parents but were displaced toward Negroes. As contrasted with most other boys, those for whom prejudice had this character proved more resistant to change in attitude. Indeed, upon contact with Negroes in camp, their prejudices deepened; those of the other boys decreased.

A vivid illustration of displaced anger being responsible for an educator's behavior toward a student was described by Hollingshead.[13] At the high school in the community he called Elmtown, a rule was in force that students who were tardy had to spend one hour in detention after school. Kathy, the daughter of a prominent family, instead of going to detention on a day when she should have, kept an appointment with a beauty parlor to have a permanent wave. When the principal mentioned the incident to the superintendent and told him the girl's mother had said Kathy needed her hair fixed for a dance at the Country Club, the superintendent told him, "Now be careful, Alfred, I do not think there is a thing we can do in this case." Later, when "Boney" Johnson, the son of a factory worker, refused to serve detention for being late, the principal sought out the boy and tried to push him into the room used for this purpose. When the boy resisted, the principal hit him. The superintendent, who came upon the scene, joined in manhandling the boy, and agreeing that he would not be allowed to come back to school unless he brought his father. The suppressed fury the two men had felt over their helplessness in enforcing the rule against children of powerful families was vented in unchecked and seemingly righteous fashion against a boy of whom they had no fear. "Boney" quit school.

Feelings other than anger also can be handled by displacement. Children in boarding schools and camps may complain about the food or the program instead of weeping over their suspicion that their parents want to get rid of them. In adolescence, a boy or girl may develop a crush on a teacher instead of yearning for love from a parent. A teacher's desire for orderliness in his personal life may be displaced into

---

[12] Paul H. Mussen, "Some Personality and Social Factors Related to Changes in Children's Attitudes toward Negroes," *Journal of Abnormal and Social Psychology,* Vol. 45 (1950), pp. 423-41.

[13] August B. Hollingshead, *Elmtown's Youth,* New York, Wiley, 1949, pp. 187-92.

a campaign for neat margins on all papers. Displacements may be much less direct and more distant, as when affection for a parent may be shown not in an attachment to a teacher, but in enthusiasm for his subject.

Many displacements are normal. Usually these are temporary and give relief from severe pressures. There is no need to worry if a child, upset by a baby brother at home, slaps a rag doll once or twice in school. There are times when almost everyone has got rid of resentments by slamming an innocent door or viciously crumpling a piece of paper. All but a few saints would probably have to plead guilty to having at one time or another taken out rage on a helpless pet or child. On the credit side, when the world looks bright and cheerful, we are all smiles, and may even unwisely overlook serious misbehavior or other problems.

When displacements are strong and persistent, when they do not solve the basic problem, they can be a source of mental difficulty. Trying to deal with the displacement itself is not a solution. The original difficulty must be discovered and solved.

Displacements, like most other mechanisms, may show in group action. Hazing by secret societies, riotous destruction in victory celebrations, and student strikes often can be traced to resentments engendered by bad school or community conditions.

COMPENSATION.   One way to deal with conflict is to seek in one area of living satisfactions which cannot be gained in another. Needs which are unmet may be gratified in a substitute field where success is more probable. Just as some students who do poorly in school concentrate on nonacademic activities, so the boy or girl who is unable to win admiration outside school may devote a disproportionate amount of time and energy to getting good marks. Compensation has also been the basis of many enduring and interesting hobbies.

Even within the confines of a single subject, teachers will sometimes observe this phenomenon. For example, in an art class a girl who has no success in other projects may be observed busily coloring very detailed geometric figures made with pencil and ruler. In a gymnasium a boy whose poor co-ordination makes him inept at other activities may try to start games of kickball at every opportunity.

Such normal substitutions of activity perform useful functions. They are part of the process whereby the round pegs locate the round holes. The task for teachers is usually one of helping children find those compensating activities which are likely to be fruitful or of seeing that the youngsters receive satisfaction in regular activities.

An example of deliberate and successful effort by teachers to produce compensation appears in a report of the work of Le Renouveau, a residential school established in France in June, 1945, to help children orphaned by World War II.[14] Among the young people was a very timid fourteen-year-old boy, who presented a problem because he often climbed the walls and roof. A part, at least, of the reason was that in order to allay great feelings of inferiority, he had to do something spectacular. The workers at the school noticed that he had a taste for music. Hoping to push him along that road of compensation, they gave him piano lessons. At the same time he began to improve in his scholastic work. Although on occasion he would go back to showing small outward signs of feeling inferior, he generally was able to turn in satisfaction to his relative mastery of the piano and scholastic work. He no longer climbed walls and roofs.

Like all other mechanisms, compensation can be carried to extremes. This usually means that the underlying problems are very severe. If the individual relies too heavily on compensation, a vicious cycle may be established. For example, a child's mother may raise so much fuss over playmates that a boy or girl spends too little time with them. Becoming socially inept, he has a more difficult time in group activities. To make up for the lost satisfaction, he may concentrate on intellectual pursuits. The more this is done, the weaker become his social skills. Eventually all desire to win companionship may be abandoned.

Sometimes the term "overcompensation" is used. This term is appropriate in cases where the gratification seeking in the compensatory field has assumed an unusual intensity and the individual concerned appears "driven." In such cases, minor setbacks may trigger exaggerated reactions.

SUBLIMATION. This often used and sometimes misunderstood term means the individual has surrendered a primitive form of satisfaction in favor of a more cultivated or socially acceptable one. A boy may escape self-criticism if he gives up a pattern of biting or kicking opponents and instead wrestles with them according to the rules of his playmates. Later, he may abandon physical combat altogether, and be

---

[14] Claude François, *Enfants Victimes de la Guerre,* Paris, Éditions Bourrelier, 1949.

content with topping their jokes in battles of wit. In both these illustrations, the boy retains his aggressiveness; the difference is in the form it takes.

Sublimation usually involves much more than a mere surface change in the way we reach our goals. Whereas in compensation one area of effort is substituted for another, in sublimation new satisfactions take the place of old, morally unacceptable ones. The goals themselves may be altered. Thus, a girl who originally wished to hurt her friends and to gain superiority over them may devote her energies to some good cause which fights evil and tries to uplift other people. To be sure, we can still detect an echo of her original tendencies: fighting evil is after all a form of combat, and uplifting implies superiority in the uplifter. Yet, from a social as well as a personal viewpoint, this is vastly more acceptable than hair-pulling contests and malicious gossiping.

Since sublimation frequently represents a constructive solution of internal conflicts, teachers often want young people to use this mechanism. However, this cannot be achieved merely by telling a youngster about a substitute satisfaction or by forcing him to go through the motions. Not too much is known of the processes leading up to sublimation; more research in this field is sorely needed. We do know that the degree and type of sublimation are products of the important human relationships in our lives. Thus, children may pick up the device of using humor when it wins approval from admired parents or friendly teachers. By contrast, a boy living in a neighborhood where toughness is admired is unlikely to sublimate his hostility feelings into activities that he and his friends would call "sissy stuff."

One other point should be made. There is a limit to the value of sublimation in a person's life. An individual who used it exclusively to the point where he was unable to get pleasure from cruder channels would be in a bad way. If a teacher holds sublimation as the goal for all children, he may demand more than they can manage at the time. Teachers may permit children to talk but prohibit moving around, although the satisfaction of vocalization is hardly adequate when muscles demand exercise. Similarly, when two children feel bitterly about each other, a game of checkers will seldom drain off their emotions.

IDENTIFICATION.   Many conflicts arise from a difference between our personalities and the demands of individuals or groups that have strong emotional meaning for us. One way to lessen such conflicts is to shift these demands from outside ourselves and incorporate them into our own set of values. In a sense, we strengthen our self-control by establishing within ourselves the codes or examples of other people. Thus, without realizing it consciously, children often judge themselves by what they believe their parents expect. Even when there is no possibility of a misdeed being discovered, they feel guilty if it runs counter to home ideals. This mechanism is the basis through which we develop our own standards of value. That is why it is essential for children to have some deeply satisfying relationships with people in their lives.

Although we ordinarily expect boys to identify with their fathers and girls with their mothers, in some aspects of living children will strongly internalize the values of the parent of the opposite sex. One area in which this is surprisingly so is in the occupational ambitions of boys. In a study made by a team of psychologists[15] among 136 high school juniors and seniors, all sons of skilled workmen, it was found that the occupational level at which the boy aimed was significantly related to his mother's original socioeconomic status, the level of her parents. This is in line with other research indicating that mothers' values have a great deal to do with boys' vocational ambitions.

Although identification with parents is often the most powerful influence of the sort, much of the effectiveness of religious leaders, teachers, and youth workers is achieved through this mechanism. (For discussion of this development during adolescence, see pages 105 to 106 in Chapter 5.) We all know of cases where admiration of a teacher has led some youngster to drop taboo behavior. As has been shown in an analysis of school compositions, by Havighurst and others[16] adolescents are especially prone to identify with figures outside their homes. Such identification is by no means limited to live individuals with whom the boy or girl has contact. Biography and even fiction have supplied heroes and heroines in whose images young people have tried to model themselves.

The demands and ideals of groups are likely to be vital sources of identification for youngsters. The emotional repugnance with which children refuse to snitch on their friends is caused by much more than fear of physical harm or ostracism; contempt is felt for this behavior because of an important standard of behavior. Although adults may not

---

[15] Gordon J. Barnett, Irving Handelsman, Lawrence H. Stewart, and Donald E. Super, "The Occupational Level Scale as a Measure of Drive," *Psychological Monographs,* Vol. 66 (1952), No. 342.

[16] Robert J. Havighurst, Myra Z. Robinson, and Mildred Dorr, "The Development of the Ideal Self in Childhood and Adolescence," *Journal of Educational Research,* Vol. 40 (1946), pp. 241-57.

be enthusiastic about youthful gang codes, their power is the same as that which gives rise to the character-strengthening behavior of religious fellowship. Concepts of sportsmanship and consideration for others are enforced through identification with group ideals.

Generally, the most solid basis for the formation of identification is considered to be a feeling of friendship and love for the person who presents those values in the life of a child. Where deep changes have been made in the values of a young person suffering from character disorders, the situation has usually involved strong, positive affective relationships with people.

Fear can also play a part in identification. Often the standards which we accept are those of a stern parent or some other person whose wrath produced fright. Identifications born of fear are often the most forceful, but they can be unstable. Not only may they be overthrown later in life, but they can be the source of considerable emotional conflict. In a study made of the way highly prejudiced college students solved certain arithmetic problems, Frenkel-Brunswik[17] found that both bigotry and mental inflexibility were found frequently among young people whose parents relied heavily on fear techniques in raising their children.

Complex Defenses

In dealing with their inner conflicts and the resultant anxiety, individuals often develop defenses a good deal more complex than those illustrated in the preceding pages. To give a sample of the real-life elaboration, we shall look briefly at two types of situation in which this becomes apparent: psychosomatic illnesses and "nervous habits."

DEVELOPING PHYSICAL AILMENTS.   From time immemorial, school children have managed to develop cramps, headaches, and colds on examination days or on lovely spring mornings when school seemed unattractive. Sometimes, of course, the excuse is an unvarnished lie or a temporary rationalization. Much more often, the pain is real, and the victim truly suffers. It is not within his power to decide to be sick or to get well again. Such events are among the most simple instances of what physicians call psychosomatic complaints, real illnesses whose origins are psychological, although they express themselves in physical symptoms.

---

[17] Else Frenkel-Brunswik, "A Study of Prejudice in Children," *Human Relations,* Vol. 1 (1948), pp. 295-306.

The individual may simply be escaping his problems by taking refuge in sickness; but the situation is sometimes quite complicated and involves other mechanisms, such as an unconscious wish to punish oneself for a hidden wickedness. A highly unusual instance involved a college student who developed fevers at examination time. Under treatment he revealed he felt guilty because he was getting a higher education at the expense of his brother; the fever was to him a retribution. The manifestations of such psychosomatic illness may be painful and disabling. Paralysis of limbs, earaches, asthma, hay fever, ulcers, nausea, backaches, and skin diseases sometimes have emotional causes. Physicians estimate that in approximately half the patients they see, psychological factors contribute heavily to physical ailments. Dealing with such problems is now a highly specialized branch of medicine.

A single type of illness may play a different role in the lives of different individuals. Some specific diseases of this type have been the subject of careful scientific scrutiny. Rarely does the pattern of causes or the psychological roots of a given disorder prove to be simple. By way of example, we shall cite here only one study[18] of a single difficulty, bronchial asthma. This usually involves an actual allergy, with psychological causes helping in varying degrees to produce the symptoms. Fine, after a very elaborate program of psychological testing, noted that among the boys in a sample of thirty such children, the psychogenic factors were more important than the physical ones. Many of these children were relatively immature, and were very dependent upon their parents, who seldom gave them physical affection. Many of these children inhibited crying more than did average youngsters. Yet they found it harder to tolerate ordinary frustrations. How could asthma arise out of such a situation? What functions did it serve? Here are a few possibilities, which would operate in varying degrees for different children. Some may have been punished for crying to the point where they would keep silent; but because of their low frustration tolerance and poor relations with their parents, they often wanted to cry. The gasping of asthmatic breathing is much like a suppressed cry; it could be a way of announcing rage while exhibiting an effort to hold it back. Then, again, as a way of claiming care from reluctant parents, so prominent an illness could be effective. It could also be a way to inconvenience, and hence punish, the mother who now had to bring in the child

---

[18] Reuben Fine, *A Quantitative Study of Personality Factors Related to Bronchial Asthma in Children,* unpublished Ph.D. dissertation, University of Southern California, 1948.

for treatment. All of these functions, and others as well, can be served by asthmatic attacks. The same type of analysis, but with emphasis upon other key factors, could be made for other illnesses in which there is a psychological component.

The one thing for teachers to remember is that a child who has frequent absences, especially where parents report that doctors are having a hard time finding the cause, is probably emotionally troubled. To punish him for his absences or to make school more unpleasant for him is more likely to add to his troubles than to solve them. Often the cause has nothing to do with school; there is something to look for elsewhere.

Even when an illness has psychological roots, there is some reason why it strikes a particular part of the body. Therefore, physicians have to deal with the physical side of the ailment. This cannot be poohpoohed. Such illnesses are not cured merely by telling the victim they are psychological. Specialists who deal with these complaints take the patient's pains and discomfort seriously and only later go into the mental and emotional causes. To laugh at the physical symptoms only arouses suspicion; genuine concern is necessary to establish the basis for cure.

"NERVOUS HABITS." Almost all individuals, adults as well as children, make use of "nervous habits." These have an amazing gamut— thumb sucking, nail biting, nose picking, hair twirling, gum chewing, smoking, doodling, scratching, and rocking. In most instances, the person feels somewhat more at ease while engaged in his or her favorite preoccupation. So much is this the case that some writers refer to them as "comfort patterns." The trend of findings is that individuals who have any quirk of this type in mild degree are as likely to be normal as those who use other mechanisms. Only when the addiction is extreme is it evidence of serious troubles, in which case it is part of a much larger disorder, which has to be tackled as a whole.

Usually, if a child or an adult is deprived of a favorite minor pastime by being punished, ridiculed, or nagged, he promptly develops a new one or the over-all problem becomes more serious. The reformed thumb sucker starts picking his nose, then chews pencils or uses his tongue to work at his teeth. Years later we may find him contentedly puffing at a pipe, cigar, or cigarette, blithely ignoring statistics relative to lung cancer or heart disease. On the other hand, a child entangled in a never-ending warfare with an adult over a "habit" of this sort may be sapped of the very energy he needs and be disturbed in the very relationships required to cope with the more basic problems behind it all. The attempt may be like picking at a scab.

Allied to the relatively benignant nervous habits are other items of behavior which handicap their possessors, annoy other people, and therefore invite attempts at correction. In this list we find stuttering, bed wetting, grimaces, and tics. All of these prove in most cases to serve important psychological functions in the lives of their victims and to be very resistant to cure. In most cases, it is wise to make use of the most expert help available for treatment, rather than to let goodhearted meddlers rush into the scene with "common-sense," and usually drastic, correctives.

To illustrate the complexity of psychological factors involved, we cite two studies in which batteries of tests were given to groups of sufferers and of normal children. In the first study,[19] 30 stutterers were compared with 30 nonstuttering brothers or sisters. For some reason, only 4 of the stutterers were girls. As a group, the stutterers did not feel they belonged in their families; they were more impulsive, yet apprehensive, in their approach to tasks and showed stronger hostilities but expected unfavorable outcomes if the aggression was expressed. In the second study,[20] 10 boys who often wet their beds during sleep were compared with 10 of the same age who were normal. In this particular sample, which was a small one, the bed wetters as a group showed more feminine identification, coupled with fear of women. Also, when asked to make up stories about a group of pictures, they tended to become preoccupied with vertical movement, either going up or coming down. Such facts as the above are merely pieces to larger puzzles. They do serve to communicate the impression that many defense patterns are elaborate to the point where no one need feel inadequate if he or she is baffled in trying to understand some behavior of children.

The subject of this chapter is the devices, called behavior mechanisms or defense mechanisms, through which people unconsciously seek to cope with anxiety, inner conflict, or threats to their self-esteem. Some of these enable the individual to overlook some aspect of himself or of the situation in which he finds himself. Others provide a means

---

[19] Arden Hans Christensen, *A Quantitative Study of Personality Dynamics in Stuttering and Non-Stuttering Siblings,* unpublished Ph.D. dissertation, University of Southern California, 1951.

[20] Joseph P. Lord, *Psychological Correlates of Nocturnal Enuresis in Male Children,* unpublished Ph.D. thesis, Harvard University, 1952.

for running away from actual or potential difficulties. In still others, the individual makes substitutions in the objects of his feelings or the nature of his goals, and thus "solves" his problems by proxy. Some of the defenses, as in the case of psychosomatic illnesses or "nervous habits," may have a very complex structure.

The behavior mechanisms which we have described in this chapter may turn up either alone or in a variety of combinations. Thus, we may find a simple denial coupled with a compensation. A sublimation may be combined with an escape into theorizing. A child with a strong hatred of a brother may drain off these feelings by debating with classmates concerning rules of conduct.

Although all of these mechanisms introduce an element of illogic into a person's living, most of the time their effect is benevolent. They provide enough protection so that the individual can devote most of his conscious effort to the problems of daily living. Only when use of the mechanisms becomes excessive or seriously disrupts his effectiveness or adequacy need the person be considered mentally ill.

Knowledge of the nature of mechanisms and the purposes they serve can be of value in two ways. It helps an individual to view behavior, his own and other people's, with good-natured understanding. Also, he can obtain clues as to what may be the deep-lying factors beneath such conduct and direct any corrective strategy toward these factors, rather than waste energy trying to suppress surface manifestations.

ADDITIONAL READINGS

Hilgard, Ernest R. *Introduction to Psychology*. 2nd ed. New York: Harcourt, Brace, 1957, Chap. 9. Describes the ways in which individuals adjust to conflict and frustration and the techniques of therapy.

Hymes, James L., Jr., *Teacher, Listen, the Children Speak*. New York: New York Committee on Mental Hygiene of the State Charities Aid Association, 1949. A pamphlet in which some types of classroom behavior troubling to teachers are explained in terms of the purposes they serve for children, with suggestions as to what teachers can do.

Kaplan, Louis, and Denis Baron. *Mental Hygiene and Life*. New York: Harper, 1952, Chap. 12. Deals with the ways in which people adjust to tension.

Katz, Barney, and George F. J. Lehner. *Mental Hygiene in Modern Living*. New York: Ronald Press, 1953, Chap. 3. An evaluative listing of defense mechanisms.

Lindgren, Henry Clay. *Psychology of Personal and Social Adjustment*. New York: American Book, 1953, Chap. 5. A very complete treatment of ways by which individuals defend themselves or escape their problems.

Shaffer, Laurance Frederic, and Edward Joseph Shoben, Jr. *The Psychology of Adjustment*. 2nd ed. Boston: Houghton Mifflin, 1956, Chaps. 6 to 10. Extensively describes adjustment mechanisms of all varieties, and documents them by means of case studies and anecdotes.

Symonds, Percival M. *The Dynamics of Human Adjustment*. New York: Appleton-Century-Crofts, 1946. Contains very complete definitions and descriptions of defense mechanisms.

AUDIO-VISUAL AIDS

Anger at Work, a 21-minute sound film produced by the University of Oklahoma, in which the displacement of anger by adults in a work setting is portrayed.

Children's Fantasies, a 21-minute sound film produced by McGraw-Hill, in which four adults debate what to think and what to do about children's fanciful imaginings.

Feeling of Hostility, a 31-minute sound film, produced by the National Film Board of Canada, in which the case study of a young woman is told with detail richly illustrating many defense mechanisms.

Meet Your Mind, a recording by William Menninger, produced by Lewellen's Productions.

chapter **5**

GROWTH

Not many years ago most people pictured human growth as a matter of continuing "habit formation," a species of individual progress in which the tree grew the way the twig was bent. According to this view, the educator's task was to encourage good conduct with praise and reward. Bad tendencies were viewed with anxiety; parents and teachers felt obliged to wipe out anything that looked like the first manifestation of an undesirable trait. This led to a vast amount of worry among grownups, not to mention terrific wear and tear on children.

During the past three decades an unusual amount of research on human development has shown the previous concepts to be inadequate. Actually, growth seems to be a matter of stages and phases, each with a specific task to fulfill. Some involve puzzling behavior. It is even to be expected that youngsters will at times act in a way which would seem highly objectionable if we did not ask two questions: (1) What purpose does it serve? (2) How long will it last? Thus, for instance, it is well known that some youngsters in their early teens seem to play fast and loose with friends. In adults this would be denounced as fickleness. Yet we know that the young people may have to act this way to find out what kinds of people they really like, and to test their feelings toward others in the process. We also know that nearly all of them soon become capable of steady and long-enduring friendships. Such patterns of developmental behavior mean that growth inevitably brings with it new problems for both children and adults.

The term "maturation" is used to refer to types of behavior which emerge into an individual's repertoire as a result of aging rather than experience, as in the first appearance of vocalization.

Growth Produces Problems

It might be taken for granted that growth means improvement and that the conduct of a child at any age would be "better" than it had been earlier. But if we expect, for example, that twelve-year-olds are easier to get along with than seven-year-olds, we will be disappointed at times. Growth involves change, and change often inserts problems into the relationships of children to the world around them, or to themselves. At home, for instance, as the child gets along with less and less sleep as he grows older, household routines are disrupted again and again. In school, the increasing interest of boys and girls in each other, which itself must be considered an advance in growth, is likely to raise a number of problems for adults as well as young people. Another instance: a girl who in the lower grades reveled in her success in jumping rope may, a few years later, still want to taste the same satisfaction, but feels a little ashamed of herself because friends call that activity childish. Now, the most important thing to her is to stand in well with those friends.

One type of problem arises when the growth task requires the child to move away from a previously mutually pleasant relationship with some grownup. Younger children are apt to be more dependent on adults than older ones are—many adults like it that way. Just as a mother may feel unrewarded when her son will no longer allow her to kiss him in public, so a teacher may be hurt when a child who once shared afterhours confidences now dashes out the door pell-mell to greet a new friend.

Another type of problem arises when growth makes a child yearn for activities which are forbidden for reasons either of safety or of custom. In an industrial arts class, for example, new troubles arise when the boys first feel up to using power-driven equipment. Experience shows that in using such tools their appraisal of real danger may not be adequate. Again, in some elementary schools, principals are irked by pressure for graduation dances. Even though some of the youngsters are as mature as Shakespeare's Juliet (she was fourteen), many American communities frown on dating "at such an early age."

A third type of problem involves internal conflict between desires to act one's age and the dictates of conscience. An adolescent, for instance, who is confronted with the task of gaining acceptance in a rather rough neighborhood may feel he ought to show sophistication by smoking, yet feel that he is doing something wrong if he smokes. Or, in the younger years, a child who has outgrown the earlier childhood pattern of tattling may still feel very guilty in joining a conspiracy of silence to protect some other child from punishment. Something within him still makes him feel he ought to be the good boy and tell the teacher. He would feel badly no matter what he did.

The phenomena of developmental change produce other problems too numerous to be analyzed in detail. Often, for instance, the tasks of a new age level may require skills and personality characteristics far beyond what a youngster has at his disposal. As a result, he may act inappropriately and fail miserably to live up to his expectations of himself. Additional troubles come into a youngster's life because of the strange blindness of adults who demand that the child act older than his age one minute and then put babyish restrictions on him the next: "You're old enough to take care of your brother now," but "You're too little to use that big saw."

GROWTH IS OFTEN DISJOINTED. There is no universal, detailed timetable for human growth. Each child is different. Always some youngsters are ahead of their age-mates, and others lag. For example, a few kindergartners are capable of recognizing words and sentences, while, in normal classes, some youngsters do not reach that level of reading until they are old enough for the third grade. Another instance: a very few girls are physiologically mature at nine; a tiny minority, not until after seventeen. For the young person who is either ahead of or behind the general procession, such differences present problems.

For most young folks, growth is uneven. Each is likely to be advanced in some areas and retarded in others. Here are two illustrations of the many thousands of possibilities: A seven-year-old may look after a younger brother with the responsibility of a ten-year-old, but react to problems involving choice with the tedious vacillation of a six-year-old. An adolescent girl may have an adult level of art expression, but show a submissiveness to teachers comparable to that of a much younger child. Teachers should, therefore, not be surprised when an "average" youngster falls below expectations in some area of conduct. The rarest of all children are those who are consistently "normal" for their age all along the line.

There is no rule as to the length of time a child remains in any one stage. A given developmental task may be accomplished more rapidly by some than by others. We see a parallel to this in physical growth, where one boy may shoot up suddenly, acquiring in a single year the growth another achieved gradually over several years. Thus, a particular girl, almost overnight, replaces shyness with poise in a group, although in the same class another girl may take two or more years to manage the transition. Similar differences can be observed at every age level.

OUTSIDE INFLUENCES AFFECT GROWTH. Most differences in growth are not inborn. A child's experiences in the early phases greatly influence how he manages the later ones. For example, if he enjoyed his first contacts with teachers in kindergarten, we would expect him to continue enjoying school even when departmentalization throws more adults into his life during a day. A child who had been nagged about sharing toys in babyhood might have added difficulties in moving into new groups of youngsters during his junior high school years.

At any stage of development, parents and teachers can make demands which create added problems at that stage. Contrariwise, by their understanding, they can greatly ease the course of development. For example, young children seem to need a great deal of muscular activity. If the school restricts this too much, added obstacles are thrown in the way of the children in developing a stable relationship with their teachers. On the other hand, if ample opportunities are provided for physical activity, the adjustment to the school may be more pleasant for all concerned. In any case, each child must be allowed the time necessary for him to complete a particular phase; attempts to speed up the accomplishment of developmental tasks are very often harmful.

The specific forms of conflict and behavior which a given developmental phase may produce are in a large measure determined by the customs and expectations of the neighborhood and community. For example, Macdonald, McGuire, and Havighurst[1] showed that young teen-agers in certain districts of Chicago were much more likely to be members of adult-sponsored youth groups than were others, who had to meet the pressures of unorganized leisure time. Davis and Havighurst,[2] in a study of child-raising practices and their effects, showed

[1] Margherita Macdonald, Carson McGuire, and Robert J. Havighurst, "Leisure Activities and Socioeconomic Status of Children," *American Journal of Sociology,* Vol. 54 (1949), pp. 505-19.

[2] Allison Davis and Robert J. Havighurst, "Social Class and Color Differences in Child-Rearing," *American Sociological Review,* Vol. 11 (1946), pp. 698-710. A more recent study along similar lines in Boston has yielded a somewhat

that "nervous habits" traceable in part to strict demands for cleanliness, were more prevalent among children of middle-class parents than those lower in the socioeconomic scale. The form that adolescence may take has shown the widest variation in different historical epochs and cultures. Anthropologists, for instance, have found several societies where the problems of adolescence, as we know them, do not exist. This fact was first brought sharply to attention by Margaret Mead in her widely read books on Samoa and New Guinea.

The Preschool Years

Psychologists and psychiatrists agree that during the first five years of life the foundations are laid for many later personality traits. During those years a person's deepest attitudes toward himself and other people are developed, and the pattern for the control of his impulses is largely established.

Because most teachers must deal with children only after those critical first years are completed, we shall treat the period very sketchily. However, those readers who have young children of their own will want to go much more thoroughly into the early phases. Moreover, teachers who have classes in home economics or family living, and all others in a position to advise young couples, owe it to themselves to secure a thorough understanding of human development during infancy, babyhood, and early childhood. They can obtain much help from the organizations and publications described in Appendix 1.

For most teachers, the important thing is to realize that characteristics which can be traced to early experiences change very slowly. In those cases in which a teacher feels the results of early patterns should be modified, it is essential to recognize that these will not yield to drastic punishment or solemn sermonizing. Rather, they require consistently patient handling in which the teacher, so to speak, partially repairs the early damage by assisting the child to accomplish in some measure tasks he should have completed satisfactorily at an earlier age. On the positive side, children who receive a good start in life usually retain their stability in meeting later problems.

---

different pattern. However, although customs within groups may change, the main point made in this study remains valid: Ways of dealing with children are related to the socioeconomic level of the parents, and the differences yield demonstrable effects. This matter will be treated in further detail in the next chapter.

RELATIONSHIP TO PEOPLE.   Perhaps the most fundamental of such tasks is that of learning to relate oneself to other people. Psychiatrists are convinced that during the very first months of life, long before an infant can talk or understand words, critical learnings about human relationships take place. Whether infants are fed promptly when hungry and are fondled lovingly or their needs arouse impatience in disinterested adults, who handle them without personal warmth, may make quite a difference in the expectations children develop toward the world of adults. Babies who feel secure are likely to become adults who enjoy other people and have an easy confidence with them.

APPRECIATION OF REALITY.   Another very important task of the early years is to develop an appreciation of reality. During their first few months, babies live in a world of seeming magic, where their cries and first words bring to them (apparently from nowhere) food, changes of clothing, and warm embraces. However, they must eventually learn to sense cause-and-effect relationships and to test the wisdom of their own actions by the results these actions bring. When the baby accomplishes this aspect of growth well, he is able to face the real world and deal with it effectively. His strength in this respect makes it possible for him to meet conflicts by using the various behavior mechanisms without losing contact with reality.

In addition, children must learn to communicate their wishes and to appraise on an increasingly realistic level what other people are likely to do. The savage impatience with which a very small child would be expected to meet every frustration of his desires must give way to acceptance of the fact that some unpleasant situations have to be endured, some wants have to be renounced, and other people's wishes have to be considered. This is the basis for later success in social living.

ATTITUDES TOWARD CULTURAL DEMANDS.   Every baby comes in contact with the demands of our culture as expressed through his parents. Through their reactions, he begins to notice that some of his behavior, even though gratifying in itself, meets with parental disapproval. At other times, actions which require effort or restraint meet with jubilation and reward. Accepting the use of the spoon, instead of uninhibited delight in manually squishing food, may draw the parents' praise. The atmosphere of acceptance and affection, or the reverse, in which such situations are met has a lot to do with the later attitudes of the child toward the rules, unwritten codes, and values of our society.

For instance, in a study Bernstein[3] conducted of fifty children at a well-baby clinic in New York, it was found that those who had received a coercive toilet training were quite apt, at the age of four, to be uncommunicative, negativistic, and immature in their behavior. It is probable that the parental conduct studied would be found symbolic of a general attitude of coercion, which could show itself in additional facets of parent-child relationships.

ATTITUDES TOWARD PARENTS AND AUTHORITIES.   Accompanying these learnings are certain strong emotional reactions to parents, which later may be generalized in attitudes toward various other authorities. At times the love children have toward mother and father is mixed with feelings of anger in reaction to the restraint or pressure which accompanies socialization. Also, before the preschool years have ended, there is often a certain amount of rivalry between boys and their fathers or girls and their mothers. In many households there are turbulent scenes in which little tots may hit at their parents, call them names, or throw temper tantrums. The wisdom with which the adults handle these situations helps determine how the child, when he gets to school, will regard his teachers and others who are in positions of authority.[4]

DEVELOPMENT OF CURIOSITY.   Curiosity and spontaneity are invaluable qualities. Their early manifestations, however, may trouble adults. The behavior involved in examining and exploring toys and animals can look like destructiveness and cruelty. Zest to discover the world may lead little folk into actual dangers. When interference becomes necessary, the problem is one of limiting harmful behavior without obliterating the zest for new experiences. If the child's activities are punished sharply and angrily, he may be left with the impression that all curiosity is dangerous or wicked. If, however, in limiting behavior,

---

[3] Arnold Bernstein, *Some Relations between Techniques of Feeding during Infancy and Certain Behavior in Childhood*, Ph.D. dissertation, Columbia University, 1952, University Microfilms Publication No. 4158.

[4] The strongest evidence upon which such statements rest is drawn from innumerable case histories, learned as individuals under treatment explored the course of their difficulties. Within recent years there have been efforts to produce more "scientific" data or to collect statistics.

For one example of such an approach, interested readers may want to examine the following monograph: G. S. Blum, "A Study of the Psychoanalytic Theory of Psychosexual Development," *Genetic Psychology Monographs*, Vol. 39 (1949), pp. 3-99.

adults show love and provide substitute opportunities, spontaneity in dealing with new things and new people can be preserved.

FORMATION OF CONSCIENCE. By the time children come to school, their consciences have already partially developed. The type of values toward which a youngster will be most sensitive are primarily dependent upon the standards of the people who mattered most in his early life and upon his relationship with them. The range of activities in which a sense of right and wrong operates will shift during the school years and in later life. Great as the variations as to content may be, the way in which a child's conscience exercises its control is largely determined during the early years. The happiest result of development is for the conscience to uphold moral values in an effective and realistic manner. The process of identification has a great deal to do with how the conscience is formed. Of great importance is whether love or terror was the dominant feeling during the process. Although some anxiety accompanies a child's desire to please his parents or to retain their love, homes differ greatly in the tone of parent-child relationship. At one extreme, some youngsters upon whom no early demands are made may as a consequence run into trouble in later life because their consciences surrender entirely to their impulses. At the other extreme are some of those who grow up in fear-ridden households and whose lives are made miserable by a panicky conscience which operates on the assumption that all satisfactory self-expression is morally suspect. The particular way in which upbringing influences conscience formation is a product of many forces. However, where a child feels safe in the good esteem of his father and mother, and they hold up definite standards he can meet, his conscience enables him to have a strong sense of right and wrong, without distorting his view of the world and himself.

SOCIAL GROWTH. The preschool years see quite a bit of progress in social development as children play together. Ordinarily, they learn to share toys, take turns, and co-operate in dramatic play based largely on household events. Their techniques of settling disagreements are still likely to be physical fighting, name calling, or appeals to adults. When no older people are present, groups larger than two are likely to be unstable. It should be realized that play serves children not only for social enjoyment but also for acting out strong feelings arising elsewhere. Thus, even though a child knows how to share toys, he may get into fights because he resents other children who remind him of his mother's preference for his brother, or because he wants to exert power over other children to balance the way he is ordered about at home. For most youngsters, such use of play is not only common but healthy. It is one of the numerous ways in which emotional stability is secured. The child who finds in social relationships not only pleasure, but a balance wheel for his emotional life, may later be able to handle without outside help problems which would be seriously disturbing to someone who had been less fortunate.

The Early School Years

In broad panorama, the early years of school see children developing in response to two main currents: On the one hand they are becoming more perfect in filling the role of children, fitting themselves better into the patterns that adults in their homes or neighborhoods set for children. On the other hand, they are learning to accommodate themselves in one way or another to such new conflicts as enter their lives. For old conflicts carried over unresolved from babyhood, they must attempt new solutions in harmony with their age.

BECOMING A BIGGER AND BETTER CHILD. Children, as well as grownups, have certain common expectations of what a child should be like and what he should be able to do. During the early school years, many children find satisfaction in gaining mastery over the skills and knowledge which their parents, their teachers, and their friends admire. They are learning to gauge rights and wrongs, to meet the expectations of their elders. They are also developing skill in dealing with adults in a more realistic way. Their grasp on the world-as-it-is is being strengthened by a growing ability to make clearer distinctions between the realm of make-believe and the domain of real people and real things. With their playmates they gain in sureness and in variety of enjoyable activities.

The first years in school, if the child is reasonably lucky, are marked by the joy of an expanding ability to cope with the world. New academic tools, such as reading, allow him to push into areas of former mystery as symbolized by the signs on stores, the headlines on newspapers, and the print in books. As he gains control over his muscles, he can feel new triumphs in playing catch, jumping rope, and making musical noises. He can feel himself less the pawn of all-knowing adults and more the captain of himself, albeit still a small self. It is in this area of growth that the school can be the child's natural ally, opening up new vistas and giving him new implements.

To some observant parents, a marked change seems to occur almost as soon as children make a successful adjustment to school. About eight months after the start of first grade in a midwestern community, Stendler and Young[5] interviewed 212 mothers. That the year had been an easier one than the previous year was reported by 112. They rated their children as showing more maturity, self-control, helpfulness, responsibility, self-confidence, and ability to get along with playmates.

The child's world, however, remains a world in which adults loom large. To please them remains an unrelenting concern; to avoid their displeasure, a prime consideration. With his increased acuity as to their demands, his picture of himself as they would like him to be becomes more sharply defined. Under pressure of both love and fear, his conscience takes fuller shape. He feels the inappropriateness of some forms of behavior in which a young child might naïvely engage, as, for instance, stealing, destroying someone else's work, talking out loud in church or public gatherings (except Saturday matinees), and openly defying adults. When he occasionally violates his own behavioral demands, he feels he has then done something wrong or daring. He is quite capable of getting temporary satisfaction out of some acts of mischief, but gains his basic security from being at peace with the standards set by adults.

He is also learning to size up adults better. Greater understanding of their demands may strengthen his conscience, but sharp-eyed observation lets him see their frailties. He is learning a whole arsenal of new tricks: how to deceive, when to ignore, where to flatter, when to throw a tantrum, how to wheedle, when to cry, and when to "act the little gentleman" or "be a little lady." This is more than a repertoire for mischief-makers. It lays the groundwork for enjoyment together in the family. It is the basis for having fun on school excursions and in the entire range of adult-supervised entertainment. This same realism in the appraisal of adults furnishes a solid foundation which enables children to sense the part which teachers, parents, policemen, and others have to play in their lives. In times of conflict, it is this awareness which helps them accept even frustrating interference without resentment or to make allowance for adult errors.

---

[5] Celia Burns Stendler and Norman Young, "Impact of First Grade Entrance upon the Socialization of the Child: Changes after Eight Months of School," *Child Development*, Vol. 22 (1951), pp. 113-22.

One of the most important functions of development at this age is to establish a clearer dividing line between reality and the world of make-believe. The young school child is quite capable of vivid day-dreams and spirited dramatic play. Indeed, such exercise of imagination remains continually important for emotional balance. Now, however, the boy or girl knows he is "just pretending," even though he may savor the delights of make-believe. He may enjoy being a deadly gunman one minute, but will meekly hurry home at his mother's call for dinner. Under normal circumstances, children will drift toward obtaining more and more of their satisfactions from undisguised reality. They relish their own mastery over things. They can take delight in getting along with real people rather than imaginary companions.

Parallel with the above development is the growth of social abilities. When good times are in order, young school children can have fun with a group of their age-mates. When anger wells, they are better able to fight. They are more capable of forming small teams and of negotiating differences of opinion, as well as employing threats, ostracism, and blackmail. In moments of serious conflict or trouble, they still seek the aid of an adult. The groups which they form do not yet have the full-fledged independence that will come in a few years. The desire to please grownups still usually overshadows even the temporary admiration of mischievous excitement. Companions who are very "naughty" or "not nice" in terms of the family or school code still are more frightening than attractive. However, at this age children definitely yearn for playmates. They feel any exclusion from the group, and can be subject to deep loneliness.

COPING WITH CONFLICTS, OLD AND NEW.   At every age level, children have to deal with some conflicts. The process of growing up involves continual changes in relationships at home. The emotions with which such changes are met may be highly colored by feelings left over from the very first years of life. Just because it is so important for the younger school children to be accepted by adults, the mixed feelings toward parents previously described may be especially disturbing to them. Accordingly, they are more likely to deal with those feelings by using one or another of the behavior mechanisms. Teachers may sometimes bear the brunt of all the negative feelings developed around the father or mother in the home. If, instead of displacement, a child resorts to reaction formation, he may become too much of a goody-goody.

The most sweeping change in a young child's life is his introduction to school itself. Here, the boy or girl meets a set of standards against which his abilities are measured in one form or another. During the first days, he may expect to read within a week, but by the end of a few months he has encountered some elements of failure or the boredom of too easy success. For most, there is the zest of genuine accomplishment. The child's picture of himself may undergo chronic jolting or be filled out with proud feelings of success. At this point the foundation may be laid for deep inferiority feelings, for conceit, for later truancies, for intellectual snobbishness, or for invaluable and calm self-confidence.

On top of all this, teachers may behave quite differently in respect to a youngster's actions than do his parents. For example, the same behavior which evoked loving laughter as "cute" in the family circle may draw an impatient frown if it interrupts a class. Or a teacher with greater knowledge of how children act may give approval to actions which parents would try to "improve." Thus, a child trying to meet the standards set by adults finds himself confronting two conflicting conceptions of how he should behave. The conflicts resulting from school may be intensified if a child's family represents a pattern of living different from that of other people with whom he is coming in contact. This is particularly true among children of low socioeconomic-status neighborhoods who go to schools which accept the role, advocated by a group of prominent and respected educators, of "teaching a middle-class culture to children from underprivileged families with a lower-class culture."[6] Thus, to a child from a home where the king's English is salted heavily with slang, a teacher's deriding of colloquialisms may undercut his natural honoring of his parents. If he accepts the teacher's standards, he may not only become a stranger in his own home, but also be torn with guilt for having assumed a position "superior" to that of his father and mother. The dilemma this creates for teachers is something to which we shall give attention later. It is a serious problem, requiring clear thinking. Throughout school life a child is bound to meet many situations which contain elements of conflict concerning ways of doing things. Differences between people are forced on his attention, and they alter his conception of himself.

Even in dealing with conflict, each age level requires a style of its own. Thus, among children in the early elementary grades, to hold one's breath in a temper tantrum means to "act like a baby," while a violent

[6] American Association of School Administrators, *Twenty-Fifth Yearbook: Schools for a New World,* Washington, 1947, p. 74.

flow of abusive words is not considered beneath their dignity. Although teachers and parents might disapprove, an eight-year-old can pick his nose without losing status with other children, yet thumb sucking would bring gibes. It is, therefore, one of the tasks of the school child to slough off inappropriate, outgrown ways of expressing emotions or even tensions, and to replace them by methods more in harmony with his age.

Preadolescence

Somewhere between the fifth and the eighth grades, teachers notice that children become harder to handle. This is the period of preadolescence, a period which from the viewpoint of experiment and research has more uncharted territory than any other stage of child development. The conduct of the children can be very puzzling. Even the nicest ones are likely to become cutups. However, there is a meaning in the weird behavior. These young people are engaged in performing two vitally important and interrelated tasks. First, they are getting rid of childish patterns, so that they can build into themselves the changes that will come with adolescence. Second, they are dropping dependence on the values of adults and molding themselves in accordance with the standards of their own groups.

GETTING READY FOR NEW ADVANCES. During the early school years, as we described a few pages back, the boy or girl is busy making himself into a bigger and better *child*. When this job has been done as well as it can be done, there is still a large gap between the resultant personality structure and that of an adult. To understand what has to happen next, we shall make use of an analogy which, although far from perfect, carries the general idea. When a caterpillar grows, it can become a bigger and better caterpillar. However, approaching perfection as a caterpillar would never make it into a butterfly. To accomplish that transition, it has to go into another phase, the pupa, in which, it is recognizable as neither a caterpillar nor a butterfly. The caterpillar structure has to disintegrate if the butterfly is ever to take wing. Somewhat similarly, the childish personality, with its dependence on adults and parent figures, has to disappear if we are to have a full-fledged grownup, standing on his own two feet and assuming responsibility for his own actions. Preadolescence is the phase during which the childhood patterns begin to be discarded in earnest.

The normal range of actions in which preadolescents engage is very wide. From time to time, they are likely to show, for more or less brief periods, qualities that are highly objectionable or that look alarmingly like symptoms of disorganization. For example, restlessness is one of the most obvious traits of this age group. Often it seems that for them to sit still is the most exquisite form of torture. At other times, they may go back to infantile habits, such as nail biting, bed wetting, or tearfulness. Old fears, apparently outgrown, come back. There may be a newly intensified preoccupation with darkness, ghosts, burglars, and the perilous world of bogeymen. There may be worry about illness and injury, alternating with foolhardy recklessness.

As a preadolescent tackles his task of freeing himself from childish, adult-oriented values, he hits out at the world of grownups. Much as he seems to fight for independence, at times he acts as though deep down he were not too sure about giving up the security of having adults tell him what to do. The confusion is shown by the difficulty many children have in talking seriously about themselves. A counselor who tries to probe beneath the surface may meet with a baffling resistance, expressed in giggles. An outsider asking the child about the conference will be told the counselor was crazy. To top it all off, the youngsters are sensitive and moody; they will writhe if parents show friends a baby photograph. They fume inwardly at such conversational gambits as, "My, how you have grown!" or "What will you be when you grow up?" Their feelings sometimes change almost from minute to minute.

In an adult, such behavior would warrant a diagnosis of severe mental disorder. In a younger child, it would be ample cause for serious worry. However, some measure of such personality disorganization is typical of the preadolescent age group. Unaccompanied by other factors, it does not represent mental ill health. What a teacher of this age level needs, in addition to vast reserves of patience, is a knowledge of the problems the youngsters are trying to solve and an understanding of why the temporary solution is at times so outlandish.

For purposes of illustration, let us look more closely at the preadolescent tendency to revel in fantasy and go mad about comic books, which provide the substance upon which daydreams can be erected. It will be recalled that one of the tasks of early childhood was to establish a clearer line between fact and fiction. Why should there now be an upsurge in fictional dramatic play and in hours spent reading highly improbable yarns?

From their nursery days, despite an ever-increasing ability to distinguish make-believe from the real world, children enjoy stories of heroes and ogres in all their many guises. Into them they can pour thoroughly disguised feelings of aggression and hostility, engendered by the demands of the adults with whom they live. Disguise is made necessary by the children's strong love for those same adults. During preadolescence the attraction of the gory reaches a new peak. Why? Impatient with the role of being a child, the preadolescent is under pressure to do more vehement battle with those who are keeping him a child, namely, his parents and teachers. Therefore, his level of hostility may be expected to rise. As a channel to drain this off with a minimum of danger to his psychological balance, comic book adventures look very inviting.

In a similar way, most of the other disturbing behavior listed above can be traced to conflicts resulting from the children's efforts to complete the developmental tasks of this period. An illustration of the strange mixture of trends was drawn by Beller[7] from a study of standards of conduct among boys. Although between the ages of nine and twelve there was a sharp increase in the ability to state norms of conduct, actual behavior did not keep up with increasing knowledge of standards. Answers to questions as to what conduct was right or wrong became more discerning, although the boys' actions did not reflect this fact.

THE TIGHTENING GRIP OF THE PEER GROUP.   Even during the early school years, it is easy to see that for children the opinions of their classmates, the prestige they have in their playmates' eyes, are important issues. During preadolescence this dependence upon the opinions of their peers shows a significant increase. This is highlighted by the development of gangs and cliques. These establish their standards in part by waging a kind of tribal warfare against adults in general and their own parents and teachers in particular. Powerful codes of behavior take shape.

The dominant themes in these codes seem to fall into three categories of purpose: (1) to demonstrate group solidarity; (2) to flaunt independence of adults; and (3) to ape the behavior of older and tougher neighborhood heroes. We would therefore expect youngsters of this age range to show an unusually vehement reaction against any and all tattling, to take pride in conduct against which adults seem to be unusually vigilant, and to egg each other on to smoking, rough talk, precocious use of make-up, etc.

[7] Emanuel K. Beller, "Two Attitude Components in Younger Boys," *Journal of Social Psychology,* Vol. 29 (1949), pp. 137-51.

Viewed from adult seats of authority, such behavior appears not only annoying but downright rebellious. It seems to be a preface to delinquency or immorality—an ominous warning that the kids are getting out of hand. Although this may be true in some instances, in general such behavior is only a preparation for assuming qualities which we value very highly when they appear: Sensitivity to group standards, courageous independence of thought, and emulation of outstanding characters are highly treasured qualities of the adult living in a democratic world. To be sure, the first forms in which these virtues are practiced may be clumsy and objectionable in content; they still remain necessary steps in a process of transition.

The solution to the problem for the teacher and parent involves a combination of humor, firmness, and long-range vision. Grownups must be able to detach their own hurt feelings from the real significance of events. On the one hand, they must be willing to sacrifice temporary popularity with the children when it is necessary to enforce clear limits on behavior. On the other hand, they must have the courage to allow a wide enough margin for transitional conduct so that personality growth can take place, even when they find it uncomfortable.

Adolescence

When the debris of preadolescence finally settles, the way may be cleared for the emergence of new personality patterns. This slow and sometimes painful process is of particular interest to educators because it is the last developmental stage over which they can have marked influence. In fact, for many young people, adolescence represents a last chance. Once they are too far beyond it, further critical changes in personality are very unlikely. Moreover, for many youngsters, the last person whose main objective is to help them in their personal development will be a high school teacher.

Adolescence itself varies greatly in accordance with national cultures, historical periods, local customs, and socioeconomic class. One variable is the attitude regarding the age at which boys and girls should marry and go to work. For example, during World War II young men who ordinarily would have been allowed to lead happily irresponsible lives as high school seniors found themselves forced to carry life-and-death responsibility in combat. And today in any large city, girls who in one section would be considered social novices might, if they lived in another area, already be married and beginning to raise families. The country-club set may be practicing social exclusiveness; the roughies, new modes of cop baiting.

THE TASK OF THE PERIOD.   The main task of adolescents is to become adults. Childish ways have to be discarded, and grown-up patterns adopted. The setting in which this takes place often makes the job a struggle. It is hard to be independent and still retain the satisfactions of living at home. It is torture to make believe you are a full-fledged adult when your family and teachers treat you as a child. It seems futile to develop well-rounded attitudes and opinions concerning religion, politics, and human relationships when you are powerless to act. When marriage must be deferred until education is completed, the onrush of sex emotion, which in itself constitutes a valid contribution to the adult personality, is likely to be a terrific hazard. Despite such conditions, the new adult personality which has been forming eventually shows itself.

As this new personality takes shape, mental health may be vitally affected. Sometimes defects traceable to earlier developmental failures are corrected in a series of rapid readjustments. Or, unfortunately, old tensions may be reinforced, and the distortions they produce become obvious and lead to serious mental illness. For most young folks, the final outcome is adequate, although the process involves some rough spots. How his parents and teachers act toward him while he is dealing with his troubles is of crucial importance to each boy and girl at this stage.

THE PROBLEMS THEY FACE.   When a group of adolescents are asked to list their problems, the range of troublesome areas seems bewildering. Within an hour, a good discussion leader can easily secure a catalogue of fifty to seventy-five tough problems. Battles at home over driving the family car are matched by worries over shyness in class. Plans for future education, choice of a vocation, and the selection of friends are all worrisome. But then, so are such apparent trivia as the sharing of sweaters by sisters, the use of the telephone, and who has the say-so in picking the television program.

All such items, mentioned as problems, are really surface outcroppings of certain basic dilemmas in the lives of adolescents. It therefore becomes important to determine what the primary source of the "real problem" behind the scenes may be. Each of the items included in lists of problems proffered by adolescents probably has one or more of the elements mentioned below as contributory factors.

One of the greatest worries of adolescents concerns their *status*. By this we mean the standing they have in the eyes of their friends, as well as of adults. Anything which they feel would mark them as "children" may make them panicky. Among their age-mates, they feel most comfortable when they know they belong to, and are accepted as, members of a group with prestige. They may fight doggedly, therefore, against their parents' efforts to make them wear clothes which would set them off from the others. In school they may be especially resentful of teachers who talk down to them. In fact, almost every detail of daily life may become a hot issue if it gets tied up with such status concerns.

The significance of these status concerns and the extent to which they permeate many relationships are illustrated by one of the reports growing out of the California Adolescent Growth Study, a project in which a number of young people were scientifically followed in their development. One device used was to set up a clubhouse in which their behavior could be watched. Here are some observations:[8]

> As the students . . . entered the ninth grade, the clubhouse became definitely a place for them to work out their own social relationships and to establish themselves with those of their own sex, and, increasingly, with those of the opposite sex. Some of the pupils who had been socially unsuccessful with their own sex up to this time redeemed themselves in the eyes of their classmates by becoming popular with the opposite sex. Those who frequented the clubhouse tried out various modes of behavior, eliminating the types of response which lessened their popularity and trying to avoid the mistakes they saw others make. The common goal was obviously to attain group approval.
>
> Adult approval or disapproval meant almost nothing to these young adolescents except as it might affect the attainment of their goal. In fact there was a noticeable resistance, not so much to authority, as our rules seldom got in the way, but simply to adults as such. Those boys and girls who were in the throes of establishing themselves socially were the most antagonistic toward adults. They manifested this attitude chiefly by shunning adults and acting as if their presence were a hindrance. Six months later these same pupils were likely to be the ones who hung around and talked to adults as if, being quite grown up now, they needed to talk and associate with other grown persons.

---

[8] Herbert R. Stolz, Mary Cover Jones, and Judith Chaffey, "The Junior High School Age," *University High School Journal*, Vol. 15 (1937), pp. 63-72. This quotation catches an aspect of adolescent development that has not been as well presented in any other report. Although it is two decades old, there is no reason to believe the basic relationship portrayed has undergone any significant change.

The significance of the needs revealed and the energy that was used in meeting them are seen in the observation of their teachers that, once these young people had achieved a satisfactory social status, they "settled down" and did better schoolwork.

With physiological maturity, the entire topic of *sex* becomes highly charged. Adolescents are likely to be worried about sex-laden daydreams, what to do on dates, and the functioning of their bodies. Parents often stress rigid taboos, which come into head-on conflict with practices urged on young people by their friends. Their own strong desires collide with their consciences. We shall return to this topic later in this chapter.

Seriously complicating the lives of many teen-agers is the *timing* of the various phases of their growth. For example, in any normal high school group there will be some boys and girls with childish builds and high-pitched voices; and in the upper elementary or junior high school grades, there will be other youngsters who are adult in form and voice. As was pointed out on page 87, such differences can be normal. Yet, they create problems at any age. For the adolescent, however, with his great sensitivity to status and with the high value placed on dating, being out of step with the growth pattern of his classmates creates especially trying problems. Those young folks whose growth is extremely rapid and condensed into an unusually short period may find additional problems in adjusting their own attitudes to the new situation their growth has created. It is typical of growth that individuals are prone to concentrate on the change, which for the moment has highest priority. Therefore, the youngster who is absorbed in the difficulties created by his own special growth pattern may temporarily slight other matters with which we might hope him to be concerned. For boys, growth which affects athletic prowess can be especially important.

In testing a group of 33 seventeen-year-old boys by getting them to tell stories evoked by a standard series of pictures, Mussen and Jones[9] found strong evidence that those who were late in maturing were likely to have feelings of inadequacy and of being rejected or dominated. They were apt to exhibit both a prolonged dependency and rebellious attitudes. By contrast, the boys who had matured early tended to be self-confidently independent and capable of taking adult roles.

---

[9] Paul Henry Mussen and Mary Cover Jones, "Self-Conceptions, Motivations, and Interpersonal Attitudes of Late- and Early-Maturing Boys," *Child Development,* Vol. 28 (1957), pp. 243-56.

For any youngster, related problems of timing can assume major dimensions. In the intellectual sphere they may influence his or her concern with larger issues of life.

The drive toward adulthood necessarily implies *emancipation*. This means a drastic change in adolescents' relationships with the very people toward whom they felt the strongest dependence in their childhood years. There is a basic striving on the part of the boy or girl to assume control of all decision making. The particular issues which may become symbolic of independence cannot be predicted, any more than the American colonists or their British governors could have predicted beforehand the significance of the Boston Tea Party. That is to say, minor specific issues, such as bedtime, the wearing of galoshes, or trivial decisions about a high school dance may lead to a tumultuous battle, only because they are tests of confidence in adolescent judgment. The young person who is continually defeated or who cannot muster courage to fight for himself encounters problems of social adjustment, especially problems of status.

The problem is well exemplified by a finding of Hutson and Kovar,[10] who asked 2,163 students in the tenth and twelfth grades of 10 four-year high schools in Western Pennsylvania to fill out a questionnaire on their attitudes toward the program of social recreation. The questionnaire showed that 694 boys and 676 girls had not attended dances. Some gave statements like this one: "My parents object to me going out and staying after twelve o'clock. If I went to parties, I'd break up the crowd. If I disobeyed my parents I wouldn't have a good time."

Even the adolescent who is successful in winning independence has problems which center around what he is to do with his feelings of love and affection for the parents, teachers, and older siblings from whose protection he has weaned himself. We may hope that those feelings will eventually persist, though in a new form. The goal of the adolescent in this respect is ordinarily not to rid himself of his parents, but to work out family ties on a basis of free give-and-take among equals. Once freed of the emotional suspicion that he has to defend his independence from tyrants, the young person will be more willing to give due weight to the value of experience in his elders. Because of the strong conflict involved, the struggle and its accompanying emotions

---

[10] Percival W. Hutson and Dan R. Kovar, "Some Problems of Senior High-School Pupils in Their Social Recreation," *Educational Administration and Supervision,* Vol. 28 (1942), pp. 503-19.

may be displaced into the school. The teacher, therefore, may get a double dose, not only through his or her role as a limiter of youthful behavior, but also as a father or mother symbol, one notch removed.

One of the most important contributions adolescence makes to the individual's final adult personality is a growth and clarification of *his picture of himself as he would like to be,* or, to use the technical term, his ego ideal. Throughout the period, this ego ideal may be modeled largely on what he thinks is the current image of what a teen-ager ought to be. In this respect, it may be a source of difficulty for school people. However, hero worship, directed toward the saints as well as the sinners, introduces into the personality structure ideals which may be of permanent effect. It is important to realize that adolescents not only identify with whole personalities but also incorporate into themselves single traits of individuals they meet in daily life whom they respect and admire. This is the point at which teachers may have their strongest influence. On the basis largely of admiration for the way the teacher treats them, the young men and women have a chance to recognize the desirability of traits which they would not have picked up from their parents or from other people in the community. It may seem a trifle fanciful to say so, but many a teacher has achieved a kind of immortality by living on in the personalities of students—and even the students' children.

A special aspect in the formation of the ego ideal may be what the individual boy chooses to make of his masculinity or the girl of her femininity. For girls, in a society which vaunts masculine values, this can be a serious problem. A not too unusual sequence in development, culminating in the appearance of happily female interests, is illustrated by a series of observations of one girl during several successive years at the Merrill-Palmer Camp.[11] At the age of ten, Barbara was vigorously good at sports and hobbies. Although she ignored boys, she aped their ideals; she wanted to be a cowboy. She was untidy and made fun of girls who primped. She organized a secret "fraternity" of girls. She was ill at ease with the men counselors. The next year, after she reached reproductive maturity and developed a figure, she organized a girls' club. Conscious of boys, she avoided being touched by them, but did get into a snow fight. At twelve, she had become interested in dancing, but did it poorly. She now teased boys. That year, Barbara planned a show full of semisophisticated humor. She primped. The next year she preferred

---

[11] Elsie Hatt Campbell, "The Social-Sex Development of Children," *Genetic Psychology Monographs,* Vol. 21 (1939), pp. 461-62.

dancing to all other activities, unabashedly liked the boys, and was flattered by their attention. She took great interest in the dresses of the women counselors.

During adolescence, a young person's *conscience* undergoes a series of changes. Acts about which he was expected to feel guilty while a child are now permitted, even expected, of him. Thus, the good little girl who would not have dared to cross prohibited highways now is urged to run errands for her mother all over town. Conflict arises where adults still cling to the more childhood-designed demands. For example, a teen-ager may not feel panic at the thought of talking back to a teacher, but parents and school staff both expect him to remain docile. Older boys and girls face a variety of new situations in which they are forced to judge for themselves, often without direct help from old heads. Here we find them using their newly mastered command of such abstractions as "justice," "fair play," and "morality." These abstractions have now at last come to have real meaning, as answers to questions on standardized intelligence tests show. Unfortunately, the adult world rarely measures up to the new ideals in their pristine purity. This introduces another source of conflict, which may show itself either in impatience with the way adults act or in overemphasized cynicism.

Another development in the conscience is the extension of old values into new areas. Foremost of the new problems, as we might expect, is the development of sex standards. Consider, for example, the girl who at five was applauded as "cute" when adults had her dance at an entertainment clad in abbreviated trunks and narrow bandeau but who is expected to feel immodest wearing an equivalent costume at sixteen.

For the adolescent, the main problem is steering himself between two opposite dangers. If he develops no new values, he may remain infantile in his level of expression or else act so impulsively that he affronts the community. On the other hand, if he cannot temper his enthusiasm for the new values with some consideration for human needs and the demands of daily reality, he may add immeasurably to the number and intensity of internal conflicts. If he rejects the group's new values completely, he may suffer rejection as a prig. Since impulses as well as values are in flux, we should expect that the adolescent will go through periods of impaired self-control.

The problems of adolescence are aggravated by the fact that social conditions and customs often prevent adolescents from *getting proper practice* in adult modes of behavior in real life. Ready in their own minds to assume moral responsibility and act as adults, they are denied many opportunities to participate in meaningful life tasks. As was pointed out in Chapter 4, they may have to resort to flight into intellectualization to work out problems which might better be handled through experience and experimentation. For those young people who grow up in economically ill-favored groups, the opposite problem arises. They are thrown into situations which demand full-fledged adult functioning without any opportunity to gain initial experience under protection. Consider, for example, the problem of the hundreds of girls under nineteen years of age who, according to United States census reports of 1940, already had families numbering five or more children. No wonder that so many adolescents of our generation and culture either carry chips on their shoulders in rebellion against prolonged exposure to infantile forms of life or else become misshapen by life pressures far beyond their maturity level.

THE CHALLENGE TO ADULTS. Since adolescent behavior can be very irritating to adults, the first task of a teacher or any other adult who deals with them is to recognize what is going on, and not to lose perspective. It is too easy to slip into suppressive measures designed to keep everything under control. That technique can well stifle necessary growth or force it into less obvious and possibly really harmful channels. Teachers may face the responsibility of coming forward as the advocates of youth and of interpreting the youngsters to the community.

A few teachers, parents, and other youth leaders may find it particularly attractive to work with adolescents. They may very much want to be "one of the kids" and to live again the dramas of romance and discovery. This may lead to an essential understanding and provide for young people a support which will greatly aid them. However, it is not a wise policy to carry this attitude to extremes. Adolescents need *adults* who can give them understanding and guidance. They are likely to be bewildered and resentful if an older person tries to live in their world without being aware of his age.

Most adults have a picture of all adolescence as being like their own. That is natural enough, since the firmest concepts we have are those derived from our own experience. However, it is a very unreliable guide, because the style of life during the teen years is subject to very sharp changes as a result of differences in time, place, and local circumstances. Yesteryear's rock-and-roll addict may be replaced by the adolescent who dances sedately to sweet music. In one community, "going steady" means that from the time she gets off the bus, a girl is accompanied in school at all free times by one boy, whose obligation ends when he puts her back on the bus in the afternoon. In another community, boys and girls are expected to engage in steady dating; in still others, they travel around in unorganized crowds with relatively weak person-to-person ties. The meaning of a specific bit of conduct will change from time to time and place to place. Therefore, all who have contact with adolescents should be appreciative of the meaning of differences. It is useless and foolhardy to try to make girls and boys behave in the fashion of one's own youth.

The real problem for adults is to work out new bases of relationship with young people as they grow toward adulthood. The older, often-pleasant ties of dependency are bound to break; close supervision and direct open protection no longer fit. We can no longer expect or demand adoration as superiors. Something new must come into the picture if adults are to remain useful figures in the development of young people. What is it? Basically, it is a form of friendship between almost-equals, one of whom still has some responsibility for the other. Adolescents expect their parents and teachers to warn them of dangerous pitfalls, to interfere in behavior which can have hurtful results, but to do so with due respect and sensitivity for their near-adult status. Curt orders, brusquely enforced, to be obeyed merely out of respect, no longer work. However, adolescents are willing to accept quite forceful interference provided it does not carry the implication they are still children.

This brings up the question of when the adult should interfere. Obviously, teachers cannot abdicate their responsibility. Yet, as already mentioned, if the school tries to overcontrol adolescents, their growth is stifled. Providing proper freedom for growth does not mean that we must stand aside and permit any young person to get himself deeply in trouble or allow one group to harm another. It does mean that when the course of a child's development seems to be leading him toward deep maladjustment, the school should step in with its counseling and guidance services, as well as its disciplinary routines. The emphasis here is on the kind of behavior which imperils the personality of the youngster, not that which is simply annoying to the school.

Granted the need for control, it should be so exercised as to provide young people with a wide range of freedom in which to develop toward adult patterns of behavior. This means, for example, that the school should give them plenty of opportunity to talk with each other, to work out *ideas,* no matter how unconventional, and even to engage in hilarious group ventures. We must be especially chary of pinning solemn trait labels, such as "irresponsible," "lazy," "disrespectful," or "antisocial," on conduct merely because it irks us. Providing young people with an opportunity to grow necessarily involves being willing to put up with a good deal of tomfoolery, noise, and plain damnfoolishness. So long as the conduct seems to be typical of that of others the same age or to be helping achieve the tasks of the period, the teacher's role is one of protection and, when necessary, guidance.

Perennially, in almost every known historical period, the older generation has been sure that youth was going to the dogs. It is the task of understanding adults to help older people see that the present crop of teen-agers, given sympathetically guided freedom, will become every bit as upstanding as, and possibly a little more courageous than, their parents. The extreme cases cited in newspaper and magazine articles on the irresponsibility or criminality of youth usually are not typical, but represent young people whose lives have been distorted by severe deprivations and mishandling during their growth, as well as by especially inauspicious conditions for adolescent development prevailing in their communities.

Two Developmental Strands

Any account of child development which stresses the characteristics of separate ages or phases is likely to leave a false impression. Missing from such a picture is the way in which what happens in one phase grows more or less gradually out of the previous phase and shades into its successor. In order to illustrate the continuity of the process, we shall give sketches of growth in two areas: sex and concepts of the self. These have been chosen not only for their intrinsic importance but also for the perspective they can give.

NORMAL DEVELOPMENT OF SEX BEHAVIOR. In the final analysis, the attitudes and actions of an adult in the area of love and sex represent a good deal more than physiological sex functioning. The forms taken by the sex impulses are largely determined by the way the individual feels toward other human beings. For example, the person who is basically unfriendly may use sex as a means of acquiring dominance or even hurting; the opposite would be true of an individual whose human relationships tended to be sympathetic and considerate. In the same way, a man or woman who regarded other human beings as means to serve him might be expected to exploit others sexually. In fact, some such people even employ the word "use" as a synonym for sexual intercourse.

Also intrinsically related to the pattern of sex behavior is the level and effectiveness of the person's own control systems. The boy or girl who is unable to control his other impulses will also have great difficulty in keeping his sexual appetites in check.

The form which love takes later in life is heavily patterned upon the early experiences in the home as love develops in relationship to parents. This accounts for the fact that many youngsters who have had outside the home some sex experiences of a type we would expect to inflict harm are often much less affected in the final analysis than anyone would have expected at the time. A home atmosphere of affection and confidence will enable a child to survive traumatic experience in any area. By the same token, when a person's sexual development takes a markedly deviant pattern, the psychologist and the psychiatrist look for the basic causes beyond the simple incidents that might appear to have begun the pattern. In this sense, then, life is all of one piece.

Long before a child can put thoughts into words, the basic groundwork for later sex attitudes has been established. The forerunners of the sensations involved in an adult sexual experience seem to be developed singly in relative isolation from the final outcome as it appears in terms of adult functioning. It seems as though children concentrate upon the discovery of gaining pleasure from different body zones at various stages of their growth. It is normal, for instance, for the very young child to gain intense gratification from feeding and the use of his mouth. Later, there is interest in the processes of elimination and the sensations related to them. Similarly, the discovery of pleasurable sensations around the genital areas accompanies normal child care.

The first obviously direct sex education takes place during the preschool years when children ask questions to satisfy their curiosities. The questions usually revolve around two main puzzles: (1) What is the difference between boys and girls? (2) How do babies get born? Children are also likely to take matters into their own hands by direct sex play, focused usually on the obvious anatomical differences. From such observations, little children are likely to gather no more than the nature of the purely external differences between the sexes. Some may, therefore, decide that boys are more desirably equipped than girls. This may easily lead to a feeling of superiority on the part of the male child or of resentment and envy in the female child. If adults do not help children understand the real nature of sex differences, such feelings may easily become the dominant note in their adult relationships. The ways in which grownups answer children's questions and react to their curiosities may establish other fundamental attitudes. For instance, a child may discover that sex can readily be used to upset adults. This first perception, as we shall see later, may provide a springboard for later conduct.

During the early school years, children begin to explore more fully the psychological and social meaning of sex roles. In the home, they begin to develop preferences for their mothers or their fathers. Mixed with the feelings of respect and admiration which many boys have for their fathers, we also find jarring undercurrents of hostility and jealousy. These may be derived from such commonplace household occurrences as the fact that the home-coming of the father acts to deprive his son of the undivided attention of the mother. The mixture of conflicting feelings may have very complicated outcomes, which can be predicted only after taking into consideration a host of factors peculiar to each home situation. One of the many possibilities, for example, is that this may lead to irritability toward the father and later toward any male teachers. On the other hand, the very guilt about this irritability may lead to fearful overdocility. It may also happen that a boy will fear his father will retaliate against him or that he will suffer loss of manhood. Similar events take place in the development of girls. The jealousies which can grow up in the home may later be echoed in an overpossessive jealousy during dating days. Another common outcome is for children to shun body contact with parents; in some cases, this type of touchiness may persist.

In dramatic play among themselves, children practice using their concepts of what men and women do. The outside world is also teaching them important lessons. Boys, for example, may be permitted greater freedom in play than girls, and are allowed to get dirty with less interference. On the other hand, a boy may learn he is expected to behave more bravely and not to cry out when hurt. Such incidents may strengthen or weaken feelings about having been born a boy or a girl. We find, for example, a significant number of grown women who resent womanhood and everything connected with it. Among girls, tomboy behavior may be a temporary reaction to the same forces. Among boys, social pressures may be brought to bear against those who behave like sissies; eagerness to reverse such deeply feared opinions may lead to overemphasis upon masculinity. Later, for some, this may lead to a penchant for making Don Juan conquests.

Although it was once believed that direct curiosity dwindled during the middle school years, except for the minority of children living in neighborhoods where they witness a good deal of sex activity, the well-known Kinsey reports on the percentages of men who recall engaging in sex play at early ages[12] seem to indicate that there is no period of uniform inactivity. According to these figures, approximately 10 per cent of all boys have engaged in some form of sex play by the age of five; 20 per cent, by seven; 29 per cent, by nine; and 37 per cent, by eleven.

During preadolescence, there may be some experimental manipulation, performed in groups. A good deal of smuttiness, vile language, and dirty story telling may make its appearance. Children who have discovered that adults are easily upset by open reference to sex may convert this knowledge into a weapon in their guerilla warfare against the grownups' world. Indeed, it may also be used in accentuating the hostility between boys and girls, which is often a feature of group life at this age level.

It is important to know that only seldom is this activity primarily sexual. Rather, it is an excellent illustration of how sex can be used to serve other ends. Nevertheless, by-products of these reactions may be translated into feelings about sex itself. The connection, for instance, between sex and dirtiness, derived from vile language and dirty story telling, may persist. If such feelings are to be counteracted, it may be extremely important that young people at this age receive calm and specific information from parents or respected teachers. Threats and other fear techniques used to stamp out unwanted activities do more harm than good. Besides giving an added fillip to the forbidden actions, they may drive youngsters into seeking and accepting wildly distorted ideas. Worse yet, the possibility of giving children helpful guidance in the very real problems of the next phase of development may be destroyed.

The result of the informal education many children give each other is an extensive knowledge of facts, coupled with an obscene vocabulary. In a study of the sex information possessed by 291 boys of middle and upper-middle socioeconomic status in a middle western city of more than one hundred thousand population, Ramsey dis-

---

[12] Alfred C. Kinsey, Wardell B. Pomeroy, and Clyde E. Martin, *Sexual Behavior in the Human Male,* Philadelphia, Saunders, 1948, p. 182.

covered that among the preadolescents at least half knew about such items as ejaculation, seminal emissions, contraception, masturbation, intercourse, and prostitution. However, a vocabulary test given to seventh- and eighth-graders revealed that—

> Vernacular terms or awkward euphemisms are employed by them to discuss reproductive system and sexual behavior. These boys would find it difficult to read the simplest printed material concerning sex and reproduction. In any sex instruction, by printed or oral methods, effort should be directed toward the development of an adequate sex vocabulary.[13]

Throughout this discussion, when statistics are given relative to boys, the reader should recognize that among girls and women, equivalent situations would be much less frequent. The difference is great enough to have led Kinsey[14] to assert:

> Many . . . women, including some high school biology teachers believe that the ninth grade boy is still too young to receive any sex instruction when, in actuality, he has a wider variety of sexual experience than most of his female teachers ever will have.

The opposite error in judgment might be made by men teachers. Especially in schools serving suburbs or middle-class neighborhoods, they might grossly overestimate the frequency of sex activities among girls.

With the advent of puberty, the physical forces of sex become manifest. When this will happen cannot be predicted for any given youngster. The range in the case of girls, for instance, shows menstruation beginning for some before the age of ten and for others in the late teens. There is a similar range for boys, although male reproductive systems rarely mature before the age of eleven. Affecting the attitudes toward these new body functions is the extent and the way in which girls have been prepared for menstruation and boys have been prepared for seminal emissions. Accompanying the appearance of these phenomena may be other occurrences. A number of young people find themselves distracted by fantasies of sex activity. For those brought up to accept predominantly Puritan moral standards, daydreams may be deeply disturbing, and may result in feelings of being very wicked. Also, youngsters

---

13 Glenn V. Ramsey, "Sex Information of Younger Boys," *American Journal of Orthopsychiatry,* Vol. 13 (1943), pp. 347-52.

14 Alfred C. Kinsey, Wardell P. Pomeroy, and Clyde E. Martin, *op. cit.,* p. 182.

are likely to seek relief from physical tensions through masturbation. A number go through temporary stages of sexual display and manipulation with members of the same sex. In a questionnaire study of 111 unmarried male college students with an average age of nineteen, Finger[15] found that 93 per cent had at some time engaged in masturbation, with the average boy beginning at thirteen. In this group, 27 per cent had had some active homosexual experience; for the average in this group, this came at the age of twelve. Intercourse had occurred in the lives of 45 per cent; the average young man among these had known 4 partners for a total of 8 contacts, with the first one at sixteen.

Figures of this type are somewhat misleading because the pattern of sex experience appears to vary tremendously from one socioeconomic level to another. This fact was one of the most important findings in the famous Kinsey studies. As illustrated in Table 1, those men who completed college were more likely as boys to have limited themselves to self-stimulation; those who never went beyond grade school, to have had more intercourse.

TABLE 1   *Types of sex outlets for boys between puberty and age fifteen; percentage of orgasm derived from each**

	GRADE IN SCHOOL ULTIMATELY COMPLETED		
SOURCE OF ORGASM	0-8	9-12	College
Masturbation	52	59	80
Nocturnal emission	2	4	12
Petting	1	1	2
Intercourse with companion	35	25	3
Homosexual contact	8	9	3

* Alfred C. Kinsey, Wardell P. Pomeroy, and Clyde E. Martin, *Sexual Behavior in the Human Male,* Philadelphia, Saunders, 1948, Chap. 10.

In some cases, unfortunately, sexual activities get linked to deeper emotional problems. Where this seems to be true, as indicated by compulsiveness or severe emotional reactions, a check-up is in order. Often the basic sex problem for young people arises out of anxieties concerning what parents may think about their activities. They may have an un-

15 Frank W. Finger, "Sex Beliefs and Practices among Male College Students," *Journal of Abnormal and Social Psychology,* Vol. 42 (1947), pp. 57-67.

realistic opinion of the relative innocence or experience of their fathers and mothers.

Many youngsters, of course, are deeply concerned about the more subtle aspects of relationships between boys and girls, men and women. Oddly, many parents and teachers are more ready to deal with physical facts than to have discussions about deep-lying feelings and intimate emotions. Despite our progress in sex education, many an adult's hesitancy echoes the observation in an old French treatise on the education of young women, "However, education does not speak of love! And that question, 'Can one speak of love to girls?' almost creates a scandal."[16]

It is important to realize that during early adolescence a child's status in his own group may be tied up with estimates of his sophistication. This may lead to very early efforts to assume such trappings of "maturity" as wearing lipstick, playing kissing games, boastful talk about sex, and dating. Frequently the emergence of real interest in the opposite sex takes the comparatively safe initial form of highly idealized romances. The object may be a radio crooner or a pin-up girl. A few young boys or girls may show a very strong attachment or crush toward some teacher. During the first stage of adolescent interest in the opposite sex, body contact in any form may still be frightening.

As adolescence begins to merge into adulthood, the end products of the entire chain of sex development begin to become clear. The young people pick up and begin to employ the social conventions regarding parties, dances, and other forms of going together. Those who have strong self-control are likely to exemplify the standards of their own parents. In any event, in most American communities, adolescents have to learn to cope with their very strong impulses. The delight in body contact which they felt as little children becomes re-established, and we see them publicly holding hands and draping arms over each other's shoulders or around each other's waists. The relative privacy afforded by darkened movie theaters, automobiles, and other rendezvous makes it inevitable that adolescents will introduce each other to necking, petting, and invitations to sexual intercourse. The greatly increased pressure of their sexual appetites becomes a problem which they must solve for themselves in one way or another.

As at an earlier age, the determination of sex conduct may be strongly influenced by psychological needs far removed from physi-

---

[16] La Vicomtesse d'Adhemar, *Nouvelle Education de la Femme dans les Classes Cultivées,* Paris, Perrin, 1898, p. 185.

ological tensions. For example, sex activity may appear more tempting if it is viewed as a daring maneuver, symbolizing independence of the adult world. A significant fraction of promiscuous girls, for example, engage in sex acts out of spitefulness directed against their parents. Other young people may find in their own particular pattern of reaction, whether it be complete continence or promiscuity, a way of making themselves feel secure and safe. A few may feel a desire to be dependent upon other people and may see in sex an avenue to reach that goal. For others, the primary consideration is status in their age group, and their actions will be guided largely by a desire to secure dates with the high-prestige figures in their world or to obtain membership in the most envied circles. Some youngsters will act out of a need to possess and dominate other people; others, out of wanting to hurt and humiliate; and still others, out of a need to demonstrate to themselves the level of their prowess or their self-control. Nor should we deny that some engage in sexual intercourse simply and solely because it is pleasurable.

CONCEPT OF SELF.   As nearly as can be discovered, an infant has no concept of himself as a separate individual organism. On the one hand, he is moved about, fondled, fed, made comfortable, without any voluntary effort of his own. On the other hand, his cries and first smiles, by a sort of magic, bring into operation forces which must seem to him as much a part of himself as the noises which issue from his throat. By adulthood this picture has changed vastly. The individual has not only established the fact that he is a distinct person with a will of his own, but has worked out the boundaries of his influence in the world around him, as well as which parts of that world are, psychologically speaking, part of him. He knows that there are many things he can do on his own volition and despite the wishes of other people. Yet very much a part of him are his relationships with other people, as he realizes when the loss of a friend or close relative makes him feel as though he had lost part of himself. Also very much part of him are certain of his clothes and possessions; a man may feel queer, "not himself," when forced to wear a dinner jacket, but figuratively expand when he gets into his hunting outfit. Then again, a person feels more himself when engaged in some activities than in others; a teacher, for example, might be untouched by criticism of a report she had made but deeply hurt by even a mild comment on her choice of words because she regarded *herself* as an expert on vocabulary.

We shall not describe one by one the separate phases which lead to the ultimate development of this adult concept of the self. As with sex development, one phase builds upon another, each phase being altered by that which preceded it. Also, the dominant tones in the final picture are quite likely to stem from the manner in which family relationships during the early days influenced the basic personality of the growing child.[17]

Individuals are likely to differ widely concerning what they regard as "the real me." Some consider that their essential selves may lie in a very restricted area; indeed, when asked, some youngsters will say their real selves are located behind their eyes, in their hearts, or at some other definite physical location. Actually, the boundaries which an individual attributes to himself may be quite flexible. These will alter with time, place, and circumstances. The clue to how he feels is indicated by his reaction, especially his touchiness to specific events, and by the relative importance he ascribes to incidents which touch on any aspects of himself. For example, most children go through a phase, usually during the early school years, when they take a rather detached attitude toward their bodies. This is shown by a total lack of concern with ordinary health rules. Later, in adolescence, youngsters may localize their feelings of self-significance in the poise of their bodies, in a special hairdo, or in litheness in dancing. In addition, a person may think of himself as including objects, relationships, and symbols which objectively look quite separate. For instance, a knife or lipstick may have a very special meaning to a particular child, as the teacher would recognize if she took the object away even temporarily. The reaction of the child would reveal that its loss may carry the same type of psychological hurt as the amputation of a finger.

In a similar fashion, young people may be specially sensitive about clothing, pets, or even such a thing as a nickname. At times an individual will feel most "himself" when utilizing some cherished skill. From his pride in his skill and his overreaction to criticism, we can guess that he regards this skill or ability as part of the central core of his personality. There are, of course, many very religious individuals who regard themselves as being essentially a soul and who look on their bodies and

---

[17] Some readers may want to look at an early report and psychological analysis of the sense of self: G. Stanley Hall, "Some Aspects of the Early Sense of Self," *American Journal of Psychology,* Vol. 9 (1897), pp. 351-95.

A more recent research effort can be read for comparison as well as contrast: Marian Radke, Helen G. Trager, and Hadassah Davis, "Social Perceptions and Attitudes of Children," *Genetic Psychology Monographs,* Vol. 40 (1949), pp. 327-447.

their physical actions as secondary. The extent to which a child will feel his essence as a distinctly separate soul will depend a good deal upon religious conditioning in the family. For teachers, it is important to be aware of what a child regards as containing a real element of himself so as not to overlook casually its significance to the youngster.

The significance of what aspects of himself an individual chooses to consider his essence appeared vividly in a study by Beilin[18] of a group of 139 high school seniors in New York City and Providence, Rhode Island. All were boys with intelligence adequate for college work; all came from homes where the fathers held steady jobs as laborers or routine white-collar workers. Eighty-six were planning to go to college; 53 were not. An analysis of their free answers to questions revealed that although both groups were ambitious to increase their earnings, the groups saw themselves from quite different perspectives. Those who planned to go to college considered personality qualities, notably drive, as individual assets. They felt the decision to continue education, far from being a postponement of present satisfactions, was seizing an opportunity for self-fulfillment. In contrast to their classmates without college ambitions, they found great satisfaction in extracurricular activities as well as in reading for pleasure.

One of the basic tasks of development is the establishment by the individual of his own identity as a separate being with a will of his own. One of the processes by which this result is reached is for each person at times to resist doing as others want him to do. One way to prove you are a distinct personality is to say No and make it stick. The first outburst of this type of negativism is likely to occur during the second and third years of life. The manner in which parents deal with it has a great deal to do with the intensity, the timing, the duration, and the tactics of subsequent negativistic phases. For most individuals, we can expect periodic surges of stubbornness, obstinacy, and disobedience. These are likely to come in preadolescence and again in later adolescence.

There is another way in which a child is likely to establish his own integrity and inviolability: by exerting power, by making things happen on *his* volition. This may show itself in many ways. Among the ways which are likely to be most puzzling if their significance is not known are those in which young people may seek to prove their indestructibility and freedom from outside forces. Thus, we very often see them take

---

[18] Harry Beilin, *Factors Affecting Occupational Choice in a Lower Socio-Economic Group*, Ph.D. dissertation, Columbia University, 1952, University Microfilms Publication No. 4556.

extraordinary risks. Some do this by deliberate and flagrant breaches of safety rules. In adolescence, the tendency will show itself in some gambling, in wild driving, and in following a regimen of burning the candle at both ends. To the individual, the point in all this is to find out whether or not he is a special, a magical, self. The extent to which an individual uses extreme measures during adolescence is usually an indication of failure to perform this basic task earlier in life. Although to the casual observer such young people may appear too cocky, the wise teacher will recognize that deep down they are unsure of themselves.

Difficult as some adults may find it to "put up with" some of this self-establishing conduct, the task is infinitely simpler than that of helping a child who has a weak notion of where he ends and the "real world" begins. Such a case in a very young girl, Olga, was reported by Rank and MacNaughton[19] from their experience at the James Jackson Putnam Children's Center in Boston. Olga was an unhappy and extremely passive looking girl whose unfocused eyes seemed not to contact people and who engaged in bizarre gesturing. When it was realized that because mental illness had taken her mother away at two crucial junctures in Olga's young life, the girl had not adequately learned to differentiate herself from her environment, a patient program to help her in this respect was included in a larger plan for her treatment. This involved such primitive games as gently bumping heads together, dodging peek-aboo fashion with a mirror, and letting her explore the therapist's person.

Along with the process of proving themselves separate, most individuals also see themselves involved in what happens to other people and to the groups to which they belong. Thus, a teacher who punishes one of a group of friends may notice that others in the group will act every bit as though they themselves had suffered. This widening of the individual's feeling of self may go to considerable lengths. Some people, especially in communities where great stress is laid on family, may be quite closely tied up with anything pertaining to their kinship. In school, particularly in the upper grades, we often try to develop a school spirit, in which the individual feels the group is part of his own identity. The eventual outcome, we often hope, will be feelings of self-involvement with the fate of one's nation and mankind in general. However, this process of widening the self may involve some problems and some dangers. These dangers are seen when school spirit runs amuck or when

---

[19] Beata Rank and Dorothy MacNaughton, "A Clinical Contribution to Early Ego Development," *Psychoanalytic Study of the Child,* Vol. 5 (1950), pp. 53-65.

identification with one racial or religious group is exploited by bigots. A similar development may lead to that curious phenomenon in which individuals actually seem to lose themselves in a group or in an intellectual or religious movement. We shudder if this loss of identity is part of mob violence; we applaud it in a group carried away by a musical masterpiece or a great speech.

The psychologically significant outcome of the processes we have just described is the development of a self-image, the individual's perception of himself as he thinks he is. The relationship of this self-image to his ego ideal, previously described, may involve some problems. One of the purposes which should be behind the school's evaluation program is to help children develop a more realistic self-image, at least one that is reasonably accurate and with which they can live. We must recognize, for example, that a girl who is really unattractive cannot be bluntly forced to recognize that fact, any more than a boy would admit to himself that he is really a slave to his older sister. This does not mean, however, that youngsters must remain completely blind to the weaker aspects of their personalities. Indeed, from the work of teachers of mentally defective children, we know that a young person can recognize that he is "dumb" but nevertheless excels in certain skills. This means that in his picture of himself, he may give little place to intellectual ability but feel his own significance lies in the area of his strength. If an individual's self-image is too far below his ego ideal, he is quite likely to be discouraged or defensive. Here, again, it helps for the teacher to get a picture of a youngster's self-image because this may explain many otherwise puzzling reactions.

Both adults and young people may have very marked attitudes toward their self-images. We all know that some people are critical of themselves, but it is equally important to recognize that some are not. These problems relating to self-insight have been of prime interest to the followers of Carl Rogers, in whose methods of counseling self-insight is a primary goal. In analyses of interview records, Sheerer[20] established in a group of ten cases that during the course of treatment an individual's evaluation of himself can be changed. Interestingly, when a person's self-evaluation changes, his evaluation of other people also shifts. Concentrating primarily upon clients who had negative feelings

---

[20] Elizabeth J. Sheerer, "An Analysis of the Relationship Between Acceptance of and Respect for Self and Acceptance of and Respect for Others in Ten Counselling Cases," *Journal of Consulting Psychology*, Vol. 13 (1949), pp. 169-75.

about themselves, Stock,[21] using similar records, found that these people had negative attitudes toward other people and groups. When their feelings changed, their attitudes toward others changed in the same direction.

For most children, attitudes toward self seem to take shape during the school years. It is to this aspect of the personality that school experience may make one of its most significant contributions. In interviews with 212 parents of first-grade children, to cite one illuminating report, Stendler and Young[22] found the following:

> In general, beginning first graders show evidences of change in self-concept in the direction of feelings of bigness and importance, according to what mothers tell us. This was true even for children who had attended nursery school or kindergarten. Preschool apparently does not represent as dramatic a shift away from home, nor does it have the prestige value for children that first grade does.

These are typical observations by the mothers interviewed: "He acts inflated now. Comes home and says, 'Boy, we sure had some hard work today!' " Or, "Considers kindergarten children quite babyish. He acts big at home and is proud of his reading. *He never showed pride before.*"

The development of the self-concept continues through the school years. By the close of adolescence, the individual has acquired a definite feeling of identity, a sense of personal uniqueness, and these feelings include the groups which have for him special meaning. Erikson[23] has described certain culminating phases of this development as being a struggle for identity.

Even though most individuals develop a generally favorable self-concept, many a person feels distaste toward one or more aspects of himself. A way for him to handle this situation is to try to disassociate himself from those aspects. Thus, we may find that a child who has engaged in some misconduct may actually feel that, at bottom, his "real me" was not involved. In adolescence, especially, we may notice an ex-

21 Dorothy Stock, "An Investigation into the Interrelations Between the Self Concept and Feelings Directed Toward Other Persons and Groups," *Journal of Consulting Psychology,* Vol. 13 (1949), pp. 176-80.

22 Celia Burns Stendler and Norman Young, "The Impact of Beginning First Grade upon Socialization as Reported by Mothers," *Child Development,* Vol. 21 (1950), pp. 241-60.

23 Erik Hamburger Erikson, "The Problem of Ego Identity," *Journal of the American Psychoanalytic Association,* Vol. 4 (1956), pp. 56-121.

tension of this splitting process. As the young person becomes part of several different groups, each with its own ideals, he may develop somewhat different personalities to fit each situation. In each he may feel very much himself, yet at times be puzzled as to the question, "Which me is really me?" The splitting may be of value in adult life, as many teachers know who would not care to carry their classroom personalities into all areas of living. But splitting of the "real me" does not solve all the problems; many young people are tormented by genuine self-doubt. They are not sure that they can approve their real selves. Some suffer from great loss of confidence. A few try to bury their self-doubt beneath brashness. Carried to the extreme, any of the processes described in this paragraph may be a sign of mental disorder.

Closely allied to the development of any child's concept of himself is his reaction to criticism. Two extremes are likely to trouble educators. On the one hand, we find many youngsters who either do not hear, do not understand, or refuse to act upon adverse comments. At the other extreme, we run across instances where a mild rebuke inexplicably touches off a flood of tears. Although we are concerned here primarily with the effects of the child's feelings about himself, it is essential to recognize that other matters can be important in these particular bits of behavior. These other elements in the reaction to criticism might include a feeling of being rejected by the critic, threats to status among his peers, and anticipated trouble at home. Always, the relationship between the youngster and the critic will affect the psychological impact of criticism. However, the observed actions of children may go beyond what these other factors would seem to imply. Thus, for example, the ignoring of criticism may be a defense if a child is trying to preserve a favorable self-image. Ignoring criticism may also be an act of negativism, designed to bolster the individual's feeling that he can resist outside pressures. If the criticism leads to tearfulness, it may signal either that a child has been defeated in an effort to maintain his integrity, or else that the criticism touched an area which was a central one in his concept of himself. The realization of the latter phenomenon is carried neatly in the slang verdict, "That hit him where he lived."

The usefulness of criticism depends not only on its accuracy and fairness and the personal relationship of the critic to the child, but also upon its timing and the degree to which it can be accepted without destroying the child's feeling of independence or his self-image and without creating too big a gap between his self-image and his ego ideal. In this respect, a teacher is much more than an umpire: he or she has to be a delicately sensitive persuader. Besides, gaining a more realistic picture of himself accomplishes only half the job for the child. He still may need help to make the changes in himself that the criticism implies. This is a task of great strategic importance, which reaches far beyond the problem of criticism itself.

For each individual there gradually emerges a set of feelings about himself that permeates almost everything he does. We will always hope that this will be marked by reasonable harmony with the real world about him and by self-acceptance. As can be seen, this outcome can be gained only by a great deal of experience and practice, some of which will be understandable to an outsider, but some of which also will look outlandish or rebellious. Although in individual conferences and in sermons delivered to groups, words may help some young people to clarify their thinking, talk alone never can do the job. What each individual needs is help and understanding as he wrestles with the world to find out who he is, what he is, and why he is.

Significance for the School

Viewing the sweep of human development necessarily raises questions regarding many school processes. Educators have several reasons for wanting to take growth phases into account. It is obviously inefficient to try to do things in school which run counter to developmental forces within children. Then again, if schools are to help create desirable adults, the points at which growth can best be influenced are important to know. As our understanding of developmental processes takes clearer shape, we can see the need for changes in educational strategy and tactics. Certain guiding ideas need additional clarification and emphasis.

HABIT FORMATION. One of the legacies left American education by Thorndike and his followers has been a great concern with those "laws of learning" which involve practice and effect. The implication has often been drawn that any species of behavior which a child uses often and from which he gains satisfaction will be more and more deeply ingrained in the personality structure. For this reason educators have nervously tried to stamp out reactions which we now know are likely to be temporary and to disappear once the developmental need for them has been satisfied.

To overcome the myopia caused by concentrating on isolated

habits, it helps to gain perspective to think of development in terms of the successful accomplishment of a series of strategic tasks. Once a task has been successfully accomplished, the individual is able to move on toward new goals. "Good" behavior which is forced upon a youngster at the wrong time and which gets in the way of development may create harmful results, no matter how long it is practiced. On the other hand, as the growing person gains experience with broad patterns of relationships which serve him well in his development, he is likely to carry these along with him as he tackles subsequent stages. By contrast, consistent use of an inappropriate pattern may lead to failure or distortion in development and make it necessary for the individual either to make up lost ground later or to go through life with a personality structure so poorly shaped that he is forced over and over again into conduct which hurts him or is socially unacceptable.

Much needless worry occurs at the points where behavior which meets a developmental need also happens to be unpleasant to adults. They fear that such conduct will become a habit. A little attention to very commonplace illustrations reveals that this need not be true; for although all babies crawl often and with satisfaction, we know this does not become a habit which troubles them as adults. So, too, the noisy jubilation of children at play is not habit-forming, but disappears of its own accord. In the same fashion, most boys outgrow the preadolescent aversion to womankind. The key word here is the verb "outgrow." Conduct fashioned to meet a developmental need is outgrown when it no longer has a purpose to serve.

The basic index, then, by which we should judge specific bits of conduct is the extent to which they are suitable to the aspect of growth upon which the young person is concentrating at the time.

DEVELOPMENTAL READINESS.   Teachers have always wanted to be efficient. Somehow, in talk about learning, the idea of speed has been linked with that of efficiency. The best teacher, some folks still think, is the one able to bring a class to a level of achievement beyond what is usually reached at their age. To agree to this viewpoint is to walk into a pitfall. In physics, the measure of efficiency is the ratio between work required and results obtained. We now know that to force learning, to teach children knowledge or skills before they are ready, yields results which do not stand up well under inspection. For one thing, both the learners and the teachers go through much unpleasantness which would not have been necessary if the tasks had been postponed until the young people were ready. Moreover, the emotional repercussions of the forcing processes are likely to distort relationships between young people and their teachers. More important, the anxiety and the failures which inevitably accompany such learning under pressure place an added burden on children and make them become preoccupied with tasks which have nothing to do, or may even interfere, with the real job they should be doing. For instance, it is a poor bargain to get children in the second grade to read one year above their true age level —a gain which experiments show is almost certain to vanish before high school—if the process hinders the development of normal cooperative social relationships which may endure throughout their school lives.

It is wise, therefore, to set our goals in terms of better accomplishment of those learnings which the young people are ready to make, and which contribute most effectively to the completion of the developmental task they are engaged in at the time.

WHEN TO INTERFERE.   As has been frequently pointed out in this chapter, children if left to themselves are almost sure to show some unpleasant and undesirable behavior as they attempt various tasks in their growth. There is danger that this fact will be interpreted to mean that if a particular course of conduct contributes to development, it is therefore sacrosanct and must be left unchanged. That is far from true. Often there are several possible courses of behavior which might equally well serve the same developmental function. Of these courses, some will be safer than others. An even more dangerous oversimplification is to argue that since children are growing, anything and everything they do must be meeting their needs and therefore should not be changed.

There are several types of conduct which we can recognize as requiring adult intervention. Some behavior has nothing whatever to do with growth; that is, it represents a problem which would concern us at any age level. For example, if a youngster is so anxious to please teachers that he stammers and becomes incoherent, we would want to get at the root of the difficulty and help him overcome it. While it is true that at certain ages youngsters are liable to be more anxious in the presence of adults than at others, such extreme behavior could not be credited to any developmental phase as such.

Another type of situation requiring adult interference involves conduct which, although it serves a developmental function, is nevertheless unsafe or harmful. For instance, if an adolescent boy joins a delinquent gang and goes with it on shoplifting expeditions, we would recognize that while his growth required him to become a member of a group, the stealing part of this picture had ominous possibilities. We would want, therefore, to help him find adequate social contacts and to eliminate the stealing. In the same way, a nine-year-old girl, in order to establish her independence, might be carrying on a successful campaign to postpone her bedtime to an unreasonable hour. To protect her health someone will have to lay down the law about bedtime, at the same time taking care that she finds other avenues for self-assertion.

In contrast are those types of behavior to which adults might as well resign themselves. For instance, a group of normal youngsters need a chance to play and make noise at some time during their day. Their piercing shrieks, no matter how uncomfortable, ought to be expected, are part of the way they learn to play together. Certainly the noise does *them* no harm. It cannot be eliminated entirely. The only problem is to find the time and place where it can be allowed most advantageously.

Most of the growth needs described in the previous sections of this chapter give rise to behavior which is irritating to adults. Up to a certain degree, it must be tolerated. Perhaps it would be better to say that grownups having professional relationships with children should attempt to develop an ability to take some pleasure in watching such conduct, so that toleration can be replaced by unirritated acceptance.

There is often a fear that children will take undue advantage of freedom and go hog-wild. Although this may happen under some circumstances, all the evidence indicates that where relationships between children and adults are good, the youngsters readily develop a feel for the limitations which make their conduct acceptable.

LIFE DESIGN IN HOME AND SCHOOL. In practical terms, knowledge of growth and development is best put to use by adults in the fashioning of the design for child living which is carried on under the auspices of either the home or the school. In all such planning, priority has to be given to growth needs. To confront children with a school program or a set of home routines which run counter to these needs is to ask for double trouble, trouble not only in getting them to do what we ask them to do, but also trouble arising from the emotional pressures we have created.

There are a number of ways in which the design for living will show itself. One may be the simple matter of scheduling—the length of time we expect children to stick with an activity. Then too, the very types of activity we expect children to engage in are vitally affected by the stage of their growth. For instance, it is as silly to expect group-conscious preadolescents to remain isolated from each other for long periods in school as it would be to expect a five-year-old in the home to remain seated at the table motionless while the grownups dawdled over coffee. In deciding what types of relaxation to encourage during intermissions between more serious pursuits, age factors can be very significant. Not only architects but teachers need to know the activity demands of each group in order to utilize the space at their command to best effect. Thus, a home with no space where children can be messy is an emotional strait jacket. So is a classroom with every available square foot occupied by seats screwed down to the floor.

The very style of day-to-day adult-child relationships must be geared to growth needs if we hope to live in reasonable peace with youngsters. A sweetness-and-light, head-patting friendliness jars the preadolescent. By the same token, demands for completely independent work might create panic in the child just beginning school.

The same principle holds true for the style of relationship we expect to exist among the children themselves; this too must be appropriate to the developmental phase of the children. Too highly competitive, individualistic a classroom atmosphere at any age level creates needless problems for children trying to win a place in their peer group. Adolescents in the upper grades of a high school can gain something from practicing large group meetings governed by the niceties of parliamentary law; so adult-like an operation would be utterly meaningless in the lower grades.

Needless to say, knowledge of growth needs furnishes us with very valuable clues concerning the curriculum and teaching methods. For some years, child needs have been the starting point of curriculum revision in a number of school systems. In such schools the topics studied, the levels of skills, and the teaching methods themselves are geared to what is known about child development. Thus we might find, for example, a core curriculum that provides not only that adolescents be given an opportunity to learn about social etiquette, but that they do so, not by taking notes from a lecture, but by arranging a number of adult-imitating social functions on their own initiative, after which "bull sessions," possibly with a teacher acting as moderator, would be held if they wished. Similarly, in a mathematics class, we might not only build upon preadolescent hobbies but encourage the youngsters to experiment with mathematical puzzles and fallacies.

At times, objective circumstances over which a teacher has no control still will force violation of the considerations we have mentioned. The question then becomes one of trying to find a balance in other spheres of a child's life. If, for example, overcrowded conditions in a classroom or janitorial bans against movable furniture lead to a restriction of physical mobility, then to redress the balance we can put up with greater noise on the playground, make opportunities for wild and free-roving play, or lengthen the recess periods beyond what we would otherwise consider advisable.

Similarly we must keep our eye on the balance between home and school. Children already thwarted in developmental expression at home, need and should be given more elbowroom in school. The old stand-by, "We treat them here the way they are used to being treated at home," would be roughly equivalent to denying children vitamins in the school lunchroom because these are missing from the foods they eat at their family dinner tables.

ADDITIONAL READINGS

Association for Supervision and Curriculum Development. *1950 Yearbook: Fostering Mental Health in Our Schools.* Washington: National Education Association, 1950, Chaps. 4 to 7. Describes major developmental tasks of childhood and what these mean for school policy and procedure.

Blos, Peter. *The Adolescent Personality.* New York: Appleton-Century-Crofts, 1941. Contains lengthy case histories of four normal adolescents.

English, O. Spurgeon, and Gerald H. J. Pearson. *Emotional Problems of Living.* New York: Norton, 1955, Chaps. 1, 3, 5, 7, and 10. A description of the development of personality at various phases, written from a Freudian viewpoint.

Fleming, C. M. *Adolescence.* New York: International Universities Press, 1949, Chap. 5. Describes and compares major theories about adolescence.

Furfey, Paul Hanly. *The Gang Age.* New York: Macmillan, 1928, Chap. 1. A pioneering description of preadolescent boys.

Havighurst, Robert J. *Developmental Tasks and Education.* Chicago: U. of Chicago Press, 1948. Explains the concept of "developmental task" and draws implications for education.

Jenkins, Gladys Gardner, Helen Shachter, and William M. Bauer. *These Are Your Children.* Chicago: Scott, Foresman, 1949, Chaps. 9 and 10.

Deals with what parents and school people can do to take into account the facts of child development.

Jones, Harold E. *Development in Adolescence.* New York: Appleton-Century-Crofts, 1943. The story of one boy, touching on all aspects of his living, is traced through the records of the Adolescent Growth Study, conducted at the University of California.

Martin, William E., and Celia Burns Stendler. *Child Behavior and Development.* New York: Harcourt, Brace, 1959, Chaps. 6 to 9. Sets forth the processes whereby children are socialized.

Mussen, Paul Henry, and John Janeway Conger. *Child Development and Personality.* New York: Harper, 1956, Chap. 10. Concentrates upon personality development during the middle-childhood years.

Olson, Willard C. *Child Development.* Boston: Heath, 1949. A comprehensive discussion of the meaning that certain facts of child development have for education.

Rogers, Carl R. *Client-Centered Therapy.* Boston: Houghton Mifflin, 1951, Chap. 5. Some observations on people's feelings about themselves as these are observed in counseling while they try to work out personal problems.

Stone, L. Joseph, and Joseph Church. *Childhood and Adolescence.* New York: Random House, 1957, Chaps. 3 to 12. A broadly conceived report on what happens in growth between birth and maturity.

Symonds, Percival M. *The Ego and the Self.* New York: Appleton-Century-Crofts, 1951, Chap. 5. A summary of the development of the individual's concept of himself.

Wattenberg, William W. *The Adolescent Years.* New York: Harcourt, Brace, 1955, Chaps. 3 to 6. Summarizes the major trends in development from the end of childhood through young adulthood.

AUDIO-VISUAL AIDS

Age of Turmoil, a 19-minute sound film produced by McGraw-Hill to give a picture of the antics of young adolescents.

Children Growing Up with Other People, a 30-minute sound film produced for the British Ministry of Education which sketches in quick summary some salient qualities of children at each age level.

Fears of Children, a 26-minute sound film produced for the Mental Health Film Board which, by concentrating on the story of a single boy, brings out reactions to strong family ties among preschool children.

From Sociable Six to Noisy Nine, a 20-minute sound film produced by Crawley Films. The title accurately indicates the purpose.

From Ten to Twelve, a 20-minute sound film presented by the Department of National Health and Welfare, Canada, in which not only major developmental trends but individual differences are made clear.

The Frustrating Fours and Fascinating Fives, a 22-minute sound film produced by Crawley Films, a somewhat oversimplified picture of the kindergarten age.

Meaning of Adolescence, a 16-minute sound film by McGraw-Hill, which makes a plea for understanding of teen-agers.

chapter **6**

INFLUENCES THAT SHAPE LIVES

As each individual goes through his developmental stages he has a series of experiences peculiar to his life alone. These alter the ways in which he accomplishes his developmental tasks. Some experiences make a particular stage easier or harder; other experiences change somewhat the task to be accomplished. Winning independence from parents, for example, is one thing for a boy in an Old World family where the father rules with a strict hand, and quite another thing for a girl in a typically American suburban home where parents are trying to be fashionably "democratic" and are at the same time competing with neighbors in a surface display of possessions and cultural "advantages." Nor is this problem the same for an only child of an invalid widow as for a youngster whose parents are forever quarreling over money matters and openly awaiting the day the child moves out of the house. Differences in life situations alter the framework for development and shape personalities.

It is to the rich variety of experiences in people's lives as well as to differences based upon inborn qualities that we owe the variety in human personality. Now and then circumstances may combine to create especially favorable or unfavorable conditions. To illustrate, here is part of the story of one lucky girl:

Theone Roberts was generally regarded as a success. In the technical high school she attended, her art work was considered very good. At home her mother was certain her good points vastly outbalanced her faults. The neighbors liked her; she was in great demand as a baby sitter. For school and church social affairs she could be sure of a date. The boys found her company very pleasant; she danced well, talked

131

easily, and respected their pocketbooks. She had several girl friends, who also enjoyed her company. The second youngest of four children, Theone had two brothers and a sister. There was some bickering in the household, especially over chores, but most of the time the teasing was good-natured.

Almost anyone would say Theone was fortunate. Healthy and attractive, she also had good physical co-ordination. Her family lived in a good neighborhood of roomy, single-family homes with enough space around them for children to play. They were on good terms with the neighbors and with their own relatives. The house was the scene of frequent informal visits and parties.

Her mother and father were a well-adjusted couple. Although Mr. Roberts seemed clearly to be the head of the household, there was no doubt that her mother played a very important role in the family. If one talked to Mr. Roberts, one learned that he felt his wife had done a splendid job in rearing the children, and that this success was very vital to him.

In the usual routine of the household, all played a part. It was easy to see that the parents set the atmosphere for real family pride. They also saw that work was shared, and made sure that the children knew the parents were pleased because of that. Each child had tasks from whose achievement he or she gained feelings of competency.

Even this brief sketch contains reference to quite a few advantages for Theone: her physique, her health, the neighborhood, the attitudes of her parents, the parents' marital adjustment, and the family spirit involving her brothers and sister. No doubt there were also problems in her life, and she undoubtedly experienced her share of frustration, disappointment, anxiety, and conflict in growing up. Yet the favorable combination of circumstances seemingly made it easier for her to take the unfavorable circumstances in her stride.

For other people, other factors might be important. In fact, it would clearly be impossible to list all the possible influences which have shaped even one life, let alone those for a large group. In this chapter we shall examine a number of life-shaping elements which are frequently found to be influential. As they did for Theone Roberts, these elements may operate to the advantage of the individual. In some cases the reverse is true. Then adults need to know how to look for the causes of trouble. Therefore in this chapter, while we shall not ignore positive, beneficial influences, we shall give somewhat more attention to possible problem-creating forces.

Inborn Characteristics

Infants show many differences at birth. Some are comparatively placid; others are active. Some prove easy to care for; others are resistant and difficult. The "easy" ones are more likely to be fondled; the "difficult" ones are more apt to be treated roughly. Within weeks, such differences in innate qualities have led to differences in treatment, and it becomes impossible to tell how much of the contrast in observed behavior is due to heredity and how much is due to variations in treatment.

It is for this reason that questions as to the role of hereditary or congenital factors in determining behavior have been the subject of debate among psychologists. Certainly, some hereditary differences are potent elements in the patterns of multiple causation underlying any child's conduct. Yet very few behavioral trends can be said to derive inevitably and irrevocably directly from the genes and chromosomes.

The weight of the evidence is that environmental forces quickly give specific shape to the qualities present at birth. Some limits seem to be set by heredity: Just as children having almost identical nutrition will show differences in height and will mature at different dates, so children brought up in similar home settings will show differences in mental adeptness and personality. In addition, some young folks are born with a predisposition to develop unfortunate conditions. Although, so far as can be proved, no one inherits mental disturbances in the same way as, for instance, eye color, some seem to be more vulnerable than others, and might suffer mental breakdown under conditions which would leave others intact.

To illustrate with findings from just one area, Bergman and Escalona[1] made a study of five young children who were especially sensitive to such stimuli as light and sound. As a result they reacted to what went on around them more violently than do most children. It was as though they lacked protection against stimulation. All five gave indications of either being or becoming mentally ill.

In some cases, specific handicaps may be present at birth. Some are visible; others may be hidden. Where the brain or nervous system is involved, the difficulty may lead to troubled behavior. Such was the case of a girl, M. M., who had a long history of apparently unmanageable misconduct. She was overactive and distractible and threw temper

---

[1] Paul Bergman and Sybille K. Escalona, "Unusual Sensitivities in Very Young Children," *Psychoanalytic Study of the Child,* Vols. 3-4 (1949), pp. 333-52.

tantrums. Because she was so hard to handle, she was institutionalized at eleven. In the course of a thorough examination, including X-ray photographs of the brain, it was discovered that one segment of her brain structure had failed to develop. Some of her misconduct could be traced to this condition; some, to the ways she had learned to react to how people acted toward her because of the way she acted.[2]

Sex Differences

There are significant differences between boys and girls that must be taken into account both in appraising conduct and in making plans. These differences have their origin in varying combinations of four major factors: (1) There are the obvious differences in anatomy and biological function. (2) Girls mature before boys. (3) The course of psychological development is such that more boys show evidence of the types of conflict symptomatized by reading or speech difficulties and, later, by delinquency. (4) Our culture has different expectations for each sex and imbues each with different values.

EARLY MATURING.   There are at least three stages in the school career of children at which the earlier maturing of girls makes a big difference. The first has to do with language development as it is reflected in reading, the skill which is a key to so much of education. As Gesell and Ilg[3] have pointed out, since girl babies begin to talk an average of two months before boy babies, an advantage in reading ability on the part of girls appears at the very start of school. As a practical result, studies of reading difficulties generally report that among children having this kind of trouble, boys outnumber girls by 2 or 3 to 1.

In the later elementary and junior high school grades, girls enter the period of rapid growth linked to physical maturity between one and two years before boys on the average. Along with this physical maturing goes an interest in grooming, different social patterns, and boy-girl attraction. From the viewpoint of classroom discipline, the girls often provide a basis of stability; the boys may seem to be silly.

---

[2] This case study is a condensation of material in the following: Leon H. Goldensohn, Ed Rucker Clardy, and Kate Levine, "Agenesis of the Corpus Callosum," *Journal of Nervous and Mental Disease,* Vol. 93 (1941), pp. 567-80.

[3] Arnold Gesell and Frances L. Ilg, *The Child from Five to Ten,* New York, Harper, 1946, p. 124.

Many a teacher would agree with the following observation advanced by Compayré[4] (although he used it as an argument against coeducation): "The development of the adolescent boy is slower. The young man takes more time than the girl to find his equilibrium. He must take years to become reasonable. The girl has this quality from the beginning."

Toward the end of schooling, the more rapid maturation of girls could place a strain on the curriculum. A small but significant fraction now marry. In one study made among 44,963 out-of-school young people in North Carolina,[5] approximately 10 per cent of the girls, but only 2 per cent of the boys, had quit school to get married. On this matter there were only slight differences between Negro and white youth. Although these young people had left school, did they have no need for further education? Will schools of the future meet this need?

PSYCHOLOGICAL DEVELOPMENT. The vital early needs of both boys and girls are met by the mother. For boys, who ultimately will feel uneasy about affection toward her and who will usually emulate their father, this can be a potent source of conflict. Evidence of the resultant problems is particularly strong between the ages of four and six, and again in adolescence. For girls, the situation is more complicated. To the extent that there may be some jealousy in the home relating to the father, this is colored by the strong tie born of early care between mother and child. For girls, other problems may be aroused by questions as to the worth of femininity in a world where men and boys are subtly accorded a desired status and extra privileges.

In adolescence, boys move more abruptly toward autonomy. They spend less time at home, and they feel less well understood. For girls, substantial contact with the home continues. Although there may be bickering, they do spend more time in talk with their mothers and tend to remain somewhat dependent. On measures of attitude toward other young people, boys moving into adolescence show little change in the esteem they accord boys and girls in general. On the other hand, young girls before puberty have a higher opinion of girls in general than do boys of boys in general, while at puberty this situation changes: girls' opinions of girls in general show a sharp decline.

These differences, plus the cultural factors to be discussed in the

---

4 Gabriel Compayré, *L'Adolescence,* Paris, Alcan, 1910.
5 Gordon W. Lovejoy, *Paths to Maturity,* Chapel Hill, University of North Carolina, 1940.

next section, lead to some important psychological differences which are visible in school. Girls appear to get along better in school. To cite one of many studies on this point, Stice[6] made a series of measures of 325 boys and girls in the fifth and eighth grades of three towns in California. Teachers rated the girls as being better adjusted than the boys. The largest differences were in self-reliance, social standards, and social skills.

By contrast, boys are more aggressive. For instance, in screening a fourth-grade class for children with emotional disturbances, Bullock and Brown[7] found that the teacher classed 43 per cent of the boys, but only 12 per cent of the girls, as aggressive. In most school situations, this quality can be quite disturbing. The inclination of many educators is to "tame" aggressive children. They would like to know how to manage boys so as to eliminate or conquer outgoing zest, especially when this appears in clashes with teachers or other children. Yet, the prevalence of these qualities seems rather to call for a policy of providing greater leeway. To the extent that boys have an inclination to be active and forceful, they will become embroiled with rules and teachers more often than girls.

The differences go deeper than mere surface appearances. In general, during the elementary school grades, boys provide more reading problems, speech difficulties, and psychologically disturbed personalities, the ratio being between 2 to 1 and 3 to 1. At adolescence, they appear as delinquents in a ratio of between 4 to 1 and 5 to 1, as compared to girls. Illustrative of such findings was a study made in six counties of Michigan.[8] In the general population of the area there were 103.3 boys to every 100 girls. Among the 1,306 children referred to the local clinic from 1948 through 1952, there were 184.1 boys for every 100 girls.

One word of warning is in order here: The above statements apply only in general. They are not to be taken as either the sole or the complete explanation when we seek to understand the behavior of a given boy or girl.

---

6 Leland David Stice, *A Comparison of Self-Evaluation, Peer Evaluation, and Standardized Test Results on Personality and Achievement Factors in the Fifth and Eighth Grades,* unpublished Ph.D. dissertation, University of California, 1948.

7 Burleen J. Bullock and William H. Brown, "Screening a Fourth Grade Class for Emotional Needs," *Understanding the Child,* Vol. 22 (1953), pp. 116-20.

8 *Differential Utilization of a Michigan Child Guidance Clinic,* Research Report No. 17, Lansing, Michigan Department of Mental Health, March, 1955.

DIFFERENCES IN CULTURAL TRAINING. In addition to those sex differences which have roots in biological factors or in the pattern of parent-child relationships, there are differences which are taught, often very subtly, by the society in which each child develops. For instance, in most American and European communities, girls are expected to be clean, to play with dolls, and to be interested in clothes. Boys are expected to be physically vigorous and to inhibit crying. Activities related to housework and child care are regarded as feminine "jobs." The masculine role, by contrast, includes making repairs and earning income. Girls and women are expected to be socially and aesthetically sensitive; men to be courageous and direct.

Anthropologists have gathered facts showing that in other cultures this picture changes so much that it is hard to find *any* sex difference, other than the biological and anatomical ones, which is not reversed in some society. For instance, there are areas where women do the heavy work while men sit around and gossip.

The early age at which children learn traditional sex roles is illustrated in Table 2, which shows the choices made from a series of pictures by 200 boys and 200 girls between the ages of four and seven. The girls, even at this age, tended to select pictures of household activities and child care; the boys, those showing physical vigor.

At later ages these differences ramify into many areas, some of which clearly affect school activities. To illustrate: In a program for testing 200 children at every grade level from the fourth through the twelfth, See[9] found that boys were more independent than girls in thought and action in both home and school activities. Girls had a greater inclination toward taking part in aesthetic and cultural leisure-time activities. They read books more extensively than did boys, and excelled them in activities requiring courtesy, unselfish service, and consideration for other groups.

In the United States, girls generally do better than boys in subjects involving language. In addition to the fact, already mentioned, that girls start to speak earlier, their superiority in language is probably also affected by our culture, as indicated by two studies made at universities. In a study of 1,050 freshmen at Indiana University, Shaffer[10]

---

9 Harold W. See, *Some Implications of Intelligence, Grade, and Sex to Certain Aspects of Pupil Attitudes and Attained Information,* unpublished Ph.D. dissertation, Indiana University, 1950.

10 John Richard Shaffer, *Relationships of Certain High School Background Factors to Achievement on a Test of English Usage by Indiana University Freshmen,* unpublished Ed.D. dissertation, Indiana University, 1951.

TABLE 2   *Subjects of pictures chosen by boys and girls**

SUBJECT	PERCENTAGE	
	Boys	*Girls*
Mother going out with father	13	23
Mother reading to child	46	31
Father drying dishes	19	34
Father at workbench	24	15
Child raking leaves	74	63
Child washing dishes	55	70
Child making a bed	30	66
Child riding a tricycle	70	57
Child playing with baby	31	56

* Source for the material from which this table was compiled: Edith Sherman Jay, *Teacher's Manual for a Book about Me,* Chicago, Science Research Associates, Inc., 1952.

noted that girls got higher scores on a test of English usage. In general, girls in the United States do better on the verbal sections of intelligence tests than on the nonverbal parts. By contrast, in giving the California Test of Mental Maturity to all students entering Ceylon University in 1950, Straus[11] discovered that the young men there did better on the language factors. A possible reason is that in Ceylon jobs in civil service, obtained through examinations, are highly valued. Also, tradition accords to verbal scholarship among men a prestige akin to that awarded athletic heroes in the United States.

Sex differences in attitudes and feeling reveal themselves, often in quite subtle ways, in a wide range of activities. One that will fascinate a connoisseur of symbolic expression is the result of an experiment in which Erikson[12] had approximately 80 boys and 80 girls at each yearly age from eleven through thirteen use a collection of blocks and toys to illustrate an "exciting" scene from an imaginary motion picture. The boys used the material to illustrate stories of height and downfall or of motion and its arrest or channelization. Girls went in for placid scenes, such as someone playing the piano. Many used the blocks to show in-

---

[11] Murray A. Straus, "Mental Ability and Cultural Needs: a Psychocultural Interpretation of the Intelligence Test Performance of Ceylon University Entrants," *American Sociological Review,* Vol. 16 (1951), pp. 371-75.

[12] E. H. Erikson, "Sex Differences in the Play Configurations of Preadolescents," *American Journal of Orthopsychiatry,* Vol. 21 (1951), pp. 667-92.

teriors which were either open or simply enclosed. Those who constructed blocked or walled-in structures concocted stories in which these were intruded upon.

It should be stressed that we are not trying here to define or describe "true" masculinity or femininity. Rather, the purpose is to help recognize differences, whatever their cause or meaning, which appear in the child population as a whole.

Physical Influences

The fact that people differ in their sizes and shapes, their strengths and their sensory abilities, is so easily taken for granted that we often overlook the psychological significance of such differences. Yet they do affect both the way children act and the way children look upon themselves.

APPEARANCE. Pretty children attract favorable comment. Ugly or dull-looking children may early be shunned by others. Parents make comparisons; strangers on the street openly voice comments. Such comparisons and comments may affect a child's outlook on life.

Some teachers have had difficulty with a few children who were judged "very cute" and who had grown used to being singled out for gushing praise. There is always a chance that such youngsters may develop an unusual amount of self-admiration. This stirs up strong feelings in adults. Some react intensely against it; some, by contrast, favor "ugly" children, who may learn to trade on the pity they arouse. Often a boy or girl who when five was "cute as a button," by eight or nine is no longer unusual. He or she then may miss being praised and may seek admiration by showing off in other ways.

When the dating age is reached, appearance can alter the trend of a youngster's life. Attractive girls, like Theone, gain easy entrance into social groups. They do not have to worry about how to spend time alone while others are having fun together. Their social popularity, even though it carries temptations, can be a stabilizing influence in their lives. The unprepossessing boy or girl, on the other hand, may find only insecurity in his social life and therefore may build a life on other foundations, seeking solace, for example, in religious or intellectual spheres. Many ordinary-looking youngsters gain social security by being pleasant, or witty, or otherwise interesting. Still others sulk, and become lonely and morose.

STRENGTH, CO-ORDINATION, AND UNUSUAL SKILLS. Throughout the school years, child society puts a high rating on strength and physical skill. This may mean a great deal in terms of who gets the toys in a kindergarten toy-pulling contest. It means even more when an older class is choosing up sides for a game. The strong will receive more admiration from children and adults; and, like pretty children, they may learn to exploit the trait which confers a temporary or superficial advantage. For some youngsters, physical skill may continue to be a source of satisfaction. For example:

An observer watching Albert would probably feel that it was fortunate that Albert was skillful with his hands. His father's drinking habits and periodic unemployment were the subject of sporadic family quarrels. From the age of seven, Albert spent as little time at home as he could when quarrels were brewing. He would arrive for his evening meal and, if the atmosphere was bleak, skip out again right away. This practice may have made his school life a little more difficult, for he had no success in such subjects as reading, spelling, or arithmetic. In the early grades, he longed for the recess period; later, the high spots in his day were in gymnasium and shop. In the neighborhood his ego fed on the admiration he won by tree climbing. Later he became a good ballplayer, but his real joy began when he started to spend his spare time around a service station. He quickly picked up mechanical information. His strong and steady hands, his good co-ordination, and his knowledge meant that he could truthfully say to himself, "I may be poor at school, but give me a motor to repair, and I'll take on the best of them." As he gained more and more satisfaction from his work, his life increasingly became organized around things rather than people.

By contrast, a physically weak boy or a boy with poor co-ordination can have a very difficult time in his teens. He may have learned to appeal to adults after defeats in childhood encounters. If he persists in this habit, he may be thoroughly isolated as a tattler or crybaby when boyhood games form. Unless he wins status in some way, he is likely to be quite lonely.

When such children fall into a pattern of whining complaints, grownups are likely to become very impatient with them. They are inclined to shove such a child away with a command that he act like a regular boy. The sad fact is that often there is nothing he would rather do if he could only learn how. With such children it is wiser for the parent or teachers to help the youngster find ways of being accepted by his group rather than to admonish him to be a regular boy.

PHYSICAL AND SENSORY HANDICAPS. Children who have serious handicaps must solve especially difficult problems. Their normal play outlets are cramped. They may meet rebuffs that make them distrustful and suspicious in new contacts. Such children may be inclined to follow one of two tempting paths. On the one hand, they may use the handicap as an excuse for remaining dependent upon others and, accordingly, may be extremely demanding. On the other hand, they may overcompensate for their weakness and drive themselves to a fierce display of self-sufficiency. If they take this last path, they may show rage at any offer of assistance, because to them it seems to be interference.

The way a disabled child handles his problems will depend in large part on how his parents act. This is as true for the child who is blind, deaf, or hard of hearing as for the child who is crippled or has lost limbs. Many such youngsters can and do achieve a healthy emotional life. This was shown clearly in a summary, made by Barker, Wright, and Gonick,[13] of studies concerning young people with impaired hearing. On many psychological measures, these youngsters on the average showed no consistent differences from normal children.

Similar results were obtained by Fitzgerald[14] when he gave a series of tests to 30 matched pairs of crippled and normal adolescents, aged thirteen to eighteen. There was great variation among both groups, with evidence that family interactions were the source of more frustration and tension than physical handicaps as such. There was a somewhat higher proportion of overprotected young people among the handicapped.

GLANDULAR AND NUTRITIONAL TROUBLES. There are some bodily disorders which directly influence behavior. Because these are hard to detect, a child may be held to blame for conduct which he cannot control. Some conditions may lead to restlessness and irritability. The victim becomes a veritable jumping jack. He would be in constant trouble with a teacher who did not like children to move around. Other types of disturbance may produce a slow-moving, apparently lazy person who is unable to speed up or to work hard. This child, unable to meet the demands of adults, would be subject to severe pressures.

---

[13] Roger G. Barker, Beatrice A. Wright, and Mollie R. Gonick, *Adjustment to Physical Handicap and Illness: A Survey of the Social Psychology of Physique and Disability,* New York, Social Science Research Council, 1945, Chap. 5.

[14] Don C. Fitzgerald, "Success-Failure and TAT Reactions of Orthopedically Handicapped and Physically Normal Adolescents," *Personality,* Vol. 1 (1951), pp. 67-83.

BODY TYPES. Within recent years, some psychologists have been interested in facts indicating that some differences in temperament are linked to body build.[15] The leaders in this movement are careful to point out that many factors besides body type affect the total pattern of behavior and that among people of identical build there is considerable variation, apparently due to nurture and environment. Although the exact relationship has yet to be traced out, some valuable clues are beginning to be made known. We shall illustrate these by citing some attributes of only one of the three major types.

One pattern of qualities which may precipitate trouble is found among young men of stocky build who are relatively heavy-muscled. The Gluecks,[16] a husband-and-wife team who have devoted their lives to research on delinquency, found that the proportion of such boys among delinquents was higher than that of boys of other body types. Sheldon had reported that such individuals are likely to prefer vigorous action, to think and act in terms of the present, to be relatively insensitive to people, and to go in for action when troubled. They would be quite likely to run afoul of the preferences for inhibition, planning in terms of the future, and emphasis upon manipulation of words, which are part of the school setting.

From a practical viewpoint, the most significant aspect of the work on body build is its implication that many striking personality attributes are deeply set and not subject to change. *If* the day ever comes when the relationship of such traits to physique has been spelled out with enough precision for teachers profitably to devote the necessary time to learning how to "type" a child by body build, we can then concern ourselves with the multitudinous details. Meanwhile, it may suffice to recognize that when a child shows a marked trend in personality, it may be more important for us to try to see that his school experiences allow for this trend than to try to force him into a new mold.

Sickness and Injury

During an illness, particularly a long or serious one, a child's life changes to a marked extent. Normally vigorous social play becomes

---

[15] Most enthusiastic in collecting evidence on this point has been W. H. Sheldon, whose early book on the subject contains a number of fascinating case studies of young men: *Varieties of Temperament,* New York, Harper, 1942.

[16] Sheldon and Eleanor Glueck, *Physique and Delinquency,* New York, Harper, 1956.

impossible. Group ties fall into disuse. On the other hand, in most homes the youngster becomes the recipient of special care from his parents. In a sense, there is a return to the satisfactions and relationships of babyhood. The conflicts between group standards and parental standards which are part of growing up may be temporarily suspended, or radically altered. For instance, look in on Charlotte, who has the measles. Four days ago she was an annoyed little girl. Her little gang had run wild in the house, and her mother had shouted for quiet and then made her friends go home. At dinner she had not been hungry, and her father clearly showed his anger because she would not eat. Her little sister had broken a favorite doll, and when Charlotte slapped her, had cried. For that, Charlotte was spanked. Today, though, things are different. For two days, the household has been hushed as Mother worried about a fever of 105°, and did all she could to stop the coughing and itching. Charlotte feels better, but the big relief is not physical. She is sure that her parents love her; she knows that they will drop anything to help her.

Psychologically, a period of illness may bring a real gain. The temptation to take refuge in illness remains with many people throughout their lives. However, most youngsters, if their days of good health are reasonably happy ones, will not yield to such temptations. While temporarily a relief, the "secondary gain" from being sick is much less attractive to the normal child than his regular work and play pursuits.

For this reason, the period of convalescence and return to school presents special challenges. As a child resumes the normal load of life activities, he must not feel too marked a contrast in the attitude of adults. He must feel that his parents and teachers still stand ready to give him special help, and yet take pleasure in watching him resume his place in his peer groups. The problem of convalescence is thus twofold: physical recovery must be protected and psychological recovery fostered. Added difficulties arise in diseases like rheumatic fever, where a prolonged period of restricted activity is needed.

The reactions to illness, as to physical handicaps, are often much less severe than many adults' "common sense" would lead them to believe. Harris,[17] for example, asked teachers to fill out a behavior-rating schedule, a personality-trait inventory, and a "nervous-habits" inventory on 58 youngsters who had polio and 58 who had not. The study was made two years after the epidemic during which the polio

---

[17] Dale B. Harris, "Behavior Ratings of Post-Polio Cases," *Journal of Consulting Psychology*, Vol. 14 (1950), pp. 381-85.

had been contracted. In general there were no significant differences between the groups. Where these did occur, they applied to items such as, "Does not have ordinary endurance."

ACCIDENTS AND OPERATIONS. Numerous young people have a deep dread of mutilation. This may originate in parental threats directed against masturbation. Children may feel that if they are wicked, they will be punished by loss of parts of their bodies. Since the many conflicts that go with growing up are almost sure to leave children with feelings that they have violated their parents' wishes, a disabling accident or an operation may produce a special panic. Unconsciously, it may be regarded as a just visitation from an angered Almighty. The damage may be exaggerated because the children fear they deserve extensive maiming. In any case, operations are frightening experiences, and some anguish is normal.

To reduce the effects of such shocks, it is useful to allow children to talk out their feelings. Realistic fears should be acknowledged, and the child assured that the adults he loves will be standing by to help see him through them. Too often the grownups are frightened or embarrassed and fall back on urging the child to "be a soldier." The nervousness their actions betray may be masked by out-and-out lies, such as, "It won't hurt." The inconsistency is especially terrifying; the lies put a strain on a child's security just when he needs it most.

Parental Attitudes

Influential as physical factors may be, for most children the most significant aspect of life is the attitude their parents have toward them.

AFFECTION. The great motive power in most lives comes from being loved. Deprived of affection in early childhood, a human being loses the will to live, the drive to please, and the reason for holding to a code of behavior. By contrast, most children owe their resilience, their basic confidence, to feelings of security at home. They have been fed, protected, and fondled. They hear their fathers and mothers talk boastfully about their achievements. When neighbors or teachers criticize, parents often wax indignant. Naturally, children do take advantage of such feelings, but much more important is the fact that there are people to whom they belong and whose good opinion is frightfully important.

One of the most dramatic illustrations in psychological literature of the strengthening influence of even one parent's love appeared in a study of vocational adjustment among some 80 individuals by Friend and Haggard.[18] In their report they give the case histories of the two men who had the worst and the best adjustments. Strangely, in many respects the two stories were identical. In both homes the man of the house frequently came home drunk and beat up his wife and children. Both husbands eventually deserted. Both of the boys had serious illnesses during their middle-childhood years. The most significant differences related to the mothers. The boy who eventually turned out well had a competent mother who built a secure home with an atmosphere of affection; the other mother proved unequal to this task. The difference between the boys was apparent in school. One managed to antagonize all his teachers; the other formed a very close and valuable friendship with a vocational education teacher, who was able to extend needed help.

Another illustration of the way affection paves the way for future successes appears in a study which Milner[19] made of the reading readiness of 108 first-graders. Those showing highest readiness came from homes where the mother took the child places and was demonstrative in showing affection, and where the father did not spank the child. That economic factors may be very important in enabling parents to express their affection was indicated by the fact that the majority of both the affection-giving homes and the high-reading-readiness scores appeared among children of middle-class origin.

When parents seem to be cold and unaffectionate, it is easy to condemn them. Yet, time and again, it will turn out that some events in their own past have blocked them from expressing their love, and that they are bewildered and angry with themselves. Out of her experience in working with parents as the chief psychiatric social worker at the Mental Hygiene Clinic of the Delaware State Hospital, Hubbard[20] wrote:

> A parent needs to share affection, fun and play of a child as well as the disciplining. Some parents, because of their own childhood, do not

---

[18] Jeannette G. Friend and Ernest A. Haggard, "Work Adjustment in Relation to Family Background," *Applied Psychology Monographs,* No. 16, 1948.

[19] Esther Milner, "A Study of the Relationship between Reading Readiness in Grade One School Children and Patterns of Parent-Child Interaction," *Child Development,* Vol. 22 (1951), pp. 95-112.

[20] Marjorie Hubbard, "Parents Come to the Mental Hygiene Clinic," *Delaware State Medical Journal,* Vol. 22 (1950), pp. 230-32.

know how to play with their children. They may treat them as far younger children than they really are, or they may expect adult behavior from a child. Sometimes parents do not feel at ease in playing with their children and tease them to the point that is no longer fun for the child, thus injuring their relationship to their child.

For an example of what may be the story of "cold" parents, let us take a look at Larry K., a seven-year-old, whose erratic behavior led to varying opinions as to his intelligence: Some teachers felt he was of average intelligence, others that he was feebleminded. Because they were worried about him, his parents went to a social agency for help.[21] Mr. K. promptly said he had been told he was too sharp, too abrupt in his manner with the boy. Mrs. K. interrupted to say she was cold, too cautious, but was not certain that this could have any effect on the boy. As the parents and counselors worked on this problem over a period of time, it became clear that the mother was a woman who was afraid to show the very deep emotions she felt; she had come from a family which never had shown emotion, and had grown up to feel that emotionality was a shameful thing, a sign of weakness. The father was a man who had to have things perfect; when he noticed any little thing about the boy he did not like, he had to correct it.

After the parents realized the source of their problems with the boy, their attitudes changed. The mother was able to say, "I didn't realize that all children must go through different periods of trying things out. I can let Larry be himself and I don't have to worry about what other people think."

This was echoed by the father's statement: "Everyone has a right to make mistakes and so do I. Larry doesn't always do what the other children do, but he's doing all right. I no longer feel my friends are trying to show me up when they talk about what their sons do."

Often, we hear a child's misconduct attributed to his being loved "too much." These are the so-called spoiled brats. True affection has no such effect. What does happen is that some parents give their children the wrong kind of loving. Such mothers and fathers may be driven by a need to act affectionate in order to please other people. They may be overeffusive, extremely generous in providing playthings, and afraid to discipline their children for fear they will lose their affection. The

---

[21] This case history is adapted from a mimeographed paper, "Family Relationships as the Generic Base in Casework," presented by Lorna Sylvester at the National Conference of Jewish Social Welfare, Atlantic City, New Jersey, June 8, 1950.

basic inconsistency is sensed by children. Children are spoiled not by genuine affection but by suspect sentimentality.

The attitudes of parents, as seen in their behavior, are a bit more complex than the term "affection" implies. The Fels Institute for the Study of Human Relations has developed a series of rating scales[22] which get at some thirty different dimensions of parent-child relationships. These include such items as warmth, sociability, criticism, understanding, and democracy. The scientific study of how such factors, and the patterns in which they combine, affect ultimate character is still in its early stages.

REJECTION.   There are many reasons—sad and understandable reasons—why a child may come into the world unwanted, a hindrance to the aims of mother or father or both. Some are "accidents," whose birth wrecked ambitious plans. Perhaps the couple had looked forward to owning a car and a house of their own, and taking glamorous vacation trips on money saved from their joint earnings, only to find that the arrival of a baby cost the wife her job, and the new expenses ate up every last cent of the father's income. Because of the child, their married life has become a drudging, tiring struggle for mere subsistence. For those men and women who picture themselves leading a life of gay pleasure, the birth of children may mean that they are "tied down," forced to follow a resented humdrum routine. Then, also, there are children born out of wedlock. This situation sometimes produces highly toned emotional complications for the adults, and these may be reflected in negative attitudes toward the child.

Some children are very trying. As infants they may need attention so often at night that mother, father, or both are driven by fatigue to outbursts of resentment. Later, some children show a willfulness or an overactivity that is irritating or that leads to quarrels with neighbors. It is not unusual to find parents who have been affectionate and understanding with all their children save one—and that one they regard as a junior edition of the Devil.

The reasons for rejection may be deeper and may involve psychological troubles. Possibly parents have failed to achieve cherished ideals; rather than admit faults in themselves they project the blame onto their children. Often people who themselves were rejected as youngsters follow the example set by their own parents; deep inside they know no

---

[22] Alfred L. Baldwin, Joan Kalhorn, and Fay H. Breese, "The Appraisal of Parent Behavior," *Psychological Monographs*, No. 299, 1949.

other way to bring up children. Unless outside help breaks the pathetic chain, rejected children may develop hostile personalities and become rejecting parents.

Rejection of a child may show itself in many ways. It may be brutally open, or it may be so skillfully disguised that almost everyone is fooled. On the one hand, life for the child may be a series of beatings and scoldings in which he is called all sorts of names. On the other hand, his parents may have as little contact with him as possible but lavish upon him gifts of wonderful toys and large sums of money. They will give him all the *things* in their power but deny him the *love* he needs so badly.

In extreme cases, a boy or girl may be neglected to the point that the courts will step in and put him into a boarding home. In more subtle instances, the child may be well clothed and fed but constantly treated with impatience. Possibly the rejection shows itself in nagging criticism; sometimes nothing he does will win wholehearted praise or smiles of approval. He may hear critical comment on traits which remind Mother or Father of the least-liked qualities of the mate. In a number of homes, the adults tend to go about their business and ignore a youngster as though he did not exist. He may always be left behind when the rest of the family do something exciting or else be brought along but made to shift for himself.

No matter in what form it expresses itself—and we have not even begun to list the possibilities—the child facing this attitude feels that he is not wanted. That is the essence of rejection.

There is no set rule as to how children deal with rejection. In extreme cases, some form of character or personality distortion is highly probable. We shall describe briefly a few of the more common types.

Hewitt and Jenkins,[23] on the basis of an elaborate statistical analysis of clinic records, found in quite a few boys from rejective homes a type of behavior which they called "unsocialized aggressive." These boys were very quarrelsome; they acted as if they were fighting the world. They showed no evidence of guilt at their misdeeds. The world was against them, and that was justification for anything they did. The boys in the study showed many variations of these qualities.

On the other hand, some children react to rejection, not by fighting back, but by pitiful attempts to find favor with adults. They may even come to welcome mistreatment because it is better than being ig-

---

[23] Lester E. Hewitt and Richard L. Jenkins, *Fundamental Patterns of Maladjustment,* Springfield, State of Illinois, 1946.

TABLE 3   *Conditions affecting allergic children*

CONDITION	PERCENTAGES AMONG	
	90 ALLERGIC CHILDREN	53 NONALLERGIC CHILDREN
Maternal rejection	98	24
Direct hostility to parents	20	83
Indirect hostility to parents	45	100
Displaced hostility in daily behavior	63	100
Hostility to self	55	20
Blocked behavior	92	17

nored. Perhaps the only time they feel they give satisfaction to their parents is when they are targets for abuse. Perennial stooges, they act as if they valued that small crumb of attention.

Another type of development was revealed by Miller and Baruch[24] in a comparison of 90 allergic and 53 nonallergic children. The results, as shown in Table 3, indicated that almost all the allergic youngsters were victims of maternal rejection. The interpretation here is that, because of either guilt or anxiety, these children could not openly show their hostility; they therefore unconsciously took advantage of allergic constitutions to dissolve the resultant tension. An allergy enables a child to annoy and hobble his parents, as well as to hurt himself.

There are many other paths a rejected child may take. Some withdraw into a dream world and eventually find refuge in insanity. Others, although possessed of good minds, may assume a cloak of stupidity. A number bide their time until they can vent their spleen upon pets or, much later in life, on children of their own. A few, receiving support from other adults, may eventually be able to come to terms with the realities of their lives and grow up as relatively well-adjusted people.

In this connection, we must be careful not to use the term "rejection" too loosely. In some social groups, children are subjected to much rough treatment, even though there is a great deal of warm love in the basic relationship with their parents. The episodes of seeming "rejection" may be widely spaced between long periods when the family have fun together. Even when strong language or cuffings are being used, there may be an undertone not too different from the playfulness of boy friends scuffling on the playground. In many cases, moreover, the parent

[24] Hyman Miller and Dorothy Baruch, "A Study of Hostility in Allergic Children," *American Journal of Orthopsychiatry,* Vol. 20 (1950), pp. 506-19.

later makes up to the child for having lost his temper. The child learns that, despite occasional violent outbursts, his parents do love him. In this knowledge he finds security.

PUNITIVENESS.   Important facets of parental feelings are reflected in the way children are disciplined, and for what. Many parents deal with problem behavior calmly and efficiently. Others, perhaps out of misinterpretation of "psychological advice," are unable to be firm. Many more wait for excuses to put on a fear-provoking display of force. The amount, kind, and consistency of interference with a child's activity all go to make up an atmosphere that leaves important traces in his personality.

A pattern that makes for trouble is one in which an atmosphere of nagging builds up through constant "reminders" and "corrections." In Table 4, drawn from a study of stutterers by Moncur,[25] the reader will recognize signs of parental impatience. The statistics are drawn from mothers' replies to a 330-item questionnaire. The children involved were all in kindergarten, first grade, or second grade. There were 42 boys and 6 girls in each group, with the groups matched for age, sex, school placement, and residential area.

In a very different pattern of family life, there is a building up toward scenes and explosions, including physical violence. An instance of this type was described by Stott[26] in a twelve-year follow-up of children who had attended the famous Merrill-Palmer nursery school. Among them was A. J., an alert boy who throughout the entire twelve years showed a consistent tendency toward a domineering and hostile bossiness. In his case, there was quarreling between his parents. The father was severe to the point where the report states, "It was not uncommon for him to spank A. three or four times in the course of a Sunday afternoon for various kinds of misdemeanors."

Consistent strictness seems to have quite a different effect from that of the type of blustering parent who so often resorts to physical punishment. A pointed example appeared in an interestingly designed study by Myers[27] in which the adjustment of 393 students was com-

---

[25] John Paul Moncur, *Environmental Factors Differentiating Stuttering Children from Non-Stuttering Children,* unpublished Ph.D. dissertation, Stanford University, 1950.

[26] Leland H. Stott, "The Persisting Effects of Early Family Experiences upon Personality Development," *Merrill-Palmer Quarterly,* Vol. 3 (1957), pp. 145-59.

[27] Theodore R. Myers, *Intra-Family Relationships and Pupil Adjustments,* New York, Bureau of Publications, Teachers College, Columbia University, 1935.

TABLE 4   *Comparison of parental discipline of stutterers and non-stutterers*

DISCIPLINARY TECHNIQUE	STUTTERERS	NONSTUTTERERS
Child threatened when naughty	33	13
Child disciplined often	27	6
Immediate response insisted upon	32	15
Child spanked for emotional behavior	13	2
Child reminded to sit up straight	27	15
Child reminded to put away toys	33	21

pared with their replies to a questionnaire concerning home conditions. Strictness on the part of fathers was reported more frequently by the better-adjusted boys and girls at all ages. However, among the seventh- and eighth-graders physical punishment was mentioned more often among the pupils whom teachers had classed as maladjusted.

There are, of course, other aspects to home discipline. We have limited ourselves here to a few of the more striking patterns for which there is research evidence.

OVERPROTECTION.   A pattern of parental attitudes about which a great deal has been written is the one called *overprotection*. Its essence is that parents, in their efforts to avoid harm, so protect a youngster that he is denied the opportunity to cope with things and people by using his own resources.

The reasons for which parents will overprotect are many and varied. One type of genesis came to light in a study by Zemlick[28] of the reactions of fifteen women toward their pregnancies and deliveries. In general, those who were most upset and anxious about pregnancy and had the hardest deliveries were the most overprotective, oversolicitous, and compulsive about their care of the baby.

Just as some children are not wanted, in other instances they may be wanted too intensely. Possibly the parents had long hoped, unsuccessfully, for a child and feared they could not have one. Then again, the mother's earlier pregnancies may have ended in miscarriages, or a previous child may have died. At any rate, once the baby finally arrives, the parents see in it the cherished answer to long-denied hopes.

In many marriages, for one reason or another, the husband does

---

[28] Maurice J. Zemlick, *Maternal Attitudes of Acceptance and Rejection during and after Pregnancy*, unpublished Ph.D. dissertation, Washington University, 1952.

not satisfy his wife's need for love or does not give her a chance to use her capacity for loving. In other cases, a woman may have unfulfilled emotional needs either to dominate other people or to sacrifice herself to them. A child may give her an outlet for these strong emotions. For this reason, it becomes extremely valuable to her. If her needs are met only by the youngster's dependence upon her, she may do all in her power to keep him from growing up.

Strange as it may seem, often the overprotection may mask what really is rejection. Unconsciously disliking the child, the mother is so horrified at her feelings that she hides them from herself and other people by being excessively careful and devoted. The reader will recognize this as an example of reaction formation.

Fathers, too, can and do overprotect. The causal factors may be quite similar. Although a father is not in as prolonged contact with children as a mother, his actions of overprotection can give rise to personality distortions.

Whatever the cause, in overprotection one or both parents, but usually the mother, spend an unusual amount of time with the child. This often has the effect of reducing the youngster's contact with other children. What social life is permitted may be so supervised that the child has little chance to learn how to get along with playmates.

Babying is frequently found. The mother may feed and dress her son or daughter beyond the age when these tasks can be performed without her help. During illness, care is excessive. Later in life, the parent may insist on choosing clothes and friends, and may act for the child in conflicts with other children, neighbors, and the school. All this adds up to a sweetly disguised strategy of preventing or forbidding the development of normal independence.

Overprotection often is a form of slavery. Sometimes the youngster is the slave: his mother or father dictates every move. The argument, "Mother [or father] knows best," is used to make him into a living puppet. Equally damaging, although in a different way, the youngster may find he has a slave at his command. His wishes are indulged, and any attempts at discipline are so feeble that a temper tantrum brings him victory.

There are, of course, numerous variations in the pattern of overprotection and of the way children act as a result, but in general the child's most serious problems arise at home and with playmates. With their parents, some are likely to be so obedient and submissive that they can hardly be called people in their own right. Others may become so demanding and disobedient that alarmed parents finally in desperation bring them to a child guidance clinic if one is available.

Such youngsters frequently have trouble with other children. Some are timid and shy; others may be unpopular because they are poor sports. A few may take to playing with younger children whom they can dominate.

Overprotected children often get along quite well in school. In a very thorough study of twenty such children—an outstanding example of research in this field—Levy[29] found that because of their unusual contact with adults, they are apt to be above average in language arts.

A teacher can easily be charmed by such a child, as was the case with a French lad described in glowing terms by Fontanel.[30] The twelve-year-old concerned was walked to school twice a day by mother or father, who wanted to protect him from the rudeness of poorly raised children. The boy walked with his father without giving in to the temptation to mingle with his fellow students. When he had difficulty with his homework, he would submit the problem after class to the teacher, imploring help in a timid voice. When the teacher put him on the right track, he would rest his hand on the teacher's and, in a charming voice, say, "Thanks, sir."

The teacher commented: "He was not the only one to ask this little service but the only one who knew how to put into the expression of his gratitude an intonation which touched my heart. How can one forbid himself a secret predilection for those exquisite natures who see in a teacher a second father and who have for him all the regard of a respectful and loving son?"

With overprotected youngsters, the main source of trouble for teachers is likely to be the parents, who may intervene in even minor difficulties. Some may protest any low grade given for work; a few may take an average mark as evidence that the school neither understands nor appreciates their darlings. As such parents tend to do many socially approved things, they may mistakenly be regarded as models whom others should follow. This is especially true if they show much concern over academic work and efficiently "co-operate" by coaching at home. Some are unusually faithful in bringing their children to school and calling for them, a type of devotion they may continue long after other parents have left boys and girls to their own devices.

---

29 David M. Levy, *Maternal Over-Protection,* New York, Columbia University Press, 1943.

30 J. Fontanel, *Nos Lycéens,* Paris, Librairie Plon, 1913.

VALUE PLACED ON SEX OF CHILD.   Mothers and fathers often have strong preferences either for boys or for girls. Traditionally many families feel it is better to produce boys. This complicates life for the many girls whose fathers or mothers encourage masculine qualities or show a preference for the boys in the family. Although not so common, some male children grow up in homes where one or both parents obviously wanted or still want girls. The parents' wishes are seldom kept secret. The boy overhears what adults say when some friend has a girl baby; he senses extra approval in the tone of comments when he does girlish things. At any rate, anxious to please mother or father, the son feels pressed to act the role of a daughter.

How a girl will act, in the more-common circumstance, depends on the interplay of many factors, not the least among them the way her parents react to any masculine ways she may show. However, the attitudes of teachers and of playmates may either tend to confirm her in a tomboy pattern or lead to an over-feminine revolt. (It should be kept in mind that many girls normally go through a tomboy phase as part of their transition to adolescence.) An occasional delinquent owes her promiscuity to an overemotionalized desire to prove herself a real woman. Some girls manage to work out a series of compromises. Thus, in adolescence, a tomboy girl may win the admiration of the most popular boys, who are attracted to her because she "talks their language."

PARENTAL AMBITIONS.   In middle-class neighborhoods teachers often see children tragically deprived of childhood play privileges as they spend hours practicing music or going to special schools because their parents are ambitious. Often such children are made to strive for goals beyond their capacities. In other cases, ambitious parents may curry favor with neighbors by acting overashamed of their children's appearance, language, or pastimes.

It is easy to feel sorry for children who, because of some handicap, have great difficulty in meeting the normal demands of ordinary life. Yet many children who are normal or even blessed with special talents may find themselves unable to meet the demands placed upon them. Their parents expect too much of them too soon. Viewed in the light of overambitious standards, the children may feel their abilities are pitifully inadequate.

The world is full of people who approached adulthood with lofty hopes for themselves. In their daydreams some pictured themselves in the future as millionaires, great artists, powerful politicians, adored saints, daring athletes, or famous scientists. Others had more moderate aims: office manager, star salesman, or foreman. Sad reality soon showed that they would have to disappoint themselves and, quite possibly, their own parents. For some, the drive to achieve great things did not die, but was transferred to their own children. Denied fame in their own right, they would gain renown through their offspring.

Events in our past histories give some of us a powerful hankering to impose our will on other human beings. Parents who are not satisfied by the domination they have acquired may want to extend it by ruling children who reach pinnacles of power. This is a double-acting type of motivation: the ambition furnishes an excuse for imposing heavy demands on sons and daughters.

Then, there are the many people who feel that they are inadequate or less worthy because of undesirable impulses. Others fear they are inferior to their brothers and sisters. By having children whom the world admires, they feel they will vindicate themselves. They may have anxieties arising from doubts about their competence as parents, or in some cases, from feelings toward children they regard as unworthy. If the children are successful, that outcome could act as insurance, a guarantee that they will be protected against criticism.

The motivation of some parents may be less devious. They may be ambitious for their children because of direct benefits they anticipate. Wealthy sons or daughters may be a source of economic security in old age. Also, the parents of admired people gain standing in the community. Vanity can be fed by showing off a child who is working up to capacity. All this is in marked contrast to the many more healthful parents who simply want to help their sons or daughters find satisfying occupations, for their own happiness.

The fields in which parents wish their children to succeed depend on the values of the grownups. Some think in terms of money; others, of social standing; and still others, of the applause of literary critics or the verdict of history. Here and there, one even finds inverted values, as in the case of the mother who brought up her sons to be feared desperadoes.

Whatever the reason, the parent takes charge of his child's life. The youngster continually hears himself compared with other children. Depending upon their sophistication, the parents may do silly things like coaching the child for intelligence tests or studying the biographies of geniuses in order to duplicate their training. They may be more subtle, and keep up a mild pressure of praise for the ultimate goal. In any case, there will be great concern in the home as the child does any learning. He is almost continually schooled in whatever arts seem wise, whether they be the niceties of etiquette or fingering the frets of a violin.

Some children submit meekly to all this. More or less deprived of the normal enjoyments of childhood, they accept the ideals of their parents. Except for the rare few who have real talent, however, sooner or later they must face failure. Here we have girls and boys who, like Karl (see pages 9 to 10) was pushed by the insistence of his parents to get exceptional grades in school, are thrown into a panic at the fact that they can earn no better than a B or Satisfactory. Perhaps they will say that they do not know how they will explain the grades to their parents; but they are equally upset at the prospect of revising their own picture of themselves. As a last resort, some go in for cheating to gain an illusion of success or to stall off unpleasant scenes at home. Others, finally recognizing defeat, have terrible feelings of inferiority or unworthiness. A number do not quite give up, but in their turn try to gain the coveted glory through their own children. Although some observers would blame the school for setting up a competitive situation or for overstressing grades, there is much more to the extreme type of distortion we are discussing. The ordinary operation of school merely provides a setting which easily confirms the pattern. However, at their most persistent, overambitious parents would try to force even a noncompetitive school pattern into one in which their children could be "first."

Instead of submitting, the children may finally meet the situation by rebellion. Their revolt may come at any time, but as we would expect, it is most common in preadolescence and adolescence. When it comes, there is often an intensity of emotion and a mixture of feelings that contrast vividly with the more guiltless, tougher attack on the whole world by the extremely rejected child. The school may see a backlash of the domestic mutiny as the boy or girl shows a perverse dislike of the parent's goal. Once in a while, the climax comes dramatically, as the youngster brings about a spasm of disciplinary incidents that end all possibility of success once and for all.

Often the revolt is less drastic or less complete. Here, the child settles with himself for lesser goals, but still attempts to please himself and his parents by trying to improve himself in the social or economic scale. The upward drive is accompanied by a growing anxiety. The intensity reflecting this may be sensed by teachers. Years later, some such individuals will pay a price for success: psychosomatic ulcers or other complaints.

In a few cases, the parental pressures may play a part in a more pathetic pattern, which is seen in mental hospitals. When McKeown[31] compared the records of 42 schizophrenics at Illinois Neuropsychiatric Institute, 42 neurotic children at that same hospital or the Institute for Juvenile Research, and 42 normal students at New Mexico Highlands University, he found that the parents of the normal children showed a great deal of encouraging behavior toward them. However, in the two "sick" groups, one or both parents not only gave little encouragement but kept up a demanding pressure through prodding and punishment to drive the child to meet rigid standards expressing the parents' needs for status. Here, we are not speaking about the ordinary ambition of parents to help children develop at their best, but an almost incessant demanding without adequate support.

By contrast with the parental attitude leading to increasing pressure, in some families an easygoing pattern prevails, or the home may deflate ambitions. In one such instance, for example, a mother refused to follow a special program of instruction for her daughter, who had been discovered to have an I.Q. of over 200. The parents felt the girl would be happiest if she married a good man and settled down to raise a family. They feared that if she knew too much, she would scare men away. Many children do take an extremely relaxed attitude toward school because of such parental attitudes.

Parental pressure or the lack of it influences the rate at which children are confronted with their several developmental tasks and the feelings with which these are approached. For example, a girl whose mother wants her to be a social success and begins to nag her about dancing and etiquette may be thrown into boy-girl relationships too soon and with too tense an attitude. Many, in self-protection or in revenge, may unduly prolong a phase of acting as tomboys, and thus evade the full force of their parents' drive.

Parental Illness

Health of parents is another factor that can make quite a difference in homes and their effects on children, as is seen in cases in which a

---

[31] James Edward McKeown, "The Behavior of Parents of Schizophrenic, Neurotic, and Normal Children," *American Journal of Sociology,* Vol. 46 (1950), pp. 175-79.

mother or father is sick. For one thing, there may be much less freedom to play, to make noise, and to have one's friends in the house. Where the onset is sudden or the illness is serious, children are likely to feel very subdued in the house. They may feel that they should not enjoy themselves; even normal, harmless fun may produce a backfire of guilt.

More serious, a sick parent can be an especially cruel tyrant. Because he is sick, he can make demands which otherwise could be fought as unreasonable. To fight back or to talk back is out of the question. In fact, any action which upsets the sick person arouses guilt. Under such circumstances, the child dare not express within the home hostility, which normally accompanies parental interference with youthful desires. If it is to come out at all, there must be a displacement. A new target, such as playmates or a teacher, must be found. If this does not happen, the guilt feelings are swallowed and turned against the person who has them. Psychiatrists have found that very severe disorders may have their roots in situations where parents express disapproval by posing as all-suffering martyrs. The effect of this on children would be equally severe whether it arose from physical illness or emotional disturbance.

If guilt feelings threaten to be too heavy, some children may take a different course. In self-protection against too much pressure and too heavy expectations, they may deny their own feelings. Then, they may act reckless or wayward.

When a child with a sick parent breaks school rules, a few unthinking disciplinarians use a particularly devilish trick. They lecture the culprit on how much the sick person will be set back when the offense is reported.

In a typical case, involving a parental illness of only short duration, trouble first showed up on the school bus. On the long ride to the Pallister Consolidated School, twelve-year-old Janet began acting like a hellion. Usually pleasant, but active, she generally took part in mild heckling of the bus driver. Now, she came aboard spoiling for a fight. She took Karen's lunch and refused to give it back, and the driver had to stop the bus and intervene. Then she made a mean joke about the purple discoloration of his skin. When her teacher took her to task, she was surly. During a recess, Janet went after Karen again, and reduced the younger child to tears. The question that puzzled her teacher was, "What has got into Janet?" She discovered the answer two weeks later, by which time Janet was her usual normal self. Janet's mother had had influenza, and had been confined to bed. Her father had made

Janet do all the cooking. He was irritable; nothing pleased him. Janet's mother had been very demanding. She had kept Janet running up and down stairs on trivial errands. What Janet needed was a chance to blow off steam, to tell someone how petty her father was and how unfair her mother had been. Lacking that opportunity, she had found her own outlets. When the need for them was gone, Janet returned to normal. We can speculate on what would have happened if the same conditions had lasted years, as they do in some homes.

Incomplete Homes

Parents mean so much in a child's life that loss of a parent may create grave problems. Many psychological difficulties have been traced to broken homes in individual cases.

The number of children from broken homes is quite large. According to statistics compiled by the Metropolitan Life Insurance Company,[32] about seven million children under eighteen in the United States are living under conditions in which one or both parents are missing. This group comprises about 16 per cent of all children.

MATERNAL DEPRIVATION.   The most serious situation arises where the mother is not present during a child's infancy, and no adequate substitute takes her place. Such conditions of maternal deprivation appear to produce serious and permanent damage. This was first described by Spitz,[33] in a study which aroused much debate: There appeared to develop a pattern of retarded development, listlessness, and dwindling energy, which often ended in mental illness or death. Since this description, much research has been done. When Glaser and Eisenberg[34] reviewed the results of 73 pertinent studies which had been completed by 1956, they concluded as follows: The combined evidence showed that where separation from the mother took place during the first year of life, the product was a general depression and retardation in growth. Where the separation occurred between the first and sixth birthdays, the child was likely to show a weak conscience. After six, separation seemed to have no deep influence.

[32] *Statistical Bulletin*, Metropolitan Life Insurance Company, Vol. 36, No. 2 (February, 1955).

[33] René A. Spitz, "Hospitalism," *Psychoanalytic Study of the Child*, Vol. 1 (1945), pp. 53-74.

[34] Kurt Glaser and Leon Eisenberg, "Maternal Deprivation," *Pediatrics*, Vol. 18 (1956), pp. 626-42.

DEATH OF A PARENT.   Here much depends upon the age of the child and the events in the household. In early childhood, when the concept of death is vague, children may seem unconcerned or even stimulated by the excitement which attends funerals. Later, as they begin to realize that the loss is permanent, they may become listless or be quite anxious in the way they cling to the remaining parent or to relatives. Eventually, as they gain security from being cared for, they make a more or less complete recovery.

Adolescents, who comprehend the meaning of death, may show extreme reactions. Often they hold themselves responsible for what has happened or brood over memories of their own disobedience or neglect. Such self-accusations are uncomfortable when faced openly; frequently, however, they are repressed, and may lead to relatively permanent damage. The young persons may seek to deny their former hostility by making a show of very intensive mourning. They may seek to punish themselves by prolonged denial of pleasures and by withdrawing from normal fun. They may project the blame for their now-loathed misdeeds upon the friends who were their partners in defiance of adults. In some cases, the dead parent is overidealized, and the youngster drives himself in pursuit of an unattainable perfection. Special problems arise where a young boy or girl tries to take the place of the lost father or mother, both in housekeeping and in disciplining younger brothers and sisters.

Adding to the influences upon the child, at all ages, is the reaction of the remaining parent. In some instances, the widow or widower may seek to make up for his loss by forming and holding an unusually strong relation to the youngsters. Such children sometimes have a difficult time in adolescence when the "silver cord" which binds them to the parent keeps them from forming normal attachments with their age-mates.

Among the problems a single parent faces is the fact that he (or she) may feel he has to be both mother and father. Trying to do both jobs, he may become confused and go to extremes. A mother may overplay her concept of the father's role and be too strict and unrelenting; a father may concentrate upon overeffusive sentimentality.

No matter how the emotional problems are handled, this situation poses very real difficulties. A woman who is both earning a living and keeping house has precious little time to spend with her children. Moreover, fatigue may make it hard to deal calmly with normal mischief. Also, a single parent is likely to be tied down: the children may feel abandoned when he or she goes to parties or engages in ordinary social life.

THE FATHER'S RETURN.   A situation which provoked considerable interest near the close of World War II and the fighting in Korea was the effect upon children of a prolonged absence of the father, followed by his return to the scene. Although such situations are commonplace during wartime, their equivalents arise for significant numbers of people during less disturbed periods. There are men who must be absent from home because of the nature of their occupations, as is true for seamen, military personnel, and engineers or construction workers on projects in primitive areas. In other cases, prolonged hospitalization or incarceration may keep a man away from his family for years.

Some notion of the possible effects can be given, thanks to a very thorough and ingenious piece of research by Stolz and a group of co-workers.[35] In the families she studied, the fathers had been separated from their first-born children by military service. The major results grew out of the fact that when the fathers returned, there were likely to be strong disagreements about child-raising methods: these men were more severe with their children than fathers who had remained home. As additional children were born, these fathers tended to consider the first child as belonging to their wives and to get along better with the other children in the family. The children who went through this series of experiences showed the effects: They had more eating problems, more sleep disturbances, and more nervous habits. In social situations they had more trouble than other children with aggression; they were either defiant or dependent on adults.

DIVORCES AND SEPARATIONS.   At current divorce rates, 1 out of every 5 or 6 children will one day go through the experience of seeing his parents' marriage dissolved. Usually, the divorce or separation is preceded by violent bickering. Children's loyalties to parents may be abused. One parent may use them as a weapon against the other. Quite often, family quarrels start in arguments over how to deal with the youngster's naughtiness. In such cases the child may actually feel he is the guilty party and that because of him the parent, usually the father, is driven from the house.

Here, for example, is the description of a boy, Jim, as he was

---

[35] Lois Meek Stolz, *Father Relations of War-Born Children,* Stanford, Stanford University Press, 1953.

seen in a permissive therapy group to which he had been referred by his teacher because of clowning, silly behavior, and scholastic backwardness:

> He was a boy who had lost confidence in and hated every adult, who was overwhelmed with guilt by his belief that he was responsible for his parents' divorce and who was filled with feelings both of worthlessness and suspiciousness. . . . His extreme unhappiness, his irrational hostility, and, most important, his complete inability to extend or receive any positive feelings were portents of the future.[36]

So drastic a result is rare, and could hardly be attributed entirely to the boy's reaction to the divorce. In such a case, there must have been considerable disturbance arising from other causes. In general, the effect of divorce and separation depends a great deal on the age of the child and the extent to which the parents involved him in their battles before, during, and after the divorce. In all cases, as in the death of a parent, the most significant factor in the long run is the relationship the remaining parent establishes with the child. Broken homes undeniably create added hazards in the development of children. However, we cannot forget that many fathers and mothers have done splendid jobs of raising children by themselves, or have made other wise arrangements for their upbringing. Scientific verification of this fact was noted in an interesting study by Haffter[37] of 210 children involved in 100 randomly selected cases in Basel between 1920 and 1944. Normal adjustment of children from broken homes did occur quite frequently. Poor adjustment was usually traceable to an unhealthy family situation, involving emotionally unstable marriage partners.

Unfortunately, such damage-producing family conditions are quite prevalent where homes have been broken. Statistical studies to this effect could be quoted almost endlessly; here we shall mention briefly only three. In a comparison between a group of 1,000 "unstable" youngsters brought to either the Clinique Annexe de Neuro-Psychiatric Infantile or the Patronage de l'Enfance in Paris and a control group from a working class district in that same city, Abramson[38] found that whereas 13 per cent of the control group came from broken homes,

---

[36] M. L. Falick, Ben Rubenstein, and Morton Levitt, "A Critical Evaluation of the Therapeutic Use of a Club in a School-Based Mental Hygiene Program," *Mental Hygiene,* Vol. 39 (1955), pp. 63-78.

[37] C. Haffter, *Kinder aus geschiedenen Ehen,* Bern, Hans Huber, 1948.

[38] Jadwiga Abramson, *L'Enfant et L'Adolescent Instabiles,* Paris, Presses Universitaires de France, 1940.

the following percentages applied to the "unstable" children: Thirty-six per cent were half or full orphans; for 10 per cent, the father was unknown; in 9 per cent of the cases he had deserted; 2 per cent of the mothers had deserted; for 9 per cent, there had been divorces; 8 per cent had stepparents; for 5 per cent, the mother was living in concubinage; and for 5 per cent, one parent was mentally ill.

Although the difficulties of the children may take almost any form, Reiss[39] showed that families characterized by separation, desertion, or divorce were unusually prevalent among 135 delinquents who, in the judgment of psychiatrists, were in trouble with the law as gang members because of weak consciences. Although they got along well on a face-to-face basis with other young folks, their too-easygoing attitudes toward questions of right and wrong made them fall easily into delinquency if it was present in their neighborhoods. This pattern is found often among children who receive little supervision. In this case, the broken home may have accounted, in part at least, for their parents' inability to give them sufficient guidance.

Another way in which broken homes affect young people is that the child may draw the conclusion that his parents must not love him, because if they did, neither would want to leave him. In reporting on the universality of feelings of rejection among children confined to the Rockland State Hospital in New York, Clardy[40] quotes one boy, institutionalized for stealing, destruction of property, and running away from home, as saying, "My parents were separated and they were having a fight for my custody. I was sent to a foster home. I thought no one wanted me and I hated everyone."

DOUBLING UP.   One aftermath of a family disaster, whether it be death, separation, or financial reverses, is that one or both parents return to the home of their own family, taking the children with them. A new set of grownups is thus forced into the children's lives. Under usual circumstances, their own parents feel constrained to insist upon more stringent standards of conduct. If the grandparents or the aunts and uncles who are more or less unwillingly providing a haven also feel that the doubling up resulted from inadequacy or misdeeds on the part of the children's own parents, the youngsters' security and loyalty

---

[39] Albert J. Reiss, Jr., "Social Correlates of Psychological Types of Delinquency," *American Sociological Review*, Vol. 17 (1952), pp. 710-18.
[40] Ed Rucker Clardy, "Dealing with Behavior Problems and Mental Disorders of School Children," *Journal of School Health*, Vol. 18 (1948), pp. 203-09.

may be shaken. Confused and resentful, the children may have to reconstruct their own private worlds.

For the child's own parents, the emotional consequences of doubling up may be very potent. They may view their child's behavior and their own actions, not in terms of the effect on the child, but in terms of how their own parents will react. The battle of the child's parents to win freedom from the grandparents may be fought out all over again as arguments about the child.

In a great many other cases, doubling up results from the need to take care of old folks. A series of three investigations by Koller[41] in heavily populated sections of Ohio during 1952 and 1953 indicated that sooner or later this situation arises for 1 family in every 4. To quote the results:

> Most three-generation households were created by the mother of the wife moving into her married daughter's home. Her past experience with household routines, the rearing of children, and other family matters led to much distress within the home. The manner with which the wife (second generation) treated her mother was very often the key to a harmonious or unhappy three-generation household.
>
> One unexpected finding was that the three-generation units studied did not last very long. Most of them lasted from one to five years although there were exceptions to the rule such as one case which had been active for thirteen years. A possible explanation for this result is that older people have a high death rate.

It must be said, however, that even one year is a long while in the life of a child. Moreover, if he had shown annoyance or resentment to a grandparent, death would be bound to stir up strong guilt.

INSTITUTIONALIZATION.   Quite a few young people are forced to adjust to another type of drastic change: a change in the grownups who influence their daily living. These are the children who are taken out of their homes and placed in institutions. Some have to spend long periods in hospitals. Others, as a result of family disasters, are placed in childcare institutions. Still others, for one reason or another, are held in detention homes or ordered to correctional institutions. Deprived of the parents with whose ways they are familiar, they must adjust to an entirely new situation.

Institutions for children vary so greatly in the way they are run

---

[41] Marvin R. Koller, "Studies of Three-Generation Households," *Marriage and Family Living,* Vol. 16 (1954), pp. 205-06.

that no over-all statement can be made as to the effects on children. However, certain factors are likely to be fairly common. One is a dilution of attention from adults. Another is the routine that becomes necessary when large numbers of young people have to be "managed." Also, the number of different adults the child must deal with is increased. In a large detention home, for example, there is not one father and one mother, but a whole corps of directors, matrons, recreation leaders, cooks, chaplains, probation officers, social workers, and psychologists. Even in a "home" for children or a boarding school, there may be the cottage parents, the directing personnel, and recreation leaders. These may go on and off duty on a shift system. There is always likely to be a turnover in personnel.

Although institutions can provide welcome safety, comfort, and security for children who have suffered disordered lives, they present emotional problems. Some children may develop a pattern of forming only loose and casual ties with grownups; others may withdraw into themselves rather than tackle the task of getting along in large groups; and there are many other possibilities. On the other hand, providing a rich group life and an educationally well-designed environment may be an asset hard to duplicate. There is an increased effort to develop institutions which serve this purpose.

The fact that institutionalization undoubtedly involves risks for many youngsters should make us especially aware of the needs of such children when we as teachers meet them. When consulted by parents regarding plans to institutionalize a child, we should help them to see the complexity of considerations going into such a decision.

Teachers who work with institutionalized children should make it their special responsibility to learn much more about the mental hygiene implications of institutional life than can be said in this short passage. They should be especially sensitive to the way the institutionalized child may feel about a situation which is "unusual," as compared to the reactions his classmates might have.

New Parents

Life not only takes parents away from some children but also gives new parents to children who had none or only one. Orphans are adopted. Widows, widowers, and divorced people remarry. Thus, quite a few children find themselves having to learn the ways of, and how to get along with, newly important grownups.

STEPPARENTS.   Beyond the already cited effects of a broken home, many children face added personality-forming events when a parent remarries and a stepparent enters the scene. This situation is so filled with possible drama that it has been made the subject of "nursery tale" plots in which the wicked stepmother has evil designs on the children. These plots may be re-enacted in less obvious form in real life. However, even in the many cases where stepparents have the best intentions in the world and act wisely, psychologically difficult problems may have to be met.

Older children may hesitate to accept the stepparent because they feel this would be disloyal to the now-lost real parent. For this reason, they may stay aloof. Not infrequently, their reaction goes further, and they may try to initiate hostilities or to make impossible demands in order to prove to themselves that they are not being unfaithful to an often highly idealized memory. In fact, the nicer the stepparent, the more severe the initial conflict may be within the child. In the case of adolescents, who are quite conscious of the sex side of marriage, overt or unspoken accusations of immorality may be leveled against the parent who remarries.

These initial conflicts may be reduced by skillful preparation of the child for the remarriage. Once the marriage has taken place and a new pattern of home life becomes routine, good relationships may emerge if the adults exercise patience. It should be realized by teachers that the fact that a child has a stepparent need not mean there is active conflict. Moreover, children may invoke the behavior mechanism of projection and unwittingly give a false impression of the attitudes and actions of the stepparent.

When the new parent brings children of his own into the marriage or when they are born later, the chance for the normal rivalry between children to be intensified into storms of wild conflict is very great. The new parent may be tempted to take sides, and acute family discord can result. Even such potentially explosive situations are not so different from other forms of sibling rivalry, which will be discussed shortly. They may require effort and patience in handling before they subside. The most important thing teachers can do in such situations is to help stepparents relax by gaining confidence and the perspective of time.

ADOPTIONS.   Now and then one encounters in psychological literature a case study in which some child developed serious problems on learning that he or she was an adopted child. Such cases only arise when the fact of adoption has not been handled wisely. The experience of child-placing agencies is that, especially when an adoption takes place during babyhood, foster children not only get along as well as other youngsters, but in many qualities resemble their foster parents more than their real parents. Usually the adopting couple is advised to tell the child he is adopted as soon as this can be understood. Adopted children, of course, do wonder about their real parents and the reasons they could not keep their children. Such pondering is frequent during the adolescent years. One child may spin fanciful yarns; another may worry about the possibility of some hereditary taint. Often they will want to talk about themselves with a friendly teacher or counselor. When an adopted child shows special behavior problems, it is wise to find out how the fact of adoption was handled originally at the time the child was curious about it. This is a matter the child may want to discuss. With help, if he needs it, the home situation can again be a source of security.

Other Adults

Few families raise their children in isolation from adults other than the parents. Often the social life of the grownups brings into the home a few relatives and close friends, who deal with the children in one way or another. Possibly they figure as an approving audience or as bringers of gifts. Often they swap advice on child-rearing methods within earshot of the youngsters. They may openly lend a hand in actual upbringing.

The most powerful of such individuals are usually the grandparents, but other relatives and adult friends of the family exert influence. Often they play very valuable roles. In times of emergency, they may take over parental functions and thus provide an extra security for the children. The approval they may give the parents and children may be stabilizing influences. Their actions and their personalities may reinforce and supplement the work of the parents.

There are times, of course, when these other grownups appear as very mixed blessings. Wanting to please them, parents are under pressure to do things differently from the way they otherwise would. The result may be domestic crusades to enforce nice table manners, shining cleanliness, and verbal respectfulness. Competition among aunts and uncles may lead to show-off behavior at family reunions or extra pressure to get good grades in school, make "good" marriages, or enter high-status occupations.

Grandparents and other adults may directly interfere. Sometimes they exercise authority by scolding or punishing the children, or by berating the parents while the youngest generation is listening. Another favorite trick is to make a play for popularity with the children by giving them forbidden gifts or winning a temporary suspension of regular discipline. This may cause trouble if it creates a split loyalty. Few children can resist the temptation to get their way by playing one group of adults off against another. If they succeed, there may be an aftermath of guilt and anxiety. There is equal danger that they may gain practice in techniques of sneaky evasion and double-dealing, which may carry over into other areas of life and make trouble later.

For adolescents, additional problems may arise when the other adults, grandparents especially, have developmental standards very different from those of the parents. Convinced that the youngest generation is well on the way to damnation, the old folks may show open consternation at behavior that the parents might be willing to accept. The possibilities for conflict are obvious.

When other grownups enter the home, a child gains an added perspective on how his parents feel toward him. When the enlarged groups have fun in which the child takes part, he may feel an increased strength in the group and learn confidence in meeting people. On the other hand, if the adults become the center of his parents' concern, he may feel he is in the way, not wanted. In some homes, parents become quite irritable with children when adult friends or relatives are present. The efforts of young folks to win a share of attention seem like annoying intrusions, to be cut short by stern measures.

By contrast, however, some children are encouraged to greet visitors and to take part in festivities. In still other homes, the children are expected to continue their own play, but know that if they want to join the adults for a while, they will receive pleasant attention. Whatever the situation may be, the relationships that parents have with other adults are influences in the lives of children.

Brothers and Sisters

A child's reaction to other children may represent a displacement of feelings toward his own siblings. ("Siblings" is a term invented to avoid more cumbersome phrases referring to brothers and sisters.) At any rate, in order to understand a youngster, it is important to know how he is treated in relation to his siblings and how he feels toward them. Often siblings have a strong bond between them and act as a team in dealing with other people.

BIRTH OF A SIBLING. How children feel about the birth of a brother or sister depends a great deal on how they were prepared for the event and how adults behave toward them. Much advice has been made public, and many parents now do a good job of preparing children for a new baby. Nevertheless, some mistakes continue to be made. In a number of cases, the impending birth is kept a secret, and the child suffers a shock because he is completely unprepared for what happens. Also, the whole affair may have been so handled that a child gets a very confused and disturbing concept of sex and sex differences. In other cases, there may have been so much advance preparation, starting many months beforehand, that the child builds up apprehensions and expectations which distort his feelings.

Even when the preparation has been well handled, children usually react strongly to the arrival of a sibling. Initially, there is bound to be a loss of attention from the parents. The mother is usually taken out of the home at least briefly, and when she comes back, she may be weak and tired. A new baby takes up much time because of the needs for feeding, diaper changing, and the like. Fathers and mothers whose sleep is broken by midnight feedings do not have as much energy to devote to older children. Even the most thoughtful visitors will be attracted to the newcomer. It is only natural that an older child will feel jealous. As attempts to regain a former status are foiled by the sheer realities of the new home pattern, the youngster may be frustrated, at a loss for what to do. Such reactions can be expected to spill over into the classroom. There may be outbursts of infantile behavior or of jealousy when a teacher is nice to other children.

An example of this type of thing was described by Moustakas[42] in a boy, Tommy, whose home world had been turned upside down. When he was four and a half, an adopted girl of thirteen was suddenly brought into the home; three months later his mother gave birth to a daughter. At school he became sulky, refused to accept limits, and showed a tendency to retreat from child groups whenever things did not go his way. During a program of treatment, he revealed that he saw the newcomers as threats. Once he learned to accept his new role in his family, his conduct in school returned to its former level.

---

[42] Clark E. Moustakas, "Situational Play Therapy with Normal Children," *Journal of Consulting Psychology,* Vol. 15 (1951), pp. 225-30.

We must not make the mistake of assuming that the birth of a sibling is sheer loss to a child. Often there is a good deal of pride in having a new baby. In the juvenile world, a youngster may gain status, as other boys and girls vie to see the newcomer, and in ministering to him insofar as the parents will permit. Later, of course, when the new baby is old enough to run around and join in play, older children may enjoy the companionship of a playmate within the home. In any case, by identifying with the parents' attitudes toward the new sibling, a child usually comes to accept the growing baby. An older brother or sister may assume the ego-satisfying role of protector.

RELATIONSHIP WITH SIBLINGS.   Eventually, in every home, the relationship between siblings settles into a more or less fixed pattern. There may be a rivalry fostered by the parents. In other cases, a tradition of bickering may develop in which the parents take sides. In some instances we see a definite master-and-servant pattern. Not infrequently, a picture of genuine mutual assistance takes shape. In all cases, so much depends upon the total number of children, the differences in ages, the sex combinations, the presence and attitudes of other playmates, as well as the attitudes and actions of parents, that few valid generalizations can be made. Differences in appearance, ability, and charm add more variations. All that can be said is that teachers may expect to find that some conduct in school will be the result of emotional reactions to siblings. It is also important to remember that arguments among children may have a realistic basis; not all quarrels between brothers and sisters necessarily reflect deep-seated sibling rivalry.

POSITION IN THE FAMILY.   The world does not look the same to a child who is competing unsuccessfully with a slightly bigger and older sibling with whom he can never catch up as it does to one who has some younger sibling whom he can excel in childhood activities. During adolescence, a girl with a slightly older brother whose friends she may be dating has different problems from those of a girl whose "kid brother" tries to upset home parties. The meaning to young folks of the almost infinite variety of sibling situations can be understood only in terms of their parents' attitudes and neighborhood conditions. An older brother who is away from home all day long playing with his friends is quite another matter from one who has no playmates. Being the youngest child of a mother who longs for an active social life is hardly the same as being the last baby of a woman who dreads the emptiness of life when her offspring are gone from home.

Much light has been thrown on the psychological effects of various sibling positions by Alfred Adler and his followers. Although the combinations of circumstances can be so varied as to defy complete classification, certain consistent trends are likely to show up in the extreme positions. For instance, the oldest child in a family is quite likely to feel secure in his or her ability to dominate situations involving other youngsters, but may also be inclined to be suspicious of possible rivals. By contrast, the youngest child is more likely to assume that he will be liked or cared for and yet feel inferior concerning his ability to compete successfully in the accomplishment of tasks. Thus, in many families, the oldest and the youngest will each show different areas of security and different areas of self-doubt. Because there are many special factors in specific homes, individual children will show considerable modification of such trends.

This is a matter on which much research has been reported. Because of the complexity of relationships, which it is difficult to control, the results usually have not been clear-cut. Here we will cite two examples. Sears,[43] in studying child-raising methods, noted that oldest children are the subjects of more anxiety on the part of their parents; in two-child families, the younger child is treated more permissively. No one knows for sure what part this plays in such findings as those of Bakan,[44] who in a study of 1,493 alcoholics arrested in Indiana, noted that youngest children contributed more than their share to the total; oldest children, less.

ONLY CHILDREN.   A great many generalizations are made about only children; scientific evidence throws many of these into question. A careful review of research in this field reveals that results recorded in one time and place are nearly always contradicted by findings in some other time and place.[45] The fact is that the effects of being the sole son or daughter also depend upon other factors. Many such children receive extra attention, have gifts lavished upon them, and have few social contacts. Some may be babied; others forced to grow up too fast. Some parents go out of their way to find companions and send children to camps, play schools, and other groups. A child may be an

---

[43] Robert R. Sears, "Ordinal Position in the Family," *American Sociological Review,* Vol. 15 (1950), pp. 397-401.

[44] David Bakan, "The Relationship Between Alcoholism and Birth Rank," *Quarterly Journal of Studies in Alcoholism,* Vol. 10 (1949), pp. 434-40.

[45] William W. Wattenberg, "Delinquency and Only Children. Study of a 'Category,'" *Journal of Abnormal and Social Psychology,* Vol. 44 (1949), pp. 356-66.

only child because his parents married late in life, or because they were divorced, or for a large variety of reasons. In each case the parents' attitudes are correspondingly different, and their treatment of the youngster reflects their feelings. For instance:

It was at a P.T.A. meeting that teachers first realized that Mrs. Goldberg was worried about Naomi. In the question period after a talk on child psychology, she asked what could be done about a seven-year-old only child who demanded attention. The speaker asked for an illustration, and Mrs. Goldberg said that Naomi dawdled so much getting dressed in the morning that she had to call to her almost every minute. The speaker replied that such conduct was quite common at that age for all children. Mrs. Goldberg thanked him, and then said, "I know I was selfish to have only one child, and I'm afraid I'll spoil her." This was all the more revealing because Naomi seemed to have no problems at all in school. The teachers realized that when Naomi reached their classes, they should give Mrs. Goldberg a chance to talk about her and to learn that they thought the girl was worthy of pride. If her fears led the mother to be inconsistent or occasionally harsh, there would be problems in the future.

Although no definite rules can be laid down, the presence or absence of other children in the family can have a deep and pervasive influence. The psychological setting may give clues to behavior.

The Larger Environment

No family lives in a vacuum; all are acted upon by social forces. These influence the family pattern and thus, indirectly, the development of children. By way of illustration, at this point we shall touch on eight items in the larger environment.

RELIGION.   The variety of religious belief is amazingly great. Even within any single denomination, families will range from the most devout to those whose religion is barely nominal. Between creeds, attitudes on such matters of real moment to children as original sin and hell are vastly different. For many families, religion is a source of abiding security; for others, the adjective "God-fearing" has literal meaning. Often, a full understanding of a child's behavior requires that one know both the content and the intensity of his religious experiences.

In many faiths there are definite statements, frequently quoted, which set forth the relationships between parent and child, and even teacher and child. Usually, the most forceful of these place obligations for respecting and honoring adults upon children. Many observers have noted that within recent decades, these articles of doctrine have been accorded less emphasis than used to be the case. Hoyland[46] echoes many other observers when he attributes this to a change in the "spirit of times." Speaking of the reputed lessening of respect for adults on the part of children, he notes:

> The parents have contributed to this by a change in their own attitude; they are not so inclined as they were to mount the high horse and lay down the law, there is more real companionship, give-and-take, and freedom of expression. The parental pedestal, where it has not disappeared altogether, is many feet lower than it used to be.

HOUSING.   The size and location of a home, although a lesser matter than many previously discussed, may have a great deal to do with people's lives. If the home is large and the neighborhood spacious, a child has space to play, room to have possessions, and privacy. On the other hand, in a crowded home children seem always underfoot, and may feel more adult irritation. Older youngsters are soon forced out of the house, and have little choice but to spend their spare time on the streets, often in contact with harmful influences. Where families live in one or two rooms or in trailers, children are bound to witness the sex act at an early age and to develop an earlier awareness of that phase of living.

MOBILITY.   A child whose family moves a great deal has some special problems to face. The one who spends his entire life in the same neighborhood and in the same school may have a more secure social life. Mobile children may feel greater insecurity in life. In each move, the comfortable routines of living are shattered. Ties to people, places, and things are broken, and new ones have to be formed. At any age it is a problem to work one's way into an already formed social group. With children, this process often involves fighting, as a new boy tests his strength against the native leaders, or delinquency, as a boy or girl seeks to win status by acts of daring directed against adults. A series of statistical studies in Syracuse showed that mobile children were more frequently delinquent than the stay-putters.[47] The child who has moved

---

46 Geoffrey Hoyland, *Religion and the Family,* London, Allen & Unwin, 1954.
47 Wallace Ludden, "Anticipating Cases of Juvenile Delinquency," *School and Society,* Vol. 59 (1944), pp. 123-26.

into a new community also has to make an adjustment to new school customs and standards.

The number of children affected by migration of one sort or another is surprisingly high. When the United States Bureau of the Census made a study[48] of this question by checking on domiciles of people in April, 1948, and April, 1949, they discovered that almost 1 child in every 5 under seventeen had moved from one house to another during the year. In almost 6 per cent of the cases, the moves had carried the children across county lines; half of these, across a state line.

As with the other factors we have discussed, the effects of mobility on the individual child depend upon other things. For some children, the results of mobility may be strengthening. It may rescue them from difficult situations. It may teach them they are adequate to cope with change, and need not feel fright at separation. Especially where several moves have been successfully managed, a feeling of trust in one's ability to find new friends and new channels of gratification wherever one goes may lead to a healthy optimism and confidence in oneself and the world.

CULTURAL DIFFERENCES.   In American society, children often must cope with significant differences in customs. The way things are done may vary for racial groups, sections of the country, nationalities, and economic classes. Such differences may lead to great pressure upon young people, especially in adolescence. A girl may assume a pattern of refusing invitations from other children because she is ashamed of her mother's foreign accent and does not want her classmates to enter her home. The *savoir-faire* of a country-club set may be erected into a standard by which "the wrong kind of people" are barred from exclusive fraternities or sororities. The members of such groups may develop a strong emotional interest in holding themselves aloof from other human beings. While teachers are naturally concerned with the heartache such situations engender, even more significant is the fact that relatively long lasting personality traits are formed as young people cope with the resultant problems.

SOCIOECONOMIC GROUPS.   The style of life to which a child is exposed varies in many communities in accordance with the social standing and economic level to which his parents and their associates belong.

---

[48] *Internal Migration in the United States: April, 1948, to April, 1949,* Bureau of the Census, Current Population Reports: Population Characteristics, March 17, 1950, Series P-20, No. 28.

There is now a vast mass of scientific evidence describing such differences in American communities. Typical of such research is a report by Volberding[49] on the out-of-school living of eleven-year-olds. In her study, middle-class children, although restricted as to play activities, showed greater social confidence and security in such situations as classrooms. Children from the lowest socioeconomic group reflected their lower prestige by showing greater insecurity. Their play activities were hampered by smaller living space.

The higher a child's family is on the socioeconomic scale, the richer has been his cultural experience, even by the time he reaches the first grade. In a study of this relationship among 710 children in the first grade of the Cedar Rapids (Iowa) public schools, Eller[50] found significant differences on a range of experiences, illustrated by such diverse items as the number of books in the house, participation in family planning, travel, ability to use a telephone, attendance at athletic contests, and number of parties attended.

As a result of these and other experiences, differences in personality arise. In a comparison of personality-test scores among 319 sixth-grade children in fifteen public schools of Washington, D.C., Maddy[51] noted that the daughters of professional men were distinctly less submissive than those of semiskilled workers and that both the sons and daughters of professional men had greater emotional stability and fewer worries.

These differences are quite visible in school. As Davis[52] has demonstrated, children of parents who work with their hands are likely to run into trouble in schoolwork and even to be rated unfairly in intelligence tests. A pair of studies on reading readiness, by Frahm[53] in Iowa and Jewell[54] in Springfield, Illinois, indicate that children from lower-class

49 Eleanor Volberding, "Out-of-School Living of Eleven-Year-Old Boys and Girls from Differing Socioeconomic Groups," *Elementary School Journal,* Vol. 49 (1949), pp. 348-53.
50 William Eller, *Relationships between Certain Socio-Economic Factors and the Experience Backgrounds of First Grade Children,* unpublished Ph.D. dissertation, State University of Iowa, 1950.
51 Nancy Ruth Maddy, "Comparison of Children's Personality Traits, Attitudes, and Intelligence with Parental Occupation," *Genetic Psychology Monographs,* Vol. 27 (1943), pp. 3-65.
52 For one of the many powerful presentations of fact by this educational leader, see the following: Allison Davis, "Socio-Economic Influences on Learning," *Phi Delta Kappan,* Vol. 32 (1951), pp. 253-56.
53 Izetta Frahm, *Reading Readiness As Conditioned by Home Background,* unpublished M.A. thesis, State University of Iowa, 1946.
54 Lucille Jewell, *A Study of the Reading Readiness of Underprivileged Children,* unpublished M.A. thesis, State University of Iowa, 1941.

or underprivileged homes tend to be less ready for reading in the first grade than more fortunate pupils.

If anything, the handicaps found in the first grade increase as children proceed through school. This shows itself in a multitude of ways. Children whose parents are low in the occupational ladder not only do poorly, but in rather large numbers become discouraged and quit school. In a study of the rewarding aspects of junior high school as these were found in the experience of 705 students in 24 homerooms of 6 different communities, Abrahamson[55] found that students with parents of high status not only received better grades and were more likely to receive favors from teachers than the others, but were better accepted by their classmates and held more school offices. The 6 schools gave a total of 18 prizes or awards: 14 went to children of upper-middle-class origin; 4, to lower-middle-class young people; not one, to a student of lower-class origin.

A very powerful factor is the difference in what parents expect of young people. In a middle-class home, a child is much more likely to be under pressure to keep clean, to act politely, and to earn good grades in school. In less demanding groups, a child may be given a much wider range of freedom so far as such niceties are concerned but be under greater pressure to fight boldly or to brave physical hurt. A boy who is not handy with his fists may have to face the open contempt of his father and mother. Thus, in each group a child may learn to fear the opinion others have of him, but the type of behavior which arouses anxiety may show tremendous variation. Such pressures may produce equally great differences in personality and in the meaning which school may have for children.

In interviews with 212 parents of first-grade children in a midwestern community, Stendler[56] found a definite relationship between their class level and their expectations for their children. Eighty per cent of the parents of upper or upper-middle status mentioned college attendance as a goal. When the little folk brought home their first report cards, only 16 per cent found their parents satisfied. Half the parents accepted the report with reservations and one-third were disappointed. It is easy to interpret Stendler's results to show that, even as

[55] Stephen Abrahamson, *A Study of the Relationship Between the Social Class Background of Junior High School Students and the Rewards and Punishments of the Junior High School*, Ph.D. dissertation, New York University, 1951, University Microfilms Publication No. 3437.

[56] Celia Burns Stendler, "Social Class Differences in Parental Attitude towards School at Grade I Level," *Child Development*, Vol. 22 (1951), pp. 37-46.

first-graders, upper-class children are under pressure to do well in school so they can go to college, and are already judged by these standards.

The particular requirements of parents vary in frequency, not only from class to class, but, within any class, from community to community. For this reason, the findings of the studies reported in this section will not be equally true for children of any class level in times and places other than where the research took place. They are suggestive and do document the point that anyone who works with children should become familiar with the pattern in his community.

There is no conclusive evidence that the total pressure of restriction on children is greater for any one class. Rather, there are differences in the points at which restrictions are imposed. To give one example, in interviews with 185 families in Dragerton, Utah, a coal-mining community, Black[57] found that parents of high social status were more demanding in regard to nursing schedule, weaning, toilet training, and work around the house. Parents of low social status in this community were restrictive about permitting the child in bed with parents, masturbation, obedience, and "talking back."

Working in a different community on the basis of intensive case studies of 21 ten- to fifteen-year-old boys and girls, Maas[58] observed that young people from lower-class homes were exposed to fewer restrictions as to cleanliness, but also had less open communication with parents. Their families were less likely to do things as groups. Although they had been dealt with permissively as infants, they had later been subjected to rigid relationships, involving fear of parental authority. They worried about neglect, and developed a strong anxiety to "be in good" with other young people, by whom most of their needs came to be gratified.

Another factor affecting parental handling is the extent to which the parents are striving to better themselves and prepare their children for a higher status. An illustration of the attitudes generated by such efforts was reported by Duvall[59] in the course of an investigation as to what qualities mothers valued in themselves. One mother told the following anecdote:

---

[57] Therel R. Black, *Child-Rearing Practices in Dragerton, Utah,* unpublished Ph.D. dissertation, University of Wisconsin, 1951.

[58] Henry S. Maas, "Some Social Class Differences in the Family Systems and Group Relations of Pre- and Early Adolescents," *Child Development,* Vol. 22 (1951), pp. 145-52.

[59] Evelyn Millis Duvall, "Conceptions of Parenthood," *American Journal of Sociology,* Vol. 52 (1946), pp. 193-203.

I never taught G—— to wash her hands after completing her toilet and one day in school she went to the washroom and when she came back the teacher asked her if she had washed her hands. She hadn't, and when she told me I was so embarrassed! Before this I had always wiped them after she washed them. Well, believe me, I taught her right then and there. That teacher must have wondered what kind of home she comes from.

In homes where the grownups are socially ambitious or are insecure, children are subjected to added pressures. Moreover, as they gain access to more new experiences, they may have to learn new social customs. Now and then, at the upper level, a woman who really wants to take care of her children may turn them over to maids in order to comply with the standards of new friends. Children may feel the effects of impersonal handling. At present, however, as a result of the prestige of the mental hygiene movement and its spread in certain social circles, some children benefit from "modern" child raising because their parents are absorbing the customs of new groups. Some of this is generally good; once in a while the result is a curious mixture of attitudes.

EMPLOYMENT POSSIBILITIES.   For adolescents looking ahead to eventual independence, the chances of getting a job may be quite significant. The working conditions prevailing in the fields in which they can get afterschool jobs or summer employment may have a lasting effect. Where little or no employment is available, some aimless restlessness can be expected. Where jobs are easy to find and yield satisfactory experiences, some young folks will cut short their school careers; others will take the first steps toward establishing good vocational attitudes.

MEDIA OF MASS COMMUNICATION.   It is easy to stir up a heated argument as to the effects of television, radio, moving pictures, and comic books. These reach into almost every home, and carry their messages to the eyes and ears of almost every child. Television, almost from the beginning, kept its juvenile audience captive for prolonged periods. One of the first studies on this[60] reported that children between six and twelve years of age watched television more than three hours per day on the average; for those over twelve, the viewing time was only half an hour less.

---

[60] John W. Riley, Frank V. Cantwell, and Katharine F. Ruttiger, "Some Observations on the Social Effects of Television," *Public Opinion Quarterly* (Summer, 1949), pp. 223-34.

The question that matters is what effect does this have? The evidence shows clearly that disturbed children, including delinquents, are above-average consumers of movies, comics, and television. They are attracted to accounts of gore and violence. Many people believe that the children's behavior is caused by the mass media. The present authors hold the opinion that serious personality disturbances have deeper causes, that the heavy consumption of exciting stories is due to such disturbances, but that some specific actions of children headed for trouble anyway can be traced directly to ideas they picked up in their reading or watching.

Because the appearance of television on the scene is fairly recent, it has been possible to trace its effects by recording at the time what children had done before and what they did after their parents purchased a set. Summarizing the effects found in these early studies, Coffin[61] reported that those heavy viewers who had poor grades in school often had had them before television.

It is difficult as yet to get concrete evidence as to specific enriching, as well as negative, effects of television. It is to be hoped that many of the general speculations on both sides of the fence will be replaced by firm evidence.

COMMUNITY CONDITIONS. Communities do differ widely in the conditions they create for young people. Moreover, there is undeniable statistical evidence of the effects of these differences. A series of studies on the moral integration of American cities was made by Angell.[62] An index measuring support of public recreation, for example, ran from a high of 11.49 in Milwaukee to a low of 1.29 in a southern state capital. That this difference is tied to conditions which influence children becomes clear when we note that in Milwaukee the number of illegitimate births per 10,000 children touched a low of 4 as contrasted with 18 in a less well integrated city. Angell also made an intensive study of a poorly integrated city, where public services were inadequate, where there was much intergroup conflict, and where less than half the citizens voted. There was more excitement over the university football team than about the soaring crime rate.

---

[61] Thomas E. Coffin, "Television's Impact on Society," *American Psychologist,* Vol. 10 (1955), pp. 630-41.

[62] Robert Cooley Angell, "The Moral Integration of American Cities," *American Journal of Sociology,* Vol. 57, No. 1 (1951), Part 2, pp. 1-140.

One factor in the effect of community conditions on children is whether there are facilities for helping parents. As was shown in the evaluation of a series of letters mailed monthly to expectant parents,[63] even printed materials can alter the extent to which fathers help with baby care, the age at which children are taken to the movies, and the procedures used in feeding. In an investigation of the practices of farm parents in Ohio, Hoeflin[64] came to this conclusion:

> This study demonstrates that there is no single factor influencing the rearing of preschool children, but that the past experience of the mother, her friends and relatives, the use of printed material about children, some of the community resources, the number of children and the position of the child in the family are all influencing elements.

In terms of resources available, we should expect that, in general, rural children would be under a handicap. Factors affecting these youngsters were the subject of a study in which Rector[65] used the eighth-grade achievement of 552 students in rural Wisconsin as a clue. As expected, children in towns and villages did better than those from the open country. Among the farm children, high attainment was found more often among children from homes where there was evidence of media of communication—telephones, daily newspapers, magazines, and comic books—and also where the children were allowed to own livestock and take part in a wide variety of 4-H projects.

Among community conditions directly and vitally affecting young people are the attitudes and actions they encounter relative to race, religion, or nationality. In a study of a junior high school in a northern city, a state capital with several automobile plants, Pepinsky[66] found evidence of social isolation of Negro youngsters. She also noted that they tended to show more aggression than others, as rated by white pupils, Negro pupils, teachers, and the school guidance worker.

Even the hard-to-define "spirit of the times" has demonstrable

---

[63] Loyd W. Rowland, "A First Evaluation of the Pierre the Pelican Mental Health Pamphlets," *Louisiana Mental Health Studies,* No. 1 (1948), pp. 1-23.

[64] Ruth Merle Hoeflin, *The Effect on Child Rearing Practices of the Various Types of Child Care Resources Used by Ohio Farm Families,* unpublished Ph.D. dissertation, Ohio State University, 1950.

[65] Franklin Eugene Rector, *Social Correlates of Eighth Grade Attainment in Two Wisconsin Counties,* unpublished Ph.D. dissertation, University of Wisconsin, 1954.

[66] Pauline Nicholas Pepinsky, *Some Psycho-Social Behavior Patterns of a Group of Negro Adolescents,* unpublished Ph.D. thesis, University of Minnesota, 1949.

effects. An example turned up in an extended piece of research in which Young[67] observed and counted "nervous habits" among a total of 1,520 students at the University of Georgia. She found that during the war years "nervous habits" were more frequently observed.

Shocks

Many of the influences we have already discussed may have a traumatic effect. That is, they may create a shock or leave psychological wounds. In the lives of numerous children, there are traumatic or shocking experiences. Young people may witness scenes of violence or death. They may be involved in fires, automobile accidents, and riots. They may be victims of brutality, sexual assault, or almost-fatal drownings. Although few people have had their lives wrecked by such experiences, if they are badly handled or if the previous development was unsatisfactory, the effect can be serious.

For example, when Sharp[68] analyzed the case histories of fifty girls who had been involved in statutory rape cases in Detroit, she came to the conclusion that those "who have been spared the ordeal of a public court trial do make a better adjustment than those who have not been spared the court experience."

Most adults are inclined to make a very common mistake in dealing with such incidents. Hoping to speed up forgetting, they stifle discussion. The effect may be that the child represses the memory of the incident and his feelings. It is usually better to allow the youngster to talk himself out, to get rid of his feelings, and to achieve a new security. When this course is followed and when the child has good relationships with the important adults in his life, the damage may be slight.

The many factors that shape lives all have consequences in the way children behave in school. By the same token, schools can have an influence in helping young people deal with those effects. Therefore, as much as it is possible to do so within the limits of practicality, teachers should attempt to discern in behavior the background outside school from which it arises.

For the purposes of mental hygiene in education, there is another implication. Often teachers learn that a child is living under conditions

---

[67] Florene M. Young, "The Incidence of Nervous Habits Observed in College Students," *Journal of Personality,* Vol. 15 (1947), pp. 309-20.
[68] Mattie Grace Sharp, *Adjustment Patterns of Girls Involved in Statutory Rape Cases,* unpublished M.A. thesis, University of Michigan, 1932.

which present unusual difficulties. Perhaps there is a divorce pending, or a new baby has been born, or the housing is very bad. Then, rather than wait for unpleasant behavior to call out special efforts to deal with the child, we may observe him quietly to see how he is dealing with his problems. Aware of the special difficulties he is facing, we may be more understanding of his actions and lend a helping hand before he becomes a serious problem either to us or to himself.

ADDITIONAL READINGS

Association for Supervision and Curriculum Development, National Education Association. *1950 Yearbook: Fostering Mental Health in Our Schools*. Washington: National Education Association, 1950, Chaps. 2 and 3. Describes the influence of families and peer groups on children.

Barker, Roger G., Beatrice A. Wright, and Mollie R. Gonick. *Adjustment to Physical Handicap and Illness*. New York: Social Science Research Council, 1946. A summary of research related to the effects of physical handicaps on personality development.

Bossard, James H. S. *Parent and Child*. Philadelphia: U. of Pennsylvania Press, 1953, Chaps. 3 to 6 and 8 to 12. A series of studies on many aspects of family living.

Havighurst, Robert J., and Bernice L. Neugarten. *Society and Education*. Boston: Allyn & Bacon, 1957, Chaps. 1 to 3. A full summary of material on the concomitants of socioeconomic class levels.

Hollingshead, August B. *Elmtown's Youth*. New York: Wiley, 1949, Chaps. 7, 10, and 14. A report on the ways socioeconomic level affected the lives of youth in a small Midwestern city.

Josselyn, Irene M. *Emotional Problems of Illness*. Chicago: Science Research Associates, 1953. A booklet containing advice to parents on dealing with illness, hospitalization, handicaps, and convalescence.

Levine, Edna S. *Youth in a Soundless World*. New York: New York U. Press, 1957. An exploration of the world of deaf children.

Martin, William E., and Celia Burns Stendler. *Child Behavior and Development*. New York: Harcourt, Brace, 1959, Chaps. 10 to 13. Shows how various socializing agents impinge upon children.

Plant, James S. *Personality and the Culture Pattern*. New York: Commonwealth Fund, 1937. Shows how certain characteristics of suburban living are reflected in children's problems.

Schaffner, Bertram. *Father Land*. New York: Columbia U. Press, 1948. A psychiatrist's effort to trace psychological forces involved in the rise of fascism to family living patterns found frequently in Germany.

Wattenberg, William W. *The Adolescent Years*. New York: Harcourt, Brace, 1955, Chaps. 7 to 13. An account of the major influences which shape adolescent personality.

AUDIO-VISUAL AIDS

Feeling of Hostility, a 30-minute sound film produced by the National Film Board of Canada, in which some effects of the early death of a girl's father are seen.

Feelings of Depression, a 31-minute sound film, showing how a boy's life was influenced by the death of his parents and his feelings toward a younger brother.

Grief, a 20-minute film produced by René A. Spitz, to illustrate the effects of maternal deprivation.

The High Wall, a 37-minute film produced by New World Productions, in which the development of violent prejudice is traced back to a boy's upbringing.

Kid Brother, a 26-minute sound film produced for the Mental Health Film Board, in which the reactions of a high school boy toward patronizing by his elder brother and domination by his father are depicted.

Preface to a Life, a 29-minute sound film available from the U.S. Public Health Service, in which four possible combinations of parental attitudes are traced in terms of how they might affect a child.

Roots of Happiness, a 25-minute sound film produced by the Puerto Rico Department of Health, emphasizing the significance of a father's behavior.

Sibling Relations and Personality, a 22-minute sound film produced by McGraw-Hill, in which many possibilities of sibling relations are shown in the context of multiplicity of causation.

chapter 7

ADJUSTMENT, MATURITY, AND NORMALITY

What are the signs of mental health? This is a very practical question. Whenever we talk about a particular child whose actions puzzle us, for example, we sooner or later make judgments that "he requires help," that "he has improved," or that "there is nothing to worry about." To do this we need some kind of yardstick. How can we think clearly about school conditions and their relation to mental hygiene unless we have certain results in mind?

To attempt a hard-and-fast definition of mental health at this point would be less fruitful than to look at the terms in which people think about it. Such thinking generally revolves around three concepts: adjustment, maturity, and normality. That is to say, when we want to say that a person is mentally healthy, we often describe him as well adjusted, mature, or normal. So far so good, except that like most glittering generalities, these words often mean quite different things to different people. In this chapter we will attempt to give these terms a little more precision.

Adjustment

We often use the term "adjustment" to describe how well a person gets along in a given situation. To some teachers this means that quiet, submissive children are well adjusted, and noisy or "bad" children are maladjusted. Similarly, in a group, anyone who causes disharmony may be accused of making a poor adjustment. In the same way, a principal or a superintendent may look at teachers from the viewpoint of how well they conform to his ideas. Industrial psychologists may be tempted to think that all workers who are satisfied with their jobs are, thereby, well adjusted.

By any such definition of adjustment, we would be forced to declare that all nonconformists, all independent thinkers, all self-asserting people are mentally unhealthy. We would have to look askance on all the great contributors to human progress and on such heroic figures as Abraham Lincoln, Mahatma Gandhi, and Socrates. Obviously, if adjustment had this implication, it would be a dubious goal, and mental hygiene would be a hindrance, not a help, in the development of mankind.

As a beginning definition, we can say that "adjustment" means "the ability of an individual to live harmoniously with his environment—physical, social, intellectual, and moral—and with himself, keeping intact his personal integrity." We need now to explore some of the implications of this definition.

BOTH THE PERSON AND THE SITUATION CAN BE CHANGED. Adjustment is not an end in itself; rather, it is a description of the relation between an individual and his environment. It does not require that a child or an adult give up his unique qualities in order to avoid creating problems for anyone else.

A well-adjusted individual may adjust as much by changing his environment to meet his individuality as by submitting to the reasonable demands of the situations in which he finds himself. On the one hand, he can avoid groups in which he would feel disturbed. By the same token, he can seek out or create settings in which he can flourish. Likewise, he may alter or modify his own abilities. He can induce his parents, his teachers, and his friends to change their demands.

For example, one physically weak boy avoids football playing and tries to gather round him a crowd of radio enthusiasts. When his father tries to get him to act as an athlete, he cleverly deflects this demand by a display of such contagious enthusiasm for the less strenuous pastime that his father joins in building radio sets. To be sure, the end product, as we witness it, is a boy who gets along very well in his environment. However, the process has involved as much change in his surroundings as in himself.

REASONABLENESS OF THE SITUATION. A corollary of all this is that adjustment is a reasonable criterion of mental health only if the demands are reasonable. For example, if a school sets up a tyrannical regime, we would expect quite a few children to adjust poorly. Similarly, if a teacher is incapable of managing the learning processes, the pupils will be upset and disorderly. What maladjustment they show is an argument for altering school situations rather than tricking the youngsters into conformity. The term to be watched in this argument is "reasonable." Its meaning must be interpreted in terms of the goal dominating the situation. Thus it is reasonable to expect soldiers to be motionless when their lives are at stake; it is not reasonable to expect children to go through equivalent torture when it serves no demonstrable function in learning or development.

An illustration of this principle confronted a school staff when a fourteen-year-old boy hurled a book at a library teacher. Still in the sixth grade, he was bored by the available books. The teacher had been "at him" to put up at least an appearance of being interested. A check of school records indicated that his I.Q. was over 120. This boy's retardation in school was the result of a feud between the principal and his parents. In each of the past two years, his mother had withdrawn him from school two weeks early to take him on a visit to her relatives. The principal had threatened to hold the boy back if he missed examinations. The mother had been unimpressed; the principal had refused to back down. No one could approve of the boy's action toward his teacher, but that he would show some strong reaction to his situation could be expected. Regardless of the history of the case, if anyone wanted this boy to adjust well to school, it would be essential to restore him to a grade where the activities were in line with his age and ability.

Neither conformity nor rebellion as such always represents adjustment or maladjustment. As a measure of mental health, adjustment means that the person is able to work out good relationships with himself and others in environments which are in harmony with his own values and which do not make unreasonable demands upon him. In intolerable situations, he will protect his integrity by fighting back or by such other measures as the situation will permit, without elevating rebellion into a goal in itself. In a democratic society, we do not want children to feel compelled to act as putty in the hands of any adult. We do want young people to be able to size up new situations and to accommodate themselves to demands in accord with their integrity.

INNER ADJUSTMENT IS INVOLVED. We are interested in much more than the way a child's surface behavior fits into his environment.

It is even more important to know how well he is getting along with himself. Are the things he is doing in harmony with his own feelings? If a person is torn by deep, unresolved conflicts, no matter how docile his behavior, he cannot be considered well adjusted. Under pressure from home, for example, some youngsters will do phenomenal school-work, but become irritable and sullen in the process. A child who meets heavy demands to gain praise at the expense of brothers, sisters, or friends may be torn by guilt at his success. By contrast, a boy or girl who is generally lively and gay need not be cause for worry even if his exuberance leads to an occasional row. A child's happiness is an important clue.

A MATTER OF DEGREE.   Adjustment is not an all-or-none quality; it is a matter of degree. Complete maladjustment is very rare; perfect adjustment is unknown. Most young people fall well in between the extremes. Our task is not to label a child as maladjusted or well adjusted but to be more specific in evaluating the intensity of his difficulty in the areas in which maladjustment expresses itself.

An interesting effort to help teachers in making this type of judgment appears in the guides prepared by the New York State Youth Commission[1] as part of a program for detecting potential delinquents early in their school careers. A series of measures on six types of adjustment items were obtained. These data were secured for 5,299 children, and, three years later, their names were checked with the files of the juvenile courts serving their communities. Of the total, 114 proved to have become delinquent. Of this 114, records showed that 77 per cent had shown evidence of poor adjustment in school, in personal traits, or both. (In general, studies indicate that the proportion of poorly adjusted children in the school population ranges from 12 to 15 per cent.)

DIFFERENCES IN VARIOUS AREAS.   As with grownups, children may show different degrees of adjustment in different areas of living. Thus, an adolescent may be deeply troubled about religion, but get along very well with the members of a church young folks' club. Some preadolescent girls may have a happy time in the family circle but may be very tense and compulsively smutty with their friends. Even highly mal-

---

[1] See, for example, this pamphlet: New York State Youth Commission, *Reducing Juvenile Delinquency: What New York State Schools Can Do,* Albany, New York State Youth Commission, 1952.

adjusted children may have one or two areas in which they are delight-fully at ease. By the same token, the best adjusted find themselves in some situations which they cannot handle.

For school people, this has a very practical implication. We can-not judge a child's whole adjustment by how he acts in school. There are some children for whom school is the only area of serious malad-justment. Low intelligence may make academic learning a dreadful experience. Occasionally teachers bring intolerable pressures to bear, or their personalities create serious conflict. We should expect, there-fore, that some children who are having trouble in school will be doing quite well in other areas of living. Parents who report this often speak the truth. In all such cases, a careful study should be made of why school is the sore spot.

School can also be the area of best adjustment. We have previously mentioned that children from some overprotective homes may do very well in school. School brings them satisfactions they can secure in no other areas of living. Often, the serious maladjustments of the child lie in home relationships. As far as the youngster is concerned, school is a low-tension area. What problems he shows in the classroom are merely spill-overs from the home, which would be cleared up if the relationships with the parents improved.

All of these situations have been verified by research reports. In a study of emotional "symptoms" observed among 239 children aged two to seven in Leicester, England, Cummings[2] listed many whose or-igin was clearly unrelated to school as well as some in which school may well have been involved.

There is some evidence that a child's happiness is influenced by how he or she compares with classmates in ability and achievement. One example was recorded by Mechem[3] in an analysis of interviews with 30 boys and 35 girls at the University of Michigan Elementary School. Their answers were rated in terms of positive "affectivity"— the degree of happiness and contentment they displayed. In general, those children who were mentally advanced had higher ratings. The key factor appeared to be the relationship between a given child's ability and that of the rest of the group. It should be pointed out that the parents of the children in this school are in the middle or upper middle

---

[2] Jean D. Cummings, "The Incidence of Emotional Symptoms in School Children," *British Journal of Educational Psychology,* Vol. 14 (1944), pp. 151-61.

[3] Elizabeth Mechem, "Affectivity and Growth in Children," *Child Development,* Vol. 14 (1943), pp. 91-115.

class, and may have placed stress on comparisons. It would be interesting to find out whether the same results would be observed in a school serving children from another social level.

"BAD" BEHAVIOR AS ADJUSTMENT.   It may seem paradoxical, but sometimes as a child's adjustment improves, his behavior becomes more unpleasant. This is by no means a general rule, but it does happen under some circumstances, particularly where the maladjustment has been marked by extreme withdrawing behavior, reaction formation, timidity, or submissiveness.

For example, Albert Evlin was an exceptionally good little boy. His teacher called him "too good." He especially shunned any bodily contact with other boys and never took part in the rough-and-tumble of the play ground. The other children took advantage of his timidity; they made his life miserable. To help him achieve a better social adjustment, his teacher teamed him with more vigorous boys in such tasks as cleaning erasers and carrying milk bottles and supplies. Eventually, as he felt safer with the other children, Albert began to get into fights. For a couple of months he was a real source of trouble. This passing phase was part of the process by which he was reaching a new adjustment to the other children. His teacher recognized the slight addition to her problems as a price she was willing to pay for watching him find his way out of his troubles. As his social adjustment improved and he became more sure of himself, his fighting dropped back to a level more typical of his age.

SUMMARY.   We must judge the adjustment of a child in terms of his whole life situation. These are the questions we have to ask: To what does he have to adjust? In which areas is his adjustment best? In which areas is it poorest? In terms of his past history, are his present levels an improvement or a step backward?

Maturity

Maturity is another of the terms we use to appraise emotional health. Too often, we think of it in the simple terms which might be applied to fruit, where we can judge ripeness by the color of the skin and the feel of the pulp. In judging the physical maturity of human beings, we have been inclined to pin our faith on such definite indexes as the composition of bones, the appearance of pubic hair, and the development of glands. Current experimental work shows, however, that even the physical picture is more complex than is generally believed.

The criteria for judging personality are especially complicated. One reason is that many adults still retain traits which are also found in children and adolescents. Would you agree that preoccupation with romance is a teen-age quality which oldsters outgrow? If you do, you must argue with Hollywood, soap-opera script-writers, and authors of great literature. Do you believe that enthusiasm for sports heroes reaches a peak in preadolescence, only to dwindle when the boys become interested in the girls? If you do, don't go near a ball park during the World Series.

A statistical summary of what adults do would be a poor measure of maturity. What usually results when a list of mature traits is drawn up is that the author describes himself or his ideals. To appreciate this difficulty, the reader might try writing descriptions of maturity as he thinks they would be given by the mother superior of a convent, a militant atheist, a union leader, and an independent farmer who had raised successfully a family of seven children. To each, "mature" would mean "good" in terms of his own value system and taste patterns.

WE CAN JUDGE MATURITY.   Keeping these cautions in mind, we can nevertheless offer a first approach to estimating whether a child is mature: if he acts like most children his age, he is mature. In general, if his behavior looks like that which is typical of much younger children from a similar background, we can safely regard him as immature. Certainly, any gross inability to function at the level of his age is immaturity.

Just what sorts of actions does this imply? An eleven-year-old boy who cannot play with other boys of the same general age range without constantly running to get the help of an adult is not acting mature in his social life. A third-grade girl who cannot dress herself is definitely not acting her age. Similarly, a high school senior who cannot work by herself but must constantly seek the approval of her teacher is not as grown up as she should be in her relations to adults.

MATURITY IS RELATIVE TO AGE.   Our standard for youngsters is the conduct of other young people. It is a bad mistake to judge children in terms of adult behavior. If we fall into that trap, we may overlook the significance of behavior that is well beyond a child's age level. If day after day a six-year-old, without pressure from adults, displays an unusual need to keep toys and books in a rigid sort of order and gets upset if this pattern of order is even slightly disturbed, we have reason to be especially watchful. It is likely that this behavior is a sign, not of unusual maturity, but of a neurotic pattern of reaction to something which disturbs his emotional equilibrium.

Some children are very docile, and easily develop traits which please their elders. Such youngsters can be trained to make a display of behavior well beyond their regular age level. Frequently, however, when they are free of adult supervision, they snap back to less advanced behavior. We must not mistake such docility for maturity. In fact, during preadolescence it is a form of immaturity.

Because children vary widely in intellectual ability, some differences in behavior are to be expected on this account. Thus, a third-grader showing interest in Greek legends or a tenth-grader in advanced algebra may not thus be showing neurotic traits, even though their interests are not typical of their classmates.

NO SINGLE SCHEDULE.   There is no single schedule which tells what conduct can be expected of all children at any age level. Not only does each child have his own unique growth pattern, but even typical behavior differs from group to group. The most extensive attempt at a scientific listing, that by Gesell and Ilg, was based largely on children who had attended a nursery school and on a number of children who went to an excellent private school. "Most . . . came from homes of good or high socioeconomic status."[4] The cultural differences are shown by such items as the following note on five-year-old table behavior. "Moreover, he frequently eats his main meal at night in the kitchen, apart from the family group . . ."[5] This obviously is a custom of a particular group of parents, which would not apply to others. The difference between groups and the general effect of individuality have been recognized by Gesell and Ilg, and the following warning wisely precedes each listing of "maturity traits" in their books: "The following maturity traits are *not* to be regarded as rigid norms nor as models. They simply illustrate the kinds of behavior . . . desirable or otherwise, which tend to occur at this age."[6]

---

[4] Arnold Gesell and Frances L. Ilg, *The Child from Five to Ten,* New York, Harper, 1936, p. 3.
[5] *Ibid.,* p. 74.
[6] *Ibid., passim.*

EVEN MALADJUSTMENTS MAY REVEAL MATURITY.   A young person's poor adjustments may tell a story of maturity. We would expect some girls in the seventh or eighth grade to be clumsy in social situations. To be sure, the emotional turmoil they undergo represents a temporary maladjustment. The point is that it is precisely the kind of maladjustment that shows they are growing up at about the right rate. However, if a senior in a high school where practically all girls were self-assured acted with similar lack of skill, we would feel justified in wondering why her social development was retarded.

Again, if a six-year-old threw a temper tantrum out of jealousy because his best friend was playing with a third child and forthwith broke up the game by smashing toys, we would recognize that he had a problem, but the form of his maladjustment could not be called immature because this is the way a six-year-old may act when he loses his temper. By contrast, if a twelve-year-old used the same way of expressing jealousy, we would suspect him of being socially immature.

Let us apply this principle to a specific case. Ruth Stewart, sixteen, gave an incorrect answer in her history class. Her teacher bitingly said that if she paid as much attention to her history text as she did to her hairdo, she might get somewhere. Ruth compressed her lips, said nothing, and sat down. After class, she walked to her locker and, without saying a word, hurled her history book at the wall. How mature was her little temper tantrum? Keeping silent in the face of adult taunts was the traditional behavior of her friends. In a neighborhood with less self-restrained patterns, she might have made excuses or argued back. However, for her setting, that part of her behavior was mature enough. How about the book-tossing episode? For a temper tantrum, hers was pretty grown-up. She did not burst into tears, stamp her feet, and pummel the air as a little child might have done. Instead, she let herself go when in an appropriate location. Although displacing her anger to a harmless book looks silly, she did give herself an outlet and a fairly satisfying one, at that. We might hope that eventually she would be able to take reprimands without getting so upset, but we could not accurately call her outburst a sign of immaturity.

SOMETIMES "IMMATURITY" MAY BE USEFUL.   Just as we appraise a poor adjustment by deciding whether it is appropriate to a young person's stage of development, so we must also pay attention to how much a relatively immature pattern of conduct contributes to the overall adjustment of the individual. There are circumstances in which acting or feeling "too young" helps to solve pressing problems. Where such immaturity is merely a delaying action, it may prepare the ground for a later advance to fuller and better-adjusted maturity.

For example, Phyllis Kepper, an attractive seventeen-year-old, bickers with boys in the style of preadolescents in her community. She seems to revel in all-girl groups and professes complete apathy toward young men. In her behavior toward boys she is far "behind schedule" —immature. But the reason for this immaturity is easily understood when you know she is the eldest daughter of a sick widow with two younger daughters. After graduation, her job in the economy of the family will be to act as breadwinner until her sisters have completed school. An open interest in boys might raise serious conflict, so she has resorted to a justifiable use of denial. As a temporary expedient, her "immaturity" in relation to boys is the basis of her adjustment in the family situation. The danger to her would come if it developed into a rigid pattern of denying interest in men.

When such "immaturity" is prolonged or interferes with new advances, it may be a sign of trouble. Edgar Constantino, eight, has never learned to play well with other children. His tactics on meeting them are to push, shove, and hit, much like socially inexperienced three- and four-year-olds. We can see why he is that way when we hear that his mother nags him whenever he comes home dirty and warns him time and again to avoid contact with "bad" children. His immature attacks, therefore, represent an adjustment to his mother's standards. However, he has stayed in this phase for almost three years and is showing no signs of change. The price he is paying to preserve his adjustment to his mother's demands is becoming too great. His teacher is justly worried, and has asked that a school social worker be assigned to the case, even though Edgar is doing well in his academic work.

EVALUATION OF REGRESSION.   Sometimes children under pressures like those Edgar is under may slide back from a level of comparative maturity for their age to a lower level. They have resorted to the behavior mechanism of regression. As was pointed out in Chapter 4, some regressions are short-lived, and disappear when the problem is solved or a more effective way of coping with it is found. In evaluating the seriousness of regression, we use standards very similar to those we applied in studying the immaturities of Phyllis and Edgar.

We can expect regression to be called out by such sudden events as the birth of a sibling or a serious disappointment in school. Also, when a child enters a new phase of development, such as preadolescence, regression may happen again. Usually, the regressive behavior in such instances is confined to relatively small areas. However, when regressions appear without any reasons of the type indicated or when they endure after most children would have given them up, then we suspect deeper troubles. In general, if the childish or infantile behavior is widespread, that is, is found in many aspects of living, it demands careful attention as an indication of decidedly poor mental health. Serious regression is a sign that expert care is needed and should be obtained as speedily as possible.

NOT AN ABSOLUTE TERM. As can be seen from the foregoing considerations, maturity is not a concept implying only two extremes, maturity and immaturity. It should be thought of as occurring in degrees and as having a different range in different areas of living. We can correctly speak of a child as being fairly mature, or rather immature, or seriously immature for his age in particular areas. To pin a label on him and declare him to be "immature" without specifying the degree or area is not helpful.

Normality

The most common of all terms used in describing mental health is "normal." Three interlocking connotations make up the usual understanding of this word. On the one hand, it is employed in its primary statistical meaning and is a synonym for "typical." Thus, we will weigh a child, measure his height, and look at a chart to see if he is "normal," that is, if his weight is close to the average for his age and height. Using the term in a slightly different sense, we look at a bit of behavior and judge whether it is what we would expect. Thus, we say it is normal for a bright child to be bored in school when a class is doing work he already knows. In this meaning, "normal" is shorthand for "His behavior doesn't surprise me."

The third use of the word represents a description in terms of healthy versus sick. In this sense, when we say a child is normal we mean that even though he may be a bit unusual and some of his conduct may be somewhat surprising, we still think he is healthy.

SOCIAL AND CULTURAL DEFINITIONS. It is in the very nature of a standard that embodies norms of conduct, individual expectations, and judgments as to the significance of conduct, that it should reflect social and cultural definitions. Thus, in some neighborhoods it is normal for little children to know and use "dirty words." In most of the United States it is normal for young and old to accumulate possessions, although we know of cultures where people take greater pride in giving things away. Among the Zuñi Indians, foot "races" are a sport in which people engage without trying to find out who is fastest; but wanting to come in first is the normal goal for most American youngsters.[7]

These differences in norms are important for teachers to understand. Many educators grew up in middle-class surroundings and many came from farm- or small-community backgrounds. The conduct they naturally regard as normal is not the same as what really is normal for children used to big-city living or for those who come from rough backgrounds. Davis[8] has shown that knife fighting is not unusual among children in some groups, although the very thought is condemned in others. Equally sharp differences in "normal" behavior hold true for cleanliness, significance of schooling, reading, sex practices, and for most other spheres of living.

NORMS ARE NOT IDOLS.   Obviously, norms need not be worshiped. In fact, we will often want to change them. In a sense, one major function of mental hygiene teaching is to alter the normal in all three senses of the term. Thus, if typical students in a high school fall into a pattern of skipping school frequently and finally quit before graduation, we would not condemn as abnormal those who attended regularly and completed the course. Rather, we would want to study the reasons for the more typical pattern so that we could take appropriate measures in the hope that eventually it would be "normal" for all to make full use of the high school facilities.

We might very well find that many extracurricular activities of importance to young people carried a substantial price tag, as was revealed in one very thorough series of investigations in Illinois.[9] Yet, to many teachers that seems quite normal. However, if it is desirable to prevent school dropouts, we have to change our idea that this situation should be passed off as "normal." Instead of being complacent, we

---

[7] Very full descriptions of such socially determined norms appear in the following: Ruth Benedict, *Patterns of Culture,* Boston, Houghton Mifflin, 1934.

[8] Allison Davis and John Dollard, *Children of Bondage,* Washington, American Council on Education, 1940.

[9] Harold C. Hand, *Principal Findings of the 1947-1948 Basic Studies of the Illinois School Curriculum Program,* Springfield, Ill., 1949.

should want teachers to get to work to bring about a situation in which it becomes normal for children of all backgrounds to have a truly equal opportunity to take part in school social life.

Again, we might find that school officials did not think it a serious indication of trouble when children started to skip school. That such an attitude can exist was also the discovery of a careful bit of research.[10] It was noted that guidance facilities are too seldom employed fully when the first "minor" truancies are reported. We would want to change the current evaluation of such behavior. Instead of simply admitting it was "relatively normal," we would still want guidance systems geared to the judgment that "something should be done about it."

CONCEPT OF "NORMALITY" HAS VALUE.   Despite all that has been said, we cannot ignore the usefulness of the concept of normality in many specific cases. Whether or not a behavior pattern is either typical or unusual, expected or surprising, often gives us valuable clues concerning the future development of a child. It is a great aid in predicting how he will react to our handling of him. Thus, if most of a youngster's conduct is typical for his stage of development and his social background, the chances are he will continue to be normal for that background. We would suspect that his basic patterns would be changed most readily by altering the atmosphere or the standards of values in the groups to which he belonged.

On the other hand, if a child is highly unusual, the nature of the abnormality may be very significant. Thus, if he is a very slow learner for his group, we can safely predict he will find school very unsatisfying unless we can make provision for his differences or place him in a special class. Again, a preadolescent boy in a tough neighborhood who shows an unusual interest in reading and lacks the usual tie-up with a gang can be expected to make an increasingly poor social adjustment. This can be reduced if he is helped to find companions who have similar aspirations. However, if another youngster constantly entertains unwarranted suspicions of other people, we may decide that we are confronted by deep psychological troubles requiring special treatment.

Abnormality is a signal that the individual should be observed carefully. The crucial question is to decide what to do. In Chapter 15 we shall discuss what the indications are that a child needs special help beyond that ordinarily available in school.

---

[10] Harold J. Dillon, *Early School Leavers,* New York, National Child Labor Committee, 1948.

IT IS NORMAL TO HAVE PROBLEMS.   Sometimes, in using the word normal to mean "healthy," enthusiasts set up impossibly high standards. They use the term as a synonym for "perfect." The truly normal person is never perfect. We might wish that children experience no psychological conflicts or problems. Yet if a youngster never showed any evidence of conflict, we should wonder if his development were normal. Each stage of development brings with it problems which are typical for different environments. The critical task is to be able to recognize when the number and intensity of the individual's problems indicate he is unusually beset with conflicts or is being overwhelmed by them. It is all too easy, for example, to shrug off real disturbances by saying, "It is normal for adolescents to have problems."

Let us look at two specific cases. Helen Munlin, twelve, is a shy little girl who blushes furiously whenever she is called upon to recite. She gets so flustered she cannot be coherent. Now, it is normal for girls of her age to be shy and even to blush easily. Yet the intensity of her troubles looks suspicious. She may need extra help. Her classmate, Albert King, on the other hand, seems brash but is running into difficulties all over the place. His fighting at home is so wild he has run away twice. He also has trouble keeping friends. He cannot keep up with classwork and clowns incessantly. Of course, no one is surprised if a boy of his age has some trouble at home, has difficulty in school, or has social problems. The combination he displays, however, is too much of a disturbance. Someone should come to his rescue. For both young people, careful appraisals should be made.

NORMAL PROBLEMS NEED HANDLING.   Merely because a problem is normal is no reason for ignoring it. The fact is that one function of schools is to help children with their normal difficulties. For example, a great many high school students get tired of formal education and long to go to work. That is perfectly normal. Because it is so normal and because a poor decision may seriously injure a career, schools wisely establish guidance systems. In the process of curriculum construction, many school systems try to find out what the normal problems of children are and then try to provide a setting in which these trouble spots can be given thoughtful attention. We pointed out in the story of the Morris boy and the snakes (pages 18–19) the fact that friction between rural children and town children is typical of many consolidated schools. But this normality did not lead the Morris boy's teacher to pooh-pooh his troubles.

THE STANDARD IS THE REAL-LIFE SITUATION. Whatever the situation, we will want to judge the normality of a child's behavior by taking into account his full real-life situation. Thus, a sickly girl living alone with a very work-weary mother (because both were deserted by an irresponsible father when the child was eight) should normally have more problems and different ones from those of physically fit classmates living in congenial families. Certainly we would expect her to show some peculiar behavior. Her teachers would want to help her find patterns which were in harmony with her age level and represented a good adjustment to her life conditions.

Signs of Mental Health

Many teachers want and need a more specific list of items which can be used in making decisions about children. Later, in Chapter 15, we shall discuss signs that a child needs extra help. Here we shall list some symptoms that indicate that he is essentially in good shape. These are of special importance when we have embarked on a program of helping a boy or girl and, after sufficient time, want to know if he or she is improving.

All the cautions previously mentioned apply here. Not all the qualities to be named will be found in all children. The age and environment have to be taken into account. And any characteristic, if carried to extremes or compulsively forced, can be a sign of emotional weakness.

HAPPINESS. The child who is in good shape seems to find life enjoyable. He finds contentment in small pleasures, and is able to take joking on the part of a friendly adult or a peer-group companion. There is a delight in humor. Also, if circumstances deny him some wished-for pleasure, he is able to obtain gratification from a handy substitute. He can see in objects, people, and activities their possibilities for meeting his needs.

RANGE OF EMOTIONS. Another good sign is that a youngster can and does display the full range of emotions when appropriate. Far from being a perpetually simpering Pollyanna, he or she will show anger as well as affection, and can become afraid, worried, anxious, or guilty. The point is that the emotions are appropriate in quality and intensity to the situation. His or her actions are usually spontaneous. Often, young people toy with powerful emotions: They expose themselves to fear, as in hearing scary stories or taking "dangerous" rides in an amusement park. They play with anger by bantering insults or having playful fights.

CONTROL OVER BEHAVIOR.   Although no youngster maintains perfect self-control or always avoids doing things that will annoy some adult, the child who is in good shape does stay within reasonable limits most of the time. He is usually able to contain his excitement in most situations. He can recognize and act upon the cues given him as to what limits do exist. In doing all this, he is able to make good use of rules and routines. He responds to the customs of any group to which he belongs. When in a group he can resist being carried away by the contagion of behavior. Also, he is reasonably immune to the efforts of others to put him in a situation where he will have to take the blame for either a silly or an expected infraction of accepted rules.

SENSITIVITY TO OTHER PEOPLE.   Another sign of good mental health in children is the ability to recognize how other people feel. There is a sensitivity to gestures and signals. On those occasions in which another person has been hurt, deprived, or inconvenienced, this shows itself in an ability to make spontaneous amends. This is one aspect of a more general concern for other people.

ABILITY TO COMMUNICATE.   Mental health is indicated not only by sensitivity to other people but also by an ability to communicate with them. When help is needed, it is sought.

EFFECTIVENESS IN WORK.   That children differ in intelligence, strength, and other capacities is recognized. Within the limits set by his abilities, the emotionally healthy child does well in tasks he tackles. When he meets mild failure, he persists until he is sure whether or not he can do the job.

GOOD APPRAISAL OF REALITY.   Such a child usually has a fairly accurate picture of what is happening around him. He has a good sense of the consequences, both good and bad, that will follow his acts. In work situations, he perceives when he needs help, and it is likely to be given. He can see the difference between the "as if" and "for real" in situations. He is realistic in facing demands for control. He recognizes the price one has to pay for being part of a group.

DEALING WITH MISTAKES. All of us make mistakes. These cannot be ignored; neither are they cause for personality disorganization. The person with good mental health is helped in facing his own errors by a faith in the possibility for future correction. When the mistake touches the realm of misdeeds, that is, violations of conscience, guilt will be felt. Where mental health is strong, this guilt will be appropriate to the misdeed. A child can cope with this guilt by seeking to make amends or by resolving to do better in the future. In fact, he may be able to secure gratification from restitution.

A GOOD SELF-CONCEPT. One of the most significant clues to good inner adjustment is the self-concept, discussed at length on pages 116 to 123. In general, the better the mental health, the more positively a person feels about himself. He sees himself as approaching his ideals, as capable in meeting demands. He obtains pleasure from the mastery of his surroundings and of his own impulses. His self-confidence helps him be resourceful under stress.

ATTITUDES TOWARD THE FUTURE. Future possibilities are quite real to the healthy child. Anticipations as to later events help him to cope with present disappointments. He can savor future pleasures and have fun making plans. His dealings with people are buoyed by trust.

INDEPENDENCE. As children mature, they begin to seek independence. The child who has achieved good adjustment is not afraid to assert the degree of independence which fits his age and the realities of his circumstances.

RESILIENCE. Mental health is indicated not only by a flexible and realistic approach to tasks but by emotional resilience. The emotionally strong child can bounce back. At appropriate times he can relax. If the pressure of events pushes him into episodes of irrationality, these evaporate quickly.

We have discussed in some detail the three concepts of adjustment, maturity, and normality. These are often used in judging both the needs of individuals and the results of efforts to aid people, either alone or in groups. All three terms, unfortunately, are too often used loosely, frequently as ways of labeling things liked or disliked.

Adjustment represents the ability of an individual to live harmoniously with his environment and with himself, keeping intact his personal integrity. It means neither spineless giving in to all demands nor stiff insistence on going one's own sweet way regardless of other people. Most important, adjusting is something the individual does for himself; it is not a series of compromises into which he is coerced more or less skillfully by parents, teachers, or counselors.

Maturity is relative to age and environment. Behavior is mature when it is appropriate to the age level, the problems, and the setting of the individual. It is not a standard of perfection, but rather an index of developmental success.

Normality, as we have seen, can have three meanings. Behavior is normal when it is typical of the group, when a great many others in similar circumstances act the same way. We can also regard conduct as normal when, even though somewhat unusual, it is what we can reasonably expect from an individual under the conditions which he confronts. Lastly, in reference to the mental health of a person, we would hesitate to call any actions, thoughts, or feelings abnormal unless they indicate marked disorder. Moreover, normal problems and difficulties are as worthy of serious attention as the abnormal.

In summary, we can say that all three of these indexes to well-being have these points in common: All should be applied to behavior, not used to label or condemn human beings. All are matters of degree rather than of absolute qualities. And in using any of them, we must take full account of the total life situation.

An important word of caution must be emphasized at this point. While a judgment as to relative adjustment, maturity, or normality of behavior may have value, it can never be a substitute for a full and objective description of how a person acts. The value of the judgment depends entirely upon its use. The ultimate goal in studying any individual or group is to work out a plan through which help can be given. A confirmed classifier might get pleasure from pinning tags on a child; a truly human educator will always ask, "What can we do?"

ADDITIONAL READINGS

Cole, Luella. *Attaining Maturity*. New York: Rinehart, 1944. A book intended to help individuals reach a level of desirable conduct.

Cunningham, Ruth, and Associates. *Understanding Group Behavior of Boys and Girls*. New York: Teachers College, Columbia U., 1951, Chap. 6.

Discusses the concept of adjustment as it applies to group reactions of children to school, and the expectations of teachers.

Honigman, John J. *Culture and Personality*. New York: Harper, 1954, Chap. 11. Develops the idea that the modal personality representing a norm of behavior varies from culture to culture.

McDaniel, Henry B. *Guidance in the Modern School*. New York: Dryden Press, 1956, Chap. 10. Presents methods for assessing student interests and adjustment.

Rasey, Marie. *Toward Maturity*. New York: Hinds, Hayden, and Eldredge, 1947. A description of children's conduct written from the viewpoint of helping them grow up.

Royce, James E. *Personality and Mental Health*. Milwaukee: Bruce, 1955, Chap. 3. Gives one description, and a relevant set of signs, for normality.

Shaffer, Laurance Frederic, and Edward Joseph Shoben, Jr. *The Psychology of Adjustment*. Boston: Houghton Mifflin, 1956, Chap. 1. Analyzes the concept of adjustment.

Stone, L. Joseph, and Joseph Church. *Childhood and Adolescence*. New York: Random House, 1957, Chap. 12. Contains a useful definition of maturity.

AUDIO-VISUAL AIDS

Shyness, a 22-minute sound film produced by the National Film Board of Canada, in which the same general symptom is seen to indicate three different levels of adjustment for three specific children.

This Is Robert, a 90-minute sound film produced by Vassar College, containing many scenes comparing the behavior of preschool children.

CLASSROOM APPLICATIONS

chapter **8**

MENTAL HYGIENE AND SCHOOL LEARNING

Schools are institutions set up by society to help the young acquire the skills, knowledge, and attitudes needed in adult living. As far as children are concerned, the main business of living in school is learning in one form or another. Most expect and want to master reading, other language arts, and number skills. They enjoy making things and expressing themselves through various artistic media. They expect to acquire interesting knowledge about the world in which they live. In addition, they take delight in developing new ways of thinking and of getting along with people. Success enables them to come closer to being the kind of children they know their adults want them to be. This is a comfortable feeling.

In the mental and emotional economy of youth, learning is a central theme. Its relation to mental health is deep and pervasive. On the one hand, success in school can be and often is emotionally strengthening. For the same reason, poorly managed learning situations which create difficulties can damage a child's stability. They can build the basis for negative self-concepts.

The relationship between learning and mental health is a two-way street. Just as the school's efficiency in enabling a child to master his environment affects mental health, so a child's mental health alters his ability to learn. For some disturbed children, the result is impaired learning ability. Others, though fewer in number, may compensate for otherwise unsatisfactory living by investing an unusually high proportion of energy in school learning. In this chapter, then, we shall focus attention on so-called subject matter learning and its place in the emotional aspects of child life.

205

Learning Contributes to Mental Health

Success in any area of living can act as an emotional tonic. Damage done to a child in his home or his neighborhood may be partially repaired by satisfactory school experiences. Since school is built around learning activities, the mastery of new skills and knowledge is the focus of such pleasant experiences. Their importance, as such, should not be undervalued.

For those people who feel that the demands of mental health require that teachers become part-time psychiatrists or full-time head-patters, this fact has important meaning. If one wants to aid a child, it is not always necessary to give him a complete psychoanalysis. A teacher may give a child the affection he needs by helping him to learn. The following little scene is probably repeated in its many variations thousands of times every day:

Ned was having trouble with decimal points in a multiplication problem. From her desk, Miss Jenks noticed the frown on his face. Walking to his seat, she asked him what was wrong; Ned said he couldn't do the problem. With patient questions she helped him figure out the answer and, in doing so, to understand the rule and the reason for it. Then she gave him another problem. Later, when he had solved it, he brought the paper to her desk. All she said was, "That's right."

Such incidents have an emotional as well as an intellectual meaning. To Ned, Miss Jenks's first approach meant that when he was making mistakes, an adult did not punish him or reject him, but stood by him. The trouble she took told him that he was pretty important as a person; at least, he was worth bothering about. The fact that he was led to find the answer for himself was a way of declaring that Miss Jenks had confidence in him and that he was justified in respecting his own ability. When his second try succeeded, the point was clinched. For all its commonplace lack of drama, the whole sequence of events was really a little poem, a poem written not in words but in matter-of-fact and eloquent actions. To Ned it meant, "She likes me." That is a grand feeling to have.

When any youngster needs affection, the simplest way for teachers to administer it is not by honeyed words or sympathetic smiles, but by friendly assistance in learning. That is the idiom of schools.

For this reason, the skills of a good teacher who can help children find success in learning are as specialized as those of a psychiatrist.

Except for social status and financial reward, they are in no way inferior. Good teaching gives boys and girls a type of support which they see as meaning they are liked and which can be accepted by many youngsters who would be frightened by more direct affection.

Although it is valuable for a teacher to have personal warmth, competence is also needed. Indeed, in the classroom and other learning situations, competence in guiding children toward success in their efforts is even more necessary than friendliness. If too little competence is felt by the learners, they may perceive personal "warmth" as giving them what they do not need, as an attempt to put them off with a second-rate substitution. In the case of adolescents, their judgment as to whether a teacher is taking them seriously is often based on how much effort he puts into helping them. For this reason, the teacher who takes a blunt, let's-get-down-to-business attitude may be highly valued.

Obviously, the relationship between competence in methods of teaching and ability to show affection is a two-way affair. It is not an either-or proposition. Most fine teachers do both things well; a few poor ones, neither. Just as a teacher's skill in helping children master subject matter may provide a groundwork for mutual fondness, so children's affection for their teacher may motivate learning. We cannot afford to forget that in the case of the very young, the first learning is done to please adults they love.[1]

LEARNING BUILDS SELF-ESTEEM.   One of the universal human needs is a feeling of adequacy, of self-respect. As a child proves to himself that he can master his environment by learning how to take care of himself, he satisfies this need. He will start doing this as soon as infancy ends, as witness the insistence with which little babies try to stand by themselves and feed themselves. Success in learning performs the same function in mental health that proteins play in an adequate diet. The need for it has to be satisfied. School, in this respect, can be a major influence.

Every teacher worthy of the name has seen the clear evidence of how children act when they have solved some puzzle or overcome some block. Eyes sparkle with the excitement of triumph. Smiles of pride glow. The effects can be seen by an outside observer who notes how the youngsters stand a bit more erect and walk a little more briskly.

---

[1] For an interesting case which illustrates this point negatively, read this study: Phyllis Blanchard, "Psychoanalytic Contributions to the Problem of Reading Disabilities," *Psychoanalytic Study of the Child,* Vol. 2 (1946), pp. 179-81.

Primary children may even break into a skipping pace on the way home to tell the good news. Older children may walk with confidence, as though each "owned the whole world." All this is the mute evidence that something grand has happened. And happen it does, thousands upon thousands of times every day.

LEARNING CAN HELP YOU "BELONG." A child whose knowledge or skills are markedly below those of other children soon has problems in group relationships. For example, if all a child's friends are reading comics and the child himself cannot read at all, he is excluded from the group. In school if one child's slowness in grasping an idea holds up the whole class, that child is made to feel the impatience of the others. On the other hand, a youngster who has learned to do things his group admires is more firmly established in his social life. Teachers show their realization of this when they help an unpopular child to display suspected ability in some field they hope the group will admire. Also, when a new child in a neighborhood shows signs of learning the local juvenile mores, the group may interpret this as a good sign and take him into their ranks to complete the process he has started.

Although it is true for most young folks' groups that the child who "shows up" the others by unusual amounts of study or by concentrating on winning the teacher's approval is unpopular, this does not mean that the opposite is true, that the child who appears "stupid" is popular. By the high school level, especially in middle-class areas where children are made conscious of the future, school accomplishment may be valued. In a questionnaire which Mather[2] gave to 443 boys and 426 girls in the high schools of Ithaca, New York, and to 90 men and 108 women attending Cornell University, in which he asked them to rate a series of twenty-five traits in the opposite sex, top rating in all groups went to "real brains." In discussing this finding, Mather said:

> It might be said that in the discussion which followed the presentation of the questionnaire, the high school group brought out that they placed "real brains" first not because they admired the book-worm— they would consider a B average sufficient for real brains—but because they want to go with a person who will amount to something; and in school, grades are the measure of one's attainment of success.

As life is now lived in our world, change is part of the culture.

---

[2] William J. Mather, Jr., "The Courtship Ideals of High School Youth," *Sociology and Social Research,* Vol. 19 (1934), pp. 166-72.

Therefore, grownups as well as children have to keep learning. In school the child may not only learn how to learn but find security in knowing he can learn. If school does this job well, he will have a relish for new situations. Instead of being defeated by new situations, he will gain gratification out of his ability to size them up and his skill in learning new ways of dealing with them.

LEARNING BUILDS CONFIDENCE.   The old saying goes, "Nothing succeeds like success." After poring over reports of experiments conducted to test the importance of success to children, the professional psychologist echoes, "How true!" The results of such experiments indicate that the attainment of success causes children to set higher and more realistic goals for themselves. Teachers are familiar with pupils who are caught in a vicious circle of failing to accomplish some task because they did not try and of not trying because they were sure they would fail. They were sure because they had failed before, probably again because they did not try. Back of that series were other experiences, reaching into the past, the first so long ago it had been forgotten. That very same cycle can be made to work the other way: Knowing the taste of success gives a pupil confidence, so that he tackles future tasks energetically and carefully enough to succeed.

If a student has had enough success, he feels that "if at first you don't succeed" you should "try, try again." He has that feeling because throughout his life that is the way it has been with him; more often than not, when he has tried to learn something, he has succeeded. When a school helps a child to learn, he grows more sure of himself; as life presents him with new problems, he is a little more likely to deal with them directly rather than to resort to some evasive behavior mechanism.

The relationship between success and self-confidence is reciprocal. Although there are a few children who are frightened by achievement because it commits them to strive for levels they feel uncomfortable contemplating, most youngsters' self-confidence is given an added boost by successes, and their favorable self-evaluation helps them tackle new tasks. This is by no means a new idea. That having a high opinion of one's self was a necessary condition for the development of high goals for one's actions was pointed out by Abbadie[3] more than two hundred and fifty years ago. Evidence that there is an interconnection has piled

---

[3] Jacques Abbadie, *L'Art de se connaître Soy-Meme*, La Haye, Chez Guillaume de Voys, 1694.

up. For instance, when Turner[4] had teachers rate two groups of high school students, one whose school marks were considerably above average and the other below average, the good achievers showed superiority in self-confidence, industry, leadership, co-operativeness, perseverance, dependability, and ambition. Clearly, the possession of such qualities makes for efficient learning. The question to ask is how much the fact that a child is meeting success helps him maintain those characteristics.

Florence and George are two stock characters almost every teacher knows. Children who act like them can be found at every grade level and in every subject. In this particular instance, they are both in the same French class. Florence got off to a bad start and never managed to catch up. Now she is listless and seems to spend much time looking out the window with a faraway frown. In a talk with the school counselor she said that she guessed she was no good at languages and wondered whether she would have any chance in college. Her own verdict on herself is, "This thing has got me down." Her reply to a pep talk is cynical disbelief. George, on the other hand, is having a wonderful time. French "comes easy" to him. In talk with the other students, he denies studying extra hard; his "alibi" is, "I just got the hang of it." He is eager to continue. When a visitor came to the school, George tried to converse in French, but the speed with which the visitor talked baffled the boy. His reaction? He asked the teacher to tell him how to get conversational experience. Of course, there is a history behind each child. Their experience in French, however, has strengthened their attitudes.

Another effect of successful learning is that a child is more able to deal with certain inner tensions. Part of all learning is due to demands made by adults on children. The tensions thus created, in normal amounts, are not harmful. By meeting the demands and resolving the inner tensions, a child becomes more stable in confronting later tasks.

LEARNING AS A VICTORY OVER ADULTS.   It is natural for children to want to test their strength against grownups. Even the most kindhearted of teachers must correct children and prevent them from following impulses which, if unchecked, would cause trouble. These very necessary restrictions are nevertheless frustrating and evoke a need to assert independence.

---

[4] Austin Henry Turner, *Factors Other Than Intelligence That Affect Success in High School,* Minneapolis, University of Minnesota Press, 1930.

Learning may be one socially useful expression of this drive. At times, many classrooms assume the psychological aspect of a battleground. Under some conditions, a student who does a notable piece of work may have a feeling that he has bested the teacher. His or her friends may act as though a point was scored for their side. Teachers may be totally unaware of such interpretations, and certainly would never want to give the impression that they feel any triumph when students do poorly. Yet young people's feelings, put into words, would often run like this, "You adults think you're *so* smart. Well, we'll show you. We'll force you to admit we're pretty darned good." Some teachers are intuitively aware of this possibility and more or less deliberately use it to drain off resentments they sense in their classes.

While the thought may be a bit uncomfortable, this aspect of learning can be useful. Its value is not to be measured in terms of the school products to which it gives rise. Rather, within limits, it is a fairly good way of handling desires to display power or to establish independence. Possibly, such expression may help to develop sublimations which will keep lives healthfully and usefully in balance. Witness the admiring phrase: "He *attacked* the lesson."

Learning Difficulties Can Cause Stress

Unfortunately, many children have trouble in school. Too often, the blame rests on inadequate teaching methods and poor curriculum construction. To the mental hygienist such difficulties are significant because they can be emotionally harmful. They may be the reason why school is the principal area of maladjustment for some youngsters. Much more frequently, learning difficulties are piled on top of troubles coming from other fields. Then, the total burden may be more than a particular boy or girl can handle with ease. In any event, failure to learn damages a child's self-esteem.

A teacher who wants children to have mentally healthful experiences must be a master of instructional methods. We all know that some teachers rely on procedures which experiments have shown are relatively inefficient. Children in such classes find it much harder to learn. Even if they are given good grades on report cards, in the day-to-day life of the classroom they repeatedly experience confusion and dissatisfaction with themselves. A teacher who is ineffectual in helping children to learn is harming their mental health, no matter how wisely he can talk about psychology.

MATURATION AND LEARNING ABILITY. One of the most widespread mistakes is to introduce the teaching of subjects or skills before children's nerves or muscles are able to respond as they should. A subject does not make sense unless the learner has had a proper background of experience. The most critical point at which such conditions cause trouble is beginning reading. A vast mass of careful investigations has established beyond question the fact that a goodly number of first-graders are not ready to read. Some cannot distinguish the small differences required to recognize letters and words: *b* is mistaken for *d; h* for *n*. Other children lack the stock of concepts needed to understand what they are asked to read.

In one of the early investigations in this field, conducted in the first grade of the Big Bend Training School, at LaSalle, Colorado, Junge[5] found that low reading readiness could cause difficulties for children of both high and low intelligence. Children who were high in intelligence but low in reading readiness were not as successful in learning reading as those who were high in both. Children low in intelligence but high in readiness met more success than children low in both.

Most up-to-date school systems now make provision for this situation. Children who are not mature enough to learn to read are placed in reading-readiness classes or are given other school experiences until they can tackle printed material with some hope of success. Nevertheless, too many beginners still are pushed into reading too soon. The result is that they experience repeated failure even when trying hard to please their teachers. Their reactions to this may poison the rest of their school years. A recent study[6] of children who quit school early has established that many had trouble in the first grade. For most of them, this meant trouble in reading. Data as to their mental development warrant the assumption that many lacked reading readiness at the time.

Similar lack of readiness may handicap learning in other subjects. Children may be asked to do arithmetic before they have adequate number concepts, or to do handwriting or particular types of art work while their fingers are incapable of making fine adjustments. In the later grades, children may be expected to understand textbooks or references beyond their reading ability. In grammar, social studies, and science lessons, they may be confronted with high-order abstractions,

5 Charlotte Wilburn Junge, *A Case Study Investigation of the Progress in Reading of a Group of First Grade Children under Conditions of Student Teaching,* unpublished M.A. thesis, State University of Iowa, 1939.
6 Harold J. Dillon, *Early School Leavers,* New York, National Child Labor Committee, 1949.

such as *modifying clause,* or *sovereignty,* or *inertia,* at the very time that intelligence-test results show they cannot define or use words like *justice.* In high school literature classes, classics are often presented to young people who have had no experience with the emotions described. In many such instances, the result is bewilderment, frustration, and self-distrust.

It should be stressed that the opposite extreme also presents dangers. Some children are ready and eager to read while in the kindergarten. Some are capable of sophisticated emotional understanding quite early. To restrict their programs may be very hurtful. In the next chapter we shall say more about such unusual learners.

OTHER DIFFICULTIES.   It would be impossible to list all the obstacles to learning found in school. Children who have physical handicaps may be left without the special provisions needed to help them learn. Many a curriculum still contains a great deal of subject matter which has no functional meaning for children. Uninspired teaching permits boredom to develop. Poor class organization or inappropriate control techniques may create a situation in which a young boy or girl who does well in school may be scorned by his group.

RESULTS OF POOR LEARNING SITUATIONS.   We are concerned here with the mental hygiene implications of such poor learning situations. In extreme cases poor learning situations are visibly reflected in the form of restlessness, disorder, and fighting. Not to be able to learn when you want to is highly frustrating. To be unable to please your teachers and parents when that is your need creates tension. Continual failure punctures self-respect and leads to lethargy.

School occupies approximately one-third of a child's waking hours during weekdays. This makes it a major area in a youngster's life. When this area is full of uneasiness and distress, the effect is likely to spread. The tension arising in the classroom can create fights outside school in play groups. It may indirectly whip up new conflicts at home, as parents try to overcome a youngster's reluctance to go to school or show anxiety over poor schoolwork. Beyond this, when learning goes badly, the child misses the strengthening effects described in the previous section.

Two studies, one done in the elementary grades and one in high school, will illustrate this point. Grams[7] made a comparison of 151

---

[7] Armin Grams, *Reading and Emotion in Lutheran School Children in the Chicago Area,* unpublished Ph.D. dissertation, Northwestern University, 1952.

retarded readers and 103 advanced ones in the first six grades of the Lutheran parochial schools of Chicago. The two groups were equated on nonverbal intelligence-test scores. The poor readers earned lower scores on a test of social and self-adjustment, gave more evidence of inner conflict, and were less often chosen as friends and work companions by their classmates.

Making a comparison between the 30 girls who ranked lowest in achievement in the Central Junior High School of St. Cloud, Minnesota, and the 30 who ranked highest, Blodgett[8] found that tests indicated the girls with low achievement also had greater feelings of inferiority and less self-confidence, and compared themselves unfavorably to other people.

Emotional Disturbance Can Hinder Learning

Of course, not all learning difficulties are due to inept teachers, poor methods, or badly constructed courses of study. Often the cause lies within the child, not in the sense that he willfully refuses to learn, but rather that he has troubles that get in the way.

One index of mental health is how well the person does in the main business of living. For adults, inefficiency at work or failures in marriage and parenthood result from personality upsets. So it is with children. When a youngster is having unusual difficulty in school, out of line with his abilities, we will often find that emotional disturbances are involved. Let us look at a few ways in which this can happen.

EMOTIONAL BLOCKS. Sometimes one subject or even a single small aspect of it creates strong emotional tensions. For example, we can take the case of a boy, Peter, who was studied by Alpert.[9] Peter's mother was a strong woman with whom he had a tendency to identify. He was struggling against this tendency. In high school, he regarded French as a feminine subject, yet envied his mother's superiority in it. On his first examination paper, he consistently masculinized all feminine nouns, and failed the test.

Commenting upon children with reading difficulties studied at

---

[8] Hariett Eleanor Blodgett, *An Experimental Approach to the Measurement of Self-Evaluation among Adolescent Girls,* Ph.D. dissertation, University of Minnesota, 1953, University Microfilms Publication No. 5521.

[9] Augusta Alpert, "Sublimation and Sexualization," *Psychoanalytic Study of the Child,* Vols. 3-4 (1949), pp. 271-78.

clinics, Rabinovitch[10] noted that although in some cases the trouble could be traced to specific defects in the brain or nervous system, for a sizable group "emotional blocking, negativism, depression, or other psychological factors interfere with the child's normal potential for learning to read."

Because of the key importance of reading, the effects of emotional blocks in learning to read have been repeatedly studied in a variety of ways. In a review of thirty-four studies in this field, Smith[11] gave this summary:

> . . . the percentage of prevalence as determined by different investigators, varies. Regardless of variance, however, all studies indicate that the incidence of emotional disturbances in retarded readers is alarmingly high.

In some cases, especially in the upper grades, the student whose difficulties are of emotional origin may be recognized because he plays a limited and rather rigidly repeated role in the group. Concentrating upon this phenomenon among students who showed high resistance in a mental hygiene class, Torrance[12] listed some such roles as: negative-devaluator, playboy, dominator, special-interest pleader. In most instances, the victim of an emotional block to learning can be recognized by the fact that performance in one subject, or one area, is unaccountably below the pupil's general level of work, that material that has been "learned" and was "known" is speedily forgotten.

Ordinary measures do not work in such cases. Customary techniques of reward and punishment are ineffective; often they merely increase the emotional tension. Once the problem is recognized as emotional, however, progress may be made if the difficulty is not too deep-seated. For speech and reading, there is a large body of professional literature on techniques.

The emotional tensions may be related not to a specific subject, but to school as a whole. An example of this sort was Richard Kane (see pages 12 to 13), for whom school was synonymous with dependence upon his father. His battle for independence was partially displaced from the home to the school. He was unable to do the work

---

[10] Ralph Rabinovitch, "Our Adolescents and Their World," *English Journal*, Vol. 44 (1955), pp. 261-68.

[11] Nila Banton Smith, "Research in Reading and the Emotions," *School and Society*, Vol. 81 (1955), pp. 8-10.

[12] Paul Torrance, "The Phenomenon of Resistance in Learning," *Journal of Abnormal and Social Psychology*, Vol. 45 (1950), pp. 592-97.

one would expect from a person with his I.Q. because he wanted to be free of school, or, rather, of his father. Until the emotional reaction to his home could be changed, there was little chance of keeping him in school. Equivalent reactions, but for different reasons, can be seen at almost every grade level.

One example of the type of forces which may be at work was brought out in an experiment by Kimball,[13] who gave what is known as an incomplete-sentences test to a group of 17 adolescent boys in residence at a preparatory school, "all of whom had a high level of intelligence as measured by both individual and group intelligence tests, and all of whom were failing in their school work." To get at attitudes toward fathers, they were asked to complete sentences such as the following: "His father ......" or "When he saw his father coming ......" Aggressive reactions were tapped in sentences like these: "If anyone bothers Carl, he ......" and "When Jack really became angry, he ......" Sources of guilt were searched for in the finishing of such sentences as these: "George was sorry after he ......" and "Roger would have given anything to forget the time he ......" The replies of the 17 underachievers were compared with those given by 100 randomly selected fellow students. Negative attitudes toward fathers were displayed by 59 per cent of the underachievers as contrasted with 29 per cent for the other students. In sentences calling for dealing with an irritant, 41 per cent of the underachieving group never mentioned aggression; a similar passivity was shown by only 13 per cent of the "normal" students. Guilt feelings resulted from aggression in 47 per cent of the underachievers and in only 13 per cent of the others. Apparently the poor learning was linked to an inability to muster the type of self-assertiveness required to learn.

Even more serious is another phenomenon, called school phobia, which is more likely to be seen in the early elementary grades, but has been known to appear as late as fourteen. The child develops so great an anxiety about school that he may not be able to attend for weeks or even months or years. When such children do attend, they are quite likely to flee in terror and go straight home to join their mothers.

A summary of eight such cases treated at the Institute for Juvenile Research in Illinois[14] pointed out that usually the boy or girl concerned

---

[13] Barbara Kimball, "The Sentence-Completion Technique in a Study of Scholastic Underachievement," *Journal of Consulting Psychology,* Vol. 16 (1952), pp. 353-58.

[14] Adelaide M. Johnson, Eugene I. Falstein, S. A. Szurek, and Margaret Svensen, "School Phobia," paper presented at the 1941 meeting of the American Orthopsychiatric Association.

has acute anxiety, resulting from either physical disease or emotional conflict. At the same time, the mother is undergoing some threat to her satisfactions. If the youngster has retained an immature dependence on his mother, the combination gives rise to school phobia. This condition calls for psychiatric treatment.

EXAMINATION PANIC. In schools where great reliance is placed on examinations, some students may make a weak showing because of the effect which examinations have on them. They react with disabling emotions, not to a subject or to school as a whole, but to situations where they are expected to exhibit knowledge or skill to people in authority. When asked to take a test or to recite, their minds may go blank. The inner tension may be so great that boys or girls in the lower grades may lose control of their bladders. The authors have observed amazing symptoms among graduate students at several universities, where, rightly or wrongly, the students felt that their entire professional future hinged upon a single examination. A few may become so panicky on oral examinations that they give incoherent answers, because their brains do not catch the meaning of even simple questions.

Recently this matter has become the subject of careful investigation, notably by Sarason and his co-workers at Yale University, who have developed an instrument designed to measure "test anxiety."[15] Because of the importance of the examinations given at about age eleven in determining the educational future of British boys and girls, the breakdown of children at examinations, known there as "flapping," has also received attention in England. Henn[16] found that in some instances youngsters appeared to suffer mental blackouts. He held the condition to be due to overanxiety, arising either from poor parent-child relationship, with emphasis upon product, so that the examination was a crisis in the child's upward mobility, or else from infantilism, resulting from a "determined and possessive mother, a sheltered existence."

In milder cases it would appear that the form of an examination may affect the amount of anxiety generated. In an evaluation of psychology courses at the University of Michigan, McKeachie[17] gave an

---

[15] Seymour B. Sarason, Kenneth S. Davidson, Frederick F. Lighthall, and R. R. Waite, "A Test Anxiety Scale for Children," *Child Development,* Vol. 29 (1958), pp. 105-13.

[16] T. R. Henn, "The Causes of Failure in Examinations," *British Medical Journal,* Vol. 2 (1951), pp. 461-71.

[17] Wilbert J. McKeachie, "Anxiety in the College Classroom," *Papers of the Michigan Academy of Science, Arts, and Letters,* Vol. 36 (1950), pp. 343-49.

objective-type examination. Some groups were given special answer sheets on which they were encouraged to explain their replies; others, as was customary, merely recorded their answers. Being allowed to give reasons for answers was reassuring to students and tended to drain off their anxiety. The result was that they secured higher scores, even though only the objective answers were scored. There is no reason to believe that similar effects would not occur at the high school or elementary school level.

When a victim of examination panic, old or young, tries to describe how he felt, it sounds as though he were concocting a very feeble excuse. However, the condition is a very real one and far from uncommon, especially in less extreme forms. The cause may be difficult to trace, as it often goes back to early family situations. However, giving the student other ways to show mastery of a subject is a minimum humane measure. Consistent kindliness by teachers may help some victims to overcome this problem.

GENERAL ANXIETY. The upbringing of many children has been so full of scoldings and ridicule that they are terrified of making mistakes. Others have had to meet such high standards that they are sure anything they do will be wrong. For even deeper psychological reasons, others suffer from "free-floating anxiety"—which has been described as feeling like "an accident looking for some place to happen." Many children of course have such feelings in much milder form.

For some youngsters, fear of ridicule may interfere with learning. These fears distract them to the point where they cannot devote full attention to ordinary school activities. A few may be so fearful of making mistakes that, to play safe, they do little or nothing. To an outside observer they may seem lazy.

Ira was such a boy. At first, teachers thought that he might have some illness that sapped his energy. He had a peculiar inability to complete any task. However, only a passing glance at the playground showed that there he was a little powerhouse. The contrast was so great that they decided he was willfully lazy. His mother offered little help; her story was that he was the same way at home. There, he never seemed to get anything right. She claimed that she and his father did all they could to give the boy high standards. The wording of her summary was revealing: "His father is at him all the time, and I'm even worse." Inasmuch as nagging and punishment had not worked at home, obviously the school should try another tack.

A clue was supplied when a student teacher was asked to watch Ira closely. She reported that he started tasks, but either destroyed his work or left it undone. Following this lead, his regular teacher waited until he was halfway through a lesson, then walked over and looked at his paper. He glanced up with the look of a dog expecting to be beaten. She said, "You have the idea," smiled, and went to another pupil. With variations, she repeated the same performance. Ira improved a little. He began to finish some tasks and take them to the teacher for approval. It was plain to see, though, that he was still very unsure of himself. His teacher was afraid to be critical when his work was faulty lest he be frightened back into his old defense. That was not a healthy situation, but a start had been made toward correcting Ira's trouble.

A high level of anxiety can have milder and more specific effects on school performance than the apparent "laziness" described above. It can and often does alter the level of aspiration, the quality of achievement for which a child strives. For instance, Gruen[18] chose the thirty-two students from the seventh and eighth grades of the University High School in Iowa City who had very high or very low scores on a personality-adjustment test. It can be assumed that those showing poor adjustment had more anxiety. She had them work on a shorthand task and tell her what they expected to do. The well-adjusted tended to set goals slightly higher than their performance. When they reached a goal, all of them raised their estimates for the next trial. The poorly adjusted were more likely to set estimates out of harmony with their ability. Some, apparently in order to protect themselves from failure and to satisfy a greater need for success, set goals much lower than their ability. Even when they did better than their estimates, 15 per cent did not change their level, and 7 per cent actually dropped it.

Another sign of general anxiety that may show up in the classroom is that a child may do very well in tasks requiring rote memory, but poorly in problem-solving tasks which put a premium on mental flexibility. In an intensive study of a small social science class of eleven at the University of Chicago, Gaier[19] discovered that in general the more anxious students had a lower performance, except for rote memory work. They spent a great deal of time thinking about themselves in negative terms.

---

[18] Emily H. Gruen, "Level of Aspiration in Relation to Personality Factors in Adolescents," *Child Development,* Vol. 16 (1945), pp. 181-88.

[19] Eugene L. Gaier, "Selected Personality Variables and the Learning Process," *Psychological Monographs,* Vol. 66, No. 349 (1952).

In a series of experiments anxiety has been deliberately induced in students, and their mental flexibility measured, by the so-called water-jar problems. In these, people are asked how they would measure exact volumes of water by pouring from one jar to another. At first the problems require four or five transfers. Later in the series, there are problems which can be solved with only one transfer as well as with the more complex pattern. Presumably the more flexibly minded person can mentally shift gears. In one experiment Cowen[20] induced anxiety by calling students back for further testing after they had taken a previous test and been told that the test would be evaluated by a board of clinicians and that those with questionable records would be called back. In a more elaborate effort to create anxiety, Harris[21] treated one group with disdain, gave them unsolvable tasks to perform, and told them that a "personality questionnaire" showed they had "strong, unconscious neurotic tendencies." Both Cowen and Harris compared the groups under stress with other groups not so treated to find out how they did on the water-jar problems. As might have been expected, anxiety reduced the mental adaptability and flexibility in both cases.

If the findings of the research cited in this section hold true generally, we would expect that youngsters who are very anxious would tend to be more hesitant in tackling tasks, would give an uneven performance, and would do poorly in work requiring mental agility. Since the cause of a high level of anxiety often is the strictness young people experienced early in life, additional severity is merely another dose of the poison that ruined their emotional health. A relaxed attitude on the part of a teacher may help the light cases. Where the anxiety is strong and persistent, treatment by specially trained workers is necessary for genuine change.

SIBLING RIVALRIES. The effects of rivalries between children from the same home may disrupt school work. Easiest to see are those examples in which a child whose older brother or sister had a highly praised school record develops a distaste for the field of the other's triumph. Unthinking parents and friends tell him too often about his elder's successes. The more he hears about it, the more antipathy he

[20] Emory L. Cowen, "Stress Reduction and Problem-Solving Rigidity," *Journal of Consulting Psychology*, Vol. 16 (1952), pp. 425-28.
[21] Robert A. Harris, *The Effects of Stress on Rigidity of Mental Set in Problem Solution*, unpublished Ph.D. dissertation, Harvard University, 1950.

develops. Escape into truancy or into other types of compensatory behavior is the finale to some such stories.

Older siblings, also, may bring their problems into the classroom. The jealousy they originally felt toward their brothers and sisters may be displaced to other children. The hostility they dare not acknowledge toward siblings may be projected upon classmates. In either event, the class group for them arouses unpleasant emotions. Their bids for praise and their suspicions distort lessons based on group discussion. For those whose difficulties are mild, a teacher's policy of fairness and of not having favorites may lower the emotional tensions.

Josephine's trouble was complicated by the fact that her tactics made her unpopular. Her social science class was so conducted that reports to the class by students were a very important feature. In the expressive slang of classmates, she was a "sharpshooter." She would listen intently, and then pounce on any imperfection. Often she asked pointedly disapproving questions. In a number of instances, it was apparent that she had distorted the meaning of what had been said. At first the teacher thought Josephine was trying to be unfair, and was deliberately using the old trick of quoting sentences or phrases out of context. Several times he broke into discussions to remind the class of exactly what the other student had said. When doing so, he curbed his irritation and emphasized pleasantly that Josephine might have honestly misunderstood.

A dramatic climax came when she made a report. Several students were obviously baiting her. When they were unfair, the teacher came to her defense, just as he had for her victims. Two days later she unexpectedly came to him and thanked him. Then she asked if she had seemed nasty. He replied that probably she had not meant to be, but she certainly had been one-sided in her attitude. She said that maybe that was why she was unpopular, and then added that she would try to act differently. When he said he would help her, she gave him a little grin. Her "Thank you" sounded sincere.

RELATIONSHIPS TO TEACHERS.   Emotional forces centering around teachers may also block learning. A teacher who is too easygoing and gives youngsters too little guidance may leave them feeling so uneasy and resentful that they cannot learn. In the same way, arbitrary and unfair discipline may arouse so strong a rage that pupils, instead of studying, will daydream endlessly about getting even or will take out their feelings in destructive attacks on each other. Some will take revenge on a hated teacher by refusing to learn. When youngsters who have had good records fail to learn, their poor showing has in it an element of revenge. After all, if only one teacher fails to teach a child who, everyone knows, learns easily, the plain implication is that the teacher is incompetent. In fact, just such evidence has been the last straw which convinced a hesitating administrator to take action against an unpopular faculty member.

The emotional teacher-pupil relationships which impede learning may affect only a few individuals. Even the best of teachers run across an occasional pupil with whom it is hard to get along. A few children who ordinarily do well in school may have trouble in a classroom which suits all the rest. Where it is at all feasible, the solution for such difficulties is to transfer the child to another group.

FRUSTRATIONS DUE TO PHYSICAL CONDITIONS. When children want to learn and physical conditions interfere, the result is a feeling of frustration. This may spread and cause a general "What's the use?" attitude which will forestall even such learning as the situation could permit. Badly overcrowded classrooms, lack of supplies, inadequate books, and bad lighting conditions may give young people an idea that they are being discriminated against, that they do not count. It is true that a few teachers may do a superb job of building a morale that will overcome such obstacles. By and large, however, many become dis-

TABLE 5   *Problems About School Checked by Chapel Hill Students*

	PERCENTAGE WHO CHECKED			
	Grade 9		Grade 12	
PROBLEM	Boys	Girls	Boys	Girls
I have difficulty keeping my mind on my studies	47	66	58	60
I have difficulty expressing myself in words	23	57	33	54
I wish I knew how to study better	33	61	54	49
I wish I could be more calm when I recite in class	40	68	29	60
I have difficulty keeping my mind on what goes on in class	33	48	38	46

pirited. Their lethargy can rapidly infect the children. The best-known antidote is for community leaders, administrators, or teachers to put on an energetic campaign to improve conditions. This evidence that the children are regarded as important, especially if results can be shown, may energize all concerned.

DISTRACTIONS. Just as friction with a teacher or bad physical conditions may distract children from learning, so do other conditions. During adolescence, for example, boys' eyes may be irresistibly drawn from their work if a woman teacher or a girl classmate wears clothing which is too revealing or is otherwise provocative.

The extent to which distraction is a problem felt by students is indicated in Table 5, which summarizes replies concerning school on the SRA Youth Inventory obtained by McDougall[22] from 279 pupils in the Chapel Hill High School, North Carolina.

In some cases, the source of distraction lies in the personal life or the private inner world of a young person. For instance, Berge[23] described an intelligent young girl of nine who began to detach herself more and more from what was being done in class. Her teacher noted that she seemed absorbed by internal preoccupations. It turned out that her mother had recently given birth to a baby brother. In connection with this event, some well-intentioned person had made the mistake of stressing too much the pain and danger of childbirth. Once the source of her secret torment was discovered and she had been reassured, her work in class improved.

When any child's scholastic life is hampered by preoccupations, which often are typified by daydreaming, it may be wise to seek the cause. In many cases it will be found within the classroom. In even more, sympathetic counseling will be needed to uncover the source.

POOR TIMING OF LEARNING ACTIVITIES. At times in the development of a child, a particular area may be highly charged with threats of conflict. If, at this time, instruction is attempted which involves the touchy spot, the youngster fends off the possible emotional consequences by developing lack of interest, by concentrating on other things, by acting silly, or by using other defense mechanisms. The topics or the

---

22 Cherie Janice McDougall, *A Study of the Problem Areas of the Students of Chapel Hill High School, Chapel Hill, North Carolina,* unpublished M.A.E. thesis, University of North Carolina, 1950.
23 André Berge, *Les Défauts de l'Enfant,* Paris, Aubier, 1953.

activities that create this reaction cannot easily be predicted in advance. Sometimes a whole group has been misjudged, as happened in the discussion of dating in Miss Devers' class, described on pages 11 to 12. Once in a while, the timing may be appropriate for most people, but poor for one or two.

A revelation concerning just such a situation was made by a group of teachers in reporting an interesting study to the 1950 annual convention of the American Psychiatric Association. In their schools at Grosse Pointe, Michigan, they had arranged to include a forty-five-minute period of free activities in the school day. In one particular class, efforts at group dramatic production had been disrupted by sabotage from a few boys. During the free-play period, two went off to a corner by themselves to play backgammon. As this continued day after day, their teacher realized that for some reason they lacked the social maturity to work well with a larger group. Fortified in her actions by the agreement of a very experienced worker with children, she let them continue this apparently unproductive pattern. Eventually the two were satiated by the game and did gain social confidence from their success with each other. They finally turned back to work with the rest of the group. Apparently the early dramatic activity came before they were ready for that type of group program; once they had achieved sufficient "social maturity," they could profit from it.

The appearance of apathy or other resistance to one portion of the curriculum is a sign of timing difficulty. It is usually wise strategy to back away from the troubled area and to approach it later when the individual or the group is emotionally better prepared. In a few cases, the touchy topic may need to be scheduled at a lower grade, where it can be taken up before emotions are too heavily involved. For instance, in some areas, social dancing can be introduced more easily at the fourth grade than in a class of preadolescents.

School Learning That Involves Maladjustment

Although most success in mastering skills and subject matter is a good thing, there are times when unusual achievement may be a source of difficulty for a child. Then, too, there are youngsters who concentrate energy on school tasks because of some maladjustment. Elsewhere in this book we have dealt with two behavior mechanisms (pages 71 to 72) which can have that effect. Young people who are having an unsatisfactory time in other areas of living may try to compensate by turning to schoolwork. Also, where a person has severe conflicts, he may try to escape them by spending an undue proportion of time and energy on work; for children that means school studies. Using school as a scene for displacement or as an escape from other problems may sometimes be the very way a youngster saves himself from more serious difficulties. When this tendency assumes undue intensity, however, something is wrong. The desirability of the school effort should not blind us to the fact that its pathological use constitutes a problem with which the child needs help. Other situations involving similar issues are described below.

DEPENDENCE ON ADULTS.   Most young people sooner or later become able to stand on their own two feet; they can make up their own minds. This trait may show itself in deciding that other activities are more interesting or more important than school. The opinions of their friends are as valuable to them as are those of their teachers.

But a few young people may be unable to achieve independence. For one reason or another, they must cling to adults. Perhaps in babyhood they lacked security in the affection of their parents. Whenever they were naughty, they lost that love, and now, later in life, they must ingratiate themselves with older persons in order to feel safe. Perhaps they were overprotected to the point where the only emotional satisfaction they dare indulge is that of being cared for by some adult.

Whatever the cause, the most important thing for them in school is to win and hold the favor of the teachers. To do so, they seek to please by performing as their instructors wish. In a sense, each bit of good work they do is a gift, or, more accurately, a bribe. Their actions carry this meaning, "See, I've done what you wanted; I've proved that your wish is my command. Now, reward me by taking me under your wing. Lift me to joy by saying you like me."

We recognize that such dependence is not a healthy personality trait in adults. Alexander and Healy[24] found it an important element in certain types of reckless stealing. On a more respectable basis, it may make people into clinging vines, unable to bear responsibility, or into compliant tools of unscrupulous "strong men." In their search for affection, these people will readily give obedience to rules and regulations without questioning.

When a boy or girl shows signs of being unusually anxious to

[24] Franz Alexander and William Healy, *Roots of Crime*, New York, Knopf, 1935.

please, we should realize we have a delicate problem on our hands. For example, if a high school girl must bring her work to almost all teachers several times for approval, or if we notice an unusual and often repeated air of strain on an adolescent's face when we are looking at his work, we might well search for further evidence of dependent attitudes. To help young people outgrow such qualities is not easy. The tactic that first comes to mind is to push them away from us and force them to act on their own judgment. This is often the worst thing to do, since they may interpret it as a rejection and merely redouble the intensity with which they yearn for approval. A more helpful course is to comply with whatever reasonable demands they may make and to show confidence in their ability to decide for themselves. If we ourselves exhibit pride in our own confidence to make decisions and to judge by our own standards, the mechanism of identification may come into play.

COMPULSIVE CONFORMISM.   By contrast, there are children whose unusual schoolwork and good conduct are inspired largely by fear. The very thought of doing any wrong or of falling below expectations arouses anxiety. As a defense against this anxiety, they must follow the letter of almost every rule, and must come as close to perfection in their work as possible. They only feel comfortable when they can find out what people expect them to do and then conform to the desired conduct. For them, rules of conduct and standards of performance are not guides to action but dictates which it is wicked to disregard. Such a personality quality is quite likely to result from child-raising methods which place reliance on fear.

There have been times in the past when this trait was highly desired, and there are some occupations today which place a premium upon it. An employer may praise it in a file clerk, an auditor, a draftsman, or a night watchman. However, the expressions "dead hand of bureaucracy" and "red-tape artists" reflect the realization that this quality kills that ability to deal effectively with new situations which is so important in a world that changes as rapidly as ours does.

Many children owe their unusually fine school performance to this unrelenting urge to conform. Knowing what is expected of them, they simply have to comply. They are quite likely to show great fear of making mistakes or to grow restless and uneasy when not told exactly what to do. A young person who acts in this way is just as unhealthy, psychologically speaking, as the one who dares not do good work for fear his gang will be down on him. The case of Karl, the unhappy prodigy, described on pages 9 to 10, contains many elements of this pattern.

Compulsive conformism may be so deeply ingrained that only a highly skilled specialist can help a child correct the difficulty. In milder cases, the classroom situation may do good. Where class control is achieved without resort to fear-inspiring techniques, young people may gradually realize that they can control their own impulses without leaning too heavily on rules.

CONCEIT. Unusual success in schoolwork, whether it is a result of emotional troubles or sheer natural ability, has some dangers for a growing person. This does not mean that we should disapprove of scholastic success or try to force our classes to a dead level of mediocrity. Rather, we should watch the unusually successful pupils and be ready to help them with the problems which may arise. One problem, for example, is the matter of social adjustment as they encounter the jealousy of other youngsters and the antischool standards of their peer group.

A particularly prevalent peril is the development of conceit. Unusual success may make some children unduly proud of themselves. They may try to hog glory or act irritatingly cocky. This cockiness not only leads to social difficulties but may tempt the victim into becoming quite self-centered. This childish trait may not be dropped but may remain in preadolescence, adolescence, and adulthood as a disturbing element of the personality structure.

However, if the very able youngster can be helped to experience the satisfaction of contributing to a group and of sharing the pleasure of a good group performance, he may learn valuable lessons. To isolate him from other children by ridicule will increase his tendency to cling to self-admiration.

This matter, and a number of related issues, will be discussed in greater detail in that section of the next chapter devoted to gifted children.

OVERLEARNING AS A SOURCE OF DIFFICULTY. Sometimes we are so impressed with a particularly fine performance in some aspect of school work that unwittingly we lead a child to practice it too often. We may tempt him to become a specialist. This may teach him to expect satisfaction from a field of endeavor for which he is not really fitted. Many a blighted career may develop.

For example, Elsie was a whiz in arithmetic. She could arrive at correct answers very rapidly. The praise this earned led her to devote more time to what used to be called mental arithmetic. She was asked to perform for visitors to the school and at a parent-teacher meeting gave a demonstration before a large audience, who applauded when she multiplied example after example of two three-place numbers in her head. She did well in other subjects but was far superior in arithmetic. By sixteen, all her friends were bored with her attempts to capture acclaim at parties; she had a hard time realizing that her forte was not a social asset. She set out to learn bookkeeping and accounting, only to find that most businesses required very simple arithmetic or else used calculating machines. The detailed work of bookkeeping was a drudgery so distasteful that she married a young man she didn't like in order to escape.

Elsie's case is an extreme illustration. However, in less glaring ways many children overlearn aspects of schoolwork in which they succeed. They would be better off if they were helped to be well rounded, and to taste satisfaction in a wide range of activities. To aid them, teachers should see that they get a tempting taste of success in several different areas. Then, they will *want* to branch out.

In trying to turn teachers' attention to the importance of youngsters' needs, some educators stress the slogan, "We teach children, not subjects." The burden of this chapter is that mastery of subjects is a very significant aspect of every child's life. We cannot teach a child without helping him to acquire knowledge and skills. We can understand children better by observing how they go about the business of learning; and when we guide them to success in schoolwork, we aid them in satisfying needs in a way which generally adds to their mental health. The truth is that schools teach *both* children *and* subjects. More accurately, subject matter is used to teach children. Neither aspect of education can be divorced from the other.

True, the emphasis and attention must always be upon the children. The subjects are a means, the medium peculiarly expected of the school. By thinking of how best to employ that medium, we advance toward our primary goal of strengthening the children.

The very core of good mental hygiene in schools is the way in which learning activities are guided. Teachers express their affection for children by aiding them to cope with the materials of schoolwork. The art of using school situations to improve mental well-being is centered in the realization that through mastering their environment, children gain freedom to develop with a minimum of distortion. In school, that environment is under professional control. Teachers can so arrange matters that the school environment is simple enough to be mastered. Thus, youngsters may gain in confidence. The successes may strengthen their ability to deal later with more complicated conditions. To that extent, they are more likely to retain emotional stability.

ADDITIONAL READINGS

Bernard, Harold W. *Mental Hygiene for Classroom Teachers*. New York: McGraw-Hill, 1952, Chap. 9. Considers the relationship between teaching methods and pupil adjustment.

Buhler, Charlotte, Faith Smitter, and Sybil Richardson. *Childhood Problems and the Teacher*. New York: Holt, 1952, Chap. 5. Describes the role of home and school in children's lives.

Burton, William H. *The Guidance of Learning Activities*. New York: Appleton-Century-Crofts, 1944. A very thoughtful presentation of the value of instructional methods.

Ephron, Beulah Kanter. *Emotional Difficulties in Reading*. New York: Julian Press, 1953, Chaps. 2 and 3. Prints records of interviews with children having reading difficulties.

Martin, William E., and Celia Burns Stendler. *Child Behavior and Development*. New York: Harcourt, Brace, 1959, Chap. 11. The part played by school in the socialization of children is touched upon.

Morse, William C., and G. Max Wingo. *Psychology and Teaching*. Chicago: Scott, Foresman, 1955, Chaps. 10 and 11. Deals with readiness for learning and the role of teaching.

Olson, Willard C. *Child Development*. Boston: Heath, 1949, Chap. 6. Forcefully presents the facts showing how, in such subjects as reading, individual maturity patterns must set the pace for schooling.

Pressey, Sidney L., and Francis P. Robinson. *Psychology and the New Education*. New York: Harper, 1944. A text in educational psychology highlighting the purposes of learners.

Robinson, Helen M. *Why Pupils Fail in Reading*. Chicago: U. of Chicago Press, 1946. A well-rounded treatment of sources of difficulty in learning this key school subject.

Stone, L. Joseph, and Joseph Church. *Childhood and Adolescence*. New York: Random House, 1957, Chap. 9. The years of childhood are described, with emphasis upon the meaning of school learning.

AUDIO-VISUAL AIDS

Good Speech for Gary, a 15-minute sound film produced by the University of Southern California, in which the effect of speech improvement on one boy is illustrated.

Learning to Understand Children, a 44-minute sound film produced by

McGraw-Hill, in which a teacher is shown finding out how to help a child.

Problem of Pupil Adjustment—The Stay-In, an 18-minute sound film produced by McGraw-Hill, in which a high school program built around student needs is described.

They All Learn to Read, a 25-minute sound film produced by Syracuse University, in which a teacher is shown organizing a classroom around individual differences in reading ability.

chapter **9**

UNUSUAL LEARNERS

As he begins to work with any class, every teacher quickly becomes aware of the range of individual differences within the group. Almost always there are a few poor learners whose need for special help may put a strain on the teacher and the group. Now and then, at the opposite extreme, is a gifted child who so outdistances the rest of the class that ordinary devices are ineffective.

In this chapter, we plan to examine the situations which such children create. We give attention first to the poor learners, the children whose difficulties perturb conscientious teachers. Then we shift our interest to the brilliant young folks concerning whom so much is now being written.

Some Basic Considerations About Poor Learners

In the educational field we confront today two extreme positions on the relationship between mental health and learning difficulties. These grow out of the recognition that emotional problems and trouble in learning are so frequently found together. The question is from which side to tackle them. One group would "solve" the emotional concomitants by manipulating educational methods and giving the child more aid in the learning process itself. The other seems to assume that if—and only if—the emotional atmosphere surrounding learning and the child's inner conflicts can be dealt with, the learning difficulties will dutifully evaporate.

It would be wonderful if life and teaching were simple enough for

231

either solution to work, but the fact is that by the time a learning difficulty becomes obvious, there has been so much interaction between the two factors that each has become a "cause" of the other and in turn has been "caused" by the other. At what point the vicious circle got started may not be easy to determine.

Fortunately, the classroom teacher often comes into the picture at the point where the predominance of one factor or the other may still be clearly visible. Moreover, the fact that the classroom teacher has control over and can vary both educational procedures and teaching atmosphere, at least while he is present, may permit a dual attack on the problem, and therefore can be of great preventive value.

To illustrate, here are examples of extreme situations: Almost everyone who has watched children in school has seen cases where, for instance, a boy or girl is having difficulty with long division. As he tries to cope with his inability to understand, he becomes panicky. His parents, seeing "bad" papers from school, begin to worry about him. He seems to be losing confidence in himself. If a psychological snapshot could be taken at this point, the picture would show a highly disturbed child whose anxiety about, or obstinate avoidance of, long division seems positively neurotic.

In such cases, it will now and then happen that the teacher hits upon a way of explaining the arithmetic process to the child which clears things up. So to speak, the child suddenly "gets the point." Now that he can do long division, the concomitants of his temporary failure go away.

By contrast, almost every teacher has also seen a child who seemingly "understands," but when it comes to solving a problem on the board, unexpectedly "forgets" everything the teacher knows he "knew." A glance at the child makes it clear he is tense and unhappy. Consciously he would say he was "trying"; clearly some inner block is disrupting his performance. Since the teacher's explanations of arithmetic processes have registered intellectually, the problem here is not one of trying to find a clearer method of teaching. Nor will the problem be solved if the teacher just acts calm and patient—behavior he may have found successful in so many other similar-looking cases. If this is a case of a true anxiety neurosis, there is no solution short of the type of specific therapy designed for that emotional disorder.

In most cases, however, the picture is much more blurred. For instance, even where the difficulty is primarily educational, the emotional products of failure may have acquired enough force so that they have to be dealt with in their own right. On the other hand, even where the emotional difficulties have been basic, their operation may have produced a deficit in knowledge and skill which will have to be taken care of by primarily educational methods, even while special therapy is working at the reduction of the emotional blocks. The two factors often have to be dealt with simultaneously rather than in succession.

Obviously, it is not the teacher's function to tackle the elimination of a child's neurosis, where there is one. The function of the teacher is both to provide educational skill and to create an emotionally supportive learning climate. This involves giving both individual help to the child and effective leadership to the class as a group. In this chapter we shall deal with the first of these functions; in Chapter 10 we shall begin the discussion of the equally important group forces.

In the first part of this chapter, we attempt to indicate some procedures for sizing up situations involving poor learners. We shall deal first with the ways in which teachers react to such students and with some typical evasive tactics which teachers may follow. Then, we shall discuss some of the clues on the basis of which working judgments have to be made. Possibilities for action will then be outlined. Throughout, we shall be thinking in terms of what can be done by the classroom teacher, rather than the function of remedial teachers, counselors, or therapists.

Teachers' Reactions to Slow Learners

Some of the feelings aroused in dealing with slow learners are disturbing; others may get in the way of success. There is no standard set of emotions felt by all teachers, but there are some which appear often enough to be worth discussing.

HELPLESSNESS. Most learning difficulties are very stubborn; they do not yield easily, whatever the treatment. If a child has a low intelligence, the chances are it will not change very much. If his troubles arise from emotional blockings of some sort, these take specialized treatment to remove. In fact, among highly trained child therapists, treatment for learning difficulties is considered a task which calls upon all their resources.

Teachers have all had courses in the psychology of learning and in methods of instruction. Ability to help children learn is the core attribute of an educator. Consequently, every child who does not learn is a challenge, if not a rebuke.

Yet if the sources of the child's troubles are not accessible, if we cannot get at them directly, the process of helping him is very likely to be unsatisfactory. Even when we make progress, it may be painfully, if not invisibly, slow. Moreover, there are bound to be setbacks.

All this can be highly frustrating. Indeed, the more conscientious the teacher, the greater the probable blow to his ego. It is all too easy to succumb to feelings of helplessness, to forget that a problem exists, to want to stop trying. In some cases, where a teacher has run through his entire string of remedies, he cannot be blamed for this despair. Just as doctors see incurably ill patients and engineers are confronted with impossible problems, so teachers must expect to be asked to work with children whose learning difficulties may not yield to now-known knowledge.

CHALLENGE TO OUR ABILITY. For the very reasons outlined above, success in helping a child with whom others have failed is a professional triumph, an event calling for self-congratulation if no other reward. Many teachers, when they find in their classes a notoriously slow learner, get to work with zealous energy. They sense an opportunity to demonstrate their prowess. They recognize that here is a chance to win status as a skillful practitioner of the teaching arts. Often when a teacher starts to help a youngster known to be "difficult," he or she has daydreams of finding the "key to the trouble" and making great leaps of progress. Thus, the teachers' own self-esteem becomes heavily involved with the progress of a child.

HOSTILITY. If the proud hopes described above are thwarted, if the child's troubles do not yield, the teacher is frustrated. This is not a minor setback; it can be a severe blow to the teacher's self-esteem. This is precisely the type of situation which creates hostility. The child who cannot be helped quickly, whose stubborn difficulties prevent the teacher from reaching a goal of professional triumph, may seem to be willfully ungrateful. At the very least, he is an obstacle in the path, and, as such, arouses aggressive feelings. At worst, he seems to be an enemy who is deliberately refusing to learn and his actions, obviously conceived in malice, deserve punishment.

Feelings of this type are not unusual. In fact, they will be felt by the very best teachers. The failure of a child to learn is most disturbing to those people who take their professional obligations most seriously, who have gone to the greatest pains to improve their skills, and who devote most of their energies to helping children.

TYPICAL EVASIVE TACTICS.   In the situation created by the reactions sketched above, many teachers are inclined to grasp at "solutions" which really solve nothing. A few of the most common ones are very briefly described below.

One attractive possibility is to find someone else to blame for the child's difficulties. Traditionally, when faced by youngsters who do not learn readily, college professors find fault with high school teaching; high school teachers detect weaknesses in elementary schools; the teachers in the upper elementary grades cast doubt upon those in the primary grades, who can always point to parental failings. In addition, it is tempting to conclude that the youngster does not belong in one's class at all. In that case, the difficulty can be dealt with by collecting evidence to back up a request for a different placement.

Another seductive evasion of the problem is to react with pity for poor bedeviled youngsters. There is here an implication that, by feeling sorry, one has discharged his obligations.

An opposite tactic is to become preoccupied with the learning problem itself. The child is no longer seen in his entirety. Indeed, some of the other children fade in one's recollections. Sometimes in describing the situation, a teacher will say not, "I have a boy [or girl] who . . .," but, "I have a poor reader. . . ." The result of such overfocusing on the one trouble intensifies the disappointment if it cannot be eliminated, and causes the teacher's dissatisfaction to spread to almost all of teaching, and perhaps the other aspects of life.

In working with a youngster with this sort of problem there is always a probability that the method used at first will yield inadequate results. Now, what to do? If a medicine has not worked, the thought will emerge that perhaps the dose should be doubled and then redoubled, and the time prolonged. If a favorite trick does not work, then we must hunt for a new magical formula. Often the end finds us trying everything in the book without giving any plan a chance.

Who can blame a teacher for wanting to turn his or her back on the problem? There are several ways to do this. One is to become angry with the child and, as a punishment, refer his case to someone else. Another is to decide that all the child wants is attention and that he should be punished by giving him none whatsoever. Although punitiveness is part of the picture in the two last-cited tactics, this does not have to be the case. It is equally possible to decide that the child is being made unhappy by his troubles in learning and therefore that, to provide a respite, everyone should make believe there is no problem. In other cases, it is discovered that the youngster has a problem in addition to his learning difficulties, and we can focus on that one. An attractive variant of the above procedure is to make use of a device which can indeed be a good one for some children: to decide that the other children can help him more than an adult and then delegate the teaching function to a bright classmate or the class as a whole.

If the possibilities being described seem cowardly or unworthy of a professional, we must hasten to point out that they do provide protection against personal self-devaluation. For many teachers, there is no possibility of gaining satisfaction from having done one's best but rather worry and chagrin when one's best does not seem to be good enough. At this point many adults become so deeply disappointed in themselves that the one area in which they feel incompetent looms so large that they may lose their sense of proportion in teaching.

The Realistic Possibilities

An important first step in dealing with poor learners is to recognize emotionally as well as intellectually that many learning difficulties are just that—*difficulties.* In some cases, the reasons a child learns slowly are linked to low mental ability of the kind for which at the present time there is no known effective corrective program. In other instances, for example in the event of emotional blockings, change is possible but is usually very slow. These situations may seem in annoying contrast to those cases where a specific difficulty disappeared almost overnight after a simple explanation or a little practice. Much as we might wish for it, there is no magic.

In dealing with the relatively stubborn situations, a teacher can make use of three major approaches. The first strategy is to develop a program of effective help. If this does not work out well, it may be wise to refer the child for specialized help. Even when this is done, there will be need for a third approach, which we shall call "supportive survival." This means that while the child remains in the classroom, even though we cannot work effectively on his problem, we can make conditions as pleasant and profitable as possible for him, for us, and for his classmates.

Effective Help

No attempt will be made here to set forth the detailed techniques of remedial education. Rather, attention will be directed to some dilemmas which may arise, to ways of sizing up difficulties, and to basic strategies.

LOOKING FOR CLUES.   Decisions as to plans for helping a child depend upon what judgments we can make as to the nature of the trouble and the reasons for it. To illustrate the types of clues which help to determine our course of action, here are four common patterns found by Bernstein[1] after an intensive study of ninth-grade students with arithmetic deficiencies at the Denby High School in Detroit. One group's difficulties seemed due entirely to gaps in their understanding of the number system; their errors showed a clear pattern, which could be traced to specific computational weaknesses. A second group, by contrast, made errors of a random variety, often "knew" something well one day but "forgot" it the next. This second pattern seemed to be related to emotional conflict. The third group gave evidence of insecurity, coupled with many gaps in understanding and poor control of the fundamental facts. For many of these, a program of working on their gaps in knowledge, when successful, aided greatly in building their self-confidence. In the fourth group, a large part of the difficulty stemmed from nervousness in test situations; they appeared to make gains in remedial instruction which could not be demonstrated on tests. For them, the observations on examination panic made in the previous chapter would seem to apply.

The type of analysis illustrated above would have to be modified considerably for other grades and other subjects. Indeed, in the very cases mentioned, a teacher would have to refine the general judgments given by Bernstein. In the remainder of this section we shall list, in respect to poor learning, a number of possible clues. In doing so, it is essential to keep in mind the possibility that several causes may be operating simultaneously. With some children, for instance, the teacher may feel as though tackling the problem is like peeling an onion. Initially, the cause of the difficulties seems clear, and some progress is made under a program which gets at that cause. As this eventually bogs down,

---

[1] Allen L. Bernstein, *A Study of Remedial Arithmetic Conducted with Ninth Grade Students,* Ed.D. dissertation, Wayne State University, 1955, University Microfilms Publication No. 13,200.

a different cause emerges as the villain in the mystery. This process may repeat itself three or four times.

In many instances a child's learning troubles are a direct result of realistic limitations. His level of intellectual functioning may be low; he may have physical handicaps. In detecting this type of situation, it is helpful if the school system routinely gives intelligence tests, readiness tests, and physical examinations. Since physical or intellectual limitations are the simplest explanation of poor work, they should always be considered. If school records do not contain the necessary information, it should be obtained by arranging for the requisite examinations. Unfortunately, there are some areas for which adequate tests are not easily available.

The next most direct possibility is that, because of previous absences or inappropriate teaching methods, the boy or girl did not get some earlier, and now necessary, skill or material. For some subjects, such as reading and arithmetic, simple diagnostic tests are on the market and can be used. Where these are not available or are difficult to obtain, teachers often detect this type of trouble either by looking over a large sample of the child's work or by having him give the reasoning behind answers. The incorrect responses will fall into a logical pattern. For example, a particular student in a foreign-language class may make errors all indicating he does not understand the different meanings involved in the several past tenses.

Another possibility is that the youngster is the victim of examination panic. The type of interview mentioned in the paragraph above will reveal that he really knows the material. The trouble arises when he is called upon to display his learning.

In yet other cases, a brief period of individual help will show that a young person is quite capable of learning in the area where his trouble appears, and can retain what he has learned. The trouble seems to be lack of interest. During a period of intensive observation, stimulated by the teacher's concern, such youngsters can move forward. But the momentum is likely to continue only if the instructor can find how to make the material serve one of the child's interests, or if he can get at the source of the apathy. An example would be a boy who dawdled over his reading, but became eager when supplied with books on space travel.

A very different type of cause is indicated by a performance pattern which is spotty as measured against the process by which most children learn. Typical examples are the girl who can spell some difficult words but gives a nonsensical response to some easy ones, the boy who apparently has mastered the reading of a passage one day but has to struggle with it on the next, and the child who develops an air of hopelessness about a segment of class activities, despite an approach involving both effort and ability. At this point we must begin to think in terms of possible emotional blockings.

In some cases, the total pattern of the child's actions and his facial expression provide clues to the nature of the emotional turmoil. Some children seem to strive pathetically at times and stall evasively at others, to try to please the teacher, and to perspire freely. These are signs of a generalized anxiety that pervades their performance. In other youngsters, there may be a pattern of behavior involving repeated acts of aggression. Their behavior is typified by outbursts of anger and orgies of blame-throwing. In such cases, we can surmise that the anger and hostility are destroying the ability to learn.

There are other cases in which information from the home may help determine the cause of the emotional upsets. In one pattern of reading retardation, described by Barber,[2] immaturity in ego development was signaled in school by a need for much supervision from the teacher and an unusual amount of seeking for help from examiners in test situations. Talks with parents revealed that many of these children needed to be waited upon at home more than others their age and seemed to be preoccupied with adjustment problems typical of younger children.

There will be many instances among children whose learning problems do not yield to ordinary educational methods, in which the nature of the emotional difficulties involved may be quite complex and obscure. For action within the normal limits of teaching, it is not necessary to trace all the causes. Indeed, this very obscurity is a hint that referral is the wisest measure. It is in those cases in which the nature of the emotional causation is clear and suggests the countermeasures that the hunt for clues pays off, provided the countermeasures lie within the teacher's domain.

For example, there are young people whose school difficulties crop up at one age level, notably in adolescence. Where the school history has been a good one and the onset of trouble is rather sudden, we can surmise that a developmental upset is at work.

In other cases, we may note that a child's troubles appear to be

---

[2] Lucille Knecht Barber, *Immature Ego Development as a Factor in Retarded Ability to Read,* Ph.D. dissertation, University of Michigan, 1952, University Microfilms Publication No. 3711.

linked to an individualistic reaction to the method used. The child's re-actions seem directed against an element in school procedure, as when a very orderly youngster seems upset by informality or a timid boy or girl "goes to pieces" under pressure.

Sometimes it is clear that what appears as a school problem is en-meshed in home relationships. It is not unusual, for example, to find high school students who go into an academic tail spin as part of their maneuvering for independence. If restrictive parents are very ambitious and have done a great deal of prodding, the child may unconsciously "get even" by finding himself unable to do schoolwork well.

There are young people for whom poor work is a real protection against having to meet high demands. For example, if a brother or sister has been notably good in school, a youngster may evade competition by declaring through action that academic proficiency is "not my line." In other cases they may feel that the ultimate escape from demanding parents is to make the case so hopeless that their elders "lay off." Sim-ilarly, in school some children will thwart pressuring by an instructor by unintentionally going on a sit-down strike.

Another variety of disturbance appears in some children whose parents have unwisely gone too far in the opposite direction. Having fun assumes a primacy in the young people's behavior pattern. They show little appreciation of a need to restrain their impulses. The result is a flighty distractibility which keeps the child so much on the move that holding him to work long enough to master a task is quite difficult.

Level of aspiration is often a clue. What a boy or girl seems to ex-pect of himself may tell a great deal. In general, healthy youngsters who have had adequate successes set levels which they are able to reach with some effort. If a child grossly underestimates or overestimates his capacity, this is a sign either that he has lacked success in previous learn-ing or is suffering from an emotional difficulty.

In a number of young people, we may find that there is a lack of effort, combined with daydreaming, which betokens a response to some potent pressure outside the main activities of the classroom. At the high school level, for instance, it is not unusual to discover a boy or girl who has fallen in love and for whom no other experience can compete with the resultant preoccupation. Many boys and girls may be completely wrapped up in problems of social status. A similar condition, with dif-ferent causes, may occur where the parents of a young child are quar-reling so much the child fears a separation. In other instances the child's energies are being sapped or his imagination captured by instruction outside school.

For a number of young people, inefficiency in learning may appear to be a road to acceptance by age-mates whom they value. They work at a level below their ability lest they become unpopular for kowtowing to adults.

THE TEACHER'S STRATEGY. In view of the variety of possible causes, as listed above, and the fact that there may be obscure elements in causative patterns, it is clear that, although, as already indicated, there are important general principles to be applied, there is no standard recipe that will treat all learning problems. Rather the teacher must piece together for each child an individual prescription, whose ingredients will be modified on the basis of experience. Below we shall list some of the possibilities which can be combined.

First of all, we can never afford to ignore the standard educational remedies which every well-trained teacher has acquired. These include special drill on fundamentals, giving practice in weak skills, asking questions, and other ways of giving help along strictly educational lines. For instance, when the instructor recognizes that a pupil may need special help, he will often take care to observe the boy or girl at work. When he sees that the youngster has hit an obstacle, he will give a hint as to next steps, show him a missing skill, or ask questions that will help the child see how to get over the hurdle.

For children who show anxiety or whose performance deteriorates under pressure, the teacher may set up individual learning situations, protected from demands. He may reassure the student, let him work at a special, lower speed, or give an opportunity to explain his answers.

The indispensable quality of patience can be all-important in working with a child who has difficulties. When a pupil recognizes that his teacher is being patient with him, this is the equivalent of reducing pressure. The youngster is less likely to become flustered, and can put his mind better to the task at hand. It may be quite important to communicate to a boy or girl the fact that, recognizing how real are the difficulties, the teacher anticipates that the two of them will have to work together for a long while before the difficulties will clear up.

Some children are not quite sure what to think of a teacher. They may see him, for example, as someone who tries to trick them into errors. They may invest a teacher with the attributes of a parent. When evidences of such misinterpretations are found, a teacher may have to take pains to make clear, both by words and actions, exactly what role he does play in relationship to the child. A special case of this need arises when we discover that parents have been "helping" the child by using tactics of demanding pressure. When this possibility exists, it may be wise to get a clear picture of how the parents operate, so that the teacher may be distinctively different. If a parent-child conflict is basic to the learning problem, the school situation must be consciously modified in order to disentangle learning from home relationships. This cannot be done unless there is some contrast between the teacher's attitude toward the child's learning activities and that communicated by the parents.

The extent to which a helping teacher should add a touch of personal warmth to his or her relationship with a boy or girl is a matter requiring the exercise of judgment. With younger pupils, and especially where the parents have been demanding, such warmth is very valuable. Freely given affection may ease insecurity and stimulate effort. There are cases, however, where personal closeness to specific youngsters is definitely not indicated; where it might cause confusion and get in the way. For example, there is always the possibility that an adolescent boy or girl may respond to an open display of fondness by developing a crush. Sexually tinged feelings are likely to disrupt learning. For some other children whose disturbance grows out of parental neglect or hostility and includes difficulties in relating to people, as well as in learning, any personal closeness may be frightening. A third type of case appears where parents have used emotional blackmail to get the young person to strive in school. Also, when a pupil is receiving psychotherapy, he is already coping with problems of relationship, which would be complicated by a close tie to a teacher. If any of these conditions prevail, an impersonal attitude may make it much easier for a child to accept and use help. It will prevent unwanted complications.

There are a number of situations in which it is important to let the youngster assume responsibility for his own work rather than to supervise him closely or set fixed demands. Where learning in school is being resisted because a child retains a negativistic attitude toward adults or as part of a preadolescent warfare on grownups, he is more likely to keep a pace that he has set for himself than one he feels is being imposed upon him. A supplementary tactic is to bring into the picture a classmate to whom the youngster looks for friendship or prestige. There are boys and girls who are positively motivated when they see other young folks respect an achievement but who would resent and resist adult help.

One of the things which happens to a pupil who has met much failure is that he is likely to become a very poor judge of his own abilities. Some grossly underestimate their own capacity; others act on a fantastic expectation of almost magical performance. A teacher working with a child whose school record is poor should first try to make a good estimate of what the youngster will be able to accomplish, and then help him become realistic about himself. There is always a temptation to play along with too high an achievement image in the belief that this is good in itself and with the expectation that it will lead to greater effort. If the teacher recognizes that children holding overhigh self-expectations usually rely not on work but on luck to reach their goals, it is easier to resist the temptation. Moreover, a high self-expectation in a less confident child frequently gives rise to anxiety and to fear of failure.

A crucial point in helping many a young person comes when the first real success is visible. At this point the teacher may well feel triumphant, and will want to let other people know what has happened. It is essential that the child receive credit for *his* achievement. If at this point he is ignored while his helper invites a chorus of praise, he may decide that his own achievement does not belong to him. He may also recognize that he is capable of making the adult gain or lose in happiness and prestige. Should this happen, control of the situation passes from the teacher to the child because he can give or withhold rewards. It is literally true that in the future the youngster can hurt the teacher by backsliding and thus casting doubt on professional prestige. This gives him a means of exacting blackmail. On the other hand, when the boy or girl feels that the success is his and learns to savor the feeling of achievement, he has good reason for putting forth effort.

Another important element in the strategy of helping is to keep the proper perspective on the relationship of the disability to the whole life pattern of the child. There are many hours of the day when most children can receive pleasure from activities not judged by school standards. Thus, although a learning weakness may loom large to a teacher, to the child it may merely be a minor annoyance in a small segment of his life. It is simpler to work on it if it is put in perspective.

Similarly, sometimes an opportunity may offer itself to make use of a child's reliance upon himself in areas where he has good, solid, positive self-concepts, and possibly to aid him in transferring this self-reliance into the area where he needs help. An illustration of this strategy is given in the case of Ronnie, a twelve-year-old boy with a series of problems, described by McGill.[3] This lad had lived with his unmarried mother until he was six, then with an aunt, and then with his father and a stepmother, of whom he was afraid. They were stern, and whipped him if he came home late. A careful study by his teacher was rather discouraging. He had an I.Q. of 78, lacked work skills and study habits, found schoolwork too difficult, felt he was not accepted by classmates, and took no part in sports. His teacher did uncover two assets: Ronnie fancied himself good in science, and he liked to paint and draw. Utilizing these as opportunities, the teacher tackled reading problems by finding him easy-to-read materials in science. She also had him make posters for the school store. His enthusiasm at this point led him into a successful attack on arithmetic.

In any such case we must be careful not to expect too much too soon, or to involve the child's good area in such a way that the unpleasantness in the region of trouble contaminates his joy in the region where he has been successful.

Most children who are having difficulties will utilize some of the defense mechanisms described in Chapter 4 to protect their self-esteem. They may concentrate upon a substitute area, take refuge in daydreams, "fool around" instead of getting down to work, or blame the teacher for their failures. In cold fact, if anyone has realistic need for defensive behavior, it is a pupil doing poorly in school. For a teacher to embark on an all-out campaign against such conduct is not only to choose a poor target for energy but to add psychological cruelty to the school situation. Accordingly, it is necessary to show tolerance for defense mechanisms, within limits. Those limits are set by the reality and strategy of learning requirements. For example, a child may be allowed to express some bitterness about teachers but not at such length as to take any large portion of the time set aside to give him individual help, or in such a way as to give himself an excuse for not learning.

In many cases, the wish to be part of the group has a powerful attraction. Some children can figuratively be sucked into a class's preoccupation with some phase of learning. If a teacher is giving such a child individual help, at times it may be wise to step aside and allow him to be caught up in group activity. For him, this allows attainment of one goal which gives zest to school.

---

[3] Maud Williams McGill, *A Study of Personality Traits Among a Group of Slow-Learning Pupils and Techniques for Improving Them,* unpublished M.A. thesis, University of North Carolina, 1950.

Referral

Not all children with learning troubles can be given effective help within the normal pattern of classroom activities, even though the teacher personally possesses all the qualities needed to handle their problems. To do the job, the teacher would need smaller class loads, different grouping, and a variety of special facilities. Some children need special class placement and teachers trained in remedial reading or speech correction. Among boys and girls suspected of being emotionally upset, there is a necessity for diagnosis, to be followed by therapy if indicated. This requires referral to school psychologists, visiting teachers, clinics, and private psychiatrists. Some of the issues involved will be discussed at length in Chapter 15.

Supportive Survival

Unhappily, when all has been tried, there will remain some children for whom in the present state of our knowledge we can find no quick, effective program of help. Also, while a child is undergoing a long program of help from an outside source, he continues to stay in the class. In addition, there are children whose learning difficulties appear linked to the reality of low learning ability. The situation this creates was illustrated in a study by Bills.[4] He had worked out a program of nondirective play therapy, which had registered significant improvement for 7 of 8 severely maladjusted retarded readers. Next, he used personality tests to locate 8 retarded readers who were not emotionally disturbed. Given the very program of play therapy which previously had worked so well, they showed no improvement.

For one reason or another, then, almost every teacher will have the problem of making a place in class activities for a child who has learning difficulties which do not yield. The teacher must learn to live with this situation and to give the child as much support as possible.

DIFFERENCES IN CHILD'S REACTION.   The first step in working out a program is to notice and think about how the boy or girl reacts to his own problem. Four basic types can be discerned; each will be discussed more fully in later sections of this chapter.

---

4 Robert E. Bills, "Play Therapy with Well-Adjusted Retarded Readers," *Journal of Consulting Psychology,* Vol. 14 (1950), pp. 246-49.

Some children show a clear-cut recognition that they are having trouble. They react to failure in school by continuing to try to do better.

A second pattern involves withdrawal from learning processes. The child not only puts out little effort, but refuses to seek help. He may go even further and develop techniques of discouraging anyone who tries to help him.

A third development may be quite the opposite. The youngster may enjoy having people take care of him. He utilizes his difficulties to place himself contentedly in a dependent relationship to adults. With teachers, he may seek and hold on to helpful attention.

The fourth, and most disturbing, pattern finds the young person becoming a serious behavior problem. In response to the frustrations of being unable to learn, he becomes aggressive, hurts other children, steals, or finds ways to take revenge on school and teachers.

GENERAL STRATEGY.   Whichever reaction a given child shows, it is important for the teacher to be realistic about the situation. This means he must recognize that the child's problems are indeed difficult ones. To create the illusion that a little help will do the trick is to deceive the child. Such youngsters soon learn not to hope, and to distrust grownups who blithely raise false hopes.

Likewise, it does little good to praise the child for performances which visibly are poor. To do so is to undermine his confidence in the teacher. If such a child is to be helped at all, he must see that an adult recognizes his difficulties for what they are, and is planning in terms of those difficulties.

WHEN THE CHILD CONTINUES TRYING.   The very fact that the youngster is struggling actively with his tasks makes it almost inevitable that his teacher will want to come to his rescue. The teacher will usually be inclined to devote much attention to him and to reward effort with good marks. Indeed, some will even find themselves doing the child's work for him. Counteracting these inclinations will be the fear that others in the class may take the standards set for the one youngster as being fair for all.

In this connection it pays to recall that in many situations children themselves will make allowances for individual weakness. Watch a game in which one of the players is recognized as being poor. The chances are that, especially if he is smaller or younger than the rest, the other players will toss the ball to him with less steam or when he is at bat, pitch him balls easy to hit. Children can and do see that it is fair for a teacher to encourage a classmate by giving hints, asking easy questions, or setting tasks that can be accomplished.

In helping a youngster to get satisfaction from school even though he continues trying to reach levels of learning beyond his operating capacity, the teacher has a first problem of protecting him from jealousy if he is given extra consideration. In some cases, however, even before he receives special attention, he may be the butt of juvenile ridicule. In this case, the teacher must be very tactful in coming to his rescue. The goal is to disentangle him from the group, not to punish the group and build their resentment at "the kid who got us all in trouble."

If a teacher finds himself spending an undue amount of time giving individual help, this has to be brought under control. Certainly, assistance should continue to be given. However, once a realistic estimate has been made of how much it can accomplish, most teachers will find it wise to limit extra attention. When this is done, a point should be made of being pleasant about the whole matter. It does no good to get angry with the child and accuse him or her of "not co-operating" or "being lazy." Rather, the basis should be that there are things that have to be done for the rest of the class.

WHEN THE POOR LEARNER ACTS DETACHED. There are quite a few poor learners, especially in the upper grades, whose actions reflect feelings that schoolwork is not worth the effort. They turn their backs on learning activities, and seek and find ego satisfaction in other areas of living.

From the viewpoint of mental health, this response is defensible. That very fact makes it a problem for teachers, who are bound to worry lest the youngster's attitudes infect his classmates. From an academic viewpoint, he is a bad example. Yet, what would be gained for him personally if he were made to feel shame about his scholastic failings?

Many such young people prove highly resistant to attempts to give them special help or to make work easy for them to accomplish. They ward off these efforts by raising higher their shield of nonchalance. They do not want to be exceptions to the school rules, because they recognize that to admit this is to declare they should be treated as patients.

The major problem teachers face here is that of the group and the group attitudes; the individual's strong defenses will protect him. There is always a temptation to punish such a youngster in order to impress the children who are working hard with a feeling that their own virtue is being rewarded. The same point can be made with less emotional turmoil if the young person is treated as an unavoidable exception, and is given activities which contribute to the class but are not academic.

Such young folks, if left to themselves, would not sit in class doing nothing; they would busy themselves in various ways. For example, some might make sketches, learn to run a projector, volunteer to carry messages, or prepare decorations. If they do these things in defiance of a teacher, this represents a potentially contagion-spreading defeat. However, if the teacher has directed these youngsters to do what they might have done anyway, there is the possibility that the class will recognize the situation as being a type of teacher-directed subgrouping. The spirit in which the teacher acts is one of realistic concession to the obvious lack of readiness in the boy or girl. To be avoided is any impression either of baffled abdication or of punitive rejection. In any case, the teacher should make sure by his attitudes that the class sees how highly he values the regular activities in which they are engaged.

A special and quite difficult problem arises if the youngster involved is a poor learner and has given up trying in only a small sub-area of schoolwork. It is more difficult for the other children to understand why he is exempt from some school demands but subject to others almost all the time. Although the basic strategy of the situation is the same, it requires greater ingenuity to put it into effect.

DEPENDENCY DEMANDS.   There are young people who enjoy being cared for, waited upon, and spoon-fed. They feel more comfortable when they are dependent upon other people. For them the extra attention received as part of teachers' efforts to help is a good in itself. They often develop subtle techniques for eliciting and rewarding the type of treatment they crave.

Many teachers' initial reaction is to like such a child very much and to be encouraged by the way he eagerly and gratefully accepts help. This gives way to irritation as the youngster becomes more openly dependent and his demands get in the way of the teachers' working properly with the rest of the class. In their annoyance, they do not recognize that the learning problem is real; instead, they may perceive it as an artificial bid for attention.

In dealing with such a child, teachers should be aware of both traps. They should recognize that it is undesirable for a child to be too dependent on any adult, and they should be equally aware that, although their own resentment is justifiable, it is no excuse for taking punitive or rejecting action.

In a way, the strategy for dealing with such a child is very similar to that which would be followed with a child who could learn well but who insisted on getting a teacher's approval for his work at every stage. The child's need for dependency is recognized, and he is given sympathetic attention on the teacher's initiative and in the teacher's own way. For instance, if the actualities permit, he might be given individualized help outside the classroom, thus relieving the teacher of pressure resulting from concern about neglect of the class.

Secondly, realistic limits to the help which is extended should be set in matter-of-fact fashion. This is done in very much the same way we would treat a child who has an inordinate need to be in the limelight. We would certainly give him his fair chance, but at times we would sit him down and point out that others in their turn deserved an equal opportunity.

BEHAVIOR PATHOLOGY.   The situation most difficult to handle well occurs when the young person has reacted to frustration from poor learning by developing behavior disorders. This can and often does raise hob with the entire group. Besides not learning himself, the child disrupts the classroom. At this point, most teachers fervently wish he or she would go away, vanish, be removed. If he is past the minimum age for compulsory attendance, it is tempting to treat him roughly enough so that he will quit. In some schools, such a boy or girl will be goaded into actions justifying his placement in a special class.

However intense the dislike such a youngster may generate, it is essential to deal with the situation as objectively as possible. One way to begin is to find out whether the bad behavior does indeed result from learning difficulties, in which case help with learning might reduce the problem. There are many highly disturbed children, however, whose learning difficulties and misconduct are both results of incomplete personality development. For these last, intensive psychological treatment is required.

If, on the other hand, there is good reason to believe that the child's misbehavior has developed after encountering trouble in learning, the possibility exists for a teacher to bring about improvement in the conduct by working on the learning. To do so, however, it is necessary to conquer the natural tendency to use disciplinary incidents as an excuse to be punitive.

However, the child's behavior cannot be ignored. It does cause trouble for the group, and the other children do need to be protected in their right to a school environment in which they can learn. Even if the teacher does tolerate, in one of these "acting-out" youngsters, a fringe of dubious behavior, this must have clear limits. The problem of how a teacher intervenes to control group and individual behavior is discussed at length in Chapter 13.

The teacher, then, should not hesitate to protect the group by setting up a strong, nonpunitive control of the offending youngster. This may require that he be removed from the group on occasion. It helps if previous arrangements have been made for his or her reception in the school office and agreements have been reached there that he needs cooling off, not a bawling out. In extreme cases in which the young person's aggression is intense, a teacher may be helpless, and special facilities are required.

Gifted Children

National concern these days spotlights the urgency of furthering the special education of intellectually gifted boys and girls, particularly those whose talents might make them scientists. Their giftedness is a valued resource. Ours is a historical epoch when scientific competition between countries may be a matter of survival.

There is a growing literature, and a rather less slowly growing body of tested knowledge, on educational techniques and administrative arrangements for working with such young people. In this book we shall not attempt to deal with any but the mental health issues, concentrating on those likely to arise in classrooms where there is one child of outstanding ability. We shall want to look at matters which influence not only the emotional well-being of his classmates but the mental health of the outstanding child himself. From a tough-minded viewpoint, this emphasis is essential; we are losing the potential value of too many young people whose latent capacity never develops into productive ability because of emotional restraints.

Giftedness, like most psychological qualities, is present in varying degrees. There is no sharp line, based on I.Q., musical talent, or artistic ability, which acts as a boundary. Some of the children with whom we shall be concerned are highly endowed; others only marginally gifted.

Teachers' Feelings

Teachers who have had gifted children in their classes, and most have had some, are often surprised that their feelings can show considerable conflict. Side by side with satisfaction and admiration, they sense annoyance and worry.

Obviously, it is highly gratifying to witness the pace at which an adept child makes use of instruction. The teacher has the satisfaction of helping the boy or girl move toward heights. However, there is bound to be some anxiety about what the brilliant performance is doing to the rest of the class. Do they feel bad by comparison? Will the difficulty, if not the impossibility, of competing successfully with an outstanding class leader be too discouraging?

If the gifted child displays that effortless quality in accomplishing ordinary tasks which is so characteristic, the teacher may even feel jealous. In the upper grades, a gifted child may easily "get" material with which the teacher once had to struggle. At this point, the teacher is likely to identify with the rest of the class. The envy may have a punitive edge; it would be justice to see a child so fortunate have to pay for his luck. There may be an unconscious search for something to criticize. For instance, the child may be set tasks clearly beyond his abilities, particularly in a field where he or she is weak, and then blamed for the induced failure. There may be a tendency to nag such children about the few things they do not do well.

A realistic worry may center on the ease with which gifted children master ordinary assignments. Are they developing bad study habits which will hamper them later? Often, the fact is that they are.

A highly endowed child offers some alluring temptations. How much good he could do if only he devoted his capacity to furthering our own values! Such a child is an especially attractive object for indoctrination in the interest field dearest to the teacher.

When a bright young person works well, his performance can produce a delight somewhat like that of a well-executed work of art. Some teachers become afraid of their own pleasure. They worry lest it harm the child or his classmates. They fear they are betraying unworthy emotions.

These and other reactions may trigger a misapplication of democratic principles on the part of the teacher. Equality of opportunity may be taken to require that people be equalized, and hence that the bright should "be cut down to size." Some teachers feel a strong need to put a gifted boy or girl in his place. They try to humble him.

An exactly opposite reaction may take place. Many of us have a hankering to be objects of wonder; more, to step out ahead of the crowd. The fast-learning child may therefore represent an aspect of ourselves we would like to have exist. Accordingly, we exult in his triumphs; we may develop an almost insatiable appetite to have him achieve our own ambitions.

On a more realistic plane, a teacher may be afraid he cannot keep up with a gifted child. The youngster may ask questions to which the instructor does not know the answers. It is entirely possible that in a class discussion this type of pupil will correct a statement on the basis of new material or a refined technicality. In any event, to keep a gifted child supplied with challenging work to do is itself a demanding task. Sometimes, teachers are reluctant to put forth the extra labor that is required.

This raises the entire question of how important it is to devote attention to the gifted. Two opposite attitudes are both likely to arise. One is that the gifted children are able to take care of themselves. God has been good to them; our efforts should be devoted to the handicapped, who need help. The contrary feeling is that the future of any civilization depends upon leaders. The gifted as potential leaders are the only members of the class who genuinely matter. To neglect them is to doom our nation. Since they are fit to rule and produce, they must be equipped for that task.

In the above listing, mention has been restricted to attitudes and feelings that give rise to trouble. Although any or all of these may be felt in mild degree by every teacher, for the majority the dominant feelings are likely to include a highly professional pride and desire to extend help and encouragement. The gifted child needs skilled assistance in making the best use of his capabilities, and this is indeed what most teachers, each in his own way, do supply.

Reactions of Gifted Children

A teacher's strategy in giving such children their needed boost will depend to some extent on how each boy or girl reacts to his own brilliance. Obviously, this will depend in large part on his personality and on how his parents behave toward him. There are many possibilities; here a few of those most frequently encountered will be described.

"SLEEPERS."   It is not unusual for a program of intelligence test-ing in schools to bring to light a child whose day-to-day work is aver-age but who has exceptional ability. These are children who early be-come sensitive to the possibility that they may have social difficulties if they become outstanding. As a result, they hide their ability. They protect themselves by taking on the coloration of a good average student.

SHOW-OFFS.   By contrast, there are very bright children, and some who are not so bright, who use their ability as a destructive tool. They not only show off and attract attention to their accomplishments, but seem to enjoy seeing other people placed in a poor position by compari-son with themselves. This attitude may not inhibit their learning, but it does create personal difficulties.

HARD-WORKING ACHIEVERS.   Others who also achieve highly may take a genuine joy in accomplishment, and work hard to get it. Their pleasure comes not so much from competitive advantage as from a feel-ing of workmanship. They put out effort, get results, and are happy.

EFFORTLESS ACHIEVERS.   For a few, achievement through work is meaningless, as contrasted with the satisfaction to be obtained from accomplishing tasks as though by a personal magic. In making the point that some self-bemused bright pupils have a need to succeed with-out effort, Klein[5] gave the following case history:

> An intelligent 17-year-old boy who was not getting the grades in high school that he needed in order to get into a good college, felt that almost anyone could get good marks if he studied hard. He left his studying to the last minute, relying on his ability to cover the whole subject in a brief period of cramming. When he got a B where he had hoped for an A, he always consoled himself that he had hardly touched a book all term, so that his B was really a great achievement. He in-sisted that if he had only studied a little he would surely have gotten all A's. He felt contempt for the pupils who had studied regularly and got high grades. They were only dullards who worked hard, he said scornfully.

EMOTIONALLY HANDICAPPED LEARNERS.   Although, in general, gifted children are more stable and show less emotional upset than the

---

[5] Emanuel Klein, "Psychoanalytic Aspects of School Problems," *Psychoanalytic Study of the Child,* Vols. 3-4 (1949), pp. 369-90.

average, they are not immune to conflicts and emotional upsets. The learning of some is far below their capacity. There is hardly a school psychologist who has not found himself confronted with a child of over 130 I.Q. who was having trouble learning to read, or at the high school level was about to quit school. The authors know of one boy with an I.Q. of 170 who, because of a combination of a slight brain injury and an unwholesome home background, was considered a candidate for an institution for the feeble-minded.

The wastage of human resources due to maladjustment among a minority of potentially gifted individuals is itself an answer to those critics of our schools who would have us forget about adjustment and concentrate upon developing intellectual talent. The talents of some young people can be released for effective living only when their adjustment problems are solved.

WANTING TO BE A "NICE GUY." Some gifted youngsters who achieve well also recognize that their performance makes them the object of envy. Without giving up the satisfaction of using their ability, they try to "buy off" criticism by proving to others that they are "nice guys." Indeed, a few go further and willingly submit to being exploited by friends. They will help other children with work, and even aid in conspiracies to raise grades by cheating.

MATTER-OF-FACT SELF-ACCEPTANCE. All studies agree that gifted children on the average are emotionally well adjusted. Many, then, are quite capable of accepting the fact that they are able to do superior work. They enjoy themselves. They are gratified by the results of their superior accomplishments.

There is an important implication in this for teachers. When dealing with gifted children, it is wise to make the initial assumption that these young people will have a zestful delight in living. They are usually able to handle well any difficulties resulting from other people's reaction to their giftedness. Unless there is clear evidence to the contrary, it may be well to trust them to find solutions to personal problems.

AMBIVALENT VACILLATION. One of the basic dilemmas facing unusually adept young people arises from the fact that they enjoy pleasing adults but fear being out of step with their classmates. Some find it difficult to set a steady course. At times they yield to the temptation of going all out to win grownups' admiration. Then, alarmed at the possibility of being considered "teacher's pet," they deliberately hold back and seek mediocre anonymity, only to be tempted again to do well.

REGRESSIVE TRENDS.   For a few gifted children, the fact that parental pressure, however benign, has led to delight in their own performance becomes a sore point in adolescence. Now, anxious to show independence, they do so by denying their ability. Indeed, some behave as though their ambition was to do poorly.

This perverse distaste for displaying ability is one of the most trying problems of educators who work with classes of the gifted. The cause of its prevalence in such groups has yet to be exactly determined. One possibility is that some children are enrolled in such classes because their parents are ambitious for them. A child may well come to resent being gifted if he feels it makes him a freak, or forces him to accept a life pattern which is childish in the sense of giving priority to pleasing adults.

DEDICATION TO AN IDEAL.   By contrast, other gifted children come to feel that their good fortune constitutes an opportunity to serve mankind, or to advance some cause. Religious young people may consider that their gift requires dedication, that it was given them for a purpose, and that it is their duty to devote their talents to high ideals.

EXAGGERATED SELF-DEMANDS.   For a few, having extra ability sets in motion an insatiable need to push themselves. Because of their successes, some overestimate their ability. They demand of themselves either a premature specialization or an all-round perfection. Some are led to narrow, too early, the area in which they are interested. They would rival the adult specialist before there is need to do so. Others act as though their pride has been injured if anyone does better than they in any area. They may pour their energies into the field where they have the least aptitude.

BOOKWORMS.   There is always the possibility that if a youngster obtains greatest gratification from his intellectual or artistic talents, his field of experience may be narrowed. He may lose opportunities to get along with his peers. In later life this may reduce his range of usefulness to those few areas in which teamwork and co-operative activity are not necessary. It may lead to vague feelings of having been cheated, and may trigger regressive trends. There is no need for this situation to arise; most gifted individuals are capable of having both the stimulation of achievement and the fun of social experience.

Group Reactions

In addition to the teacher's attitude and the child's own feelings, there is a third element of the classroom situation: the reaction of the class. This has twin aspects which are of concern to teachers: (1) how it will affect the gifted child and (2) how it will influence his classmates' work.

ENVIOUS ADMIRATION.   The most common reaction is a combination of admiration and envy. Attracted by good accomplishment, some children will want to be friends. Wishing to be like the admired boy or girl, others will feel hostility fed by envy. In any case, many a child will be less gratified by his own achievement because it is now pale by comparison. A number will avoid the imputation that the contrast is one of merit by deciding that the gifted youngster is "just lucky."

INCREASE IN DEMANDS.   The adept child's merit in schoolwork may be conceded, but demands may be made that he prove he is "one of us." It is as though he were suspected of having gone over to the grownup enemy. He therefore confronts, especially in preadolescence, a continuous loyalty investigation. He may be provoked to engage in behavior unacceptable to teachers to prove that he is a "regular fellow."

EXPLOITATION.   The other children may be tempted to exploit the gifted one. Not only may he be expected to help them with schoolwork, and to make it easier for them to solve other problems, but his good relations with adults may be made an asset for the group. In tough neighborhoods, he may be expected to act as a defense counsel, or "mouthpiece," for delinquents. In any area, he may represent the group by being fresh to the teacher in a manner which would draw disciplining for an ordinary child. The others get satisfaction from seeing him get away with what they could not afford to do. Later, his exploit may be used as a self-justifying argument to avoid guilt.

DISPLACEMENT.   The emotions which might be directed toward a talented child may instead be fastened on the teacher. Instead of showing jealousy, his classmates may make extra demands that the teacher be fair to everyone. They may let the teacher know that they want added attention. Especially in the lower grades, a teacher may find that with a gifted boy or girl in the class, a good social climate is harder to secure.

EXEMPTION FROM ORDINARY DEMANDS. To maintain their own self-respect, the classmates of a gifted child may consider him to be in a special category. They may compete with each other, but not worry about the gifted one. His work is not a standard they attempt to meet. This device does have the additional merit of protecting the gifted child from ordinary jealousies.

IMPUTATION OF SHOW-OFF MOTIVATION. As another way of protecting themselves, the classmates may decide that the brilliant youngster is only a show-off. By implication they declare that if they were motivated by so unworthy a goal, they could do equally well. This tactic is likely to be accompanied by ostracism, social rejection, or scapegoating.

ACCEPTANCE AS GROUP CHAMPION. Quite the reverse often happens. The class regards a splendid achiever as reflecting credit on the group to which he belongs. Like a champion athlete, he is "our" hero. Each child can identify with him, feel the better because he is in "our" class. This pattern of reaction frees the gifted child to accomplish superbly, and win social approbation in doing so.

HAPPY ACCEPTANCE. Short of hero worship, there are other patterns by which gifted youngsters can have a happy peer-group life. Many of them are as skillful in managing their social life as they are in their intellectual or artistic lives. By showing culturally approved modesty, being pleasantly helpful, and displaying ingenuity in leisure-time fun, they find a gay spot in group structure.

The Teacher's Strategy

What is the role to be played by teachers in respect to gifted children? Obviously, there is the instructional task of challenging them, of meeting their need for individualization of work. There is also the job of helping the child taste gratification from the use of his talents. There is the management of class morale so that all find incentive for self-development.

While most exceptionally able pupils handle themselves well, some mismanage their relationships with classmates to a point beyond any possibility of help from a teacher. In other classes, reactions in the direction either of popularity or of ostracism may be exaggerated, but the teacher can have a decided influence.

An important first step in working with a gifted child is to evaluate the actual present balance of forces in his life. One has to avoid the temptation of acting on stereotypes. Despite popular legends, many a brilliant child is quite happy with his talent. He may need help, however, in developing age-adequate relationships with other children or with adults. The point is that such judgments should be made for each individual in terms of himself, his needs, and his setting.

A similar objectivity and judiciousness should govern the use of praise and of criticism. It is too easy to overreact, either by giving excessive praise or by finding fault. Each performance should be judged on its merits, in terms of the child's ability.

One point at which special leeway can be allowed is in behavior designed to win peer approval. If a gifted child makes an effort to win social acceptability by helping other youngsters or by showing dislike for minor rules, a teacher may prefer to encourage his maneuvers within the limits clearly needed for good group atmosphere. Thus, the child might be allowed to aid classmates with problems, but not on tests or papers utilized for grading purposes.

If such a child engages in behavior incidents requiring correction, this should be given without dragging his brilliance into the picture. Comments such as, *"You* should know better!" are not particularly helpful. Neither are remarks beginning, "If any *other* child had done this, I. . . ." With the exceptions suggested by the previous paragraph, any bit of conduct should be considered on its own basis.

Most important, however, is the matter of individualizing classroom work sufficiently so that a child can utilize his talents. He should not be kept at assignments he has already mastered. Rather, he should be given opportunities to work at different tasks, to explore difficult tangents, or to deepen his understandings. The atmosphere should be one of giving him the joy of using his ability, rather than of turning out showy performances for which his teachers can take the bows. There is much more to be done than merely preventing boredom. Giving a gifted child a quantity of work to do is no substitute for challenging him with a higher level.

A teacher should try to build a feeling that the child's brilliance is as much a fact as any other fact. It should be accepted as any other quality. It is pointless and inappropriate for a teacher to compete personally with him, or to go to the opposite extreme and show deference.

When individualized work is given, its level should be realistic in terms of the youngster's abilities. When he is given tasks which will make him extend himself, it should be made clear that he will be accorded help when he needs it. The teacher should obviously stand ready to assist him in achieving success. This will encourage him to continue raising his sights.

It must also be recognized that, however gifted a child may be, he is still a child. He still has to achieve the developmental tasks on the road to adulthood. For instance, in preadolescence he has to learn to be less childish; in adolescence, to be comfortable with the opposite sex. He still needs to win emotional independence. In these and allied respects, his developmental needs are not significantly altered by his being talented. Although in intellectual or aesthetic realms, he may be quite adult, his social relationships may be appropriately childish. In these areas, a teacher should treat him as any other young person.

A technique which needs to be thought through, in the light of what has just been said, is that of utilizing gifted children as assistant teachers. Many can be kept interested and busy, to their own and their classmates' benefit, by having them act as tutors or "resource people" for classmates. This can be a very useful device. At least two cautions should be observed, however. First, it is no substitute for providing the child with the challenge of work which tests his true ability. The fact that an exceptionally able pupil is enjoying this role does not excuse his teacher from trying to give him learning tasks of appropriately high level to do himself. Second, it is necessary for the teacher to observe how the individual's reactions affect his own social standing and the group atmosphere.

In working with gifted children, a teacher may easily be seduced into gaining concentrated gratification from the child's progress. There is a trap in this reaction: it makes it more difficult for the teacher to be objective in working with the child and his classmates, and it may hinder the child's efforts to establish appropriate relationships with classmates.

Lastly, all must recognize that the gifted child is not immune to problems. These may be entirely unrelated to his giftedness. He or she may be hostile, or dependent, or anxious. At home he may be deprived, or overindulged. If a gifted child has emotional difficulties, he can use help. Indeed, it is always possible that a school program for aiding children to become better adjusted will release the energies of seemingly "ordinary" children so that they can reach new levels.

In this chapter we have dealt with the problems of teachers who find in their classes children who are either exceptionally slow or unusually bright. These are young people who often will benefit if their teachers learn how to give them extra help within the limits set by the necessity of dealing with the larger group.

In each instance we have devoted considerable space to some of the feelings which trouble teachers confronted with exceptional learners. This was done for the purpose of helping each teacher recognize that, whether the reaction be considered "good" or "bad," it is so universal that it need be a source of neither guilt nor pride. The goal should be that of achieving a workmanlike objectivity in which the focus is kept on the child and his reactions.

Although much remains to be discovered, our present knowledge does make it possible to help many exceptional children learn better. In this respect, the mental health goal of good adjustment and the social goal of educational efficiency, far from being inconsistent, are best approached along a common route.

ADDITIONAL READINGS

Blos, Peter. *The Adolescent Personality*. New York: Appleton-Century-Crofts, 1941, pp. 113-219. A full case study of a very bright boy.

Bond, Guy L., and Miles A. Tinker. *Reading Difficulties: Their Diagnosis and Correction*. New York: Appleton-Century-Crofts, 1957. Written for classroom teachers, this book has sections on diagnosis and remedial treatment.

Buhler, Charlotte, Faith Smitter, and Sybil Richardson. *Childhood Problems and the Teacher*. New York: Holt, 1952, Chap. 6. Patterns related to scholastic problems are discussed.

Hildreth, Gertrude H. *Educating Gifted Children at Hunter College Elementary School*. New York: Harper, 1952. Reports from a well-conducted special school for outstanding pupils.

Rogers, Dorothy. *Mental Hygiene in Elementary Education*. Boston: Houghton Mifflin, 1957, Chap. 14. Discusses ways in which teachers can help children who are "different."

Witty, Paul. *The Gifted Child*. Boston: Heath, 1951. A compilation of material dealing with education of the gifted.

AUDIO-VISUAL AIDS

Discovering Individual Differences, a 25-minute sound film produced by
McGraw-Hill, in which a skillful teacher explains to a student what
clues helped her develop plans for five children with problems.

chapter 10

GROUP LIFE IN THE CLASSROOM

There is all the difference in the world between dealing with people (old or young) one at a time and working with them in groups of thirty or forty. Yet most of our organized knowledge about human beings is derived from situations where they were studied as individuals isolated from everyone but the observer. This is particularly true in the field of mental hygiene, where so much of our information grows out of what psychiatrists have learned as they dealt with their patients in individual conferences.

Slowly, however, experimenters are beginning to accumulate accurate information about what happens to individuals when they are members of a group. Fortunately, because children are more readily available, what scientists have been learning quite often involves children of school age. In this chapter we shall discuss some of the findings of group research as they apply to teaching.

Sociometric Studies

Here and there one hears of teachers who use sociograms or friendship charts. They ask children to state preferences for other members of the class by responding to such questions as these: Who would you want to sit near you? With whom do you want to work in the chemistry laboratory? Which children in this class would you like to have spend the weekend at your house? Which boys or girls do you like least?

On the basis of the answers, a diagram is constructed (see accompanying figure). Such a chart can give a teacher some insight into social relationships among children. However, care should be taken to use a fairly wide range of questions, because experience has shown that groupings based on play activities may be quite different from those based on seating preferences or study. Furthermore, there is a big difference between knowing the distribution of affection or the popularity ratings in a classroom and planning what to do about them. Nothing would be worse than too direct an approach, exposing children to an embarrassing discussion of their group positions. Youngsters may react poorly to naïve, open urgings to be nicer to unchosen children. It is important to remember that the causes of any particular sociometric pattern may be much more complex than the chart can convey, and

FRIENDSHIP CHART OF A SMALL GROUP

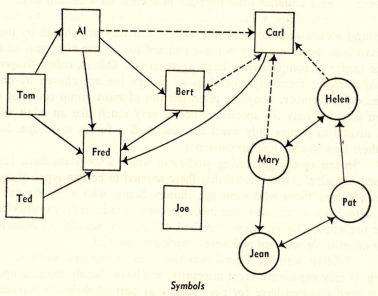

Symbols

A ←————— B   B chooses A, but A does not mention B
A ←————→ B   A and B choose each other
A ——————→ B   A dislikes B
A ←— —— —→ B   A and B dislike each other

Explanation

There is a clique centering around Fred, as leader.
Al is a fringer in this group; only Tom has chosen him.
Ted and Joe are both isolates; neither has been chosen by other youngsters.
Carl is a reject; two boys and two girls dislike him, and he has no friends.
There are two pairs of mutually chosen girl friends: Mary and Helen, and Jean and Pat.

that no plan of action for dealing with it is contained in the analysis of the chart.

A large number of sociometric studies has revealed that natural friendship groups among children are usually small; five or six is generally the largest combination in a class, with occasional groupings of seven or eight. That is to say, although we can think of a room of forty children as a group which operates as a whole, it is an artificial unit. Left to themselves, without a framework imposed by adults or by the rules of a game such as football, young people prefer working in small gatherings. One implication of this fact is that a teacher must be aware that in many situations a schoolroom is really composed of many sub-groups with varying relations to each other. Rivalry among them, for instance, may underlie what happens in a class on a certain day.

Children differ widely in the extent to which they enter these natural groups and the frequency with which they are chosen by their classmates. Some are very popular and are likely year after year to be the center of comparatively large aggregations. Others, called *fringers,* may consider themselves members of groups but are chosen by only one other member. They are often left out of most group activities or are included only for special purposes, very much like an adult who is invited to parties only when the rest need a fourth at bridge. Still others lead an even lonelier existence.

In one of the pioneering studies in which sociograms have been used, Bronfenbrenner[1] noted that there seemed to be two types of children among those who were not chosen. Some, who might be called *isolates,* were so colorless and inconspicuous as to be simply overlooked or neglected. Others, whom we shall call *rejects,* manifested offensive or undesirable behavior and were consciously disliked.

Children who are forced into the roles of fringers, isolates, and rejects may experience great insecurity. We have already touched upon the need children have for peer groups as part of their development. If a youngster does not have membership in one of the class groups and does not belong to a group outside school, he is growing up under difficulties. This is a signal for the teacher to observe closely, to figure out the why of the situation, and to develop a plan for coping with the fundamental problems of the group and the youngster. Sociograms, by making an instructor aware of the young people who need such assistance, serve an invaluable function.

---

[1] Urie Bronfenbrenner, *Social Status, Structure and Development in Classroom Groups,* unpublished Ph.D. dissertation, University of Michigan, 1942.

By providing evidence with some objectivity, sociograms may make for wiser decisions in areas where speculation has hitherto been dominant. For instance, when Johnson[2] studied 25 classes (5 at each grade level from one through five) where there were no special classes for mentally handicapped youngsters, he found that those with low I.Q.'s were selected less often than, and rejected more often by, their classmates. In general, the lower a child's I.Q., the worse was the social situation he faced. In view of the finding by Flanders[3] that anxiety about social relationships can disrupt learning, we would suspect that keeping mentally retarded children in regular classes would not only lead to social troubles, but would lower the possibility of their learning very much. In Flanders' words, "Student behavior associated with interpersonal anxiety takes priority over behavior oriented toward the achievement problem."

A similar type of evidence, involving the social effects and, presumably, the academic repercussions of nonpromotion policies, has been gathered by Goodlad.[4] He compared fifty-five first-graders who had been held back with a control group, equated on mental age, chronological age, and achievement, who had been promoted. There was a distinct difference in social adjustment. The nonpromoted children tended to reject more of their classmates, and were not as often chosen by them.

In utilizing sociograms, there are a number of cautions to be kept in mind. For instance, the friendship groups among children are continually changing. It would be a sad mistake for a teacher to assume that a class sociogram made at the start of a year held true three months later. A series of friendship charts, showing the changes in group organization, may be amazingly useful. For one thing, it tells the teacher how the group is developing in terms of shifts in the structure of subgroups. Furthermore, it may throw light upon conditions which would otherwise be puzzling. In one case,[5] for example, it was found that an apparently popular leader was the cause of considerable bad feeling.

---

2 George Orville Johnson, *A Study of the Social Position of Mentally-Handicapped Children in the Regular Grades,* Ed.D. dissertation, University of Illinois, 1950, University Microfilms Publication No. 1664.

3 Ned A. Flanders, "Personal-Social Anxiety as a Factor in Experimental Learning Situations," *Journal of Educational Research,* Vol. 45 (1951), pp. 100-10.

4 John I. Goodlad, "Some Effects of Promotion and Non-Promotion upon Social and Personal Adjustment of Children," *Journal of Experimental Education,* Vol. 22 (1954), pp. 301-28.

5 Staff of the Division of Child Development and Teacher Personnel, American Council on Education, *Helping Teachers Understand Children,* Washington, American Council on Education, 1945, Chap. 10.

Examining a series of sociograms, the teacher noticed that in each one the girl was at the center of a different group. Equally significant, there was rejection between members of the group to which she now belonged and those of her last-previous coterie. This discovery led the teacher to recognize a hitherto unsuspected source of group friction, to clear the air, and to make a careful study of the girl to help her gratify her group needs in more normal ways.

The friendship chart is only one technique for getting a picture of group structure. When the same information is obtained by observing a class as it engages in free play, forms into table groups in the lunchroom, or splits into natural subgroups on leaving the school building, the teacher is saved from difficulties arising from the chartmaking procedure. There is less temptation to discuss the chart with the class, because they have not been made curious by being asked for choices. To analyze the reasons for popularity, isolation, or rejection with a class may do damage to some children.

When attempting to secure sociograms, it is wise to remember that the more specific the basis of the choice, the clearer is the meaning. For example, a word like "friend" is used by some children to describe anyone who has ever given them candy; others reserve it for someone with whom they have a deep relationship.

Also, there is a big difference between popularity and influence. Not all children who are frequently chosen by others are leaders. Indeed, one can find children so imbued with the importance of having friends that they shape their actions so as to retain popularity. Such a boy or girl, for instance, would be afraid to befriend a child of low status. A genuine leader, by contrast, would be willing to do so, and could alter the group's reception of an otherwise unpopular classmate.

The Group as an Organism

Even though a school class is an artificially large aggregation, it nevertheless has a unity of its own. We are not here falling into the exploded fallacy that any group has a "group mind." However, individual children act differently in one class from the way they do in another. Teachers recognize this and will speak of a class group as having a distinctive personality. At any one grade level and in any one subject, and with the same teacher, one class may enter well into discussion; another, be apathetic; a third, be boisterous; and a fourth, be tense with feuds. In the teachers' lunchroom, the word goes down the line: "Watch out for this year's sixth grade—they're hellers!" or "That junior class is the swellest bunch of kids I've ever had."

What creates the differences between groups? The complete answer cannot be given yet. However, we do know that any group is somewhat like an organism. It creates conditions such that its member parts will behave in certain ways because they belong to it; at the same time the manner in which the parts function affects the whole. Thus, a girl who is very unsure of herself and likely to challenge a teacher may calm down if she is in a class with an easygoing tradition. In another group, challenging a teacher may set up an irritation which alters the group.

A very effective demonstration of this quality was shown by an experiment which Merei[6] conducted among nursery school children in Hungary. He had small groups play together until they had established a traditional pattern. Then he would introduce a child of known leadership ability. The initial efforts of the leader to entice the others into playing his favorite game almost always failed. Most leaders then fell into the pattern of the group—which, however, gradually changed its ways under the leader's influence.

The great differences between class groups have a very practical effect upon what may be done for disturbed children. Skill in placing the child in the correct group may mean a great deal for his mental health. Some youngsters, for example, may become overstimulated in a group where other children would be calmed. Frequently, a partial solution to a child's difficulties may be found in transferring him from one class to another. When this is being considered, it is essential to estimate what the effect of the new group is likely to be. By the same token, in trying to figure out the reasons for problem behavior, some attention is wisely given to the effect of the group on the child.

Cliques and Subgroups

One factor which gives each class its own peculiar characteristics is the particular pattern of cliques and subgroups which it contains. The formation of subgroups in any aggregation as large as the average class is inevitable. The questions are, How many will form? On what basis? How will they feel toward each other?

In the lower grades, one frequent basis of clique formation is

---

[6] Ferenc Merei, "Group Leadership and Institutionalization," *Human Relations,* Vol. 2 (1949), pp. 23-29.

ordinary proximity. Children who sit near each other or are in the same small work group are quite likely to become friends. Often the primary factor is where the youngsters live. Those whose homes are on the same street or who follow the same route to school form groups. In small towns, as illustrated in the case of the Morris boy (pages 18 to 19), the children who live in town are considered different from those brought from the rural areas in buses. Sometimes this division is merely a fact, and does not influence group life very much. In other cases such differences loom large in the children's feelings about each other. In a Texas town of five thousand, to give a concrete illustration, Bonney[7] found that town students were much more frequently chosen as friends than bus students. Worst off were all groups of rural girls. They showed greater preference for town girls than for each other, and no other group, either boys or girls, preferred rural girls. These girls did not even choose one another. To alter such a situation would require thoughtful planning by a teacher. Some of the relationships might change in response to judicious seating and working arrangements, and tact used, based on awareness of the facts about the feelings of the children and groups toward each other.

Among older children, similarities in play interest and abilities begin to play a part. You may, for example, find a trio of vigorous boys who spend much of their time dashing about on bicycles, while a pair who could not keep up with them have found solace in watching television together. A teacher may be able to help an isolate at this age level by having him demonstrate some interest or ability that intrigues a few of his classmates.

Wellman's observations[8] of 113 junior high school students at the Lincoln School of Teachers College indicate that girl friends tend to be alike in scholastic characteristics. Among boys, physical stature, as well as intelligence and age, is important.

By adolescence, adult society is placing its imprint on clique formation, which is now likely to be patterned after divisions in the grown-up community. At this age level, we find cliques derived from attendance at the same church, from race membership, or from economic class. Where adults enjoy feelings of exclusiveness, the adolescent

---

[7] M. E. Bonney, "A Sociometric Study of the Peer Acceptance of Rural Students in Three Consolidated High Schools," *Educational Administration and Supervision*, Vol. 37 (1951), pp. 234-40.

[8] Beth Wellman, "The School Child's Choice of Companions," *Journal of Educational Research*, Vol. 14 (1926), pp. 126-32.

cliques may be organized as secret societies. However, group formation on the basis of similarities in other interests continues. To counteract patterns which may create bitter feelings and acts of discrimination, teachers may have to use their influence skillfully to strengthen those groupings based on less socially hazardous interests. Here athletic teams, dramatic groups, subject clubs, and junior auxiliaries of civic organizations can be important. It is essential, though, to see that these are not captured by any exclusive racial group, economic class, or secret society.

There are other very significant bases for subgroup formation. Psychological needs come into play. A clique may arise because its members are different in ways which meet their mutual needs. For example, a small group may gather around a boy with a very active imagination for creative dramatic play because he furnishes them with an excitement they can get only from him. The group may contain several who willingly play the less pleasant roles in the games. Their participation, in turn, helps him satisfy his need to be bossy. Similarly, a girl with a need to establish herself as grown-up by telling many filthy jokes may enjoy the companionship of a group which is satisfying its sex curiosity by listening to her and asking questions.

The problem for a teacher who wants to appraise the effects of subgroups either on the class as a whole or on a single individual is to estimate the purposes the small groups serve. For example, if a high school class is upset by a group of girls who seem to specialize in malicious gossip, one would want to know the relationship of these girls to other cliques. If it turned out that they had been excluded from dating by strongly organized secret sororities, one possible strategy would be to see if through school social activities the inequality could be partially redressed. If the center of the group is a leader whose parents are unusually strict in forbidding dates, we may be able to whittle down the group through finding opportunities for most members to enter boy-girl activities. However, we would still have the problem of helping the leader deal with her individual conflicts.

The existence of subgroups carries with it the possibility that a teacher may unwittingly line up with one clique. For instance, a teacher who hates gossip could easily see the above-mentioned group of gossipers as something to be destroyed, whereas one who had herself suffered from a social freeze-out might take on the job of helping them to humble the sorority girls. Any such alignment brings into play on a large scale all the evils of having a teacher's pet.

When a small group displays behavior that shows its members have problems, some teachers feel helpless. But there are many ways of coping with the difficulty. In fact, with some modifications all the influence techniques to be described in Chapters 12 and 13 can be applied to groups.

Role Concepts and Expectations

In one way or another, many groups give rise to something approaching a division of labor. Thus, one girl may be expected to act as the wit who initiates verbal dart throwing at boys; another may be the expert at wheedling permission from parents for the rest to get away from home; and a third may be the patient butt of practical jokes. The specialized function of an individual within a group is called a role.

Such sharp delineation of function is found more frequently among adolescents, but may be observed even in play groups among primary school children. The significant thing is that the group's own expectations have a decided power. A particular youngster feels impelled to play the role his group feels he has assumed. Thus, among older children, a leader may take on a boldness in confronting adults which he would not exhibit but for the presence of his friends. Even leadership may differ, depending on the circumstances. For example, in a group of adolescent boys, one may be pushed forward to make the initial approach to strange girls, but another may feel that his "department" is thinking up ways of killing time when nothing definite is in view.

Among juvenile gangs which develop an organization for delinquency, such subdivision of roles may reach a great length. For example, the group may have one or more "brains," who provide ideas to the apparent leader. In battles with rival gangs, the command may go to one who is expected to show daring. A physically weaker member may serve as the gang's spy or information service. There may even be one or two "punks," young fellows who are seemingly tolerated because they act as errand boys or as an admiring audience for others.

In the classroom, this phenomenon may lead to conduct which is hard to change unless its cause is understood. For example, a boy or girl may be "bad" partly because he is living up to a previous reputation. Another may be the pride of the class as a cartoonist, whose caricatures of teachers are put on display when the group insists. At times these roles may lead to classroom conduct which pleases teachers. In any event, it is important to find out how other class members expect a youngster to behave. He may be unable to change a course of conduct unless he is either helped to build a new reputation or is given a chance to make a fresh start in a new setting.

An unexpected illustration of the power of role expectations grew out of a series of conferences at a junior high school, concerned with a boy we shall call Emil. The boy had been in a series of fights in the hallways, but his manner of flailing at opponents and of making excuses after the incidents quickly changed the teachers' anger to impotent laughter. However, he exhausted their patience when he dictated to a girl a letter addressed to a friend in the Army in which he described events at parties in the crudest of language. The mothers of the girls mentioned in the letter refused to take it seriously when they learned that Emil was the author. Shortly after the furor subsided, he transferred to another junior high school. Curious to find out how he was doing, his former principal visited his new school several months later. She was quite surprised to discover he had been in no trouble. In fact, he was regarded as a quiet boy. His explanation was that his new classmates did not expect him to "act crazy."

Role expectations affect group behavior as well as individual conduct. In a school situation, a particular clique or a particular class may develop a strong concept of how it is expected to act. For instance, in a suburban school system, one class took pride in a tradition of being hard on teachers, and despite the misgivings of a minority devoted considerable ingenuity to driving new teachers and substitutes from the school. In many schools the stability of the student group is supported by the tradition that the senior class will assume the role of protecting younger groups.

Some Group Roles

We have discussed the power exerted by various group expectations. Now we want to look at a few roles which we often find within a group.

LEADERS.   From ancient times, men have been fascinated by the power of leaders. Plato's *Republic* and Machiavelli's *The Prince* are only two in a long series of treatises on how leaders should be trained and how they should act. The fact is that, wherever a group of human beings are acting together, one is almost sure to stand out by giving instructions, settling disputes, co-ordinating activity, or setting an example which others follow.

The distribution of leadership differs from group to group. In some, the role shifts from one child to another, depending upon activities. In others, there is a single strongly entrenched leader. That leadership may be a product of the situation rather than the inevitable appearance of a personality trait is indicated by a review which Krumboltz[9] made of fifty-seven studies following up leaders in high school and college extracurricular activities. No conclusive evidence was found that such activity either did or did not have a relationship to adult leadership. It cannot be proved that a person active in high school will tend to remain equally active in college. There is relatively conclusive evidence, however, that college extracurricular participation is indicative of future leadership.

Even more significant is the range of different psychological functions which leaders perform, and the bases upon which leadership is founded. After analyzing 124 studies on leadership, Stogdill[10] reported that, as indicated by uniformly positive results in 15 or more researches, the average leader exceeds the average member of his group in the following respects: (1) intelligence, (2) scholarship, (3) dependability in exercising responsibilities, (4) activity and social participation, and (5) socioeconomic status. The studies were in firm agreement that the qualities and skills required in a leader are largely determined by the demands of the situation in which he is to function as a leader.

Here, by way of illustration, are some results of an analysis of leaders in grades nine through eleven at the Horace Mann School for Girls, in New York, as made by Flemming.[11] In this group, composed mostly of girls from well-to-do families, four types of leadership emerged. Some were leaders because they were entertaining; others because they were brilliant; still others because they represented a cultured talent; and a fourth group because they were fair. The qualities possessed in varying degrees appeared to be compounded of four factors: fairness, originality, liveliness, and a pleasant voice. Obviously, different qualities would have headed a list for leaders of delinquent boys.

Ability, whether it be sheer physical strength or intellectual skill, may give rise to leadership, especially in groups organized to accom-

9 John D. Krumboltz, "The Relationship of Extracurricular Participation to Leadership Criteria," *Personnel and Guidance Journal*, Vol. 35 (1957), pp. 307-14.

10 Ralph M. Stogdill, "Personal Factors Associated with Leadership: A Survey of the Literature," *Journal of Psychology*, Vol. 25 (1948), pp. 35-71.

11 Edwin G. Flemming, "A Factor Analysis of the Personality of High School Leaders," *Journal of Applied Psychology*, Vol. 19 (1935), pp. 596-605.

plish a definite purpose, as in a ball-playing aggregation or a class committee. More often, youthful leaders are distinguished by their psychological understanding of the others; some heads of juvenile gangs can give a penetrating analysis of their followers which a highly trained psychologist might envy. Frequently, the leader acts for the group as a sort of embodied conscience who represents the group's ideals. The followers may feel relieved of responsibility for acts which involve conflict with either adult standards or the juvenile code.[12] Teachers meet this phenomenon when they hear the alibi, "He told me to do it."

It is essential to realize that the leader is at least in part a product of group forces. As was illustrated in the experiment cited on page 267, he is not the all-powerful free agent people assume. Teachers will do well to employ the influence of youthful leaders more than is now customarily the case. However, in doing so we must recognize their limitations.

We must recognize also that there is a big difference between a natural leader and one to whom someone has delegated power. So, too, it is a mistake to assume that the brightest and most proficient students are leaders. In juvenile groups, the bases for selection of leaders are often quite different from those adults could officially approve. It is very tempting to overlook this fact and to appoint a child we like to be leader of an activity. Such an appointment may solve certain specific problems but it usually does not change the influence patterns which govern all other activities. At certain ages and in certain neighborhood groups, a teacher may create a problem beyond what a child can handle by confronting him with the dilemma of loyalty to an assigned supervisory task as opposed to loyalty to his natural group code.

One of the trickiest problems for school people arises when the group leader turns out to be a tough customer who exploits his position, and who represents antisocial values. When this occurs, educators may be caught in a conflict between respect for democracy and responsibility. If the undesirable leader has been elected to office, the dilemma is truly devilish.

A first step in dealing with this situation is to analyze the sources of such a leader's power. Often it will turn out to be a form of double-edged blackmail. By threats he gets other children to support him; then he uses this support to blackmail adults into concessions to the group, made because of him. By becoming the authoritative source of

---

[12] See Paul Deutschberger, "The Structure of Dominance," *American Journal of Orthopsychiatry*, Vol. 17 (1947), pp. 343-51.

communication as to what each group is actually going to do, he becomes indispensable to both.

If a monopoly on communication is bolstering a harmful leader,
a wise preliminary move is to develop open and wide channels. This is
usually a necessary move, but rarely is it sufficient. Usually it will be
necessary for the adults in the situation to move directly against the
leader. Before this can be done, it is essential to be sure that the evidence against him is firm, and that the moves being planned will be sure
to win. Schemes which are stimulating in fantasy but which leave the
bad leader in the saddle make everything worse. However, if it is necessary to destroy his influence, this must be done wholeheartedly.

There is often a tendency in such situations to try to build a juvenile fifth column, which is masterminded by an ingenious teacher. It is
unfair to place youngsters in positions where they can, with truth, be
condemned as tattletales. It is even more unfair to ask them to buck
pressures which are frightening adults. Therefore, in the initial attacks
adults must participate openly, and make clear the values which impelled their decision. If, as the situation develops, young people band
together and want to take over the campaign to unseat a young tyrant,
they should be allowed to do so. Only in this way will a new leadership
of their own come into being.

ADVOCATES. In some groups one finds youngsters who, though
they may lack the leader's sensitivity toward people or his boldness in
action, are more facile with words or ideas. These youngsters may be
cast in the role of defending the group against charges from adults or
rival gangs. They play a part analogous to that of lawyers or diplomats.
In their own eyes and in the view of the group, they are expected to be
masters of the alibi, the rationalization, and the clever negotiation.
Where some child assumes this role with zest, adults may mistake him
for the leader.

CLOWNS. A great many juvenile groups have their court jesters.
These are boys or girls who are expected to supply mirth. Sometimes,
but by no means always, they are markedly fat or thin, very tall or
short, or else they are below par in skill. By combining humor with self-
display they win a place in the group. Their clowning provides a diver-
sion when the group has nothing more serious to do. It may act as a
thin veneer for feelings of inferiority. At times when the group wish
to attack a teacher but are afraid to do so, the clown may express the

group's hostility by undermining classroom control. Children may clown for many reasons, most of them rooted in individual psychological problems. The group expectations, where these are involved, may be only one portion of the explanation.

Accordingly, in situations where something needs to be done about a child's clowning it is important to have at least a hunch why that particular child was enticed to take a clown's role. For instance, there are occasions when a group's needs are being poorly met. An imaginative young person, who is sensitive to the unrest and has a flair for action, may clown in order to dissolve tension, to prevent an outbreak of bickering, or to call a halt to adult restrictions self-righteously imposed. If the clown has, in fact, rescued the group from a worsening situation, an attack on him for clowning will backfire. Basically, the solution is to correct the situation, and only then to find some means to give the youngster attention in a nonclowning role.

In some cases, the clown is a socially clumsy, insensitive child who happens to arouse merriment at some opportune time. His first successes are self-intoxicating. Lacking judgment and hungering for approbation, he continues his antics even when they are ill-timed and disruptive. This situation calls for the careful timing of intervention by adults, and will be discussed in Chapter 13.

In other instances, the clown may be a rather suggestible child who is seduced into silly behavior by other children. The blame for his behavior really rests on the group. It may assist the child for a teacher to help him see how he has been placed in a false position.

"FALL GUYS."   Many juvenile groups carry with them a boy or girl whose ineptness or mistakes can be blamed for most failures. The presence of such a "fall guy" gives the others a great psychological security. In some cases he is expected not only to take the blame within the group but also to accept penalties imposed by adults. He may even get a perverse satisfaction from this role. In dealing with group behavior, teachers should be alert to this possibility. The other children are more likely to be amused than impressed by measures directed at a scapegoat.

The fall guy may be unaware of how easily he can be induced to get in trouble. Often he gets a subtle security from feeling that he is incompetent and therefore no demands will be made of him. In this sense, he hardly takes himself seriously, and hopes no one else will expect him to try to amount to anything.

An example of the group attitudes toward fall guys was furnished by an incident in a detention home. Three boys were washing dishes in a kitchen. They noticed a police officer walking across the yard, three floors beneath them. One said, "Man, would he hop if we dropped a bottle near him." One of the others did just that.

When supervisors rushed to the kitchen, they found two of the lads convulsed with laughter, pointing to the third and gasping, "Did you see what that dope did?"

The interesting aspect is that in a group where tattling is treason, the fall guy is considered such a "dope" that his misdeeds are not protected. Indeed they are considered so stupid as not to count as true crimes worthy of secrecy. This in itself is clear evidence that it is useless for adults to give excessive punishment.

To cure a fall guy of his penchant for failures is a difficult task, and one about which little has been written. From the viewpoint of maintaining a good classroom situation, the point of attack is the individual or group which puts him up to his delinquencies.

INSTIGATORS. Often responsible for the deeds of a fall guy, but usually covering a wider range of activities, are boys and girls who cause trouble but keep clear of direct involvement. They may be skillful in setting the stage for fights; they suggest pranks; they spread gossip. Here is a simple illustration of one at work:

Three girls, whom we shall call Jackie, Lorna, and Kate, were on the playground. Jackie pushed Lorna against Kate. Kate shoved back. Jackie then said to Lorna, "Don't let her push you around like that." With this she again pushed Lorna against Kate.

When Kate told Lorna to stop, Jackie told Lorna, "You must learn to stick up for yourself." With that advice, she again pushed the two girls together. When Kate impatiently shoved Lorna away, Lorna slapped Kate's face. Soon the two girls were furiously clawing at each other.

When a teacher told Jackie that Lorna accused her of starting the fight, Jackie said, "I didn't do anything. I was just telling her not to be so easy."

Some instigators are much more subtle. In any event, when a teacher has a class in which there is more ill feeling and fighting than is customary for the neighborhood, it is wise to start looking for an instigator. By getting full details on who told what to whom before an incident, it may be possible to discover who the child may be.

The basic tactic in dealing with an instigator is to unmask him and make his tactics clear to the group. This will not always change the youngster, but may protect the group. It is essential that the teacher be sure that the accusation is true and that it will be backed by testimony from enough other children so that the group will be convinced.

The chances are that a thoroughgoing instigator will be a fairly smooth operator who causes no other problem. In a sense, he solves his own inner problems by using other youngsters as live props to work them out. He rarely feels guilt. In fact, he has usually convinced himself that what he is doing is for the good of his victims. What is more, his victims are likely to consider him a friend. This is one reason why it is necessary to have overwhelming evidence. If this is not done, his victims will back him up, and the group may consider him a martyr.

The purpose of exposing his tactics is twofold. First, if he comes to recognize that social disapproval is attached as much to starting trouble as to being an active participant, there is a possibility that his own conscience will begin to cover new territory. Secondly, for others in the group there is a valuable lesson in learning how to disengage themselves from people who want to get them into difficulties. In some cases a teacher might encourage a class discussion of how to meet the gambits of a skilled instigator.

Group Atmosphere and Group Morale

Another significant attribute of groups is their "general feeling tone," or emotional climate. Teachers seek to create a good atmosphere in a classroom. Administrators strive for similar goals in terms of a school or a whole system. They realize that if the group atmosphere is bad, problems keep bubbling up which would appear less frequently if the atmosphere were healthier.

In early studies by experimenters, the term "social climate" was used to indicate differences in power structure and leadership techniques and in the subsequent characteristics groups develop under these two influences. A pioneering experiment by Lippitt, conducted under the inspiration of Kurt Lewin, illustrates the influence of the social climate created by different leadership techniques.[13] The experimenters placed boys' clubs under various leaders, each of whom was instructed

---

[13] Ronald Lippitt, "An Experimental Study of the Effect of Democratic and Authoritarian Group Atmospheres," *University of Iowa Studies of Child Welfare*, Vol. 16 (1940), pp. 43-195.

to use one of three general methods: (1) autocratic, in which the leader gave detailed directions and did not take part in work, (2) democratic, in which the leader acted as a consultant but promoted decision making by the group and took part in the work, and (3) laissez-faire, in which the leaders neither gave directions nor took part. In the democratic atmosphere, the boys worked efficiently, co-operated well and got into few fights with each other. The laissez-faire climate produced much desultory activity and led to considerable aggression. The autocratic groups had a tendency either to show poor work habits and much fighting or to work with apparent efficiency, which quickly dissolved when the leader left the room. When the method of leadership was changed, the same group of boys would display great differences in behavior.

Although these results suggest general ideas as to group leadership, it should be remembered that the experiment applies directly to small groups of American preadolescents. How much difference it would make if the children were adolescents or of primary school age has not been shown. In a similar experiment done in England with mentally retarded boys,[14] it appeared that laissez-faire leadership resulted in more aggression than either strict or friendly supervision.

One hypothesis has been that the more a leader intervenes, the more frustrating the group is to its members. There is some evidence that frustrations are less likely to arouse strong feelings if they seem to be inevitable and impersonal. On the other hand, when rules are arbitrary, they are more likely to be resented. To get at this issue, Pastore[15] presented 131 college students with two sets of frustrating situations. In one set, actions were depicted as unjustifiable or arbitrary: for example, "Your instructor springs an unexpected and difficult examination for which you are unprepared." In the other set, the frustration had an element of justification: for example, "Your instructor gives a difficult examination for which you are poorly prepared." The responses to the arbitrary frustrations involved more anger than to the justified set.

The result of the factors mentioned and others yet to be discussed is to create a "group atmosphere." This term was coined primarily to refer to the general feeling tone of people in a group toward each other, and to some of the attitudes they reveal in their behavior. There are many types of climate or atmosphere which may pervade a classroom.

---

14 J. Tizard and N. O'Connor, "The Occupational Adaptation of High Grade Mental Defectives," *Lancet* (September 27, 1952), pp. 620-32.

15 Nicholas Pastore, "The Role of Arbitrariness in the Frustration-Aggression Hypothesis," *Journal of Abnormal and Social Psychology*, Vol. 47 (1952), 728-31.

The tendency of a class may be to think in terms of punishing, of making its recalcitrant members squirm, or of humbling other groups. By contrast, there are other classes in which teamwork seems to come very easily, where the inclination is to work together and to think of other classes as augmenting the teamwork. Still another of the many possible climates is one of low energy, where the prevailing attitude is, "What's the use?"

To the mental hygienist, such differences in group atmosphere are quite important. Where relative harmony reigns, youngsters are able to develop with less conflict. When they must work out their problems in an atmosphere heavy with pressure, added burdens are placed on them. Moreover, differences in group atmosphere give rise to differences not only in the type of difficulty with which young people must cope but also in the type of solutions to those difficulties which appear to work.

Here, for example, is the report of a teacher on a boy who had been sent for one hour a week to a small group especially designed to have an atmosphere of freedom and understanding:[16]

> When Dick first came to school, he appeared frightened and so timid he cried. His father was very wise to bring him in before the children came. He was shown the games and supplies but it took him a long time before Dick asked for anything. He just sat in his seat day after day until something was placed in his hands. His best friend ordered him about and he accepted anything from him. He drew beautifully, but was not relaxed for many months. Group work was wonderful for Dick because in a small group he is recognized and he began to assert himself a little. Now he is able to fight back for himself and really has established himself as a recognized individual in the classroom. He is witty and has so much to offer the other children. He is still quiet but can fight back when the occasion arises. I think Dick has to be handled very carefully next term. He might be a wonderful leader if the teacher can recognize his assets and at the same time cope with a very sensitive nature.

When, as often happens, two teachers have different impressions of the same child, it may be that each is seeing a contrasting reaction resulting from a difference in group atmosphere. In such cases it may be wise to arrange, when there is a choice, to let the child spend as much time as possible in the group where he works best with other children.

---

[16] Bureau of Educational Research, Board of Education of the City of New York, *Final Report of Study of Mental Hygiene Project at Public School 33, Manhattan,* New York, 1949, mimeographed document.

ACTIVITY STRUCTURE.   One of the ingredients which change group climate is the nature of the activities. Some, such as free art activities, call for little intervention on the part of a teacher. Others, such as a teacher-directed step-by-step "solution" of a geometry proposition, have to be closely controlled. A pioneer analysis of this variable was a study by Gump and others[17] of two activity settings at a camp. Over a three-hour period, observers watched 9 boys in two different activities: swimming and a cook-out. In swimming, boys were under few restrictions. At the cookout, there were delays while the fire was built and the food prepared. While the group was swimming, counselors had to intervene 8 times; during the cook-out, 39 times.

Although we do not have comparable analyses of typical classroom activities, this experiment would suggest that if a teacher finds himself spending an undue amount of energy keeping a class in line, it may arise from what the children are being required to do. For instance, any action done in unison would probably require greater direction than one in which each can go at his own pace.

FOCUS OF ATTENTION.   Another way of looking at a group is to ask who or what is most important in it. In educational literature, the terms "learner-centered" and "teacher-centered" denote such qualities. Several efforts have been made to measure this aspect. One that has proved useful for research purposes was devised by Withall.[18] In teacher-centered groups, a large proportion of the teacher's response to incidents fall into the following categories:

1. Directive or hortative statements with the intent to have the pupil follow a recommended course of action.

2. Reproving or deprecating remarks intended to deter the pupil from continued indulgence in present "unaccepted" behavior.

3. Self-supporting remarks of teacher intended to sustain or justify the teacher's position or course of action.

By contrast, in a learner-centered classroom, the bulk of the teacher's remarks will serve the following purposes:

1. Learner-supportive statements that have the intent of reassuring or commending the pupil.

---

[17] Paul Gump, Phil Schoggen, and Fritz Redl, "The Camp Milieu and Its Immediate Effects," *Journal of Social Issues,* Vol. 13 (1957), pp. 40-46.

[18] John Withall, "The Development of a Technique for the Measurement of Social-Emotional Climate in the Classroom," *Journal of Experimental Education,* Vol. 17 (1949), pp. 347-61.

2. Acceptant and clarifying statements having an intent to convey to the pupil the feeling that he is understood and to help him elucidate his ideas and feelings.

3. Problem-structuring statements or questions which proffer information or raise questions about the problem in an objective manner with the intent of facilitating the learner's problem solving.

Where the choice is between the alternatives described by these criteria, it would appear, on the evidence, that the emotional climate is better in learner-centered groups, and that the subject-matter achievement is on a par.

The present authors suspect there is another dimension to the situation. In some groups there is relatively little concern with the relationships; all energy is channeled into the problem or task at hand. In this sense such groups are *task-oriented*. This is a matter which calls for further research.

GROUP MORALE. Although both the leadership and the group composition are highly significant, the morale of a class is also influenced by relationships between groups and by community conditions. We see such morale differences in assembly behavior, where some classes develop higher self-discipline and others may act ashamed. Similarly, community boasting or other behavior may raise school spirit to flaming heat. School people will often try to give membership in a school a genuine emotional meaning for young people. However, this cannot be done by lectures alone. In fact, if the appeals are on emotionally false premises, an atmosphere of cynicism or clowning may appear. At the opposite extreme, overdeveloped group pride may cause trouble. The task is to help the children to domesticate the high spirit and to use it constructively. This is especially true where nearby communities have had bitter rivalries or where nationality or racial differences embitter the contact between neighborhoods in big cities.

From a mental health viewpoint, the question is not so much how to get morale, but the basis on which it is secured and what it does to the pupils. For instance, in some groups the result of strong cohesion is that life is made miserable for anyone who dares to be "different." A child who raises questions about the worth of a group activity becomes highly unpopular. There can develop a type of vigilantism which is the antithesis of an educational atmosphere. This does not have to happen. If the group's morale includes pride in socially valid helpfulness and in search for answers, the effects may be sound educationally and contribute to good mental health.

The phenomenon of group morale has become the focus of many studies and experiments. To be sensitive to conditions which endanger good morale and to be skilled in the techniques of strengthening and repairing it are assets of all good group leaders, including teachers and principals.

Some Typical Dynamics

The very existence of a group makes possible the development of psychological forces which would otherwise not come into being. Conditions from either within or without may create new chains of events. A full description of group dynamics is not yet possible, because research in this area is comparatively young. However, for the sake of illustration, we will describe eight types of situation upon which some observation has been made.

CONTAGION OF BEHAVIOR. In deciding what to do about a particular youngster's conduct in a classroom, teachers must estimate whether it is likely to spread. Where poor behavior is certain to be contagious, we may be justified in taking rather firm action; however, if there is no such danger, we can safely resort to such techniques as planful ignoring and other low-pressure devices, while avoiding the risks involved in punishments, threats, banishment from the group, and emergency measures.

This whole problem of contagion of behavior within groups is just beginning to receive concentrated scientific attention. Definite findings cannot be quoted. However, certain tentative conclusions may be of help in the classroom.

Where behavior gives expression to impulses which are shared by several children and which they are not intent upon controlling, it may sweep through a group. Thus, if some child breaks a pencil point and noisily resharpens it, a class which is bored or has been kept immobile too long may be seized by an epidemic of the same kind of noisemaking. The reason for the epidemic is that the children have built up the need to move around and to be relieved of their tension by a chance to manipulate something. However, they have hitherto kept to their seats because their consciences somehow insisted that they stay within the limits of teacher-approved behavior, no matter how unpleasant a duty that might become. The openly demonstrated courage of the child who broke the ice by seeking release for himself acts as a stimulant for similar behavior in all the others. On the other hand, if a boy in the fourth grade started crawling on the floor, most classes would not follow suit. Few nine-year-olds have a strong "need" to act like babies in this way.

Another factor in contagion is the way in which an act is performed. Where the child who is breaking the ice shows a fearless or exuberant attitude, his behavior is more likely to spread. On the other hand, if he displays evidence of fear or guilt, few will be tempted to follow his lead. Thus, if a girl confidently puts her foot out to trip up another member of the class and smiles triumphantly at her success, such tripping-up episodes may well be repeated by others, provided, of course, there are no special feelings involved, such as sympathy of the group with the victim. However, if she acted in a sneaky fashion and seemed genuinely worried or upset afterwards, contagion would not be likely.

A third factor is the standing of the first perpetrator within the group. For example, if the tripping was done by a girl whom the rest admired or who had a reputation for daring that several envied, the temptation to ape her would be high. On the other hand, if she was unpopular or was regarded as a pitiful screwball, her actions would be without direct effect.

In a laboratory study[19] where boys were observed as they worked in pairs at boring tasks, the actions of one boy of each pair (a secret confederate of the experimenters) were varied systematically. It was found that contagion from the confederate to the other was more likely to appear when the confederate's actions showed a way of escaping from an unpleasant state of affairs. Other qualities of actions which proved likely to spread were that they reduced the possibility that a youngster would be disapproved by his peers, that they reduced the fear of dangerous consequences, and that they made apparent the satisfaction to be gained. Interestingly, in this situation it was found that "good" behavior also is contagious. Where the paid confederate stuck to the assigned task, his action clearly bolstered forces making for restraint on the part of the other boy.

There are other elements in contagion which have not been explored fully enough to warrant generalization. The seating or working arrangement of a group may limit the spread of behavior. The level of

---

[19] Daniel Grosser, Norman Polansky, and Ronald Lippitt, "A Laboratory Study of Behavioral Contagion," *Human Relations*, Vol. 4 (1951), pp. 115-42.

boredom, the amount of restlessness, and less easily described qualities of group atmosphere, some of them temporary, exert influence. That is why an action which is ignored at one time may create an epidemic in the same group on another occasion.

Desirable as well as unpleasant conduct may spread by contagion. Thus, in a class which has developed a tradition of showing a low opinion of poetry, for example, a well-liked boy or girl may set off serious discussion by making an obviously interested comment.[20]

SCAPEGOATING. When a group is under pressure or is meeting many frustrations, it is likely to displace its feelings of hostility upon an unpopular individual or subgroup. Because this phenomenon can play a critical part in the development of social prejudices, it has been the subject of much psychological thought and study.

From the mental hygiene point of view, scapegoating of this kind is not only a symptom of poor emotional health conditions within a group, but is especially serious in its effects upon the victims. Too often, the child against whom the others turn is one whose original unpopularity can be traced to manifestations of considerable internal tension. For example, the scapegoat may be chosen because he or she is dirty, or smelly, or cruel. On the surface, one might think that the victim was selected because his behavior was unpleasant. However, we can readily understand that his conduct may be a repercussion of bad home conditions or of personal conflicts poorly handled. Such a child would be least able to cope with the concentrated social pressures the class then brings to bear.

When a school group exhibits a tendency to be cruel to its least popular members or when there is evidence of great friction between subgroups, we may suspect that scapegoating is taking place. This calls for a careful examination of school procedures to see whether they are creating undue pressure or are leading to many interferences with the achievement of children's needs. It is always wise to remember that at times the pressures on children arise from community conditions which the school cannot directly control. In the case of Mr. Lawrence's Rhoda (see pages 7 to 9) the group probably "needed" a scapegoat, not because of anything in his class, but because of the many frustrations they

---

[20] For a theoretical formulation of material on contagion, see the following: Fritz Redl, "The Phenomenon of Contagion and 'Shock Effect' in Group Therapy," in K. R. Eisler, *Searchlights on Delinquency,* New York, International Universities Press, 1949.

had previously encountered because of their "slowness." The scapegoat need not always be a youngster who was initially disliked. Under pressure, a group will produce a scapegoat; nearly anyone may be picked for that role.

In some puzzling instances, signs of scapegoating may appear in groups which have unusually strong spirit. Light on this situation has been given by Festinger[21] and his co-workers, who found that in highly cohesive groups, members who differ significantly from the rest are put under pressure to conform. To retain "good standing" an individual at one extreme is likely to "redefine group boundaries" to exclude those at the opposite extreme. For instance, if a class with strong pride has a pattern of doing average work, the members might try to use persuasion on those who did very little work or did a great deal. A youngster under pressure for doing too little might distract this attention by "riding" a gifted boy or girl. Thus, if a teacher notices that the source of scapegoating is a deviant child or clique, the countermeasures would be directed not toward the group as a whole but toward the initiators.

The handling of episodes involving scapegoating needs especially careful attention. Clumsy attempts to handle the problem too directly sometimes may increase the dislike of the group for the scapegoated member, or may tempt scapegoats to exploit their involuntary role for secondary gains in terms of leader protection.

CULTIVATION OF MASCOTS. A very interesting phenomenon occurs in some groups in which a youngster is included whom the others regard as different from themselves but in a way which makes them feel superior in a nonpunitive style. They make him a mascot. We see this clearly in the cases of undersized children or handicapped ones. The same thing is also found where there are one or two members of a minority group. The mascot is then taken into the group with apparent affection, is allowed to move with the group provided he keeps to his role, and is often displayed by the group. Among adolescents, for example, the mascot may be asked to perform in the name of the group, but would never be considered an acceptable date. On the surface, this looks much less harmful than open prejudice or discrimination. For the individual, however, it may carry heavy problems. He may be every bit as irked at not being taken seriously in many aspects of group life, his

---

21 Leon Festinger, Harold B. Gerard, Bernard Nymovitch, Harold H. Kelley, and Bert Raven, "The Influence Process in the Presence of Extreme Deviates," *Human Relations,* Vol. 5 (1952), pp. 327-46.

self-respect may be as heavily threatened, but he is denied any reason for open rebellion. He may also submit to all this and develop a vain personality, thus becoming a person easily duped into being a "sucker."

A case in point is Sheldon, a roly-poly who enjoys being a member of a rough, athletic crowd. He has a good sense of humor, which often leads him to invent amusing antics directed toward adults. Because he is so comic, the group accepts him instead of scorning him. Even though his appearance and softness represent the exact opposite of their ego ideals, they are not ashamed of him. What abuse is directed his way is marginal; this he is expected to take in fun. However, in contests and in making decisions he is not considered fully a member of the group. As Sheldon learned to play the mascot, he flourished. This formerly retiring fat boy seemingly became unworried about his shape or ineptness. After a while, though, he did resent the fact that no matter where he went with the group, he could play only one role in its proceedings.

There are other reasons for mascot status besides physical defect or ethnic-group membership. The mascot may be a fall guy whom the others like enough so that they reward him during interim periods. Or, again, especially where the child in question is much younger or less experienced than the rest, he may serve to remind them of their triumph over their own previous developmental phases.

ISOLATION OF TEACHERS' PETS.   Under many conditions, people react strongly to the feeling that someone else has a privileged position as a result of favoritism. A few may want to compete with the favorite or displace him, and others may fawn upon him in order to share in his "influence." However, this situation usually creates jealousy and a desire to get even.

Many groups act as though a large proportion of the members considered the favorite guilty of disloyalty. They bring strong pressures to bear to exact penalties for the treason or to force the teacher's pet to return to an undistinguished membership in the group. On the one hand, they may discourage him with jibes or even fisticuffs. On the other, they may pointedly "include him out" of confidential discussions.

Occasionally, the resentment of a class may be directed against the teacher, rather than the favored child. Although it may be focused on the favoritism, this is not always the case. Their criticism may come to the surface in a displacement and concentrate on other actions of the teacher. For instance, if a teacher has praised the way his pet prepared for a test, there may be an outbreak of complaints about the test.

Much that has been said above also applies if, instead of favoring a single individual, the teacher accords special privileges to a clique or other subgroup within the class. Additional reactions have been suggested by an experiment in which Thibault[22] studied what happened when one group of boys were consistently given attractive roles in play as compared to another, which he called a low-status group. The favored group took their privileges in silence. In the low-status segment, those boys who were at the center tended to have greater cohesion; the others tried to get away from the group. Interestingly, when protests were followed by corrective action, bickering increased.

For teachers wanting to help individual children who have difficulties, an important consideration is always the fear that special attention may make the boy or girl seem to be a teacher's pet. The amount and kind of resentment developed seem to depend a great deal upon the class atmosphere, the teacher's relationships to the group, the way in which the attention is given, and the way in which the child acts toward the others. For example, in a class where the teacher rules with an iron hand and is feared by the group, a pupil who is excused from the most disliked activity and sneers at the rest is almost sure to feel the full weight of a wrath which will be as cruel as possible. On the other hand, a popular teacher whose class is pervaded by an atmosphere of mutual helpfulness can go to considerable lengths to give special consideration to a child the others recognize as needing approval without exposing the "favorite" to any serious risk.

MUTUAL SUPPORT AND PROTECTION.   The reader must not get the idea that most group dynamics are harmful or cause problems for teachers. Most of the time, membership in a group is an emotionally strengthening experience. This is so much the case that specialists who work with seriously troubled children find that it is possible to achieve cures in properly managed groups that could not be obtained as fully in other ways.

When any young person who genuinely belongs to a group gets in trouble or needs help, the others are almost sure to come to his rescue. Teachers meet one aspect of this process when children cover up for each other, refuse to tell tales, or else extend aid during recitations or examinations. Outside school, a youngster who is "in bad" with a teacher will be given not only sympathy but a good deal of advice on

---

22 John Thibault, "An Experimental Study of the Cohesiveness of Underprivileged Groups," *Human Relations,* Vol. 3 (1950), pp. 256-78.

how to "get around him." A girl who dances poorly will be given hours of patient lessons by her friends.

This aspect of group life is one which can be very profitably used to aid children who need help. Classmates, out of group feeling, are often quite willing to lend each other a helping hand. If a youngster belongs to a strongly knit subgroup, his immediate friends will often make great efforts. At this point the teacher can do much good by guiding the group to discover ways of helping him. Because of their limited experience, they might not think of the very possibilities about which they could become most enthusiastic. They may be pleased and proud when a teacher gives them ideas they can adopt. The point is that powerful group forces stand ready to aid us; the trick is to know how and when to use them. Here, again, clumsy handling can be harmful. It is not good for a child to be made to feel he is a "group project." Support from friends has no such implication and is therefore especially helpful.

REACTIONS TO STRANGERS.   Sooner or later in the life of every group a stranger appears. He may be a new child to be absorbed, or an adult who has come to observe or to "supervise." The appearance of a stranger often alters the situation. No matter how strongly the teacher or the visitor may want it, no group will always act "naturally" when an unknown person is present. Even classes in constantly observed experimental schools may act a little differently when alone with their teachers than when they know they are being watched.

One effect of a stranger is to increase group tension. This is shown by the fact that both teacher and children are more conscious of their actions. There is bound to be either an increase in show-off behavior or else greater restraint. Usually, both things happen at once; some children become more active, and others more inhibited.

If the stranger is a new child, the group behavior may be a mixture of two tendencies. On the one hand, the group code may be exhibited in exaggerated form, as though to tell the newcomer how he is expected to act. Where the group prizes rebellious behavior, there may be an outburst of rule breaking; where co-operation is a keynote, the welcoming of the new child may seem unnecessarily effusive. At the same time, there are bids to test out the new member. These may range all the way from invitations to fight on the way home from school to skillful attempts to draw him out in conversation. Within the subgroups, there may be stirrings of rivalry or jealousy. At its most obvious we see this in a high school class where the more insecure girls eye a new girl's clothes, hairdo, and mannerisms, or watch the boys' faces to decide if she is going to be a menace in dating competition and, if so, what weak points they can dwell upon with their best friends.

A special condition in some groups is failure to absorb some child into the group. He then becomes a perpetual stranger. The same kind of thing may happen to a teacher. One sign of this situation is that, although the group takes the person for granted most of the time, on special occasions it becomes self-conscious in his presence. This may be evidenced by covert glances in his direction. The existence of such a condition calls for deep consideration by a teacher.

When the stranger is a supervisor who, the children feel, is judging the teacher, they may react largely in terms of the relationships within the class. In those cases where the group thinks the teacher is genuinely *its* teacher, a real part of the group, we may see all the mechanisms of support and protection come into play. They may then outdo themselves in putting on a performance calculated to please the observer. On the other hand, if hostility is strong, the class may passively resist efforts to show off its strong points.

Other factors, of course, enter the picture. Subgroups may react to the visitor without reference to the teacher. Rivalries may be accentuated and give rise to grimaces of boredom or deprecation, or other efforts to distract the visitor's attention. In a competitive group, self-display may go to embarrassing extremes. At times almost every teacher is chagrined at what the class has done in the presence of a visitor. Always it is wise to think over the conduct displayed. The behavior which appears under strain can be a valuable clue to conditions which are well hidden under ordinary circumstances. There may be a problem of communicating to the class the teacher's attitudes toward it and also his expectations as to their behavior. This matter will be discussed further in the next chapter.

GROUP DISINTEGRATION.   Few things can make a teacher feel more futile than to have a group go to pieces. At the extreme we have classes which have no cohesion, which must be treated as just so many individuals working at cross-purposes or as an undisciplined mob, living from moment to moment. Such disintegration may appear in well-knit groups for short periods of time; in other groups it is the typical state of affairs.

There are quite a few conditions which can lead to group disintegration. Long periods of empty waiting, for example, can lead to unco-ordinated disorder. Children, if confronted with tasks they cannot accomplish, may vent their frustration in bickering that can wreck any possibility of teamwork.

A poor group structure may leave a class very vulnerable. For instance, if warfare among cliques is so strong that no solution appears likely, the members will see no point in trying to work together. Also, if the teacher and the class are estranged, unable to understand each other, disintegration can speedily result. Teaching methods which create too much competition or which give rise to strong tensions can have a similar outcome.

Psychological security is important for good group life. When a group is confronted by an unexpected change, as, for instance, when teachers are shifted without preparation, the group structure may be jolted. Exposure to frequent changes in leader, meeting place, activities, or organization will destroy cohesion. Asking the group to work on a poorly explained assignment can have the same effect.

The level of success and of activity both have a powerful influence. A group which is working on the incorrect assumption that it can do a job it eventually finds is way beyond its ability, or which is trying to stay interested in something too simple, will lose its enthusiasm and may dissolve into a conglomeration of disgusted or bored individuals. Similarly, if the members have no opportunity to receive an emotional pickup following the completion of an activity, they may lose momentum. It is also a bad thing for a group if one portion of it is a sort of slum area in which there is too little activity or too few achievements.

Direct or implied criticism may be fatal under some conditions. For example, a teacher who violates the dignity of young people, especially during the teen years, may find that classes refuse to jell into any group structure. Embedding a cohesive group in a larger mass which overwhelms it may set the stage for disintegration. For instance, an orderly group can lose its morale if surrounded by disorderly groups at an assembly.

From the mental hygiene viewpoint, we are as interested in how such situations can influence young people as in the control problems disintegration produces. When a group goes to pieces, life becomes very insecure and perilous for its members. The experience is a highly unpleasant one. The weaker members can be very seriously disturbed.

Group disintegration always has a cause. When it begins to become evident, that should be a signal for very thoughtful rethinking of all plans concerning the group.

COMMUNICATION PATTERNS. A crucial aspect of classes at the upper levels is the pattern by which members first learn of important events. A child who is in possession of information as to what is going to happen gains prestige. An individual who is always the last to know will be disgruntled.

Although in the lower grades teachers usually make important announcements to the class as a whole, in secondary schools where teachers have less time with any one class, some young people will act as special transmission lines. For instance, a boy may approach a teacher after class or even in the hallways and say, "The kids are wondering whether our next examination will be like the last one."

Taking advantage of the situation, the teacher may say, "Tell them to be sure to know the next three chapters; we'll have a hundred true-false questions on that material." A few youngsters may repeatedly proffer information to the teacher, and give messages to their classmates.

In situations where a few are "in the know" and others are not, the morale of the ones with information is likely to be good. Since they are the ones with whom the teacher has most contact, he may have an illusion that all the pupils like the situation. However, many of the others may come to feel they do not belong. Often unfavorable rumors spread among them, a sign that they can easily become hostile to the class.

To avoid this type of problem, it is wise to make announcements of any importance directly to an entire class rather than through the grapevine.

Desegregation

No discussion of group forces in the classroom these days can be complete without commenting upon the problems encountered by teachers in schools where integration of racially separated school groups has taken place or, in all sections of the country, where population movement has added a new ethnic group to the school's clientele. The issues are complex, but have received well-informed attention.[23]

The basic problem in the classroom is how to get the children to live together despite the fact that many have prejudicial stereotypes.

---

[23] For a full discussion of the psychiatric aspects of such situations and prevalent emotional reactions, the reader is referred to the following bulletin: "Psychiatric Aspects of School Desegregation," New York, Group for the Advancement of Psychiatry, 1957.

The essence of the difficulty is that when one child looks at a child from another group, he sees him or her not so much as an individual in his own right but as "typical" of the group to which he belongs. This depersonalizes the individual. There are situations, as when a person is actually serving as representative of a group, where this type of reaction is appropriate. Usually however, whether the stereotype is negative or positive, it does confuse any effort to deal with realities.

From a mental health viewpoint, the impact of the situation must be considered in terms of the needs of individuals, rather than defined in philosophical or political terms.

When desegregation or racial change is taking place, there is a tendency to relate all events to that fact. It is held to be the primary cause of behavior and of problems that occur in classrooms at any time. On the part of educators, there may be pressure to "prove" that now there are no problems. This is unrealistic. In many classrooms there are combinations of individuals which lead to trouble. Race is not the only factor in a healthy grouping. The added pressure of racial feelings can hardly be expected miraculously to cure all the things that normally can go wrong.

It must be recognized that children *do* develop tremendous amounts of prejudice when this serves their psychological needs. If there is heavy pressure upon them, they may find solace in looking down on other people. If the classroom atmosphere leads to uneasiness, prejudices against some pupils may emerge.

If, as is often the case, there are strong feelings in the community, children may expect the teachers to take sides. For this reason, and in order to reduce any insecurities, it is essential to avoid any ambiguities in group management. The classroom regulations should be made clear; their application, fair and uniform.

A special problem may arise when the teacher belongs to a minority group. It is very tempting to reason that if the children of that minority group would only show eminence in behavior and achievement, this would lead to a reduction in prejudice against them. Because most minorities are at a socioeconomic disadvantage and because this is usually accompanied by lower verbal facility and more free-flowing aggression, however, the normal behavior of many will chagrin a teacher at times. It is unfair to children if they are made to act as representatives of a cause—if they are forced to carry social change. They should be given a level of expectation in accord with reality.

The most touchy of problems has to do with fighting. In view of the fact that children will engage in combat regardless of race, it is essential that teachers look at each incident in terms of the usual causes of fighting, and help the other children to adopt the same attitude. To avoid an unnecessary addition of pseudoracial issues to the picture, be careful to get the whole story. Then, if one must act as umpire in the dispute, base decisions on what happened and see to it that all participants are aware, for instance, that John hit Bob because he had taken John's money, not because Bob was white or Negro, as the case may be.

There are two tricky problems for a teacher belonging to the majority group.[24] One arises from sensitivity lest customary intervention directed toward a minority-group child be interpreted as discrimination. To counteract this possible impression, the teacher may refrain from necessary measures. In other cases, where he fears unfair accusation from children or their parents, he may preface his actions by an overdiligent collecting of evidence, as though preparing a court case. At the other extreme, in an effort to show how free of prejudice he is, the teacher may push himself into dwelling upon good qualities or establishing a patronizing smoothness in necessary personal relationships. To counteract these trends, the teachers should keep in mind that children prefer to be considered without reference to group membership. In view of the very real difficulties involved, teachers can gain a good deal by talking things over with each other.

The Power of the Group Code

Watch any children's group closely and you will see that actions are guided by a set of unwritten rules and regulations. These rules determine how games are to be played. They also set a standard concerning how children will talk about school. Adolescents are bound by juvenile conventions as to clothing, spare time group activities, and modes of social routines. Best known is that juvenile commandment, "Thou shalt not tattle."

At this point we must state very strongly a fact which has been implicit in much that has been said previously. The standards of conduct derived from juvenile-group forces are very powerful. After the first few grades in school, they are likely to be much more influential than most educators like to believe. In a head-on collision between the group

---

[24] Here we mean not the numerical majority in the school or immediate community, but the racial, national, or religious group dominant in the nation as a whole.

standards and the teachers' code, the juvenile code is more likely to prevail, although its triumph is usually masked. By bringing the full force of adult coercion to bear, we can almost always gain a surface appearance of having won our way. However, the surface is deceptive. It is generally the product of defense mechanisms by which young people evade conflict. Beneath the surface, the youngsters' concealed but lasting attitudes are formed by the dynamics of their own groups.

The Key Importance of the Teacher

For all that has been said, the teacher is still in a central position as the adult leader of a class, and the groups react to how the teacher's role is handled, although there are cases where even a genius would be helpless in the face of bad group dynamics. The social-climates experiment of Lippitt (page 277) showed not merely how children's groups acted in certain atmospheres but that those atmospheres can be influenced by adult leaders. In a very detailed series of observations in classrooms,[25] Anderson and his co-workers showed how emotional chain reactions are set in motion by teachers. Where the teacher relied largely on dominating techniques, evidences of conflict multiplied; but where more co-operation evoking methods were employed, spontaneity and social contributions were more frequent. Moreover, the longer a class was with a teacher, the greater was the effect. Furthermore, when a class changed teachers, the conditions disappeared, to be replaced by those found in classes which the new teacher had had before.

The forces which are at work in young people's groups are influenced by the entire setting in which they operate. A significant aspect of that setting is the teacher. The experimental evidence is clear and unequivocal. Teachers, either with deliberate forethought and intuitive skill or by unthinking action, affect the context which molds group life in the room.

In this chapter we have tried to picture some of the forces which operate in classrooms. Classes are groups of children rather than collections of isolated individuals. As large groups, they are divided into sub-

---

[25] Harold H. Anderson and Joseph E. Brewer, "Studies of Teachers' Classroom Personalities, II," *Applied Psychology Monographs,* No. 8 (1946).

Harold H. Anderson, Joseph E. Brewer, and Mary Frances Reed, "Studies of Teachers' Classroom Personalities, III," *Applied Psychology Monographs,* No. 11 (1946).

groups and cliques, each with its own structure and its own traditions. Under these circumstances, group psychological forces come into play and profoundly influence the individuals. The pattern of currents and crosscurrents is largely determined by the group characteristics, in the development of which the teacher plays the key role.

ADDITIONAL READINGS

Association for Supervision and Curriculum Development. *1950 Yearbook: Fostering Mental Health in Our Schools.* Washington: National Education Association, 1950, Chaps. 13, 16, and 17. Good material on the use of friendship charts in schools.

Barker, Roger G., Jacob S. Kounin, and Herbert F. Wright. *Child Behavior and Development.* New York: McGraw-Hill, 1943, Chaps. 27 to 30. Good summaries of early research in group dynamics.

Cantor, Nathaniel. *Dynamics of Learning.* Buffalo: Foster & Stewart, 1946. An account of a learning situation typified by student-centered teaching.

Cunningham, Ruth, and Associates. *Understanding Group Behavior of Boys and Girls.* New York: Teachers College, Columbia U., 1951, Chaps. 2 to 5. Contains interesting information on classroom interactions as they came to light in a study by teachers in Denver.

Group for the Advancement of Psychiatry. *Psychiatric Aspects of School Desegregation.* New York: Group for the Advancement of Psychiatry, 1957. A bulletin dealing with issues involved in racial problems.

Hollingshead, August B. *Elmtown's Youth.* New York: Wiley, 1949, Chap. 9. A description of the cliques in an American high school.

Morse, William C., and G. Max Wingo. *Psychology and Teaching.* Chicago: Scott, Foresman, 1955, Chap. 9. A basic discussion of how learning is affected by group forces.

Prescott, Daniel A. *The Child in the Educative Process.* New York: McGraw-Hill, 1957, Chap. 9. Treats of methods for analyzing group dynamics in a classroom.

Richardson, J. E., J. F. Forrester, J. K. Shukla, and P. J. Higginbotham. *Studies in the Social Psychology of Adolescence.* London: Routledge & Kegan Paul, 1951, Part 1. A full report of an experiment with sociometrics and small-group technique in a London school.

Wittenberg, Rudolph M. *So You Want to Help People.* New York: Association Press, 1947. A very well written book designed to be used in the training of volunteer youth groups.

AUDIO-VISUAL AIDS

A Day in the Life of a Five-Year-Old, an 18-minute sound film produced by the Metropolitan School Study Council, showing the effects of a good kindergarten atmosphere.

Experimental Studies in the Social Climate of Groups, a 33-minute sound film produced by the Iowa Child Welfare Research Station, showing scenes and data from the Lippitt-White experiment on effects of leadership.

Maintaining Classroom Discipline, a 20-minute sound film produced by McGraw-Hill, the first half of which illustrates the dynamics of behavioral contagion.

The Other Fellow's Feelings, a 10-minute sound film produced by Young America Films, in which a teasing incident leads to cruel scapegoating.

The Outsider, a 10-minute sound film produced by Young America Films, in which the plight of an isolate and the abilities of a leader are shown.

chapter **11**

THE PSYCHOLOGICAL ROLES OF TEACHERS

The emotional well-being of young people can be expressed to a large extent in terms of their relationships with adults. First, of course, are parents. Second only to parents are teachers. During school days, close to one-third of a youngster's waking hours are spent in school. During these hours, in addition to the group influences we have previously discussed, the important people in his life are the instructional staff, whose influence may be felt in direct person-to-person contact or, more indirectly, in terms of classroom atmosphere. Parent after parent has watched a child who was bitter and resentful under the teacher in one room display gay interest in another room under another teacher.

For these reasons, no true mental hygiene of education can be written without turning the spotlight on the psychological part played by teachers in the development of children. It is simple to recognize that some grownups are good for most children, others are harmful for many. Yet, even their friends cannot be sure which of them will click and which will not. Some do not ever quite do the job they want so badly to do. Others surprise themselves and form superbly good relationships with youngsters.

The Roles Teachers Are Expected to Fulfill

Let's look at you. You are the teacher. We are not trying to be silly when we ask, "Who are you?" You think you know. You are the man or woman who likes children and enjoys watching them learn. Perhaps part of you is your memory of the fun you have laughing with your friends, reading magazines, or buying new clothes. Possibly, as you plan your lessons, you feel a real thrill in your own mastery of the subject. That, and a great deal more, is you.

What do the children see? To some you are just another grownup who, they feel certain, is going to dislike them. To others, you are, by tradition, a dry-as-dust old fogey. To most, you are another nice person they are sure will be fun. If there are forty children in your room, each will be reacting to his own private image; there will be forty different versions of you. Some will be gross libels; others will be sheer flattery.

What do children expect of you? That depends upon their age, neighborhood traditions, what you teach, and several other variables. In Table 6, drawn from a study which the Survey Research Center at the University of Michigan made for the Boy Scouts of America,[1] there are some facts as to what adolescent boys expect of adult leaders. The percentages are based on more than three hundred boys at each age level.

As soon as any teacher steps into a roomful of young folks, he or she assumes various roles. In some teachers, we can see the change in facial expressions and posture as they cross the threshold. They have their own ideas as to what a teacher should be like. However, often they find themselves playing a part that is more or less forced on them.

As far as children are concerned, a large part of a teacher's life is veiled in mystery. Even for those periods when the class is together, the whole area of professional purposes and motives is perceived dimly, if at all. Therefore, it frequently happens that as the youngsters talk with each other, they fill in the voids in their own knowledge with myths and legends. For example, many members of a class may have fantasies, sometimes shared with one another, in which the teacher craftily thinks up traps to catch them in misdeeds. After disciplinary episodes, groups may regale themselves with unrealistic scenes in which they hale their temporarily hated leader before the school board. Ordinary social pleasantries between men and women faculty members may be the seeds from which adolescents concoct a scarlet-tinged love story. Most of such group-stimulated fantasies never come to the teacher's attention. When they do, we may find it essential to correct skillfully those which may cause trouble, but can well be amused by those which are harmless.

In addition to the images which children have in their minds, there are a wide variety of roles which a teacher will be expected to play in their lives. There will also be roles which the teacher considers part of

---

[1] Survey Research Center, Institute for Social Research, University of Michigan, *A Study of Adolescent Boys,* New Brunswick (N. J.), Boy Scouts of America, 1955.

his being a teacher. Some of these can be described as functions which have to be performed. Others may be thought of as psychological services to be rendered. In the list which follows, both conceptions of "role" are deliberately admixed. Let us look at some of these.

REPRESENTATIVE OF SOCIETY.   Teachers often fulfill the function of the adult who represents to children the values which the community wishes to inculcate. By precept and example, we try to develop the moral attitudes, the thinking patterns, the life goals which we feel make for good citizens, living a good life. In this role, we are more or less faithful mirrors of the society in which we live.

JUDGES AND SCREENERS.   Marking systems, report cards, promotion schemes, and the day-to-day work of conducting class sessions and correcting papers imply another role. In this role, we are judges who pass upon not only the products of learning but also the quality of a youngster's personality. Diplomas are viewed as stamps of approval. Teachers are expected to screen out the "unworthy" who do not "deserve" to pass into the next grade or the next school. In many neighborhoods, school is considered the stairway which can lead a child upward into a social class above his parents. Teachers, so to speak, stand on each landing and determine who may enter the next flight of stairs. Some teachers find the role irksome; others accept it as a matter of course. However we feel about it, children and their parents either hope or fear we will form opinions upon which they or other people can act.

There are some teachers who may consider this part of their activities a major source of gratification. It provides them with many chances to be "an angel with a flaming sword." The narrowness with

TABLE 6   *Relation of age of boy to conception of function of an adult leader*

CONCEPTION OF LEADER	PERCENTAGE STATING CONCEPTION		
	Age 14	*Age 15*	*Age 16*
An organizer and initiator	52	53	35
An authority, maintaining order and supervision	46	49	63
A helper, giving advice and aid but not dominating	45	47	60

which they play the role is all the harder to detect because it is cloaked with talk of discipline, rigor, and justice.

SOURCE OF KNOWLEDGE.   An instructor is expected to be a living textbook from which one can get information. How often we acknowledge that good teachers must know their stuff! Listen to almost any class and note how often children ask questions and are given answers. There can be little doubt that both children and teachers agree that this role is a proper one.

HELPER IN THE LEARNING PROCESS.   When either an individual child or a group encounters some difficulty in learning, the teacher is looked to for help in overcoming the obstacle. We ask leading questions; we have children go over the problem step by step; we conduct a discussion. When finally the light of understanding, which one psychologist neatly called the "Aha! reaction," dawns on a child's face, the instructor feels successful. Equally, parents and children judge teachers' worth by their ability to do this job.

REFEREE.   When young people find themselves in disagreement, they will often carry the dispute to an adult for decision. This is especially true in those arguments which may lead to combat, whether these be disputes for toys in the kindergarten or noisy battles over a hairsplitting decision on the basketball court. Then, every teacher is expected to be a Solomon. At this point, the instructor is valued for the fairness of the verdict or the skill with which differences are reconciled. It is almost impossible to escape being cast in this role; the problem is to carry it off well.

DETECTIVE.   Even among the nicest of children, belongings will disappear, injuries will be inflicted, and rules will be broken. The victims and the bystanders now wait for the damage to be rectified, the culprit punished, and security restored. Here is another role that cannot be evaded, although it is all too easy to overdo. For a period, some children value the teacher as a one-man or one-woman criminal investigation squad. Prestige may rest upon success in restoring stolen property to its rightful owners or in reassuring the group that law and order are being preserved.

Failure of a teacher to play this role when it is needed may leave the child community to face excitement, fury, or anxiety they do not know how to handle. It may delay the opportunity to give help to a child who badly needs it. For, no matter how much a teacher may shrink from this role and prefer to bet on developing confidence and trust in the children, there is no denying that a child who steals, for instance, cannot be helped until we know who he is.

Blundering in this role may lead to unwise use of third-degree methods or mass punishment. There is also the danger that a class may be made too conscious of this function by overelaborate measures to prevent cheating.

OBJECT OF IDENTIFICATION.   As has been previously discussed, one way children deal with conflicts is by identification with some respected person. Teachers very often perform the very critical psychological function of serving as objects for this process. Young people may take over such surface traits as a manner of walking or mode of grooming; they may equally well incorporate within themselves methods of dealing with people. Through values expressed in punishment or reward, voiced in words, or illustrated in actions, teachers serve as models after whom some class members pattern themselves.

LIMITER OF ANXIETY.   In the process of growing up and learning to control their impulses, many children develop anxiety. They may be deeply afraid that if left to their own devices, they are bound to do wrong. They may worry lest they be unprotected and fall victim to unimaginable harm. They may find that naughty conduct by other children weakens their ability to control their own impulses. Almost all children have such feelings to some degree. Unconsciously, they look to their teachers to reduce their anxiety. By setting limits to permissible behavior, by acting with a confident and competent air, by dealing with "bad" behavior in an understanding way, teachers can meet these expectations. We must note, of course, that some teachers, by building an atmosphere of rigid severity or by stern threats, have seriously increased anxiety for some children. At the opposite extreme, others create uncertainty by failing to set limits, even when these are sorely needed to enable a child to develop self-control.

Teachers also can play a part in allaying less deep-seated anxieties, such as fear of failure, poor grades, shyness, and parental disapproval. Children worry about many things. Teachers can help them to reduce needless apprehensiveness.

EGO-SUPPORTER.   Another weakening condition almost all children display at times is a lack of confidence in themselves. As life presents them with one developmental task after another, they may feel inadequate. When they falter, they may look to a teacher to help them muster their resources and to give them assurance. Teachers who see that each child tastes success and that each feels sure of the teacher's confidence perform this role well. However, we must admit that the traditions of some school systems encourage teachers to stand by while slow-learning children destroy themselves in futile efforts to meet unrelenting academic standards, and that some educators even add to the damage by expressions of suspicion, hostility, or contempt.

GROUP LEADER.   By its very nature, formal education involves groups. Teachers are expected to provide guidance so that groups achieve harmony in functioning and efficiency in reaching group goals. This is the field of classroom management. Adeptness in its arts is an attribute which most teachers value. Children as well as administrators depend upon it.

The effects of the teacher's success or failure as a group leader are universally recognized as both significant and difficult to pin down. When Reed[2] followed 129 children and 4 teachers over a two-year period by observing and rating behavior, she found that each teacher tended to continue certain patterns of leadership, even with different children. The children tended to change their behavior patterns as they went from teacher to teacher. Those teachers who gave leadership by integrating rather than dominating the group were more likely to have classes in which children were spontaneous and showed initiative.

PARENT SURROGATE.   For many children, teachers may act somewhat as parents. We see this in very open form when kindergartners throng around the teacher, making bids for affection, or when, at a higher age level, a high school girl seeks personal advice of the kind usually sought from a mother. Emotional attitudes toward real parents may be displaced onto teachers. A sizable number of youngsters are unable to react objectively to instructors because their thinking processes are distorted by their feelings toward their parents, which they generalize toward all adults in authority. Legally, in many states, teachers are

---

2 Mary Frances Reed, *A Consecutive Study of the School Room Behavior of Children in Relation to the Teachers' Dominative and Socially Integrative Contacts,* unpublished Ph.D. dissertation, University of Illinois, 1941.

vested with the power of parents while children are in their charge. Psychologically speaking, this is much more than a legalistic fiction. Even though they may not in the least want to do so, members of the educational profession act as parents.

CORRECTIVE TO PARENTS.   In many children, there are emotional conflicts resulting from parental attitudes. Some youngsters are under pressure to achieve beyond their ability; others have been brutalized. We recall one boy whose parents wanted him to be a tough and ruthlessly successful competitor, who enjoyed taking advantage of "suckers." For many youngsters, teachers perform the valuable function of representing attitudes and principles different from those of parents. In this way teachers may round out or correct a child's picture of the world and the people in it. As with other roles mentioned here, there is a risk both in overplaying this role and in avoiding it completely lest it interfere with teaching.

TARGET FOR HOSTILITY FEELINGS.   Learning the ways of civilization inevitably exposes every child to frustration. Adults must forbid him to give free rein to all his impulses, and also compel him to do some things he does not want to do. The result is that, just as inevitably, young people develop feelings of hostility toward grownups. The intensity of the resentments will vary from time to time. The shape they take will depend upon the skill with which grownups have acted toward children. For many, the hostilities have been terrifically deepened by rejection at home, by parental overdomination, or by community pressure. One outlet children have for these feelings is to vent them against teachers. This outlet is psychologically attractive because it involves no conflict with the deep-seated feeling that one should love one's parents. Therefore, we would expect that many teachers must cope with some juvenile ill will that has nothing whatever to do with the teacher's personality or procedures. Because the hostility may be undeserved, it often hurts badly unless its origin is realized. There is no escaping this role; the best we can do is to fill it in such a way that children learn how to express their hostility feelings in more socially acceptable and conflict-free ways.

Here we are talking about a normal process of displacing some feelings of hostility upon adults who guide a child's growth. The extreme forms of hostility found in some delinquent neighborhoods, which break out in acts of vandalism or physical attack perpetrated in mob action, or the lashing out of severely disturbed children, are special cases and contain factors entirely different from what is referred to here.

INDIVIDUAL FRIEND AND CONFIDANT.   Much more heart-warming are those instances in which a young person chooses a teacher to serve as a friend or a confidant. Because of the pleasures which can be involved, many educators behave so as to increase the likelihood of such incidents. Although there is danger that a child's social development may be stunted if he substitutes friendships with grownups for the more typical relationships with his age-mates, warm personal ties with a teacher may have a definite place in rounding out children's worlds. Young people feel instinctively that life will be more pleasant if they and their instructors share confidence in and good feeling for each other. A good teacher is almost always a good friend to many children.

Here, it is not necessary to fear that all children will use as an excuse for license in the classroom the fact that the teacher wants to help them with personal problems. On the other hand, it is well to be watchful lest we fail to refer to specialists a child who needs a more specialized type of professional help.

OBJECT OF AFFECTION AND CRUSHES.   Just as most adults need to have someone to love, so also do young people. We must naturally expect, therefore, that the ordinary friendly feelings in a class will sometimes take on a special force for some youngsters. These may be as innocuous as a first-grader's little gifts to a beloved instructor, or as potentially dangerous as a high school girl's truly romantic infatuation with a male faculty member. Whatever the age level, these feelings express psychological needs that are as real as, and may have as little to do with the teacher's personality as, the hostility which we discussed earlier. Here, too, the task is to deal with matters so that the children learn to handle their feelings in an appropriate manner.

IMPLICATIONS.   The roles we have listed here by no means exhaust the possibilities. For example, nothing has been said of the part teachers play as entertainers, as conciliators, or as ogres invoked by parents to control children. Also little has been said about such teaching roles as task-setter, frustrator, and helper with problems, which may result in such comments as, "He was a tough old bird, but he really taught me." Enough has been brought out, however, to highlight certain fundamental considerations. One is that teachers play a great many different roles in the lives of children. The second is that, although a teacher may prefer to accent one role and to eliminate others, he has little freedom of choice. Every role we have discussed is one in which some children will cast almost every teacher. This is so because in each situation the role is a mixture of four considerations: (1) the images projected by the children, (2) the expectations of the profession, (3) the personal intent of the teacher, and (4) the demands of the larger community. Avoid this condition, we cannot. The art is to handle it as well as possible.

The totality of how the roles are taken by a teacher contributes substantially to the relationship between teacher and children. From it, young people develop an expectation of how their instructor will react. If this perception is one which is steady and consistent, if it is colored by helpfulness, mutual respect, and fondness, the details matter rather little. On the other hand, a basically good relationship can be disturbed by neglecting a necessary role, by inappropriate behavior in crisis situations, or by mistakes in such roles as detective and confidant. In a sense, the basic relationship is so important a matter that many details of classroom administration and many lists of teacher competences are by comparison gimmicks and trivia.

The fact that teachers have to play specific roles still leaves each quite free to decide how to play them. Thus the job of being referee in a dispute can be handled with stern coldness or accompanied by bitter denunciation of peer-group standards. Or, by contrast, the teacher may draw the group into free consultation. The task can be performed with a dozen different attitudes. Indeed, a teacher may assume any number of roles and yet in each display a consistent feeling toward children. This is the common denominator. Permeating all is the real nature of the teacher's interest in and attitude toward children. The effect of the roles upon youngsters is highly colored by this.

It is also important to realize that each teacher is likely to feel more comfortable in some roles than in others. Such personal predilections may interfere with a proper balance. It is very easy to get into a rut and spend too much time doing one part of the teaching job. The requirement at this point is for the teacher to assess the objective need for the role in terms of the needs of each situation.

In dealing with the existence of role expectations, teachers face a number of problems. Some are created by the difficulty of dealing with unfamiliar or disliked activities. A lopsided distribution of roles can cause trouble; sometimes classwork might go more smoothly if the teacher could attempt greater versatility.

Miss Landman, for example, was a top-notch organizer. She taught in a school district where transiency was high. Sensing the fact that the children had been moved around too often and longed for security, she provided schedules which told them what to expect every minute of the day. They liked that. She gave them one large area in their lives where they felt sure they knew what would happen next. They knew they could depend on her, and that was a real solace. The only trouble was that she devoted almost all her time to the business of devising and enforcing rules. She was afraid to make exceptions. The squalor of the neighborhood and the untidiness of the children made her avoid any close contact. The thought of being friendly made her feel unclean. Therefore, when children needed a confidant or reassurance, they found her cold to them. In the end they developed a strong distaste for her classes. With each new group she started out well but had trouble later. For her, teaching became a rather dreary, mechanical business.

Another group of problems is created by poor playing of the several roles. For example, if the standards of society are portrayed on a level children cannot understand or in a context which ignores their needs, it may be confusing rather than helpful. If the teacher corrects errors in a harsh manner, his pupils may feel that rules are weapons to be used against children. In any case, there will be times when teachers know what they intend to do, but the young people are confused. By their actions or words, children will reveal almost fantastic misconceptions. When this happens, it is very easy for annoyance to reach an explosion point. Actually, loss of temper by the teacher accomplishes nothing; the group needs an explanation so they can understand what is going on. The problems of communication in the classroom are discussed in the next section of this chapter.

More intricate difficulties may be created by a bad combination of needs in a class. For example, in a particular high school class we may find that almost all the young people need the teacher as a confidant, but that five really want a policeman. If their need is ignored, they will very likely show much problem behavior. On the other hand, if the teacher turns into a policeman to give the five security, the rest of the class will be restive and resentful. When a teacher finds it difficult to make a good choice of roles, it is wise to look closely at the group composition. This may provide a clue.

In working out such problems, it is also well to recognize that the children's reaction to roles is often indirect. The trouble may pop up at an unexpected point. Thus, difficulty in developing a free discussion may be a repercussion of anxiety created by poor use of the detective role on a previous day. In any event, when a class is showing signs of insecurity or friction, it is well to look closely at the way in which the teacher performs the needed roles.

In making such a survey, account must be taken of the age level of the children. The demands upon teachers vary in accordance with developmental phases. Thus, during the early years of school, because children are still largely preoccupied with their relationships to adults and with learning to meet the standards of the grown-up world, they are inclined to expect teachers to help them with such problems. At this stage, they are more likely to make heavy demands that teachers substitute for parents and that they function as judges and referee disputes. They look for a stronger leadership than older children do, one which will control group processes to limit anxiety.

Although many of these demands persist during the preadolescent years, the power of the peer culture enforces a shift in emphasis. For example, fewer problems are brought to the teacher to be refereed. On the other hand, the growing warfare with the adult world may require a clearer target for hostility feelings.

By the high school years, further shifts become apparent. Young people who are forming an image of themselves as adults may feel greater need for objects of identification. Those who plan to make vocational use of learning may place increasing value on the teacher as a source of knowledge. Also, with the appearance of more adult love impulses, crushes are likely to show greater intensity.

In view of such trends, rural teachers who must deal with a wide span of ages face special problems. Clearly, it is necessary to establish different types of relationship with the different age groups in the room. This calls for a greater versatility and for extra sensitivity in reacting to individuals. There is always danger that the teacher may find it so pleasant to meet the demands of one age level that the children who are older or younger are largely ignored.

Communication

As was mentioned a few paragraphs ago, children may display misconceptions concerning the role played by a teacher. This highlights a significant point: the effect of what a teacher does is determined not exclusively by his intentions but by what is perceived by the young people, what is communicated. The consequences of a course of action depend upon what message it is seen to carry. Because faulty communication can result in misunderstanding and distorted perception, our prime concern will be with ways in which this may occur. There are three areas in which communication may break down: (1) how the child perceives the teacher; (2) how the teacher perceives the child; (3) how the children perceive each other. Moreover, there are two kinds of communication, both of which are subject to breakdown: communication of *specific content* and communication of *attitudes*.

In talking to children, it should be obvious that the language used must be suitable: the vocabulary and sentence structure must be understood. Since one never can take it for granted that this is the case, it is always important to find out from a few children what they understood. Inaccuracies in children's responses may be reason for working on improved communication, not mistakes to be punished.

In many instances, our attitudes are poorly interpreted. This may occur through a species of psychological mumbling on our part. The actions which convey the attitudes may have an abortive quality. If, for example, a teacher wants children to know they can come to him for help with learning difficulties but feels ashamed at the prospect that they might consider him a soft sentimentalist, his invitations may be given with a touch of sarcasm, which is discouraging to a hesitant child.

At times, however, trouble appears because the adult is confused as to what he is doing. For instance, many teachers think of themselves as permissive, when in fact they give assent only after having been cajoled. To the children they appear to be weak; their "permissiveness" is seen as a grudging concession.

The confusion, of course, may reside in the young people, in their misinterpretation of the teacher's intent. A common source of such misconceptions is, for example, pressure for good manners, which children may view as picayune fault-finding. When a teacher checks up frequently on a child who needs help, he may see this as evidence of suspicion and lack of confidence. Informality combined with easygoing standards may appear to some children as unfriendly disinterest in their welfare.

A frequent source of communication failure is a teacher's misperception of a child's intent and his resultant faulty reply. For instance, the teacher may see disrespect in ways of addressing him, ways which would have been impertinence on the part of children where he grew up, but which are basically respectful for the school neighborhood. Also, anxiety may cause some children to freeze or to put on a supercilious face. In circumstances where the teacher expects them to quake, these actions may be interpreted as silly indifference. Again, in some settings children may break school rules in an impulsive effort to be helpful. If they are punished for the rule breaking but not given credit for the helpfulness, they will feel the teacher is petty.

In some instances, the subtle messages carried by postural gestures, facial expressions, and vocal intonations are misread. For example, a few children have faces which at rest look sullen. If they are dealt with as though causelessly resentful, they cannot make out what an adult is trying to do.

At times every teacher feels it necessary to make believe that he or she is reacting rather differently than is the case. For instance, juvenile ingenuity often takes an amusing turn. A teacher may recognize that he must show serious interest in an explanation which he may later repeat with wholesome laughter in the privacy of a luncheon table. A teacher may feel he ought to show righteous indignation at an infraction that he doesn't consider horribly serious. Some of this play acting is necessary and good. However, it is limited in the extent to which it is effective. On the whole, the more a teacher can be emotionally sincere, the better.

Many teachers have great confidence in their intuitive ability to detect lying and guilt. There is a great deal of folklore, such as the generalization that a liar has shifty eyes. Although there will be cases in which a basically honest child cannot look one straight in the face while fibbing, there are more exceptions than we think. A child whom we falsely accuse knows that he is innocent. If we insist that we know he is guilty, the message that he gets is that we are stupid, pigheaded, and unfair.

The intuition on which we rely is a sensitivity to small clues, which comes from our past experience. Intuition is thus least reliable when the teacher has grown up in a different social setting from that of his or her present pupils. If this is the case, then it is most important to find out how children are reacting to the words and actions of the teacher which are based on this intuition. A similar condition prevails when a teacher has been switched from one grade level to another.

At what point should a teacher give deliberate thought to communication and some of the possible defects mentioned thus far? In clear fact, many teachers go along for years without worrying about how well they are putting messages across. Is this a sign of blindness or ineptness? Not at all. But, should difficulty begin to appear, should children act in unexpected fashion, or should it be necessary to keep up a nerve-eroding pressure, then communication is worth investigating. When trying to get to the roots of trouble, remember the possibility that psychological static is fouling communication. Check for the types of difficulty mentioned above.

Just as communication difficulties may roil teacher-pupil relationships, so they may spoil social contacts among the children. In some cases in which a teacher is trying to deal with social tension among students, the source may be found in poor communication among them. For instance, when a newcomer appears on the scene, the other pupils may leave him alone to get used to the situation. One child may see this as ostracism. Yet if they were to show curiosity, another child might feel he was being put on the spot. In other instances, imitation may be seen as ridicule where it is intended merely as friendly banter. In all such cases, a teacher may be helpful by showing the angry or hurt child that he has misread his classmates' intent. In this case the teacher plays a new role: that of communication clarifier.

Effects of Group Differences

The extent to which a teacher may effectively play various roles is altered by differences in sex, race, socioeconomic level, and other group factors. No clear and universal rules can be given. Rather, the important consideration is how these differences are met. Where a teacher has established good rapport with a class, the differences may have no effect.

The community attitude must also be considered. If prejudices or antagonisms are strong, they may infect the children or the teacher and make it more difficult for the teacher to override the troublesome effects.

It is easy, for instance, to assume that in the early grades women may be more effective as mother substitutes for both boys and girls, but in later grades might be weak as objects of identification for boys. This, however, would be much more true in a neighborhood full of father-dominated homes than in a suburb whose standards were set by feminine leaders. Also, a vigorous woman might well set up a relationship which would let her play all roles for boys, whereas a lackluster man might fail.

The same thing is true for racial, religious, nationality, and economic differences. Where community conditions are good or teachers have developed helpful attitudes, such differences may have no effect. But the contrary may be true if, for example, either the teacher or the class is conscious of race differences; then an instructor is bound to face problems if he and the children are of different races. The teacher may then be seen not as a representative of society as a whole, but as a representative of one race. (Also, children of a minority group may reflect majority attitudes in reacting to a teacher of their own race.) The teacher in turn is likely to deal with the class in terms of meeting race solidarity in the group or of coping with any antagonisms which may exist. The teacher should be aware that for some he may be used as a target of hostility feelings, and therefore be less efficient as an object of identification; for other children he may become overly important, although they cannot say so. In this situation, the subtle emotional roles of parent surrogate or object of affection may also have added complications for both teacher and children. Counterbalancing such tendencies are others related to prestige when the teacher is of the majority race. Children coming from homes in which parents show a desire to move upward or to get along with an advantageously placed racial group, might react quite differently. They might display a greater desire to please or to be admired. They might be much less ready to engage in hostile actions than they would with a teacher of their own racial group. They might study the teachers carefully in order to identify with them more closely.

Similar considerations arise in connection with nationality and religious differences. Although these are usually not as potent, community attitudes and parental feelings are reflected by children. In some cases, elements of suspicion may make for difficulties unless they are recognized. The teacher may be seen by the children, initially, in terms of stereotypes inculcated by the home. Again, prestige feelings can come into play. In most instances, such differences are of little moment in the lower grades. Adolescents are likely to be more conscious of them.

Economic differences also can extend influence. A middle-class teacher working in a community inhabited largely by unskilled laborers will sometimes find that he is accorded unusually high respect. Ambitious parents may want him to have great influence upon their children. He may be cast in the role of prophet, interpreter, or protector. But the opposite may also happen: older children may show a resentment, common to some parents, toward people with "easy" jobs. In order to understand what lies behind children's actions, it may be essential to think about such effects.

In wealthy areas, a teacher may occasionally be cast in the role of servant or governess. The lower standing may make it safer for children to use their instructors as targets for hostility feelings. However, because of the lower status, teachers may be treated with great politeness: one is not rude to a servant; he is not important enough for that. However, his word carries little weight in any issue which conflicts with parental policies.

A special situation, which cannot be explored at length, arises in parochial schools where teachers belong to religious orders. They are expected to assume additional roles as religious leaders and to exemplify some degree of saintliness.

Admixture and Separation of Roles

Because teachers have many roles to play there are bound to be some mix-ups. The same teacher who is a friend or a confidant is also a referee in quarrels and the target of the group's hostility feelings. During the course of a single hour, the same grownup may act as a group leader, then play detective in uncovering failure to do homework, only to turn around and help the culprit later in overcoming his learning difficulties.

Quite often, the mixture of roles makes for efficiency. One role prepares the ground for another. Thus, the adult who limits a child's anxiety or who supports his ego may thereby gain power as a parent surrogate and be able to represent adult society with more helpful impact. The teacher who acts as a confidant or as an efficient source of knowledge may more easily become an object of identification. Fairness as a judge or a referee may bolster the teacher as a group leader.

It is equally true that the roles may interfere with each other. For example, a teacher who has been acting as an ego supporter to build up a child's self-confidence may destroy his own good work when he shifts to the role of judge and gives a low mark.

In the face of such conflicts, either the class or the teacher may seek a separation of the roles. This may sometimes be accomplished by confining each to a particular time or area. Thus, during a discussion the teacher may concentrate on being the voice of society, but during a specially designated conference period accept confidences without rebuke. A science teacher may act almost solely as a helper in the laboratory periods but be expected to play policeman during final examinations.

The existence of such role confusions has been recognized, especially as it affects the counseling function. Quite a few schools have a guidance staff without disciplinary duties. This type of specialization is often wise.

In schools where children meet several teachers in the course of a day, there may arise another, unseen type of specialization that can produce special problems. A very common one appears when one teacher concentrates on policeman roles and operates by fear-producing methods, while another specializes in being a friend. The pent-up pressure produced by the first roars through the safety valve provided by the second. The trouble encountered by the friendly teacher may be falsely attributed to the role he has taken, rather than to the fact that the other teacher has built up resentments but has done nothing about them.

Where particular conditions seem to require specialization, the problems should be given careful thought. However, as a general principle, all teachers need to perform all roles well.

Disentangling Role Confusions

If teachers now and then find they are working at cross-purposes with themselves, who can wonder that children are sometimes troubled by the confusion in roles? Let us not, however, fall into the error of assuming all conflict in roles is harmful. Most children are used to similar situations in their homes. There, a girl's mother may act as confidant one minute, only to scold her daughter a little later for some shortcoming. Young people who are reasonably well adjusted can take the usual inconsistencies of a schoolroom in stride.

For disturbed children, however, such role conflicts may be damaging. Their needs for affection, for example, may be so intense that when a teacher, as detective, catches them in a misdeed, they feel he does not like them. They are thrown into confusion by normal inconsistencies. For this reason, in projects designed to help troubled youngsters, avoidance of role confusion constitutes a separate task. Occasionally, it may become important to distribute roles which would be too confusing to a youngster if performed by one and the same person. These roles are therefore given to several people, who, however, must then work in close co-operation and on the basis of a very clear strategy. In dealing with emotionally disturbed children in a classroom, teachers may be wise to make sure they perform the roles each child most needs. Incidents requiring someone to act in a conflicting capacity might be met by an assistant principal, a special counselor, or other designated person.

Sudden and drastic changes in role may upset even normal children. Teachers may shift their viewpoint toward a class greatly without being aware of the effect. Thus, in response to administrative or community pressure, an instructor who has been absorbing the youngster's hostility feelings with equanimity may suddenly decide that the group is deficient in respect for authority and then clamp down in a way which completely reverses the tone he has been setting. Similar sharp inconsistencies show themselves when a teacher or a class is having a "bad day" or when behavior passes the limits of individual tolerance.

A teacher who provides a reasonably consistent tone which the children can predict may give them added security. Even where a teacher appears cold or crabby, the consistency may help youngsters adjust well to the unpleasant aspects of classroom life with him or her. Here is an example in which the value of consistency was not recognized and, therefore, wrong conclusions were drawn:

When Bill Johnson first came to teach at the Hudson Grove High School, he was determined to exemplify democracy in action. He started off by setting up a student court to handle any infractions of classroom rules, he organized class sessions on a parliamentary pattern, with a student chairman in charge, and he had the group ballot on the topics to be studied. However, when the class took two weeks on "preliminaries," he began to get nervous. One day there was a name-calling incident. He intervened with a firm, "I'll take care of this," and ordered the offender banished from the room for three days. However, to show that the court had not been supplanted, he had them deal with three instances of tardiness.

Later in the year, when a few of the boys joked about his interest in Miss Spellman, the art teacher, he grinned and said he thought she was very nice. A week later he began to worry about the growing familiarity, and the next time her name was mentioned, sternly upbraided them. Making his life even tougher was a sardonic comment from Mr. Langer, the other social studies teacher. Langer's teaching procedure was simplicity itself: He told his classes what pages to read each week in an assigned text, gave them a weekly true-false test, announced the grades, and called in the "weak sisters" for "pep talks," which consisted mostly of warnings that they would fail unless they improved. Regularly he did fail 10 per cent of every class. Bill Johnson was really crushed when he overheard some students in one of his classes talking about Mr. Langer. The verdict of the group was shown in general agreement with Bob Kilmore's statement: "Old man Langer is O.K. At least, you know where you stand with him. This Johnson keeps changing signals all the time." The next year, Bill Johnson adopted Mr. Langer's system. What he did not realize was that the students wanted only consistency, and that he could have worked out his own ideas in a way that would have given it to them.

Other effects of role confusions may be reduced somewhat by bringing them out in the open. Thus, if the teacher who has been giving a child much support has to indicate that the youngster is still doing objectively poor work, a conference in which the situation is explained and confidence in improvement is expressed may help. Similarly, when a teacher, as referee in a dispute, has to render a decision against a child who looks to him for affection, this can be accompanied by praise for sportsmanship at the time.

Role Hierarchies: Place of the Principal

In almost all large organizations, there are hierarchies; that is, there are several ranks of leaders. Thus, the chief executive of a city does most of his work by directing the department heads. Many of these, as, for example, the fire commissioner, give leadership to district or bureau officials, who in turn deal more or less directly with the men or women who do the actual work. The top officials are expected to assume roles of decision making and supervision much heavier than those in the lower ranks. The latter may be looked to for more personal relationships with individuals. Along with hierarchy in authority goes a system of role concepts, which varies in accordance with the tradition of the organization. In some, the chief is presumed to be aloof, a coldhearted and efficient upholder of standards. In others, the highest official acts as a morale-building glad-hander who fights for the welfare of the group, while a middle rank takes on the tough tasks of making inspections and enforcing unpopular regulations. The combinations vary.

The typical hierarchy in large school systems calls for a superintendent, assistants in charge of various functions, regional superintendents to do the trouble shooting and deal with local problems, the principals who give leadership to individual schools, and the teachers. All share in common the effect which, directly or indirectly, they have on children. We shall deal, however, only with the principals and a few of the roles they play which in one way or another are felt by youngsters in the classroom. As was done earlier when the roles of teachers were catalogued, we are combining job descriptions with statements of psychological services performed.

BUFFER BETWEEN SCHOOL AND COMMUNITY.   Teachers may look to the principal to handle problems involving parents or local pressure groups. Traditionally, he or she is supposed to smooth out conflicts. If the principal fails in this function and shifts the responsibility to teachers, morale suffers.

PROTECTOR OF TEACHERS AND PUPILS.   With the buffer role goes the idea that the principal acts as a big father or mother who safeguards everyone from dangers. These may be such physical dangers as traffic hazards. They may be social, as when a group of youngsters runs afoul of the police or local merchants. Teachers often hope that the principal will go to bat for them with higher authorities, on matters ranging all the way from requests for transfer to professional conflicts with "the downtown office."

Where this role is performed well, the result is to reduce anxieties among the faculty and the student body. In times of major or minor crises, it gives rise to a type of leadership in which direct appeals to the teachers or the students carry overwhelming force. Where the principal is inadequate, feelings of insecurity may spread and seriously interfere with efficiency in teaching or in learning.

TONE SETTER.   The manner in which the principal deals with teachers or with youngsters is highly contagious. The psychological power of the principalship almost guarantees that most teachers will identify with the principal and carry his attitudes into their classrooms. Thus, if the principal takes a relaxed attitude toward the mistakes which teachers are bound to make, they in turn will be less tense and more likely to be sympathetic wtih the vagaries of their pupils. On the other hand, if he goes in for violent temper tantrums, we would not be surprised to hear many teachers trying to control their classes by screaming or by being ruthlessly tough. Reread the account of Mr. Brown's school (pages 14 to 15) and notice how quickly Miss Keith reflected his impatience.

By contrast, there are many good principals who know how to inject genuine friendliness into a school. Such a one was Mrs. Morgan of the Queen School. She was a very warm, motherly woman with a fine sense of humor. Even a casual visitor could sense the spirit of the school. Supervisors liked to go there. When they entered a room, the teacher was likely to show a friendly smile rather than forced efficiency. The children looked relaxed. The P.T.A. also seemed to have fun. They organized a child-study group, and talked very openly about their problems with their children. The fact that Mrs. Morgan was there made it easier for them to talk.

Her reputation spread, and when the Spring School became a problem, she was transferred to take care of the trouble. Two years later, although there had been no shift of teachers, the Queen School was quite different. The new principal, Mr. Turner, was a jittery, hard-driving leader. Now halls seemed much more quiet, a bit like a hospital. A visitor could sense the tension. The P.T.A. lost membership and went back to a routine of talks on travel and world affairs.

THE "BIG BOSS" WHO CANNOT BE DEFIED. The principal's office is often the place to which stubborn disciplinary problems are sent. The fact that the principal has greater prestige and is respected by the teachers invests him or her with a psychological aura. He or she, being distant from the scene of trouble, may be considered impartial. Youngsters expect him to stand by the values of the entire school. For certain children a few words from the principal may therefore carry great force. A boy or girl who loses his self-control and defies a teacher often can regain self-control after a suitable talking-to by the head of the school. Although in some schools this function is overworked to the point where it weakens the ability of teachers or becomes ineffective because the most difficult children become too familiar with it, nevertheless it has a real place in the well-rounded treatment of children.

LAST COURT OF APPEAL. Every executive is also a chief magistrate. He is presumed to be above the personal animosities which flare into disputes between people. Therefore, when either a teacher or a child feels that injustice is being done, the case winds up in the principal's office. The important thing for all concerned is not so much the decision that is finally made, but the opportunity to tell their stories and have their feelings recognized. Teachers expect that the principal will either back them up or else announce a solution that will give them the appearance of victory. The children, or their parents, expect that some-thing will be worked out to warrant feelings of security and self-esteem.

OGRE AND MUTUAL ENEMY.   As the highest local authority, prin-cipals of necessity are also targets for the hostility feelings of teachers, parents, and children. They are bound to inspire some fear. Therefore, at times, teachers and pupils will band together to do things which pro-tect them as a group from either a real or a legendary displeasure. Valuable class cohesion may arise in this fashion. However, if teachers overplay terror of the principal, the result may be emotionally dis-turbing.

PEACE-KEEPER.   The principal is also expected to head off pos-sible conflicts. In this role, a type of strategic leadership is implied. Teachers, parents, and others bring him information that indicates trouble may be brewing. Their hope is that he can determine how to remove the grounds for an impending clash. He talks, cajoles, and works out compromises. Here is how one possible conflict was avoided:

When teachers at the Midvalley High School heard a rumor that a local minister was planning to launch a crusade against sex education and alleged immorality among students, they told Mr. Nelson, the prin-cipal. He in turn called a private meeting of all the pastors in town. At the meeting he emphasized that the high school staff was anxious to do everything possible to bolster moral values in the student body and to prepare the young people for eventual family living. He would like the group to make suggestions for any changes in present courses or for new programs. There were several additional meetings at which in-formation was given in answer to questions. Several said later that they had been under a misapprehension as to what one of the teachers had been telling her class. They also reviewed some films giving sex in-formation, and selected one as being generally acceptable. The rumored attack on the school never took place.

OTHER ROLES.   There are a great many other roles which are part of the job into which the school leader is thrust or which he takes upon himself. In all of them, his educational function is to help set the stage so that pupils and teachers may engage in learning activities with a maximum chance of success. From the mental hygiene viewpoint, this implies that he seeks to reduce needless frustration and to create an atmosphere low in tension.

Substitute Teaching

Many teachers are initiated into the profession by serving as substitutes for a year or two. Quite an initiation it is! The psychological roles of the substitute are quite different from those of a regular teacher, and are harder to handle. From a mental hygiene viewpoint, substitutes who are with classes for a relatively short time will have a rather weak influence on the emotional development of children, unless they make outrageous blunders. Much more significant in the long run is the effect of the experiences upon the mental health and future teaching personalities of the substitutes themselves. Relatively little has been written on the problems to be faced. Consequently, in meeting frequent emergencies, they learn to rely on techniques which achieve superficial results. These techniques may be carried over later into more stable situations in which they may be harmful.

A class whose regular teacher fails to appear is bound to feel some insecurity, much as would a child whose mother has gone away and left him in the care of a stranger. Therefore, the first demand placed on substitutes, especially in the lower grades, is to re-establish familiar routines and to make the children feel safe. The fact that the substitute lacks knowledge of what the class has been doing and how the regular teacher has dealt with particular children makes this rather difficult.

Among preadolescents, who may be inclined toward organized hostility against adults, the appearance of a substitute presents an almost overpowering temptation. Shorn of the power that goes with giving grades, knowing parents, or having regular relationships with the children, the substitute is an ideal target. He or she may represent the tribal enemy unarmed. The inevitable outbreaks have left many a substitute shaken badly, and more than one has decided that he was too incompetent to stay in the profession.

There are other roles which the substitute may be expected to play. Where the classwork was of a nature that an outsider could not pick up easily, the group may expect most work to cease while the time is made to pass enjoyably in interesting activities. A substitute may be valued principally as an entertainer.

Substitutes do not have to face the aftermath of their actions in the same way as regular teachers. This may be an advantage, because there is a correspondingly greater freedom of action. However, it does create false evaluations of the techniques used because there is little opportunity to learn from experience what the long-time effects may be.

One perennial substitute, for example, made a practice of entering a room, slamming the door, and then strutting to the desk while the children sat in stunned silence. In a loud voice, she would announce, "I am a substitute. I suppose you think you're going to have fun. The one who is going to have most fun stand up right now!" As might be expected, not one startled child moved. Then, slamming a book on the desk top, she crowed, "Good! Then we understand each other! You're not going to have fun!" This substitute reported that her technique always worked. She also made it a personal policy never to stay with a class more than three days. She was quite sincere, however, in recommending her approach without reservation to all young teachers she encountered.

The situation met by a substitute always reflects in large part the relationships between the class and the regular teacher. Where these relationships have been marked by deep resentment, even the most skillful of substitutes cannot avoid either having a difficult time coping with the displaced hostility or being idolized to an unrealistic degree. On the other hand, in a school with a relaxed atmosphere of confidence between the teachers and children, the substitute may be taken easily into the previous relationship.

The feelings the substitutes have toward themselves and the situation may alter relationships. Some see themselves almost as animal trainers courageously stepping into a den of snarling lions, armed only with a lesson plan or a bristling tongue. Others may feel a need to achieve stardom by putting on a brilliant display of teaching technique. Still others may specialize in finding fault, picking up trouble indicators, or acquiring a stock of gossip by which to bolster themselves. A few even expect to be scapegoats, to make a mess of things, and to take the blame for a series of errors.

Whatever the situation, however, it is important to realize that success or failure in substituting is not necessarily a true sign of future teaching ability.

Student Teaching

Almost universally, teachers serve an apprenticeship in student teaching of some sort. This experience is assumed to help familiarize the student with classroom situations. It is also regarded as the ultimate test of teaching ability.

The combinations of personal qualities which make for success in student teaching are quite different from those which have influenced the students' previous educational experience. For instance, in a study by Carlin[3] of 237 graduates of the Central Michigan College of Education, it was found that, whereas students' grades in their education courses were best predicted by scores on the language section of an intelligence test, success in student teaching was better predicted by self-adjustment scores on the California Test of Personality. Some students who do very well in most of their classes have trouble in student teaching. Also, a few who have difficulty in academic work find success coming easily at last when they start teaching.

The psychological role of the student teacher is somewhat different from that of the regular teacher. For example, instead of reacting to him or her as they would to a parent, some children see the student as an older brother or sister. Because the student lacks the authority of a "real" teacher, he is a safer target for hostility feelings. Yet, because he is young and relatively powerless, he makes a safer confidant. Also, because they may see the student teacher as a learner like themselves, students may have a feeling of fellowship in any predicaments which occur. This may make them unusually tactful and helpful, especially in critical situations. Many student teachers succeed in sharing their pupils' attitudes to a degree which they will never be able to duplicate later.

The role the children assign to the student teacher will reflect their sensing of the relationship between the apprentice and the supervising teacher. If they feel their regular teacher is jealous of the student, they may be inclined to play the two off against each other. On the other hand, if they feel the supervising teacher does not have confidence in the student but wants to protect him from the class, they will behave very differently. Where the supervising teacher and the student get along well on a basis of apparent equality, some classes may show no difference in behavior or attitudes, whichever teacher is in charge of the room.

RELATIONS WITH SUPERVISING TEACHER. Not only does the student teacher have to learn to deal with the realities of teaching; he or she is also forming important relationships with the adult immediately

---

[3] Leslie Orville Carlin, *A Comparison of the College Marks by 312 of the June, 1950, Graduating Seniors at Central Michigan College of Education with Their Battery of Guidance Tests and Inventory Percentile Scores,* unpublished Ed.D. field study, Colorado State College of Education, 1951.

responsible for the classroom. Titles vary: in different locales this teacher is called a critic, a supervising teacher, or a co-operating teacher. To many students, especially those who give primary consideration to earning good grades, getting along with this teacher is perhaps more important than doing a good job with the children. At any rate, the experiences of student teaching are influenced by the interpersonal relationships at this point.

In an attempt to depict the satisfactions and dissatisfactions which arise in student-teaching situations, Huey[4] interviewed fifty-three student teachers. In order of frequency, the principal sources of satisfaction were these: professional opportunities, relationships with children, personal relationships with the co-operating teacher, help received, professional relationships with the co-operating teacher, and the co-operating teacher's method of teaching and working with children. The following were the four chief sources of dissatisfaction: restriction of professional opportunities, co-operating teacher's poor method of working with children, lack of planning in the professional relationship with the co-operating teacher, and disciplinary problems.

A particularly trying situation arises where the co-operating teacher is unusually effective as a result of a highly personal style of teaching. If this does not suit well the personality patterns of a student teacher, the main learning is a futile sense of inferiority.

RELATIONSHIPS WITH CHILDREN.   The dynamics of group formation which we discussed in Chapter 10 will greatly influence the student teacher. For example, if he seems to ally himself with the children against the critic teacher and readily joins in childish recreation, there is always the danger that the group may act as though the student teacher were really one of its members who is trying to get a special position. Then, out of the jealousies engendered, they may turn against him. On the other hand, if they regard the student teacher as a genuine member of the group, in whose success all can take pride, the class may go to considerable lengths to protect him. More than one student teacher has been pleasantly surprised to see a class put on an impressive performance when a supervisor was observing.

The matter of control is always difficult. Some student teachers, out of fear, play the tyrant. In some groups this may work surprisingly

---

[4] J. Francis Huey, *Interpersonal Relationships between Student Teachers and Their Cooperating Teachers,* Ed.D. dissertation, New York University, 1952, University Microfilms Publication No. 4,544.

well; the pupils may appreciate having their mischievous impulses checked. Often, of course, the reaction is exactly the opposite: the insecurity behind the tyranny is sensed, and the resentment bred by stern measures combines with the resultant uneasiness to produce wild misbehavior, which grows worse as the tyranny is clamped down more frantically.

Although student teaching is regarded as one of the best indexes of future instructional ability, it is not the only indication. For some students and in some critic teachers' classes, it is a poor index. The differences between the roles taken by regular teachers and those thrust upon student teachers are significant. Accordingly, we find some teachers who do poorly as student teachers but brilliantly when they have classes of their own.

BEING A SUPERVISING TEACHER.   The position of supervising teacher has its own complications. Therefore we might expect to find some really wonderful teachers who are badly upset or who do very poorly in this role. Now and then, a quite average teacher proves to be a splendid supervising teacher. One trap that catches some of them is that they show so much affection and take so strong an interest in the student teacher that the class becomes very jealous. As a result the relationship between the supervising teacher and the pupils is poisoned. Pupils also may take their resentment out on the student teacher.

There are quite a few other trouble-breeding possibilities. For instance, now and then a supervising teacher feels very jealous of the youthfulness, fresh looks, or gaiety of a student; the reaction may be to squelch with criticism or load with extra tasks. At times the opposite type of jealousy may interfere: the older teacher may resent it when the children show affection for the student. Human personalities being as complicated as they are, the supervising teacher may recognize this jealousy and feel very guilty. The guilt in turn may create problems whenever there is a decision to be made in class. Conferences with a student teacher under such circumstances may be tense and strained.

As always, there is a chance that the teacher-student-class triangle may revive emotional hang-overs of early family difficulties. Less deep, but every bit as trying, are those cases in which the supervising teacher is resentful of the student's college. Then we are very likely to see a battle for the loyalty of the student. The introductory conference with the student may be opened with those ominous words, "Now, honey, you just forget everything they taught you at Blank. I've been teaching twenty years and I'll see that you learn to handle these kids."

The position of supervising teacher may also affect a teacher's standing with colleagues. Some of the teacher's colleagues may react by making snide remarks aimed at him, or by giving additional and conflicting advice to the student teacher.

In brief, the student-teaching situation has its own emotional traps. The student has the task of trying to figure out the cross-currents. The truly helpful supervising teacher and the college's supervisors have the duty of assisting the apprentice and each other in working out solutions.

In this chapter we have examined the psychological roles fulfilled by teachers. These are many and varied, ranging from policeman to parent surrogate. The roles are influenced by many significant factors of age, sex, race, and social status. From the viewpoint of helping children develop emotional stability, it is essential that teachers know the feelings and expectations which children have toward them.

Additional role expectations give tone to the work of other school people. The substitute, the student teacher, the critic teacher, and the new teacher, all must cope with special roles. These may vary in accordance with the tradition of the school system and the customs of young people. Teachers of special subjects may find they have to operate in terms of customary anticipations. Thus, a boys' gym teacher or shop teacher may have to be a he-man idol for identification, or a music teacher may be granted extra leeway in showing exuberance. Always there are tasks considered the peculiar province of principals and counselors.

The threads which hold these roles together and which reduce the confusion are the general relationships between children and teachers. Friendliness or harshness, patience or impatience, humor or acidity can mark the way all the roles are played. For the emotional health of pupils and teachers alike, it is best that teachers be able to exemplify attitudes of helpfulness in all the roles they have to play.

ADDITIONAL READINGS

Bernard, Harold W. *Mental Hygiene for Classroom Teachers*. New York: McGraw-Hill, 1952, Chap. 6. Gives examples of some ways in which teachers' personalities may influence pupil behavior.

Bruce, William F., and A. John Holden, Jr. *The Teacher's Personal Development.* New York: Holt, 1957, Chap. 12. Reactions of teachers to classroom situations are considered.

Bush, Robert Nelson. *The Teacher-Pupil Relationship.* Englewood Cliffs, N. J.: Prentice-Hall, 1954, Chap. 2. Sets forth a case study of the relationships observed between a teacher and the children in her class.

Cronbach, Lee J. *Educational Psychology.* New York: Harcourt, Brace, 1954, Chap. 15. An insightful discussion of the classroom-leadership aspects of teaching.

Kyte, George C. *The Principal at Work.* Boston: Ginn, 1941. Deals with some of the roles which principals have to play.

National Society for the Study of Education. *Fifty-Fourth Yearbook, Part II: Mental Health in Modern Education.* Chicago: National Society for the Study of Education, 1955, Chap. 14. The focus is on what teacher education can contribute to meeting mental health needs.

Peterson, Houston. *Great Teachers.* New Brunswick, N. J.: Rutgers U. Press, 1946. Sketches of a number of outstanding teachers.

Prescott, Daniel A. *The Child in the Educative Process.* New York: McGraw-Hill, 1957, Chap. 1. A thought-evoking statement of the teacher's task.

Rogers, Dorothy. *Mental Hygiene in Elementary Education.* Boston: Houghton Mifflin, 1957, Chap. 3. Discusses the role of teachers in preventing and treating maladjustment.

AUDIO-VISUAL AIDS

Effective Learning in the Elementary School, a 20-minute sound film produced by McGraw-Hill, in which a teacher is shown working skillfully with a class.

Passion for Life, an 85-minute film with dialogue in French, subtitles in English, available from Brandon Films. The central figure is a teacher whose conception of his role contrasts sharply with the norm.

chapter **12**

DIAGNOSTIC THINKING IN THE CLASSROOM

By the time they have reached this point in the book some readers will feel disheartened. The task of teaching which may once have seemed so simple stands revealed as full of complexities. The interlocking networks of relationships which exist in a classroom may now appear to be a devilish spider web designed to entangle teachers. Too many may feel baffled by the possibility that anything they may do can turn out to be a mistake.

To counteract such feelings, there is bound to be a demand that the mental hygienist give some definite, helpful answers. What can a teacher do in a classroom? How can the principles of mental health be put to work?

Although no one general statement can tell a teacher exactly how to handle each of the highly specific situations that can arise, it is possible to outline general approaches with which to meet the challenge of difficult situations. With practice, such ways of tackling problems can become second nature. As they gradually do so, insight concerning the complex interplay of psychological forces can become a source of professional security rather than a threat to personal adequacy.

To illustrate the pattern of diagnostic thinking[1] in the quick-as-a-wink setting of an ordinary classroom crisis, let us study a teacher in action.

As the third grade worked on some arithmetic problems, Miss

---

[1] By the term "diagnostic thinking" the authors refer to all the complexity of thought and observation which go into "sizing up a situation for what is in it" and, from the various possibilities, deciding on the most suitable way of dealing with it. The term here is not limited to labeling a disease with its proper name, a usage frequently applied in a medical frame of reference.

Queen noticed tears streaming down George's face. He was a frail boy, quiet but well liked by the others. Her first thought was that he was sick. She asked him if anything hurt him. He said, "No." His voice sounded embarrassed, but he did not look sick and did not sound as though he were in pain. Her next guess was that maybe he had had an "accident." His denial sounded convincing. During the exchange she noticed that he shot a look toward Harry, who had been watching with a scowl on his face. When Miss Queen looked around the class, Harry instantly began working on his arithmetic with unaccustomed vigor. Her hunch was that there had been some set-to between the boys, but, knowing the juvenile code against tattling, she kept the guess to herself. However, she did want more information, and pressed George to tell her what was wrong. Even as she did so, it seemed as though the rest of the class was too quiet; she suspected that they knew something. George finally faltered that he had lost his lunch money. Miss Queen was sure Harry had taken it.

Her conclusions made sense to her, but the question was, What should she do? Lend George the money? That would solve nothing, and she could always do it later in time to see that he had a good meal. Force him to tell the whole story? That would turn the class against him and give Harry social reinforcement outside school. Browbeat Harry or some other child into telling the truth? They would still blame George. She decided she had to show that George was not a tattletale and yet let Harry find out that the actions she suspected had social consequences. She had to let the class see she could protect all of them. Harry was overage for the class, and was using his size to get power, but that problem could be tackled later. A vivid lesson now might make him more ready to accept her help later, especially if she did not attack him directly.

All these considerations flashed through her mind while listening to George. One possibility occurred to her, and she decided to take a chance. She told the class that George had lost his lunch money and good-naturedly admonished him to be more careful. When the arithmetic papers were collected, she said she had to go to the office and asked them to help George find his money while she was gone. To make the request more striking, she dwelt a bit on how it feels to sit hungry in class all afternoon.

As she had hoped, no sooner was the door closed behind her than there was a noisy outburst. She was never sure but thought she heard voices shouting, "Give it back to him." At any rate, when she returned in five minutes the class was quiet, George had thirty cents on his desk, and Harry was drawing something on a piece of paper. All she said was, "You found his money? That's good."

There was no point in forcing anyone to think up fibs. Miss Queen remembered, of course, to work on the problem of helping Harry find ways of using his size for better purposes.

The Concept of Diagnostic Thinking

In this simple case, Miss Queen illustrated the procedures involved in diagnostic thinking. This is the habit of mind which enables physicians, automobile repairmen, and industrial trouble shooters to locate the causes of difficulties and work out plans of action. The essential characteristic of such thinking is that it is primarily concerned with determining the nature of a situation, figuring out the constellation of factors which produced it, and finding the point of attack. With a mind open to the meaning of developments, the practitioner proceeds into action as quickly as possible.

THE FIRST HUNCH.   As any difficulty arises, those who face it almost immediately form a hunch as to its meaning and the appropriate remedy. Such hunches are rarely reasoned. Rather, they represent the echoes of a person's previous experiences. Beginning teachers may react in terms of how previous teachers behaved toward them, and of their own feelings as students under similar conditions. The veteran has a backlog of experience, having dealt with a wide variety of conditions. Before logical thought can be brought to bear, these memories emerge and suggest a theory as to why a child or a class is behaving in a particular way and what strategy will probably work. Miss Queen, for some reason, first thought that perhaps George was sick.

Whether or not this first hunch turns out to be correct, it constitutes an essential step in the process of working out a solution. By giving a focus to the collection of observations and to thought processes, it prevents aimlessness. Because each child is different from all others and no two situations are ever exactly alike, the first hunch will almost always need to be modified. It is not a sacrosanct goal but a point of departure. In the illustration given, Miss Queen had to drop her first two guesses before she finally hit a promising lead.

EXERCISING SUBSURFACE CURIOSITY.   In testing the first hunch, the next step is to bring to bear the facts we already know and those which we can gather readily by observation. We try to determine the hidden factors in the situation. Miss Queen, for instance, gave much weight to children's aversion to tattling. This is the point at which we use our information concerning psychological dynamics. Here is where we apply facts concerning behavior at different stages of development. In the light of all our knowledge, we try to check our first hunch for harmony with possible explanations. Sometimes the hunch holds up under examination. Sometimes it must be completely discarded, and a new one developed, as Miss Queen's experience showed quite clearly. More often, the first hunch has to be amplified or altered.

To give another illustration: A seven-year-old boy complains to the teacher that he has been hurt by a youngster who always seems to be getting into fights. An obvious first hunch would be that here was another in a series of aggressions by a boy already unpopular for his quarreling. An investigation might reveal, however, that the victim was one of a group who had been taunting the "bully." Here we are dealing with a somewhat different situation than was at first suspected. The aggressor is being made into a scapegoat. Now, the problem is seen as one of finding ways to guide the group into a more constructive attitude toward a boy already wrestling with serious problems.

THE MEANING OF CONDUCT AS A GUIDE TO ACTION.   Even when we may not know the cause of a bit of conduct, we may still see some meaning in it. Lest this seem like a hairsplitting distinction, let us look at a simple illustration: In the course of a group discussion, a boy walks to the door with quick, tense strides, and slams the door when he leaves. Now, we cannot know on the basis of so few facts the *cause* of his action but we can see a clear *meaning*—that he was angry or disturbed. Whatever caused the boy to slam the door at this particular moment, or whatever led to door slamming as his technique of acting out resentment, may not be known at the time. To know, however, whether his slamming the door "meant" that he was ashamed, embarrassed, fearful of further taunting by other children, angry at the teacher, jealous, or what not, would be an important first clue to look for, and the answer can often be read directly from the way the door was slammed and the circumstances which led up to the incident. Although the full pattern of causation is not known, it is possible to take a first step on the basis of our understanding of the meaning of conduct. For Miss Queen, the ways Harry and the class acted were her important clues. Our knowledge of psychological principles enables us to decide what added facts we need to know. As these are interpreted, we can begin taking steps which stand a fair chance of being helpful.

ACTION TESTS THE HYPOTHESIS.   In any case, as soon as we feel reasonably confident of our hunches, we act upon them. Such action is regarded as a test of the accuracy of our estimates, rather than as a course of behavior to which we are irrevocably committed. This is done in the same spirit in which the doctor who suspects that a patient's headaches are due to eyestrain prescribes glasses. If the headaches then vanish, he feels satisfied he was right; if they persist, he looks for other causes.

Grace Arthur, in her book *Tutoring as Therapy,*[2] describes a boy, Sandy, who often played hooky. An analysis of test scores led to the hunch that his actions were a compensation for defects in reading and spelling. It was felt that since he had normal intelligence and showed no signs of other disturbance, individual remedial tutoring would do the trick. A teacher was employed to help him. As soon as he could compete with the rest of his class, he stopped being truant.

When a hypothesis is tested by action, it is sometimes found that a person's hunches are wrong or incomplete. For instance, a girl with a very good high school record began to misbehave in the mathematics class. The teacher first suspected the difficulty was due to shame over a poor grasp of basic concepts. However, a proffer of special help was rejected with some little heat. Since this had happened in only one class, the teacher decided that the first guess was wrong and that there must be some emotional reaction to math. A sympathetic high school counselor found that the girl was reacting against pressure from her father for her to become an engineer—part of the father's efforts to cover his disappointment at not having a son.

REVISING ESTIMATES AS EVENTS UNFOLD.   An essential characteristic of true diagnostic thinking is that it is flexible. As events unfold, we change our hunches and hypotheses. Our estimates are revised, not only by what happens as a result of our own treatment, but also by developments in the individual or the group. Thus, in a fifth-grade class, we might have a boy who seemed to enjoy disrupting the flow of a lesson by getting into an argument with the teacher or a popular class member on some minor point. A friendship chart might give the information that the boy

---

[2] New York, the Commonwealth Fund, 1946, p. 17.

was an isolate. We might know that his father had the reputation in the town of a truculent lone wolf. Our diagnosis, based on these facts, could be that the boy identified with his father and was also being cold-shouldered by the children, and that his argumentativeness was both cause and effect of this situation. Therefore, we would do what we could to get him accepted by the other children. Assume we were reasonably successful. Now, having won some friends, he continues to badger the teacher but not his classmates, several of whom seem to enjoy his antics. Our diagnosis would change to fit this new situation. Quite possibly, he was making a better social adjustment but had taken the lead in his juvenile group's warfare against adults, as represented by the teacher.

One further word of advice: Remember that a youngster or a group, if given a chance, will often work out problems without interference. For many individuals, trouble is a signal to bring their own resources to bear. An opportunity to think about what is happening or to talk it out in the presence of an attentive leader is all they need. The wise teacher senses those situations in which the child or the group can gather added strength by being left free to work out a solution. Miss Queen, for instance, wisely realized that she could count on her class to settle the immediate problem of getting Harry to return the money.

More Illustrations

All that has been said above may seem a little glib and vague. The tactics, of necessity, have been described in very general terms. They offer small satisfaction to a teacher who wants to know precisely what to do. To make the meaning somewhat more clear, we will give a few more illustrations of how these tactics have been used in concrete situations.

A ROOM BECOMES RESTLESS. The sophomores at Jefferson High were making a study of occupations in various local industries. Committees had gathered facts and had been presenting reports to the class. Interest had been high. Today, Betty was telling about the bus company. A bright girl, she had taken the initiative in the committee. The teacher had wondered whether Betty had not been highhanded and done all the work herself without giving the others a chance. Her report, though, was a masterpiece; she had obviously done a thorough job of getting facts from her father, who was treasurer of the company. She spoke with the smooth confidence of a self-assured executive addressing a meeting of yes men. As she proceeded, however, the class became restive. The movable chairs creaked as students shifted their weights; an unusual undertone of whispers or mutters could be heard.

What was the cause? Did the students resent the usually popular Betty's tone of superiority? Were they bored with the contents? Were the committee members expressing their discontent with her hogging of the work? All this was possible. The teacher also recalled that the company had almost had a strike that summer, and that some students came from homes of bus company employees. Was the restlessness an echo of that conflict?

Whatever the exact reason, it looked as though the dominating flow of her report was forcing quite a few class members to bottle up observations they were itching to make. If that were the case, the cure for the restlessness was to find a way to break into her report. It might be possible to do that in such a way as to avoid throwing her on the defensive; the firm way she was talking suggested that she was afraid of that potentiality.

As she finished telling about the maintenance shops, the teacher broke in with, "Betty, your report is so full of facts that it might be better to take it up one section at a time. I think Joe's father has been a repairman quite a while. Maybe he can give us an idea of what training that job required."

Joe was glad to take the opportunity. A lively discussion followed. Betty was at first impatient, but was drawn in to answer some questions. No mention was made of labor troubles. Apparently, the restlessness was not due to that so much as to her monopolizing the subject. The remainder of her report was given in short snatches. Although it was not completed that hour, the feeling as the class left the room seemed good.

CHILDREN FLARE UP AT EACH OTHER.   There was a clatter as Tim and his chair went sprawling onto the floor. Miriam stood over him, shouting "Freshy!"

Miss Silver told them to stop the fighting. She picked Tim up, told him he was not hurt, and started to find out what had happened. Just then, trouble popped in another part of the room. Fred gave a cry of pain. Miss Silver turned to find him and another boy rolling in furious combat. When she separated them, their alibis were vindictively voiced:

"He spit on me!"

"He kicked my foot!"

Such occurrences had been frequent ever since the class had begun a circus unit. The idea for the unit had come to Miss Silver when she noticed posters advertising a circus in the neighborhood store windows. She was sure her third-graders would jump at the chance to put on a show of their own. Indeed, there had been an excited clapping of hands when she had broached the idea. She told them that they would make their own circus and that each one could be whatever he wanted. She put out a supply of construction paper and told them to begin making costumes.

She had been reading some articles on the effects of too much domination of children by teachers. Since she wanted to do things the right way, she was determined not to interfere with the children's own ideas on the unit. When they came for advice, she told them to do whatever they wanted. The results were bad, she had never seen so much fighting and name calling.

The pattern of behavior did not fit Miss Silver's conviction that aggression is a product of frustration, as her texts had said; obviously she was not forcing the children to conform to her standards. Yet, something was keeping them from enjoying the experience. She could see they were not happy. Why? What was the matter? It was not the fault of the class, because up until then the group had worked well both in class and on the playground. Her first hunch grew out of a talk she had had earlier when Fred asked what kinds of animals they had in the circus. To her surprise she found out he had never seen a circus. She asked the whole class; three quarters said the same thing. Her conclusion was that they were frustrated because they lacked knowledge of what to do. To counteract this condition, she had brought in a collection of circus books and pictures. The flare-ups subsided for a while, but soon started again.

Next she had noticed that costume making was proving too hard. George had wanted to be an elephant, but failed dismally at fashioning a trunk out of the one piece of paper which was his allotment. The wonderful ideas of the others met similar fates. In the terms of psychology texts, their level of aspiration was unrealistically high. They had set goals far beyond either their skill or the materials available. Miss Silver felt that might explain all the evidence of frustration. Accordingly, she had announced that they could bring any materials they wanted from home.

The fights involving Tim, Miriam, and Fred came on the day of "culminating activity," the circus itself. The children arrived with a choice collection of cowboy accessories, Indian suits, and the like. However, they seemed to have no idea of what to do. They switched roles constantly: Kathy, for example, was a clown one minute, a trained horse the next, and ended by being an airplane. Once again, the group disintegrated in ill-tempered bickering.

When the principal came in to see the promised show, Miss Silver was ready to cry with vexation. In a friendly way afterwards, the principal quoted to her that part of the Lippitt experiment (pages 277-78) describing the frustrating effects of laissez-faire leadership.

Miss Silver promised herself that she would try another unit based on pupil purposes. Next time, she will make sure that the children have previous experience with the subject matter, that adequate supplies are available, that any construction required is within the ability of the pupils, and that there is sufficient planning by the class so that they feel some security. Certainly, another such debacle would not be good for the emotional health of the class, much less her own.

A CHILD TEARS UP HIS WORK.   The new first-grade teacher at the Corcoran School thought she would start off by trying to have the children enjoy being in her room. Remembering that children like big-muscle activity, she spent the first week in games, rhythm-band activity, and finger painting, instead of following the local custom of introducing primers the very first day. Although they seemed a very willing group of children and appeared to enjoy each activity when it was at its height, between activity peaks there was a growing undercurrent of disorder.

The new teacher's perplexity was brought to a head on the third day by something Eddie did. She had noticed him very early. Somewhat shy and anxious to please, he had come into the room carrying a shiny box full of pencils, crayons, rulers, and all the other gewgaws dear to fond parents. He was surrounded by a group of admirers, apparently friends from last year's kindergarten. At lunch the kindergarten teacher mentioned him as a dependable little leader. At the conclusion of a finger-painting session, he brought up a liberally smeared design. The new teacher told him it was very pretty and he could take it home. The look on his face was most peculiar, as though he thought she might be joking. What he said was equally enigmatic: "Oh, pooh!"

Eddie dutifully carried the rolled paper away with him. Watching from the window, the teacher was surprised to see him rip it to shreds, which he flung into the gutter. Then, he gaily joined some friends in a chaotic running race. A little while later the kindergarten class emerged from the building, each child proudly holding a crude basket made of paper. Some of her first-graders yelled a chant about "kindergarten babies."

The new teacher had learned enough psychology to realize that to Eddie the work he destroyed might be a symbol of something he disliked. The attitude of her class toward the kindergartners and the fact that those children had been taking work home suggested one possibility: Eddie had felt that he was being treated as a "baby," and his pride in his first-grade status was being threatened. The whole thing seemed childish and silly to the teacher.

A few thoughts later, it did not seem so silly. Maybe it was a clue to the growing disorder, the strange discontent that was troubling the class. Perhaps the activities of the first days were too much like kindergarten. Of course, Eddie's reaction was childish, but then first-graders are children. It could be that the reading and the other things that the new teacher considered work would be regarded at first as proud evidences of a long-awaited superiority.

When the first-graders came into their room the fourth day, there was a big pile of books on the teacher's desk. She noticed an immediate spark of interest. The room was quiet for once. When the books were passed out, there was an eager look on Eddie's face. The others looked equally impressed with themselves. That day the new teacher introduced the class to other "regular" subjects. She was surprised at their avid responses.

She knew that soon individual differences would take effect, and that sooner or later some would lose enthusiasm. The incident made her realize, though, that statements concerning the power of children's curiosity were true after all. She wondered a little now why she had felt otherwise. She realized that she should take into account the children's own expectations of what learning meant, in addition to her educated concept of the right technique. Anyway, she concluded, teaching might turn out to be more pleasant than she had expected.

"EVERYONE" CHEATS ON A TEST.   It was close to the end of the third marking period, and almost all the teachers at the Buchanan High School were giving tests. That week's issue of a national picture magazine had an article showing how students at several colleges cheated on examinations. Several teachers were quite upset and bitter at the possibility that the article might put ideas into Buchanan students' heads. Jack Pullen, the assistant football coach, who had been a very popular student leader seven years before and who was still regarded by the staff as an overgrown schoolboy, was frankly amused by all the fuss. He confided to Miss Johnson, a young science teacher: "Those old goats don't know the half of it. If every kid who cheated around here this week got caught and expelled, you could count the rest on your lovely little fingers."

Miss Johnson, however, was not amused. The thought that her students could be dishonest went against the grain. She had to admit to herself she was shocked; she just couldn't believe that what Mr. Pullen had said was true. In her own classes she used an informal honor system; after giving out the exam, she sat at her desk and, without looking up, corrected papers or worked on records.

To prove that Pullen was wrong, she feigned her usual casualness, but watched closely. A curved mirror set up on the demonstration desk gave her a good view of part of the class without anyone suspecting he was being observed. Within ten minutes she was thoroughly disheartened. Two of the girls had open textbooks hidden among papers on the shelf underneath their desks. The way notes were secretly passed from one student to another, answered, returned, and read in chain letter fashion reminded her of a film in which prisoners had plotted a mass escape. Out of the corner of her eye, she saw several students look at her, and when they were sure she was not watching, copy answers from the brighter members of the class. With the exception of Alice Wilkins, whom she had always disliked because of her prissy mannerisms, these bright youngsters were holding their pens in an awkward fashion that Miss Johnson realized was adopted to make such copying easier.

As her anger mounted, her first impulse was to pounce on one of the offenders and make an example of him. For a moment she debated with herself as to whom she could pick. Then she realized that would be unfair. Her next idea was to stop the examination, and denounce the whole class. That raised another question: Why penalize her students just because Pullen had tipped her off and she had been more observant?

The problem was obviously too big for her to tackle alone. This thing must be going on throughout the school. That thought settled her mind as to what to do. She would take it up with Miss Cump, the principal. There was no point in making an incident. Miss Johnson recalled having heard someone say something about how a wise teacher has to know what not to see. So she carefully refrained from any further watching that might let the students know what she had discovered.

When Miss Johnson told her tale, Miss Cump was not the least bit surprised. She had suspected that the curriculum and the emphasis on grades were putting too much pressure on many students. Miss Johnson's story convinced her that the problem needed to be faced by the faculty. In a short while committees composed of respected teachers were at work.

They made a series of suggestions which led to quite a bit of discussion. The content of several courses was changed to put more stress on topics related to the vocational goals of most students. Teachers planned to secure student effort on the basis of the usefulness of the material rather than fear of examinations. Although exams were still given, they were followed by sessions in which the results were used for remedial purposes.

A TEACHER'S PET ENCOUNTERS JEERS. Olga was Miss Elton's favorite pupil. The girl, a fourth-grader, was one of those alert, happy youngsters who work hard, learn easily, and are generally pleasant. One day, when the rest of the class had been apathetic, she came through with a very clear explanation of an arithmetic problem. Miss Elton turned to the class and said, "That is the kind of answer I like to hear. Why don't the rest of you do things the way Olga does?"

Before this speech was half finished, Miss Elton wanted to bite off her tongue. The other children seemed stonily quiet; a number glared at Olga. Miss Elton realized that she had made an error and that Olga would have rough sledding. Sure enough, on the way home, she saw a little circle jeering at Olga. The girl was angry and in tears. Miss Elton felt very bad, but did not know what to do. She drove past the group without being noticed by them.

The next day, Olga acted quite distant. She avoided Miss Elton and did not volunteer in class. However, she did work on problems at her seat. During a short quiz, Miss Elton saw her whisper an answer to Doris, who sat in front. The following day she came late, and gave a weak excuse in a belligerent voice. Miss Elton told her to stay after school, a traditional penalty at the school. Olga obeyed, but bristled defiance. Miss Elton did not know how to approach the girl. As she puzzled over the affair, the teacher reviewed what she knew of the girl. All the information pointed clearly to the fact that Olga was a stable youngster who had good sense and knew how to get along with her fellow pupils. Her actions were well calculated to overcome the reputation of being a teacher's pet. Miss Elton figured that the girl could undoubtedly work out her present problem by herself. After five minutes, Miss Elton excused her with a friendly injunction to be her usual pleasant self. She asked whether Olga's mother would be worried if she came home late. Olga replied that she usually played with some friends and was not expected home until dinnertime.

Two days later, Olga lingered for a moment after dismissal to tell Miss Elton she was sorry for having been snippy. Then she ran to join her friends. Within a week, Olga was again taking an interested part in class activities. The only noticeable differences were that she seemed to spend more time helping her friends and that she seemed to hold back giving answers to problems when several others had made errors. Miss Elton had been correct in her guess that the girl would work things out satisfactorily.

OVERDOING A GOOD THING.   Mr. Schultz had an uneasy feeling about modern education. He was sure that, especially in arithmetic, many members of his third-grade class could do better work than was now the case. It was his idea that if he insisted they do every problem in their workbook, their mastery would become complete.

The immediate response of the class tended to justify his hunch that they had been pampered and really wanted to work harder. When there were too many problems to be completed on class time, he made them finish assignments at home. There was no immediate objection to this; indeed, a few parents went out of their way to compliment him for making the children get down to business.

Of course, a few of the children with low mental-test scores began to flounder. This he had expected. The thing that worried him was what happened to a group of four bright boys who had done quite well in arithmetic the previous year. None of them now finished the assigned work in school. To spur them, he gave them low marks. He was surprised that they did even less work; their showing became worse.

The turning point came after two of the mothers came to school. Mr. Schultz had been expecting complaints from a minority. The second interview in the principal's office surprised him. The mother began by saying she and her husband had hired a tutor to work with the boy. They were concerned because the tutoring time plus the homework had cut into his time with friends. The tutor had told them, moreover, that the boy was good in arithmetic. Mr. Schultz replied that he marked solely on the basis of papers done in school; the principal backed him. The mother left saying she would tell the tutor to concentrate on speed.

After she had gone, the principal told Mr. Schultz that he had had an earlier visit from a mother who had requested that her son be transferred to another teacher. This request had been granted. The principal asked if he could come to the classroom to see what was going on.

Two days later, Mr. Schultz was confronted with some facts that made him think. The principal pointed out that the boys did know the required arithmetical processes and facts, but that the problem was their listlessness; they did not complete the amount of work assigned. The principal also revealed that the one boy who had been transferred was now doing "A" work.

Although Mr. Schultz was at first inclined to feel the principal was another weak-kneed dupe of progressive education, he had to admit that the principal had backed him fully when the mother was present. Moreover, he could see for himself that the boys' enthusiasm for arithmetic had been lost, although they had been good in the subject. When he checked, he found that although his low marks were justified on the basis of work not completed, they did not reflect the boys' understanding.

He decided that if he gave less work and tried praise for correct answers, he might reverse the downward trend. The response of the boys to this new tactic was surprisingly good. He was a trifle miffed when two of them gave credit for their better grades to their fathers, who had been helping them with homework. For the future, Mr. Schultz made a mental note that insisting on too much quantity can get in the way of giving credit for quality.

The Strategy of Timing

The use of diagnostic thinking may be complicated by the fact that in psychological matters timing is very important. Often the appropriate action is not a single act, but a series of acts. It is essential that we not only decide what to do but when to do it. For example, if a new boy in a class starts to clown in a way which is winning the admiration of the other children, our tactics have to be carefully timed. If the particular circumstances indicate that he is being successful in winning popularity, we might deliberately ignore his antics for a while. For one thing, it would be hazardous to turn the group against him. Indeed, if he became socially accepted, his reason for clowning might vanish, and we would want to let that possibility develop. Moreover, a head-on clash over clowning while it was novel and popular might make him a martyr and fix the pattern in his repertoire. Therefore we would wait. If the clowning continued, as soon as the class began to become impatient with him (as they surely would), we could take decisive measures to stop him in class, and follow up those measures with an interview, in which he would be much more willing than earlier to discuss how to win the approval of his classmates. Thus, the early policy of avoiding action would be an essential feature of the long-time strategy of moving vigorously when the class feelings and his own needs had developed to the point where we could be effective.

Here is another illustration of a situation where timing can be crucial: Miss Philips had been making a special effort to win Ralph's confidence. The boy had a bad reputation in the school. He was quarrelsome and had many fights. When warned about him at the beginning of the year, she had said that with everyone against him, the boy needed a friend. She had been very pleasant to him, and lately he had shown signs of gratitude. That is why her heart sank when the children came in from lunch all excited with a story that he had almost killed another boy because that boy had pushed Ralph's little sister. Soon Ralph appeared on the scene, pushed into the room by two indignant teachers. They grimly announced, "Here's your dear, sweet little Ralph."

Their story was that he had beaten Jack McQuade with a stick and hurt him badly. Ralph kept shouting, "He had no right to pick on a girl."

Soon an angry shouting contest was in full swing. The teachers were repeating over and over again, "You almost killed him."

Ralph changed his angry chant to, "Nobody can pick on my sister."

Several things were clear to Miss Philips: First, Ralph was getting in deeper water all the time. Second, he was too excited to understand anything. Third, she must satisfy the other teachers that she would take action. Fourth, Ralph and his classmates must get it clear that mayhem could not be condoned. Fifth, Ralph must continue to feel she was on his side. Obviously, the last two vital points could not be made until he was calm. Even then, she would have to do some hard thinking.

The first step, though, was to break up the angry scene then raging. She moved between Ralph and the other teachers. To them she said crisply, "I'll take care of this." She turned to Ralph and told him to take his seat. Then she stepped out into the hall with her colleagues, closed the door, and let them tell her what they had heard and what they thought she should do, until at last they were all talked out and went to their rooms.

In her own room, there was Ralph anxious to tell his side of the story. The class excitedly corroborated his claim that Jack McQuade had really been mean to his sister. They wanted, however, to add gory details about the stick beating. That, Miss Philips cut short, and gave the class a solemn lecture on law and order. She told them how terrible life would be if everyone took to beating or shooting anyone they thought had wronged them. Deliberately she encouraged the group to work out their excitement in fantasies of disorderly chaos. As the discussion shifted from the immediate incident, Ralph became quiet and then thoughtful. She was sure he was beginning to wonder what would be done to him. He looked at her searchingly, as if to find out what she thought of him.

The class soon had said all they had to say. She gave them some work to do, and re-established the usual routine. During the first recess period she motioned to Ralph to come to her, and told him, "You and I had better find out if Jack is hurt badly." On the way to the office, he showed his worry. He stressed that he had meant only to scare Jack. In the office, Miss Philips took the lead. The principal assured her that there had been no serious injuries. Miss Philips firmly said in Ralph's hearing that the boy was truly sorry, that this time he had learned his lesson, and that she would personally guarantee his future good behavior.

After class she had a long talk with him. He told her how the other children had picked on him and how mad it made him to see the same thing start happening to his sister. She sympathized with him but pointedly repeated that his beating of Jack had been wrong. She dwelt a bit on possible consequences. That done, she listened as he told about how mean Jack and other children had been and how he felt about them. He began to blubber. Just at that point the two other teachers looked into the room. Seeing him in tears apparently satisfied them. Gradually, he calmed down again. She ended the interview by telling him that the next time anything happened he should tell her. Not that she thought he ever would, but she wanted to be sure he knew she was his friend, and she hoped that would make him think twice about starting another incident, which, he now could see, would put her in a bad light for having come to his rescue. In this whole pattern, she was quite wise in so timing her actions that he first had time to get over his excitement; she let him feel anxious just long enough for it to have an effect, so that he then could relax in the confidence of her backing and be in a proper frame of mind for the final interview.

In analyzing the several incidents in this chapter, it is worth while to indicate once again what they have in common. Perhaps it is easiest at first to point out some things that none of these teachers had done. None had handled the situation solely in terms of his or her own feelings. Rather, they reacted to what the children were doing. None had relied upon a single act to do everything; rather, each had made use of several measures. None had applied a stock solution; instead, they had worked out a new plan to meet a new situation. None had wandered off into an interpretation about children in general; rather, each had worked in terms of specific causes and effects operating upon the individual children as he knew them.

Through these examples we have tried to give concrete illustrations showing how teachers used diagnostic thinking to cope with mental health aspects of classroom problems. The first hunches which arose as a situation developed were subjected to examination on the basis of known facts and psychological principles. Lacking complete information as to all the causes operating in a situation, the teachers relied upon the youngsters' behavior to furnish them with clues. In the light of the best estimate which could be made as to the forces at work, a program for dealing with the situation was developed. The changes in the situation after the program was applied tested the accuracy of the estimates. The analysis was flexible; it was changed as new developments threw more light on the situation.

ADDITIONAL READINGS

Cantor, Nathaniel. *The Dynamics of Learning.* Buffalo: Foster & Stewart, 1946. An account of the development of a student-centered learning environment.

Cunningham, Ruth, and Associates. *Understanding Group Behavior of Boys and Girls.* New York: Bureau of Publications, Teachers College, Columbia U., 1951, Chap. 6. Develops the idea of group adjustment, what situations reveal it, and how groups can be guided.

Hymes, James L., Jr. *Behavior and Misbehavior.* Englewood Cliffs, N. J.: Prentice-Hall, 1955, Chap. 3. Concentrates on cases where discipline is necessary as a basic corrective.

National Society for the Study of Education. *Fifty-Fourth Yearbook, Part II: Mental Health In Modern Education.* Chicago: U. of Chicago Press, 1955, Chap. 9. Discusses mental health practices appropriate to the intermediate grades.

Prescott, Daniel. *The Child in the Educative Process.* New York: McGraw-Hill, 1957, Chap. 5. How to interpret behavior is the subject of this chapter.

Rogers, Dorothy. *Mental Hygiene in Elementary Education.* Boston: Houghton Mifflin, 1957, Chaps. 11 and 12. Describes ways to study children.

Wittenberg, Rudolph. *So You Want to Help People.* New York: Association Press, 1947, Chap. 2. Describes the criteria by which a leader can judge what is good for a group.

AUDIO-VISUAL AIDS

Each Child Is Different, a 15-minute sound film, produced by McGraw-Hill, in which some causes of individual behavior are depicted.

Individual Differences, a 22-minute sound film, produced by McGraw-Hill,

in which a student teacher is told of the clues used in working out
strategies for helping five children.

Problem Children, a 20-minute sound film, produced by the Ohio Department of Mental Health, showing how a teacher dealt with an aggressive boy and a very shy one, both in the same class.

chapter **13**

INFLUENCE TECHNIQUES

Many teachers regard the area of discipline and leadership as the one in which they have received least help from educational science. For instance, when Graham[1] questioned secondary school teachers with less than three years' teaching experience, 46 per cent criticized their training for not having given them instruction in handling discipline problems.

The teachers described in Chapter 12 used a wide variety of techniques in handling various situations. Some behavior they deliberately ignored. Sometimes they stepped in and redirected a class. When necessary, they had talks with children. The scope of possible devices ranges all the way from expelling "incorrigible" children to playing a traditional chord on the piano as a signal for quiet in the kindergarten; from giving lectures to holding gripe sessions; from easing tensions with jokes to conducting private conferences.

In this chapter we want to focus attention on the techniques which teachers employ to influence present and future behavior and to handle conduct in day-to-day situations. These techniques can be likened to a kit of tools. The question a teacher faces is when and how to use each. The effect of the devices depends upon the clarity with which they are employed, a matter to which more attention will be devoted later.

The decisions which a teacher makes as to technique must take a number of factors into consideration. One of these is the existence of certain administrative understandings. For instance, whether or not a child should be sent to the office depends upon what it has been agreed will be

---

[1] Ralph William Graham, *Secondary School Teachers' Criticisms of Their College Preparation for Teaching,* unpublished Ed.D. dissertation, University of Southern California, 1952.

his reception there. Decisions also depend upon the personality of the teacher; some measures may be unsuitable because they would seem unnatural for a particular person. For instance, humor comes easily from some people, but sounds forced and corny on the lips of others. Additional considerations appear in the following description of a commonplace incident.

Steve was one of those restless jumping jacks whose ill-considered activity can and does upset a room. This particular morning, Miss Ulrich had three times asked him not to disturb various classwork groups. He had managed somehow to get in the way of other children who were busy on their own projects. At last she put him in a seat, gave him some colored chalk and paper, and told him to stay there. Now, here he was making straight for the pencil sharpener, apparently oblivious of the fact that he was walking over a long sheet of paper on which a committee had sketched the outlines for a mural. Regardless of the long-range job of getting at the roots of the restlessness, to begin with, Miss Ulrich had to find some way of coping with the disturbing behavior right now.

There were, of course, a great many possibilities. She could frighten him by shouting an order to go back to his seat. She could punish him by keeping him in the room during the playground period. She could give him a lecture on the importance of rules. She could send him to the principal's office. She could ask him to leave the room. She could return him to his seat and find work so interesting to him that he would not want to wander again. She could ignore the incident. She could promise him a reward if he went the rest of the day without getting in anyone's way. She could give him one last chance and threaten dire consequences if he created another disturbance.

Yes, there were a great many things she could do. From the numerous possibilities she had to choose the one which would not only ensure order in the classroom but also be most helpful to the child. To accomplish both purposes, she must give some thought to such questions as these: (1) Why is Steve acting as he is? (2) What does the class think? (3) What is his relationship with the teacher? (4) How will he react to whatever method is used? (5) How will it affect his relationships with the teacher and the class?

Here are a few examples of how the answers to the first of these questions would influence the final decision. If Steve were a boy whose overactivity was due to some physical cause, obviously it would be pointless to punish him; Miss Ulrich would have to find him some other activity in which he could do much moving around. On the other hand, if he were merely trying to make a splash in the juvenile world by "getting away with murder," firm handling would be in order. Then, Miss Ulrich might use either an immediate penalty or the one-last-chance-and-dire-threat combination. However, if she felt that this would confer martyrdom and she was also sure that the others would not want to ape his rebellion, she might decide to ignore him and thus deny him the satisfaction of attention. By contrast, if his restlessness was due to boredom, then none of these methods would be appropriate, and she would be well repaid for a successful effort to help him find some classroom activity that would absorb his attention.

Two Preliminary Considerations

Before entering on a detailed discussion of influence techniques, it is desirable to identify two basic considerations which teachers will do well to keep in mind whenever they exercise such techniques.

CLARITY.   The effectiveness of influence techniques depends upon how clear children are as to the issues involved. This generalization has been given experimental backing by the results of research in which Gump and Kounin[2] examined the effects of teachers' actions upon the children not directly involved. In using any device to eliminate misconduct, teachers always hope to influence not only the child involved but also the rest of the class. The question is, What produces these effects? Gump and Kounin classified kindergarten teachers' interventions in terms of the clarity, the firmness, or the roughness shown. They found that the more clearly the teacher defined the issue, the more all children were favorably influenced. Firmness seemed to increase conformity only for guilty children. Roughness "did not direct behavior—it merely disturbed it."

For the purposes of the above-mentioned research, "roughness" was defined as the showing of irritation and hostility toward the deviant child, indulging in overfirm physical handling, and giving vent to angry words and looks. "Firmness" related to acts or other ways of increasing the "I mean it" quality of what happened. This could be done by "following through," by utilizing emphatic speech, gesture, or posture, and by approaching, touching, or guiding the little offender. Clarity was developed

---

[2] Paul V. Gump and Jacob S. Kounin, "Effects of Teachers' Methods of Controlling Misconduct upon Kindergarten Children," paper delivered at the American Psychological Association meeting, August, 1957.

by telling exactly what was wrong: "Don't hit other children," as contrasted to, "Stop that!" It also was developed by stating standards, as, "We don't fight in the kindergarten." In addition, it was important to tell the child how to stop his deviant conduct, as, "Fold your hands and look at me."

Although this research applies specifically to kindergarten children during the initial weeks of school, there is good reason for thinking that the principles involved may operate at other grade levels.

THE AUTHORITY HIERARCHY. Throughout the remainder of this chapter we shall be primarily concerned with actions to be taken by classroom teachers. However, it is important to realize that children do react to prestige and authority. Some children, who might ignore what a teacher does or says, are genuinely impressed by a principal or assistant principal. How and when this power should be used is a matter on which there should be understanding between teachers and administrators.

A Variety of Techniques

Too often, when people talk about methods of influencing conduct, the discussion bogs down on punishment and various ingenious ways of administering pressure. Actual observation of a group of good teachers will show that they have a wide repertoire of techniques for providing leadership for groups and for helping children develop better social behavior patterns in school. More than twenty different procedures can be identified, and they will be discussed.[3]

These stopgap measures, so important to group leaders, do not readily fall into any simple set of categories. At the risk of some oversimplification, we have here grouped them, for purposes of study, into four classifications. Of these, one set is based primarily on the assumption that children want to live up to or get along with the standards of conduct expected by their parents and teachers. Lapses may be due to the fact that at times young people forget themselves or that their impulses, for a brief period, overpower their self-control. When this is true, a respected teacher may help by calling their attention either to the lapse or

---

[3] This list is based upon an analysis made in connection with the operation of Pioneer House, a treatment home for highly disturbed children, as first reported in the following: Fritz Redl and David Wineman, *Controls from Within,* Glencoe, Ill., Free Press, 1952, Chap. 3. [This material now is also found in the following: Fritz Redl and David Wineman, *The Aggressive Child,* Glencoe, Ill., Free Press, 1957.]

to the standards. Then the young people recover self-control and work out their own solutions. The outstanding characteristic of such techniques is that they support and strengthen a child's ability to help himself. We shall discuss these in greater detail under the heading *supporting self-control.*

The second general class of influence techniques works by removing those difficulties in a situation which the children cannot master on their own. The teacher may, so to speak, "run interference" for the youngsters by smoothing out objective obstacles, changing a program, or otherwise modifying the situation. These techniques we shall group under *situational assistance.*

The third type of influence technique involves guidance in developing an ability to deal realistically with problems. Although many difficulties arise as a result of the interplay of unconscious forces, there is always some room for a person's sense of cause and effect to work. All techniques designed to help the child solve his own problems to this end seem to rely upon talk and discussion. The goal is to help the child see his actions in a new light. These may be classified under *reality and value appraisal.*

The fourth type of technique bears some similarity to the conditioning of reflexes. By the pleasantness or unpleasantness of our response to what a child does or may want to do, we seek to develop a reaction which serves as a guide to action. Such methods may be considered under the heading *invoking the pleasure-pain principle.*

Supporting Self-Control

As was pointed out in Chapter 3, where we discussed children's control over their conduct, much misbehavior is not really motivated by a desire to be disagreeable. It often results simply from a temporary lapse of the individual's control systems. There are a number of techniques which are designed to support young people in regaining the ability to fit in with the desired classroom pattern.

These techniques share several advantages. Because all are low-pressure methods, the teacher avoids the problem of having to deal with the aggression which forceful interventions produce. When they are used, the child retains his autonomy. In this group of techniques, acts are often stopped before an offense has been completed. These techniques serve to communicate values without putting the teacher in the position of having to administer penalties.

SIGNALS. A trick most teachers have learned is to catch the eye of a child beginning to get into mischief. Then a mildly disapproving warning is flashed by some signal—shaking the head, frowning, waving a finger, or clearing the throat. The signal is all that is needed. So to speak, it calls attention to the fact that what is going on should be controlled. After the signal is received, the child does the controlling by his own volition. Although this technique may lose its force if invoked too often for trivial matters, it does prevent many incidents from growing to proportions that can cause difficulty. It stops unwanted behavior by mobilizing the youngster's own powers of control. Thus the complications of outside pressure are avoided.

Signals are usually most effective in the early stages of misconduct or when an ordinarily normal and well-controlled child has literally forgotten himself. For instance, they are traditionally used to recapture wandering attention, to stop irrelevant chatter, or to end minor horseplay. When the unwanted behavior is due to strong emotions, to powerful impulses out of control, or to a persistent source of dissatisfaction, they either do not work or else have to be repeated so often as to be ridiculous.

For instance, Bill Connolly was having trouble with his Scout troop. The boys had only two pieces of rope for knot-tying exercises. Those not at work kept making a row by unorganized wrestling, spontaneous games of tag, and the like. Every so often Bill blew his whistle. The disturbances would then stop, only to start a few minutes later. The meeting ended in a frenzy of exasperated whistle blowing as the boys raced wildly through the halls. All the signals in the world cannot help youngsters in an intolerable situation.

By contrast, Ed Smith and his buddies, who liked science, were entranced by a comic book they had added to their joint collection earlier that day. They did not notice that Miss Barkley had started a table demonstration. She cleared her throat. Ed heard the sound, gave a little start, and put the book away. That was the end of the incident.

PROXIMITY CONTROL. A rather similar technique is employed on the many occasions when children are tempted to do something they know they should not do. If the teacher moves close to them, they are better able to control their wrong impulses. This works not so much because they fear detection as because they draw added strength from the teacher's nearness. Perhaps the proximity makes it more likely that any identification which may exist will go into action. Many teachers recognize this mechanism and use it wisely by putting a youngster with weak self-control in a seat close to the desk or chair the teacher usually occupies, unless some other reason, such as the fact that "honor" is attached to that location, makes it impractical.

An extension of this technique consists of a friendly, steadying gesture. For some children this has an almost magical quality; they act as though a current of self-control has flowed through the area of contact. This procedure works best with younger children, but may sometimes be appropriate in special situations involving adolescents. For example, if a boy in a gym class has been accidentally struck by a fellow player and is struggling not to fly into a rage, a friendly pat on the shoulder may help him win his battle. It should be emphasized, however, that in the upper grades and in high schools physical contact between a teacher and a young person can be risky. As has been previously mentioned, children at this age are sometimes very sensitive to body contact. Also, when a child is angry at an adult or is in a stage where too-close friendship with grownups causes a loss of face, this method may backfire.

INTEREST BOOSTING. When a young person begins to show boredom with a task, some teachers will go over to him and look at his work. A few words convey their interest. This simple step changes somewhat the value the youngster puts on his work. The result is a renewed burst of energy. For a while, the wandering attention is checked; the young person concentrates on the task at hand. In this way, any misconduct which might have arisen from boredom and restlessness is prevented.

This procedure will work well when the child's control systems are in good shape, and when the faltering of interest is caused by mild discontent with sticking to one task. It will not work when the child is emotionally troubled or when the boredom is the result of genuine inability to succeed with the work. Also, if the required period of concentration is beyond the attention span for the age level, the number of children needing this type of stimulation would be so great that the teacher would be worn to the proverbial frazzle trying to reach all of them.

HUMOR. Laughter can serve several useful functions. When a youngster is engaging in undesirable conduct resulting from thoughtlessness or other minor reasons, a benign joke may call his attention to the lapse. At the same time, the humor reassures him that he has no immediate cause for anxiety. His answering laugh is a return signal that he appreciates both points. It is an unspoken promise that he will be more careful in the future.

Now and then when some child openly defies a teacher, the class becomes electric with suspense. As far as the other children are concerned, quite often all they need is reassurance that the teacher is in effective control and that their own resources are ample to cope with any contagion effects. By handling the incident with humor, the teacher retains leadership of the group while wiping out the anxiety which the defiance may have created in the class.

Here we are speaking only of a genial and kindly use of humor. Where there is an edge of sarcasm or ridicule, however, the technique is no longer humor but becomes really a form of revenge or punishment, and should be considered as such. To illustrate a wise type of humor, we shall describe what happened when Mr. Landis returned to his room to find a portrait of himself on the board. The quiet in the room and the exaggerated angle of the ears both made it clear that the artist's intent was ridicule. Mr. Landis inspected the portrait with an air of obviously feigned appreciation. Then he shook his head in mock disagreement, erased the ears, and sketched in two a good deal larger. There was relieved laughter from the class. Even the unknown artist felt better. There were no more portraits that year. More significant, the young people agreed that he was a good fellow and felt much less desire to attack him. Children usually consider humor evidence of imperturbability based on security. This is a far cry from the fear of some teachers that humor may be taken as a sign of weakness.

PLANFUL IGNORING. A feature of such incidents as the one just mentioned is that the offense or the offender is ignored. Under some conditions, such deliberate ignoring of misbehavior, even though disapproval is tacitly implied, enables a youngster to reduce the inner tensions driving him to create disturbances. This is especially true when children do something out of sheer curiosity to find out what will happen next, or try misdeeds in order to get themselves noticed. In the upper grades, it may be socially worth while to "get the teacher's goat."

The wise teacher learns to estimate the significance of such happenings. For example: An overage boy in the fifth grade is openly disregarding the arithmetic lesson and is making a slingshot in full view of his classmates. Two basic questions have to be asked: Will he go on to other and more flagrant behavior to precipitate a scene? Will the behavior spread to other members of the class? If the answer to both questions is No, it may be wise to do nothing at the time. When a young person gets no result from such a bid to "get a rise" from the teacher, the behavior may soon be dropped. Of course, the boy's needs, revealed in what he has done, must be recognized for later action.

Annoying behavior may also be the result of poor self-control resulting from deep difficulties, immaturity, or physical abnormality. The teacher may therefore be unable to help the child with the immediate misconduct. The classroom problem is rather to help the other children resist contagion effects. Also, there is the problem of helping them work out a way of dealing with the unfortunate offender without increasing his problems. By ignoring his actions, the teacher may set the stage for solving both problems. The fact that the teacher is not disturbed implies confidence in the group. That confidence strengthens self-control. At the same time, by preventing anxiety, it reduces the chances that the group may seek a scapegoat for its unpleasant feelings. By setting an example, the teacher indicates how the group itself may act toward the offender. This method presents no answer to the basic problem, but is merely a way of handling a momentary situation. What we are referring to here is the kind of ignoring which represents a deliberate choice of procedure.

For instance, in Miss Hovland's fifth-grade class, Walter was flicking balls of paper on his desktop. He and two children near him looked up occasionally and expectantly at the teacher. She glanced at what Walter was doing, and then called on another child in the class discussion. After one more feeble flip, Walter gave up his effort to distract her attention. His next move was to enter the discussion. Miss Hovland made no comment.

By contrast, in some situations a teacher may not know how to deal with a situation or may be reluctant to take needed action. Uncertain as to what to do, he does nothing. The hesitancy communicated by this type of ignoring will incite children to test the limits of behavior. It leads to an upsurge in disorder.

The technique of ignoring always depends very much on the situation. It can be used only when we can afford to ignore what is happening.

IRRITABILITY DRAIN-OFF. Many incidents involving annoying classroom conduct arise because one or more of the youngsters are dissatisfied with some aspect of school or of group life. Not knowing what to do about their feelings, they engage in rebellious, aggressive behavior or lose interest in the work. If these feelings could be drained off, the young folks might be able to regain control over themselves.

An experiment illustrating this technique in action has been performed by Thibault and Coules.[4] They devised situations in which hostility was aroused by the contents of a note which one person passed to another. Some individuals who received such notes were given a chance to express their hostility; others were not. Those who did express their feelings proved later to be more friendly to the original sender.

In a group situation, the holding of a gripe session can work wonders in accomplishing this goal. It is important to realize that to the participants the real good comes from being able to tell freely how they feel. The teacher's proper role is to encourage honest discussion and to help the young people express themselves. If the leader tries to stifle complaints with a barrage of self-justification or pounces on anyone for talking frankly, the session may do more harm than good. The purpose of such discussions is to reduce tension, not increase it. Like the other techniques, the gripe session is not an all-conquering trick. It is best used to cope with a temporary state of tension.

ADVANTAGES AND DISADVANTAGES OF THE "SUPPORTIVE TECH-NIQUES." All these techniques share the advantage that they can stop undesired acts while in the making. Therefore, they may forestall the problem of what to do about a completed violation. They reinforce and communicate the values upon which desired behavior is based; yet they avoid the kinds of interference which arouse aggression. More than is true for other procedures, these allow a child to retain his personal autonomy and to modify his conduct on his own.

It is important to realize that the usefulness of this group of techniques is limited to cases where the ego is still in the saddle. They do not work when individual or group excitement becomes too strong. Moreover, if they are used constantly, children may feel they are being picked on. Overuse also robs the child of his autonomy; it makes him feel like a puppet receiving constant instructions. The child may think the teacher is suspicious of him and does not trust him.

In general, these are the measures of first choice. Where they work, little else is needed. If they fail, other procedures are in order, and can be introduced without confusion. Failure of low-pressure methods to maintain order in a group is a sign that there is need to bring to bear the type of diagnostic thinking described in the previous chapter.

---

[4] John W. Thibault and John Coules, "The Role of Communication in the Reduction of Interpersonal Hostility," *Journal of Abnormal and Social Psychology,* Vol. 47 (1952), pp. 770-77.

Situational Assistance

Somewhat different in their theoretical base are the techniques for dealing with problems which arise out of children's inability to cope with the
difficulty of a situation. Again the assumption is made that something in
most youngsters generally impels them toward doing the right thing.
However, where analysis indicates that an aspect of the situation makes
them want to be bad, or that they are having trouble, not because of
temporary lapses or slightly inadequate self-control, but because outside
forces make them unable to control themselves, the teacher's active assistance as a guide or trouble shooter is required.

HELPING OVER HURDLES.   Much disorder in schools arises because
youngsters do not know how to cope with some phase of the work. For
example, a first-grade class might dissolve in confusion if a teacher,
about to go to the office, told them, "Keep yourselves busy by making
up examples." Similarly, a high school class committee may engage in
random mischief if they lack know-how in bringing together individual
findings to make a group report. By helping young people over such
hurdles, a teacher can save them from frustration and anxiety, and thus
eliminate inappropriate behavior.

Another time that children may need a little expert help is when
they have had difficulty with a teacher or with other children. Then, help
in "saving face" may head off further trouble. If the child's unwanted
conduct in a particular incident can be traced to an exceptional instance
of inability to do the work at hand, a teacher can help him with the
specific task itself, and thus avert future trouble. For instance, if a boy
is disorderly because of inability to do one operation involved in an
arithmetic problem, the teacher's point of attack is to help with that
operation, rather than to make an issue of the misconduct connected
with the lad's anxiety about his work.

RESTRUCTURING THE SITUATION.   One problem that sometimes
arises is a growing restlessness because the group have been sitting still
too long. Frequently, also, the children become "wild," overstimulated,
or overexcited. Rather than to concentrate attention on the restlessness
or overexcitement, it may be wise to change the nature of the activity or
to give the group a new center for attention. By such means we can
change the quality of the situation. This is a technique for dissolving a

real or impending disturbance by setting up an entirely new economy of needs, goals, and frustrations. For example, when a necessary review lesson becomes boring, teachers may turn the session into a simulated television quiz program. A straggling group of primary children may be brought to cohesion by the idea, "Let's pretend we're soldiers on parade." Rather than be drawn into a battle over the by-products of poor curriculum development, we can tackle the cause of the trouble and work out new activities that will cause less strain on everyone in the class, the teacher included.

SUPPORT FROM ROUTINES. Concern lest schools overregiment children and thus stifle the initiative so vital to scientific inquiry brings the use of routines under scrutiny. In this connection, it may be too easy to lose sight of the helpful aspects of set procedures.

In some groups, trouble arises simply because the young people cannot manage themselves when they do not know what is expected of them. In order to check impulses which can lead to trouble, they need some support in the form of expectations which they are to meet. The establishment of a group pattern of doing things meets this need. Routines are most wisely used where the situation would otherwise be too complex or too tempting, where too many people or too much danger is involved.

A very common cause of disorder lies in the fact that children may have nothing to do at the start of school while a class is gathering but work has not officially begun. To avoid this, many teachers set up a routine, assigning "belltime" tasks to keep everyone occupied until regular work can capture their attention.

In some situations, as when kindergartners are playing with a fascinating toy or high school boys are shooting baskets, there are likely to be quarrels over the sharing of an object. If a simple routine is established which governs the transfer of the desired thing, the teacher may not have to intervene; the problem takes care of itself.

NONPUNITIVE EXILE. Sometimes events may take such a turn that the behavior of the group hampers a youngster's ability to control himself. The opposite also happens: for a while a single child, by kicking, shrieking, name calling, or other uncontrolled conduct, may cause group turmoil. In either case, the final outcome is a situation which is exciting and untenable. Then, the child must be removed for his own good as well as for the order of the class. The adjective "nonpunitive" is used deliberately to indicate that such removal is not to be considered punishment. Both the offender and the group are shown that the exile is imposed to help the young person and the group to regain self control. A display of anger during the ejection defeats the purpose. It is important, in any event, to have some idea of what the child can or will do while outside the room. Also, an opportunity should be created afterward to deal with the feelings of the banished youngster and of the group.

Too often in this type of incident the parting words the banished child hears are, "Don't come back until you can behave yourself." This smacks of punishment and faultfinding. Rather, the emphasis should be on "getting over it."

In a fifth-grade class Bill Roth "got the giggles." He made several efforts to stop, but each time a titter from someone or the memory of what he had done set him off again. At the conclusion of one spasm of squeaks and gasps, his teacher gently told him to go out of the room until he was sure he could quiet down. Of course, he was not surprised to be banished. In fact, he was inwardly grateful. After fifteen minutes and a few abortive giggles, he returned to the room. Nothing further needed to be done.

The extent to which the principal's office can be used for this purpose is a matter of some importance. In many schools there are helpful understandings on this point. Ideally, it should be known by all that a child can be sent to the office with a note. If it indicates that he has been banished from the classroom to regain self-control, then the secretary will allow him to sit undisturbed, and he will not be subjected to scoldings or ridicule.

USE OF RESTRAINT.   Now and then a child so loses his head that his actions threaten to harm other members of the group. In such emergencies he must be physically restrained; there is no other alternative. There is no implication here of punishment; the restraint has to be entirely a protective action. It is important, therefore, that the young person be held firmly but not roughly. Shaking, hitting, or scolding him only makes it harder to convey our intent. No one can draw rational conclusions when upset. Hurting a child in any fashion produces more aggression. Accordingly, for the good of the berserk individual and for the stability of the rest of the group, nothing which involves real menace or hostile intent should be done. The restraint must not be made an excuse for triumphant revenge on the part of the teacher. If such incidents are handled well and interpreted properly to the other children, it will increase the security of all concerned. However, when a child is so mixed up that physical restraint is needed, he is clearly in need of specialized help, beyond what a classroom can provide. Restraint is not therapy; it is only a measure for handling a specific incident.

In public discussions, the fact that both restraint and corporal punishment are physical leads to confusion between the two. Psychologically speaking, from the viewpoint of the child there is a world of difference between being held by a supportive adult during a temper tantrum and being sent to the principal's office for a paddling or being manhandled by an irate grownup opponent.

REMOVING SEDUCTIVE OBJECTS. There are objects which have a strong appeal to children. There are young people who are strongly tempted to handle them. Put the two near each other, and the child's attention wanders, or the object is misused. At the very least, other children are distracted. At worst, costly damage is done.

If misuse is occurring, then child and object must be gently parted. Even knowing that this may happen will give some youngsters a feeling of security in resisting forbidden acts. The object should be removed only when its seductive power is too strong. Then, be sure that the youngster understands that his loss of possession is temporary. The how is very important. It is essential to avoid displaying hostility either to the pupil or the object, tempting though that might be. It may be well to let the youngster know that you do want him to have fun through using the object in the proper way at the appropriate time and place.

ANTICIPATORY PLANNING. Some situations are hard for children to manage because they arise unexpectedly or involve temptations to overstimulation. To wait for trouble to arise can be inefficient. Often a little description of what the situation may be like and what limitations may be anticipated will enable the group to be more relaxed in the face of whatever overstimulating elements may be present. For example, now and then a teacher takes a class on a trip or excursion. By describing in advance what the trip will be like, what the dangers may be, and how other people will expect the group to act, later confusion can be prevented. Tension is forestalled. Care must be taken, however, that this anticipatory talking over is not overdone to the degree that it spoils the fascination of the experience itself.

For many student teachers, the minute when a supervisor comes in the door to evaluate is likely to be a rough one. Some know they will be thrown off stride. Their uneasiness may affect the children. It does help if the class not only knows in advance that a supervisor will arrive but has rehearsed the routine of greeting, introducing, and seating the visitor. These mechanics may set a fortunate tone for subsequent class activities.

ADVANTAGES AND DISADVANTAGES OF SITUATIONAL ASSISTANCE. Anticipatory planning is often more helpful than forceful intervention. This, and the other forms of situational assistance, prevent trouble. They enable children to learn good patterns of control without arousing the conflicts which come when things get out of hand.

Counterbalancing the obvious advantages is the fact that by facilely smoothing over present difficulties, the adult lulls himself into thinking he has solved long-range problems. It is easy to overlook deep-rooted needs because momentary trouble has been avoided. In concentrating upon these techniques, the teacher may add confusingly to his goals for the group. In addition, the young people may become overdependent upon the teacher. Rather than meet complexities with their own resources, they may expect the teacher to protect them from all difficulties.

Yet, in moderate amounts, situational assistance has great strength. It frees energy for learning. It reduces confusion. Attention can be given to the task at hand, rather than concentrated on resisting temptations. Situational assistance may counterbalance whatever is amiss in the learning situation. We cannot forget that the realities of school may be too complex for some boys and girls to manage. If the teacher has done a good job of providing situational assistance, this may underscore the fact that his actions are permeated by a desire to be helpful to the class. This perception, if forceful intervention later becomes necessary, will increase the possibility that the class will react to its benign intent. Thus, they may learn that even the negative experiences in life can be benevolently designed. To give priority to situational assistance prevents the energy waste of blame throwing. Mental ingenuity can be used for anticipatory planning rather than justifying past actions.

Reality and Value Appraisal

One of the goals of education is to enable people to increase the areas in which they can be guided by intelligence and conscience rather than by blind impulse, fear, or prejudice. Special interest therefore attaches to those techniques by which we appeal to children's sense of fairness and strengthen their ability to see the consequences of their actions.

DIRECT APPEALS.   Often behavior in the classroom may be guided by showing the children the connection between conduct and its consequences, or its relationship to standards they hold. This can usually be done concisely in a sentence or two. There are many things to which we can appeal. For instance, a noisy room may be quieted by pointing out that no one can hear what others are saying. During a session of planning for a trip, horseplay can be stopped by mentioning that it may prevent completion of plans. The judgment, "That wouldn't be fair," may prevent a group from ganging up on a weaker child. Sometimes we invoke school spirit or class spirit.

The effectiveness of any appeal depends upon whether the basis for it has a genuine relation to the issue involved, whether the youngsters are sensitive to the invoked connection, and whether the appeal is appropriate to the role of the teacher. Thus, if properly presented by a teacher the class likes, a plea to be fair to an unpopular youngster may produce the desired results. By contrast, an attempt to quiet loud behavior of preadolescent boys with the question, "Don't you want to be little gentlemen?" will have no effect because that ambition does not belong to the group code for the age. A plea based on such an argument may fall on puzzled or amazed ears.

Care should be used not to overwork this device. It gains its effectiveness, not only from the argument and the class attitude toward the person making the appeal, but also from the drama attached to a comparatively rare event. This is seen in the solemnity of a class which is listening to a brief sermon from a teacher who gives but few.

CRITICISM AND ENCOURAGEMENT.   Another common device is a teacher-conducted analysis of a child's actions. This may be done either in private or within the hearing of the entire class. We are not referring now to scoldings or to tirades designed to inspire fear or create embarrassment. Nor do we mean soothing encomiums solely designed to make the children "feel good." Rather, we are discussing those efforts, usually made in a helpful spirit, to give a child or a group greater insight into the adequacy of their conduct. Properly managed, such criticism or encouragement can be an effective teaching device. However, a teacher has to be very sensitive to the relationship between himself and the youngster, the general attitude of the child toward corrections, and the way this will affect the role of the child in the group. Some children have basic attitudes which prevent them from remaining emotionally calm when they fail to win unconditional adult approval.

In both criticism and encouragement, one appeals to the child's perception of his self-image. We indicate the distance between what he wants to be and what he is. In criticism, we deal with the shortfalls; in encouragement, with closing the gap. In both cases, we hope this will serve as stimulus for his continuing to work.

The mere fact that a statement may be clearly true is no excuse for using it if it does emotional damage. One purpose of criticism is that, by pointing out how far a child falls short of a goal, we stimulate him to strive harder. This can only hold true when the goal is within the child's reach. The problem, from the viewpoint of mental hygiene, is whether the effect of the criticism is to produce frustration or stimulation. If a child has strong inferiority feelings, we must bear in mind the probability that criticism may make him stop trying.

At this point we must realize that in reacting to criticism youngsters employ the full range of behavior mechanisms. If they feel that the intent of the criticism is hostile to their personal values, or that the encouragement is patronizing condescension which humiliates them, they will turn a deaf ear, or deliberately "show the teacher" by doing the opposite of what is wanted, or go into a private panic.

Public censure is likely to be harmful, especially if it is seen by a child as an attack on him or as likely to lower his prestige in the group. On the other hand, if the teacher is obviously friendly, if the child feels secure in his class group, and if the criticism is an objective evaluation devoid of blame, the class and the youngster may see it as merely an explanation from which all are expected to profit.

Illustrative of a very frequent and valid use of public criticism is the following incident: George Allison, a popular and confident boy, was playing shortstop. A high fly ball was hit into the territory of William Davis, who often missed catches. George went charging in, and William, seeing him coming, hesitated. George, afraid he would run into William, also stopped. The ball fell between them. After the game, Mike Kelso, the coach, called the team together to discuss what had happened. First, he praised George for his good playing throughout the game. Then, he had a good word to say about players who backed up each other on any play. He told George that whenever he saw a teammate under a fly, it was better to take a chance on an error than to risk what actually happened. He continued talking about how to act in case of doubt. It was now apparent that the remarks were meant as instructions for all players. George suggested some simple signals to be used in the future. As the team went home, there was good feeling among all of them.

In some situations teachers using more democratic methods may have the entire class take part in the encouragement or criticism. This can be and often is a very valuable experience for youngsters. Of course, care should be taken to provide an atmosphere of support, and to use tact. The fact that the criticism or encouragement is coming from the group rather than from the adult is not in itself a guarantee against the perils mentioned above. The danger points to watch out for are (1) use of the procedure to pounce on a scapegoat, (2) the production of embarrassment or anger, (3) the encouraging of feuding cliques, (4) the bringing in of extraneous issues, (5) battle heat among the discussants, and (6) collective overexpectation as to results.

DEFINING LIMITS.   Children need to know what is expected of them —what the rules of the game are. Perhaps the simplest way that this is done is by establishing prohibitions and granting permissions. At times, all that must be done is to answer queries with a Yes or a No. If the Yes is a free judgment, if it implies no concession to a fear of griping or extortion, it tells a class they are in safe territory. Where a No is required, it can be given calmly and firmly, without being aggressive or challenging.

Some of the misbehavior children show is often closely connected to their trying to determine limits of behavior. This is not always undesirable, as it is one way in which learning takes place. It is not always necessary, however, to treat each act of permitting or forbidding as though it were a major lesson. There is no need for a teacher to explain every action. Sometimes, putting one's foot down does the entire job.

What we are talking about here is how teachers indicate the limits of behavior; enforcing those limits is a separate issue. For that purpose teachers will use the entire range of influence techniques described in this chapter. Confusion between the two leads some teachers to accompany the setting of limits with long speeches full of threats, which imply that they expect the limits to be violated. Later, when we write about threats, the dangers in this approach will be discussed.

Some limits do not so much have to be "set" as taken for granted. Clarity depends upon the firm consistency with which the teacher prevents the class from trespassing upon them. For example, if children are dropping books to make noise, obviously they should be told to stop. There is no need here for a ten-minute lecture on how noise distracts people who are working. The children know this.

Where it is necessary to explain limits, the arguments used will vary with the real nature of the issue at hand. Thus, children would consider it legitimate for a teacher to tell them to stop a jocular exchange and go back to work, without a long disquisition about how fun is "all right in its place." On the other hand, if an issue involves a school rule, such as not leaving the building without parents' written permission, it is better to explain this as a regulation rather than as a personal decision of the teacher.

If there is a change in the situation, as when a shop class stops work to have a discussion, the class may have to be reminded of what new limits will prevail. Limits are guidelines, not guarantees. Teachers should not feel they have failed in setting limits well, just because misbehavior still occurs. A considerable part of the task of an adult is to help children live within prescribed limits.

The art of talking with children and helping them talk with each other is a very important one for teachers to master. Some teachers fall into the habit of using a special tone of voice. The implied condescension can be quite irritating. In fact, youngsters in the upper grades may be so infuriated by this trait that their anger toward the teacher may nullify what he has to say. When the teacher's words and manner of speech carry a feeling that equals are taking part in a discussion interesting to all, a much happier effect is secured.

POSTSITUATIONAL FOLLOW-UP. The meanings attached to an incident require some time to take shape. Immediately after something has happened, emotions may be so strong that rational thinking is difficult. However, once the excitement has calmed down, the individual or the group may need to rearrange their feelings. For example, Alice Bishop has been used to volunteering correct answers in history. To give others a chance, the teacher has pointedly ignored her upraised hand. Now the problem may be to help Alice draw two conclusions which she might not reach on her own: (1) the teacher is not irritated with her and (2) she should herself limit the extent of her volunteering. A group situation may need similar handling. For instance, if the borrowing of personal supplies begins to approach stealing in a group old enough intellectually to understand, the teacher may have to step in forcefully and put a stop to all borrowing for a while. Afterward, there should be a chance for the children to talk over with the teacher the reasons for his action, to help them clarify their own feelings. Such a session is not a lecture or a scolding. It is a way of helping the children work out for themselves their relationships to each other and to the teacher. It helps them reason out the standards on which they will act in the future.

The principle involved here is analogous to the familiar finding of educational psychology that transfer of learning is much more likely to occur if you teach to get it than if you hope it will happen. Just because a teacher knows the implications of his actions does not mean that the children see them.

MARGINAL USE OF INTERPRETATION. As has been mentioned often, children's conduct may spring from motives they do not understand. This is true, for example, if emotions are displaced or impulses projected. When the behavior mechanisms involve very powerful impulses or arise out of damaging experiences in early childhood, helping a child to discover their source is a long-time job requiring highly specialized treatment. However, there are times in a classroom situation when a child can gain control over his actions if he is given some insight into their meaning. A high school class may be growing restless as lunch hour nears. By merely saying, "I know you're all getting tired and hungry, but we have to finish the lesson," the teacher may enable them to get hold of themselves. Again, a fifth-grade boy who gets into a playground fight with a brighter youngster may be helped to see that his fistic onslaught is merely an attempt to get even for a defeat in academic competition. The readiness of the child to accept such insight without being too much disturbed must be carefully appraised in advance.

An interesting account of this technique in action appears in an article by Maas.[5] A ninth-grade class became involved in a feud. One student verbally attacked the student chairman. He was joined by two others. A fifth youngster defended the chairman.

In the discussion, the first attacker said that the chairman had not organized the work well. The teacher wondered aloud whether this was criticism of the chairman or of her for not having taken over the lesson. One of the attackers followed this up by remarking that they ought to have a teacher competent enough to teach class herself. The teacher asked if others felt the same way. A girl replied that some people always needed a person to show them how to do things. Discussion turned to how uncomfortable any one might feel who wanted direction and did not get it.

"He might even get real mad and fight with someone—like Rob and Lou did," one said.

After more discussion, someone said, "Well, let's get back to work."

The setting for this type of technique in other instances may be

[5] Henry S. Maas, "Applying Group Therapy to Classroom Practice," *Mental Hygiene,* Vol. 35 (1951), pp. 250-59.

a private interview. The goals and techniques of talks with children will be discussed at length in the second half of Chapter 16.

ADVANTAGES AND DISADVANTAGES OF REALITY AND VALUE APPRAISAL. One disadvantage of these techniques is that, because adults tend to feel quite pleased with themselves when they have made a stirring appeal to values, there is a temptation to use such appeals even when they are not warranted. Also, one cannot appeal to something which is not there. In many instances, the values which we want to invoke or the sense of reality are either weak or absent. When emotional reactions take over, as when a child is sulking, this absence may be temporary. However, it may dominate the scene at the very time the teacher is talking.

On the advantage side, these techniques imply an autonomy in children, and actually help develop the very values and feel for reality which we want to have govern their behavior. A youngster who is always handled by outside techniques cannot be expected to develop. The techniques we have been discussing imply a trust in the young person's ability to move ahead.

Invoking the Pleasure-Pain Principle

Another category of influence techniques consists of those in which the teacher deliberately produces pleasant or unpleasant feelings to "teach a lesson." The hope is that a pleasant experience will induce a child to repeat desirable conduct; an unpleasant one, to avoid unwanted behavior. To teach youngsters what we expect, and to get them to act as we wish, we hold out rewards, make threats, and extend praise or blame. Or we employ punishment to produce fear of consequences, to create an inner anxiety which will add to the power of conscience, or otherwise to help the youngster learn more appropriate control of his behavior.

REWARDS AND PROMISES. Teachers are often told to use a "positive approach" to influence behavior. The fact that a child receives a reward shows him that his conduct is acceptable. In addition, rewards tend to build a positive self-concept. The traditional wisdom of teachers in this respect is thoroughly justified.

Promises are in effect the holding out of future rewards. From a mental health point of view, they presuppose that a given child can make use of anticipation of the future to counteract the frustrations of a present situation. In a sense they are a promised wage to be given for the effort of the present moment. But the ability of children to make use of promises cannot be taken for granted. Indeed, children with delinquent or other behavior disturbances are known to be poorly equipped in this respect. Teachers should not be surprised if well-intentioned promises do not work.

As with any other influence measure, of course, one must be aware that under specific circumstances the use of rewards carries risks. Teachers know that too great reliance on extrinsic stimulation is perilous. The danger is that by stressing the reward or promise we may drown out natural motivations and thus render artificial a situation where better management would help children see the satisfaction inherent in doing good work for its own sake. This type of artificiality is especially apt to arise when rewards are given in accordance with some mechanical system. Then, the reward takes on the psychological aspect of a wage rather than a token of esteem. Another danger arises when jealousy about the reward sets a few children apart from the rest. When this occurs, those who are set apart bear the brunt of juvenile criticism; in terms of their social relationships, receiving a reward is then an unpleasant experience. A third danger is that if the reward can be achieved by only a few and is beyond the reach of most, it loses all value. A fourth peril arises when a reward system is so constructed that so many are deprived of winning that it is really a means of punishing. It is surprising but true that a too-elaborate system of rewards may be as productive of anxiety and fear as punishment is commonly credited to be. As long as these dangers are kept in mind, however, reward stands as a preferred means of achieving good results for appropriate purposes.

THREATS. In order to get pupils to do something which does not immediately attract them, teachers may announce that undesired consequences will result from failure to do the work. Or, to prevent unwanted behavior, threats of punishment may be used. This technique often works, but it has dangers.

For one thing, if the teacher does not have full control of all aspects of the situation, children may escape or evade the conditions established. For example, instead of working on problems, they can produce apparently acceptable results by cheating. They may conceal their misconduct or produce plausible alibis. In some instances they may elect to disobey the instructions and take the consequences. If punishment is not then forthcoming or if it proves less unpleasant than expected, the teacher's control may be seriously weakened. Empty threats are always perilous.

This is even more true when some youngster may make a bid for juvenile fame by calling the teacher's bluff.

There is always a danger that threats may work too well. The effect of threatening is to produce anxiety. Although mild doses of anxiety can be taken without damage and can serve as guides to behavior for normal children, they can work havoc with children who are unsure of their relationships with adults. To some children, any threat carries a warning of rejection by adults and sends them searching frantically for some behavior mechanism by which to evade the situation. As anxiety is increased by sterner threats, the effect produced becomes worse and worse. Within recent years psychological research has produced a number of studies which reveal that excessive anxiety interferes with learning. Increasing the pressure on a class is poor strategy from every point of view.

What is intended as a threat does not always have that effect. To some children it may be a challenge to a battle of wits and stealth. To some emotionally disturbed children, including many prone to delinquency, threats have no real meaning because such children have a very weak sense of futurity, as was pointed out previously in connection with promises. They live in the here and now.

Before leaving the negative aspects of threats, a word should be said about the very natural tendency of adults to give voice to utterly unrealistic menaces. They may speak of expulsion, calling the police, or ominous disasters "when you get out in the world." Children usually spot these for what they are, outbursts of emotion. Actually, such outpourings are verbalized fantasies in which the grownup tells the world what, at the moment, he would like to have happen to the children. To be sure, the threats are rarely carried out, but they do tell more than is intended. They can terrify insecure children. They are very unfair to the other people who are supposed to do the alleged punishing in the future.

There is quite a difference between threats which require a person to take punitive action and statements which merely map out natural consequences. The second situation has altogether different implications. Even here, however, the presumed consequences should not be described with hostility. It is also important to recognize that children's grasp of consequences changes with age. In a study by Long, [6] 10 boys and 10 girls aged six, the same numbers aged eight, and the same numbers aged

---

[6] Eleanor Ruth Long, *A Study of Children's Appreciation of Consequences,* unpublished Ph.D. dissertation, University of Toronto, 1938.

ten were interviewed as to what might happen in ten different situations. The typical six-year-old gave a single consequence. About half the eight-year-olds could see that in some cases an action could lead to several consequences. Only half the ten-year-olds gave chains in which an incident had a result which in turn led to a second or even a third consequence.

In view of all that has been said about the dangers, do threats have any legitimate function? Under proper circumstances, the answer is Yes. If a teacher whose basic affection the children are sure of makes a firm statement as to what he will do in case of certain conduct, the self-control of emotionally healthy children may be strengthened.

PRAISE AND BLAME.   Less striking, perhaps, is the type of pressure represented by praise or blame which applies to the person rather than the act. Here the teacher seeks to mold conduct by making the child feel good or bad about himself. Such an approach presupposes both that a child wants to enhance his self-image and that the present relationship with the teacher is meaningful in this respect. Usually, this is only partially true. For many young people, the need for approbation is great; the possibility of meeting disapproval arouses anxiety. Inner tension is reduced when they find they have pleased a teacher. Their goal is not so much to develop or express standards of their own. Rather they want to find out what adults expect of them; they automatically think the expectation is "good." The main value of blame may be to make sure that a child finds his conduct unacceptable and holds himself accountable for it.

Certainly, when an adult is respected, clarification of his expectations does play a big part in the children's development of their standards of value. A number of cautions must be observed in the use of praise or blame. The behavior praised or censured must actually have taken place. If questions of intent are at issue, it is essential that the estimate of this be fairly accurate. The child will know of gross errors. A child praised for being considerate will know what he had in mind; a child condemned for being sneaky will have an idea of what he was doing.

In any case, for a teacher's evaluation to have impact, he must have the respect of the class. This respect is impaired when the children get the impression that the praised child is a teacher's pet, or the blamed one the victim of hostility. The group situation must be such that the young person's social relationships are not impaired by the praise or strengthened by the blame, as might occur in a group of preadolescents united in antagonism to a particular school regime. In this connection, the basis on which praise is awarded can be very significant. Praise given because conduct is comfortable for adults or is a goody-goody departure from peer-group norms is almost sure to get children in trouble sooner or later with their classmates. Care should be taken, also, lest in a particular group blame aimed at a vulnerable youngster may make his position in the group untenable. Either of these effects of praise or blame increases emotional conflict instead of reducing it.

Overpraising may have a number of unfortunate effects: it may, for instance, make children too dependent on adult interpretation or may rob them of spontaneity. Wrong forms of blame can turn the issue into a personal one or serve as an incentive to irritate the teacher in the future. Finally, as was mentioned in the discussion of appeals, the basis on which praise or blame is given should be in harmony with the issue at hand.

PUNISHMENT.   We shall define punishment as the planful infliction of an unpleasant experience for the purpose of modifying future behavior. That is to say, the action of the teacher in professionally levying a penalty is the result of deliberate forethought aimed at producing a desirable change. Punishment is always unpleasant; the person being corrected always suffers some type of hurt or loss.

Note carefully that this definition rules out instances where a teacher, in the heat of anger, lashes out at a child. We consider such action as an adult temper tantrum, not as professionally administered punishment. The very display of personal anger makes it all too tempting for a child to ward off the whole incident as just another case of adult crankiness. We likewise rule out the instances where a child is made to suffer because someone wants to balance accounts with him on the ancient principle of an eye for an eye. From the point of view we are taking, that is revenge, not punishment.

More About Punishment

The discussion of influence techniques in the previous sections of this chapter could do little more than mention a few salient features of each. To give a fuller picture of the considerations teachers might well hold in mind, we shall deal with one of these techniques in greater detail. Because so much debate among educators touches on punishment, we have selected that technique for more extended treatment.

SOME ILLUSTRATIONS.   First, let us look at a few situations in which teachers have used punishment. In each it is easy to see why this technique was employed. Yet, we have questions about each one.

Mario Pellegrino was a safety patrol boy, and was very proud of wearing the white belt that went with the job. One day he was very late for his morning class. His teacher, looking out the window, saw him in the playground, climbing up the pole for the big swings. When she called to him he looked startled and then ran to a school entrance. After he came into the room, she reminded him of the instructions for patrol boys, announced that he was suspended from the patrol for the rest of the week, and ordered him to surrender the belt. As he brought it to her, he hung his head.

In view of his reaction to discovery and scolding, we can reasonably ask these questions: What was gained by taking his belt away? Would a one-day suspension have been as useful as suspension for one week? How will he regard the whole affair at the end of the week? Could the point have been driven home just as well by one of the twenty-one other techniques?

A traditional technique, used with many variations, has been described in these words by a fifteen-year-old boy immediately after leaving an English public school: "Thomas' method of punishment was a very good one, as he thought. The boys had to read a certain passage of history, and then rewrite it in their own words."[7]

We wonder what this technique, called "one hundred lines of history," did to students' attitudes toward history. Did they regard it as a field of study or an instrument of malevolence?

Miss Jackson had introduced her kindergarten class to finger painting. She had been very careful to explain that the paints were to be used only on paper and had made sure that all understood. Next day there was a commotion in the part of the room where the finger painting was going on; Janet was trying to smear some black paint on Helen's blond hair. When Janet saw Miss Jackson looking at her, she stopped and went back to the table where the paper was. Miss Jackson shook her and told her not to use the paints any more that day. Janet burst into tears.

Our questions here are these: When the signal interference had

---

[7] E. L. Black, "Why Do They Like It?" *Educational Documents* 1 [no other publication data].

worked, why did Miss Jackson go on to more drastic measures? What was the effect of the shaking? What did Janet's crying indicate—remorse, fright, or futile rage?

Mr. Mooner, the gym teacher, really meant what he said about sports being preparation for good citizenship. During one of the basket-ball team's big games, he noticed that Joe Kolodny stood on the Central High center's foot during a jump for the ball. The referee did not see the foul, and Joe smirked with satisfaction as the play ended in a basket. Mooner took Joe out of the game. When Joe heard his coach say that the play was dirty basketball for which he would be benched for the rest of the game, the boy flushed and sullenly went to the locker room to get dressed. He wondered how he would explain the incident to his girl friend.

Here, we cannot help but wonder what will happen next. What does Mr. Mooner expect Joe to do? What will the rest of the team do, and why? Will Joe find some excuse to quit the team or will he stay on it and become a clean player?

WHAT DO WE WANT TO HAPPEN?   Punishment exerts a constructive influence under certain conditions, which need to be clearly appreciated. First, the behavior which draws punishment often has involved some initial conflict; that is to say, there has been some internal struggle between the child's impulses and his self-control. He has a feeling that what he did was not right. Second, the person who does the punishing should be someone who the child feels really likes him and upon whom he depends for affection. Third, the nature of the punishment must be such as to be felt by the child as a natural, or at least understandable, consequence of what he did.

Under these conditions, the anger aroused by the unpleasant experience of the punishment is internalized. Since the punisher is a person the child loves or whom he does not consciously dare challenge, the anger must eventually turn inward and be directed against that portion of the child responsible for the offending action. It is as though the conscience, which was originally defeated, can now turn around and say, "See what you got for not minding me!" In the future, therefore, any tendency likely to re-create the original conflict is met with vigilance. As was explained in Chapter 4, such a situation can bring the behavior mechanism of identification into play, and the type of behavior involved now becomes more strongly forbidden by the child himself.

Another purpose of punishment is to show a child standards of behavior we want to have him emphasize. In those cases, the punishment is meant to set the stage for a postsituational follow-up. The real job of helping children work out their feelings and "learn their lesson" is a task in itself. It cannot be taken for granted as an automatic result of punishment.

WHAT CAN GO WRONG? The conditions necessary for effective punishment are much less likely to be present than most people would like to believe. Sometimes the child either has no sense of wrongdoing or else cannot control his actions. Very often, the person who does the punishing has such a bad relationship with the child that the anger aroused can flash outward with wholehearted force. Then, too, the nature of the punishment may be unfair or inappropriate. Let us now look at some things that can go wrong.

The anger at the punishment may fail to be connected with the point at issue. This can happen when the youngster has no idea of what he did that was wrong. Sometimes the social situation may make the real crime seem to be getting caught, as happens if many students cheat but only one is detected and penalized.

If the punishment is too severe or is unfair, the anger aroused may be too much for the youngster to handle. This can also happen where the bonds of affection are weak. Under such circumstances, the youngster may either become angry directly with the punisher or displace his rage and work it off on a scapegoat or other victim. Naturally, any desirable internal effect is weakened. The result is more likely to be a feud than a strengthening of conscience. This explains why so many delinquents are children who have been repeatedly subjected to violent beatings by parents whom they loathe.

Another condition which encourages the outward expression of anger exists if the act of punishing was done in a spirit of hot rage. The child then sees his teacher or parent, not as someone whose love he wants to hold, but as a person who hates him. Aggression which is met with counteraggression is fortified, not weakened. A child who has been subdued in a shouting contest may feel deflated but hardly guilty. Administering punishment with a cold and impersonal air—the opposite extreme of adult reaction—may be equally infuriating to young people. It seems to convey the impression that the adult is uninterested in their feelings or is using them as props with which to demonstrate an issue of "justice."

For children who feel insecure with adults or who are overdependent, punishment may produce panic rather than anger. The realization that they have lost affection so frightens them that they are disorganized. For such children, there is little chance for self-insight to develop. If there is any likelihood that a child will react in this fashion, it is wise to try to handle the problem with one of the other techniques which have been listed.

Another highly undesirable result is the development of so much anxiety and guilt that the child either loses his independence or develops neurotic patterns. We have already mentioned the effects of child-raising methods based on fear. Often this outcome reflects the failure of adults to realize the importance of dealing with the aftermath of punishment. The wounds left by any incident should certainly be treated later; as a very minimum, the child should be given reassurance that he still retains the affection of his parent or teacher. When this is done, the adult should show a clear-cut concern about the misbehavior, express earnest disapproval, and make it clear that his major worry is the child. There should be no triumphant crowing over the young person's predicament.

Punishment almost always has by-products. Unless these are weighed in advance, they may nullify any good that could have been accomplished. Thus, if we unwittingly give a child a martyr's crown in the eyes of his friends, our "punishment" has acted as a reward. Similarly, if a child takes our action to mean we are barring him from a whole area, when we thought only to indicate disapproval of one way of acting, we may lose far more than can be regained. For example, if we were trying to get a boy to take part in active sports, it would be folly to penalize him for his first errors in that field. That might lead him to give up the whole business as involving too much risk.

In some cases, punishment is sheer cruelty because the child either is unable to understand the reason for it or else is incapable of controlling his actions. A great many possibilities are compressed in the two general terms "unable to understand the reason" and "incapable of controlling." There are such obvious impediments as intellectual slowness on the one hand or nervous disorders, like chorea, on the other. Here are a few more. Inability to grasp the values of a teacher may be a product of a neighborhood environment; some children, for example, just cannot comprehend why a teacher gets excited about a crap game. Also, a child may use any or all of the denial mechanisms to keep knowledge of wrongdoing from himself. On the other hand, lack of proper training or experience, as well as physical and mental disorders, can hamper efforts to meet adult standards. What, for example, could be more tragic than to deny a child physical activities during recess because he was restless during a class as a result of malnutrition, glandular imbalance, or some other condition over which he has no power? Yet that very type of gross stupidity appears thousands of times every year.

Too much punishment may eventually harden a child. Particularly during his striving for independence, each attempt to make him feel guilty reduces his capacity to feel guilt. The final product is a person who regards punishment as a challenge to show how much he can take. This type of casehardened young person is found among the most severely punished delinquents.

Another personality distortion created by unwise reliance on punishment is found in the "cash-and-carry" delinquent, who feels that anything he may do is justified by his willingness to take his medicine afterward. If punished for something they did not do, such youngsters feel the world owes them a free offense. Within the authors' experience, the extreme case of this "cash-and-carry" punishment was a boy who reported each day to the principal's office to be paddled before school began in the morning. The assumption was that he would do something during the day to "deserve" it. Of course, he usually obliged. What the ritual was supposed to accomplish remains a mystery.

A distortion that appears, at first mention, to be more rare than it really is arises when a boy's or girl's behavior is allowed to continue until he clearly deserves punishment. That is, the adult does not use such devices as signals to stop an activity which is becoming seriously wrong. Instead, he waits until an offense has been committed and then, in the postaction situation, triumphantly levies a penalty. This happens when a parent or teacher dislikes a child. Watching incidents of this type develop, the observer gets the uncomfortable impression that the adult is pleased by the opportunity for hostile action which the child's offense "requires." In some cases, one can find evidence that the adult gave subtle incitement.

Still another cause of ineffectual or harmful results is a penalty which is too drawn out or is deferred. So long a delay intervenes between the incident and the "punishment" that the child's feelings of guilt have evaporated; he experiences the punishment only as a hostile frustration, not as an educational act. If there is such a delay, of course, the most likely effect is to destroy any positive relationship which may have existed between teacher and pupil. Another error is to have the penalty cover so long a range of time that by the end of the period there is no longer any psychological connection between the penalty now being suffered and the original offense for which it was imposed.

CAUTIONS.   In view of the high risk of undesirable results, punishment should be employed rarely, and then only with the greatest caution. As a very minimum, what we hope to accomplish should be clear in our minds. This means that there should be some solid reason for believing a particular child really benefits from it. Too often, the decision is made on the spur of the moment because an adult simply can no longer stand a type of conduct or the personality of a particular offender. In truth, the real purpose is to relieve tension in the teacher or parent. If that is the case, then the problem is to find some way of establishing emotional balance without damaging children in the process.

Frequently, the decision to punish is based on the fact that what the youngster did deserves a penalty, and that all agree that punishment would be fair. Obviously, any punishment imposed without being fair would be highly unwise. However, those conditions do not answer the question, "Will it do any good?" which must be asked. There is a vast difference between having earned a rebuke and being able to profit from it. If we are thinking in terms of influencing future behavior, then we must concentrate on that latter consideration. If planful ignoring, signals, or restructuring the situation will do the job better for a particular child, those are the tools we should use.

We must always be aware of the fact that punishment rarely ends an incident. Having inflicted a wound, we are duty-bound to see that it gets healed. Properly handled by a postsituational follow-up, punishment may leave the relationship between a child and a teacher stronger than ever. However, this means that there must be a chance for the child to talk out his hurt or for the teacher to let him know how he stands.

Unless the aftermath is watched, we can often be deceived into believing we have achieved results which we have not. Children are quite likely to show surface deference and good behavior after any such incident. Inwardly, they may be seething with contempt or be bitter at injustice. Aggressive feelings driven underground may turn up in fights among children.

Here is an illustration of how punishment which looks as though it had worked may have striking side effects. Albert Kolen was new to the Grant School and was trying very hard to become a member of the tough little gang on his block. To show off, he ineptly challenged the teacher by demanding, "Why should I?" when he was asked to carry a message for her to the principal's office.

Infuriated, she upbraided him violently and denied him recess. As she put it, "I showed him who was boss, and that settled that." In fact, the entire class was considerably more polite to her for the rest of the week.

But there were other effects. Albert was really a shy boy. He felt after the teacher's actions that trying to impress the other boys was fraught with peril. He therefore did not try to, and became an isolate. Also, he was so frightened of the teacher, he could not bring himself to volunteer answers to questions he knew. When she did call upon him, he stammered.

The necessity for weighing effects requires that attention be given to all changes which follow any use of punishment. This means that not only do we keep an eye on the individual but we must also consider how his relationship with his teacher has been affected and what has happened to his standing in his group. In our follow-up, we may want to mitigate the disapproval of his classmates, for example, if that is likely to force him into further misconduct.

CORPORAL PUNISHMENT.   One of the perennial debates among educators in a few sections of the country centers on the use of physical punishment. A number of states and cities very wisely have made physical punishment illegal. In such school systems both teachers and children survive very nicely. The fact is that whippings, slappings, beltings, and paddlings can accomplish nothing that cannot be achieved better by some other method. The very conditions which physical punishment involves violate the known requisites for producing a psychologically justifiable result. Pain, whether produced quickly by a blow with a ruler or slowly by forcing a child to stand still in one place, invites anger, or panic, or bravado, which accomplish nothing. In addition, by using force, teachers set an example which preaches eloquently that deep down they believe might is right, and that size or brawn mean more than logic or wisdom. Corporal punishment is a denial of everything an educator should stand for.

In a review of what has been happening in Canadian schools, Johnson[8] found that up until 1880 heavy reliance was placed on corporal

---

[8] F. Henry Johnson, *Changing Conceptions of Discipline and Pupil-Teacher Relations in Canadian Schools,* unpublished Ph.D. dissertation, University of Toronto, 1952.

punishment. A questionnaire given in 1950 to 174 teachers from British Columbia revealed that, although it is still used, the frequency is fairly low: In the course of a year in the schools of Vancouver there are an average of 9 incidents per 100 elementary school pupils; 10 per 100 junior high school pupils; and 1 per 100 senior high school students. For those young people who are referred to the principal, physical punishment is less used than private reprimands, loss of privileges, and detention. The principals prefer using remedial measures such as talking over problems in private, interviewing parents, and encouraging interest in extracurricular activities. The principals declared they were fostering prevention in the form of keeping youngsters busy, making the school an attractive place, and exhibiting good work.

In attempting to find a rationalization for physical force, some educators point to its use in certain families. The implication is that a schoolroom and a family are psychologically identical. Although we can point out many similarities, it is important to recognize that conditions in many homes permit parents to make errors which the children can survive simply because over the years those same parents have fed the children, tenderly nursed them through illnesses, played with them, and built up so strong a feeling of security that a spanking, a violent outburst of anger, or a nasty quarrel can be taken in stride. Although every teacher has some psychological attributes of a parent, the aspect which is lacking is that deep background of years of relationship. The extent to which punishment depends upon just that background makes its use much more risky in schools than it is in a family. Moreover, even in a family setting, punishment is so tricky a technique that thoughtful parents are very careful in its use.

In connection with the argument that some children are dangerous and need "restraint," the reader is referred to pages 356-57, where we discussed this matter. In those schools where there are really potentially dangerous children, it would seem wiser to provide adequate personnel capable of restraining children who need it than to give everyone a license to use the dubious measure of physical punishment.

TIMING.   A very frequent source of mistakes is poor timing. We have already mentioned how too long a gap between incident and penalty can produce unwanted results. It is equally important to realize that punishment administered when a child is in a sulk or a tantrum, or is otherwise "out of his head," is worse than wasted. The very insight to which we hope to appeal is out of commission.

Also, unpleasantness that lasts too long wears thin as punishment and gradually seems like arbitrary, hostile malice. This is particularly apt to be the risk in taking away privileges. To make such a penalty seem impressive, we often make the period too long. Also, as the child deals with the situation by devices of denial or compensation, he may convert the deprivation into a temporary advantage. When an individual or a group is barred from activity, boredom and restlessness set in; the stage is ready for new mischief. The development of classroom activities will sometimes make us want to reverse our verdict: for example, a child exiled from class as a punishment may be the very one we would especially want to take along on a class trip.

We will always want to take into account what we know of the child's total life situation. Thus, if a child has just had upsetting run-ins with some other teacher, further punishment is questionable; a child can digest just so much in the course of a day. So, too, a child who has just moved, had a baby born into the family, lost a parent, or suffered other drastic change, may be too full of problems to profit from punishment, even though the punishment is deserved.

MASS PUNISHMENT. Occasionally events may tempt a teacher to punish the class as a group. This may happen when the infraction of rules was actually a group phenomenon; that is, when the children urged each other on and practically all joined in the fun. Or some offense may have been committed by one or two who cannot be detected, and the teacher penalizes everyone in the hope of either forcing the others to tattle on the culprit or of turning the group against him.

These are two very different conditions. In the first set, much of what was said about individual punishment holds true. If the relationship between the group and the teacher is good and if the group misbehavior took place only after conflict or was accompanied by guilt feelings for many children, the effect may be somewhat similar. However, mass punishment even under such ideal conditions is more risky than individual chastisement. For one thing, it may have quite different effects upon the ringleader, the boy or girl who joined in the fun halfheartedly, the one who suggested the misbehavior but actually did nothing, or the one who was entirely innocent.

Even less can be said for the technique of penalizing a group for the teacher's inability to discover a wrongdoer. The anger created by the punishment is as likely to be directed against the teacher as against the real culprit. The children may become little vigilantes, imposing a lynch law of their own. Or, the conflict between respect for grownups and loyalty to the peer group may be sharpened.

"DEMOCRATIC" PUNISHMENT BY THE GROUP. A common practice in many schools is to turn punishment over to the class group or to vest its exercise in juvenile juries, student courts, or similar groups. On a less dramatic scale, a teacher may involve the children in making plans and decisions about action concerning a wrongdoer or in setting up punishment policies and methods. As a teaching device for children who will live in a democracy, this can be a valuable experience.

As can be seen from the general discussions of punishment, there are some cautions to be observed. First of all, even when the fact of fairness is guaranteed, the problem of whether or not the punishment is helpful to the individual remains as complex as before. Children might think it fair, for example, to forbid a bicycle-rule violator to use his bike for a week, but will they or the teacher be aware of new difficulties this may create for him? Also, if the children do not have much solidarity as a group, the effect of the whole procedure may be merely to legalize scapegoating or clique domination. The effect that punishment by the group has on the social relationships of a punished youngster must always be watched. This may call for a postsituational follow-up by the teacher. The very formalization of group verdict rendering may lead to legalism at the expense of individual leeway. More dangerous in many cases is the possibility that teachers might allow groups to get the impression that punishment is the only technique for dealing with problems and that punishment solves most issues.

All the above points are cautions for the teacher to keep in mind as young people learn the justice-dispensing phase of democracy. They are not arguments against its use.

ROLE DISTRIBUTION. Who should do the punishing? The usual answer may be that the teacher should always take on this unpleasant chore. However, there are certain situations where it may be wise to send a child to the principal or to bring a parent or even a counselor into the picture. The demands of reality may require that the values reflected in declaring certain conduct out of bounds need to be reinforced by some other person in addition to the teacher. In some cases, this other person may have prestige in a child's eyes which the teacher does not possess. Although too frequent use of punishing by someone outside the classroom can weaken the teacher in children's eyes, the evidence that the teacher is not an isolated spoilsport may enhance his status if the children have been uncertain about it. The principal has two significant attributes not recognized in teachers. Because he is less intimately linked in a personal way to classroom events, children are less likely to consider punishment from him as due to animosity, real or fancied. Also, he is the protector of order for the whole school; punishment by him therefore has a higher sanction than that given by someone seen as responsible for classroom events about which "nobody else" knows.

There are a great many techniques teachers may use to influence behavior and guide personality development. No single one can honestly be called the best. The trick of the teaching trade is to learn to use all of them wisely and in each situation to choose the combination most likely to be most effective and safest for youngsters' emotional development. In any situation there are more ways out than the one a teacher thinks of first. It is easy to get into a rut and to use the same technique so often that, although once useful, it becomes meaningless.

Always, the teacher has the task of evaluating what has happened. The ever-present danger is that he may allow himself to be dazzled by immediate effects and thus fail to investigate what may be happening beneath the surface. In addition, there is need to appreciate the fact that, in teaching, one problem inevitably follows the solution to another. Therefore we can reasonably ask after each incident, "What new problems has this created?" Only rarely will the answer be "None."

The several techniques require skill in use. The important factors so frequently are the spirit expressed in what was done and the clarity with which the issues were stated. If the attitude is one of genuinely helping children develop greater emotional stability, deeper confidence in themselves, and less conflict ridden self-control, then even some mistakes in the selection of techniques will not be disastrous. A teacher the children know likes them can make some errors without doing serious damage.

Timing is often a major consideration in developing strategy. The thing that will work well two seconds after an incident may be foolhardy the next day. Often, the good teacher spars for time in which to let emotions subside.

The various devices are often used in combination. Reread the story of Mr. Lawrence (pages 7 to 9). Note that, as soon as he realized what was happening, he attempted to suppress criticism of Rhoda with a signal. When this failed, he removed her from the situation by nonpunitive exile. Then, he set about clarifying values in a postsituational follow-up.

There are a number of very prevalent dangers that it is well to avoid. One is the tendency, when a method has failed, to try bigger and bigger doses of the same method. Failure of a plan should, rather, be taken as a sign that a totally new approach is required. We must always be on the lookout lest we add to the insecurity of children or produce extra conflicts in them. Over the long run, so much depends on the relationships of children to their teachers and their friends that we must take alarm at any steady decrease in positive relationships or any increase in hostility. We do not want to drive children into solitude nor to make life less rich for them. Neither do we want to increase their total burden of guilt, anxiety, or aggression.

Occasionally teachers have to take positive steps to stop some behavior. Then, it helps to remember what the child is really like, and to act in terms of what would or would not aggravate the situation. Naturally, at times the first move may be a false one. It is still possible to repair the mistake by a later action or to choose a wiser action next time. Wrong handling is rarely disastrous in its effects on a child or a group if it is only occasional, but it can be serious if it is made a matter of principle or if it is repeated persistently.

ADDITIONAL READING

Association for Supervision and Curriculum Development, National Education Association. *1950 Yearbook: Fostering Mental Health in Our Schools*. Washington: National Education Association, 1950, Chaps. 11 and 18. Contains substantial treatment of reward, punishment, and techniques for accepting and clarifying children's feelings.

Cutts, Norma E., and Nicholas Moseley. *Teaching the Disorderly Pupil*. New York: Longmans, Green, 1957, Chap. 3. Deals specifically with the problem of using punishment on troublesome children.

Highfield, M. E., and A. Pincent. *A Survey of Rewards and Punishments in Schools*. London: Newnes Educational Publishing Company, 1952. A study of the situation affecting disciplinary methods in British schools.

Horrocks, John E. *Psychology of Adolescence*. Boston: Houghton Mifflin, 1951, Chap. 16. The case study of a girl, Mary Marlowe, which reveals some limitations on interpretation.

Hurlock, Elizabeth B. *Modern Ways with Children*. New York: McGraw-Hill, 1943. A discussion of discipline in the home, intended for parents.

Hymes, James L., Jr. *Behavior and Misbehavior*. Englewood Cliffs, N. J.: Prentice-Hall, 1955, Chap. 2. A description of disciplinary procedures for use with normal children.

Redl, Fritz, and David Wineman. *Controls from Within.* Glencoe: Free Press, 1952, Chap. 3. A discussion of influence techniques upon which much of the material in this chapter was based.

Wittenberg, Rudolph M. *So You Want to Help People.* New York: Association Press, 1947, Chap. 7. A critical account of the tendency of adults to rely too much on talk.

AUDIO-VISUAL AIDS

We Plan Together, a 20-minute sound film produced by the Horace Mann-Lincoln School of Teachers College, showing a discussion meant to evaluate (criticize and encourage) the work of pupils.

chapter **14**

SOME COMMON DILEMMAS TEACHERS FACE

Few people enjoy being in a position where no course of action open to them seems completely right. Such a condition may be faced by many beginning teachers, for example, during the first days, because they may feel that they should keep their rooms quiet or "everyone" will think they are poor teachers. Yet, in obtaining quiet, they may fear to do psychological damage by frustrating the children. For experienced teachers, similar dilemmas exist. Mental health principles seem so often to praise actions or situations which run counter to what teachers usually have been trained to admire.

For those whose preparation has been completed since the early 1950's, an opposite problem arises. Changes in educational goals and emphases may seem to call for ignoring psychological insights which have proved very useful. Indeed, many dilemmas arise from the fact that the educational sciences are growing rapidly and that new ways of applying principles keep coming on the scene and calling into question existing practices, which, too, have a basis in established fact.

The questions raised by these seeming contradictions are very serious ones. What becomes of discipline in a mentally healthy classroom? What happens to such basic concepts as authority and respect for teachers? How far can we follow the shibboleths of "permissiveness" or "high standards," whichever happens to be considered modern? What about the techniques of evoking laughter? How far must a teacher go in showing affection to children? What is implied by "understanding children"? Are consistency, fairness, and justice still virtues? What should be done about report cards, grades, and marks? What behavior should we worry about? How can we devote adequate attention to individuals and at the same time fulfill our obligations to an entire class? Is it all right for teachers to get angry at children?

In the pages which follow, we shall try to examine these dilemmas. By doing so, we hope to clarify major concepts related to mental health in education. In some cases, we shall find that misinterpretations and confusions have created conflicts where none really exist. In other instances, however, there are genuine difficulties, which can be solved best in terms of the peculiarities of specific situations.

Discipline

A chaotic, disorganized classroom in which children can do no learning because there is so much noise that they cannot think, will find no defenders among mental hygienists. For a child, to spend all day in a room where he cannot carry through any activity because other children interfere with him is a frustrating experience. It creates emotional disturbances. Bad discipline of this type is also bad for mental health.

There is disagreement, however, between mental hygienists and some other educators concerning the opposite extreme, that of rigid discipline. One can still find schools in which children are expected to act as robots who have surrendered full control of their every action to an all-powerful teacher. They are supposed to sit ramrod stiff in tomb-like silence, ready to spring into obedient action at the command, but only at the command, of the adult who sits enthroned at the front of the room. Such a concept of discipline the mental hygienist decries as harmful to children and teachers alike. It can be defended only by strenuously ignoring a solid mass of scientific evidence.

Fortunately, very few teachers are troubled about seeking to maintain either extreme of discipline. The dilemmas arise in that broad intermediate zone where effective group functioning requires relatively light restrictions on individual children. Here the teacher must make decision after decision as to whether it is better to allow some young person greater freedom of action or to restrict particular bits of conduct in order to obtain more efficiency in group learning. To develop standards of group behavior, the teacher brings the influence techniques into play.

There is an ideal answer, a fantasy image. Where children are all concentrating on a task and have accepted those standards of conduct required for effective progress, there would be no problem. Such a situation would provide a wonderful setting for each individual's psychological development.

The trouble is that such ideal conditions are difficult to approximate in real life. On the one hand, school authorities insist upon regulations no group of normal children would impose on themselves. The requirements of most courses of study will not evoke equal interest in all children at any one time. On the other hand, some children come to school with a load of psychological problems that find expression in conduct which, if unchecked, would disrupt the functioning of any group.

Under real-life conditions, therefore, the problem is to help children develop standards of conduct in the classroom which make for the best possible conditions for learning and development. Actually, those methods which produce least internal conflict are best for educational purposes. A child whose mental life is disturbed is usually handicapped in learning. There is no real conflict between the modern professional educator and the mental hygienist as far as the need for discipline is concerned. On fundamentals, both agree.

Indeed, by taking into account the psychological principles of human development and group psychology, the concept of discipline can be clearly conceived. One caution should be stressed. In any situation involving orderliness, we should always try to find out what else is happening. Pleasing surface behavior can be bought at too high a price. We should at least know what it is costing. To this end, we need to exercise quite a bit of subsurface curiosity. Also, in seeking a good level of order, we must recognize the wide variety of influence techniques which can be used and the different effects each may produce. In a nutshell, the mental hygienist has no quarrel with good discipline, but would emphasize that the type of order the teacher is trying to establish and the means being used to support it should not be injurious to the sound emotional development of children.

Respect and Authority

To the questions, "Should children respect their teachers?" and, "Should they respect principals?" practically all educators would answer, "Yes." However, they might mean quite different things. Some would want to force children to show a surface deference, no matter how they really felt. Others would mean that children should be scared of the teachers and principal. Still others would denounce such ideas as undemocratic but insist that educators should so conduct themselves that young people would admire them and look up to them.

At the very outset, it must be pointed out that attitudes toward authority can have deep roots. During the early years of childhood, strong and often mixed emotional reactions develop toward parents. The mechanism of displacement operates to attach these same reactions later to other representatives of authority. Therefore, educators must recognize that in this respect children are not blank slates. Rather, by the time youngsters reach school, attitudes toward authority have been deeply ingrained in personality structures. This has two implications: First, the attitudes may be highly resistant to change by ordinary pedagogical methods; second, the meaning of children's actions cannot be interpreted solely in terms of the immediate situation but must be viewed over a longer life span. The place of adult authority in a child's life may be quite different during preadolescence from what it was in early childhood or will be in full adolescence.

In the light of mental hygiene principles, it is especially important not to mistake surface behavior for inner reality. With relatively little skill almost any teacher or principal can coerce youngsters into showing signs of admiration. Beneath this mask, there can be, and frequently is, mocking contempt or surly hostility. The more an adult insists upon the outward forms of deference, the more likely that the triumph will be hollow. In fact, children may well interpret such demands as meaning the teacher or principal is more interested in himself than in them. Pomposity is always a little ludicrous. Children are as quick to spot it as they would a Homburg hat which invites snowballing.

In more immediate terms, much concern about "respect" involves misinterpretations of purpose and motives. It is very easy to read into children's actions an intent which a child would not harbor but an adult would. For example, children will ask personal questions without any idea that these will be taken as invasions of customary privacy. Simple curiosity can be mistaken for prying disrespect. Anyone can make a few mistakes in evaluating such conduct, but children will correctly feel that an adult who makes frequent misjudgments and who is always harping on respect is really a weak, uncertain person.

Educators often have reasons for worrying about respect. Much uneasiness is ingrained by traditional advice during student days and the inauguration into the profession. Many fear that if they do not act tough, they will be open to all sorts of trouble. They take the term respect to imply a sort of bulletproof shield that alone can save their professional skins. To lose respect, therefore, carries the threat of being unprotected. Actually, the issues are not that simple. Too much of the argument is based on carrying the case to absurd extremes. The real question is not whether or not children will esteem their principal and teachers. Rather, we must think in terms of what kinds of respect are desirable, how they can be attained, and what the several ways of achieving respect do to children.

Often fear of "loss of respect" assumes exaggerated proportions in a teacher's mind. He may fear that to tolerate even a minor bit of insubordination, to admit to an error, or to leave unpunished the "fresh" behavior of an excited child will destroy the fabric of respect. Experience shows such fears are not warranted. Real teacher-pupil relationships are made of sturdier stuff. "Respect" that would crumble so easily couldn't have been worth much to begin with.

The role of authority in education raises many questions. Involved are matters of social philosophy. Obviously, school policies would be quite different in a dictatorship, a colonial educational system for "natives," and a liberal democracy. We have considered only the latter situation.

We must recall that automatic respect for authority is of dubious merit. In a world where several systems of authority are in bitter conflict, we would not want young people to grow into adults who willingly obeyed everyone who said he should be followed.

Permissiveness versus Toughness

An amazing sequence of flip-flops on the "proper" attitude to take toward children has been presented to parents and teachers by "experts" during the past two decades. In the late 1940's and early 1950's, the idea of habit training was figuratively dumped into the lake of oblivion. Parents and teachers were told that the modern thing to do was to be permissive, to accept children without making any demands on them. By 1955, a return swing of the child-psychology pendulum appeared among adults looking for the "latest thing." This stressed the need for discipline and control, even to the point of rather extreme demands for punishment. When the launching of the first sputniks in 1957 revealed to the general public that Soviet schools were turning out capable scientists, a call for imitation of their rather tough attitudes toward children in schools became popular.

For a while teachers had asked this question: "In order to practice good mental hygiene, must I let children do everything they want?" More recently, some have had to ask a new one: "Are tough attitudes, reputedly needed to attain high standards, the best signs that schools are doing a good job?"

First let us examine how the concept of unrestricted permissiveness developed. For one thing, it is often stressed as a good policy for dealing with infants *during the first year*. Many pediatricians and psychiatrists advise that at that time a child be fed when he is hungry, rather than according to an arbitrary schedule. Also, they feel a baby's personality structure is strengthened when adults respond to demands for cuddling, and do not try to restrict elimination of bodily wastes.

Another origin of the idea grows out of some oversimplifications of ideas useful in psychotherapy. The false idea is widespread that if a child in treatment is allowed complete freedom to do whatever he wants, then he will automatically get well. This is not the case. However, for strategic reasons, in the treatment of special disturbances, it does become necessary to permit a child a much wider range of behavior than is allowed in a classroom. For example, by allowing a wide scope for impulse expression, the therapist can set the stage for the child to bring out into the open those feelings which are at the roots of his difficulties. Also, where the trouble was caused in part by too heavy an inhibition of impulses in childhood, permissiveness may counteract the effects. Even in these cases, however, realistic limits to behavior are maintained by the therapist and are recognized as necessary.

Beyond the days of infancy, restrictions are a part of living. Some are obviously necessary in school. Children are not injured by knowing what adults expect them to do and what their friends demand of them. In fact, within limits such realizations make for psychological health. It is as unpleasant to have grownups ignore you as to have them nag you all the time. A teacher who let children do everything they wanted would leave them every bit as unhappy as one who had a rule for everything.

There is no debate, then, on the subject of *absolute* permissiveness in the classroom. It would not be a mentally healthful policy. The serious questions are along another line. These have to do with the criteria which tell us when to step in and how to intervene.

Once the necessity of giving young people guides for social living has been recognized, permissiveness has an important place in school thinking. We are referring here to a basic attitude toward the needs of young people. In theory, at least, we have left behind the old days when a medicine was considered good only if it tasted bad, and a teacher was an old-fashioned policeman, the tougher the better. However, from those days there still persists a frame of mind holding that schools should

find a way of saying No to anything out of the ordinary routine that children want to do. By contrast, we would urge the opposite tendency. In
the absence of really good reasons for imposing restrictions, it is healthy
to let children work on the problems which are important to them and
to express the feelings which have the most meaning for them.

A special consideration must be given to dealing with behavior
which is an outgrowth of some deeper trouble, such as the impulsiveness
of a child from a turbulent home. At this point teachers often need
greater symptom tolerance. They are sometimes afraid that to tolerate
behavior of this sort might be interpreted as approval. Such fear is unfounded. In their own minds, children know the difference between the
teacher's "putting up with" something and actually approving of it. It
is possible to face an action which we do not like without having to
muster all our resources to wipe it out. Children can sense that the
teacher disapproves of behavior even when he uses low-pressure influence techniques. Too often the extinction of behavior is made a moral
issue when the question is simply one of educational or therapeutic
technique.

Aside from the impact of the sputniks, the trend toward a tougher-
minded approach to education is rooted in undeniable facts. For many
years gifted children in most schools were not encouraged to strive toward their highest possible achievement; some developed poor work
habits. By contrast, in certain European school systems the *survivors* of
programs which are very demanding show a comparative advantage in
strictly academic work over the average American high school graduate.

From the mental health point of view, there can be little question
of the value of encouraging gifted individuals to build realistic self-
concepts, and of challenging them so that they find school exciting. The
problem, from this viewpoint, is not only what happens to the gifted in
any proposed program, but what happens to *all* children. Standards
which are good for the gifted can be destructive for an average young
person.

The issue here need not be placed in either-or terms. A valid solution can be built on careful individualization of instruction within each
classroom.

Humor, Sarcasm, and Irony

Laughter, which can add so much to human enjoyment, is a fascinating
subject. We have already mentioned its use as a release for tension. It

can and does serve other purposes. It may be a vicious attack on someone else, as when a group whoops with glee when a disliked child makes
a stupid mistake, or when derisive scorn explodes at a youngster whom a
teacher has made ridiculous. It may bind a group more closely, as when
they affectionately acknowledge the foibles of favorite members. It may
be applause for a victor, as when the victim of a joke turns the tables on
would-be tormenters, or when in a contest of wit someone "tops the gag."

Teachers frequently face dilemmas in invoking laughter. On the
one hand they hear that pupils like those instructors who have a sense
of humor. On the other hand, they are warned against losing the respect
of the children. To complete the circle of conflicting advice, they are
told that sarcasm should never be used against a child.

In evaluating any use of humor, the essential consideration is the
purpose it serves. The revealing questions are: What does the teacher
hope to do? Why are the children laughing? At whom are they laughing?
How will it affect him? What is the general attitude that is being communicated to the children?

If the teacher is using humor to create a jovial atmosphere in the
group, that is quite a different matter from efforts basically intended
to display the teacher's own brilliance of personality. A witticism designed to dissolve a disciplinary incident is by no means the same thing
as one intended to shrivel the soul of a juvenile offender. As in so many
other matters in education, the specific technique is not half as important
as the spirit in which it is used. If a teacher genuinely likes children and
they feel it, the use of humor will present few problems.

In general terms, wit which represents self-display by a teacher or
which attacks an individual class member or group is dubious, to say the
least. This is particularly true of sarcasm. When "successful," it produces
at best a short-lived triumph. The teacher, having won an unequal
contest, leaves the victim not only angry but with many outlets for his
anger. Of these the most typical is a daydream in which he tells off the
teacher. His friends are quite likely to join him after class in building up
imaginary incidents in which he or they now top the gag of the absent
teacher. If his classmates, instead of rallying to him, echo a teacher's gibe,
he can do battle with them. In any case, his own actions which led up
to the "punishment" can be easily forgotten in the welter of emotion for
which the sarcasm set the stage. Of course, sharp-tongued teachers may
so inspire fear of sarcasm that children are very careful to avoid giving
offense. This, however, is merely another form of terror, whose emotional consequences few would dare defend.

On quite a different plane are those classrooms, particularly in the upper grades, where a teacher customarily uses banter to ease tension or to produce good-natured relationships. Essentially, this is more a spontaneous expression of the teacher's own personality than a thought-out technique. The playful exchange of witty and not-too-pointed criticisms is an accepted feature of many American social getherings. Teachers who employ this device are likely to use words which seem sarcastic, but are more inclined to address their remarks to the young person involved. They do not try to evoke scorn from the class as a whole. Another distinguishing feature is that the youngster is permitted to acknowledge the criticism with a respectful wisecrack. In effect, such sarcasm acts more as a signal than as a punishment.

Miss Barry's eighth-grade class, to cite an illustration, was in the midst of a social studies lesson when Tim O'Neil entered the room. "Don't tell me your alarm clock didn't go off again!" she said. There was a ripple of chuckling from the class, and eyes turned to Tim.

"No, it went off too soon, and I went back to sleep," was his reply. All laughed. Then he said, "I'm sorry I'm late. The real reason is we were out of bread, and I had to get some for breakfast. I'll see it doesn't happen again."

Humor can serve other functions. It may show to a group that the teacher has a sense of perspective. For the teacher and the class it may act as a shield against aggression. By preventing anyone from suffering emotional injury when some child engages in hostile activity, it reduces the likelihood of anger being produced or of counteraggression aggravating the episode. Many an event which otherwise could lead to a deep feud may have its poison removed by a well-timed jest.

Humor about himself has aided many a teacher in some situation where he had to admit that he had been in error. Now and then a teacher does have to accept defeat. Perhaps he has made a statement that was factually wrong. Then again, a child may have been wrongly accused of some misdeed. Once in a while, a rule or a regulation proves unworkable. Accepting such reverses with humor not only preserves the esteem children feel for the teacher, but also reduces the tension and uneasiness many children suffer when an adult's position is being shaken.

Display of Affection

Over and over again, in publications addressed to teachers, mental hygienists make the point that many children suffer from lack of affection and that this deficiency may be partially remedied in school. Such advice often seems ludicrously unrealistic. At first sight, it flies right in the face of such time-honored warnings as these: "Teachers should not have pets." "Favoritism has no place in the classroom." "A teacher should not become emotionally involved with a student."

Part of the difficulty stems from a false concept of what fondness for a child implies. It does not mean head patting, kissing, or cooing words of romantic endearment. It does not mean long speeches full of honeyed praise. It does not mean giving one child a monopoly of classroom privileges. The other part of the difficulty stems from the unspoken theory that the classroom is so soaked in competition that friendship shown one child must be given at the expense of the others. That is not necessarily the case. Neither of these assumptions need apply.

Within the setting of regular classrooms, there are ways a teacher can give a child affection without creating jealousy or getting him in trouble with age-mates. Through many little actions, a teacher can convey the idea that he likes a boy or girl. Efforts to understand a youngster tell that he is valued. If the teacher is bothered when a pupil misunderstands what was said or done, there is a meaning: the child's ideas are important to the teacher.

There are other ways in which a youngster can learn that he is "in good" with his teacher. This realization is created when he sees that the teacher pays attention to him and that this attention is marked by smiles rather than frowns or suspicious squints. A favorable attitude is communicated if, when things go wrong, he is invited to tell his side of the story, instead of being dared to produce an alibi disbelieved in advance. Even more telling, when he is in some trouble, the teacher can show either an implied or outspoken sympathy with his predicament.

There are other traditional signs of fondness. Notice taken of his health, his clothes, his hobbies, and events in his family can mean worlds to an otherwise ignored boy or girl. Another thing all of us expect of the people who like us is a chance to talk about ourselves and our interests. This does not have to mean long conferences after school; it can happen very informally while walking through the halls, strolling on the way to school, or watching the other children on the playground. A teacher displays affection by helping a child work out difficulties in learning or extend his abilities to higher levels of achievement.

In all of these actions, the familiar doctrine is that it is not so much what teachers do, but how they do it. An affectionate interest in young people can be conveyed while limits are being set to behavior, while the teacher is interfering with unwise or harmful actions, and even when punishment is being administered.

Some children will not be satisfied with such measures. They may be so seriously disturbed that they demand more affection or attention than can be given in the regular context of the classroom. Others may be wrestling with home situations where there is intense rivalry with other children. They see everything in a competitive context. Their striving is not so much for more affection as for *the most* attention. To meet their demands may involve damage to other children or destruction of a healthy group atmosphere. In larger school systems, help may be available from specialized facilities for the worst cases. In small communities and rural areas this source of rescue may be absent. In such situations a choice may have to be made between unsatisfactory alternatives. No teacher can give every young person all the attention he wants. Even warding off undue bids for attention, however, can be done in such a way that it conveys to the child the affectionate interest of the teacher.

Understanding Children

The trickiest dilemma for teachers arises from the demand that they "understand" children. There is an old French proverb to the effect that to understand is to forgive. This may falsely be taken to imply that if we truly understood why a child acted as he did, then we would have to approve his every action. Pushing this reasoning to its absurdity, we could never find it in our hearts to punish or interfere with anyone, and therefore all schools would disintegrate into wild bedlam. That would be terrible. To prevent it, should we flee to the opposite absurdity and say that the less teachers understand human behavior, the more efficient they will be?

Let us look at a few concrete cases. Fred is not doing his arithmetic but is looking sadly out the window. His teacher learns that Fred's father was fired the day before, and Fred is worried. Understanding one cause for his abstractedness, does she do nothing?

Meg is given to outbursts in which she hurls vile epithets at other girls. Part of her background is that she is a cruelly treated daughter of an unwed woman reputed to be a prostitute. Knowing this, does Meg's teacher ignore the tirades?

In a mining town, a politician has managed to organize inhabitants of Finnish descent into a dominant faction. In the high school, this group's children are systematically freezing other students out of all offices. Because they suspect the inspiration of the students' actions, do the high school staff merely fold their hands? Do they tacitly encourage the children involved?

The answer to each question is No. In each case, the teachers gained two things by knowing the background of the incidents. On the one hand, they were better able to judge the significance of what was happening. On the other hand, they could work out a plan of action that had some chance of achieving success. To be sure, attitudes of unalloyed condemnation would have to be abandoned. But those would have been useless anyway.

Many teachers find that when the background of an incident is realized, it may lead them to veto the course of action that first popped into their heads. We also note that when a problem is brought to an "expert," he may weigh the pros and cons instead of suggesting a simple solution. All this combines to create the impression that the better one understands an event, the more he is likely to shilly-shally. In actuality, understanding does not have to create indecision. It can and usually does lead to a better-conceived course of action.

In many cases, the problem is not that teachers know too much, but that important facts are difficult to uncover.[1] Always the hope is that if we really understand children, their behavior will make sense; we can figure out what has led up to their present conduct. We can put ourselves in their places and sense how they must have felt. We can see ourselves acting as they did. Even more important, we can make pretty good guesses as to what may happen next and how our plans will influence future developments.

Understanding may sometimes change our ideas as to the desirability of a situation or pattern of behavior. Some actions we would otherwise condemn, we may see in a different light. On the other hand, behavior we might ordinarily approve may be seen to have factors we want to correct. However, some undesirable things remain undesirable, no matter how well we understand them. Our knowledge merely helps us to act more effectively in correcting them. For teachers, a very significant by-product of increased understanding was brought to light in an experiment by Wilkinson and Ojemann.[2] They found that as teachers

---

[1] For a presentation of this aspect of the problem, see Celia Burns Stendler, "How Well Do Elementary School Teachers Understand Child Behavior?" *Journal of Educational Psychology,* Vol. 40 (1949), pp. 489-98.

[2] Frances R. Wilkinson and Ralph H. Ojemann, "The Effect on Pupil Growth of an Increase in Teacher's Understanding of Pupil Behavior," *Journal of Experimental Education,* Vol. 8 (1939), pp. 143-47.

gained insight into factors underlying behavior, conflict in the class-room decreased, and the pupils did better in their schoolwork. Subsequent studies have verified this effect.

Consistency

There are very different theories behind the oft-repeated plea that adults who deal with children be consistent in their actions. Believers in psychologies which stress habit formation rely heavily on a steady pressure of rewards and punishments to achieve desired results. From this viewpoint, adult inconsistency dilutes the pressure and thereby produces inefficiency. For a child, extreme variability in adult behavior can lead to great insecurity. Thus, if a teacher who seems to encourage pupils to ask critical questions suddenly reverses himself by calling the queries "impertinent," there is bound to be confusion. Those children who have a strong need to please adults will be especially shaken by such inconsistency.

Mental hygienists would sympathize with the feelings of many teachers that perfect consistency is impossible to expect. The normal ups and downs in emotions to which all human beings are subject cannot be ruthlessly ironed out in teachers. To attempt to do so would destroy that spontaneity which is at the root of the warmest personal relationships. Through their previous experience with grownups, most children come to accept a normal range of inconsistency.

It is very important to realize that any pattern of action is altered by the setting in which it takes place. By overstressing certain surface consistencies, a teacher may lose sight of basic emotional effects. For example, in moments of group elation children expect some relaxation of conduct standards. A teacher who on the plea of consistency in enforcing classroom regulations destroyed the spirit of a pre-Christmas party would be guilty of a deeper emotional inconsistency.

Worship of "consistency" can do most harm when a teacher has made a rash decision or embarked on a dubious course of action. For instance, in an impoverished neighborhood children may have been barred from physical activities because they did not have gym shoes; it is later discovered that their parents really could not afford the extra expense. Then the teacher faces an unpleasant choice. Should he permit an exception (and thus back down on his ruling) or hold to the original rule in the name of consistency? The latter alternative often leads to harmful conflict, even within those children who want to like and respect the teacher. It is much better to set matters right and start off on the firmer foundation built by admitting the error and changing the rule to one that is reasonable.

Fairness and Justice

Almost without exception, studies of the qualities which children most desire in their teachers show "fairness" at the top of the list. Young people dislike favoritism, which breeds jealousy. They naturally loathe the feeling that a teacher is "down on" them or is "riding" them. Teachers usually agree, intellectually at least, with this standard. Many like to think of themselves as exercising the impartiality of a judge or a referee. To counteract any efforts to sway their emotions, some rely heavily on mechanical marking systems. The popularity of objective tests is due largely to the fact that they permit teachers to furnish strong evidence against any charge of partiality.

From a mental hygiene viewpoint, it is essential that the relationships between teachers and students be fair. The existence in any group of a teacher's pet makes for trouble. Such a situation arouses feelings of jealousy, hostility, and guilt. These can add seriously to the weight of conflict with which children must deal.

While there is thus no quarrel with the basic notion of fairness and justice, there can be valid argument concerning the way it may be carried out in practice. Children being very different from each other, an objective standard may be psychologically unfair. Justice might appear to be served when two high school students are equally praised for reports of equal merit. However, if one report represented hours of work by a slow-learning boy while the other was dashed off in a few minutes by a brilliant youngster, it would be fundamentally unjust not to recognize the first for the triumph it really is. The same thing applies to all phases of conduct. Thus for a girl from a conventional home to pull hair in a playground quarrel might be quite a different thing from the same behavior in a girl from a neighborhood where street scenes involving physical battles between women drew appreciative audiences. The capacity for self-control of children from an identical background also varies.

Scrupulous uniformity in rewards and punishments can also lead to psychological injustice. A public reprimand might bring one girl to tears and leave another disdainful. Going home with an art-room valentine for his mother might bring elation to a child of ambitious parents but create shame in another trying to act as nonchalant about school as his big brother.

Children also vary in their needs for approval and for attention. It makes as much sense for a teacher to try to treat all children exactly alike as it would to insist that an irrigation project deliver exactly as much water per acre to a flooded swamp as to a parched farm. In a classroom, then, fairness and justice are better served by taking account of individual differences. The old boast, "I treat them all alike," is a confession of psychological blindness.

In attempting to allow for individual variations, the troublesome problem is to do so in such a way that the children and their parents understand the reasons. At best, there will be difficulties. Very ambitious parents may want their offspring given the accolade "First in the class." Children with exceptional needs for approval or those who are solving conflicts by projection may press the teacher to single them out for praise or to punish some classmate who has not behaved perfectly. In the face of such demands, it may be necessary for teachers to comfort themselves with the thought that their own self-respect is more important than an attempt to win universal applause at the expense of the less articulate children.

Much of the pressure for rigid justice is a product of competitive atmospheres. The less teachers employ comparisons between children to motivate desired conduct, the more they are free to deal with youngsters on an individual basis. Experience has shown that it is possible to foster a group spirit which gives the leader a wide range in meeting the needs of individual members. Normal children can see the fairness and justice of a teacher treating members of a group in accordance with their abilities and their problems.

In choosing a course of action, it is well to recognize that fairness is a minimum condition. Often there is a choice among several possibilities, all of them fair. Then the important consideration is what each will accomplish. Thus, if a little girl is discovered to have taken and eaten some goodies another child has hidden in a desk, it might seem that, among the several possibilities, justice could be served as well by giving her a vehement reprimand in the presence of the class as by having her work out with the victim some plan of restitution that would satisfy both. However, the reprimand might be quite likely to lead to a social isolation that would do harm in the long run. The planning of restitution, if feasible, could have the opposite effect. The decision should be made in terms of what each course of action will do in each specific case. For a group of children to witness a teacher respecting individual differences underlines an important value.

Report Cards, Grades, and Marks

The worst part of teaching for many conscientious people is the assignment of grades or marks, especially when these go home on report cards. Then, all the considerations discussed above come to a head. Debates over the form and use of report cards dot professional journals. The brainpower devoted to devising new marking systems and modifying old ones is overwhelming. Yet, except in a few communities where unusual skill has been applied to building parental acceptance of descriptive techniques rather than letter or number systems, the basic dilemma finds no satisfying solution.[3] If grades are based on any objective system, they are psychologically unfair in the sense that differences in effort may not be recognized. If the system is founded on relationship between individual capacity and performance, it seems to breed a different species of injustice: the same grade may be received by children doing different qualities of work.

The whole process of assigning grades is so filled with possibilities for increasing emotional conflict among children as well as teachers that it remains a bugaboo. As the fatal day approaches, evidences of insecurity mount: young people become extra good, apple polishing increases, and anxiety is openly displayed. The defensiveness of some teachers breaks out in a rash of symptoms, ranging from casehardened insouciance to nervous indigestion. Teacher and youngsters alike often dread report-card day. The techniques used to inform the young people of the results go all the way from chip-on-the-shoulder defiance through hit-and-run sneakiness to plaintive interviews. To thoughtful adults, the glee of those pupils who "did well" is more than counterbalanced by the scenes in less fortunate homes. Here, a "co-operative" parent administers a beating, cuts an allowance, or indulges in a third-degree interrogation. There, to avoid a scene a parent's signature is forged. Elsewhere, ambitions crumble amidst sorrow or vows of vengeance.

Of course, there is a bright side to all this. Many children, and adults, too, like to have their work judged. They use grades and marks as guides for self-evaluation. There are many boys and girls who are capable of earning good grades, and who do so. They look forward to report cards.

---

[3] For a description of the development of a parent-teacher conference plan, see Prudence Cutwright, "Planning for Child Growth Through Parent-Teacher Conferences," in *For Parents Particularly*, Washington, Association for Childhood Education International, 1950.

They know that the teachers' marks will bolster pride. Indeed, some work hard and want some evidence that virtue indeed receives a reward. The report card is that reward.

Also, a great many parents value the teachers' judgment of a child. Of course, they like this judgment best when it tells them good news. One of the authors worked intensively with a group of parents studying the reporting system of schools in a suburb. Most of the fathers worked in large corporations where competition for status was highly organized. They felt that a similar experience would be good for their children.

The facts of life are such that both within the educational profession and in most communities enough people see value in all the grading paraphernalia so that most readers of this book will have to assign marks. In fact, for those who are reading it in connection with a college course, both their study of mental health principles and their relationships with instructors are almost certain to be distorted by the realization that they will be graded.

In the face of the prevalent reality situation, the job of the mental-health-conscious teacher is to use his or her wits to help young people and their parents make the most constructive use of whatever marking system is in force. The real issues are how to use marks, how parents react, and how to make the system more reasonable. There is a purpose to helping a child judge his abilities and deal with that phase of reality. For example, school grades may help in making a more intelligent choice of a vocation. Always, it is essential to give emotional first aid to those who may be injured. This will usually mean time devoted to conferences with both children and parents. If we are to give first priority to helping the young people, discussions which include information as to grades are best held before publication, even though this may result in pressure for changing grades.

Too often the tenor of such conferences is one of defense, with the teacher trying to justify the grade or win the assent of the child. Rather, the focus should be on the emotional reactions of the children. The teacher's attention should be concentrated on noting evidences of anxiety, snobbishness, and the like. Very frequently the problem is not the child's feelings about the marks as such; the youngster is really worried about what his parents may say or do. Then it is rather callous to let the child shoulder the full burden of explanation and interpretation. It may be more humane and more effective to deal directly with the parents; when this is done before grades go home, both children and parents are spared scenes which can be not only painful but quite damaging.

The real problems in many cases go considerably beyond the grades as such. The crucial issue may be not so much the evaluation of academic work or character traits as the strengthening of social relationships within the class or the management of attitudes concerning schools and teachers. Also, the grading may be symbolic of strategies in teaching which should really be questioned. Then, we may have to recognize, for instance, that heavy concentration on grades may be destroying motivation needed in the daily work processes of the school. Where everyone is counting on the threat of poor grades to keep a class interested and active, the development of plans geared to child needs may be slighted.

Before leaving this problem-laden topic, one fallacy should be exploded. In some schools, systems are set up on the assumption that young people experience success and failure in school only on the day report cards are given out or promotions are announced. Some such arrangements may be called "no-failure" systems. The term is absolute nonsense. Feelings about schoolwork are built solidly as a result of day-to-day experiences. It is bootless to tell a child who knows he gets most problems wrong that he is doing satisfactory work. The unpleasantness and repeated frustrations do not disappear without a trace just because the report card bears an S or a B or some other mystic symbol.

Children do need to know how they stand. Such knowledge can be ego-supporting, whether it is pleasant or unpleasant, *if* care is given to how it is imparted. Is there a better way than marks and report cards for schools to perform their evaluating function? The answer is Yes. A number of schools rely upon parent-teacher conferences to communicate information about the young people. In these, planning takes precedence over rendering verdicts. That is as it should be. This method can only work well, however, when the staff is given adequate time for it and there is a good basis of parent-teacher co-operation.

What Is Problem Behavior?

One of the pioneer studies on mental hygiene in education[4] brought to light the fact that more than thirty years ago teachers considered open violation of rules or moral standards to be the most serious type of conduct. By contrast, mental hygienists then were more likely to worry about such behavior as shyness or excessive daydreaming, which might be symptoms of mental illness. There is now evidence that three decades

---

[4] E. K. Wickman, *Children's Behavior and Teachers' Attitudes,* New York, Commonwealth Fund, 1928.

of education in both groups have led to some significant changes in attitudes. Teachers now are thinking and dealing more effectively with the whole child.[5]

It is only natural that teachers should be most ready to worry about behavior that threatens the order of a classroom or interferes with learning. Principals and supervisors are still likely to judge success or failure in teaching on the basis of ability to maintain discipline and inculcate subject matter. Anything that prevents a teacher from attaining these goals is a problem. When a professional reputation is at stake, who would not concentrate upon what seems to be the source of danger?

As more and more parents and educators become aware of the significance of mental health, however, the standards by which teachers are evaluated are shifting. More weight is therefore being given to behavior which shows that a child is a problem to himself or his close associates. To be sure, some of this behavior may be of the antisocial variety which overtly disrupts the classroom. However, much is of the type which represents unusually great use of the mechanisms of denial, withdrawal, and substitution described in Chapter 4. In these terms, even though the conduct may not violate classroom niceties, it is regarded as problem behavior if it signals that the victim is dealing inadequately with his conflicts or that he is wrestling with conflicts which are severe or numerous.

By the same token, a whole group may engage in problem behavior. Teachers will certainly bend their energy to cope with group conflict which is openly disturbing. But equally worthy of attention are such phenomena as, for instance, group apathy, inability to discuss complaints or irritations, and scapegoating of all varieties.

The Group versus the Individual

Stated as the extremes in an either-or choice, if a teacher devotes adequate attention to individual children, the rest of the group suffer; if he is to give adequate energy to group leadership, he must ignore individuals as such. Both extremes make poor sense. Yet it is possible to find both of them in practice.

A related problem concerns the objectives which guide day-to-day activities. Is the teacher to judge his success in terms of the knowledge, skills, and attitudes acquired by the group, or does he now see himself

[5] E. C. Hunter, "Changes in Teachers' Attitudes Toward Children's Behavior over the Last Thirty Years," *Mental Hygiene,* Vol. 41 (1957), pp. 3-10.

as a therapist who "cures" troubled children of their ills or, perhaps, as a special tutor for a gifted few? An example of the confusion this creates was documented in a report of a project in New York schools[6] where inclusion in special small groups was arranged for children not doing well in kindergarten or first grade. One of the stated purposes was "wherever possible, to explore the underlying factors which cause certain children to adjust poorly, working with fears and hostilities, through reassurance, acceptance, and interpretation levelled at the 5-year-old's range of understanding."

Commenting upon this purpose, the final evaluation report noted:

". . . some confusion seems to have developed as to which orientation to work from. In direct help to children, the emphasis seems to have been to work with children in ways a teacher can. However, introducing an objective like the . . . above clouds this direction. As an extension of educational procedures in individualization, the project showed what a sensitive teacher could do with a small group in giving them a supportive environment and an opportunity for release. As a cross between a teacher's work and group therapy, however, it tended to cause confusion in the minds of both teachers and workers. In a number of cases where clinical attention would have been desirable, inclusion in the project appeared to have been considered an adequate substitute."

While agreeing that a teacher should not attempt the concentrated attention to a single child which would be given by a psychiatrist or other therapist, or the exclusive attention of a personal tutor, we need not go to the opposite viewpoint of saying that he never should attempt any such activity. The plain fact is that good teachers in all ages have given individuals interested help, and have added thereby to their effectiveness with groups.

In every school day, there are opportunities to note and attend to individual boys or girls. Many an effective interchange has occurred while the teacher was walking in hallways, in a meeting on the playground, or at the teacher's desk during recess periods, while a class was gathering, or after it had been dismissed. During class periods, there are times when children are busy reading or working. Then, a teacher can devote time to remedial work or to conferences with individuals.

When teachers make use of these opportunities, the group does not

---

[6] *Final Report of Study of Mental Hygiene Project at Public School 33, Manhattan,* New York, Bureau of Educational Research, Board of Education of the City of New York, 1949, p. 54.

suffer. Indeed, such individual help may prevent individuals from doing things which would disrupt a group. Conversely, if the group activities are going well, individuals' need for special attention will be reduced.

Of course, there will always be some children whose needs cannot be met within the time and energy a teacher can find while dealing with a class. For instance, there was the moody girl who came from a home where the father, mentally ill, was given to sadistic outbursts. The mother was afraid to ask for his commitment, although relief workers were refusing to give the family money unless she did so. A situation as involved as this would not yield to any line of action open to the teacher alone. The solution, from a classroom standpoint, would have to be one which left the teacher's energy free for the entire class, at the necessary price of leaving the girl's needs to be satisfied, if at all, by other people.

How Good or Bad Is It to Get Angry?

Popular theories about the wisdom of an adult getting angry with children fall into three categories:

1. It is *always* bad to get angry because
    (a) It scares the children.
    (b) It makes them think we do not like them.
    (c) It may interfere with the adult's judgment as to what is really needed.
    (d) It isn't nice to be so "subjective."
    (e) The proper attitude is to be cool as a refrigerated cucumber.
2. It is good for children because
    (a) Sometimes they deserve it.
    (b) It shows them what the limits of behavior are.
    (c) It shows them the adult is interested in their welfare.
    (d) It is better for children to know that adults are real people, not cool, calculating machines.
3. Anger is natural, it is part of reality. Therefore, if an adult is angry, he should do what comes naturally.

LIMITS TO POPULAR THEORIES.   As so frequently happens, each of the above-outlined theories has in it a kernel of truth, but there is much more to the story.

The fact that anger frightens children can be perfectly acceptable *if* the fear is well handled, if it comes in mild doses, and if it is geared to reality. The rub is this question: Which anger rattles children just the right way instead of producing panic, fury, counteraggression, or a feeling of being hated and no good?

Of course, under some conditions anger may make children feel they are not liked. However, if the anger is well modulated, clearly related to issues, and produced by a person known to like them, boys and girls are perfectly able to interpret it correctly as a signal that their behavior is off the beam and not as a sign of rejection. In fact, nothing makes children feel more uncared for than a cool disinterest in what they do. On the other hand, an irritable adult, flooded by aggressive rage, yelling at a youngster who is unsure of his acceptance, can hardly convey the impression he likes children or even communicate what is at issue.

It is true that anger shows young people the limits of behavior. Yet in many cases obviously a temper tantrum is not the best way of accomplishing this. The fact that anger shows what the adult disapproves does not guarantee that it helps children to identify with the value the adult gets angry about or to control their behavior accordingly. How many people are in such good psychological shape that they can learn from the experience of having a value rubbed in with fury? For many children, and especially for disturbed ones, the sight of an angry adult is quite likely to stir up past images of the same sort. These get in the way of an awareness of the issue at hand. An adult's angry face or voice is not much good as a tool for repairing a child's defective control system.

The fact that it is normal and understandable for a person to get angry is hardly a clinching argument. It is also normal to feel sentimental. Does that mean we would hug and coddle a cute little ragamuffin while he was snatching our purse? The "naturalness" of our feeling has nothing to do with the professional issue: How much anger should be *shown* to the child? What action is really needed to help him with *his* life?

A FEW TIPS FOR CLEAR THINKING.   Without getting into all the clinical problems related to anger, here are a few ideas which may help when thinking about the issue:

When talking with someone about the "role of anger," be sure all concerned are talking about the same thing. The following are all quite different: irritation at the discomfort produced by a child's behavior, even though we know he cannot help it; fury at our own embarrassment over being helpless, even though we ought to know better; forceful vigor, needed to show a child that certain behavior is wrong and that he cannot get away with it, even though the reason for our anger is that we love him and hate to see him act as he did; indignant wrath at somebody's tampering with our values; fury as a direct result of panic and fear, as when an adult shrieks at a child who has barely escaped being hit by a car after he disobeyed warnings; the irritable disgruntledness of an adult who hates all brats to begin with, and barks at anything that disturbs his comfort; the triumphant vengefulness of someone engaged in a power struggle and eager to put the other fellow in his place; and an impassioned demonstration to an invisible audience of other adults that we are really people who stand for law and order, even though our helplessness at the moment doesn't make that clear. All of the above are very different, one from the other, yet each is what someone may refer to when talking about the "anger" of an educator.

When people raise the question of whether anger is all right, they forget to add a question as to what an adult does with his anger. Even where anger would be natural and justified, there is still the problem of whether it should be conveyed at that moment to a youngster. Certainly, the anger should not be allowed to determine what should be *done*.

Sometimes anger may have to be put on. There are occasions when a mild display of definite irritation is in order to mark the unacceptability of behavior for a confused child. This has to be done even though anger is not felt. The ability to come up with just the right amount of constructively angry gestures, without being swept away oneself in the process, is an important educational skill in its own right.

In dealing with disturbed children, there are some special questions: Even if anger is justified, can the child benefit from it? Will the teacher's angry face trigger memories of the adults who have mistreated the child? If the child is excited, can he perceive the anger? If so, will it stir up too much counteraggression for any useful purpose? The heavier the interference with behavior, the less one can afford to show any anger at all with disturbed young people. Interference and limiting produces either panic or aggression; where the child's ego is weak, it may already be strained to the limit. Of course, there are times when it is perfectly all right for the boys and girls to notice that their actions make even you, who have been so patient with them, angry. Even then, the question of what should be done or decided upon must never be answered on the basis of anger. To keep judgment free, even when quantities of anger are welling up within us, is a prime requisite for work with disturbed boys and girls. It is as important as a "steady hand" in surgery.

The guilt many teachers feel about getting angry can be a liability as well as an asset. If we have, in fact, let rage interfere with what was educationally wise, being guilty can be good. That is, if our reaction to the gnawing of conscience makes us ready to have better insight, our future handling of incidents will be improved. However, in some cases the guilt itself gets in the way of wise handling of children. Here are a few common errors: Some adults do not dare interfere with pupils' behavior because the adults are afraid they will get angry. Some are so ashamed of having been angry that they are overpermissive in the next few instances of mischief. A few bother the children by unnatural apologizing or interminable rationalizing. More common, perhaps, is the effort to deny feeling ashamed by arguing that the anger was "good for them" or to try to deny or argue it away in talking with the child.

Since each person is different, each of us has to find his own way of assuaging his anger when he becomes angrier than he should. One way is to locate those life problems which arouse too much anger. Knowing at least that "this is *my* problem" makes it easier to avoid letting the anger interfere in important decisions. Or else, count up to ten, and interfere *before* you work up too much rage. There are other devices: Avoid the situation, get busy doing something else, develop a manageable psychosomatic complaint, make a speech denouncing mental hygienists, or write a paper, "How to Stay Calm."

In this chapter we have discussed several dilemmas teachers face when they try to reconcile mental health principles with traditional values of the teaching profession. What mental hygiene can do is to throw added light upon old professional problems. At no point need a teacher surrender professional standards in order to practice good mental hygiene. Rather, as we give thought to the problems of classroom management, we find that objectivity and good will can enable us to unravel more and more difficulties. Also, while employing our new knowledge, we remain human beings whose personal reactions will cause us some concern. Portions of these reactions we can learn to manage with equanimity.

For many of the dilemmas outlined in this chapter, there are no single, simple, general solutions. The problems confront teachers in the form of specific situations in which there are also side issues. Accordingly, each teacher will have to face the problems in terms of their details, analyze their most pertinent aspects, and try out his own possible solutions.

ADDITIONAL READINGS

Association for Supervision and Curriculum Development. *1950 Yearbook: Fostering Mental Health in Our Schools.* Washington: National Education Association, 1950, Chap. 18. Discusses the reactions of teachers as they seek to accept and clarify children's feelings.

Buhler, Charlotte, Faith Smitter, and Sybil Richardson. *Childhood Problems and the Teacher.* New York: Holt, 1952, Chap. 11. Deals with teachers' reactions to situational difficulties.

Burnham, William H. *Great Teachers and Mental Hygiene.* New York: Appleton-Century-Crofts, 1926. Describes Socrates, Jesus, Roger Bacon, Trotzendorf, Comenius, and G. Stanley Hall as educators and mental hygienists.

Hymes, James L., Jr. *Discipline.* New York: Bureau of Publications, Teachers College, Columbia U., 1949. A pamphlet dealing with feelings about discipline.

Ives, Olive M. *A Critique of Teachers' Ratings of High School Boys as an Indication of Later Neuropsychiatric Rejection for the Armed Services.* New York: Bureau of Publications, Teachers College, Columbia U., 1949. A research report which casts doubt on the ability of teachers to rate children accurately.

National Society for the Study of Education. *Fifty-Fourth Yearbook, Part I: Modern Philosophies and Education.* Chicago: U. of Chicago Press, 1955, Chap. 1. Gets at a number of current issues in education.

National Society for the Study of Education. *Fifty-Seventh Yearbook, Part II: Education for the Gifted.* Chicago: U. of Chicago Press, 1958, Chap. 1. Comments on the issues involved in decisions as to what to do about gifted children.

Olson, Willard C. *Child Development.* Boston: Heath, 1949, Chap. 4 and pp. 310-21. Discusses the implications of research on growth with respect to school practices and grading.

Rogers, Dorothy. *Mental Hygiene in Elementary Education.* Boston: Houghton Mifflin, 1957, Chap. 18. Indicates the directions in thinking required for a sounder philosophy of mental hygiene in elementary education.

Sheviakov, George V., Fritz Redl, and Sybil K. Richardson. *Discipline for Today's Children and Youth.* Rev. ed. Washington: National Education Association, 1956. A booklet which deals with problems of both goal and method for classroom leadership.

Wittenberg, Rudolph M. *So You Want to Help People.* New York: Association Press, 1947, Chap. 3. Raises questions as to objectives for many
activities in groups.

Wrinkle, W. L. *Improving Marking and Reporting Practices in Elementary
and Secondary Schools.* New York: Rinehart, 1947. A discussion of the
entire question of marks and report cards.

AUDIO-VISUAL AIDS

When Should Grown-Ups Stop Fights? A 17-minute sound film produced by
the Department of Child Study at Vassar in which situations are depicted
for the audience to discuss.

PART D

SPECIAL PROBLEMS

chapter **15**

CHILDREN WHO NEED SPECIAL HELP

The longer mental and emotional disorders go without adequate treatment, the greater the possibility they will become more serious. In state after state, child guidance facilities have been established on the theory that if such difficulties are dealt with in youth, many people can be saved from mental illness and blighted lives.

Teachers occupy a strategic point in the life histories of seriously disturbed children. They are often the first adults children meet who can bring an objective attitude to their contacts with the youngsters. Teachers may be the only trained people who ever observe an individual's conduct. Therefore, their skill in detecting deep-rooted difficulties and in taking the steps which will bring competent help may be decisive in the life of many a child.

At facilities for psychological treatment, workers very often notice, when they get the history of a seriously disturbed boy or girl, that it was a teacher who first recognized the difficulty and worked with the child.

When investigations are made into the past history of adults who have become criminals or psychological casualties, evidence of their peculiarities can usually be found in their early years. Reread the story of Jean Warpatch (pages 16 to 17), the girl who became mentally ill. Her teachers recalled quite a few symptoms that could have told them she was in trouble. Her constant daydreaming, the peculiar quality of her relationship to her mother, and the violence of her emotional outburst were clues to difficulties which, if cared for, need not have resulted in hospitalization.

In addition to those young people whose behavior indicates severe conflicts, there are others who need specialized help. These include boys and girls with exceptionally low intelligence and those afflicted with poor hearing, loss of sight, nervous disorders, and other physical handicaps. Their problems in learning and social adjustment may require the skill of specially trained teachers and the facilities of special schools. In many classes there are children with mild disturbances which would be lessened if they were only brought to the attention of a school counselor for assistance.

The number of children needing help is rather high. In one early survey conducted jointly by the Division of Mental Hygiene of the Ohio State Department of Public Welfare, the Ohio State University, and the Ohio Agricultural Experiment Station,[1] it was found that among 1,500 school children studied, 19 per cent were poorly adjusted. Quite independently, the same figure was noted in a survey of 788 children in 131 classes in 17 schools of Battle Creek, Michigan.[2] There, approximately 2 per cent were discovered to be severely maladjusted; another 17 per cent showed some indications of poor adjustment.

Spotting Children Who Need Extra Help

The signs that a child needs extra help with his problems are not always clear. Luckiest in a way are those youngsters who try to solve their difficulties by engaging in open misconduct. They become problems in a manner so obvious that they cannot be ignored. They may drive parents and teachers to desperation. Their fate then depends upon whether adults understand what to do. Such children may be mishandled; they are not ignored. More pitiful are those whose troubles show in behavior patterns adults are not forced to notice. They may be entirely overlooked. It is for them that teachers should be especially alert. What are the indications of their needs?

PERSISTENCE OF DIFFICULTY.   All children engage in some unusual conduct. From time to time, almost all will have periods when they misbehave, act a bit queerly, display nervous habits, or indulge in daydreaming. The conduct which puzzles adults comes and goes. The seriously disturbed child, by contrast, is likely to have difficulties which

[1] A. R. Mangus, *Personality Adjustment of School Children,* Columbus, State of Ohio, 1948.
[2] Gwen Andrew, "Health Survey Estimates Emotional Adjustment of School Children," *Mental Hygiene Bulletin,* Vol. 9 (1951), pp. 11-12.

last for long periods. For example, he or she may be very timid about playing with other children, not for a few weeks at the start of kindergarten, but for months on end. If stealing is part of the unusual conduct, it will not be limited to a few episodes but will occur over a period of years. A particular symptom, such as thumb sucking, may disappear but some other behavior problem takes its place. The child who has persistent difficulty in his social relationships usually needs special help.

BEHAVIOR WHICH DOES NOT YIELD TO USUAL MEASURES. Teachers ordinarily become quite skillful in dealing with problem behavior of normal children. They can usually eliminate ordinary infractions of classroom discipline. A lonely child can be helped to find friends by teaming him with other children in work projects. Daydreaming can be reduced by finding activities that enlist interest. Only exceptional children do not respond to the normal range of classroom management. When a teacher who has had fairly consistent success in handling a particular type of behavior is at wit's end over one child, there is a strong suspicion that the youngster needs special help.

From the viewpoint of schools, the major areas are likely to be learning difficulties, especially in reading, and conduct disturbances. As is shown in Table 7, which reports statistics analyzing 1,267 cases referred over an eight-year period for some form of personal service by

TABLE 7   *Analysis of 1,267 children referred for special help by Santa Barbara schools*

RANK	PROBLEM	NUMBER	PER CENT
1	Reading	204	16.1
2	School behavior	132	10.4
3	Physical problems	116	9.2
4	Mental defect	91	7.2
5	Social acceleration	90	7.1

the Department of Child Guidance of the Santa Barbara, California, city schools,[3] reading and school behavior accounted for one-quarter of all cases.

A persistent inability to learn may reflect not emotional troubles,

---

[3] Charlotte Dickinson Elmott, *The Development of a Mental Hygiene Program in the Santa Barbara City Schools,* unpublished Ed.D. dissertation, Stanford University, 1944.

but mental retardation. If there is any question, diagnosis by a trained person is necessary. There seems to be quite an overlap between these two types of difficulty. In some cases, a child suffers from both poor learning ability and emotional disturbances. In others, emotional difficulties so seriously limit his intellectual functioning that he is classed as mentally defective. Although carefully obtained data might not yet verify the particular estimate by Brown,[4] given in a description of a program for mentally retarded students in a high school in Floral Park, New York, it is well to take the opinion seriously:

> If the children in our program are typical of the country as a whole (and there are many evidences for believing that they are), it may be conservatively estimated that at least half of the adolescents in the country who are labeled retarded or mentally deficient would not have been so designated if they had had the services of a child guidance clinic at the beginning of their school life.

COMPULSIVE CONDUCT. Seriously disturbed children often engage in compulsive conduct. That is, they simply cannot help doing certain things, even though there is no good rational reason, and they themselves may be puzzled as to why they do it. Such compulsive acts may range quite widely in nature. At one extreme we might find a high school student who is badly upset at a minor tear in his notebook cover and insists on buying a new one. At another extreme is the youngster who cannot resist acting surly even to a friendly teacher. What we are saying is that a child who is under unusual pressure from within to do odd things not demanded by outside conditions is the victim of psychological forces beyond the scope of regular classroom handling.

WEAK REALIZATION OF REALITY. Even more alarming is behavior which is poorly related to what is really going on around the youngster. Excessive daydreaming is an often-stressed symptom. So are abnormal amounts of unfounded suspicion, inappropriate rage, or one-sided romance. These are all signs that a young person's actions are being determined by largely imaginary conceptions. Something is getting in the way of his seeing people as they are or of his judging their motives with anything approaching accuracy. Loss of contact with reality and inability to re-establish such contact is the clearest sign of

---

[4] Frederick W. Brown, "A Psychotherapeutically Oriented Coeducational Program for Mentally Retarded Adolescents in a Comprehensive High School," *Mental Hygiene*, Vol. 39 (1955), pp. 246-70.

mental disease. The seriousness of such conduct depends, of course, on age. The younger the child, the more leeway we must grant in our interpretation.

Illustrative of the weaker appraisal of reality by disturbed young people are the results of a study by Rosen[5] carried on in a camp for normal middle-class boys and one for disturbed delinquent boys referred by social agencies. The nondelinquents very quickly became accurate in estimating how they stood in terms of social power. The disturbed boys were quite inaccurate at first. Within this second group, the relatively well-adjusted boys were more accurate in judging their own power position than those judged to be emotionally troubled.

PASSIVITY.   Among boys especially, unusual passivity or docility may indicate troubles. The tendency has been to worry about aggressiveness. Of course, when we see the extreme of hostility and hate, we recognize that something is very wrong. However, there is now good evidence that mild, controlled aggressiveness makes for success in learning. Recently, Sontag and his co-workers[6] reported that children who at the age of six were rated high in aggressiveness, self-initiation, and competitiveness tended to gain in intelligence during the elementary school years. The absence of these qualities is good cause for concern. Passivity in its more extreme manifestations is a sign of trouble.

EXISTENCE OF OBJECTIVE DIFFICULTIES.   It is another sign that a child should be considered in need of extra help if the conditions of his life are imposing heavy psychological burdens. The situations described in Chapter 6 illustrate what some of these might be. It seems evident, for example, that if a youngster comes from a home in which the father frequently beats him and his mother, we should be especially alert. It is quite likely that at some point in his life he will have to learn to live with his feelings about such events. If so, trained counselors or psychotherapists may be highly valuable to him. The same thing applies, for instance, to a boy or girl whose age, physique, or learning ability differs markedly from that of his classmates. We know such objective difficulties increase the possibilities of psychic turmoil. Any

---

[5] Sidney Rosen, *Social Power and Interpersonal Adjustment,* Ph.D. dissertation, University of Michigan, 1952, University Microfilms Publication No. 3798.

[6] Lester W. Sontag, Charles T. Baker, and Virginia L. Nelson, "Mental Growth and Personality: A Longitudinal Study," *Monographs of the Society for Research in Child Development,* Vol. 23 (1958), Serial No. 68.

strong indication that the young person is using harmful means of coping with his heavy problems is an additional sign that special assistance might need to be invoked.

Tests and Their Use

The routine in dealing with children who have problems is to subject them to a battery of tests and examinations. These will usually be given by a school psychologist or other trained person. The need for this should be talked out with the child, his parents, or both, since an apprehensive youngster may be thrown into a panic by a sudden and unexplained barrage of tests. His emotional antipathy or suspicion may otherwise utterly invalidate the results.

In cases involving either extreme apathy or restlessness, a complete medical examination is essential. Physical abnormalities may be at the root of what seem to be mental difficulties. For instance, what looks like laziness may be related to kidney conditions; obstinacy, to loss of hearing. It is wise to consider such possibilities. Where physical abnormalities are found, medical correction must accompany any program of aid. In any event, it is well to know the extent to which physical ill health is entwined with other problems.

The timing of the necessary examinations, as well as the adequate preparation of children and parents for the purpose, must receive careful consideration. Our desire for additional facts must not blind us to the possibility that the procedure for securing them can, if mishandled, arouse emotional reactions that would hinder us in giving future help.

Of the psychological tests, intelligence scales are most universally used. In most school systems, scores on early group tests are in the child's file. The results may provide valuable clues, but cannot always be taken at face value. If the tests were given carelessly, as sometimes happens, the scores can be wildly inaccurate. Also, if a child was ill or under strain, the scores may be too low. If intellectual ability is an important consideration, no decision concerning a disturbed child should ever be made on the basis of a group-test score. An individual test should be given by a well-trained psychologist. Sometimes, if intelligence is unsuspectedly high, simple corrective measures in school, as by providing a higher level of work, may be all that is needed. Very low scores, if carefully verified, may point to placement in special classes or in institutions. Of course, in any such drastic step many other factors have to be weighed. Finally, if a child's intelligence is in the normal range, but he does work of poor caliber, a search for special disabilities or emotional problems is indicated.

Tests of a child's social adjustment may be given in a classroom. These include the friendship charts mentioned in Chapter 10 and the Guess Who test, in which children are given descriptions of various personality qualities or behavior patterns and are asked to name those who resemble the descriptions.[7] They may help locate children who lack friends in the particular class or who suffer from a poor reputation among other children.

In the junior high school grades and above, it is possible to obtain pencil-and-paper tests of personality or emotional instability. Of these, probably one of the more useful is the Mooney Problem Check List,[8] which will help a teacher realize the areas in which a youngster faces trouble. On the test, children check off statements describing problems which they feel. Obviously, a young person who has many more problems than the rest of the group may need extra help.

There are other tests which help provide information on special abilities and on personality structure. These include projective tests, such as the Rorschach and Thematic Apperception tests, which throw light on basic personality qualities. Which tests to use is best decided by trained clinical psychologists. The administration of the tests and their accurate interpretation also require considerable training. Like treatment itself, this is a field for experts. Where it is required, such testing is part of the program of child study clinics.

In using the results of any testing program, teachers will often have to deal with the anxieties of children or their parents. Test scores, like other professional information, should not be made public. When there is good reason to let a child or a parent learn the results, the possible emotional reactions must be considered.

Limits on Teachers' Effectiveness

What we have just said brings up the whole question of the extent to which teachers can enter into the treatment of children with grave

[7] Hugh Hartshorne, M. A. May, and F. K. Shuttleworth, *Studies in Service and Self-Control,* Macmillan, 1929.

[8] Ross L. Mooney and Mary A. Price, *Problem Check List, Manual, Form for Junior High School,* Ohio State University Press, 1948.

Ross L. Mooney and Mary A. Price, *Problem Check List, Manual, High School Form,* Ohio State University Press, 1948.

Mary A. Price, Ralph E. Bender, and Ross L. Mooney, *Problem Check List, Manual, Rural Youth Form,* Ohio State University Press, 1948.

problems. Often this does not appear to be a serious question because the work of teaching large classes leaves no time or energy for other duties. However, an occasional administrator may feel that, once teachers have studied mental hygiene, they should be able to deal with all children. Some teachers even take mental hygiene courses with this assumption in mind. Their pride or self-respect may be hurt when they "fail" with any child. Therefore, they would like to be completely self-sufficient and take care of every difficulty that affects their classes.

There is a great deal that teachers can do for children. The bulk of this book has been devoted to matters involved in promoting the mental health of children in school. Conditions which lead to this goal for all children do aid those with serious problems. However, when a youngster has troubles so serious or so deep that ordinary measures do not work, special treatment is required. The limits of a teacher's effectiveness in conducting this work should be clearly recognized by teachers and administrators alike.

NEED FOR SPECIALIZED KNOWLEDGE.   Ability to treat mental difficulties requires a tremendous mass of highly specialized knowledge. Psychiatrists usually have to follow a program of study which occupies between seven and ten years after college graduation. Clinical psychologists and psychiatric social workers who work in teams along with psychiatrists must take intensive courses for two to five years. All are expected to work under supervision for up to five years.

These requirements are far from arbitrary. To deal with emotionally disturbed children, one must be able to recognize the signs of specific types of difficulty, must know the detailed application of various methods of treatment, and must have received careful schooling in the meaning of changes in behavior. Many topics which were summarized by a single paragraph in this book are the subjects of large volumes which are must reading for a therapist. It would be unfair to expect teachers to master this knowledge in addition to all they need to know about subject matter, methods of instruction, and classroom management.

CHILDREN'S CONCEPTS OF ROLES.   Even if a teacher had mastered the knowledge and skills required for treatment, children who were in his class might not be able to establish with him those relationships which are necessary in dealing with deep emotional conflicts. For purposes of therapy, it is often necessary for a grownup to play a highly special role in a child's life. Among other things, the child must see the therapist as a person who not only understands, but does not condemn, violent feelings. With proper training many a teacher could play such a role for a child outside his class. The question is whether a member of his class would accept him in this type of relationship.

As was pointed out in Chapter 11, teachers are cast in such roles of authority as judge, referee, representative of society, and detective. To reveal one's deepest feelings freely to such figures may be difficult. What is at issue here is not the skill or flexibility of the teacher, but the ability of children to understand that the person who in one setting has to act one way can, in another setting, be an entirely different person. As was stated previously, most normal children can adapt to moderate inconsistencies of role by adults, but highly disturbed children do not adjust so readily. Since it is just these relatively inflexible youngsters who would be under treatment and who would be most likely to hold to an unrealistic rigidity in their concepts of the teacher's role, we can see the difficulties which would prevent their ever seeing their own teachers in a light essential for therapy.

If by concentrated effort a teacher were to assume the role of therapist for a child, this could put serious obstacles in the way of classroom activities. What would happen, for example, when the child under treatment got into arguments with other children? If the teacher always backed him, the group would be disrupted. If, to maintain a tradition of fairness, the teacher showed disapproval of objectively unreasonable demands, the relationship necessary for treatment might be disturbed, especially if treatment were in the early stages.

This discussion applies specifically to "treatment" in the sense of delving into deep-lying unconscious motivations and conflicts or engaging in the other arts of psychiatry. There is, of course, much every teacher can do, short of such measures. Considerable help can be given to individual children without disturbing relationships in the class.

EMOTIONAL INVOLVEMENT OF THE TEACHER. Not only would a child be emotionally confused by an attempt at treatment by a teacher; the teacher himself would be in danger of becoming so emotionally involved in the success of the cure that his personal mental health might suffer. Here is a concrete example: Miss Chelsea was a wonderful kindergarten teacher. After a series of mental hygiene workshops in which she had shown an unusual grasp of the ideas presented, her principal put into her class a boy whom another kindergarten teacher had declared "impossible." Miss Chelsea felt that if she did not succeed with the boy, her failure would set back the mental hygiene movement. That one boy occupied the center of her attention in her thinking about the class. Without realizing it, she began to think of the other children not so much as individuals with their own needs but as instruments for satisfying his needs. The class as a group suffered, and before long she felt that she was losing her usefulness as a teacher. Within six months she was on the verge of a nervous collapse. Examination of the boy disclosed that he was the victim of a severe mental disorder with which even the most highly trained psychiatrists often fail.

A related possibility is that, when the teacher has his heart set on "curing" a child, signs of progress bring delight. Conversely, if the child backslides or relapses, the teacher feels bad. Some disturbed children may sense that this gives them control over the teacher; they can exercise a species of blackmail. If such a situation reaches the point where the teacher is afraid that necessary class actions may produce a setback, if the teacher really becomes more afraid of what the child may do than the child is concerned about the teacher, this is good neither for the child, the teacher, nor the class.

Handling of Symptoms

The above considerations apply to the temptation, which a teacher frequently faces, to assume responsibility for the *treatment* of a disturbed child. They do not settle the question of what to do about such a child while he is in a class. Obviously, the teacher has to do something. Even the act of attempting to ignore him has its effects, not only on the youngster, but on the class. There is no known way of being utterly neutral toward another human being.

In general, by dealing wisely with the behavior which is a symptom of the young person's disturbance, a teacher may help him. Although such handling of symptoms does not produce a cure, it may relieve the child of some emotional pressure. At the minimum, it may keep him from getting worse. On the positive side, it may increase the probability of success in treatment being undertaken by outside agencies.

What does the phrase "wise handling of symptoms" imply? Let us look at an example: Alice was a pale, timid little second-grader who became terribly upset whenever she thought she had done something wrong. She burst into tears when a paper she was writing fell to the floor and was smudged. She became sick and vomited the day the class was given a group intelligence test. There were many such incidents. What should her teacher do? Scold her for her failures? Lecture her on her lack of realism? Obviously, such actions will not alter her basic anxiety; words or actions of reassurance and sympathy are what she needs. In the smudged-paper episode, her teacher could let her know that the work done before the accident was recognized and admired. Alice might be assured that it was not necessary to do the paper over again, but informed that if it would make her feel better, she could do so. The anxiety she attached to the incident would thus be drained off, rather than derided or suppressed. This action, however, would not prevent future outcroppings of her anxiety. That would probably require extended treatment.

In other cases, the way the teacher and children react to the symptom may either create or prevent additional problems. An obvious instance has been pointed out by Shanks[9] in the case of children who have convulsions. Often these incidents are treated in a way to make the child feel isolated and unwanted in the group. Thus, social difficulties may be piled on top of physical ones.

The Usual Process of Treatment

In this chapter we have frequently referred to "treatment." What does "treatment" involve? Aside from those cases in which physical ailments are dealt with by surgery or medicine, treatment usually means that the child and his parents go through processes leading to emotional re-education. The details vary in accordance with the theory upon which the agency or individual therapist operates, but certain conditions are almost universal. These conditions require that the child, his parents, or both develop a unique relationship with the person giving treatment, that they bring into the open the feelings which underlie their behavior, and that they work out new patterns of conduct.

A teacher who has helped bring a child into treatment which proves successful will have the pleasure of seeing improvement take place. As changes occur in the youngster's happiness, as he makes better use of his potential, the teacher will know that something has been done which affects the future. In addition, while treatment is under way it is comforting for the teacher to know that his problems can be shared with someone else. Most good therapists have a healthy respect for teachers and work well with them.

A word of caution is in order. The processes of treatment are far

---

[9] Robert A. Shanks, "Convulsions in Childhood and Their Relation to Epilepsy," *Glasgow Medical Journal,* Vol. 32 (1951), pp. 257-67.

from smooth or easy. Often they are highly disturbing. Neither children nor adults enjoy facing the fact that they have impulses they regard as wicked. They are loath to give up behavior patterns that have saved them from conscious conflict. As a result, all the phenomena of resistance to which we referred in Chapter 2 come into play. At times, the child's conduct will grow worse before it gets better. Rarely is there steady improvement. On the contrary, there probably will be a series of ups and downs. It is not unusual to find that the very worst episodes come just before the child finally accepts new patterns of conduct.

The resistance of the parents may be even more dogged. Often they bring the child for treatment on the assumption that he is to blame for his conduct. Almost inevitably, they begin to realize that their own relationships to the child, their own attitudes, and their own behavior are coming under review. Their resistance can well take the form of doubting the competence of the clinic or therapist. They may be deeply eager to end what for them is an unexpectedly annoying experience.

Teachers may sometimes share the parents' attitudes to some extent. Even though they may understand why a child has been placed in special treatment, they may nevertheless feel that the very fact of referral carries an implication that they have failed. Or they may have hoped that treatment would speedily eliminate problem behavior. When this does not happen but, instead, the child seems to require more attention, they feel let down. Unthinkingly, clinics may contribute to such feelings. Some clinics do a very poor job of communicating with schools. In any case, teachers have the right to ask for a discussion with the clinic of their problems with youngsters.

In view of these mixed feelings on the part of all concerned, there is a strong temptation to withdraw a child from treatment either during periods when his conduct worsens or when the first slight signs of improvement appear. This action terminates the unpleasant pressures which the treatment process generates. It may give teachers and parents a salve for their wounded self-esteem; after all, if the expert has failed with a child or the problem can be made to seem too slight for extended treatment, who can point a finger of accusation at them? In actual fact, the sudden termination of treatment under such circumstances may leave the child worse than if nothing had been started; moreover, it will seriously reduce the possibility that subsequent treatment will be successful. Later therapists might find his memories of this experience led the child to shy away from them or to fear that confiding in them would lead to another disrupted relationship.

The Time Element in Personality Change

Children who are so badly disturbed as to develop severe forms of delinquency, neurosis or other disorder are the products of years of intensive miseducation, most of it during the preschool period. Their basic personality qualities have become ingrained through years of persistent practice. They cannot be changed in a day.

Treatment of disturbed children is almost always a lengthy affair. It is a matter of months and sometimes years before the processes of emotional re-education can be completed. Therefore, much patience must be exercised. Months may drag by in which nothing seems to happen, although beneath the surface the child is preparing himself to face new facts and form new behavior patterns.

A corollary of the need for lengthy treatment is that not only must we look with suspicion upon treatments which promise unusually swift results, but also we must warn against the temptation to withdraw a youngster from treatment because he "no longer needs it." The ups as well as the downs in the curative processes may be seized upon as excuses for ending the experience. Indeed, one study[10] of cases referred for psychiatric treatment revealed that one of the most frequent excuses given for not following recommendations was that the person had "improved" and therefore treatment was pointless.

There is a pitiful shortage of facilities for the psychological treatment of children. Consequently, reputable practitioners in this field, desirous as they are of catching up with a backlog of untreated cases, have no motive for prolonging any case beyond what is necessary. If a child does not need their facilities, they will say so. If his difficulties are mild and can be cured swiftly, therapists are elated and will promptly discharge him. If they are failing with him and see no hope of success, they will recommend the most practicable disposal of the case. Teachers should be very chary of supporting parents, should they wish to interrupt the treatment process.

Fortunately, time also can be an ally. Some processes, begun in school, may continue and show results years later. Life may bring new corrective forces into play. For instance, in 1925 Mary Adams tested 40 boys from the Opportunity School in Columbus, Ohio. In 1943,

---

[10] Bernard C. Meyer, "Obstacles Encountered in Recommending Psychotherapy: A Follow-Up Study of 400 Cases," *Journal of Mt. Sinai Hospital, N. Y.,* Vol. 15 (1948), pp. 90-96.

Muensch[11] located and tested 8 of the group. There had been a significant increase in their I.Q.'s; the average had risen from about 65 to slightly over 80. In life they had shown gains beyond what would have been predicted when they were boys. Of the 8, 7 were married, none had a court record, 6 had held the same job more than two years, and every one had life insurance.

Sources of Outside Help

How does one go about securing extra help for children who need it? What sources are available? What can one expect such sources to do? These are the practical questions of any teacher who finds that a member of the class may require especially skilled assistance.

The facilities vary somewhat from community to community, depending upon such local conditions as budget resources, history of school organization, and effectiveness of various pressure groups. In most large cities, a full complement of services is usually available, although these are rarely adequate to deal with all needs. In rural areas, some facilities may be completely lacking or they may be provided on only a county- or state-wide basis, which makes necessary a heavy expenditure of time and travel.

SCHOOL SOCIAL WORKERS.   Often the first resource within a school system is the school social worker; in some communities the position still carries the title "visiting teacher." Although the training of social workers has varied widely, this worker is expected to be equipped to deal intelligently with children whose school difficulties arise out of home conditions or who may benefit from referral to specialized services available in the community. In communities where the school-social-worker service is adequate and workers are well trained, presumably the only step a teacher has to take for a child who needs extra help is to call for the school social worker, who should be able to make such further arrangements as are possible.

Generally, the first thing the school social worker does is to collect information needed for a decision as to the course of action. He or she should know what resources the community contains, the various organizations' policies as to cases they will accept, and the steps necessary for completing a referral. Thus, for example, if a child appeared to suffer

---

[11] George A. Muensch, "A Follow-Up of Mental Defectives after Eighteen Years," *Journal of Abnormal and Social Psychology,* Vol. 39 (1944), pp. 407-18.

from emotional disturbances, the school social worker would ordinarily make arrangements to have the difficulty diagnosed. If treatment were necessary, the next step would be to secure the parents' consent and have the child accepted at the proper clinic. On the other hand, if the youngster's difficulties had grown out of his parents' mistaken attitudes toward school, the worker might adjust the situation by a series of interviews with the pupil and the parents. In an extreme case, where a hopelessly bad home environment existed, the worker might merely call the case to the attention of whichever organization handled the preparation of neglect proceedings before the local court.

Making an analysis of the actual doings of a sample of school social workers, Hourihan[12] found that their principal activities involved working with children, parents, other social personnel, and community resources. They had casework interviews with children, and tackled problems by environmental modification, psychological support, clarification, and insight development. They acted as chief liaison between school personnel and community agencies.

The school social worker, then, is basically a trouble shooter and expediter in cases involving individual children. In practice, because of the fact that there are usually more problems than can be handled, local rules are set up limiting the activities of school social workers to certain types of cases or to a quota of cases from each school. However, their help is wisely invoked wherever serious psychological difficulties are suspected.

SCHOOL PSYCHOLOGISTS.   Although differently trained, school psychologists do many of the same things as school social workers. The major difference is that the psychologist knows how to give tests and interpret the results. His services ought to be brought into the picture when there is a question of a youngster's ability to learn. Many psychologists can detect boys and girls who require intensive treatment. Once they have done this specialized part of their job, many will go on to the business of talking with parents or counseling with children. They will also complete arrangements for treatment with clinics, hospitals, and private practitioners.

SCHOOL COUNSELORS OR GUIDANCE DEPARTMENTS.   Another resource within many schools, especially at the secondary level, is the

---

12 Joseph P. Hourihan, *The Duties and Responsibilities of the Visiting Teacher,* unpublished Ed.D. dissertation, Wayne State University, 1952.

school counselor or the guidance department. In many of the smaller communities and in some rural areas, the counselors may be the best-trained people locally available to deal with disturbed children. Where counselors are included in a school's personnel, informal arrangements for securing their aid for youngsters usually work well. The teacher who is concerned about a young person may have to do no more than speak to the counselor and, if the case seems suitable, make an appointment for the youngster. In some instances, the guidance people prefer to have the students take the initiative. Where counselors have been well trained, they will know the limits of their own ability and will refer serious cases to clinics or other agencies. Often, the problems of an adolescent can be worked out quite well on the basis of a few consultations with skilled counselors. This is especially true when the problem is of recent origin.

CHILD GUIDANCE CLINICS. Organizations for diagnosing and dealing with children's serious mental disturbances take a number of forms. A few school systems have well-equipped child study bureaus or psychological clinics. More often the facilities are independent of the school system, operated either by other governmental bodies or as privately supported agencies. They may be called child guidance clinics, children's centers, or by other titles. In a number of cases, the establishments are adjuncts of a juvenile court.

Whatever the formal title, the setup frequently follows a standard pattern. It consists of a team including a psychiatrist, one or more psychologists, and one or more specially trained social workers. The division of labor among them varies from place to place, but usually the psychiatrist acts as director. He supplies medical knowledge and takes a leading role in deciding what is wrong with a particular youngster and in developing the course of treatment. The psychologists give and interpret tests, which provide valuable information, and may sometimes conduct treatment in co-operation with the psychiatrists. The social workers may take responsibility for helping parents to see their part in aiding the child. In addition the social workers may obtain important facts about the home life of the children and work directly with youngsters as therapists.

There is a serious shortage of psychiatrists trained to work with young people. For this reason, and because many communities do not realize the need for child guidance clinics, the quantity of resources is insufficient. Almost all clinics are heavily overloaded. As a result, they have to limit the number and type of problems they can accept. They sometimes have long waiting lists, and, except in genuine emergencies, months may intervene between the date a child is referred to them and the time that treatment begins.

Child study bureaus attached to school systems will usually examine a youngster upon request from designated school personnel. This ordinarily means that the teacher must call the case to the attention of either the principal, a counselor, the school psychologist, or the school social worker, although in some instances the teachers may be authorized to act on their own. Customarily, school child study bureaus devote most of their time to conducting a careful study of the youngster and to making recommendations. These recommendations may take the form of authorizing transfer to special classes or special schools when that is required. More often, the child is returned to his regular class and suggestions are made to be observed by the teacher or the school social worker. Remedial work related to school subjects, as for example the correction of reading or speech problems, may be undertaken by the bureau. (In small school systems unable to support a child study bureau, there may be a number of teachers trained in remedial-reading procedures.) Where long treatment is indicated, the case is often passed on to an outside child guidance clinic.

For very good reasons, clinics will not treat a child without the consent of parents except on court order. Such consent may be legally necessary. In any case, the chances of success hinge upon co-operation from the youngster's home. Therefore, most clinics will not work with a child merely upon request from a teacher. Completing the necessary arrangements consequently involves enlisting the support of parents. Where the services of visiting teachers or school social workers are available, a classroom teacher will usually find that they may be able to handle the whole matter of referral with greater satisfaction to all concerned.

In all but the largest communities, there may be additional problems. Usually a fairly large population base is considered necessary to maintain a child guidance clinic. Therefore, such clinics as are available may be located in a county or regional center, or else may be provided on a traveling basis, under which they are open at a county or regional center only on certain days. A good deal of correspondence may be necessary to complete arrangements. Here again, having these details handled by a school social worker or an administrator may save the classroom teacher many headaches.

This inconvenience has a drastic effect on the utilization of resources distant from a community. For instance, when a study was made of the 1,306 clients who had utilized the Lansing Child Guidance Clinic from

1948 through 1952,[13] it was found that the rate of utilization was four times as great in Ingham County, where the clinic was located, as in counties more than twenty miles away. In a county forty miles distant, the rate was less than a twentieth of the Ingham rate.

FAMILY AGENCIES AND OTHER SOCIAL AGENCIES.   Another resource to which teachers can turn is the network of social agencies, children's aid societies, and public welfare bureaus. All these agencies are likely to be staffed with workers who have training in helping families work out their problems. Quite often, an improvement in home conditions will help a child cope with or reduce his own troubles. Also, even though the youngster needs individual treatment, it usually cannot succeed, or even begin, until his parents are prepared. A trained social worker can do a great deal in solving the problems of timing and of completing referrals when necessary.

Social agencies often have policies which guide them in accepting cases. Some limit their cases to a particular religious group; others do not accept cases where financial support may be necessary; still others shy away from situations involving children where divorce proceedings are in progress or where court action may have to be taken against parents. Knowing these policies is the business of social workers rather than teachers. Also, many agencies require that the potential clients voluntarily request aid. For these reasons, a classroom teacher is well advised to secure the assistance of school social workers. Where this help is not available, it is best to obtain advice directly from the offices of the nearest council of social agencies or community chest.

SPECIAL CLASSES AND SCHOOLS.   Quite often a child's need cannot be met in an ordinary classroom, but he could benefit from special classes of one kind or another. In large school systems there may be special facilities for children with defective hearing or sight, for physically handicapped youngsters, for those with low learning ability, for victims of nervous or physical disorders, and for boys and girls presenting difficult behavior problems. In rural areas and small systems, these special facilities, if they exist, may be centralized on a county-, regional-, or state-wide basis. To prevent inappropriate use of special classes, there are usually special safeguards. Medical or psychological examinations may be required. Inevitably, there is some red tape. Although much of this is best

---

[13] *Differential Utilization of the Facilities of a Michigan Child Guidance Clinic,* Lansing, Michigan Department of Mental Health, Research Report No. 17, 1955.

handled by the child study bureau, or the principal, or the county superintendent, forms may have to be filled out giving the teacher's observations. A small amount of work well done at this point may pay rich dividends afterwards in terms of peace of mind for teacher and pupil alike.

There has been a tendency recently in some localities to reduce the number of special classes. The feeling is that handicapped or gifted children must be able to get along with average people, and that the special class is a species of segregation. It should be pointed out that the legitimate goal sought by having unusual youngsters in regular classes can be reached only if skill is used in dealing with the real social difficulties. When Johnson[14] used sociometric tests to study twenty-five classes, each with one or more children having I.Q.'s below 70, in communities without special classes, he found evidence of social difficulties. The mentally retarded children were less accepted by other children than their classmates; they were more often rejected. It should be pointed out that there always will be some children who need special classes.

Relationship With Specialized Helpers

In the vast majority of cases, while the child or his family is receiving help from a school social worker, psychologist, counselor, clinic, or social agency, he remains in his regular class. This means that the teacher and the other helpers must tackle the problem of working together. A child will naturally be aided by co-operative efforts; conflict may cause damage. Therefore, good relationships among the several adults dealing with the child become especially important.

It is easy to say that all concerned should co-operate. However, very real obstacles can and do get in the way. Not the least of these stem from attitudes of the specialized helpers, who may discount the importance of teachers or be suspicious of them. Some specialists, who should have learned better, neglect to keep in touch with teachers. A few, because of harmful preconceptions or bitter experiences with unwise teachers, assume that all teachers are subject-matter-centered, punitive, rigid personalities with a callous disregard for children's feelings. Accordingly, at times communication between the teacher and the other helpers may be faulty.

---

[14] George Orville Johnson, *A Study of the Social Position of Mentally-Handicapped Children in Regular Classes,* Ed.D. dissertation, University of Illinois, 1950, University Microfilms Publication No. 1,664.

Whatever the situation may be, whether the teacher is openly welcomed as a collaborator among equals or grudgingly accepted as a partner out of necessity, the primary consideration must be the best interests of the child. Several considerations may be crucial here.

SUPPLYING INFORMATION.   The first step in building genuine collaboration is taken when information as to a child is forwarded to the clinic, social agency, or other source of help. The most helpful way to do this is to state the facts about the youngster in concrete, specific terms. If a general trait is described with adjectives or adverbs, these take on meaning when illustrated by typical incidents or anecdotes. Estimates of the frequency and intensity of the behavior round out the picture.

RESPECTING PRIVACY.   Whenever people are receiving special help, many facts about them become known to those giving the help. The child or parent has to feel free and safe to talk about his most private thoughts and experiences. The sacredness of such confidences has been protected for ages by medical ethics and legal tradition. Disclosure of confidential information will not only set back the treatment of the individual immediately affected, but will prevent others from accepting help. A single secret carelessly aired can do irreparable harm.

As a general rule, therefore, persons conducting treatment will share information only to the extent that it is necessary. Even then, they will discuss a case with a teacher only in general terms and will withhold detailed facts which, although interesting, are not needed for wise handling of the child. Such policies reflect, not suspicion, but a wise caution that is amply justified.

Among the facts which a teacher will learn, however, are some that would make juicy gossip and many more that are highly intriguing. A child or a parent, in the course of conferences with a respected teacher, will reveal items that he would not want to have widely known. These may be shared with other professional workers who need to know them. Beyond such guarded professional disclosure, however, it is a good rule to keep all information strictly confidential. It should not be used to spice conversation in the teachers' lunchroom. Hints should not be dropped to anyone in the community. Certainly such facts should never be alluded to when reproving a child or dealing with a classroom incident.

CO-OPERATIVE ROLE DISTRIBUTION.   All persons dealing with a child who needs special help should respect the roles that others fulfill for the child. Thus, the school social workers, if well trained, will not say or do anything to undermine the youngster's confidence in his teacher's ability. They should not attempt, for instance, to discipline a child for classroom infractions or to interfere with grading procedures. By the same token, a classroom teacher should not try to draw out confidences concerning home relationships which the child may be giving to a clinic worker.

The wisest procedure for arriving at co-operation is to hold a case conference of all the people who are working with the child. At such a conference, there can be a considered agreement as to who shall do what. We have already discussed the effects of role confusion on disturbed children. By deliberately assigning different tasks to different people, this confusion may be reduced. If such a solution is reached, it is essential that it be carried out in good faith. Thus, for example, it might be decided that one teacher may help a child over special learning difficulties but otherwise hold him to the conduct standards expected of all other members of the class.

MUTUAL SUPPORT. It is especially important that neither the teacher nor the special helper permit himself to be used to counteract the influence of the other. Children or their parents may try to get a clinic worker, for instance, to support a complaint against a teacher. When resistance to treatment runs high, parents may attempt to get teachers to agree that they should stop the treatment or ignore its requirements. In the same spirit that ethical physicians, whatever their professional disagreements, uphold a patient's faith in his own doctor, a teacher should support confidence in the psychiatrists, psychologists, and social workers who are dealing with a child or his parents. These special workers, in their turn, should be expected to return the support. Failure of any member of the team to follow this rule is ample reason for a vigorous direct protest. It is no excuse, however, for engaging in retaliation in kind through the person being helped. In this connection it is important to realize that disturbed people do not give accurate reports. To find support for their own resistance, they may be driven to create a feud that has little or no basis in objective fact.

Many children who come to school have problems which cannot be handled adequately in the course of regular school activities. They need special help of one sort or another. The skillful teacher will recognize such youngsters and will help bring to them the assistance they require.

Such action, far from being a confession of failure, is the exercise of a higher competence. There can be a special pride in watching a youngster thrive because we knew enough to find for him the resource from which he is drawing strength.

ADDITIONAL READINGS

Australian Council for Educational Research. *The Adjustment of Youth.* Melbourne: Melbourne U. Press, 1951, Chaps. 7 and 9. Describes youth welfare services and the activities of social workers in England and the United States.

Buhler, Charlotte, Faith Smitter, and Sybil Richardson. *Childhood Problems and the Teacher.* New York: Holt, 1952, Chap. 14. Discusses how psychologists can collaborate with the school.

Burns, Charles L. C. *Mental Health in Childhood.* Chicago: Fides Publishers Association, 1956, Chaps. 1, 2, and 6. Briefly discusses the use of child guidance facilities and residential treatment.

Fenton, Norman. *Mental Hygiene in School Practice.* Stanford: Stanford U. Press, 1943. Thoughtfully describes many of the issues involved in helping disturbed children in school.

Getz, Steven B., and Elizabeth Lodge Rees. *The Mentally Ill Child.* Springfield: Thomas, 1957. This book, written for parents with emotionally disturbed youngsters, is of value not only for its content but as an illustration of how to present matters to parents.

Hamilton, Gordon. *Psychotherapy in Child Guidance.* New York: Appleton-Century-Crofts, 1947. Intended for study by therapists, this book will give an accurate picture of how and why a child in treatment is handled.

Hamrin, Shirley A. *Counseling Adolescents.* Chicago: Science Research Associates, 1950, Chap. 6. Examples of three counseling interviews give concrete ideas as to what is involved in a counselor's work.

Pearson, Gerald H. J. *Emotional Disorders of Children.* New York: Norton, 1949. Devoted to the diagnosis and description of emotional disorder in children, this text contains many of the signs by which professionals decide what is wrong with a child.

Shaffer, Laurance Frederic, and Edward Joseph Shoben, Jr. *The Psychology of Adjustment.* Boston: Houghton Mifflin, 1956, Chap. 16. Sets forth processes in psychological treatment.

Stone, L. Joseph, and Joseph Church. *Childhood and Adolescence.* New York: Random House, 1957, Chap. 13. Presents a picture of some disturbances in development.

Symonds, Percival M. *The Ego and the Self.* New York: Appleton-Century-Crofts, 1951, Chap. 10. Describes one group of signs of psychological trouble.

Waller, Willard, and Reuben Hill. *The Family.* New York: Dryden Press,

1951, Chap. 21. Insightful treatment of family crises and family adjustments.

Wittenberg, Rudolph M. *So You Want to Help People.* New York: Association Press, 1947, Chap. 6. Deals with the problem of making referrals.

AUDIO-VISUAL AIDS

Angry Boy, a 33-minute sound film produced by the Mental Health Film Board, built around the treatment at a child guidance clinic of a boy caught stealing in school.

The Counselor's Day, an 8-minute sound film produced by McGraw-Hill, illustrating the type of problems with which counselors deal.

Face of Youth, a 25-minute sound film produced by the University of Wisconsin, in which a public health nurse helps a mother whose son is being treated at a clinic.

Family Affair, a 30-minute sound film produced by the Family Service Association of America to demonstrate by a concrete case what is done in social casework.

The Quiet One, a 67-minute sound film produced by Athena Films to show a program of residential treatment for highly disturbed boys.

Step by Step, a 20-minute sound film produced by the City College of New York to illustrate the activities of youth workers who deal with gangs.

chapter **16**

HELPING CHILDREN DEVELOP INSIGHT

Knowledge and understanding of oneself and of others has long been recognized as an important goal of education.[1] In this chapter we shall treat of ways by which it is hoped to deepen children's insight into human behavior. This insight can take two directions. On the one hand, we can concentrate on understanding the cause-and-effect relationships in other people's behavior. On the other, we can attain greater self-knowledge. These two aspects are not in opposition. Often, progress toward one goal makes it easier to reach the other. There is a vital interplay between them; it is easier to understand yourself if you know the roots of people's reactions in general. Knowledge of yourself can clarify perceptions of others.

Why Insight is Desirable

Generally, though we find praise for insight, it is not a good in its own right. It is a means by which important ends can be achieved. The value of any new insight must be judged in terms of its effects, both immediate and indirect. In the case of children, it must be appropriate to their age.

Insight is especially worth while when it fits into or implements a person's purposes. *If* he needs it and *when* he needs it are important concerns.

In groups, there are often periods when difficulties can be over-

---

[1] For instance, in his list of essential knowledge, Diderot included the following: "La Morale, pour se connoître soi-même et les autres, ce que l'on peut et ce que l'on doit dans les cas divers, où il plaît à la Providence de nous placer."—*De l'Éducation Publique,* Amsterdam, 1763, p. 7.

come if the members have a keen appreciation of each other, or if they can understand why certain conditions have arisen. Some aspects of this were discussed in Chapter 13 when we described the influence technique dubbed "marginal interpretation."

Another positive effect of some insights is that they produce comfort when the child or grownup recognizes the universality of some reaction about which he has worried. Often, when a group is discussing common quirks, the room will be swept by relieved laughter. This is indicative of a happy salutary effect.

Related to the above, insight can help an individual develop a more positive self-image or self-concept. Many individuals are in difficulties because they see themselves as bad, inadequate, unworthy. A goal of much counseling is to improve this self-concept. When insight aids in this respect, it is good.

There are conditions under which an individual cannot surrender an inadequate behavior pattern until he sees what it is linked to within himself or how other people react to it. Such insight becomes a phase in the strategy of re-education or of therapy. It should be pointed out that insight does not automatically lead to this happy result; success depends on the need the person has for his inappropriate behavior. But, if the need is weak, insight is a powerful tool.

In the Classroom

The classroom can present a number of opportunities for children to learn about themselves and other people.[2] There are several arrangements under which curricular provision may be made. Units taught as part of a course in health or in home and family living may deal with emotions, mental hygiene, child raising or boy-girl relationships. Sometimes, a conference period or home-room period is used for the purpose. Where a "core" organization is employed, the entire class may deal with personal problems or engage in "group guidance."

However, there are many instances where, instead of setting a fixed time in the curriculum, teachers seize opportunities provided by topics in the regular curriculum. Discussions of citizenship in the social studies or analysis of how people behaved in historical episodes or of the effects of

---

[2] For an analysis of four very promising programs, see the following: Committee on Preventive Psychiatry of the Group for the Advancement of Psychiatry, *Promotion of Mental Health in the Primary and Secondary Schools: An Evaluation of Four Projects,* Topeka, Kansas, Group for the Advancement of Psychiatry, 1951.

other cultures may open up consideration of human behavior at any grade level. Similarly, at various ages children may discuss why characters behaved as they did in literary works, ranging from *The Ugly Duckling* to *Hamlet*.

PROBLEM-SOLVING DISCUSSIONS.   Whatever the curricular arrangement, the most effective programs are those which lead to *problem solving* through group discussion. The teacher works with the group to establish a tradition of free give-and-take of expression about personal difficulties and feelings. In some cases, printed materials or short talks by the teacher are used to give a focus for the discussion. In one type of program, little anecdotes of situations in which common emotions are dramatically involved are read by or to the class. In another, the class reads stories which stop before a satisfactory ending, and the teacher then invites them to tell or act out how the incident would develop. In still other cases, a more informal setting is used: the teacher leads the class into talking about classroom incidents or their own experiences. In all of these, the goal is to gain expression through informal discussion.

LECTURES AND PRESENTATIONS.   Many efforts are more didactic. They are built around telling and studying. The class reads material explaining how people react. The teacher delivers lectures and shows moving pictures. The class procedure is in no way different from what it would be in dealing with traditional subjects. Knowledge is sought; understanding is tested. Often there is moralizing; the teacher persuades the group to take what he feels is a desirable attitude toward certain events of daily living.

This type of program often raises problems. At times what happens, in fact, is that a "mental health" reason is used to give a modern sugar-coating to ideas it would be hard to sell in their original form. This is merely a nice-sounding propaganda trick, a value swindle. Usually the pupils will recognize the goal of persuasion, and be politely resistant. This sequence of events is more likely to be ineffective than harmful. However, it may create a confused notion of what is meant by mental health. Even then, if opportunity is given for true discussion, there may be gains in emotional insight.

AUDIO-VISUAL AIDS.   The area of promoting self-understanding and good social relations has been very attractive to producers of educational films. A wide and varied selection is available for teachers at every grade level. Three major types can be recognized:

Quite a few films are designed to teach and illustrate *social skills*. Because these rarely refer to psychological forces, they may be considered superficial. However, for adolescents who are concerned with improving their techniques for getting along with people, these films can have great value. Once they have acquired social know-how, some young people who apparently have been isolates may find the courage to be more outgoing.

There is a large assortment of *moralizing* movies. These usually preach some virtue, real or alleged. Sometimes this is done honestly and effectively. In other instances, an improbable dramatic line held together by poetically licensed coincidence is used to make the point. Worst of all are those films which hold up to ridicule young people who represent such qualities as procrastination. By producing scorn and guilt, they are likely to deepen the difficulties of already vulnerable boys and girls.

Most useful are films deliberately structured as *discussion starters*. These usually picture a dilemma or a problem, leave the solution open, and invite the class to tell what they think.

ROLE PLAYING.   Another technique which is often effective is that of *role playing*. Here, the class decides on a problem it wants to discuss. Members of the group either volunteer or are designated to play the parts of the people involved. After the situation and the characters have been described, these young people then enact the scene as they think it would develop. They put themselves in the place of the real people and think up their own lines as the action develops. Discussion can center on how accurately the class thinks they took the roles, how others might have acted in the same circumstances, and how they felt. This procedure is both exhilarating and penetrating.

COMMON FEELINGS OF TEACHERS.   Whatever the nature of the procedure used, how it will work out depends very much on teachers' feelings. For that reason, we shall look at common feelings among teachers.

On the positive side, many find that the class sessions devoted to helping children develop insight are very rewarding. Statements made by children and actions which reflect those statements give reason for believing that ideas and attitudes likely to accomplish permanent good have grown. Here, for example, are some statements made by high school students in counseling interviews or in written evaluations of small-group discussions, reported by Driver:[3]

> It is good to know others have worries and problems like you.
>
> I could feel just like the ones in the sociodramas—could see both points of view.
>
> Before this I couldn't stand up in English class and give book reports. Now I can, and have given two in succession.

Usually, in any plan that permits discussion, teachers will learn many valuable things about the boys and girls, items of a type rarely brought to light in cumulative folders. Details regarding home and work situations, relationships within the family, and reactions to school events, all are given as background for questions as well as opinions and ideas. Many teachers enjoy knowing students well; classes devoting time to self-understanding hardly can be equaled for reaching that goal.

In the frank give-and-take of discussion, new channels of communication are opened. With knowledge and understanding, fears and misconceptions vanish. Facts known about the young people enable a teacher to see meaning in statements and also to find ways to make his meanings clear in conferences and in group activities. This can be immensely satisfying.

Along with these satisfactions, indeed as a price to be paid for them, are worries and risks. Many teachers fear the power of psychological insight. They regard certain topics as dwelling in a protective zone of privacy. They fear that if there is too much self-revelation children will be injured.

More realistic is a reluctance to get into areas where the teacher senses that it will be hard to come up with a "right" answer, one that adults would officially approve. For instance, a young person may describe incidents at home where a mother or father sets restrictions based on a difficult-to-defend lack of confidence in a child's ability. If, instead of backing the parent's viewpoint, the class concentrates on helping the youngster develop a strategy for correcting the misapprehensions, a teacher may be nervous about his own role in even listening. Behind this may be a feeling that adults should be loyal to each other and that if the young people talk about what happened in class, some touchy grownup will protest. There may be horror at the possibility that we are working at cross-purposes with other adults.

---

[3] Helen I. Driver, "Learning Self and Social Adjustments through Small-Group Discussion," *Mental Hygiene,* Vol. 36 (1952), pp. 600-06.

Oddly, another fear is that the program will work too well, that in the area of understanding people the children will become too sharp, and that they will see through the teacher. Recognition of human motivation is seen as a two-edged sword. Not only can it be used by young people to change aspects of themselves; it may give them a mastery over people they do not like. As they learn that everyone has problems, the children will come to see that this holds true also for the teacher. They can use their knowledge to score in a game of who dominates whom.

There is an allied and very tempting possibility. The topics chosen and the direction in which discussion is steered may be affected by the teacher's problems. The hidden goal may be to get the support of the children or the tonic of their assent. Thus, a man or woman who simply must be agreeable, who cannot hold an opinion which is unpopular, and who feels shaken by the realization that in so acting he betrays his own identity, may entice a class into dwelling upon ways of getting along with people. He may evoke and bask in praise of the importance of avoiding arguments.

Where the class contains one child whose actions or patterns of conduct are a source of trouble or concern, there is the temptation to aim the discussion at that youngster. A good class in human relations will be useful to everyone. If its purpose is limited to helping one individual, discussion will be distorted.

PROBLEMS LIKELY TO ARISE.   Many of the feelings described above have a realistic base. As in any kind of teaching or discussion leading, there are problems. In this section we shall touch on some of the more common ones and indicate lines of solution.

A teacher may feel responsible for whatever direction the discussion may take. Here, it may be wise to develop an atmosphere of permissiveness for discussion, so that the class members recognize that they influence the choice of topics.

The concepts the young people may seem to need to work on a problem may be recognized as involving psychological vocabulary, or the children may regard the ideas as farfetched. It may help matters if the teacher works at the task of translating psychological terms into the students' vocabulary and of finding illustrations from events likely to have been witnessed by the young people.

A child we may be trying to reach may not see that the point under discussion applies to him or her. This means he is not ready to make personal use of the insight. Rather than becoming annoyed, we should learn to be thankful for the children's defenses as permitting what insight they can achieve without disturbance.

In the course of a discussion, the young people may act silly. This is a natural reaction to embarrassment. It may be a sign of discomfort because they are not used to hearing certain problems aired. The best course is usually to let the discussion move along. Rarely is it wise to interrupt or stop the class as a disciplinary measure.

At points some children will be concerned about value implications and will take a goody-goody turn in their remarks. They may feel that as children in a classroom their job is to find an answer the teacher likes. This means that the teacher has the tough task of disentangling this kind of discussion from other types of class procedure. The purposes of the discussion and the criteria for evaluating its success must be clarified.

Sometimes the teacher may have to fish for a contribution which will enable him to point out that in *this discussion* he wants the class to tell how they feel. For example, if a class is talking about anger, the teacher might ask if he has ever done anything that made them angry at him. If some pupil mentioned that he became annoyed when the teacher put pressure on the class to finish work, the teacher could then draw him out on the subject, instead of becoming defensive. The child could be praised for making the class session more honest.

There is always a likelihood that some youngsters will be tempted to test the limits, to find out how far they can go. This is to be expected. If they broach topics the teacher feels cannot be touched on, this should be stated calmly. If language or actions go beyond what should be permitted, the appropriate influence technique should be brought into play.

On occasion, a boy or girl may raise a very personal issue, one which it might be unwise to pursue in public or which would not interest the rest of the group. The simplest thing here is to invite the individual to talk with the teacher later in private.

When an opportunity is given for free discussion, inevitably questions will be raised which could put the teacher in an embarrassing position with parents, other teachers, the police, or a religious leader. A sharp-witted boy or girl may ask a question designed to trap the teacher into taking sides in a family, school, or community argument. For instance, a high school class might ask a teacher what time he felt boys and girls should come home from Saturday night dates. As a preliminary step in such situations, the question should be turned back to the group. The various opinions should be summarized. Then, if he wishes, the teacher may add his own thoughts on the subject. There is no rule that the teacher must answer every question. In general, the teacher should maintain group loyalty to other adults, but not do so in a mean, angry, or punitive style.

When role playing is used, occasionally it will move into directions which touch upon deep, unconscious motivations. This is a real danger, which arises when the role-played incidents go on for a long period. It is a good idea to make a practice of stopping all role playing as soon as the class has witnessed enough to start a good discussion of the issue.

Some children may use the setting of discussion to attack and criticize members of the class. They may turn upon a scapegoat. Clearly the teacher should protect the victim. The problem is to avoid punishing the others, using their actions as an excuse for withdrawing discussion privileges, or spoiling the atmosphere. This usually can be done by halting the attack, reminding the class of the purpose of the discussion, and suggesting a line of thought they can profitably pursue.

For example, after a series of arguments on the playground, in which Ted was the center of trouble, one of the girls interjected into an English class the question, "Wouldn't it be a good idea to talk about the way small men want to be like Napoleon and boss everyone around?" (Ted was the shortest boy in the class.) The question itself was not too far outside the scope of the class, which did often spend time on psychological questions. However, the smirks and the glances at Ted indicated that the question was designed to hurt him. The teacher replied that rarely can any person's behavior be accounted for by one isolated fact. Then he said, "It would be a good idea to look at all the causes which might make a person aggressive. Let's see how complete a list we can make."

A very different source of pressure which can cause problems arises when it appears necessary to "cover" so much territory in so short a period that little can be said. First, it is essential to keep in mind that there is no merit in running up a long list of issues which have been brushed so lightly that they have had no effect. Good discussion thrives in a low-pressure, leisurely atmosphere. The teacher has a direct responsibility at this point. The use of such aids as moving pictures and role playing should be carefully timed to free plenty of time for talk.

Occasionally, at the very beginning of a discussion, there may be a long, dead pause. The young people are either collecting their thoughts or warily waiting to see what happens. If the teacher gets nervous about the silence and starts talking, there is risk that the period may develop either a monologue, or a question-and-answer pattern. If, on the other hand, he deliberately waits out the group, sooner or later some child will find the silence unbearable and will speak. Often, a sign of the mounting pressure of silence is that there will be a rippling of giggles. Then, almost always, a boy or girl will make a tentative remark, and if the teacher turns this back to the group for its opinions, discussion will be under way.

Informal Talks with Children

Every teacher is likely to be asked for advice by some child. Every teacher will probably hold some informal talks with boys or girls about problems in learning or behavior in class. The goal often is to help a youngster clarify some issue or gain insight.

Here, it will be noticed, we are not attempting a technical treatment of counseling, especially as it is directed to therapy. We shall be concerned with the type of individual interviews, usually brief, which all teachers hold. We shall not try to deal with formal counseling and will not get into questions related to intensive relationships where the goal is akin to therapy. (That is a matter requiring a full book, at the very least.[4]) However, on a more immediate and informal level, much of value can be done for young people.

TOPICS INVOLVED. Many of the questions that children want to discuss are basically educational. They involve questions of fact as to data, where information may be located, what the rules of the school are, and what the requirements of other teachers are. Unless these questions are a disguise for personal problems, they can be handled simply by clearly giving facts.

A similar range of questions has to do with facts about vocations. In some cases, a teacher will know the facts and can give them. In other cases, there will be someone in the school or the community who is a better resource. In that case, the boy or girl can be told whom to see.

Of course, there will be times when it is apparent that a question about educational or vocational issues is really a thin disguise for a personal problem. In other cases, the child openly brings up a problem he is seeking to solve. This is one type of situation in which we shall be interested here. For the teacher, this presents a fruitful opportunity to aid an individual.

---

4 For a discussion of interviewing pointed at a child's current problems, see the following: Fritz Redl, *Strategy and Techniques of the Life Space Interview*, Washington, National Institute of Mental Health, 1958, hectographed document.

Not all children with whom a teacher has informal talks come with questions. Some have been invited, and others ordered to talk over some incident. They have had trouble in a lesson, they failed to do home assignments, they acted up. Perhaps the teacher in whose class the incident occurred is the one who does the interviewing. It is always likely that where an incident happened in another teacher's room, the child is told to see a teacher who has a special relation to him due either to personal contact or school organization.

There will be instances where a child has been told to see the teacher by his parents. Once in a while, a police officer, a clergyman, a youth group leader, or some other adult may have suggested the interview either to the young person or to the teacher.

Whatever the circumstances, the teacher finds himself face to face with a youngster who needs help. Now, questions are asked, events described, feelings are told, explanations are given. One goal may be to help the child understand better how other people have acted or will act. Most important, he may move toward a clearer perception of himself and why he acts as he does. In the end we hope he will be able to make and carry out better plans for himself.

COMMON FEELINGS OF TEACHERS.   The most common feeling of all when confronted by a child wanting assistance is that it is nice to be able to give it. Few activities are more a source of pride than those in which directly or indirectly we make life better for someone else.

For those who like children, such talks are a wonderful way of showing fondness. It is "better" than teaching because here is one activity in which there is no need to give marks or otherwise frustrate youngsters. Because of the friendly relationships implicit in personal conferences, there is greater likelihood that one will emerge as the teacher the children like. It also implies a superiority to other teachers, who may not understand the children so well.

Mixed with these ego-inflating feelings are others of uncertainty, worry, and anger. There is always the possibility that the final result of the talks may be disappointing. No one can measure up to all the needs of all the situations about which teachers are consulted. Often a situation will reveal realities which are overwhelming.

The reactions of children to talks are not always those of immediate pleasure or openmouthed admiration. If we give advice, sometimes they fail to act on it. This is irritating. If they expected an easy answer, they may resent the questions asked as we seek to explore important aspects of the problem. Sometimes they sit or stand with impassive, expression-less faces, or else seem too facile in their agreement. We are bound to wonder what they really think.

If a child seemed to get a great deal from a talk with us, we may recognize how much more there is yet to be done for him and become afraid that the limits set by our power and function in his life may prevent our giving all the help he needs. Our pride may later be dashed if untoward events reveal that the gains we thought we had made were transitory.

REALISTIC GOALS.   In this section we shall discuss principally the question of what can be considered legitimate levels of aspiration for teachers in helping children through informal interviews. Some issues of technique will be touched upon later.

Helping a child find a way of attacking his problem usually is useful. If he is ready, he can then work out his own plans to conquer a difficulty. As the old saw goes, sometimes a person cannot see the forest for the trees. A teacher, in conversation with a troubled child, may be able to help him see the pattern of his problem and find a course of action that can change this, rather than get deeper into difficulties by reacting to minor details.

In many cases, what a youngster needs is a map of reality. He cannot solve his problems until he recognizes what the issues really are. For instance, some children get into difficulties because their expression of their need for affection is to borrow things. If a teacher can help them see that people generally dislike to lose possessions, one source of social difficulty can be eliminated.

There will be cases where the problem is one revealing deep troubles. Here, if the outcome of an informal conference sees the young person going for help to one of the better-equipped resources in the community, a major forward step has been taken. This usually involves more than telling about the preferred resource. A youngster will often have doubts that need to be settled, and misunderstandings that require correction.

There are situations in which, so to speak, there is not a problem which needs to be solved but strong feelings that could be a problem if nothing were done about them. Here, by providing a safe time and place in which hot emotions can be ventilated, a teacher has done exactly what needed to be done. In an interview, a child may rage or cry. The ending may be put into words or left unexpressed: "Now, I feel better." That is that.

The feelings that need expression may be a short distance beneath the surface. A teacher may notice that a child looks moody, appears sulky, is anxious or scared, or is weeping. Now, a friendly comment, an invitation to tell what is bothering him, may unlock pent-up concerns. Even if nothing more occurs than that the boy or girl finds words to tell himself how he feels, this is a big step. In addition, the invitation gives the youngster the realization he has supporting friends, and is worthy of support. This is an asset upon which he may build.

Now and then, the facts which emerge indicate that a child's difficulties grow out of his inability to communicate or deal appropriately with some adult. Now, if the teacher to whom he talks can serve as an ambassador for him, matters can be adjusted.

In other instances, two opposing trends may be impelling a boy or girl in conflicting directions. As he talks, his ambivalence or indecision becomes apparent. He may be looking to the teacher for judgment. To an extent, the adult can umpire the psychic dispute as it pertains to concrete issues.

Frequently, the young person will be working toward a solution of his problems. He needs a setting in which he can put the major considerations into words. The role of the teacher here may be to listen and to ask questions which help the youngster to find his own answers.

There will be instances in almost every child's life when he is disturbed by anxiety and guilt. For instance, a hitherto passive child has been angered by the unfairness with which a bullying safety patrol boy treated a kindergarten child, and reported him. However, he found his anger upsetting; hearing the culprit punished made him feel guilty. Obviously, such extreme reactions have a deep meaning. This we could hardly untangle. However, if the child can talk with someone he trusts, his feelings will be calmed. Everything will seem all right again. This service is valid for itself.

Many children must live with circumstances they cannot change. For instance, if a boy has a sister suffering from cerebral palsy, his parents are likely to pay more attention to her than to him. They are likely to feel he is "the lucky one." If he feels jealous of the attention she gets, he is probably also aware that his feelings would be looked upon as unworthy. He may see himself as being petty. It may help him to talk about the situation and how he feels. He may regain a sense of proportion in respect to his self-concept. He may be helped to accept the inevitable.

Looking back on the preceding paragraphs, the reader will see that there is a great deal teachers can do through informal conferences with children. He will also recognize that some children will come with needs beyond those described above. Where there is no quick or ready solution, the teacher should seek out, and talk the problem over with, the best-equipped person who is available.

THE TALKS "THEY DON'T WANT."   All the above concerns talks where the children have taken the initiative or where their readiness for help is close to the surface. Another and more difficult category arises when either the teacher or another person recognizes that the child needs to develop insight, but the child either sees no need for it or is openly defiant. In some of these situations, the teacher may even be requested to give him a talking-to as a disciplinary measure.

The initial recalcitrance may be deceptive. If a child was expecting punitiveness or rejection, and sees that the teacher is seriously interested in his predicament and is ready to listen to his side of the story, the tough front may be abandoned. Should this happen, the later stages of the conference will be similar to those described in the pages above.

In other cases, the mere fact that the teacher represents a value position to which the child originally had not given weight has a delayed-action effect. At the moment it may even appear that no communication has taken place, and we cannot be sure we have been heard. However, as the child thinks things over later when he is calm, the incident may sink in, and he may readjust his thinking. Occasionally, he may even seek an opportunity to talk things out.

Timing can be an important issue. Although it is clearly unwise to expect any communication while emotions are boiling, yet it is a mistake to delay any expression so long that all feeling has evaporated. During the heat of events it may be possible to make a very brief comment and set definite arrangements to "talk matters over" at a later time. This is especially indicated when the presence of other children and the nature of the incident produces the additional complication of loss of face.

We must never forget that deep down children are favorably impressed by incidents showing that an adult is concerned about them and considers them worth effort. Even if nothing more is accomplished than to leave this impression, a positive step has been taken. There may have to be a long succession of such incidents in some cases before even the faintest glimmer of tangible response can emerge. This is a difficult thing for adults to perceive, and the lack of immediate response from a child they are trying to help can be more infuriating than open aggression.

SOME TIPS FOR INFORMAL TALKS.   In areas involving feelings, children may not know the answers to questions. Perhaps some elements of the problem are unconscious; perhaps they cannot use terminology or abstract ideas. In any event, one must be patient in getting at the facts.

It helps to understand what a child is trying to say if one has him describe concrete situations. For instance, if a girl tells you she is afraid to talk to people, have her picture for you a few situations in which she was afraid. You may discover then that all involve making requests of women in authoritative positions. This may be quite different from what you would have taken to be the meaning of "afraid to talk to people."

When a child does not talk, and sits silent, apparently uncertain, it may be a good idea to say something first. Such anticipatory verbalization should not be mere pleasantries. Rather, you can tell him what you already know, or you can make a guess as to what is the matter. This will open up the question to be discussed. His correction of inaccuracies will not only clarify issues but give him evidences that you are open-minded and helpful. Besides, it may be the one incentive that makes it possible for him to start talking.

In cases where the interview is part of the process of umpiring a dispute, of arriving at a judgment, it is well not to summarize too soon. A boy or girl may begin to bring in irrelevant facts or issues. That you may see listening to these as a waste of time is not as crucial as the child's need to feel that he is being heard. The impact of any decision you may have to recommend will be increased if each child feels sure that you have grasped and understood all the facts that child regards as germane.

As was implied above, some conferences involve young folks who are engaged in disputes or those who feel they have been treated unwisely or unfairly. If you are to be helpful, it is well not to take sides too soon. Although it requires effort, care should be taken not to show impatience when you feel the young person talking to you was in the wrong or to overidentify with him if you feel he was justified. There is such a thing as sympathetic listening that will not be perceived as taking sides. It is essential not to show triumphant glee at a child's recital of other people's mistakes. In this whole field it is difficult to give highly specific advice. One must be flexible and seek to be as sensitive to nuances of expression as possible.

The handling of confidential information raises serious problems. Each child must know that you use discretion in regard to information given to you. However, there are some facts upon which you will have to act, and there is some information which it would make you accessory to delinquency to guard as a secret. In regard to such information, one must be frank and aboveboard. For example, if a child begins to give information that must be brought to the attention of a parent, another teacher, a clinic, or some authority, you may have to interrupt and say, "If you are to continue, you will have to let me talk this over with ————." When children tell of some misdeed and request, "Promise you won't tell," it may be best to refuse to promise. Instead, you can say you will tell only if it is necessary. Appeal to them to trust you to do what will help most in the long pull.

At times, a worried child will ask for information about others which is confidential. This should not be given. Point out that he would not want you to violate the secrecy of any confidential information you had about him.

Another tricky situation arises when a child asks for your judgment on some point where an honest answer would hurt. For instance, a boy with very low intelligence scores and a poor scholastic record, but anxious to live up to the college-going tradition of an ambitious suburb, may ask whether by trying hard in high school he could get into medical school. Obviously, one would not blurt out, "You are too dumb." Neither could one say, "Yes." In such instances, the teacher gives the individual what support he can without being dishonest. In the case cited, he might point out to the boy those assets he really had which would be of vocational value, and also remind him of how difficult he found academic work.

Often, as he gains confidence in a teacher, a boy or girl will tell more about himself than he can face comfortably. So to speak, the dam of reticence has collapsed, and all kinds of thoughts which trouble him come flooding out. There is always a temptation to exploit such a situation by probing for deeper and even juicier facts. Instead, here is a place where it is essential to make clear to the young person exactly what your role is, and to encourage him to limit what he tells you to what you need to know to help him in ways appropriate to that role.

Among the problems to be faced is the possibility of emotional involvement on the part of the child. Most dangerous are young people who are paranoid. These are boys or girls who often spread convincingly damaging stories about other people. They are likely to feel that teachers or classmates are unfairly critical of them. In any case they are full of contagious suspicion. They are very likely to interpret any friendly gesture as a trap. Whether it comes from a teacher of their sex or the opposite sex, they invest it with sexual overtones, which they violently repulse.

Paranoids cannot be talked out of their difficulties; this is a form of emotional disorder which is extremely stubborn as to cure, and certainly its treatment is not a realistic objective in a class situation. The person who befriends a paranoid is likely to be his or her next victim. The only advice which makes sense seems harsh: if you suspect a child is paranoid, refer him to another resource and steer clear of him.

More recognizable are those instances where a boy or girl develops a crush on a teacher. Sometimes, the existence of yearning is the reason the young person finds excuses to ask for conferences; sometimes, the sharing of confidences and the resurgence of strong emotions, which is part of talking about oneself, step up the intensity of the attachment. In either case the teacher will become aware of this intensity in face-to-face situations. At this point it is essential to make clear to the young person the limitations on conferences and the goals of the teacher. Then, the youngster should be transferred to someone for counseling.

There will be a few isolated occasions when interviews with a pupil involve a probing for facts needed before help can be given. These are much like interrogations which would take place in a court or similar situation. The usual interviewing techniques do not work here. In any event, success is unlikely if the child is in a panic, or is self-centeredly tough and has a weak conscience. The fact of such failure does not condemn the line of hard questioning which is required. Many teachers are uncomfortable when faced with this task, or do it poorly. When this is the case, they should turn the task over to someone who is good at it.

In cases where the progress of the interview arouses anger or impatience in the teacher, it is important to guard against complicating the situation by demands for "respect," good posture, or a polite attitude. Some children will begin to communicate after they have expressed resistance in some form or other. The value of getting them to communicate at all is worth passing up the chance to teach them a lesson.

It is very important to keep one's role clarified. Not only the children but other teachers and administrators should know what you are doing. This not only saves embarrassment but prevents the development of situations forcing an inconsistency or vacillation which could be damaging to the young people.

Insight as to one's own motives and other people's actions is extremely valuable. Increasing it will strengthen the mental health of young people. It will reduce some present problems and serve to help handle future situations.

Within recent years there has been substantial experimentation with programs for making psychological insight a direct objective of classes. These go under various labels—adjustment, home and family living, and preventive psychiatry. The label is not important. What is valuable is to give pupils and students the opportunity to discuss and think about their reaction patterns and the behavior of others. The results have been most heartening.

Always, good teachers have held private conferences with youngsters who were troubled by difficulties. By keeping roles clear and giving thought to the realities of motivation, teachers can give added value to a traditional function.

Every child who gains in ability to understand people in general and himself in particular represents a valid contribution to the sum total of a school's impact upon living today and in the future.

ADDITIONAL READINGS

Bullis, H. Edmund. *Human Relations in the Classroom, Course II.* Wilmington: Delaware State Society for Mental Hygiene, 1948. A textbook and discussion guide for use at the junior high school level. Two other courses are available from the same source.

Gordon, Ira J. *The Teacher As A Guidance Worker.* New York: Harper, 1956, Chap. 8. A rather full discussion of counseling by teachers.

Krugman, Morris, ed. *Orthopsychiatry and the School.* New York: American Orthopsychiatric Association, 1958, pp. 159-68. Deals with preventive mental hygiene in the schools.

Lane, Howard, and Mary Beauchamp. *Human Relations in Teaching.* Englewood Cliffs, N. J.: Prentice-Hall, 1955, Chap. 17. Draws attention to psychological considerations as these affect the development of group discussion and the use of role playing.

McDaniel, Henry B., with G. A. Shaftel. *Guidance in the Modern School.* New York: Dryden Press, 1956, Chaps. 3 and 15. Discusses counseling at the elementary school level and also group guidance.

Martinson, Ruth, and Henry Smallenburg. *Guidance in Elementary Schools.* Englewood Cliffs, N. J.: Prentice-Hall, 1958. Sets forth the various guidance functions of elementary school personnel.

Miel, Alice, and Peggy Brogan. *More Than Social Studies.* Englewood Cliffs, N. J.: Prentice-Hall, 1957, Chap. 8. Treats of ways to help children feel good about themselves.

Ojemann, Ralph H., ed. *Four Basic Aspects of Preventive Psychiatry.* Iowa City: State U. of Iowa, 1957, Chap. 4. Orville G. Brim, Jr., summarizes recent research findings as to the effect on children of programs transmitting human development materials.

AUDIO-VISUAL AIDS

First Lessons, a 22-minute sound film produced by the Iowa Mental Health
Authority, illustrating a class discussion concerning the causes of behavior.

Diagnosing and Planning Adjustments, a 12-minute sound film produced by
McGraw-Hill, showing a counselor in action.

Role Playing in Human Relations Training, a 25-minute sound film produced by the National Education Association, which demonstrates several uses of role-playing procedures.

chapter 17

WORKING WITH PARENTS

Very few really important problems involving children can be solved adequately without bringing their parents into the picture. (For children without parents, this means the adults who substitute in the parental role.) Most serious difficulties involve home relationships. Accordingly, teachers and parents usually have to work together to get at the meaning of unusual behavior. In those cases where a child needs extra help, it may be impossible to do anything unless parents take the initiative in bringing him to a clinic or in presenting their own family difficulties to a family service agency. A legal minimum is parental consent; practically, this is meaningless unless co-operation develops.

It is quite important, therefore, that teachers learn how to work with parents. This is true even in handling the life problems of normal children. To this task teachers must bring disciplined effort. Direct scientific study of the problems involved is in its infancy. Teachers must rely largely on the working tools developed in several fields, notably the casework methods in social work.

Underlying Feelings and Role Concepts

When we wanted to depict the relations between teachers and their classes, we began by describing the roles which teachers played or which children expected them to play. Now, in order to understand the psychological forces operating in parent-teacher conferences, we shall list some of the role concepts and feelings which may determine how each may view the other. Some of these concepts and feelings can get in the way; others may produce illusions; still others may smooth the path to success.

In many communities, both teachers and parents are used to seeing each other as mutually interested in the children. To teachers who have had that type of experience, the thought that parent-teacher relationships are a problem area will seem outlandish. For other teachers in less happy situations parents appear as prejudiced, obstinate people who either cannot or will not understand simple facts about their children.[1] In this latter case and others like it, the whole area of parent-teacher relationships presents numerous crucial problems. It is in solving these that the analysis of role expectations can shed revealing light.

ROLES IN WHICH TEACHERS CAST PARENTS.   In some cases a teacher may look on parents as instruments to be used in strengthening his or her own policies. The parents are called to school to be told what to do. Their role is to carry out orders; too frequently, to administer punishments that will hurt worse than anything the teacher could do. In other instances, the parents may be accepted as equals, partners in a conspiracy designed to keep Youth in check.

Often, deeper feelings come into play. Teachers, like other people, may yearn for approval. In an interview with parents they may want nothing more than appreciation, someone to confirm their pride in achievement. On the other hand, when a teacher has had difficulty with a child, it is easy to look for someone else to blame. What better scapegoat than the parents? In such a case, in an interview the teacher might be impelled to put the parents in the wrong.

There is evidence that the approval desired by teachers may be quite personal. Jenkins and Lippitt[2] asked teachers in one New England community questions like "What do parents do that teachers like?" and then, in interviewing parents, turned the question around: "What do teachers do that parents like?" The answers indicate that many teachers see parents as potential adult friends. By contrast, parents see teachers, not so much as potential friends, but as persons whose primary importance lies in their ability to help children and who are seeking parental co-operation.

Many teachers feel uneasy at the prospect of meeting parents. This,

---

[1] For a summary of differences in viewpoint brought to light in four different communities working in connection with the National Conference on Family Life, see the following: Muriel W. Brown, *Partners in Education*, Washington, Association for Childhood Education International, 1950, Chap. 4.

[2] David H. Jenkins and Ronald Lippitt, *Interpersonal Perceptions of Teachers, Students, and Parents*, Washington, Division of Adult Education Service, National Education Association, 1951.

too, is very understandable. Their feelings of sureness and control may be shaken. They see in the parents rivals for the affection of the children or powers who may nullify school authority.

The tendency to see parents as the epitome of power not only has an ancient history but involves complicated personal and religious overtones, as witnessed in the following quotation from a sixteenth-century work on political science.[3]

> The right government of the Father and the children, consisteth of the good use of the power which God (himself the Father of nature) hath given to the Father over his owne children. . . . This word Power, is common unto all such as have power to command over others, either publickly or privately. So the Prince (saith *Seneca*) hath power over his children, the Master over his schollers, the captaine over his souldiers, and the Lord over his slaves. But of all these the right and power to command, is not by nature given to any be-side the Father, who is the true Image of the great Almightie God the Father of all things.

Very powerful feelings may be evoked by parents. All people, teachers included, are inclined to react to any authority figure somewhat after the way they did toward their own parents. Echoes of childhood rebellion or deference mock the tones of confidence with which they would like to speak. For example:

June Wilson, teaching her first year in Evansdale, had rehearsed in her own mind what she wanted to say to Robert Townsend's parents. The boy was very timid; he seemed afraid to undertake new tasks. In a conversation with him, precipitated by an anxious inquiry as to his probable grade on the first report card, she had learned his father had promised him a dollar for every E. (In Evansdale's scheme of things, E stood for Excellent.) She wanted to tell his folks that they had a very good boy and that they would help him best by putting less pressure on him. The night of the first P.T.A. meeting she looked for them. As she waited around, feeling a little out of things, she saw a burly, confident man talking familiarly with the principal, who then pointed to her. The man came over with his wife and announced heartily, "I'm Bob's father, and I want to meet the teacher my boy likes so much."

Somehow, his manner and his appearance took the wind out of her sails. She felt as she had as a little girl when her father had praised her. Her resolution to explain about Robert evaporated. Disheartened at herself, she heard her voice faltering, "He's a wonderful little boy."

---

[3] J. Bodin, *The Six Bookes of a Commonweale*, London, G. Bishop, 1609, p. 20.

Mr. Townsend glowed with pleasure as she told how well the boy had mastered reading. She seemed unable to find an opening to broach the question of the timidity; she was afraid to see Mr. Townsend's smiles turn to frowns. In fact, she felt like finding a hiding place to get away from him. The interview seemed almost a complete frustration for her. The turning point came when Mrs. Townsend left them to greet some friends. Then, unexpectedly, Mr. Townsend's voice took on a confidential tone and he said, "He worries me when he acts like a little 'fraidy cat.' Does he do that in school?" Relieved, she launched into her little speech, but padded it with a few extra compliments. He listened with evident interest and nodded agreement several times. Even at that, when he left to join his wife, Miss Wilson was surprised at how her heart was pounding and her palms were drenched with perspiration.

Another type of role expectation appears when parents are of different race, nationality background, or economic class. If the school regards itself as an agency for winning the children over to a "higher" standard of values, the parents may be considered as representatives of an inferior or an enemy culture. In this case, the purpose of interviews is to conquer or outwit the enemy. Typically, in such situations the school staff will use the phrase "handling parents."

The teachers of the Van Buren School, for instance, looked upon their mothers' club as a necessary evil. The principal explained that it was wise to have some channel through which to reach parents. Besides, he pointed out, not all the people were hopeless. Therefore, he made a practice of personally inviting the mothers who impressed him most to be active in the club. He always sat with the executive committee and chose the slate of officers, who were duly elected. He made sure that all meetings had a full program. Each class would put on a dance, or a skit, or a quiz program. The teachers dutifully attended, and made sure to say something nice to the mothers of children in their room. It was generally agreed that the club was well in hand.

There is not always conflict in parent-teacher relationships. Many a teacher regards parents as helpless laymen who, with the best intentions in the world, blunder along through ignorance. In such a relationship, the teacher treats parents as another set of pupils to be given help.

Ideally, an entirely different set of role concepts should prevail. Parents can be teachers' partners in finding out about children and in developing plans to help them. This ideal is being approximated in many cases. The number of situations in which it is the dominant theme is hearteningly large.

HOW PARENTS MAY FEEL.   The feelings which parents may bring to interviews with teachers are varied and mixed. In many instances they too look forward to conferences as situations in which they can sit down comfortably to learn more about their children, and can find allies for improving conditions at home and in school. But in every community, there are some parents whose attitudes are quite different. A part of what underlies their reactions was brought out in a study by Futter.[4] He asked parents in Alameda, California, to answer a questionnaire. Those parents who were known to have poor relations with school gave the following reasons for being hesitant about visiting school:

1. The teachers would make things harder for a child if his parents tried to interfere.
2. Teachers never change their minds.
3. Teachers think there is only one side to a story; they will not listen to a parent.
4. Teachers are too busy.

Obviously, most of these parents felt that teachers are unfriendly and unsympathetic. Such feelings have very personal origins. When parents such as these enter a school building, some feel awed and resentful. When they were children, school may have been the scene of unpleasant failures. The memories come alive again, and they see in the children's teacher an old foe. Others, out of hostility toward authority, are irked by school teachers because they are symbols of power.

Illustrative of many such were Tom Brown and his wife. They had been asked to come to school to talk about Jerry's truancy. Tom was bitter because he had to lose a half-day's pay, but the attendance officer had been insistent. The night before Tom had fumed, "Who do they think they are? I'll tell them where to get off."

At school they had listened for a while to the long list of Jerry's misdemeanors. Then Tom had lost his temper. He had listed some of the stupid things teachers had done, and given alibis to cover up some of Jerry's absences. The principal had been very firm. He had said that unless Jerry mended his ways, the boy would be in trouble. Any more truancies, and he would turn the case over to the courts. The Browns promised to co-operate.

Outside the school, Mrs. Brown indignantly exploded, "Did you ever?"

[4] Irvin Charles Futter, *Parent-Teacher Relations*, unpublished Ed.D. dissertation, Stanford University, 1950.

Tom grumped, "The boy's O.K., a chip off the old block."

That spring he took Jerry on a hunting trip. Mrs. Brown phoned the school to say that her mother had died and the whole family had to go to the funeral, in a distant city. The family often chortled at how they'd put one over on the school.

In the presence of authority, many people go on the defensive, rather than attack. Accordingly, we would expect some parents to listen to a teacher with their minds set to find loopholes, think up alibis, and concoct excuses. Others may see in teachers a threatening power to be cajoled. Such people are inclined to agree with anything and to make any promises that will avoid trouble. For them, "sweet talk" is not a technique but a state of mind.

To quite a few people, the independence which their family has achieved is a symbol of their own personal battles for emancipation from their parents. They may see in the school an enemy threatening to enslave them once again. Their dominant feeling is one of defensiveness. They enter a conference determined to assert their own independence. Others feel jealous of teachers, as rivals for the loyalty of their children.

Many parents harbor the fear that they themselves do not measure up to what they fancy is the school's standard. A number have repressed feelings of hostility toward their offspring. Many have given rein to impulses which prevented their giving their children as much time, or as much affection, as they felt they should. Almost all have felt themselves criticized by their own parents, by articles in magazines, by television lectures. In short, they are uneasy. They have an uncomfortable feeling that the teachers have found them out. In an interview, they see not another human being so much as an embodiment of their own bad conscience.

For one reason or another, then, many mothers or fathers coming to school really do not want to listen and hear what may be said. To prevent this, they may build up a towering rage. Called to school, they pile up anger to the point where no criticism can penetrate. They arrive on the scene, deliver a blast, and, if possible, rush out in triumph. Another technique is to armor themselves with a fine shield of disdain for schools and teachers. Then, no matter what is said, they discount it in advance. They may look down on teachers as "sweet young things" who have no right to give advice to an "old hand" with children. Another neat parry is to declaim inwardly about "old maids" who "know nothing of life." Men teachers are shrugged aside with that shopworn aphorism, "Those who can, do; those who can't, teach."

Among families which are diligently ambitious and rising in the socioeconomic scale, teachers may be discounted as belonging to a lower order of people. Sometimes this is done on the basis of relative social prestige, and sometimes because being in so unremunerative a field is taken as evidence of different values. This group of parents includes some who are especially suspicious of modern education and others who support it intelligently. They may be avid consumers of magazines and books which discuss education. In an interview the critics would combine a wary alertness against being put upon with an eager readiness to get in a few licks to reform the educationists.

It would be a serious error, however, to assume that most parents are necessarily hostile or defensive. Many look on teachers as instruments they can use for their own purposes. They may think of the school as a supplementary arm of the home to carry out home policies. In poorer neighborhoods, many accept the idea that a teacher may inculcate in children a set of "higher standards" and thus fulfill the parents' ambitions. In the guerilla warfare between the Adult World and Youth, a number see the teachers as learned co-conspirators. Once in a while, in a battle at home over the bringing-up of children, the mother or father may try to use the weight of the school's influence against his or her mate.

FEELINGS CREATED BY COMMUNITY CONDITIONS.   Many of the feelings brought to parent-teacher conferences by both parties are the products of community conditions. Long-standing customs may set a pattern involving expectations of one sort or another. For example, in many schools teachers only seek conferences when there is trouble. A parent receiving a request to go to school immediately assumes that his child has done something wrong. Genuinely co-operative attitudes are rare in such circumstances. Anticipations of criticism from teachers and alibis from parents also obstruct interviews when there is an old tradition that the school is a reform organization engaged in a weary battle to correct the errors or low standards of parents.

There are some schools where administrators or teachers have discouraged, or prevented the formation of, parent organizations. This may be done in a spirit of protecting the school from "interference" on the part of "busybodies." Reflecting their colleagues' expectations, teachers will be inclined to fall back on secretiveness or arbitrary fiat. Even when this does not occur, parents will be influenced by suspicions about the school and its personnel. They may assume a chip-on-the-shoulder inclination to fight for their children or to vanquish the "know-it-alls "

In any case, the free flow of ideas may be impeded by the feeling that one must be cautious in dealings with an adversary.

At the other extreme, a community may go too far in accepting the notion that the superior training and experience of educators will enable the school to solve most problems. An atmosphere of dependency may prevail. In response to this, principal and teachers, confident of themselves, may freely give advice to parents who are perhaps too ready and willing to listen. Mothers and even fathers may bring their own family problems to school to be solved.

Politeness may mask the true situation. A pattern of apparent cooperation may have been ingrained through years of practice. For instance, in some towns one still finds that teachers are invited to dinner or tea at the homes of their pupils. In a great many more, a few days may be set aside as an open house, when parents visit the school. Although such contacts may furnish opportunity for genuine sharing of ideas, some participants merely go through the motions of what is really a stilted, empty ritual. Teachers and parents may be anxious merely to comply with surface amenities.

Underlying the spirit displayed in individual interviews may be very generalized feelings, resulting from how the community regards its schools. If the belief is widespread that the school system is an adjunct of a political machine, shot through with graft and patronage, parents will be more inclined to bring pressure, rely on cajolery, or suspect favoritism. Where folks believe the schools are poor and the teachers incompetent, they may discount in advance any suggestions put forth in conferences. On the other hand, in those many districts where people feel proud of the schools and respect the teachers, parents may look forward to opportunities to discuss their children with the staff.

A number of fortunate communities benefit from a tradition of mutual confidence and helpfulness. Through years of happy experience in working together, teachers and parents have developed a spirit of give-and-take; feelings of partnership are the rule rather than the exception. Tensions are at a minimum when mothers or fathers talk about their children. While such a condition is an invaluable asset to all affected, the children are the chief beneficiaries.

Interview Techniques

Whatever the setting, the heart of parent-teacher co-operation lies in the interviews or conferences in which both meet to talk together and work out problems. If the interviews are unsatisfactory, little good can be accomplished. On the other hand, if they increase confidence and promote understanding, the groundwork is laid for further advances.

FOUNDATIONS FOR UNDERSTANDING.   An interview is successful only to the extent that two minds have met and that *both* parties feel they not only understand but are understood. A sermon, an argument, or a scolding is not an interview. If either the teacher or the parent takes complete charge, talks down the other, or skillfully evades the main issues, little has been achieved. Under such circumstances self-satisfaction may bloom, but it can be maintained only by denying the reality of the fact that the other person remains basically unchanged.

In the preceding pages, we have described at length the feelings and role concepts which may prevail at the beginning of an interview. Of necessity, we have stressed those conditions which can hamper genuine co-operation, not because they are more common, but because interviews may fail if they are ignored. When meeting parents, teachers need to be aware of the feelings which might get in the way. Once these are recognized, they can be overcome. This means teachers can keep an eye on their own attitudes. Knowing also how the parents may feel, they can speak and act in a way to reduce, neutralize, or change unfavorable feelings. Also, they can make more realistic guesses as to how much can be accomplished and how long it will take.

Illustrative of the products of good interviewing are the following types of remarks obtained by Zudick[5] in reply to a questionnaire used to discover the result of a full day devoted to conferences with parents of a class for mentally retarded boys at the Marxhausen School in Detroit:

1. I understand my boy's problems better than before.
2. I know how I can help my boy after talking to his teachers.
3. I know what kind of work my boy can do after visiting the classrooms.
4. I understand better why my boy is in a special school.

OBTAINING GENUINE COMMUNICATION.   The first principle of good interviewing is to let the other fellow talk when he wishes to. Let him say what he wants to get said. Having spoken his piece, he is more likely to feel appreciated. The more he can explain his problems, the better we

---

[5] Leonard Zudick, "A Conference Program *with* Parents of the Mentally Handicapped," *Exceptional Children,* Vol. 21 (1955), pp. 260-63, 272.

can understand him and the more he feels understood. Time spent listening attentively saves time which would otherwise be wasted in futile arguments and blunders resulting from misunderstanding. Having to hold his tongue may be frustrating to the teacher, but as a professionally trained person, he can get his satisfactions from long-term accomplishment. This principle should not, however, be carried to such an extreme that the teacher feels compelled to be passive and show absolutely no reaction in an interview.

The primary purpose of letting parents do most of the talking is to let their feelings come out. That in doing so they will make errors of fact, give colored information, or repeat unfounded charges is a relatively minor matter. To deny or correct these aberrations too soon is to get into arguments which halt the progress of the interview. Once resentment, anger, fear, or suspicion has been expressed, its psychological force is reduced. When parents realize that their feelings have been recognized and appreciated, they are more apt to consider that mutual respect is possible.

Many parents are handicapped by a relative weakness in the use of language. While this would give teachers an advantage in a debate, it is a handicap in an interview. At times, therefore, a teacher must do more than listen; he must give parents active help. They need assistance in saying what they want to say. When this help is extended, the feeling of being understood is strengthened. The foundations for genuine co-operation are made more firm.

A hazard in achieving a full meeting of minds is the fact that many parents espouse patterns of living which to a number of teachers are strange or inferior. These styles of life are so much a part of the parent that to speak critically of them is to condemn the person. That, at least, is the way the parent will feel. A frown of contempt, a snort of disdain, or a short lecture, no matter how well intentioned or supposedly deserved, will throw the parent back into self-justification and will block the interview. The person has to be accepted as he is if talk about his children is to get anywhere. Problems which may arise when parents are of superior status have been discussed elsewhere.

Being a mother or a father always involves some difficulties. Practically all parents are at times irritated with their offspring. Just as teachers appreciate administrators who understand their problems, so a parent rates highly those teachers who sympathize with his or her troubles and resultant attitudes toward children. An interview in which such sympathy becomes apparent may set the stage for wholehearted co-operation.

Here is an illustration of how good rapport can be established. As the children began filing into the room, Mrs. Schwartz saw an untidy, poorly dressed woman hovering outside the doorway. The teacher asked if she could be of help. The woman introduced herself as Paul's mother. Mrs. Schwartz said she was glad to see her, and said it with genuine warmth. Then she gave the class some work to do, told Miss Green in the class next door that because of a very important conference she would be out of the room, and ushered Paul's mother into the teachers' makeshift lounge, where there were some easy chairs. Paul's mother had come to complain that Paul was being attacked by other boys, who were also getting him in trouble. Mrs. Schwartz felt like objecting to these statements, as Paul was definitely the leader in much mischief. However, she said she wanted to hear more.

Paul's mother had a great deal more to say. Most of it dealt with how harried she was. In the course of a few minutes, she had told how hard she worked, how Paul was a good boy but got on her nerves so that she spanked him regularly. She also revealed that her husband was running around with another woman. All the while, Mrs. Schwartz listened. During the brief interludes in the story, she indicated that she felt life had been hard for Paul's mother. The turn in the interview came abruptly. After a moment of speculative silence, Paul's mother leaned forward confidentially and said, "Tell me, Paul is not a happy boy, is he?" Then they talked about Paul. His mother had suspected that he was headed for serious trouble. Apparently, though, she had wanted to be sure she was with a friend before she was willing to reveal the depth of her worry. From then on she openly sought help. In later interviews Mrs. Schwartz was able to work out with her a variety of definite steps to be taken on both sides.

A particularly tough problem is presented by parents who come to school to coerce or persuade teachers to grant requests for specific privileges or special treatment for their children. Here we have the mother or father who wants his or her son or daughter to have a part in a play, to be given better marks, to be double-promoted, or to be allowed to leave school early. They may insist on telling what discipline should be meted out to someone else's child. Although it is essential to give them a sympathetic hearing, it is equally important to be clear as to the existence and nature of school policies. A firm declaration of intent to follow those policies, coupled with a willingness to discuss other ways of helping the child, will usually turn the conference into more productive channels.

EXTENDING ADVICE AND SUGGESTIONS.   The eventual outcome of any parent-teacher conference is joint planning for the children. Parents will often be able to make suggestions that the teacher may find helpful. They also may expect the teacher to help them with their problems. The teacher may have advice in mind. As mutual confidence becomes established, the give-and-take of suggestions is bound to occur. The way this is done may determine the extent of success.

To give useful help, the teacher must have some awareness of the over-all life situation of the parents. For example, it is bootless to tell a mother to give her son a place to study without distraction if the family consists of seven people living in two rooms. A woman who has to work, on the other hand, may be grateful for suggestions on the supervision of her children while she is not at home if the realistic problems entailed in her having to work are taken into account.

In extending suggestions it is wise to concentrate on one strategic spot. Inasmuch as a child who is having trouble usually has several areas of difficulty, it is hard to avoid mentioning all of them and giving a whole list of suggestions. This usually results only in confusion and a scattering of energy. For example, in the case of Jerry (read again pages 6-7) one might talk with his mother solely in terms of how pressure at home on language usage might be relaxed. It would be desirable to avoid telling her what you think could be done about his choice of playmates, his penchant for comic books, or her conflict with her husband. As was pointed out on page 242, the goal would be to disentangle his schoolwork from the emotional crosscurrents in the home.

Where some condition over which parents have control is an important source of difficulty, it may be necessary to make them aware of the ill effects. A certain amount of criticism may become inevitable. The problem is one of timing; criticism can have the desired effect only when the parent is ready to accept it.

When advice has to be given, it should be specific, not vague. To illustrate, many parents would not know what to do to "give the girl more attention." By contrast, the same point would be much more likely to be carried out if couched in terms of making sure she has time to talk about her day at the dinner table, taking her shopping for clothes, and chatting with her during opportunities provided as she worked with her mother in the kitchen.

In the same spirit, when talking about possible future developments, give realistic appraisals rather than far-reaching diagnoses. Thus, it makes more sense to say, "If Ted does not have more chance to play with other children after school, he may have an unhappy time in the fourth grade," than to predict, "If he keeps on being so self-centered, he may wind up in the electric chair."

So far, we have gone on the assumption that in the interview a teacher will have reached a fairly good understanding of the forces at work and will have suggestions clearly in mind. That is not always the case. No teacher can know everything. It rarely hurts to let parents know that we recognize that fact. If an interview has developed properly, both parties will feel free to show their uncertainties. Such honesty encourages further joint search for cogent facts and additional co-operative planning.

One word of warning is in order here: When interviewing parents, teachers should be on guard against the temptation of stepping out of the role of teacher and into the role of a social worker or therapist, whose energies would be given to settling the parents' personal problems.

SOME TYPICAL TRAPS. In view of the many different motives with which parents and teachers enter interviews, it is quite easy for discussion to be sidetracked. The flow of conversation may be diverted into by-paths or may take a harmful turn. Some of the traps are sufficiently common so that they can be recognized and avoided.

A typical trap is to lure the teacher into a discussion of philosophical generalities. As time slips by in "high-level" talk, the specific problems escape careful consideration. Thus, instead of exploring the possible reasons why her eleven-year-old son has several times knocked down smaller children with his bicycle on the way to school, a mother might prefer to hear the teacher's views on competitive athletics, a new system of phonetic reading, or whether children should be allowed to talk back to their parents. If these issues have anything to do with the boy's trouble, they should be discussed in terms of the specific connection. If there is no relevance, the teacher should politely refuse to rise to the bait.

A more difficult trap to avoid is a parent's request for an extended bill of particulars against a child. A teacher should not allow himself to be cast in the role of a squealer. If this happens, the parent may avoid all consideration of basic causes, and escape responsibility merely by punishing the youngster or else by holding a private inquisition in which he is cleared. What a young person has done is less significant than why he did it. Piling up complaints distracts attention from the main point.

In families where there is any large amount of quarreling or con-flict—and that situation is quite common—a mother or father may hope to enlist the teacher on his or her side. The attempt may be as barefaced as in the statement, "I tell Susan to go to bed at 8:30, but my husband lets her stay up later. Don't you think I'm right?" Or it may be more tricky as in the question, "What time should a nine-year-old girl go to bed?" The conflict may be between parents and child, as in this type of request, "I want you to tell her that she must bring you a note from me that she went to bed on time." The variations are infinite in number. In cases of this sort, definite verdicts and promises must be avoided, and the discussion shifted to other aspects of the problem. It may be worth while to work out ways the combatants can reconcile their differences on the point in question.

Neighborhood quarrels offer similar traps. One or more parents may come to school to complain against one child or a group. There may be attempts to get special rules passed. Again, an effort may be made to get a verdict to a query like this, "What do you think of a woman who beats her fifteen-year-old daughter with a strap?" All such questions should be met with a request for further details. When it becomes apparent that the incident or situation does not directly involve the persons being interviewed, there should be either a refusal to be drawn into the quarrel on the grounds that all the facts are not known or else a consideration of ways of reaching a satisfactory solution for the dispute. As soon as possible, the interview should be brought back to matters directly related to the parent's own youngster.

Less dangerous in terms of large-scale mischief are efforts to obtain the teacher's opinion of other children or to find out how two children compare. To meet such requests, however, rarely does any good; moreover it can and often does create hard feelings which spoil parent-teacher relations.

This same wariness should apply to criticisms of other teachers. Just as children will try to play off one parent against the other, parents may enjoy creating division in the school faculty. They will sometimes bring to one staff member highly colored recitals of another's defects. To support such criticisms merely undermines the other teacher and prepares the ground for reprisals. Often, the account is full of exaggerations and distortions. Even if it sounds plausible, the safest course is to express surprise and to mention known good points of the colleague. Here, again, attention should be redirected to the main object of the interview.

When a teacher, in the course of building good relationships as a foundation for co-operative planning, shows himself to be sympathetic and generally approving, parents may now and then attempt to get specific support for poor techniques of handling particular problems. Often, such specific approval cannot be given in good conscience. For example, a mother may say that because her son brought home a report card showing only average grades, she took away his allowance for a month, barred him from watching television, and forbade him to play with his friends. Obviously, it would be harmful to praise this excessive penalty and to invite its repetition. Such incidents can be handled by approving the mother's desire to have her son do well and at the same time indicating that the specific measure is one to be talked over at greater length. Then, when the ground for joint planning has been prepared, the criticisms and suggestions for alternative handling could be discussed.

Even with the most skillful interviewing techniques, a parent may find that the search for causes and the development of effort-involving plans is so irksome that he wants to cut the process short. Others may hold to the idea that the conference is a negotiating session. Whatever the reason, they may seek to satisfy the teacher by making a superficial deal. In return for the teacher's approval, they will agree to do something which actually leaves the basic difficulty untouched. For instance, after episodes involving stealing or destruction of property, parents frequently say that if the youngsters are given another chance, they will pay for the damage. All such deals should be refused unless and until there is evidence of a careful search for underlying factors and a sincere effort to take genuinely remedial action. This does not mean more drastic punishment, but rather planning to meet the emotional needs of the young people in better fashion.

Respecting Privacy

All information received in the course of interviews must be considered confidential, to be used only for professional purposes. The background of this principle as it affects treatment by specialized agencies was discussed in Chapter XV. Here we shall deal with special factors likely to arise in conferences with parents.

Facts obtained in the course of interviews with parents should be neither revealed to children nor used against them. Thus, if a mother discloses that her high school daughter is keeping very late hours, a teacher should not refer to that fact in criticizing a poorly done bit of homework. If a youngster feels that his parents are getting him in trouble with his teachers, family relationships may be weakened at the very time when they need repair. Moreover, if parents learn that such incidents have taken place, their co-operation with the school will be impaired.

Conferences with parents should not be held in the presence of a young person unless there is a very good reason for him to be present. Certainly, a boy or girl should not be threatened with punishment through his parents. A thoughtful parent would never talk as frankly about his children in their presence as he would in a carefully guarded professional interview. Consider, for example, what would happen in the case of a mother who came to school to complain that a teacher was not making enough allowance for the fact that her daughter had a withered arm. In the daughter's presence, could she discuss freely the girl's attempts to conceal the handicap? Could she agree to a plan that implied a need for change in her own attitude toward the girl?

Children and their parents are entitled to privacy in their relationships. Law courts recognize as inviolable the confidences between husbands and wives. By what right, then, can a teacher or principal try to rip away this protection by forcing children and parents to testify against each other in joint conferences? When conflict in the home is revealed by interviews with either a parent or a child, the problems should be discussed in separate conferences. Neither should be betrayed by a revelation of his statements to the other. The ultimate goal, joint planning by all concerned, is not reached by any such path. Eventually, if the interviews are handled properly, a good relationship should develop. Once in a while, a third party may aid in the process; more often it will be concluded in privacy. Family problems ultimately must be solved within the family.

When parents are to be interviewed, it is often wise to inform the child and to let him know the purpose of the conference. In some instances, especially those arising in a counseling or guidance service, where a youngster feels that a teacher has been a special friend in whom he has confided, it may even be desirable to obtain the young person's permission to talk with his parents.

Whatever the outcome of the interviews, all that has been learned in them remains the property of the parents or the children who did the talking. The interviews were for their benefit alone. Where it is professionally necessary, information may be transmitted confidentially to other professional workers who will work with the family or the child. As far as other people are concerned, whether they be friends or colleagues, the rule should be underlined in words harsh with urgency: Keep your mouth shut.

Home Visits

Local customs differ as to home visits by teachers. In some communities they never take place. In others at the opposite extreme, they may be a matter of ritual. Usually, unless special provision is made, parent-teacher interviews take place in the school building; very rarely, in homes or outside school hours.

Where teachers' visits have an element of rarity or novelty, advance preparation is important. A sudden unannounced call may arouse alarm or anger. In any case, neighborhood customs must be observed. This means that appointments should be made in the same way as for other social engagements, and that a preliminary talk about the purpose of the anticipated discussion will have cleared away fears. A brusque announcement may create anxiety or hostility; a leisurely telephone chat can set the stage for a welcome.

Whenever parents know that a teacher is going to visit them, they are almost sure to try to find out what to expect. The most likely information source is the child. Accordingly, youngsters should be told why the teacher is visiting the home, and what the visit means. This information should be given in rather specific terms. To do otherwise may lead to unfavorable effects.

In fact, any vague notice given too far in advance is likely to create anxiety. For instance, to tell a mother that you want to talk to her about Dorothy's "problems" merely provides a wide field for worried speculation. On the other hand, to tell her that the girl has been daydreaming in class and that you hoped that the two of you might be able to find out the reason would at least narrow the area for her and give her an idea of the probable tenor of the visit. (This assumes that the mother can be relied upon not to take drastic punitive action upon receiving the news.) In those places where a policy of visits to all homes is being inaugurated, it is well to explain that fact to children and parents alike.

More and more schools have discovered that seeing parents only when there is trouble is a dubious procedure. Accordingly, arrangements are made to bring teachers and parents together in a pleasant setting as early as possible in the children's school careers. In some cases, teachers go on duty a week or two before classes begin, and spend part of that time in a regular program of home visits. Such schemes work very well.

A rather common mistake is for teachers to *threaten* to make home visits. In the heat of some classroom incident, they will tell a child that if he repeats his "bad" behavior, they will go to see his parents. The plain meaning is vividly conveyed. Thereafter, to children all future home visits by the teachers are regarded as punishments. This attitude is almost certain to reach the parents. They, too, will look upon a teacher's visit as a disciplinary action rather than a planning conference. Under such circumstances little good can be achieved.

By contrast, the most fruitful approach is for the teacher to act very much as a friendly guest, who has come to enjoy a bit of talk. Anything even suggesting an inspection, an appraisal of the housekeeping, or an attempt to pry may arouse a hostile reaction. The visitor must be sensitive to the community's style of life and must act the part of a social visitor as it is customarily played in the community. Although home visits have a purpose beyond socializing, that purpose cannot be achieved if the parents feel they are being kept at a distance. A successful home visit is a form of neighboring, with all that word implies.

It helps sometimes to reconstruct a scene from the other person's viewpoint. Here, for instance, is how a visit from the teacher looked to Celia Carleton's parents. Celia, age seven, came bouncing in from school with the news, "Mrs. Dalton is coming to our house."

Mrs. Carleton, recalling her own school days, had a sinking feeling. "What have you done?" she demanded.

Celia, well coached at school, said, "Mrs. Dalton is visiting the parents of all the children in our class. She's already been to George Vandermeer's. She said to tell you she'll drop in Thursday night if you will be home, and I told her you would." Celia seemed proud of her efficiency.

That evening at dinner, Mrs. Carleton broke the news to her husband. They debated what could be behind the visit. Finally, he phoned the Vandermeers. They said that the visit to them had been really only a pleasant social call. They told the Carletons not to worry because Mrs. Dalton was nice as could be, a "real homebody."

Despite all these reassurances, Mrs. Carleton went into a frenzy of house cleaning. At the table there were little debates as to what to serve, how to conceal the spots on the big easy chair, and what Mr. Carleton should wear. As the appointed hour drew near, the Carletons sat stiffly waiting. They were relieved when the bell jingled.

Mrs. Dalton introduced herself, talked to Celia about something she had done very well in school, and inquired about the history of a very old Bible. Soon Mrs. Carleton had opened the volume and was proudly telling of the ancestors whose births, marriages, and deaths were

recorded on the inside cover. Mr. Carleton deprecated the enthusiasm
for ancestors and was rewarded with a knowing smile.

The inspection of the Bible led into talk about Mrs. Dalton's childhood community and people she had known. A little later, Celia was
sent to bed. The way she obeyed opened a conversation about her and
how she was doing in school. Mrs. Carleton waited for criticism, but none
came. She brought up the question of Celia's poor penmanship, but the
teacher said that there was nothing to worry about there. In fact, she
politely vetoed the suggestion that Mrs. Carleton coach the girl, and said
it was more important for children to play. This led to some questions
from Mr. Carleton regarding what the school was doing. The teacher
explained the reasons for some recent innovations. The Carletons, now
relaxed, reminisced about their school days. A little later, Mrs. Dalton
took her leave. The Carletons held a brief post-mortem in which they
agreed that they had made a good impression and that Mrs. Dalton was
a very friendly soul. Later, if need be, they would confide in her without
any qualms.

A picture of a different type of home visit, one concerning a serious
problem, has been given by Lane.[6] In this case, the visit was made by a
social worker as part of a program to reach families with children who
seemed headed for serious trouble. Mrs. A's grandson, Martin, had been
misbehaving in school. A letter had been sent, asking her to come to the
office, but she had not responded. A second letter was sent telling her
she would receive a visit, which took place a week after she failed to
keep the office appointment. Here is what the worker reported:

> Mrs. A was awaiting my arrival, and was a bit shy in meeting me. We
> sat in a rather cluttered, clean kitchen. Here and there attempts had
> been made to make the place more presentable. Mrs. A knew of me
> through [the school], and let me know she had stopped by to see [the
> school authorities] the other day, after receiving my letter about the
> home visit, and she had been helped to understand why I was coming.
> I recognized how hard it sometimes is to begin with a new person from
> an unknown agency, and asked her if her not keeping the office
> appointment had been due to her uncertainty about who we were and
> what we did. She nodded agreement to this and said that she had
> thought we would take Martin away from her. I agreed then that not
> coming had been valid, and appreciated this opportunity to tell her

---

6 Lionel C. Lane, "Strengthening the Child's Home; Application of 'Aggressive'
Casework in Preventive Services to the Family and to Children in Their Own
Homes," paper presented at the New York State Conference of Social Work,
November 12, 1951.

more about us. Actually we are interested in helping families remain together, if at all possible, and that was why I had come. At this I felt Mrs. A's warmth toward me and her interest was apparent now. She referred to Martin, telling me he was out working as a shoe shine boy, and then she admitted advising him to stay away from home so that he would miss my visit. I understood her reasons for this, but asked if we could get together to help Martin. I knew about some of the school difficulties Martin had, and wondered if he didn't feel uncomfortable about some of the things he did. Mrs. A admitted not always being able to understand him, but felt he was a good boy and some of his problems stemmed from feelings about his height. We talked of this and other related problems and Mrs. A reviewed at length the tragedy of her daughter's death and her desire to do all she could for the children.

I gave her recognition for all she is doing under trying conditions. I broached the subject of office appointments, and she assured me that Martin would be coming in next week, if I gave him an appointment, now that she knew what we wanted. She was still unsure about her own participation, but agreed to discuss this later on, after we had begun with Martin.

Preparing for a Clinic Referral

For many teachers, an especially trying problem is that of talking with parents whose children need to be referred to a child guidance clinic or some other special agency. At such times, teachers may face the always difficult task of breaking the news about a serious condition. In addition, there is the whole problem of securing necessary consent and then laying the groundwork for genuine co-operation.

One helpful attitude is to sell the agency as a new member of a partnership to help the child. For example, a teacher might say that he needs more help in working with the youngster and then, after showing why this is so, go on to indicate that a specific clinic or social agency can aid both the parent and himself. Needless to say, this implies that the main subject of such an interview is the child and his troubles; not his misdeeds or symptoms, but the weight of his unsolved or unfathomed problems.

Although attention should be kept concentrated on the child, the parents' feelings about the referral must be handled. Often parents will be inclined to resist the idea. They will react with feelings of worry, anger, and shame. They may feel a need for self-justification. Whatever the situation, they should be allowed, even encouraged, to pour out their emotions. Then, they must be helped to see that their fears, hostilities, or self-accusations are natural enough, but should not stand in the way of helping the child to meet his problems.

Quite a few parents in such circumstances will at first deny that their sons or daughters need extra help. Such denials have to be countered with a direct and realistic statement as to why referral is recommended. For instance, if a child shows evidence of deep troubles, an unwilling parent may have to be told, "Your Charlie may be a very sick boy," and then given the evidence.

Sticking to one's guns at the same time that the parents' feelings about the situation are being sympathetically received calls for single-mindedness and courage. Tempting as it may be to please the parents, there must be no backing down on the main point—the child needs help that the clinic can give.

It is much easier to do this job well if the parent does not feel that the referral involves or implies criticism. For many teachers, especially those most likely to want to secure help for children, it is difficult to avoid subtle signals that in fact they do feel the parents are to blame. Here teachers may be hampered by an attitude described by Szurek:[7]

> Persons attracted to therapeutic work with children's problems often have a basic overidentification with the child. This attitude seems to imply that the parent is the enemy of the child; that the parent should be shamed or subtly coerced into a more generous and kindly treatment of the child; or that the child must be protected against the bottomless hatred of the parent. Most persons who bring their children to psychiatric clinics are already self-critical, although defensive, and this overidentification of the therapist with the child only tends to increase the parents' conflict.

Certainly, in dealing with parents, referral should never be used as a threat. Rather, parents should be helped to realize that their own problems are appreciated. If they fear they made errors in child raising, there was a reason for what they did, a humanly understandable reason. Now, they can find a new basis for feeling that they are good parents and have cause for pride. Going through with the referral can bring them grounds for greater self-respect.

We must remember that the goal of referral is successful treatment, which requires a long period of co-operation between the parents and the

---

[7] S. A. Szurek, "Problems around Psychotherapy with Children," *Journal of Pediatrics*, Vol. 37 (1950), pp. 671-78.

new agency. Therefore, we must not lead them to expect miracles. Rather, we must build very realistic expectations. In advance, parents should be given a fairly good notion of their probable reception by the clinic, the length of any waiting period, the probable duration and success of treatment, and the ups and downs to be expected.

Once a referral is made, teachers should support their new partners. In conferences with the parents, teachers should display faith in the training and judgment of the clinic workers. Never should they directly or indirectly support the parents in terminating treatment before it is completed.

It should be kept in mind that parents of children with serious problems very often have their own problems. Even if they are eager to co-operate in plans to aid their children, they may find it very difficult to do so. Their own inner conflicts may be the real reason they now have emotionally troubled youngsters. Events in the course of treatment for their children may disturb them. If they want to pour out their hurt feelings, that is one thing. However, if they want to interrupt extra help for their children and seek the support of the school in doing so, in all but the most exceptional cases the answer should be a direct warning that such action would not be for the good of the child and that the parents alone will be responsible for the consequences.

Whether the parents co-operate fully or not, it is wise to show follow-up interest without seeming to pry. This will give them a chance to bolster their pride. It will reassure them as to their standing. In cases where resistance to treatment is rising, it will give them a chance to talk out their feelings.

Parents in Groups

Parent-teacher organizations, mothers' clubs, or similar groups are found in many school systems. In a group setting much can be done which will influence the mental well-being of children. The good that can come out of such organizations is obvious. Sometimes, as a result of errors, this good is not fully achieved. A teacher who is working with such groups, a principal whom they may consult, or a speaker who appears at meetings should keep a few things in mind lest progress be impeded.

Any group is likely to contain cliques which get along only with some friction. For a teacher or principal to become allied with any one clique is a serious mistake. This will not only cut lines of communication within the organization but will also poison the atmosphere of such in-

TABLE 8   *Attitude toward classes in child care for parents*

GROUP	PERCENTAGES		
	In favor	*Opposed*	*Undecided*
People of college education	69.7	18.2	12.1
High school graduates	51.8	24.8	23.4
Democrats	62.8	15.1	22.1
Republicans	52.9	20.6	26.5
Veterans	70.5	18.0	11.5
Union members	52.2	30.4	17.4

dividual interviews as teachers may hold later with parents of either clique.

It is always tempting to mention particular children to the group. This should be done very carefully. Few people are so tactless as to speak of a child's "bad" qualities in a public meeting. However, feelings may be as badly hurt when one or two children are singled out for praise. As soon as this is done, most proud parents want to have the group told about their children. Moreover, we should remember that the parents we want to have at the meetings are not only those whose children are bright and doing well, but those whose children have troubles which can best be tackled by co-operative planning. If praise for a few star performers will alienate them, as it may, it does more harm than good.

It is important to recognize that there is a growing public awareness of the need for learning more about children. This is illustrated in Table 8, which reports the answers of citizens in Peekskill, New York, to the question, asked by Hedlund,[8] "Would you be in favor of spending public money to add the following service to those now offered by the Peekskill Public Schools: Training in child care for parents of young children?"

Parents' groups do most good when they have a genial atmosphere. Actually, they represent a transplanting into the school of the neighborhood's feelings. Therefore, it is the cultural amenities of that neighborhood which should prevail. An attempt to use the group to teach parents "better" ways of social living is likely to backfire. If members feel stilted and ill at ease, they will embrace excuses for staying away.

Another common error derives from fears that the parents will

[8] Paul A. Hedlund, *Measuring Public Opinion on School Issues,* unpublished Ed.D. project, Teachers College, Columbia University, 1947.

meddle in school affairs. To prevent this, a school administrator may get the group involved in fund-raising activities or in securing things for the school. Once in a while, someone will see in a meeting merely a nice batch of votes. To be sure, instruction in a school goes more smoothly if there are extra projectors or playback machines; the school auditorium looks lovelier with new curtains or new drapes; and politicians who depend on parent support may vote better budgets. However, the real work of such groups is to bring about co-operative action for the children. It is better to deal directly with this possibility and to show appreciation for the parents' interest in their sons and daughters than to divert the group into time-consuming side issues.

Parents and teachers are tempted to rely heavily on outside speakers in planning programs. Although some experts can add spice to a meeting and may initially stimulate attendance, it should be emphasized that often more good is accomplished by a discussion in which the experience of the parents and teachers can be pooled. Every group contains some people who, if given the opportunity and encouragement, make excellent discussion leaders.

The existence of parents' groups is a golden opportunity. If they can be encouraged to concentrate on child study, problems arising in home situations can be reduced. Mental health instruction is most effective when it is being applied in parent-child relationships. In any community there are many resources from which parents may secure help. Teachers and principals may not only be of direct assistance but may also help the groups to find and use other sources of help and information.

The ultimate measure which schools may take to strengthen a child's mental health is to work with his parents. The goals are to improve home conditions by increasing the parents' understanding of their children and to obtain better school conditions by giving teachers new insights. Working with parents is a two-way affair in which mutual respect is essential. When this is obtained, then life may become much more livable for young people. They will benefit from co-operative planning instead of being torn by conflict as their grownups work at cross-purposes.

ADDITIONAL READINGS

Baruch, Dorothy W. *Parents and Children Go to School.* Chicago: Scott, Foresman, 1939. A book on school-parent relations.
Brown, Muriel W. *Partners in Education.* Washington: Association for

Childhood Education International, 1950. Discusses parent-teacher relationships.

Buhler, Charlotte, Faith Smitter, and Sybil Richardson. *Childhood Problems and the Teacher*. New York: Holt, 1952, Chap. 12. Case illustrations point up some basic principles of working with parents.

Cunningham, Ruth, and Associates. *Understanding Group Behavior of Boys and Girls*. New York: Teachers College, Columbia U., 1951, Chap. 10. Tells about co-operative relations between school and parents built up in the course of a study in Denver.

Gabbard, Hazel F. *Working with Parents*. U. S. Office of Education, Bulletin No. 7, 1948. Washington: Government Printing Office, 1950. A handbook which can serve as a source of suggestions.

Gruenberg, Sidonie. *We, the Parents*. New York: Harper, 1939. A book designed to bring greater understanding to parents.

Hymes, James L., Jr. *Effective Home-School Relations*. Englewood Cliffs, N. J.: Prentice-Hall, 1953. A book describing what teachers can do.

Jenkins, David H., and Ronald Lippitt. *Interpersonal Perceptions of Teachers, Students and Parents*. Washington: Division of Adult Education Service, National Education Association, 1951. A booklet reporting a research to ferret out how each of the groups named saw the others and thought it was seen by the others.

Langdon, Grace, and Irving W. Stout. *Teacher-Parent Interviews*. Englewood Cliffs, N. J.: Prentice-Hall, 1954. Several types of interviews are analyzed and suggestions for improving them are offered.

Lee, J. Murray, and Dorris May Lee. *The Child and His Development*. New York: Appleton-Century-Crofts, 1958, Chap. 18. The topic here is parent-teacher relations.

Lindgren, Henry Clay. *Mental Health in Education*. New York: Holt, 1954, Chap. 14. Relations with parents are considered.

McQuinn, Jim, and Dorothy McQuinn. *Parents Can't Win*. New York: Pellegrini & Cudahy, 1947. A collection of cartoons depicting problems of parenthood.

Staff Members of the Child Study Association of America. *Parents' Questions*. New York: Harper, 1947. Deals with matters of frequent concern to parents.

AUDIO-VISUAL AIDS

Farewell to Childhood, a 25-minute sound film produced by the North Carolina Board of Health, in which the concern of parents about their adolescent daughter and her counselor at school is portrayed.

chapter **18**

TEACHERS' PROBLEMS

In our modern world, each occupation and way of life poses its own special psychological problems and has its own special advantages. The farmer cultivating a field in comparative solitude, the salesman being jolly no matter how he feels inside, the factory worker staying on good terms with the other girls in her department, the housewife dusting mournfully while listening to a soap opera, the live-wire advertising executive nursing ulcers—all have unique satisfactions and yet all wrestle with more or less troublesome difficulties pertaining to their past and their present. Although some people simply drift into an occupation and a way of life, for most of us there were motivations which influenced the choice of a life pattern. These may help to make the working part of life a source of deep pleasure; they may also lead to dissatisfactions, which may be a part of that pattern as it works out. In practically every occupation, moreover, there are relationships with other people which contain elements of both enjoyment and tension.[1]

Over and beyond the normal range of problems most people face, there are special problems arising in certain occupations and professions where the individual's main working tool is his own personality. Just as a carpenter uses a hammer and nails to build the frame of a house, so the physician uses his manner of behavior to create confidence and to arouse the sense of urgency that will make a patient follow his advice. The professional man or woman consciously modifies his personality to

---

[1] For one illustration of the many studies designed to find the link between personality and job satisfaction, see the following report on people engaged in routine clerical work: Solis L. Kates, "Rorschach Responses Related to Vocational Interests and Job Satisfaction," *Psychological Monographs,* Vol. 64 (1950), No. 309.

obtain results for the good of his client. In this sense, then, teaching is a profession and carries with it the special mental health problems and opportunities of all such occupations. It involves its own strains on personal inclinations.

The significance of "personality" as an indispensable factor in good teaching has long been recognized. Sometimes we find it expressed in off-the-cuff terms, full of hopes and prejudices; a statement from eighteenth-century France, for example, held that ideal teachers would be found among "those young ladies of quality who, having good birth, sensitivity, and a certain education, combine the most noble heart with a cultivated mind and are free of that taste for trifles which renders most women unfit for so important a task."[2] Equally sweeping judgments are still found, though stated in "modern" terms.

Somewhat more objectively and scientifically, we get pictures like that drawn by Bush[3] after an intensive study of eight teachers at a small private boys' school in western United States. Although each teacher has his own unique pattern of characteristics, Bush came to the following general conclusion:

> This study suggests that student-teacher relationships are at a maximum of effectiveness when a teacher is well-adjusted to his job, likes his students personally, spends much time counseling with them, understands them and their problems, knows them individually and thinks they are academically well adjusted.

Among the millions of teachers in the world, a large number discover that their occupation makes life more interesting and more worth living. But even though the good points outweigh the bad, the unfortunate aspects are still annoying. Very much as a man or woman complains of having constant headaches, although the pain endures but an hour or two in a week, the dissatisfactions of teachers are more likely to be talked about and thought about than the moments of comfort and pleasure. For this reason this chapter will deal largely with troublesome aspects of teachers' professional lives. It will be useful, however, to look first at some of the reasons for entering the teaching profession. This will help to portray the motivations which are at work—both those which teaching will ultimately satisfy and those which are doomed to go unmet when expectations prove unrealistic.

---

[2] *Plan Général d'Institution, particulièrement destiné pour la Jeunesse du Ressort de Parlement de Bourgogne,* Dijon, Chez Causse, 1763.

[3] Robert Nelson Bush, *A Study of Student-Teacher Relationships,* unpublished Ed.D. dissertation, Stanford University, 1941.

Reasons for Choice of Teaching

A person's choice of occupation frequently has a good deal of high ardor behind it. The motivations for the selection are deeply planted in the personality structure. They may have much to do with the satisfaction he gets out of adult living. Certainly, they profoundly influence the way he works. In perusing the list below, the reader must realize that it is rare for a person to become a teacher for any single one of the reasons named or for all of them combined. Most teachers make their choice out of a combination of motives. The list is not a complete one nor is it in order of frequency or importance; undoubtedly there are teachers whose choice could not be accounted for by any of the motives given. However, all are reasonably common.

STATUS.   Teaching, for many people, is a symbol of middle-class status. It is a respectable job, and in every survey of public opinion ranks well toward the top of respected occupations. Many teachers seek the field because it means they will have a secure standing among their acquaintances.

FAMILY PRESSURE.   Linked with the above is the fact that the status of teaching may be valued by the family; having a son or daughter become a teacher may be a family ambition. For many, then, going into teaching is a way of retaining the affection of their parents. Some accept the goal as their own, and wholeheartedly enter the field. Others may have been divided in their preference, but, as a final demonstration that they were good boys and good girls, have done as they were told.

LOVE FOR SUBJECT FIELD.   In school, especially high school or college, a number of youngsters develop real affection for some field of study. This may be a field in which they have done particularly well or which has some special appeal. Teaching is often the most likely way in which to make a living while continuing with the beloved subject.

IDENTIFICATION WITH A FORMER TEACHER.   Interest in a subject is often the result of having identified with a teacher of that subject. In any event, many young people have admired some teacher, often a relative or friend of the family, frequently one who taught them. Admiration gives way to the wish to be like that person. Entering the same profession can be a step in that direction.

LOVE OF CHILDREN.   A significant number of men and women enjoy being with young people. They may find that they are skillful at working with children and that they enjoy the experience. Perhaps an opportunity to teach a Sunday school class, act as counselor at a camp, or lead a youth group has been for them a self-revealing experience. Many girls like to care for babies; caring for children may symbolize a more complete womanhood. Being a teacher is a way of having children to love.

FUN IN TEACHING.   There are many occasions inside and outside school when young people instruct each other. In high school groups, there is always a certain amount of informal tutoring. Young people teach each other how to play games, and in long bull sessions work out the meaning of ideas. Some discover that they enjoy intellectual leadership. Just as a girl "fooling around" in a kitchen may gain a joy from craftsmanship in cooking, so others come to relish success in helping people to learn, and turn to the teaching profession as a lifework.

HELPING TO BUILD A BETTER WORLD.   One of youth's most precious qualities is the idealism which makes them want to fight evil and reform the world. That wish lives on for many people. Some continue to feel it as the most important thing in life. The fact that each generation of children becomes the next generation of parents and citizens invests teaching with practical significance as a way of improving the world.

SELF-SACRIFICE FOR AN IDEAL.   For some, the desire to make the world better is coupled with a need to devote themselves to an ideal or a way of life. They feel that they must renounce some of the worldly pleasures. Consequently, some willingly accept popular beliefs that teachers are poorly paid or unlikely to marry, and enter teaching in a spirit of self-sacrifice. We cannot forget that huge systems of parochial schools, notably those maintained by Roman Catholics, are staffed with members of teaching orders, men and women who are expressing their religious fervor by embracing ascetic ways and devoting themselves to the instruction of youth.

CORRECTING THE SHORTCOMINGS OF ONE'S OWN PAST.   During the years of development, quite a few people have encountered unsatisfactory environments or poor relationships with grownups. These dissatisfactions may have left a mark upon them; they may feel a need to go back and rewrite that chapter in their history. Teaching may be a way to do just that. For example, one encounters teachers who were hurt by poor methods used when they went to school. Some act as though their main reason for teaching is to show their former instructors how the job should be done. Another illustration is offered by the men or women still tortured by guilt over past quarrels with brothers or sisters. They now use teaching as a way of being nice to other young people and thus making up for acts or feelings about which they are guilty.

RELIVING CHILDHOOD PATTERNS.   It may be pleasant to be an adult, but in a number of lives some period of early development may have yielded more satisfactions or been marked by fewer conflicts than any subsequent phase. A chance to relive that earlier period seems inviting. Without surrendering dangerously to regression, a teacher has that opportunity. This is often the reason why a teacher has a marked preference for one age group. Thus, for instance, a high school coach can live over and over again the glories of his own triumphs on the basketball court. The same thing applies to all grade levels. As was pointed out earlier, the ability to feel at one with youngsters may be a highly valuable quality for teachers.

DESIRE FOR AFFECTION.   A large number of adults are starved for affection. They enjoy the feeling that someone is fond of them. A teacher has contact with many children and knows that they are likely to return good feeling. This possibility makes the educational profession especially attractive for some persons.

NEED FOR SECURITY.   As recent studies of college students have revealed, an increasing number of educated men and women are showing a preoccupation with mankind's old search for security. Teaching offers steady employment and, in many districts, the possibility of a pension. Furthermore, tenure regulations provide extra protection. Such safety is highly valued.

HALFWAY HOUSE TO OTHER AMBITION.   Because of the security and the steady income, we find that teaching attracts a number of people who have other ambitions but want to be assured of a livelihood. A number of young people work out life plans in which the first step is to become a teacher; the next step, to go to some other field. Such plans frequently work well, as may be illustrated by the fact that every recent Congress of the United States has included at least ten former teachers.

More typical, perhaps, is the young lady who was intent on becoming a great writer, but went into teaching so she would be "able to eat." A number of such people enjoy teaching and remain in the field; others fail to reach their original goal and make the best of the situation; still others leave the teaching field.

NEED FOR POWER AND GROUP LEADERSHIP.   Many people feel complete only when they can exercise influence, when they can see other people affected by what they do. Although teaching would never satisfy a Napoleon, it does promise many chances for leadership. Furthermore, the youthfulness of a school's clientele makes the establishment of power a certainty. Even though there are some teachers who do hate children and get satisfaction from making their lives miserable, the exercise of power in schools is usually felt as being for the good of the children. It does not entail the direct destructiveness and ruthless competition which make the winning of domination a source of moral conflict in some other occupations.

In a study of qualities linked to effectiveness in teaching, Ryans[4] reported that a dominant personality was found among teachers rated as effective. Here is his description of that characteristic:

> *Dominant.* People scoring high on this factor think of themselves as leaders, capable of taking initiative and responsibility. They are *not* domineering. They enjoy public speaking, organizing social activities, promoting projects, and persuading others.

GUARANTEED SUPERIORITY.   To a rather large group, another attraction is that in the classroom the teacher is clearly the most well informed, the most mature, and the most skillful person. The man or woman who has inferiority feelings, who doubts his own worth, can be reassured day after day during school hours. It is a guarantee that there will be one area in life where he is the best.

A similar analysis could be made for any other profession. A study of why psychologists become psychologists might yield equally fascinating or uncomfortable discoveries. Our purpose, however, is not to compare professions or to debunk claims to virtue, but to understand teachers' motivations. What led a person to enter a profession is sig-

---

[4] David G. Ryans, "A Study of the Extent of Association of Certain Professional and Personal Data with Judged Effectiveness of Teacher Behavior," *Journal of Experimental Education,* Vol. 20 (1951), pp. 67-77.

nificant only if it increases our understanding of his present actions and feelings.

The Changes Time Brings

The psychological forces that make a teacher choose his or her vocation may not remain fixed; often they continue to change and develop. The psychological meaning the job has also shifts as one becomes immersed in the day-to-day work. For a great many education students, becoming a teacher is a goal; once that goal is reached, they need to find something else at which to aim. Perhaps in their daydreams the moment they face a class is the point where they end the story with the fairy-tale tagline, "They lived happily ever after." In this section we want to look at a few of the possible outcomes arising when the motivations we have been describing collide with the realities of teachers' lives.

SATISFACTORY ADJUSTMENT TO THE REALITIES.   It is important to realize that each of the motives we have listed for joining the educational profession may serve as a start for a happy and useful professional life. What matters is the way the reason is applied. In some instances the reason for choosing the profession blends into a sublimation, which we have already shown to be a way of turning possibly harmful impulses into praiseworthy life patterns. Or a teacher may integrate his principal reason for entering the profession into a larger and more complex structure of goals and ideals. The end product can be a well-rounded life in and out of school.

The prevalence of this development, in which teaching becomes one facet of a rounded, satisfactory life, is indicated in a study by Cohart.[5] She had the classroom conduct of a total of more than two hundred kindergarten, first-grade, and second-grade teachers in Connecticut and New York rated by principals and supervisors. The teachers were divided into the highest 20 per cent, a middle 60 per cent, and the lowest 20 per cent. All were given two personality tests. The results, as they were interpreted, showed that the very good teachers were emotionally more secure. They had greater maturity, more interest in

---

[5] Mary Cohart, *The Differential Value of the Group Rorschach and the MMPI in the Evaluation of Teacher Personality,* unpublished Ph.D. dissertation, Yale University, 1952.

people, and a larger capacity for channeling impulses into constructive forms of activity.

Here, in the form of an individual's story, is an example of a good adjustment involving teaching:

When Frances Davis was a little girl even her mother thought she was bossy. In play groups, it was she who decided what games her playmates would play. She was either the mother, the nurse, or the teacher in games of make-believe. Throughout her school career, she almost always took the lead in activities. Once in a while there were quarrels, and she would be left alone. From these she learned to watch the way she gave directions and to be careful to build up the self-esteem of her friends. She became not less dominating but more adroit. To everyone it seemed natural for her to go into teaching. At first she repeated her old mistake of being too bossy, but again learned quickly from the way children reacted. Today if you were to see her walk into a classroom, you would realize that she knows exactly what she wants to do. She is clearly happy on her "home grounds." She has learned to enjoy being responsible for a group which is working happily and which she is adroitly helping to overcome obstacles. Among the faculty she has the reputation of being an excellent and considerate chairman of committees. Everyone agrees that when she is involved in any project, things move smoothly. Each year as the summer vacation draws to an end, she looks forward to the opening of school.

Like Frances Davis, many teachers gain satisfaction from teaching while giving priority to the growth needs of young learners. In their lives they have a balanced feeling of well-being. For such people, the inevitable conflicts and frustrations of the job represent a price they are willing and able to pay for having a happy time at work. Indeed, for some, paying the price may enhance the personal significance of their life patterns. It is only thus that we can account for such apparent anomalies as teachers who turn down more remunerative administrative posts, those who seek out the unusually difficult groups of problem children, and those who fight to postpone retirement on well-earned pensions.

When Frierson[6] made a study of turnover among 145 graduates in elementary education from Ohio State University from 1941 to 1947, she found the major sources of satisfaction they listed were—

---

[6] Marguerite Shepard Frierson, *A Study of Mental Health Problems as They Have Related to Turnover among One Hundred Forty-Five Elementary Teachers,* unpublished Ph.D. dissertation, Ohio State University, 1950.

1. Love of children
2. Interest in the development of children through guidance
3. Pleasant association with other teachers
4. Appreciative attitude of students
5. Freedom to experiment with new ideas
6. Co-operation from parents and other adults in the community
7. Favorable geographical location

There are thus some fortunate teachers for whom life's changes bring increasing satisfactions. For them, the reality is richer than their first hopes, excitement increases with knowledge and skill, and they see more in children than they had dreamed. To such lucky individuals, teaching may be an ever better balance wheel for mental health. For the many others, teaching may be a source of difficulty.

CONFLICT BETWEEN EXPECTATION AND REALITY. At times, of course, the motives which draw a person into teaching make for trouble. In some instances, the underlying motives create personal pressures which make it impossible to give priority to the needs of children or which lead to hostile interference with children's growth patterns. Thus, a teacher who seeks affection and goes out of her way to be nice to children may feel bitter when their preoccupation with each other makes them seem ungrateful toward her. The bitterness may lead to an inclination to punish them by increasing the number or severity of restrictions.

For others, the job itself is quite likely to prove unsatisfying. For example, the person who wanted to influence or improve children may be irked by the fact that youngsters with low I.Q.'s seemingly refuse to learn. In such instances, disappointment is inevitable; the sad ending of the story sees a soured man or woman either quitting the profession or, worse yet, dragging along wearily and cynically through the years, venting spite on hapless youngsters and colleagues.

Other reasons for becoming a teacher may prove a handicap. The wish to be popular may make teachers into "softies" who cannot bring themselves to risk resentment by placing needed limits on undesired behavior. The unfortunate victims either fail to overcome the frustrations inherent in the work or establish a one-sided relationship to children which invites chaos and poor learning. For all these people, teaching may threaten to poison life.

In many cases, the effects are far less drastic. Among a person's many needs, most may be well met by teaching, and yet one item in the total pattern may cause some strain. Such, for instance, was the case with a teacher, F, described by Pinkham.[7] In general, she enjoyed teaching and was outstanding in her knowledge of the students in her typing classes. However, she knew more about the students she liked most than those she liked least. The latter proved to be "lazy" students, those who seemed to lack effort and persistently required prodding. These qualities she found both annoying and difficult to understand.

Another, and probably more prevalent, situation occurs when the work of teaching is pleasurable, but teachers find themselves economically undervalued. They discover they have the social status they wanted but not the money to go with it. In a study of superintendents, Seeman[8] noted that this combination tended to make an individual set himself apart from other people. He would begin to restrict his personal social life to others in the same profession. He also was likely to resist changes and to take a dominating attitude in his work. The prevalence of this situation was noted in a study by Naramore.[9] In a questionnaire study reaching one out of every ten classroom teachers in Connecticut, he found that although most teachers were generally satisfied with their jobs, fifty-nine per cent felt that salaries were inadequate.

One of the most obvious changes that teaching experience brings is the realization that the teacher's work involves much more than people think it does. There are reports to write, obdurate parents to interview, lunchrooms to supervise, and standards to meet. Lesson plans go to pieces against the hard rocks of psychological reality. When the bubble breaks, the victim moans, "Why didn't someone tell me it would be like this?" Then comes the hard work of rearranging ideas and ideals to fit the professional world as it is.

It is at this point that many quit. In a study of a group of 543 young women qualified to teach home economics, Coppola[10] found that the

---

[7] Fred O. Pinkham, *Teacher Performance in Pupil-Teacher Relationships,* unpublished Ed.D. dissertation, Stanford University, 1950.

[8] Melvin Seeman, *A Status Factor Approach to Leadership,* Columbus, Personnel Research Board, Ohio State University, 1950.

[9] Lloyd S. Naramore, Sr., *An Inquiry into the Attitudes of Classroom Teachers in Public Schools toward Some Professional Problems,* unpublished Ph.D. dissertation, Yale University, 1951.

[10] Theresa M. Coppola, *Dominant Factors Influencing Acceptance of Home Economics Teaching Positions by Young Women Trained for the Profession,* unpublished Ed.D. dissertation, Syracuse University, 1951.

second year after graduation 155 had no position. Of these, 63 per cent did not want to teach. Major reasons for this decision included these: the young women felt too many demands were made of them, they thought teaching took too much time, and they felt they could not be successful teachers.

In an analysis of the difficulties reported during their first year of teaching by 95 beginning secondary school teachers from the Appalachian State Teachers College in North Carolina, Wey[11] found the three most frequent types of problems were (1) control and discipline, (2) adjusting to deficiencies in facilities, and (3) personal living problems connected with their assignments.

The comparatively low pay, particularly in view of the scale of living which our culture expects teachers to exemplify, makes many seek and hold additional employment. In replies received to questionnaires mailed to 15 per cent of the teachers in Detroit and its suburbs, Berry[12] found that 76 per cent of the men and 21 per cent of the women reported income from outside employment. "Economic necessity" was the most frequent reason given. The majority (67 per cent) of the group with outside employment were married. Clearly, a life pattern in which leisure time and opportunity for reading are curtailed may become quite wearying.

In all these ways, the romance many once attached to teaching rubs off. Intimacy with teachers and teaching destroys illusions and misapprehensions. This is not always a bad thing, but it does make problems for a number of people. Naturally, if they can work out a good adjustment to their changed and more realistic concept, they may gain an even deeper satisfaction.

For a number of teachers, the reality of working with children is far from being a shock. Rather, they find their first years full of excitement. As they meet challenges to their intellectual or emotional mastery, they glow with pride. As new discoveries follow each other, they figuratively eat, drink, dream, and talk teaching. Unfortunately, this does not always last. Gradually they get used to children and work out stock

[11] Herbert W. Wey, "A Study of the Difficulties of Student-Teachers and Beginning Teachers in the Secondary Schools as a Basis for the Improvement of Teacher Education," *Educational Administration and Supervision,* Vol. 37 (1951), pp. 98-107.

[12] James David Berry, *The Socio-Economic Status of the Classroom Teacher in Detroit with Especial Emphasis on Extra-Contractual Income and Its Implications,* Ed.D. dissertation, Wayne University, 1952, University Microfilms Publication No. 4297.

techniques for problems which daily become more familiar. The fine excitement ebbs, and in its place there can come the boredom of dreary routine.

MODIFICATION OF MOTIVES.   The processes of psychological growth continue to work throughout an individual's life. As we grow older, our needs change. Accordingly, the satisfactions which we once craved and which led us into teaching may become less important as new needs clamor to be satisfied. Possibly, the same old need may grow in a way which cannot be satisfied in the classroom. For example, the desire to have power over people, which once made managing a class look like fun, now may demand a wider field for conquest.

Then again, the need we once thought to satisfy by teaching may be met in other ways. Teaching loses its emotional significance as it becomes a side issue. Thus, for instance, the young man or woman who once was starved for affection and counted on getting it from children may develop a circle of companions whose close friendship is more warming than the affection of children. Now the ties of a juvenile group seem pallid, unworthy of effort.

The meaning which children may have in an adult's personal life may also change. One example, which has been overemphasized in popular literature, is that of the young woman who originally saw in her pupils the foreshadows of sons or daughters she expected to have, but gradually comes to see in them bitter reminders that life has denied her hopes for romance. Much more commonplace is the almost universal situation, previously described, of children taking on the qualities of obstacles standing in the way of professional success.

Administrative changes can take their toll. A teacher who once found satisfaction in working with one age group or in a particular assignment may fall victim to professional opinions which attribute greater prestige to another age group or a different type of teaching. Then, either on his own volition or on the initiative of an administrator, he may leave the type of teaching in which he was happy and move into a post where satisfaction is lost. The actual situation may not be recognized; instead the feelings of discouragement may be directed against teaching as an occupation.

Other community pressures may also force teachers into roles they do not want. The basketball coach who revels in working with a team may make his own life miserable trying to be a witty luncheon-club speaker. The gay, enthusiastic new teacher may hate herself when she has to become a stern disciplinarian. The tenderhearted counselor may feel a deep dishonesty in assuming, toward children of a minority group, a casehardened cynicism, which he begins to accept because it is displayed by "everyone who really matters."

Although in every school system there are some teachers whose lives center around their work, others discover that there is much more to living. Instead of finding their spare time filled with thoughts of teaching, they find that problems from outside school intrude into the classroom hours. If there was ever an expectation that teaching would meet most of life's needs, it evaporates.

Illustrative of the hazards of change is the story of Calvin Muir, a once-proud music teacher. When he first came to Blainesburg, his popularity and his joy grew by leaps and bounds. He liked adolescents, he basked in the praise of the superintendent, and he expanded at the sound of his first bands playing well. For a few years, that was all he wanted. Whether it was the urging of his wife or his own self-intoxication at being hailed by his fellow citizens, no one knew for sure, but when he was in his early thirties he began to hunger for bigger worlds to conquer. Money bulked larger in his talk. He became jealous of the athletic coach, he insisted on entering state music competitions, and he began giving music lessons in his spare time. To forestall interference from the superintendent, he organized a group of friends and parents to back him in battles within the school board. He became a wily, ruthless fighter who was the storm center of several nasty fights. Two superintendents who fought against him had to resign. Yet his satisfaction faded as he lost friends in the faculty. Bitterest blow of all, no band of his ever won a first prize. To bolster his self-importance he began to circulate fictions of triumphs elsewhere. He now spends his summers playing in orchestras in summer resorts, and frantically tries to develop schemes which will produce lucrative work or fame in show business.

Common Frustrations in Teaching

The problems pictured in the previous pages are highly personal in the sense that they pertain to motivations which will vary from individual to individual. No matter how successfully teachers may adjust to changes in motivation or to the conflict between their hopes and reality, there are a number of frustrations and problems which are almost universal. In one way or another, these must be faced by practically all members of the teaching profession.

ASSUMING A "FALSE" PERSONALITY.   In the interest of maintaining a desired classroom atmosphere, most teachers find themselves at times either concealing their true feelings or simulating attitudes they do not really have. They may act cheerful or confident when they are really worried or frightened. They may feign interest in materials with which they are bored. They may work up enthusiasm for youthful productions they regard as ludicrous. In short, they assume in the classroom a personality which is bound to be somewhat artificial, put on consciously because it helps with the job. By the same token, impulses which could be allowed freedom elsewhere must be blocked in the classroom.

SOME TYPICAL CONFLICTS.   Teachers who have true professional spirit recognize that the needs of the children should have priority over their own personal wants. This is bound to produce some conflict. At times the contradictions are obvious and dramatic, as they are when a kindergarten teacher with a headache longs for quiet but leads the children in exuberant play because she knows they need plenty of activity. Holding her irritability in check is quite a strain, and we would not be surprised if once in a while she lost a battle with herself. Sometimes the conflict is not quite so obvious; a teacher, angered at some piece of juvenile nastiness, may force himself to inhibit his urge to hand out punishment, and instead deliberately ignore an incident or with forced calm divert the offender to other activity.

For reasons often hard to determine, some child may tempt a teacher to be unfair. Possibly a girl belongs to a nationality, race, or religion against which the teacher cannot help but harbor prejudice. Possibly a face or mannerism awakens echoes of some unpleasant event in the past. Perhaps the child's life symbolizes a pattern of pleasure which was denied to the teacher. The opposite may also be true—a teacher may find his heart going out to a youngster he finds especially appealing. Yet along with such feelings runs the conscious realization that it is bad to be unfair or to have pets, that this could create problems for both the child and the class. The teacher, then, is left struggling with the dilemma of how to handle his feelings and still live up to ideals of fair play and justice.

In schools where teachers come in contact with children very different from themselves in upbringing, there are the additional problems of accepting the differences without surrendering the teachers' own values. For instance, an ardent prohibitionist may have to meet without repugnance parents who, she knows, drink heavily, see them as partners working sincerely for the benefit of their children, and still hold true to her feelings about the use of alcohol. Differences in moral codes, different standards of cleanliness, and different social customs may be troublesome to many fine people.

Another problem requiring restraint occurs in a school where the staff is divided into warring factions or where one or more members of the staff are disliked. Most teachers would agree that such divisions should not be aired before children. Yet it is only facing facts to state that when one adult is angered at another, he will want to vent that anger, and is likely to find relief in making either open complaints or sly digs. We might agree such a tendency ought not to exist, but it does. Holding it in check is necessary, but that very action means bottling up emotional pressure.

THWARTED AIMS.   In their daydreams many teachers have seen themselves doing wonders in raising levels of skill and knowledge. Scores on objective tests or examinations are considered the simplest measures of such success. Often, the principal or the community will judge a teacher by those standards. Unfortunately, not all children oblige by learning easily. Some have low learning ability; others are not interested; still others suffer from emotional upsets. For those teachers who keep their eyes fixed on set subject-matter standards, the children seem to stand in the way. They take on the psychological aspect of being obstacles, obstinate barriers to success. Not only are the teachers frustrated, but the children are the source of their frustrations. The emotional toll for teacher and students alike can be very high.

Even when a teacher's aims are seen in terms of personality development for the children, failure may be unmistakable at times. His ambitions for the children in his room may outrun his power to accomplish what he hopes. For instance, Alma was an intelligent girl who, her teacher thought, could become a bright and socially alert secretary if only she had a little ambition. Despite several heart-to-heart talks, the girl blithely left school on her seventeenth birthday to become an unskilled domestic servant. Every such incident—and they are frequent—means dissatisfaction for a teacher. Stubborn reality makes this type of frustration an inevitable part of education.

It is very difficult to judge success in helping children to develop and grow. There are no clear criteria to tell us what has been accomplished. Many a day, some teachers have gone home wondering what really happened, whether some incident was helpful or harmful. Truly, success can be invisible, and that is small satisfaction.

One possible effect of this was mentioned by Terrien[13] who made a study of approximately 10 per cent of all the teachers in the New Haven, Connecticut, schools. He noted—

> The teachers in this sample frequently mentioned as a disadvantage of their work the fact that all their efforts depended on someone else, and that they had no way to measure the results of their work. . . . The tendency for teachers to be dogmatic and authoritarian may be, in part, compensation for this lack of observable results of their best efforts.

Objective conditions may raise obstacles. Too many teachers have too many children in their classes. Too often, there is too little equipment. When a teacher knows what can be done under good conditions, the poor results achieved in unfavorable conditions are irksome. Equally disturbing is being forced to use procedures which are second-rate. The new teacher in a standpat system who has to do things he knows are ineffective, or worse than ineffective, finds teaching a moral trial. When community pressures or expectations force a staff to ignore their own professional understanding, the result is a new set of frustrations. Yet, across the country, there are thousands of educators itching to make improvements and to try out new ideas, who have to hold themselves back in the face of subtle pressures or stern edicts.

WHAT PART OF YOURSELF CAN YOU BE?   An age-old barrier to happiness for teachers has been the tradition that they must set an example to youth, and therefore must accept stringent limitations on their personal lives. In large cities, such demands rarely operate away from the school, but they are still strict in many smaller communities. However, even if boards of education were to grant complete freedom, many teachers would still feel constrained. They would recognize that some children would choose them as objects of identification and, consequently, would want to exemplify especially high standards of conduct.

This condition has a deep psychological meaning. Teachers put themselves under pressure to exhibit that part of their personalities

---

13 Frederic William Terrien, *The Behavior System and Occupational Type Associated with Teaching,* unpublished Ph.D. dissertation, Yale University, 1950.

which they feel is in accord with community ideals and to deny other aspects from which they feel they could gain satisfaction. The internal pressure is itself a source of dissatisfaction. This accounts for some rather strange behavior from teachers on vacation away from the school's environment. At such times many will deny that they are teachers, or if "trapped" into an admission will feel very ill at ease. Oddly, in view of all this, vacationing teachers are a rather well-behaved lot. Some go so far as to be disappointed with themselves because, even when free of restrictions, what escapades they do manage are often pretty tame and decorous.

AMOUNT OF FRUSTRATION. The amount of personal frustration varies from individual to individual and from situation to situation. Some school systems are so full of blocks and barriers that teachers leave them as soon as possible. There are schools which experience almost a complete turnover of teaching staff every year. Others, by contrast, are such happy places to work that vacancies are rare. Especially irritating to many are the large number of interruptions. A teacher who has settled down with a class is often "surprised" by a call to the office or an unanticipated visit from an official or a parent, or confronts some other obstacle to continued work with the class.[14]

The mere fact that teaching involves some frustrations does not mean it is likely to produce mental illness in teachers. Every occupation has its share of difficulties. Rather, we must recognize that the existence of frustration implies mechanisms for dealing with any conflict to which it could give rise. Overcoming handicaps and learning to live with necessary frustrations can give added spice to the business of teaching. The significant factor for each individual is the way in which the frustrations are met. Knowing they exist may enable us to use our intelligence better in dealing with them.

What Can We Do About It?

No one can expect to get from a book the solution to a very deep dissatisfaction. Each individual being very different from every other, there can be no pat solution that will work for everyone. For this reason a trained psychologist snorts at books which purport to solve all personal problems. These books will help a few people, but will leave others un-

---

[14] For data on this type of situation, read the following: Alice V. Keliher, "A Day in the Life of the Teacher," *Mental Hygiene,* Vol. 34 (1950), pp. 455-64.

touched or even worse off than before. There are, however, some general strategies which, with intelligent variations, have aided quite a few adults in facing dissatisfactions.

DEVELOP SELF-AWARENESS. The better a person understands himself, the less likely he is to be tossed about by events over which he has no control. This does not mean that every adult should psychoanalyze himself. In fact, complete self-understanding is not possible. However, a greater degree of self-awareness can usually be obtained. This is often basic to any attempt to deal intelligently with problems of living. For instance, a teacher in Flint, Michigan, whom Holmlund[15] called Miss X, had difficulty with one boy in her classes. Worry exhausted her to the point where she could not sleep. Recognizing her need for help, the principal referred her to a program for the study of children. In the course of understanding the boy, Miss X began to recognize her own emotional reactions. In her words, "I soon found out that the trouble was not with the students but with me. I found I was releasing my own frustrations and anxieties upon them." With this insight, problems became more manageable for her.

SEEK SATISFACTIONS ELSEWHERE. Very much a part of any self-awareness is knowledge of some of the satisfactions one hopes to attain through teaching. If these expectations run counter to school realities or if they would produce conflict with professional ethics, then there is a chance to remedy the trouble by seeking those satisfactions elsewhere in living. In this manner one can drain off some of the pressures causing difficulty. Thus, a man who yearned for friendly participation in young adolescents' groups, a participation which was denied because of the roles in which a community's young people cast their junior high school teachers, might be able to find what he wanted by acting as a scoutmaster.

DELIBERATE EXPOSURE TO NEW EXPERIENCES. When life becomes drab and unsatisfactory, a new experience can have a tonic effect. More important, many of us are prone to fall into routines which once were satisfactory and in which we find security. Deliberately broadening one's range of activity may introduce a new and valuable element

---

[15] Walter S. Holmlund, "Flint's Plan for the In-Service Training of Teachers in Child Growth and Development," *Journal of Teacher Education,* Vol. 3 (1952), pp. 50-52.

into the life pattern. It is for this reason that many school systems wisely provide opportunities for exchange teaching and for sabbatical leaves devoted to study or travel.

RE-EVALUATE TOTAL LOAD.   In any case, it is a good idea once in a while to get away from daily pressures and then go over one's total life pattern. Some people have problems because they are giving themselves too little to do; others are busy at those things which yield less satisfaction than activities that have been crowded out; still others have spread themselves so thin that they give themselves no chance to gain satisfaction from anything. A re-evaluation of such patterns may provide the clue to happier living. To cite a very simple illustration, now and then a teacher falls into a pattern of teaching which requires classes to produce so many papers and tests that almost all the time is spent grading papers. Once this is recognized as a source of trouble, a shift to other methods may release time to be spent on more interesting professional reading, visiting with friends, or play going.

STUDY SOMEONE WITH MORE DIFFICULT PROBLEMS.   Some restlessness is caused by failure to live up to the standards one has built in daydreams. It helps, therefore, to compare oneself, not only with those who seem to be better off, but also with those facing more difficult problems. The purpose is not so much to develop a Pollyanna-like attitude as to get perspective. Also, the techniques which are working for someone with a heavier burden may be suggestive.

EVALUATE DISSATISFACTIONS.   Dissatisfaction itself is worth examining. How widespread is it? How serious? How much of a problem? Obviously, to be irked at one minor aspect of living is quite a different matter from feeling distaste for everything that happens all day long. A mild irritation has a meaning which cannot be compared with a profound loathing for an entire life pattern. It is one thing to look forward to a chance to complain to one's friend; it is something quite different to wish one were dead. The degree and extent of one's dissatisfactions must be faced. Not to be overlooked is the possibility that the real object for discontent is not teaching itself, but some condition or relationship elsewhere. The cause of dissatisfaction may be in the private life of the teacher, displaced to the professional situation.

LOOK FOR HELP ON SPECIFIC QUESTIONS.   Often, a good part of a person's troubles seem to stem from a single problem he cannot solve.

Not infrequently, a teacher's life is made miserable by an inability to work with a particular child or to handle one aspect of teaching. If such be the case, it would seem wise to get help on that specific point.

Elaine Cotton, for example, was bothered by her inability to get any spontaneous art work from Miss Hawkins' fifth-graders. Each time she was scheduled to be in the room she planned to stimulate a free discussion out of which projects would be developed. But each time she found herself delivering a monologue and then assigning formal exercises. The children seemed scared or stiff or just plain uninterested. Her failure with this one group made her feel like pretending sickness on days she was to come to Miss Hawkins' class. Finally, in desperation, she mentioned the problem to Mrs. Johnson, the principal.

Mrs. Johnson smiled and said, "For goodness' sakes, don't let that get you down. Miss Hawkins believes in running her room so that the children are scared to peep. Don't expect to get any discussion there. You just go in with some interesting things for them to do and start right off by telling them what to do. After they are all at work, talk to them one at a time. But I doubt if you will get very far. It is too bad, but she has only a year to go."

Miss Cotton already felt better. She did try Mrs. Johnson's suggestion. Gradually, she broke through the children's wall of fear. They would, rather pathetically, come up to her in the hall or after class, and ask permission to try out their own ideas. She took real pleasure in these little measures of success.

TALK IT OVER WITH FRIENDS. So much of any person's life is bound up with other people that it is often impossible to work out a problem by one's self. Just talking about a problem with friends often clarifies the problem. Sometimes, of course, the friends can give active help, but even when this is not the case, talking may provide relief. In addition, it can lead to insight and self-awareness.

GET PROFESSIONAL HELP. Where the nature or the intensity of the difficulties is beyond the point where friends can assist, it may be the height of wisdom to seek professional help. Depending upon the situation, one can utilize the resources of qualified counseling services, social agencies, mental hygiene clinics, or psychiatrists.

STIMULATE GROUP DISCUSSION. As one would suspect, the problems of all teachers are rather similar. Therefore, the pooling of ideas and experiences may help all concerned. The "gripe sessions" in a teachers' cafeteria can have a salutary influence from the point of view of mental health. Even more valuable is systematic and organized consideration of problems, making use of qualified leaders.

DEVELOP SUPPLEMENTARY AREAS.   At times, the solution to boredom or frustration may involve the planned development of new areas of life. Group action may enable several people to provide each other with the needed activities. Teachers, because of their training in group processes, often do play a large role in such community enterprises. Professional organizations have done yeoman's service, both by directly tackling causes of dissatisfaction and by enabling members to meet some of their own needs through committee work, social gatherings, the operation of co-operatives, and other satisfying experiences.

Social action performs another valuable function by helping individual teachers to separate issues. Thus, a campaign for tenure may help some to see that their dissatisfaction with teaching is a result of anxiety derived from staff relationships, rather than a product of classroom relationships.

RECOGNIZE NEW POSSIBILITIES IN TEACHING.   When dissatisfaction seems to grow out of a low level of living outside school, many teachers have repaired the situation by looking for and discovering new possibilities in teaching. This is one of the happy results of many curriculum workshops and experimental programs. Child study groups in school systems can be quite effective in this way. Unfortunately, some standpatters, by hostility to such programs, will unknowingly deprive themselves of the opportunity to find new sources of stimulation in their own classrooms.

Significance of Staff Relations

We must not make the mistake of supposing that all teachers' mental health problems center on the children. Actually, for many there is more personal significance in relationships with other staff members. Many transfers are motivated by a desire to join a more congenial group. For quite a few teachers, the decision to stay in the profession or leave it hinges upon the satisfactions they get out of their faculty associations.

In many communities, teachers are important in the social life of one another. Upon interviewing 358 men teachers in four counties of Iowa, Edwards[16] discovered that 44 per cent of the guests in their homes were in the same profession. Of the men with whom they preferred to spend their leisure time, 45 per cent were in school work.

In an investigation of factors affecting how long teachers stayed on the job in the Appalachian Highlands area of Kentucky, Gray[17] noted that the longest tenure was in the consolidated schools. He conjectured that the more favorable social situation of daily contact with other teachers was the reason.

Unfortunately, the effect is not always favorable. When Kvaraceus[18] asked sixty-seven graduate students in a mental hygiene course at the University of Illinois to check a list of hazards they had encountered in their own firsthand experience, 43 per cent mentioned conflicting personalities among teachers, and 41 per cent jealousies among school personnel. Clearly, many teachers react strongly to their relationships with colleagues.

WHAT OTHER TEACHERS MEAN TO US.   One aspect of such relations is how the teachers see each other. Just as children cast their teachers in various psychological roles, and teachers similarly see children as filling certain needs, so each teacher may endow the others with various characteristics. For instance, one teacher may see others as rivals, as contestants in a competition. Again, one member of a faculty may seek to find someone to help and protect her, someone she can lean upon. An experienced teacher may try to cast newcomers in the role of worshipful apprentices or as novices who are bound to make fools of themselves. A new teacher may tremble before self-assured or dominative colleagues on the supposition that they are faultfinders. Some of these expectations have deep roots in a person's make-up. Their pattern may often be analyzed with profit.

GROUP SPIRIT.   The ways in which the relations we have been describing finally work out depend upon the general tone or group

---

[16] Nathan Amos Edwards, *Sociology of Teaching II: A Study of the Male Classroom Teacher,* Ph.D. dissertation, State University of Iowa, 1952, University Microfilms Publication No. 4061.

[17] Wayne T. Gray, "Factors Affecting Teacher Tenure in the Appalachian Highlands," *Rural Sociology,* Vol. 13 (1948), pp. 295-307.

[18] W. C. Kvaraceus, "Mental Health Hazards Facing Teachers," *Phi Delta Kappan,* Vol. 32 (1951), pp. 349-50.

spirit of the faculty. In some schools, bickering and faultfinding are traditional. In others, especially in some big systems, there is no group life worth mentioning. In still others, there is an atmosphere of warm companionship. In some buildings one can almost feel the tension; in others, there is easygoing relaxation. Obviously, a bad psychological climate imperils the mental and emotional health of the staff. It is not something to be shrugged off. Rather, it is a serious problem to be tackled with all the resources that can be mustered.

FINDING ONE'S PLACE IN THE GROUP.   One of the big tasks of many teachers is to find their places in the faculty group. For some this involves the problem of retaining their own personalities and ideals. On the one hand, they like to be liked by the others. On the other hand, they want to be distinct personalities. The extent to which a group enforces uniformity and the way it reacts to differences are matters which have great weight for individual members. A teacher having difficulties may want to think out his personal strategy in this respect.

SURFACE CALLOUSNESS.   For many new teachers a special problem may be the tone of conversations about children. There are many experienced teachers who sound very hard-boiled, if not cynical. Teaching, with all its frustrations, does create some hostility toward youngsters. This may be drained off in tough talk, leaving the adult more ready to display affection in the classroom. However, the talk may disturb the conscience of someone not familiar with its true significance.

FEELINGS ABOUT ROLE EXPECTATIONS.   As we pointed out in our discussion of children's groups, a group is quite likely to "type" its members. This frequently happens in a school staff. Whether or not what is expected of any individual is based on reality or on legend, the several expectations make for either adjustment or friction. For instance, how would you like to be the teacher everyone assumed would ask laughably silly questions at staff meetings? Read once again the account on pages 20 to 21 of the Kilroy Junior High School and note how each staff member took a different viewpoint. Such pressures and tensions may be reduced by giving careful consideration to feelings about a role, or ways of creating a new one.

CONFLICT AMONG DISCIPLINES.   In many school staffs there is a certain amount of rivalry or competition among the different disciplines represented. For instance, the teachers may express resentment at the school social workers, who, they think, have an easy job, never take difficult cases, and make projects out of simple situations. The school social workers may regard the teachers as punitive creatures who cannot be trusted with information. If such rivalry leads to a jockeying for position at the expense of children, it will be bad for all concerned. If this is happening, there is good reason for each group to review its relations with the others, looking not for self-justification but for ways of reassuring colleagues.

Similar situations may prevail within the teaching staff itself, as in a tendency to derogate health education teachers, shop teachers, or those teaching classes for the mentally retarded.

Some Things Principals Can Do

As in all group processes, the development of intrastaff relations often reflects the personality and the methods of the leader. However, a principal has to deal with some forces which are rarely given adequate weight. For instance, the many frustrations inevitably involved in teaching are bound to create some aggressive feelings. These feelings are quite likely to be displaced against the school administration.

The extent of these reactions is illustrated by replies which O'Malley[19] received from 125 teachers who replied to a questionnaire asking them to list the most irritating or annoying situation they had experienced since beginning to teach. High on the list were these complaints: (1) that the principal showed no appreciation for the work done by the teacher but constantly nagged about minor matters and (2) that there was no cooperation from the principal or supervisor on matters of discipline. To an extent, there probably was a reality behind these complaints. However, we well might surmise that the principals' actions were seized upon as a convenient outlet for irritations built up elsewhere during the school day.

A principal who understands mental health principles will recognize what is happening and will see a useful role in playing the target, rather than get angry and crack down on his staff. A thoroughgoing mental hygiene for school administrators remains to be written. At this point we shall comment—all too briefly—on a few steps a principal can take to aid teachers.

---

[19] Kathleen E. O'Malley, *A Psychological Study of the Annoyances or Irritations of Teachers,* unpublished Ph.D. dissertation, New York University, 1935.

KEEP ROUTINES TO A MINIMUM.   Unnecessary restrictions which have to be enforced increase the number of conflicts between teachers and their classes, and raise the probability of tension.

LISTEN.   Much talk helps relieve the speaker's feelings. The principal who can listen instead of arguing or trying to squelch complaints helps relieve tension.

USE DEMOCRATIC PROCESSES.   As shown in the Lippitt experiments on group atmospheres, democratic, as opposed to dictatorial, procedures reduce the harmful outcropping of aggression.

RESPECT ESTABLISHED HIERARCHIES.   Where there are established channels for dealing with problems or for supplying supervisory suggestions, the principal should respect them. Many adults find it nerve-racking to try to serve two masters or to please two different people. For instance, in high schools it would be unwise to have a principal giving instructions to a teacher in contradiction to those established by the department head.

BACK UP TEACHERS.   Nothing destroys morale faster than for a principal to fail the teachers when they expect his support. Low morale is an outgrowth of their insecurity. This does not mean that a principal should abdicate use of his own judgment and do exactly what any one teacher demands. Certainly, the principal should not feel bound to let himself be used as a club against children or parents. It does mean using his prestige to help teachers out of difficulties, as when a parent complains about them. A clear reality, which requires effort in this connection, is that a teacher, like anyone else, needs the confidence of a superior much more when the teacher is on shaky ground than when he is clearly in the right. In cases where the teacher is clearly in the wrong, or where the principal is under pressure to compound injustice to a child, "backing up the teacher" may take the form of extricating him from the situation in a manner designed to "save face" for him.

MINIMIZE THE EVILS OF CLIQUES.   When cliques form, the principal should recognize the probability of rivalry. It is as bad for a teacher or a group of friends to be the principal's pet as for a child to be teacher's pet. The less-favored group will naturally feel dissatisfaction with the situation.

SHOW EQUANIMITY WHEN MISTAKES ARE MADE. The less upset the principal acts when a teacher makes a mistake, the less anxiety will the teacher feel. Although many will never be able to get over being tense at the possibility of error, a relaxed atmosphere will reduce the severity of this type of reaction.

ESTABLISH FRIENDLY RELATIONS WITH THE COMMUNITY. By building good rapport with community leaders, a principal can reduce some of the pressures upon teachers. This will ease one source of dissatisfaction and divided feelings.

KEEP DETAIL IN ITS PLACE. There is enough normal conflict for a teacher in the relationships with children without adding to it by over-emphasizing details. It is hard enough for a teacher truly to give priority to the needs of children. If the school office insists that priority instead be given to records or other routine matters, pressures can approach the intolerable.

BE FLEXIBLE. When new problems are met effectively in new ways instead of being forced into old, ill-fitting procedures, teachers feel more sure of themselves.

GIVE CRITICISMS IN PRIVATE. The task of correcting ill-advised procedures and of influencing teachers' conduct involves all the elements discussed in connection with the techniques teachers use to influence their classes. In addition, a teacher's prestige with colleagues and students is very important. Accordingly, when criticism is necessary, it should be delivered in private conferences.

RECOGNITION OF PARENTAL ROLES. People who work with children may have more need than others to feel close to an authority figure. To some extent, every principal must act toward members of the school staff as would a protecting father or mother.

APPRECIATE ROLE AS EXAMPLE-SETTER. In contacts with children and parents, the principal sets an example. To the extent that he is respected and liked the teachers will identify with him. Hence, if his emotional management of daily situations is wise, the wisdom will spread. If he remains cheerful under attack or when confronting problems, unafraid of admitting mistakes, and capable of dealing with juvenile misconduct without paling with alarm or throwing a tantrum, the same qualities are bolstered in the staff. The practice-what-you-preach strategy is of paramount importance.

In dealing with problems, principals reflect their own personality structures. To get at what combinations seem to lead to good personal relations, Sachs[20] used a pair of personality tests with 14 male elementary school principals in the San Francisco Bay area. Four of these had been classed as facilitating interpersonal relations; 4, as hindering them. The "facilitators" did show quite a bit of anxiety and uncertainty, but were sensitive, tended to question authority, needed people, and had solved family troubles by reaching out toward people. The "hinderers" often established social distance from other people and took a moralistic tone in dealing with issues. They disliked change and dealt with people on a manipulative level.

Like all professions, teaching carries with it a number of conflicts. To cope with these effectively requires that all concerned apply scientific methods and skills to the study, not only of the children, but also of teachers and the administrative staff.

The key role in the mental health of teachers is played by the school board and the superintendent. There is an emotional chain reaction in every school system, which carries feelings and patterns of action from the central office to the individual classrooms. Where the top administrator acts in accordance with good mental health practices, these are more likely to pervade all aspects of the school system. Conversely, if "headquarters" is a place of high tension, teachers will have to shoulder an extra burden in applying psychological knowledge to their dealings with children and parents.

ADDITIONAL READINGS

Bruce, William F., and A. John Holden, Jr. *The Teacher's Personal Development*. New York: Holt, 1957, Chaps. 11 to 14. Describes factors in the total life pattern of teachers.

Donovan, Frances R. *The Schoolma'am*. New York: Frederick A. Stokes, 1938. An impressionistic account of the characteristics and reactions of people who become school teachers.

Havighurst, Robert J., and Bernice L. Neugarten. *Society and Education*. Boston: Allyn & Bacon, 1957, Part 4. Summarizes data on the social

---

[20] Benjamin M. Sachs, *Selected Personality Factors as Related to Ability to Facilitate Interpersonal and Intragroup Relations in the Case of Certain School Administrators*, unpublished Ph.D. dissertation, University of California, 1952.

origins, social roles, careers, and classroom activities of professional educators.

Heaton, Kenneth L., William G. Camp, and Paul B. Diederich. *Professional Education for Experienced Teachers.* Chicago: U. of Chicago Press, 1940. Discusses the educational needs of teachers familiar with problems in schools.

Jersild, Arthur T. *When Teachers Face Themselves.* New York: Bureau of Publications, Teachers College, Columbia U., 1955. Sketches emotional factors in the lives of teachers, such as anxiety, loneliness, sex, hostility, and compassion.

National Society for the Study of Education. *Forty-Third Yearbook, Part I: Adolescence.* Chicago: U. of Chicago Press, 1944, Chap. 15. Discusses the principles of in-service teacher development in secondary schools from the viewpoint of the administrator's role.

Prall, Charles E., and C. Leslie Cushman. *Teacher Education in Service.* Washington: American Council on Education, 1944. Deals with the on-the-job education of teachers.

Roethlisberger, F. J., and William Dickson. *Management and the Worker.* Cambridge, Mass.: Harvard U. Press, 1939. A report on experimentation with factors influencing good morale in industry.

Stiles, Lindley J., ed. *The Teacher's Role in American Society.* New York: Harper, 1957, Chaps. 4 and 5. Cites case studies depicting patterns of reacting to professional problems as these relate to social origins of teachers.

Wittenberg, Rudolph M. *So You Want to Help People.* New York: Association Press, 1947, Chap. 2. Echoes the reactions of group leaders to events common among young people.

AUDIO-VISUAL AIDS

Planning for Personal and Professional Growth, a 19-minute sound film produced by McGraw-Hill, in which influences upon the happiness of teachers are illustrated.

Who Will Teach Your Child? a 25-minute sound film produced by the National Film Board of Canada, in which community reactions to teachers and education are stressed.

chapter 19

LIMITATIONS OF MENTAL HYGIENE IN EDUCATION

A history of American education could be written in terms of "movements" and "emphases." During each such movement in the past, articles enthusiastically describing the thinking behind the new set of ideas flooded the educational magazines. No convention or institute program could be complete unless it included a talk by an apostle of the "new emphasis." Educational leaders, to stay in style, had to parrot the vocabulary. The road to fame for a modish teacher or administrator was to put the new ideas into practice and report the results.

During the upsweep of each movement, its advocates were likely to become overenthusiastic. Somehow, the impression would be created that they had found the answers to all significant educational problems. Many experienced teachers can no doubt recall the surges of interest in objective tests, the project method, creativity, "progressive education," and integration of subject matter.

The onslaught of each group of enthusiasts sooner or later drew an adverse reaction. Some of this reaction could always be expected from standpatters who hated to be disturbed in their old routines. However, experience also brought the realization that there were other problems in schools which the new movement left untouched. Then, as the initial excitement subsided, another "new emphasis" would appear on the horizon. The band-wagon followers would rush to the growing parade, and the older movement would wane. A few faithful followers would remain behind to continue work along the older lines, but the attention of the profession would be elsewhere.

This process has never been entirely useless. Each wave has left behind it a solid residue which has become part of the educational scene. Thus, we still make much use of standardized tests, encourage creative work, use many ideas first emphasized by the "progressives," and work toward better integration of subject matter. To that extent, such waves of enthusiasm have served an important function.

The introduction of mental health ideas to education has followed this pattern closely. In the late 1940's and early 1950's, there was a fascination with how the insights of psychiatry could throw light on educational problems. There was great enthusiasm about the possibility that schools could stem the rising flood of people entering mental hospitals. Although educators are now tending to become preoccupied with criticisms of schools and to turn their attention to programs for gifted children, much of the loyalty to mental health thinking remains, and the scientific evidence on which it is based continues to accumulate. For this reason, it is important to make clear the limitations of mental hygiene in education. If these limitations are clearly set down, some enthusiasts may be spared a destructive disillusionment. The possible help which can be brought to youngsters is too important to be imperiled by overinflated claims or absurdities.

Mental Health Is Only Part of Education

The role of teachers is larger than that of preserving mental health. During the course of any day, a teacher's mind will necessarily be occupied with a great many considerations, all of them important and valid parts of his job. Some will involve protecting physical health; others, guiding learning activities; and still others, routine classroom management. To be sure, the way the teacher carries out these tasks may affect the emotional well-being of the children. But the basic conceptual tools he is employing, even though they may be used in line with mental health principles, are derived from other fields of thought.

Perhaps another way of putting the matter is to say that education cannot be dissolved into mental hygiene. Education involves emotional learnings, but it also must be concerned with such matters as reading skills, number ability, scientific thinking, vocational techniques, aesthetic appreciations, and the thousand and one other aspects of personal and group competence needed to live fully in our present-day world. In addition, schools take some responsibility for the development of social skills, character, and work habits. Building enthusiasm for a democratic way of life is a major objective. Certainly the mental health of pupils may be influenced by how schools seek these objectives. In gaining them, however, each field of education has its own theoretical principles and its own know-how.

A teacher must know a great deal more than mental hygiene. In a gymnasium, for instance, a teacher must be experienced in safety precautions and competent in giving first aid for injuries; he must know the tricks of helping young people master game skills and must be able to make good use of space and equipment. A kindergarten teacher must have a working knowledge of children's literature and know a variety of rhythmical games; she must be able to plan a varied schedule and be capable of expressing herself in vocabulary children can understand. A high school principal must be a master of schedule construction, give leadership to faculty meetings, deal with civic organizations, and know how to evaluate lunchroom service. So it goes. The capable educator is a man or woman with many skills. The most fundamental skills involve leadership of groups engaged in learning.

Any talk about "understanding" children, therefore, must be related to the context in which the term is to be used. In schools, that context is composed largely of formal education. A teacher sees the emotional reactions of children as the youngsters study foreign languages, become acquainted with carpenters' tools, try to understand long division, or work at drawing pictures. As far as the children are concerned, these educational activities are the reason for school. Parents share this belief. Recognizing that teachers will spend more time improving their mastery of subject matter or learning how to encourage learning than they do reading books on mental health simply means accepting reality. This does not mean, of course, that we can safely ignore the mental health of young people in school. It does mean that a teacher is very wise to give a great deal of attention to other aspects of educational activity.

Sometimes what we can learn about children may be irrelevant to the business at hand. For example, the symbolisms in art productions can be intensively studied, and, with expert knowledge, yield a great deal of highly interesting information concerning the unconscious motivations of children. Such findings can be of value to a specialist conducting therapy with a child. But for all practical purposes, they usually have little value in deciding how to help make better use of drawing techniques. Similarly, an observant math teacher can get clues about very deep formative influences upon young people, but find himself unable to use this information in any aspect of classroom work. To concentrate energy on such probing at the risk of mismanaging learning activities can be highly inefficient. Of course, if a child's problems need understanding, we must look at them more deeply; but random excursions into personality analysis are no substitute for competence in teaching.

Mental Health Reaches Beyond the School

Many implications of mental hygiene involve much more than school experiences. The mental and emotional health of young people is influenced by forces over which schools in a free country can have no direct control. Therefore the schools cannot safely give the impression that they will take full responsibility for solving the mental or emotional difficulties of young people. Educational institutions recognize this fact by working to secure co-operation from parents, churches, civic organizations, social work and recreational agencies, and clinics. The limits to what schools can actually do must be recognized. To illustrate this point we shall comment briefly on three aspects of such limitations: the difficulties inherent in changing the attitudes of the children's families, the difficulties in changing the personalities of the school staff, and the power of cultural forces.

LIMITATIONS ON CHANGING FAMILIES. Time and again, we encounter problems arising from a child's reaction to the way his family is treating him. Any complete solution to his mental health difficulties or to the problems he creates for other children would require a change in his family's attitude. While we will always want to do our utmost in this respect, as was pointed out in Chapter 17, we are bound to meet difficulties. There is no magic by which a teacher can change a family.

On purely legal grounds, we cannot force any family to do what we want it to do. Unless parents are guilty of extreme neglect or blatant cruelty, they have the right to manage their families as they see fit. They have the right to their own ideas on child raising, and no one can deprive them of the liberty to put their ideas into practice. In the eyes of the law, anyone who seeks to invade a home and tell people how to live their lives is a trespasser. Parents can stand on their rights whenever they wish. In a democracy this is as it should be. The outsider, no matter how well trained, can use the arts of persuasion, but that is all.

If we are realistic, we recognize that the way parents act may be the result of deeply imbedded emotional patterns. This is especially true when parents are literally unable to use advice with which they might agree. The processes of change are not easy; even with the best co-operation they may take a long time. Moreover, if the parents are basically satisfied with themselves or else feel too threatened by the thought of self-examination, even the most highly trained experts may have to give up. At the very least, they may have to mark time until matters become bad enough so that the parents become anxious to find help.

In view of these facts, the school can often do nothing directly to change a particular home situation. This is a limitation on the practice of mental hygiene which we must recognize. It does not prevent us from giving some help to the children affected, but it does interfere with the fullest use of mental health knowledge.

LIMITATIONS ON CHANGING SCHOOL PERSONNEL.   Another very real limitation to mental hygiene is that the personality needs of each teacher may lead him to do some things that are not good for children. Most of us are most sensitive to such imperfections when we see them in colleagues or administrators of whom we disapprove. These people cannot all be fired, and many will not "listen to reason."

Even when a teacher wants to change his reactions to children, there is no magic by which this can be done immediately. By long and patient self-education, a great many teachers today are dealing with children much more admirably than they have in the past. Indeed, the whole point of writing a book like this one is to help them get still closer to perfection. Yet, with the best intentions in the world, almost all are going to fall a bit short of that goal.

The steps in individual personality change are slow and uncertain. This is especially true when an adult is trying to do the job himself. A few enthusiasts have urged that all teachers be psychoanalyzed. Regardless of the theoretical questions about the merit of this proposal, it is clearly impracticable. If all the psychiatrists in the United States were psychoanalysts (which they are not) and every one gave all his time to working with teachers, less than 4 per cent of the teaching profession could be reached at any one time. Moreover, the customary charges would be more than most beginning teachers are paid per year.

The fact is that teaching will continue to be in the hands of a good cross section of the educated population. The teaching staff will, therefore, have an ordinary range of conflicts and problems. These problems will limit to some extent the degree to which mental health information will be used in schools. Those teachers and administrators who fortunately are able to accept that knowledge must recognize that for many years they will have to work with colleagues who are handicapped to some extent. Here, as in dealing with hostile or passive families, the major requirement is patience and understanding. If change comes it will be the result of persuasion, both by word and by example. Here, as in other matters, there is no sure magic, no short cut. All of us must live with colleagues who do not share our principles or our tastes.

POWER OF THE CULTURE. The society in which we live influences everyone in it. To some extent it shapes young people in ways which add to their conflicts and their anxiety. Teachers inevitably have to cope with the product of the culture. This is very visible when generally accepted attitudes toward one group in a community impinge upon the children. To take but one example, within recent years schools in areas within the continental United States having a large Puerto Rican population have had to contend with serious difficulties. The way this group is treated tends to produce economic deprivation, discouragement, and aggression. One illustration of the effects appeared in a study which Beauchamp and her students[1] made of a neighborhood on the Lower East Side of Manhattan Island. In cases where the school records of junior high school students showed they had received two intelligence tests at different times, there was a decrease of 5 or more I.Q. points between the first and second tests for approximately one-fourth of all Puerto Rican youngsters. For none was there an equivalent increase. So sharp a decrease is very unusual; it implies a negative or lethargic attitude which would create great problems for teachers, and is probably linked to the attitudes these youngsters encounter from all sides. In this group, approximately 1 child in every 5 needed, but lacked, dental care or eyeglasses or both—a sign of the financial problems and poor living conditions of their parents.

Affecting all members of our culture, and frequently setting limits to the effectiveness of mental health techniques, are such tendencies as ambition for material possessions, a high value on independence among adolescent boys, and a demand for popularity and social resourcefulness in girls. Other illustrations appear in Chapter 6.

OTHER SOCIAL INFLUENCES. Social conditions, economic forces, and other strong influences often limit what can be done. For instance, we can trace some of the effects of broken homes but stand helpless be-

---

[1] Mary Beauchamp and Associates, *Building Neighborliness,* New York, Center for Human Relations and Community Studies, 1957.

fore the social conditions which are destroying family unity. We might study what comics, radio, and television are doing to children, but be unable to modify the economic forces which influence a publisher's decision as to what to print or a sponsor's choice of what he will put on the air. We stand relatively powerless to control international events, even while we realize their sweeping effects.

The mental hygienist may often give very sound advice to schools on how to set up appropriate services for children or how classes might better be handled, and yet be unable to counteract the effect of the school budget, the shortage of trained psychiatrists, the cost of altering a building, community pressures for an honor roll system, or the personal needs of community leaders.

The way around this weakness may be to have problems tackled by teams, on which the mental hygienist is one member. For the time being, however, we must recognize that there are practical restrictions to the use of mental health knowledge in schools. The extent to which these limitations can be pushed back depends upon the ingenuity and determination of countless teachers, administrators, and, especially, interested citizens.

Limitations on Mental Hygiene as a Science

Even if the limitations we have been describing did not exist, we would still have to acknowledge that the sciences upon which we must draw are far from complete. The scientific study of human personality is very young. On many questions we cannot speak with finality. The theoretical basis for action is only partially formed, so that there are obvious limits to what schools can do to help children.

WIDE GAPS IN OUR KNOWLEDGE. On many questions, the proved evidence is still unsatisfactory. There is much we need to know, much on which we can only speculate. For example, the meaning of some adolescent behavior is still so unclear that even the most skillful experts have difficulty in deciding whether or not it is a symptom of serious disturbance. We have barely made a beginning in learning how and why particular kinds of behavior spread in a group. We cannot tell for sure why two children growing up in the same home and apparently faced with the same parental attention or neglect may turn out differently. It is still a puzzle why so few girls who are victims of extreme parental rejection develop the violent, individualistic aggressive patterns found so often in boys from the same background. The number of such problems is very great.

WIDE GAPS IN KNOW-HOW.   Even more of a limitation are the wide areas in which no tested techniques are known. These missing techniques range all the way from how to handle rather ordinary classroom problems to methods of therapy for certain personality distortions. For example, readers of this book must have been struck by how much remains to be learned about conducting interviews with parents, about discussing a child's conduct with the youngster, and about the way teachers can deal with their own dissatisfactions with teaching. Similarly, many world-famous psychiatrists will openly confess that when an unwanted child becomes an adult unable to form attachments to other people, they are usually helpless to correct his condition.

The fact is that the job of applying mental health knowledge is still at the stage in which the average teacher has to rely on his own ingenuity much of the time. While this does limit what we can accomplish, it also means that those who try to work out problems can have the pleasure and satisfaction of being pioneers. If one is occasionally at sea for want of tested techniques, he can at least taste the pleasures of discovery and communication with fellow explorers.

CONTRADICTIONS BETWEEN SCHOOLS OF THOUGHT.   It is to be expected that in the current state of the mental health sciences there will be contradictions between various authorities or schools of thought. Gradually, of course, as knowledge increases, such contradictions will grow fewer. For instance, the old debate as to whether people ever act under the influence of unconscious motivations has now been settled; the evidence of such motivation is well established. On other questions, however, differences of opinion still exist. This means that there can be legitimate debate on the best course to follow to help a particular child or to improve a given situation. The educator has no choice but to use his best judgment and to improve that judgment by enlarging his own experience. Some errors will be made; but the only way to avoid them is to do nothing, and that is likely to be an even worse decision.

DISGUISED TRADITIONS.   There is always a tendency for some people who do not want to change their practices to hold to their old opinions but disguise them. This is a species of rationalization against which we have to be on guard. Some people are inclined to try to sell their own values or favorite concepts by pinning on a label, "This is good for mental health." Therefore, not all recommendations made in the name of mental hygiene are properly so labeled. Incidentally, both psychologists and psychiatrists of outstanding reputation yield to this temptation. The fact that such a tendency can exist means that school people must proceed with greater care and with somewhat less certainty than they might wish.

VAGUENESS IN CRITERIA OF NORMALITY.   Another limitation on the use of mental hygiene is that precise criteria of normal mental and emotional health do not now exist. As was pointed out earlier, we can recognize certain clear-cut types of illness and can act upon rather general indications of health. However, we have no sure-fire apparatus comparable to thermometers, devices for measuring basal metabolism, or blood-pressure gauges. This means we are limited, but not helpless. Like any group of pioneers, we can make the best of what we have. This is not a new condition for educators. Long before they had standardized tests, school people did a pretty fair job of helping young people toward the achievements those tests can now measure.

DIFFICULTY OF BEING CONCRETE ABOUT PSYCHOLOGICAL PROBLEMS.   In some ways the most irritating of all limitations is the fact that it is very hard to be concrete in talking about psychological problems. A psychological problem cannot be felt or touched. It is deep, intangible, and complex. It shows itself only through behavior and then in many disguises. This means that often we have no choice but to proceed in the face of uncertainties. Only as experience accumulates can the guesses become more accurate. This has already happened in some areas, but the limitation still exists, and it looks as though we shall have to live with it for many years.

TIME NECESSARY FOR COMPLETE EXPERIMENTATION.   In addition, there is a severe limitation on the value of today's experiments. The desired end which we hope to achieve through education is, in part, a better or more adequate type of parent-to-child relationship. For instance, we would like to feel that some of the measures we take will result in a new generation of parents who will get their children off to a better start toward mental health. That very goal means we cannot know the result of what we are doing until today's youngsters are grown. That being so, truly complete experiments may often have to be planned in terms of decades; even where the desired goal is less remote, sound experiments require long years. Thus, our knowledge is bound to grow rather slowly.

A Look Ahead

We have pictured some of the realities that limit the use of mental health ideas in schools. It is equally important to stress that all these realities are elastic; they can be changed. In the present state of affairs, the sincere professional who wishes to incorporate mental health concepts into his activities will find that those same concepts make very hard demands upon him. Far from finding his life made more peaceful, new insights reveal to him that he will have to work harder, try harder, and fight harder than he would wish. As he labors under a heavy load today, he will have to help create the conditions that are needed to do a creditable professional job for future classes and future generations.

Let it be said regretfully but boldly that mental hygiene does not simplify matters or guarantee peace of mind for teachers. But teachers can find security in the knowledge that they are doing their utmost to bring new light into the emotional lives of all their children. Each of us can taste the enduring satisfaction of knowing we have helped bring to future generations a deeper purpose in living, and added effectiveness in achieving those purposes. The fact that in doing so we put forth disciplined effort will season our satisfaction.

We can hope that tomorrow's teachers will move more skillfully and surefootedly to add to the knowledge and skill of their pupils. Children will grow toward adulthood with added zest and firmer integrity. By applying what we know about mental hygiene today, each of us can take some steps, however tentative, toward bringing bits of that future into our present schools.

ADDITIONAL READINGS

Buhler, Charlotte, Faith Smitter, and Sybil Richardson. *Childhood Problems and the Teacher*. New York: Holt, 1952, Chap. 14. Gives perspective on the contribution psychologists can make to the adjustment of children.

Chamberlain, Leo M., and Leslie W. Kindred. *The Teacher and School Organization*. Englewood Cliffs, N. J.: Prentice-Hall, 1949. A book making clear the role individual teachers can play in respect to school policy.

National Society for the Study of Education. *Fifty-Fourth Yearbook, Part II: Mental Health in Modern Education.* Chicago: U. of Chicago Press, 1955, Chap. 6. Treats of the role of the community in both the production and prevention of emotional strain.

Rogers, Dorothy. *Mental Hygiene in Elementary Education.* Boston: Houghton Mifflin, 1957, Chap. 18. Examines factors cogent to a sounder philosophy of mental hygiene in teaching.

Stiles, Lindley J., ed. *The Teacher's Role in American Society.* New York: Harper, 1957, Chap. 11. Discusses the extent to which teachers can formulate educational policy.

Strang, Ruth. *The Adolescent Views Himself.* New York: McGraw-Hill, 1957, Chap. 2. Summarizes some impacts of social forces on adolescents.

Strode, Josephine. *Social Insight through Short Stories.* New York: Harper, 1946. A book of short stories designed to make the reader aware of the complexities involved in changing people's lives.

AUDIO-VISUAL AIDS

What Is Your Opinion about Popular Psychology?, a 10-minute sound film produced by the National Film Board of Canada in which questions are raised about the impact of psychological understanding.

APPENDIXES

appendix 1

SOURCES OF ADDITIONAL HELP
AND INFORMATION

A single course or a single book on mental hygiene can at best give only the most general knowledge in a very important field. If at all successful, it will provide a taste for new satisfactions, which can be obtained by developing and deepening the understanding of why children act as they do and of what forces are at work in the classroom. Each person will want to extend his knowledge along lines of his own choice. Furthermore, each will want to draw upon existing resources in putting ideas into practice.

Fortunately, there are many sources of additional help and information. National organizations devoted to mental health provide a wide range of assistance. There are several fine periodicals which publish articles ranging from technical reports to simply worded expositions of new ideas. There are series of pamphlets which deal with various topics in an interesting fashion. Organizations operating on a state or community level hold conferences and arrange opportunities for discussion. Some bring together people who are ready to campaign for new facilities. Often, a local clinic will act as a center for education, as well as a resource for the referral of youngsters. A number of school systems have organized in-service training programs.

As interest in mental health grows and develops, the organizational scene also changes. For efficiency, some groups join forces and unify their structure; others add to their services. New publications and new facilities are inaugurated. As this is being written, new film series are in production, and several state organizations are working out new programs. This pace of change is likely to continue. Therefore, the accounts given below will require some alteration almost from the moment of publication.

Periodicals

A large number of publications report research findings, scientific discussions, or specific application of mental health principles to teaching. In this section we shall discuss briefly a few magazines which are devoted in large part to this field. It must be recognized, however, that much good and useful material is also published in general educational magazines. Articles in these may be located by looking under "mental hygiene" or related headings in the *Education Index,* which can be found on the reference shelves of almost all libraries. The front pages of that publication also contain an up-to-date listing of all major periodicals in the field of education. A similar listing of psychological periodicals appears in the annual index number of *Psychological Abstracts,* a periodical which summarizes each year approximately eight thousand articles, monographs, and books in psychology and allied fields. Summaries of current research concerning children can be found in *Child Development Abstracts.* A teacher or a school group planning to subscribe to a publication would be well advised to consult a professional librarian to supplement the list below.

Mental Hygiene (Quarterly, National Association for Mental Health, 10 Columbus Circle, New York 19, N. Y., $6.00).[1] This general publication usually contains over one hundred fifty pages per issue. The articles vary widely in content, but all are concerned with some aspect of mental hygiene. It is of great value in keeping up to date on trends in thinking and on new developments in facilities and objectives. It includes a section giving news of other organizations working in the field.

Human Relations (Quarterly, Research Center for Group Dynamics, University of Michigan, Ann Arbor, Mich., $8.00). Jointly sponsored by the Tavistock Institute in England and the Research Center for Group Dynamics, this is one of the most important technical magazines reporting pioneer work in the experimental development and application of psychology and allied sciences. The contributions are

---

[1] Addresses given in this appendix are those of the business or subscription office. Both the address and subscription price in each instance are those existing in 1959.

international in scope, and there is a strong tendency to give priority to work involving groups.

Psychiatry (Quarterly, 1703 Rhode Island Avenue, N.W., Washington 8, D. C., $10.00). Addressed to readers with a high level of knowledge and understanding, this publication describes itself as a journal of interpersonal relations. Many articles are dedicated to the application of psychiatric principles to other fields.

Social Casework (Quarterly, Family Service Association of America, 215 Fourth Avenue, New York 3, N. Y., $4.00). Social workers have become increasingly concerned with the operation of psychological forces in creating problems for the clients they serve. Their professional literature, and this journal in particular, give a great deal of attention to methods of working with people who have such difficulties and who come to the attention of social agencies.

American Journal of Orthopsychiatry (Quarterly, 209 Longworth Avenue, Boston 15, Mass., $10.00). Another professional journal of high caliber, this magazine deals with the mental and emotional disturbances of children, and with methods of treatment and rehabilitation. The bulk of contributions consists of papers delivered at the annual meetings of the American Orthopsychiatric Association. Especially interesting are the verbatim reports of symposia and of discussions which follow the presentation of certain papers.

Journal of Social Issues (Quarterly, Association Press, 291 Broadway, New York 7, N. Y., $4.00). This journal is the official publication of the Society for the Psychological Study of Social Issues, a group of social psychologists, sociologists, anthropologists, and allied social scientists with a special interest in research on the psychological aspects of social problems. Each number deals with a single social issue, which often is related to mental health.

Child Study (Quarterly, 132 East 74th Street, New York 21, N. Y., $2.50). Addressed to parents, teachers, social workers, public health workers, and others who have contacts with children, this quarterly contains many articles by specialists. These are held to standards of scientific accuracy, and are written in a style which makes them of maximum practical usefulness. There are a number of regular departments dealing with parents' questions, suggestions for study groups, reports of scientific findings, book reviews, children's books, and television programs.

Personnel and Guidance Journal (Monthly, 1534 O Street, N.W., Washington 5, D. C., $7.00). Articles dealing with aspects of counseling, many having to do with school problems, appear in this periodical.

Pamphlet Series

Because organizations interested in mental hygiene are so eager to get their message across to parents and teachers, many have made a special effort to produce effective pamphlets. As a result, there are a large number of very brief and easily read treatments of significant problems. The speed with which such items can be produced means that any listing such as that below will be incomplete within a short time. For that reason, we list here only a few organizations which have published series of interest to teachers, parents, or study groups. Anyone wishing to compile a complete list can do so by using the *Vertical File Index,* a reference series carried by most large libraries. From time to time the National Institute of Mental Health, a division of the U. S. Public Health Service, publishes an up-to-date catalogue of pamphlets and reprints.

An unusual and highly valuable service is provided by an organization called Human Relations Aids, a division of Mental Health Materials Center, Inc. Located in Room 713, at 1790 Broadway, New York 19, it sends to subscribers a series of packets which contain recently published pamphlets, mental health plays, and information on moving pictures. Further information can be secured by writing their office.

Public Affairs Pamphlets (Public Affairs Committee, 22 East 38th Street, New York 16, N. Y.). This is a series, now numbering more than two hundred pamphlets, on a wide variety of questions of general public interest. Several items in the list deal directly with mental health and with problems affecting children or child raising. Quite frequently, the more recent numbers are stocked in public libraries.

Children's Bureau Booklets (Children's Bureau, Department of Health, Education, and Welfare, Washington 25, D. C.). For a number of years, the Children's Bureau has put out an inexpensive series of booklets designed to help parents understand their young people. Separate publications, regularly revised to include new findings, deal with prenatal care, early infancy, the preschool years, middle childhood, and adolescence. They stress emotional as well as physical care.

Parent-Teacher Series (Bureau of Publications, Teachers College, Columbia University, New York 27, N. Y.). This series is keyed to a somewhat more highly educated audience than those previously mentioned. The specific interests of educators are more directly taken into account.

Science Research Associates Booklets (57 West Grand Avenue, Chicago 10, Ill.). This organization produces tests and other materials used in guidance programs. Among its ventures is a series of booklets designed to be read by high school students or to be used as the basis for classes dealing with adjustment.

Audio-Visual Aids

Films, plays, and tape recordings are frequently of great use, not only for teaching purposes but to form the core of a meeting or a series of meetings. The success achieved by the first really good films has encouraged the production of more. Here we shall list a number of the more active producing organizations. Although distributors' addresses are given here, it is often easier to rent educational films from the film library of a state university. In some cases, the official state mental hygiene commission also has a collection. In the larger cities, public libraries may stock films which are loaned to organizations holding meetings.

National Film Board of Canada. Unusually effective and psychologically accurate films on mental health subjects have been produced by the National Film Board of Canada. There are series depicting normal development in children at various ages, types of emotional troubles, and resources for treatment. Recently, a series of portraits of adolescents in action has been released. The films are distributed in the United States by the McGraw-Hill Publishing Company.

Federal Radio Committee, U. S. Office of Education. A loan service for radio transcriptions and tape recordings is operated by the Federal Radio Committee of the U. S. Office of Education. Inquiries should be addressed to the Committee at the Department of Health, Education, and Welfare, Washington 25, D. C.

Mental Health Film Board. This nonprofit association, composed of psychiatrists and public health officers, has as its sole aim the production of films on human relations. Its productions span the range of mental health ideas. The address is 166 East 38th Street, New York 16, N. Y.

Vassar College. Based largely on scenes filmed in the Vassar College nursery school and psychological laboratories, a number of excellent studies bearing on child psychology have been produced. The emphasis is on normal personality development. Some have been aimed at the general public; others are geared to the training of psychologists.

McGraw-Hill Publishing Company, Inc. This firm has prepared a number of motion pictures to be used with certain textbooks. Films bearing upon mental hygiene are included in the series on hygiene, student teaching, child development, family life, and adolescence.

Coronet. A commercial producer, this company has a long list of films for classroom use. At each age level there are some which would be useful in starting discussions on mental health topics. The company's general offices are at 65 East South Water Street, Chicago, Ill.

American Theater Wing. Easily produced one-act plays, dealing mostly with child raising and family issues, have been developed by this group. Parent groups, especially, have enjoyed putting these on at meetings. The scripts are available at low cost; staging is simple, and no elaborate sets are required. Producing packets can be secured by writing to Human Relations Aids, 1790 Broadway, New York 19, N. Y.

National Organizations

Individuals and groups making plans for study or action can often obtain considerable assistance from those national organizations which deal with mental health directly or whose interest in children, parents, or teachers gives them an incentive to render assistance to programs designed to improve family living or to raise educational standards. In this appendix we have already referred to the *U. S. Children's Bureau* and the *National Institute of Mental Health*. In addition to their fine publications, both of these federal agencies carry on many other activities. They will furnish consultants, provide backing for demonstration projects, and give advice on programs. We have also referred to the *National Association for Mental Health*. This, too, does a great deal more than issue educational materials. It gives direct support to local groups tackling problems in the realm of mental health. In addition to these organizations, there are a number of others from which various kinds of assistance may be secured. As in other sections of this appendix, there is no pretense that the list below is at all comprehensive. Rather, it gives a representative sample of different types of organization.

Child Study Association of America. This group has been active in the field of parent education for over sixty years. In addition to publishing pamphlets and the magazine *Child Study,* it supplies speakers for meetings, compiles carefully evaluated lists of books for children and parents, maintains a family counseling service, and provides an information service on schools and camps. The national headquarters is at 132 East 74th Street, New York 21, N. Y.

Group for the Advancement of Psychiatry. This is an organization of psychiatrists. Its many committees make intensive studies of questions related to their field, which are usually published in carefully developed booklets. It has issued several reports dealing with important educational issues. The headquarters is at 1790 Broadway, New York 19, N. Y.

National Congress of Parents and Teachers. Through its magazine, *The National Parent-Teacher,* and its study outlines the National Congress of Parents and Teachers has done a great deal to stimulate discussion of mental health considerations influencing children. The local units of this national organization are the P.T.A. groups in countless schools.

National education organizations. Teachers' organizations, through their programs and publications, have done their bit in spreading key ideas. Although neither the National Education Association nor the American Federation of Teachers concentrates on mental hygiene as such, both have carried its lessons to their members. Moreover, the divisions and the local organizations affiliated with both have held meetings at which mental hygiene was the main theme.

Local Resources

In many cases, an individual or a school group wishing to increase its effectiveness in promoting mental health will receive help most fully from some local public service or organization. This help may be in the form of assistance in organizing or staffing an in-service education program. In other cases, it may be in giving effective direction to a campaign to secure needed facilities. A roll call of the types of organization from which help might be obtained may aid some readers in locating needed services.

State mental health departments. The vast majority of states have a department devoted to mental health. Although the main duty of such a department is likely to be the supervision of mental hospitals and child guidance clinics, many provide speakers for meetings, consultants for educational programs, and films for gatherings.

State departments of education. The state department of education may be of great assistance. Sometimes it will provide expert aid in setting up guidance facilities or in inaugurating a school-psychologist or visiting-teacher program. Financial aid for in-service education projects may be within its province. The range of services varies greatly from state to state, but when one is making plans to improve mental health conditions in a school system, the state department of education should not be neglected.

Mental health societies. Most states have a mental health society—a group of public-spirited citizens who are working to improve facilities and spread information. Such groups usually have local chapters in the larger cities and counties. The pressure they can bring to bear may be a real asset in securing needed public services or in obtaining a budget allowance for a program. These groups usually can obtain speakers and furnish literature.

Public libraries. People often forget libraries when they are making plans for a program. The usefulness of librarians in providing reading lists is obvious. Sometimes they can do a great deal more. The reference librarian can be a source of invaluable information as to the identity and address of other organizations. He may be able to provide facts and figures which would take days to obtain without his help. In addition, the library may have a collection of films or records.

Councils of social agencies. Another key source of information is the local council of social agencies or community chest. The workers there may be able to locate very speedily the agency which can be of most service to a particular child or his family. They will also know how to make a referral with the most satisfaction to all concerned. For in-service education programs, the social workers may prove to be invaluable.

Institutions of higher learning. Much more likely to be drawn upon is the local college, university, or teacher-training institution. Some will provide psychological services. Many are willing to provide staff members as consultants or to send them out as speakers. Often arrangements can be made for an organized program of in-service education.

Clinics and child study bureaus. The staff at a child guidance clinic or child study bureau usually will have its hands full doing its own job. However, the members can usually see the value of aiding teachers to do a better job of helping disturbed children and recognizing those who need specialized help. The staff can be persuaded to act as resource people in in-service education programs, to serve as consultants in setting up new school facilities, and to speak before teachers' meetings and parents' groups.

Psychiatrists and hospital staffs. Serving in capacities similar to the members of child guidance clinics, workers at mental hospitals can sometimes be induced to assist school mental hygiene activities. To an increasing extent, psychiatrists in private practice may do similar jobs. At any rate, neither group should be overlooked. In dealing with anyone in private practice, it is a wise precaution to secure first a list of qualified physicians from the local medical association, mental health society, or psychiatrists' organization.

Local psychological associations. Although psychologists are not as strongly organized as physicians, help in securing qualified personnel can often be obtained from the local psychological association. Always, before arrangements are made with a psychologist in private practice, the psychologist's standing should be checked with the local organization.

appendix **2**

MEANING OF SPECIAL TERMS

In preparing this book the authors have deliberately avoided, insofar as possible, the use of technical terms frequently employed in psychological and psychiatric literature. Where ordinary expressions could accurately convey the intended meaning, the "two-cent words" have been used. Terms not within the common experience of most people have been employed only when they were necessary to avoid cumbersome sentences or inaccurate statements. While this procedure makes the book easier to read and understand, the authors realize that many readers will want to master a more specialized vocabulary. As they delve into other works, readers will find expressions with which they may be unfamiliar. For the benefit of those who wish to get a better grasp of frequently used psychiatric terms, the following glossary is provided.[1]

Acting out. This phrase refers to the expression in action of powerful feelings or emotional conflicts. Teachers are most likely to hear it in connection with children whose behavior is typified by outbursts of destructive rage.

Aggression. This much-used word has several meanings. Often regarded as "a tendency toward hostility involving physical or other injury to people," it can also take the form of efforts to impose one's will on several aspects of the social environment. Aggression may range in intensity from mild expostulation all the way to murder.

Alter ego (see also *psychodrama* and *role playing*). A term used

---

[1] A brief, readable booklet entitled *A Psychiatric Glossary,* published in 1957 by the Committee on Public Information of the American Psychiatric Association ($1.00) is useful for this same purpose.

to describe a person who, in the presence of a second person, acts the part of that individual in a psychodrama or in other role-playing techniques.

Ambivalence. The technical term for the mixture of conflicting emotions directed toward a person or situation. Usually there are components of both love and hate. This is a very common condition.

Anal character. This refers to the behavioral residue in adult life of unresolved difficulties from the anal phase (see below). This behavior is characterized by such traits as obstinacy, stinginess, and orderliness.

Anal phase. Employed mostly in Freudian descriptions of child development, this phrase refers to the period, frequently beginning during the second six months of the infant's first year, in which he becomes sensitive to the processes of defecation and toilet training.

Anxiety. A feeling of uneasiness or apprehension, usually a result of inner tension or conflict, the object of which is vague or unknown.

Aphasia. A technical term which covers various disorders centering in inability to understand or to use language.

Association. The psychological term used to describe the process whereby two situations become linked in our nervous system, so that the reaction to one arouses the reaction to the other.

Birth trauma. The shock of being born. This phrase is used largely by psychologists who have been influenced by the thinking of Otto Rank, who regarded the birth trauma as a very significant cause of later anxieties.

Blocking. Difficulties in memory or in other intellectual processes, such as reading, caused by emotional reactions, often unconscious.

Boarding home. A home in which children are placed by their own parents, by social agencies, or by court order under a temporary arrangement where money is paid to the couple in charge.

Castration complex. In the course of psychoanalysis it is often found that a complex of emotional reactions is derived from a boy's childhood fears that he may be shorn of his distinctive masculine genital apparatus. The phrase "castration complex" describes not only the fear of castration but all the reactions which have arisen from it and are associated with it.

Catharsis. A Greek word which means "cleansing," this term describes the action of a person who is pouring out an account of something that troubles him. This is often regarded as a health-building process on the theory that expressing certain emotions robs them of their damage-breeding power.

Cathexis. This technical term means the sum of the energy or emotional reaction which is invested in an action or a relationship. The word itself is a translation into Greek of the German word *Besetzung,* which Freud employed when he wrote about feelings of love being bestowed upon an object. The normal adult cathexis of love is to a person of the opposite sex, but inappropriate cathexes may occur.

Clinic team. A combination of skills is usually required in agencies dealing with the emotional or mental problems of individuals. For this reason, clinics are usually organized around teams, consisting of a psychiatrist, one or more psychologists, and one or more psychiatric social workers.

Clinical. When used in connection with psychological matters, this adjective refers to the concentration of attention upon the disturbed behavior of single individuals and groups (as "clinical" evidence, "clinical" psychology, "clinical" experience, and so on).

Complex. A group or pattern of feelings, ideas, and other psychological reactions which are linked together by a common cause. Examples described in this glossary are castration complex, Oedipus complex, and inferiority complex.

Compulsion. A type of behavior, often repetitious, in which the individual feels driven to do something, even though there is no outside necessity. Compulsions range from symbolic behavior in which the individual is aware of the irrationality to less obvious and often socially approved conduct, such as fastidious neatness.

Contagion. By analogy with the spread of disease, this term describes the spread of psychological reactions or behavior among members of a group.

Conversion. An adjective used to characterize neuroses or hysterias in which body phenomena appear as symptoms. The mental problem is thus converted into a physical symptom. Headaches and paralyses of psychological origin are common examples.

Cycloid. This adjective is used to describe those mental disturbances characterized by a more or less periodic rising and falling of emotional tone. The extreme is the so-called manic-depressive psychosis in which the victim may go through long intervals of excitement and high energy output which alternate with depressive phases showing the opposite condition. There are many variations, some individuals, for example, displaying depression alternating with a normal level.

Death wish. Mostly unconscious or unrecognized in barefaced form by their possessors, wishes for the deaths of other persons are commonly uncovered in the course of psychotherapy.

Delusion. A false belief upon which the individual acts or founds reactions.

Dementia praecox. A form of mental illness characterized by extreme withdrawal to a point at which the victim lives apparently in a dream world without recognition of what is happening around him. The literal meaning is that the person shows in his early years the "loss of mind" found among some very old people. It is now usually called schizophrenia.

Displacement. This behavior mechanism, described more fully in Chapter 4, involves the shifting of an emotional reaction from its true object or area to one involving less conflict for the individual.

Domination. Domination represents the winning of control over other people. It is usually seen as a series of acts by which one person's will is imposed more or less adroitly over other human beings, but may also include inanimate objects.

Ego. In the terminology of Freudian theory, the ego is that part of the personality which is in contact with the world of reality and which is capable of dealing with consequences.

Ego ideal. A part of the person's control and value systems, the ego ideal can be considered the individual's picture of himself as he would like to be.

Extrovert. Originally emphasized by Jung, the term refers to an individual whose tendency is to turn outward rather than inward in coping with his needs. It implies preoccupation with action, things, people, and the external environment, rather than with one's own emotions, feelings, and fantasies.

Fantasy. A form of imaginative activity in which the individual constructs daydreams or otherwise lives in a world of make-believe which has little or no relation to reality.

Field theory. A very general term, this phrase is used to classify those psychological systems in which behavior is considered the result of various forces generated within a specific situation. There is an analogy here to physics; for example, the behavior of a compass is described in terms of a magnetic *field.* The contrast is with atomistic theories in which conduct is traced to the combination of single, isolated causes. The late Kurt Lewin did some of the most penetrating pioneer thinking in applying field concepts to the dynamics of personality.

Fixation. The condition whereby some people revert to an early phase of their development or appear to be arrested at a particular earlier growth stage, so that they can keep working on some task that has not been accomplished. It may show itself as an actual halt in the developmental process or as an inclination to regress to a particular point as a defense against anxiety.

Free-floating anxiety. Strong feelings of uneasiness or anxiety which do not seem to be attached to any definite threat to the individual.

Frustration. A condition which arises when an individual finds himself in a situation where a basic need cannot be met or where progress toward a goal is blocked. The verb "frustrate" means to create such a situation around an individual.

Group therapy. A wide variety of specific techniques for treating disturbed individuals is included in the general category of group therapy. The distinctive features are that the patients are handled in groups instead of individually and that reliance is placed on psychological forces generated in the group to take care of at least part of the process of cure or improvement.

Hallucination. Often considered a symptom of serious disorder, a hallucination is an episode in which the person actually experiences as a real perception what in fact has no corresponding stimulus in the outside world. It may involve auditory, tactile, and other sensory reactions.

Homeostasis. There are certain equilibriums, such as the maintenance of body temperature, necessary for survival. The term for the processes by which these balances automatically maintain themselves is homeostasis. By analogy, this idea is applied to the maintenance of psychological relationships.

Hypnoanalysis. This is one of a number of so-called short-cut methods of psychotherapy. Its distinctive feature is that the individual is placed in a more or less deep hypnotic state and then is induced to talk about himself and the origins of his present difficulties.

Hysteria. In popular use, hysteria means wild emotional reaction or an overexcited state. When used by psychiatrists, it refers to forms of mental disturbance characterized by inappropriate reactions, distortion of reality in favor of one's own unconscious fantasies or emotions, and emotional overreaction. It may show itself in quite a few forms, including paralysis, inability to see, and anesthesia.

Id. A key concept of Freudian theory, the id is that part of the personality composed of the individual's primitive drives. In this book we have used the terms "impulses" and "impulse system" as synonyms.

Individual psychology. This is the title given by Alfred Adler and his followers to their system of psychological theory and its resultant implications for treatment.

Inferiority complex. In those individuals beset by deep fear of inadequacy, there may develop an elaborate structure of emotional reactions and behavior mechanisms by which the individual tries to defend his self-image. Such a tendency to consider oneself a priori inferior may be called an "inferiority complex." It was first described by Alfred Adler.

Inhibition. This term is used in a number of psychological systems. It describes a reaction which has the effect of blocking some behavior which the individual would otherwise be able to perform.

Introjection. The technical term for the act of taking into oneself the presumed value systems of parents and other powerful figures. This process is important in the development of conscience.

Introvert. The opposite of extrovert, this term refers to individuals who show a tendency to seek satisfaction for their needs by turning inward. They are likely to be preoccupied with their own feelings, fantasies, and thought processes, at the expense of maintaining contact with outside reality.

Libido. A term employed by Freud to designate a person's drives to love or the love energy which is directed to an object. In many situations it is practically identical with the meaning of the word "love."

Lobotomy. An operation performed on the brain in an effort to cure or relieve certain mental illnesses. Its use has been almost entirely discontinued.

Masculine protest. This phrase is used by followers of Alfred Adler in describing the emotional reactions of women against their own feelings about the desirability of being men. By extension, it refers to all protest against weakness or inferiority.

Masochism. Seeking injury at the hands of a loved person. This noun is also given the more generalized meaning of securing pleasure from humiliation or misfortune.

Menarche. A term frequently found in books on adolescence, this refers to the onset of the menstrual cycle.

Narcosis. A medical term for sleeplike states.

Narcosynthesis. A method of treatment in which the patient is put into a type of half-sleep by means of various drugs. In this state, he is able to recall and talk about events and feelings which otherwise would be beyond access. The psychiatrist then tries to help him deal more effectively with the problems thus revealed.

Neurosis. Several words are used to describe types or degrees of mental illness. A neurosis may be considered a maladjustment which creates serious problems for a person who is nevertheless living sufficiently in contact with reality to be considered sane. A neurosis may be so mild as to be considered just normal trouble or so severe as to incapacitate its victim for effective living. In neurosis the individual's reactions to present situations are distorted by emotions carried over from his past.

Nondirective counseling. Also called the "client-centered" approach by its chief protagonist, Carl Rogers, this method of dealing with emotional problems stresses interviews in which the counselor does a minimum of directing or guiding of the interview but instead mirrors the client's feelings. The goal is to permit the client to achieve self-insight and make plans for himself.

Obsession. An idea or group of related ideas which force themselves on an individual's consciousness even in the face of deliberate attempts at suppression.

Occupational therapy. This is a kind of treatment, used in ordinary hospitals as well as mental institutions, in which the patients are given work of a nature which aids their recovery.

Oedipal period. In the Freudian scheme of personality development, the Oedipal period is that phase of growth which occurs between the ages of three and six during which the child develops a strong attachment to the parent of the opposite sex, accompanied by rivalry, hostility, and jealousy directed against the parent of the same sex.

Oedipus complex. The conflicts of the Oedipal period can have very serious emotional repercussions. The constellation of behavior mechanisms and emotional reactions generated by these conflicts when inadequately resolved is termed the Oedipus complex.

Oral phase. According to Freud, this is the first phase of development, occupying the period of early infancy. Its outstanding quality is that the developing human being finds most of his needs concentrated in sucking and related activity of the mouth. Contacts with other humans tend to center on that same body zone.

Orthopsychiatry. The literal meaning of this term refers to that branch of psychiatry concerned with straightening or re-educating the individual. In this sense it is analogous to orthopedics or orthodontia. In practice, it has come to mean the name of one professional organization, the American Orthopsychiatric Association, which deals with psychiatric problems of young people. The group emphasizes the team approach by psychiatrists, social workers, psychologists, and educators.

Outpatient clinic. A service center available to patients who are not confined to a hospital.

Overprotection. This noun is used to describe a situation in child raising in which the youngster is denied normal activities and normal social contacts because of parental fears. Although it looks like the opposite of rejection, it is frequently a reaction formation against it.

Paranoia. The tendency to harbor unfounded suspicions or delusions that other people are trying to harm the victim. At its extreme, it is a species of insanity typified by feelings of persecution and is sometimes combined with other forms of psychosis. In a mild form it is a very common symptom of emotional conflict. (See the description of projection in Chapter 4.)

Perceptual defense. A term used by some psychologists to describe situations where conscious recognition of a sight or sound is blocked, delayed, or distorted to protect the individual against a threat to his self-esteem or emotional equilibrium. It is a special case of the mechanism of denial.

Persona. Much used in the psychological system of Jung, this word has the sense of mask or outer surface of the personality.

Phallic. Derived from the Greek word for the masculine sex organ, this adjective is used to refer to qualities derived from or directly related to the sex organs.

Phallic period. This phase of personality development occurs in early childhood, during which time sex curiosity is high and there is interest in the sex organs as such. In chronological sequence it very largely overlaps the Oedipal period.

Play therapy. In working with children who have emotional disturbances, specialists find that in play with toys, children's feelings are revealed and new patterns can be explored. Such play can do for youngsters what the use of the verbal-interview technique does for adults.

Pleasure principle. The tendency of human beings to govern their actions by seeking comfort or a relief from tensions is sometimes labeled the pleasure principle.

Projective tests. A number of tests are now being used in which the individual is asked to tell what he sees, hears, or imagines in a series of standard situations. The theory is that the individual projects into the test situation various aspects of his own personality. The most widely known is the ink blot (Rorschach) test.

Psychiatric social work. That branch of social work concentrating upon the problems of emotionally disturbed people in hospital or clinic settings.

Psychiatry. That branch of medicine having to do with mental and emotional problems. A psychiatrist is a physician who has specialized in this field.

Psychoanalysis. A type of treatment in which a person to be cured of mental or emotional troubles explores his own psychic life by free association under the guidance of a psychoanalyst. Almost all psychoanalysts are full-fledged psychiatrists who have had intensive training in this method and the theory behind it. There are a few nonphysicians, known as lay analysts, who are recognized as qualified to conduct psychoanalysis with children or special groups. The founder of psychoanalysis was Sigmund Freud.

Psychodrama. Role playing used in connection with individual therapy is known as psychodrama. The dominant focus for the spontaneous dramas is the inner feelings and conflicts of the patient, who may take part, act as director, or be an interested observer. J. L. Moreno is its foremost practitioner.

Psychodynamics. A word which designates the complex interaction of motivation and behavior. The purpose of investigating psychodynamics is to understand the roots of people's actions and feelings.

Psychosis. The most serious and disabling forms of mental illness are known as psychoses. A person with a psychosis has lost effective contact with the world of reality.

Psychosomatic. This much-used adjective describes a bodily illness which has all or part of its origin in psychological conditions.

Psychotherapy. This term embraces forms of mental treatment which depend upon psychological methods, in contradistinction to those which employ surgery, shock, drugs, or other physical or chemical means.

Reality. As used in relation to mental problems, reality means the people, things, and relationships which actually exist and to which the normal individual is expected to react with reasonably accurate perception and behavior.

Reality testing. The process by which a person learns to adapt his behavior patterns and control his impulsive expressions in terms of their probable consequences.

Recreational therapy. Those procedures whereby a mentally or physically sick individual is helped toward health by his taking part in games, sports, hobbies, and other recreation.

Regression. Behavior representing a retreat to an earlier phase of development.

Rejection. This term covers those situations in which an individual is disowned, ignored, or otherwise treated in a way to deny normal affectional ties. Its most frequent reference is to the types of home situation outlined on pages 147-50.

Repression. A behavior mechanism by which a person puts out of his consciousness desires, feelings, or memories which would be disturbing.

Resistance. This term is used to describe the total effort of a person to avoid facing facts or the uncovering of unconscious reactions which would create uneasiness or demand change in important behavior patterns.

Rigidity. The opposite of flexibility, rigidity is used to describe personality structures which resist change or which do not readily adapt to changing situations. Often regarded as a defense against anxiety, rigidity is also used in field-theory dynamics to describe people whose behavior in one area of living is little influenced by changes in other areas.

Role playing. In a number of situations people may be helped to gain insight regarding themselves and other individuals by acting the part of some other person. Similar to techniques used in psychodrama or sociodrama, these role-playing procedures are used in general education to stimulate group discussion, as well as in mental treatment. Role playing is a specific technique. The term is not to be confused with the metaphor "play the role," which describes an individual's specific function within a group, as explained in Chapter 10.

Rorschach test. A famous test consisting of a series of so-called ink blots, the Rorschach test is used to assess personality structure. The person taking the test tells or writes what he sees in the ink blots.

Sadism. Sadism is a general term used to describe those reactions which involve getting pleasure from hurting people or other living things. The word is most frequently employed to denote cruelty combined with sexual gratification.

Schizoid. This adjective describes people or conduct which resembles milder forms of schizophrenia.

Schizophrenia. That form of mental disease in which the individual withdraws or becomes insulated from the world around him. Schizophrenia is a psychosis which can take several different forms. (See *dementia praecox.*)

Screen memory. A memory which the individual consciously recognizes but which serves to cover up a linked recollection which he would find unpleasant or anxiety-provoking.

Shock therapy. Many people who have mental disorders are submitted to electrical, chemical, or physical shocks. Such treatment is called shock therapy.

Sibling. Children of the same parents are called siblings. The word is used to avoid the more cumbersome phrase, "brothers, sisters, or brothers and sisters."

Sibling rivalry. Originally intended to describe the competition between siblings for the affection of their parents and for power over each other, this phrase is used to connote the whole range of hostile feelings which is one part of the relationship among siblings.

Social work. This is a broad field of endeavor in which such agencies as family service societies, settlement houses, and other organizations for human betterment aid persons who need help.

Sociodrama. A type of role playing designed to give participants an insight into such social forces as prejudice, leadership patterns, organizational pressures, and the like. Its chief proponent is J. L. Moreno.

Sociogram. A chart depicting the social relationships among members of a group. The friendship charts mentioned on pages 262-66 are one type.

Sociometry. This term denotes the science of measuring relationships within groups. Most research in this field appears in the magazine of the same name.

Spastic. This adjective, sometimes also used as a noun, refers to motor behavior dominated by unco-ordinated jerky movements, usually as a result of brain injuries.

Structuring. This term is mainly used in connection with field theories. It refers to that quality of a situation which endows it with goals for individuals, limits within which they must conduct themselves, and procedures by which the goals may be reached. Structuring also involves defining the roles of the participants by the group leader or by the consensus of the group members themselves.

Subception. This word was invented to describe situations in which an individual reacts to a stimulus without having consciously perceived it.

Sublimation. The process whereby a primitive impulse or drive finally is converted into a socially acceptable form. Much more is said about this concept on pages 76 to 77.

Superego. Roughly synonymous with "conscience," the superego is the technical term used in Freudian theory to describe that aspect of a person's control system which embodies the prohibitions and the positive values of his parents and other influential figures in his life.

Surrogate. An individual who serves as the psychological substitute for, or the target of displacement of feelings toward, someone else, usually a parent or sibling.

Symptom. A manifestation of a condition as distinguished from the condition itself. Thus, a fever is a symptom of an infection; the infection is the condition caused by the presence of attacking micro-organisms.

Taboo. A strongly enforced social or cultural prohibition. The term is taken from practices in primitive tribes.

Thematic Apperception Test (TAT). First developed by Murray, this is a type of projective test in which the person is shown a series of pictures and asked to tell stories about them.

Therapeutic. Medical shorthand for describing any procedure whose purpose is to cure. The word "therapy" means an attempt to cure or an effort to find and use a remedy.

Tic. An involuntary movement or muscular action over which the victim has no control. Typical tics are blinking, jerky hand movements, and spasmodic grimaces.

Transference. In the course of a psychoanalysis, the patient begins to displace onto the analyst emotions derived from his childhood. This process is called transference.

Traumatic. Experiences that are likely to be followed by an emotional injury. "Trauma" is a Greek word meaning "wound."

Unconscious. That portion of a person's psyche or "mind" which contains all thoughts, feelings, or memories which have been repressed or otherwise lost to consciousness. The term is also used as an adjective. The fact that the individual is unaware of the contents of the unconscious does not mean they are inactive.

Voyeurism. A strong desire to see or watch sexual phenomena; "Peeping Tom" activity.

INDEX

Note: For convenience, the names of those characters in the illustrative cases in Chapter 1 to whom reference is made in later chapters are indexed here, with italics used to distinguish them from the real persons indexed.

Johnson, Adelaide M., 216
Johnson, F. Henry, 375
Johnson, George Orville, 265, 429
Johnson, Louise Snyder, 40
jokes, 350
Jones, Harold E., 129
Jones, Mary Cover, 102, 103
Josselyn, Irene M., 182
Journal of Social Issues, 521
Jung, C. G., 531
Junge, Charlotte W., 212
junior high schools, 103, 176, 268, 271, 376, 417
justice, 106, 395-96
  See also fairness
juvenile courts, 426

Kalhorn, Joan, 147
Kaplan, Louis, 83
Karl, 9-10, 156, 226
Kates, Solis L., 477
Katz, Barney, 83
Keliher, Alice V., 493
Kelley, Harold H., 285
Kentucky, 498
kicking, 76
Kimball, Barbara, 216
kindergarten, 66, 87, 88, 302, 335, 346, 506
Kindred, Leslie W., 514
Kinsey, Alfred C., 112, 113, 114
kinship, 119
kissing, 115
Klein, Emanuel, 253
knowledge, 39
  source of, 300
Koller, Marvin R., 164
Kounin, Jacob S., 295, 346
Kovar, Dan R., 104
Krugman, Morris, 450
Krumboltz, John D., 272
Kvaraceus, W. C., 498
Kyte, George C., 325

labels, 39
laissez-faire leadership, 221, 278
  example of, 332-34
Lane, Howard, 450
Lane, Lionel C., 470
Langdon, Grace, 21, 476
language, 137-38, 153, 308
Lansing, Mich., 427
LaSalle, Col., 212
late-maturers, 103-04
latency, 112
laughter, 350-51, 388-90, 435
Lawrence, Mr., 7-9, 68, 284, 379
Lazarus, Richard S., 62
laziness, 52, 109, 218, 416, 486

leaders, 252, 265, 266, 267, 270, 271-74, 277, 347
  adult, 298
  group, 302
  teachers, 482
leadership, 35, 210, 351
learner-centered groups, 280-81
learning, 55-56, 71, 156, 186, 265, 358, 366, 384, 391, 491
  forced, 124-25
  help in, 300
  mental health and, 205-29
learning difficulties, 162, 211-14, 231-50, 413, 463
  example of, 6-7
leaving school, example of, 12-13
  See also drop-outs
lectures, 21, 31, 158, 281, 344, 345, 436
Lee, Dorris May, 476
Lee, J. Murray, 476
Lehner, George F. J., 83
Leicester, 188
leisure, 88
Levine, Edna S., 182
Levine, Kate, 134
Levitt, Morton, 162
Levy, David M., 153
Lewin, Kurt, 277, 532
libido, 534
librarians, 526
life patterns, 495
Lighthall, Frederick F., 217
limits, 91-92, 100, 169, 199, 249, 250, 301, 387, 391-92, 403, 404, 485
  defining, 361
  testing of, 440
Lincoln School, 268
Lindgren, Henry Clay, 40, 83, 476
Lippitt, Ronald, 277, 283, 294, 334, 453, 476
lipstick, 115
listening, 447, 501
listlessness, 160, 210, 339
  See also depression
literature, 69, 213
liveliness, 272
lobotomy, 534
local resources, 525-27
Long, Eleanor Ruth, 366
Lord, Joseph P., 82
love, 47, 79, 92, 109, 115, 148, 225, 240, 304
  need for, 152
Lovejoy, Gordon W., 135
lovers, 72
lower classes, 107, 175, 176
luck, belief in, 28, 243
Ludden, Wallace, 173
Lulu, Mabel Thorn, 33
Lutheran parochial schools, 214

I   8
J   9
K   0
L   1